Fodor's

THE COMPLETE GUIDE TO CARIBBEAN CRUISES

4th Edition

Fodor's Travel Publications   New York, Toronto, London, Sydney, Auckland
www.fodors.com

FODOR'S THE COMPLETE GUIDE TO CARIBBEAN CRUISES
Editor: Douglas Stallings

Writer: Linda Coffman

Editorial Contributors: Carol M. Bareuther, John Bigley, Sirkka Huish, Marlise Kast, Lynda Lohr, Elise Meyer, Paris Permenter, Vernon O'Reilly Ramesar, Heather Rodino, Paul Rubio, Ramona Settle, Jordan Simon, Eileen Robinson Smith, Roberta Sotonoff, Jane E. Zarem

Production Editor: Carrie Parker
Maps & Illustrations: Mark Stroud, Moon Street Cartography; David Lindroth, Inc.; Ed Jacobus, *cartographers;* Bob Blake, Rebecca Baer, *map editors;* William Wu, *information graphics*
Design: Fabrizio La Rocca, *creative director;* Guido Caroti, *art director;* Tina Malaney, Chie Ushio, Nora Rosansky, Jessica Walsh, *designers;* Melanie Marin, *associate director of photography*
Cover Photo: Royal Caribbean International
Production Manager: Angela L. McLean

4th Edition

ISBN 978-0-679-00973-3

ISSN 1558-819X

SPECIAL SALES

This book is available at special discounts for bulk purchases for sales promotions or premiums. Special editions, including personalized covers, excerpts of existing books, and corporate imprints, can be created in large quantities for special needs. For more information, write to Special Markets/Premium Sales, 1745 Broadway, MD 3-2, New York, NY 10019, or e-mail specialmarkets@randomhouse.com.

AN IMPORTANT TIP & AN INVITATION

Although all prices, opening times, and other details in this book are based on information supplied to us at press time, changes occur all the time in the travel world, and Fodor's cannot accept responsibility for facts that become outdated or for inadvertent errors or omissions. So **always confirm information when it matters,** especially if you're making a detour to visit a specific place. Your experiences—positive and negative— matter to us. If we have missed or misstated something, **please write to us.** Share your opinion instantly through our online feedback center at fodors.com/contact-us.

PRINTED IN THE UNITED STATES OF AMERICA

10 9 8 7 6 5 4 3 2 1

CONTENTS

CONTENTS

MAPS

ABOUT THIS BOOK

Our Ratings

At Fodor's, we spend considerable time choosing the best places in a destination so you don't have to. By default, anything we recommend in this book is worth visiting. But some sights, properties, and experiences are so great that we've recognized them with additional accolades. Orange **Fodor's Choice** stars indicate our top recommendations; black stars highlight places we deem **Highly Recommended**; and **Best Bets** call attention to top properties in various categories. Disagree with any of our choices? Care to nominate a new place? Visit our feedback center at www.fodors.com/feedback.

Hotels

Hotels have private bath, phone, and TV, and do not offer meals unless we specify that in the review. We always list facilities but not whether you'll be charged an extra fee to use them.

> For expanded hotel reviews, visit **Fodors.com**

Restaurants

Unless we state otherwise, restaurants are open for lunch and dinner daily. We mention dress only when there's a specific requirement and reservations only when they're essential or not accepted—it's always best to book ahead.

Credit Cards

We assume that restaurants and hotels accept credit cards. If not, we'll note it in the review.

Budget Well

Hotel and restaurant price categories from ¢ to $$$$ are defined in the opening pages of the respective chapters. For attractions, we always give standard adult admission fees; reductions are usually available for children, students, and senior citizens.

Listings
★ Fodor's Choice
★ Highly recommended
⊠ Physical address
✛ Directions or Map coordinates
🕮 Mailing address
☎ Telephone
🖷 Fax
⊕ On the Web

🖉 E-mail
🎟 Admission fee
🕓 Open/closed times
Ⓜ Metro stations
▭ No credit cards

Hotels & Restaurants
🏨 Hotel
🗦 Number of rooms
ⓒ Facilities
🍽 Meal plans
✗ Restaurant
🍴 Reservations
👔 Dress code
⤵ Smoking

Outdoors
🏌 Golf
⛺ Camping

Other
🕐 Family-friendly
⇨ See also
⊠ Branch address
☞ Take note

THE BEST OF CRUISING

Best Suites at Sea

If you want the best accommodations at sea, then look for the plushest suites. The highest-category cabins on today's cruise ships are stocked with extra amenities and services, offering much more room than the typical cruise ship cabin. While the prices are high, you certainly get what you pay for when you book the best.

■ **Cunard Lines' *Queen Mary 2*.** Fit for a queen, or anyone who wants to be treated like one, each of the two Grand Duplex apartments covers 2,250 square feet. The tastefully decorated main level is connected to the upstairs bedroom and bath by a gently curving staircase. Have the butler serve your guests predinner cocktails as you make a grand entrance.

■ **Norwegian Cruise Line's Jewel-class ships and *Norwegian Epic*.** High atop each ship, Garden Villas or Courtyard Villas are the ultimate seagoing digs. More apartments than suites, they have bedrooms and bathrooms offering all the comforts of home—if your home is posh—and the private gardens are idyllic retreats.

■ **Oceania Cruises' *Marina*.** Spanning the width of the ship, Owner's Suites are decorated in furnishings by Ralph Lauren Home and include a private fitness room. After a workout, guests have two whirlpool tubs to relax in—one in the master bath and the other on the spacious verandah.

■ **Silversea Cruises' *Silver Spirit*.** Owner's Suites are the largest suites on board, and have an ideal midship location, stylish furnishings, and plenty of room to entertain guests for cocktails or a complete dinner party.

Best Regular Cabins

Cruise ship accommodations are not created equal; however, you don't have to book the highest-priced cabin to have a comfortable cruise. The following cruise lines offer something a bit above the ordinary for the kind of prices the typical cruiser can afford.

■ **Carnival Cruise Line.** Consistently large by cruise industry standards and with plenty of storage space, Carnival cabins are spacious for two and surprisingly roomy for families. A basket of sample-size goodies in the bathroom often includes new products, such as cinnamon-flavor toothpaste.

■ **Disney Cruise Line.** It's no surprise that cabins are suitable for families of two, three, four, and even five—they were designed especially for them. Whimsical Disney touches in the decor are sure to delight passengers of all ages.

■ **Holland America Line.** Comfort is key, and all cabins have the types of conveniences we take for granted at home. DVD and CD players, flat-screen televisions, lighted magnifying makeup mirrors, and baskets of fresh fruit are unexpected bonuses in all categories.

■ **Princess Cruises.** On all but their small ships, Princess accommodations get our nod for spacious comfort and plenty of storage. Walk-in closets in most are an unexpected and efficient use of space away from the main entry door.

Best Bathrooms Afloat

Let's face it: cruise ship bathrooms aren't usually noted for their roominess or luxury. However, there are exceptions. Here's a rundown of our very favorite bathrooms on the high seas.

- **Disney Cruise Line.** A bath-and-a-half configuration makes these bathrooms ideal for families. One bathroom has a sink and toilet, the other a sink and shower or tub/shower combo—perfect for families.

- **Regent Seven Seas Cruises.** Without a doubt, the marble bathrooms with separate shower and full-size tub on *Seven Seas Voyager* and *Seven Seas Navigator* are totally pampering.

- **Seabourn Cruise Line.** Although not the biggest shipboard bathrooms, unless you pick the newer *Seabourn Sojourn, Seabourn Quest,* or *Seabourn Odyssey,* Seabourn's bath amenities are nonetheless deluxe. Just ask and your stewardess will draw your bath using deluxe products of your choice from the *Pure Pampering* menu.

- **Silversea Cruises.** Double vanities, marble-clad showers, separate tubs, and fluffy, oversize towels are luxurious appointments, even in standard suites. Top suites add whirlpool jets to the tub for total bathing decadence.

Best Ships for Romantics

There's something about being on the open ocean under a blanket of thousands of stars that gets your heart racing. Whether you're planning your honeymoon or just a quiet getaway for two, these are the ships you should consider above all others.

- **Princess Cruises.** Television's former "Love Boats" still deliver romance. In fact, they will deliver Ultimate Dining on your balcony for champagne breakfast or dinner, and, if your fantasy includes a wedding at sea performed by the captain, their ships can deliver that dream as well.

- **Regent Seven Seas Cruises'** *Seven Seas Navigator.* The intimacy of a small ship. the features of a big ship, and comfortably appointed all-suite accommodations make *Seven Seas Navigator* a favorite of couples. In the elegant Prime 7 restaurant the steak and seafood cuisine is sublime—perfect for a quiet dinner for two.

- **SeaDream Yacht Club's** *SeaDream I* and *II.* Luxurious, intimate settings include snug alcoves for private dining alfresco, a Caviar & Champagne Splash party in the surf, and the feel of being a guest on a private yacht. Suites feature Belgian bed linens, and bathrooms have a to-die-for shower large enough for two with multijet massaging showerheads.

- **Star Clippers.** For sheer enchantment, you can't beat stargazing side-by-side on deck chairs with billowing white sails overhead and the thrill of skimming across the sea. Star Clippers ships are intimate sailing vessels, with friendly, unobtrusive service and cozy accommodations.

Best Cruise Lines for Families

A cruise vacation is ideal for families with children. With a safe environment and enough facilities and activities to keep everyone amused, parents can relax and kids can have fun. Put these cruise lines at the top of your list when you want to bring the kids along.

■ **Carnival Cruise Line.** Kid- and teen-friendly spaces packed with toys, games, and activities—combined with nonstop adult action—mean a vacation that offers something to everyone.

■ **Disney Cruise Line.** Disney works its legendary magic by creating not only top-notch youth programs but also activities with adult appeal as well. Add a dash of pixie dust, the only fireworks display at sea, and appearances by Mickey Mouse, and there's a lot of family fun to share.

■ **Norwegian Cruise Line.** Facilities for teens and tots on the newest ships have to be seen to be believed. Water parks, playrooms, and discos are elaborate, and even picky kids should find the active programs enticing.

■ **Royal Caribbean International.** Well-conceived areas for children and teens, plus sports facilities that invite active family members to play together, are bonuses for parents who want to spend quality family time with the kids.

Best Cruise Lines for Water Sports

When you'd prefer to spend more time under or in the water than onshore, you want a cruise line with a strong water-sports program. These lines will keep you both wet and happy.

■ **Norwegian Cruise Line.** Underwater program pioneers, NCL's Dive-In instructors offer easy-to-learn snorkel lessons in the shipboard pool or at excursion sites. Even those who aren't certified can get a taste of scuba-diving thrills under direct supervision of instructors.

■ **Star Clippers.** Only *Royal Clipper* has a stern-located water-sports marina, but the entire fleet features motorized launches to offer water sports such as banana boating, sunfish sailing, waterskiing, and windsurfing. Extensive scuba diving and snorkel programs are available for novice and experienced divers alike.

■ **Windstar Cruises, SeaDream Yacht Club, and Seabourn Cruise Line.** Water-sports marinas are dropped from the stern of each ship for passengers to participate in kayaking, waterskiing, windsurfing, and Jet Skiing to their hearts' content. Add to that the integrated pools on Seabourn's marinas and you have the perfect Caribbean swimming hole. Weather and sea conditions permitting, of course.

Best Spas Afloat

Some cruisers are more interested in a hot-stone massage or a facial than a midnight buffet. Happily, gone are the days when the most you could expect was a new bouffant hairdo and tips. Today's ships offer better-equipped spas with more services than at any time in the history of cruising. Our favorites can go head-to-head with the best of the landlocked variety.

■ **Celebrity Cruise Line Spas.** Attractive, tranquil decor and a full complement of wraps, massages, and deluxe treatments are features of all AquaSpas; however, only Millennium-class ships feature complimentary bubbly saltwater thalassotherapy pools to melt away tension. AquaClass accommodations on most ships feature spa amenities and dining in Blu Restaurant.

■ **Disney Cruise Line.** Spa Villas provide nirvana at sea for couples. Relax on an open-air veranda after a foot exfoliation and some whirlpool time before moving inside to adjacent tables for side-by-side massages. A tea ceremony is a charming finale. (Singles are welcome to indulge in the Spa Villa experience as well!)

■ **Norwegian Cruise Line's Dawn- and Jewel-class.** Massages and facials take a backseat to the elaborate pleasures of long, long indoor lap pools, soothing whirlpools, and indoor relaxation areas worthy of a fine European spa resort.

■ ***Queen Mary 2.*** Canyon Ranch operates this plush spa on board Cunard Line's flagship. In addition to offering a wide range of massages and spa treatments, the Aqua Therapy Centre facilities are simply the finest afloat. For a daily fee, you have access to the huge therapy pool, reflexology basins, herbal or Finnish saunas, steam room, and sensory showers.

Best Sports and Fitness Centers

If you'd rather lift something more than a mai tai or play something more strenuous than shuffleboard, then consider booking a cruise on a ship with a full-service health club. No longer does a shipboard gym mean a treadmill and some dumbbells in a small room deep in the hull. These days, some shipborne fitness centers are as well outfitted as your gym at home, and they probably come with much better views. We can especially recommend the following.

■ **Carnival Cruise Line's Spirit Class.** Multilevel gyms afford a view of the sea from nearly every stair stepper, treadmill, and exercise cycle. After your individual workout or aerobics class, a tropical therapy-style pool, saunas, and steam rooms offer relaxation with equally good sea views.

■ **Princess Cruises' Grand Class.** Stationary bicycles, treadmills, and step, rowing, and weight machines are positioned for wide-open views of sea and sky during cardiovascular workouts. Laps in the waterfall-generated, swim-against-the-current pool also provide a stimulating workout.

■ **Royal Caribbean's Voyager-, Freedom-, and Oasis-Class.** Huge and well-equipped gyms and exercise classes are second-string players next to full-size outdoor basketball courts, rock-climbing walls, and the unique experience of ice-skating at sea. The addition of full-size Everlast boxing rings to Freedom-class gyms gives new meaning to "working up a sweat."

Best Entertainment at Sea

The quality of cruise ship entertainment is higher these days than it has ever been. You're likely to find a Las Vegas–quality revue or Broadway–quality show on most cruise ships. Still, some lines stand out with their offerings. These are our favorites.

■ **Carnival Cruise Lines.** Flash, dazzle, and special effects worthy of Las Vegas are backdrops for the talented teams of entertainers in Carnival production shows. Guest entertainers include some of the most hilarious comedians at sea.

■ **Disney Cruise Line.** No one knows how to please audience members of all ages like the folks at Disney, and their shipboard showmanship draws standing-room-only crowds and thunderous applause. A magical fireworks display—the only fireworks at sea—is a wondrous and well-loved event.

■ **Norwegian Cruise Line.** Professional shows star highly polished artists, who often include adagio dance pairs and accomplished gymnasts. Performances by Chicago's Second City players are highlights throughout the fleet. Norwegian Epic offers some of the most elaborate and unique entertainment afloat. Not only does the ship offer comedy by Second City, a fleet staple, but it also showcases authentic Vegas-style acts such as Blue Man Group, Legends in Concert (the original live tribute artist show), and Howl at the Moon (a full out rock show centered around two dueling baby grand pianos).

Best Specialty Restaurants

Virtually every cruise line now offers reservations-only specialty restaurants, which prepare restaurant-quality meals for a special cover charge. Many of these tables are hard to come by, a testament to their quality and imaginative cuisine. Here are the lines that stand apart, offering specialty restaurants that are well worth planning ahead for.

■ **Carnival Cruise Lines.** When Carnival introduced supper clubs, the line took shipboard dining to a new level with a sophisticated ambience and the ingredients for outstanding meals at sea. Anyone familiar with big-city steak houses will recognize the presentation of a tray displaying the evening's entrées.

■ **Celebrity Cruises.** Decorated with authentic ocean-liner artifacts, exquisite Murano-glass fixtures, and rich furnishings, the upscale restaurants on Millennium-class ships offer tableside food preparation, classical music, and food that is described in hushed tones. Going even a step further, Solstice-class ships each house six specialty restaurants and cafés, including a crêperie.

■ **Crystal Cruises.** Asian-theme restaurants on Crystal ships receive rave reviews for the beautifully prepared dishes, including ultrafresh sushi. Presentation is as beautiful as the divine food. If you aren't adept with chopsticks, no one will raise an eyebrow if you use a fork.

■ **Cunard Line's** *Queen Mary 2.* Cuisine in the Todd English Restaurant, named for the famed chef and restaurateur, is as otherworldly as the exotic Moroccan surroundings in which it is served. The small cover charge for lunch or dinner would hardly be sufficient for a tip at his *Olives*

Best Regular Dining Room Cuisine

With more than 2,000 passengers, today's large cruise ships simply can't offer elegant restaurant-quality food on such a vast scale. However, most cruise lines do manage to provide good food to their passengers. A few do even better, and you may be surprised to find that they aren't always the most luxurious lines.

■ **Carnival Cruise Line.** Yes, Carnival! The line offers what is possibly the best mainstream dining experience at sea. The waiters still take time out to dance and sing, but the food is tasty, more sensibly portioned, and nicely presented. Plus, everyone's favorite Chocolate Melting Cake is on the dessert menu every night!

■ **Holland America Line.** Gone is the reputation for bland food designed for senior passengers. Under the leadership of Master Chef Rudi Sodamin, the culinary staff creates dishes high in quality and taste.

■ **SeaDream Yacht Club.** A true gourmet meal is hard to come by on land, let alone at sea, but SeaDream chefs accomplish just such a feat. With only 112 passengers on board, every meal is individually prepared.

■ **Silversea Cruises.** It's hard not to get exactly the meal you want on a Silversea ship. Special requests are handled with aplomb, and the pasta dishes are authentic and *squisito*.

Best Access for Travelers with Disabilities

The U.S. Supreme Court ruled in 2005 that all cruise lines that call on U.S. ports must make some effort to make their ships more accessible to travelers with disabilities. While it's unlikely that every nook and cranny of every ship will ever be fully accommodating to passengers with mobility problems, some lines have already made great strides in the right direction.

■ **Celebrity Cruises.** While the accommodations designed for accessibility are some of the best at sea, equally as desirable are the line's "easy" shore excursions aimed at expanding the number of in-port tour options available to guests with mobility issues.

■ **Holland America Line.** In the forefront of accessible cruise travel, Holland America offers a variety of services to passengers with mobility, sight, and breathing impairments. Shore tenders are equipped with wheelchair-accessible platforms that simplify transferring wheelchairs and scooters.

■ **Princess Cruises.** Not only are accessible staterooms and suites available in a wide range of categories, but Princess takes care also to provide shoreside wheelchair access to appropriate tours on vehicles equipped with lifts.

■ **Silversea Cruises.** Suites designed for accessibility are limited, but the ships are small and easy to navigate with wide, wide passageways and elevators that reach all decks. Public rooms with broad entryways are clustered together aft, and the distance between them is small.

Best Shops on Board

The need to shop doesn't fade away with the receding coastline, and many cruise lines have now made the experience of onboard shopping a more pleasant one. The best have taken things a step further.

- **Carnival Cruise Line.** You'll find a great selection of popular logo souvenirs, many of them priced under $10, as well as low-priced liquor and sundries and sales on some nifty high-end baubles and trinkets.
- **Celebrity Solstice-class ships.** With 19 shops and boutiques to browse, these ships provide the most extensive retail therapy at sea. There's little you won't find, including designer sunglasses, high-end jewelry and home furnishings, "grass" soled flip-flops in the Lawn Club Shop, and luggage to take it all home.
- **Crystal Cruises.** Signature apparel, sportswear, formal wear, and luxury cosmetics are all available in thousands of square feet of exclusive boutiques. A favorite is the Crystal Home Collection, featuring the Bistro's Guy Buffet porcelain tableware.
- **Princess Cruise Line.** Should you have the misfortune of lost or delayed luggage, you're in luck. Princess shipboard boutiques are stocked with nearly everything you need to carry on in style.

Best Service

When you go away on a relaxing cruise vacation, you want to be pampered and waited on. While service in all ships is pretty good these days, it's a given that with more than 2,000 passengers, large ships just can't give the same kind of personalized service as smaller ships. So it shouldn't be surprising that the best service at sea is on cruise lines that operate smaller ships.

- **Seabourn Cruise Line.** It just doesn't get any better than this. From the moment you step aboard staff members know your name, quickly learn your preferences, and consider no request too small or too outlandish to be considered for your comfort. Gracious service is sincere and offered with genuine warmth and courtesy.
- **Regent Seven Seas Cruises.** Staff efforts go almost unnoticed, yet even out-of-the-ordinary requests are handled with ease. Butlers provide personalized service to guests in the top-category suites.
- **SeaDream Yacht Club.** A Corona with no lime, extra juice in your rum punch—whatever your preference, it will be remembered by all servers on board. They seem to network behind the scenes to ensure perfection.
- **Silversea Cruises.** The mostly European staff doesn't seem to understand the word "no." Every attempt is made to satisfy even the most unusual request, even if it means buying a bottle of guava juice in the next port of call. Every suite has a butler to cater to your needs.

Best Fun and Funky Activities

Being on vacation means having fun. While you may be able to amuse yourself, your fellow passengers sometimes need a little push. The best activities get passengers involved in the fun and give them an opportunity to let loose a bit. We don't claim these are always the most sophisticated activities at sea, but they will make you smile.

■ **Carnival Contests.** As wacky to watch as they are to participate in, the knobby knees and hairy chest competitions are something of a throwback, but you have to love the enthusiasm.

■ **Celebrity Solstice-class Ships Lawn Club.** Hone your short game on the only real grass putting greens on the high seas. The half acre of turf above the water also provides a sea of green for genteel games of croquet, lawn games, picnics, and simple barefoot strolls.

■ **The Costa Toga Party.** Do as the Romans did—dress up in a toga (supplies and accessories provided on board) and join in the Bacchanal. Peel a grape for your significant other.

■ **Disney "Pirates in the Caribbean" Deck Party.** Even Captain Hook smiles on a Disney cruise, and nowhere is that more evident than at this fun deck party. Full of high energy and high spirits, we won't spoil the surprise of how Mickey makes his exciting entrance, but the grand finale is the only fireworks show presented from on board a cruise ship while at sea.

Best Shore Excursions

Taking a cruise doesn't mean staying on the ship all the time. The real draw of a cruise is that it gives you the opportunity to visit more places in a single vacation than you might have been able to get to on your own. You can always go snorkeling or take a tour of a rum factory, but the best shore excursions will be remembered long after you've gone back to your regular grind.

■ **The America's Club 12-Meter Regatta, St. Maarten.** Not only is it a thrill to sail on one of these super-fast yachts, but you can join in to crew the vessel for a real America's Cup–style race. Consistently popular, this one should definitely be booked on board as it will be sold out once you go ashore.

■ **Cave Tubing, Belize.** Explore isolated caves where the ancient Maya were said to have conducted religious ceremonies. The current moves your inner tube as you leisurely drift along the waterways connecting jungle caverns.

■ **Rain Forest Aerial Tram, Panama Canal.** Whiz through the treetops for the approximately 20-minute ascent through the forest canopy. Guides provide an explanation of the complex ecosystem and point out wildlife along the way.

■ **Stingray City, Grand Cayman.** Playful and lively as kittens, the stingrays await visitors on an offshore sandbar reached only by boat. Help your guides feed them while you pet their velvety bodies, and you'll be rewarded with gentle rubbing.

Best Enrichment Programs

All travel is enlightening, but if you wish to return home with more than souvenir photos and a suntan, you might want to explore the variety of enrichment programs currently offered by cruise lines. As outlined on the lines' Web sites, most curricula are available year-round, but the specific courses and lecturers may change. These are the ones we've found most inspirational and entertaining.

■ **Crystal Cruises.** Discover your inner artist by learning to play piano in the Crystal Cruises Creative Learning Institute. Expert instruction and lectures can be found in the areas of Arts & Entertainment; Business & Technology; Lifestyle, Wellness; and Wine & Food. Consistently popular is the Computer University@Sea program, which teaches computer basics as well as advanced techniques.

■ **Cunard Line.** After a trip through the heavens in the only planetarium at sea, on board *Queen Mary 2* you can attend lectures presented by Oxford University luminaries and other guest speakers on topics from diplomacy to interior design, or delve into classes ranging from computers to wine appreciation, foreign languages to photography. You can even study acting with graduates of the Royal Academy of Dramatic Art.

■ **Holland America Line.** The Explorations Speaker Series features lecturers whose topics may cover the wildlife, history, or culture of worldwide destinations; other subjects of interest might include astronomy, ocean-liner history, wellness, or personal finance. For hands-on cooking and computer classes, each ship has a Culinary Arts Center and Digital Workshop.

Best Beds

A good night's sleep is important to a feeling of well-being, so why would anyone want to sleep on a lumpy mattress outfitted with pancake-thin pillows and scratchy sheets? No one does. Hotels have been in the process of offering upgraded beds and bedding for years. Cruise lines have now joined the wave, and these are our favorites.

■ **Carnival Cruise Lines.** The Carnival Comfort Bed features a thick spring mattress, a downlike nonallergenic pillow, high-quality sheets and pillowcases, and a 100% hypoallergenic down duvet covered by a satiny cotton-blend duvet cover.

■ **Holland America Line.** The Mariner's Dream bed is an extra-thick Sealy innerspring pillow-top mattress. Hypoallergenic poly or goose-down pillows and cuddly down blankets are covered in 300-thread-count sheets with a soft, sateen finish.

■ **Oceania Cruises.** Inaugurating the bed wars at sea with its "Tranquility Bed" and upping the comfort with the "Prestige Tranquility Bed," Oceania has outfitted all accommodations with high-quality mattresses, 350-thread-count Egyptian cotton linens, silk-cut duvets, and goose-down pillows.

■ **Silversea Cruises.** Topped with a memory foam cover, mattresses feature a spring system with a soft and firm side that can be reversed to suit your preference. Down duvets, a choice of nine pillow types, and 300 thread-count Egyptian cotton linens insure sweet dreams.

Cruising:
The Basics

WORD OF MOUTH

"There is just something about stepping on board a cruise ship that takes me away from everyday living. How fortunate we are to be able to enjoy such luxuries."

—Anne G.

"We have never had a bad cruise; some are just more memorable and enjoyable than others."

—George H.

The words *value* and *cruise* may not sound like they belong in the same sentence, let alone the same conversation, but if you haven't considered a cruise vacation lately, you might be surprised. A cruise can be less expensive than staying home and a lot more relaxing. Mundane, everyday chores are forgotten as crewmembers take care of everything from cleaning your cabin to washing the dishes. Breakfast in bed? Just ask and it's yours. A cruise sounds too good to be true, but it isn't. And sailing away on your ship of dreams is more affordable—and enjoyable—than ever.

Over lunch at the Lido buffet on our first cruise, I scanned the ship's daily newsletter and found myself in seagoing heaven before I'd even gone out to sea. Not only would I not be cooking or cleaning, but I had my choice of fun and exciting ways to spend the days and evenings on board. Morning walks on the promenade deck led to aerobics before breakfast. After lunch there were lectures and trivia games. Every night was like Saturday night—dressing for dinner, seeing a show, and dancing until the wee hours. My husband Mel's agenda was a bit different. His sea days were spent lounging at the pool. Clearly, he enjoyed relaxing while the captain did the driving.

We found ourselves attended to by an excellent service staff in first-class surroundings and fed multiple-course meals, all for a single, affordable fare. Our only obligation was to enjoy ourselves as the luxurious cruise ship sped from one port of call to the next. Once ashore, we took in the sights, shopped, and discovered a variety of Caribbean cultures. Instead of uncomfortable island-hopping by plane—been there, done that—we visited several destinations while our needs were catered to in high style.

Mel and I enjoy meeting new people, and we made friends for life on our first cruise. Many more years—and cruises—have followed, and

CARIBBEAN CRUISING MILESTONES

| 1966 | **Norwegian Caribbean Line** (now Norwegian Cruise Line) begins offering seven-night cruises from then-obscure Port of Miami. | 1972 | **Carnival Cruise Lines'** "Fun Ship" fleet is launched with a single converted ocean liner that runs aground off Miami's Dodge Island during its inaugural voyage. | 1975 | *The Love Boat* television series, starring Princess Cruises' *Pacific Princess*, introduces the idea of cruise vacations to millions of weekly fans. |

we've met more people along the way. We still receive holiday greetings from a newlywed couple who conceived their first child during a rather fateful honeymoon cruise. Over the years, I have met hundreds of other passengers through Internet Web sites I have hosted, and it's always a pleasure to answer their questions and possibly see them on a cruise ship. My love of cruises has forever changed my travel habits. All clichés aside, there is nothing like a cruise.

WHAT IS CRUISING?

Ocean travel in the early decades of the 20th century was just another means of getting to a destination. Ships were the only practical way of traveling from one continent to another. Even so, venerable ocean liners such as the *Normandie* offered an occasional round-trip pleasure cruise to exotic locales like Brazil for the pre-Lenten Carnaval.

However, early cruisers didn't have the comforts of today as they steamed toward the unfamiliar. As on *Normandie,* it was common to find air-conditioned comfort only in ships' first-class dining rooms. However, they could at least find relief from Rio's heat in one of that era's few outdoor swimming pools at sea. (At that time, if an ocean liner had a permanent swimming pool at all, it was often indoors and deep in the hull.)

Carnival Cruise Line executives like to reminisce about the tiny gyms on their early ships, which were converted ocean liners, and then point to how far ship designs have evolved. I remember those ships well. It was even difficult to find the casino on Carnival's first Fun Ship, the *Mardi Gras,* let alone the indoor swimming pool. You won't find claustrophobic natatoriums or ill-equipped, windowless gyms on today's modern cruise ships. Designed for contemporary travelers and tastes, these vessels carry passengers amid conveniences unheard of in the heyday of the North Atlantic ocean liner or even on board the earliest ships permanently dedicated to cruising.

There's a lot to like on cruise ships these days. Nearly everything about cruises has changed, from the presence of air-conditioning and roomier cabins to the ever longer list of activities. In the old days, entertainment was staid, and there was no cruise director to lead the merriment. In truth, passengers were usually required to entertain themselves, with

| 1978 | After sailing for less than a decade, **Royal Caribbean** "stretches" *Song of Norway*—cutting it in half and inserting a new middle section. | 1979 | In an unprecedented move, **Norwegian Cruise Line** purchases the SS *France* and rechristens it SS *Norway,* the largest cruise liner to sail from Miami at the time. | 1988 | **Holland America Line,** one of the most revered names in passenger shipping, is purchased by Carnival Corporation. |

after-dinner cigars, brandy, and cards for the gentlemen in a smoking room, conversation for the ladies in a separate drawing room.

As cruising evolved, swimming pools and pool games became common, and the position of cruise director grew to be the most visible in the hierarchy of shipboard staff. These days, as the average age of cruise passengers drops, more attention is focused on keeping people active. Gyms and spas have grown in size, with today's emphasis on healthy living. Menus now offer lighter fare as well as vegetarian dishes.

By night, lavish production shows, cabaret acts, comedy shows, and classical concerts are staged for your enjoyment. Discos and dance clubs rock into the early morning hours. And on most ships there's no cover charge or ticket to purchase—all are included in your fare. No one dresses to dine every night anymore, and even traditional formal dinners can be skipped if the casual dining option is more to your liking.

If you ask six couples what they enjoyed most about their Caribbean cruise vacation, you are likely to get a dozen different responses. Nearly everyone raves about the meals, an opportunity to sample unfamiliar dishes with the assurance that if you don't like something, you can get something else simply by asking. The gracious, nonstop service and attention to detail often come as a surprise to first-time cruisers, who may not be used to a server taking their tray at the end of the buffet line and showing them to a table. Many cruisers appreciate the ease of unpacking only once and settling into accommodations that visit a variety of destinations.

As you might have guessed, it's the unique social atmosphere that appeals most to me. I rarely encounter the same level of sociability at resorts Mel and I visit, where we typically live out of a suitcase and seldom meet fellow travelers.

Today's cruise ships are lively and luxurious floating resorts that offer something to satisfy the expectations of almost everyone, but each cruise line and cruise ship is different. Most people find that selecting the right cruise is a bit more complicated than booking a land-based resort vacation.

The more you know about cruise travel, the better prepared you will be when the time comes to make your choices. Unfortunately, while cruises have come a long way from the days when ships were viewed as the travel

---

| 1990 | With a refitted vessel from its budget Fantasy Cruises line, the Chandris family of Greek shipping prominence launches **Celebrity Cruises,** a premium cruising option. | 1991 | A boyhood dream for Michael Krafft becomes a cruise line reality when **Star Clippers** sails onto the scene with the tallest clipper ships ever built. | 1998 | The *Magic* and *Wonder* of Walt Disney's beloved resort vacations go to sea with the launch of **Disney Cruise Line.** |

1

pick of well-heeled, newlywed, or nearly dead passengers, misconceptions still abound. Most disappointments—and the inevitable complaints—are the result of misunderstandings that stem from unmet expectations. Having the right information debunks the most persistent myths.

My goal is to help you make the right decisions so the cruise you select will be the best fit for you. If you're taking the family, you don't want to sail on a ship without a good children's program. Nor would you be happiest on a ship without a casino if your favorite vacation spot up to now has been Las Vegas. You need the tools to select the proper wardrobe and desirable accommodations. In this book, we'll do our comparison shopping together. We'll give you the dimensions of every cabin category and outline the amenities of every ship plying Caribbean waters so you can pick the cruise ship that fits your needs. Planning to sail away is fun, and I want you to enjoy cruises as much as I do.

Now, let's get started.

WHAT'S ON THE SHIP?

Some people fear they won't know the ropes and will stand out as a first-timer. While some passengers are certain to be repeat cruisers, the majority are in the same boat, so to speak, and will be cruising for the first time. Keep in mind that most of today's larger cruise ships have the same basic arrangement. Once on board, you will encounter a reception area and shore excursion desk, very likely centrally located in a multideck atrium or lobby. Explore a bit further, and you will discover lounges, a main restaurant, buffet restaurant, showroom, Internet–business center, boutiques, photo shop, library, spa, and a gym. Cabins are lined up along quiet passageways. And that is just inside.

Out on open decks there are swimming pools, hot tubs, bars, and a plethora of deck chairs. You're likely to find a deck dedicated to sports with courts for volleyball and basketball. Some ships take the facilities up a notch and include waterslides, miniature golf, in-line skating tracks, rock-climbing walls, and even a surf simulator or bowling alley. For joggers there's the outdoor promenade deck or a designated track for running and walking. Children and teens have their own playrooms, swimming pools, video arcades, and, in some cases, lounges and party

| 2001 | As a testament to their 20-year appeal, the diminutive Sea Goddess ships are rebuilt in luxurious fashion for the SeaDream Yacht Club. | 2003 | Carnival Corporation acquires **Princess Cruises**, foiling an attempt by Royal Caribbean to become the world's largest cruise company. | 2009 | **Royal Caribbean** launches the world's largest purpose-built cruise ship, *Oasis of the Seas*. Its sister ship, *Allure of the Seas,* made its debut in 2010. |

rooms. The hottest trend at sea is an adults-only retreat complete with spa-style amenities. Deck plans and signage point the way to all the features. Still, it may take a couple of hours—or possibly even a couple of days—to get your bearings.

WHAT A CRUISE COSTS

More than 15 million people embarked on cruises in 2010, and most of them sailed on ships that were designed and launched in the previous decade. A massive shipbuilding program commenced in the early 1990s, and with so many new ships—more than 100 new ships were introduced between 2000 and the end of 2010—cruise lines had a lot of berths to fill and did so by pricing their cruises attractively. Fares in recent years, which could be found as low as $50 per person, per night, are reminiscent of those offered in the 1980s. Even factoring in inflation, you can see that cruises are actually selling for less today than they did 25 years ago, even as the ships and amenities are far superior.

It's no secret that the entire travel industry has suffered tremendously during the recent global recession. With flights more expensive and with fewer seats, more Americans take to the highways on domestic road trips. Cruise lines are in an enviable position compared to resorts, to which travelers might have to fly; if passengers can't fly to traditional embarkation ports, ships can be moved to where passengers are able to reach them by car, and in the past decade, the cruise industry has done exactly that. Continuing low cruise fares, new ships, and accessible home ports have combined to make cruises more popular than ever.

But—and there's always a but—the economic downturn that began in late 2008 also put a damper on cruise travel, which has resulted in continuing low fares, particularly on many Caribbean routes. New, more feature-filled ships, including Royal Caribbean's massive *Oasis of the Seas* and *Allure of the Seas* and NCL's *Norwegian Epic* have been able to capture higher fares, which has been good for the cruise industry. But the good news for cruise consumers is that deals are still out there—even on some of the newest ships, which continue to be priced less than they were in 1990, especially in the Caribbean. As you will see, when you crunch the numbers to compare the total cost of a cruise to that of a traditional resort vacation, a cruise compares favorably.

ADD-ONS

Most cruises are *not* all-inclusive and have never been. Although low fares have brought cruise vacations within the realm of reality for many people who could only fantasize about them in the past, those same rock-bottom fares can cause consternation to passengers on tight budgets when they factor in the extras. Increasingly, cruise lines devise creative ways to entice passengers to spend additional money once on board their dream ships. In the industry, it's called "onboard revenue enhancement," and *charge, charge, charge* is the mantra; if you heed it, you can see the cost of your cruise vacation rising faster than a helicopter over a Caribbean island volcano.

Although your cruise ticket price includes a lot—accommodations, food, entertainment, taxes, and port charges are covered in the ticket price—there are also many add-ons. Air fare, tips, shore excursions, travel insurance, passports, cocktails, soft drinks, and even bottled water can increase the bottom line. Some of these add-ons (spa visits, alcoholic drinks, specialty restaurants) are purely optional and can be easily avoided; others (tips, travel to the port, and passports) cannot. Holding down the add-on expenses is not easy; after all, the cruise is your vacation, which you deserve, and you want it to be special. But there are ways to minimize those costs. To get the true picture of what you can expect before your budget floats out of sight, you must consider those extras.

In addition to transportation to your port of embarkation, which is usually not included in the cruise fare these days, there are a few costs that are often overlooked but that add to your overall cruise costs. Before leaving home, consider the cost of passports or passport cards (now required for some travel to the Caribbean) and travel insurance (optional, but highly recommended).

ADDING UP THE COST OF THE EXTRAS

The majority of on-board extras are strictly discretionary. For instance, whether to purchase alcoholic beverages or cappuccino is your choice, and no one will blink an eye if you shy away from the casino or spa. However, it's unlikely you will be able to avoid all extras. Bottled water seems to be an unavoidable expense these days, and tipping isn't optional. Although the extras greatly enhance the overall experience of a cruise, they can quickly add up and exceed your initial budget if you're not careful. Even if you're frugal, you should expect to pay at least $100 (and often much more) beyond the cost of your cruise for tips and incidentals.

Cruise passengers are often caught in something of a catch-22 situation: you must either pay a higher fare up front for a more-luxurious cruise or pay for nonincluded items later. Just as you may compare the cost of a cruise vacation to a resort vacation, consider the cost of a less-inclusive mainstream cruise versus the cost of a more-inclusive luxury cruise. In addition to the added comfort, you may decide—by determining and budgeting for your personal priorities in advance—that there's not so much difference between the cost of a truly all-inclusive luxury cruise and a less-inclusive mainstream cruise, particularly if you prefer suite accommodations. Of course, it all depends on the cabin category you book and your individual spending habits. Read the fine print in your chosen cruise line's brochure, and you should face no spending bombshells once you are on board.

CUTTING YOUR BAR TAB DOWN TO SIZE

Bar drinks and wine typically cost about what you would expect to pay at a nice lounge or restaurant in a resort or big city in the United States. Unless you really want a souvenir glass to take home, order tropical umbrella drinks in regular glasses—the keepsake glasses cost extra. Wine by the bottle is a more economical choice at dinner than

What Things Cost On Board

Here's a list of what some of the most popular extras cost on board a ship.

Gratuities: $10–$15 per person, per day

Cocktails: $5.75–$9

Wine by the glass: $5.50–$9

Alcoholic coffee drinks: $5–$6

Beer: $5–$6

Bottled water: $2.50–$4

Sodas: $1.25–$2

Specialty ice cream and coffee: $4–$6

Alternative restaurants: $4–$75 per person

Cell phone calls: $2.50–$5 per minute

Shore excursions: $25–$110

Dry cleaning: $7–$11 per piece (50% of these prices for pressing)

Laundry: $1–$4 per piece

Spa treatments: $100–$175

Salon services: $30–$100

Personal training: $75–$90 per hour

Special exercise classes: $10–$12 per class

Casino gambling: 5¢–$10 for slot machines; $5 and up for table games

Bingo: $5–$10 per card for multiple games in each session

Video arcade games: $1–$2 per game

Photographs: $7–$20 each

Internet access: 35¢–$1 per minute

Medical treatment: $75 and up, depending on treatment

---

ordering it by the glass, and any wine you don't finish will be kept for you and served the next night. Gifts of wine or champagne ordered from the cruise line (either by you, a friend, or your travel agent) can be taken to the dining room. Wine from any other source will incur a corkage fee that can run up to $15 per bottle.

Whether to BYOB is a hotly debated issue. Many cruise lines look the other way at soft drinks and bottled water toted aboard by arriving passengers, but most lines do not allow passengers to bring alcoholic beverages on board. Duty-free liquor purchased ashore will be collected when you return to the ship and held until the last night aboard, when it's delivered to your cabin. Similarly, liquor purchases from the ship's own duty-free store will be held until the last night. You will usually be allowed to bring aboard a bottle of wine or champagne for a special occasion in your carry-on when you initially board the ship, but do not even think of carting on a case of beer.

Tap water is always plentiful and free. Why not bring along a powdered drink mix for a flavorful and refreshing change? An insulated cup or mug makes it easy to prepare and keep chilled—cabin stewards fill ice buckets in passenger staterooms at least twice a day. You can also order up a pitcher of fruit juice with your room service breakfast and keep what's left for later; juices are a healthy choice and complimentary with meals (there's usually a charge for juice if you order it at the bar).

In lounges, request the less-expensive bar-brand mixed drinks or the reduced-price drink of the day. On some ships discounted beverage cards for unlimited fountain soft drinks are available for approximately $5 a day for children and $6.50 a day for adults. Be sure to attend the Captain's Welcome Aboard Party, where complimentary drinks are often served. If you're a repeat passenger, do not miss the repeaters' get-together for the same reason.

SHIP SIZES

Although all ships share certain similarities, there's one distinct difference that can be as important as any other single factor in whether you enjoy your cruise: ship size. Choosing the right ship is quite possibly the most important decision you can make when booking your cruise, and your lifestyle and expectations should be major considerations when making this choice. This is one time when size matters and can make or break your vacation.

The size of the ship affects every other aspect of the cruise: entertainment and dining options, the kind of activities you'll be offered, and even the ports of call you can visit. It stands to reason that the larger the ship, the more room there is for features like alternative dining venues, huge show lounges and casinos, elaborate swimming pools, and expansive spa and fitness facilities. This has to be balanced by the fact that there are intriguing ports of call that only smaller ships can visit because of docking or tendering considerations. Keep your priorities in mind while you're examining cruise line brochures.

Large ships start at approximately 70,000 tons and go up in size from there. These are the ships that have more than 1,800 passengers and often carry as many as 3,600-plus cruisers. They are the megaships that include the bells and whistles modern passengers have come to associate with a cruise. Larger ships offer nonstop activities designed for all interests; they have high-energy Las Vegas– or Broadway-style music revues; a wider variety of restaurants and lounges; dance clubs and discos; well-rounded children's programs; and more. Royal Caribbean's extra-large megaship vessels even include rock-climbing walls, ice-skating rinks, miniature golf courses, and surfing simulators. Carnival's megaships have some of the largest casinos and most lavish spas and exercise facilities afloat.

Midsize ships range from approximately 25,000 to 70,000 tons and carry between 400 and 1,700 passengers. There's no lack of entertainment and features on these ships, but they tend not to have some of the more extravagant facilities. Alternative dining is generally an option, and in addition to the traditional daytime activities, there will be ample nightlife, a casino, shows, and a spa. By necessity, they are usually on a smaller scale but no less satisfying. Although there are more ships this size in premium and luxury fleets, some older Carnival ships also fall within this range. The most upscale midsize ships have a higher passenger-space ratio, meaning there's more room per person than on a larger ship. It's usually not difficult to find a deck chair by

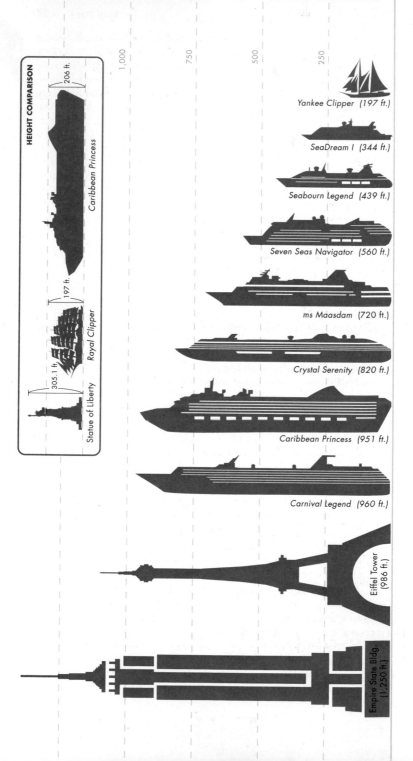

HEIGHT COMPARISON

206 ft.

Caribbean Princess

197 ft.

Royal Clipper

305.1 ft.

Statue of Liberty

1,000

750

500

250

Yankee Clipper (197 ft.)

SeaDream I (344 ft.)

Seabourn Legend (439 ft.)

Seven Seas Navigator (560 ft.)

ms Maasdam (720 ft.)

Crystal Serenity (820 ft.)

Caribbean Princess (951 ft.)

Carnival Legend (960 ft.)

Eiffel Tower (986 ft.)

Empire State Bldg. (1,250 ft.)

1

the pool on a sunny day. Smack in the middle of this range is Regent Seven Seas Cruise's *Seven Seas Voyager,* which has one of the highest passenger-space ratios on the seas; if you cruise on this ship, you may wonder where everyone is.

Small ships range from megayachts and sailing vessels of less than 5,000 tons to ships of about 25,000 tons. These ships may have as few as 70 passengers or as many as 350. On smaller vessels, passengers tend to entertain themselves rather than be entertained. Lounges on small ships are more intimate, and the only entertainment is usually done cabaret-style. Intriguing itineraries are more often the focus of the voyage and often include some ports of call such as Mustique or Bequia, which are not suited for larger ships. Restaurants often accommodate all guests in a single open seating. On board luxurious small ships, gracious service and fine dining are paramount, and your table is likely to be set with signature china, European crystal, and heavy silver, and covered with Belgian linens. Good things do come in small packages; a well-kept secret is that Windstar Cruises' superyacht *Wind Surf* has one of the largest spas at sea relative to her size.

TYPES OF CRUISE LINES

Just as cruise ships differ by size and style, so do the cruise lines themselves, and finding a cruise line that matches your personality is as important as finding the right ship. Some cruise lines cater to families, others to couples, active singles, and even food and wine aficionados. Each cruise line has a unique personality that will appeal to different lifestyles. Selecting the right one can mean the difference between struggling with unmet expectations and enjoying the vacation of a lifetime.

Some of the differences are subtle, but today's cruise lines still fall into three basic categories: Mainstream, Premium, and Luxury.

MAINSTREAM LINES
What you'll find. Mainstream cruise lines usually have a little something for everyone:

- Ships tend to be the big, bigger, and biggest at sea, carrying the highest number of passengers per available space.

- Ship decor runs the gamut from glitz and glitter to nautical kitsch.

- Staterooms range from inside cabins for three and four to a variety of outside cabin configurations with or without balconies. Top-notch suites may or may not come with numerous extra amenities.

- Schedules include enough activities to keep even the most hyperactive passenger content. Expect to find deck sports and pool games, team trivia and scavenger-hunt contests, bingo, golf lessons, karaoke, fitness classes, a high-tech gym, and full-service spa.

- Entertainment tends to be high-energy, Las Vegas–style production shows; you can always find a variety of lounges and discos for dancing; and in the liveliest piano bars everyone might be encouraged to sing along.

CRUISING FAMILY TREE

CARNIVAL CORPORATION

Carnival Cruise Lines: Founded in 1972 by Israeli-born Ted Arison, who got his feet wet at Norwegian Caribbean Line, Carnival's "Fun Ship" fleet of 21 ships is now the largest afloat.

Costa Cruises: Costa's name first appeared in 1854, when Italian founder Giacomo Costa began trading olive oil by sea, and grew to include passenger ships in 1947. Carnival completed a buy-out of the cruise line in 2000.

Cunard Line: Samuel Cunard founded the venerable line in 1839 to carry mail and passengers between Great Britain and North America. After a succession of owners, the company's stability was assured when Carnival bought it in 1998.

Holland America Line: Since 1873, the Dutch company has roamed the globe, carrying passengers and goods worldwide and operating its first vacation cruise in 1895. In 1989 the premium line was purchased by Carnival.

Princess Cruises: Founded by Stanley McDonald in 1965 to carry cruisers from California to Mexico, Princess burst into prominence in 1977 as star of television's The Love Boat. In 2003 Princess joined the list of Carnival-owned cruise lines.

The Yachts of Seabourn: Norwegian industrialist and luxury cruise pioneer Atle Brynestad founded Seabourn in 1987. Partially owned by Carnival since 1991, the line was acquired in full by Carnival in 1999.

DISNEY CORPORATION

Disney Cruise Line: When Disney launched their first ship in 1998, the cruise line had an instant winner with family fun and entertainment for all ages. Even Walt Disney's most beloved character, Mickey Mouse, sails on every cruise.

EASYGROUP

easyCruise: Launched in 2005 by serial entrepreneur Stelios Haji-Ioannou, no-frills easyCruise was designed for the backpacking and hostel set. It fills a niche somewhere between a budget line and flexible passenger ferry.

ROYAL CARIBBEAN CRUISES, LTD.

Celebrity Cruises: Greek shipping tycoon John D. Chandris founded premium Celebrity Cruises in 1989, in essence replacing a previous budget venture, Chandris-Fantasy Cruises. Celebrity was acquired by Royal Caribbean Cruises, Ltd. in 1997. A new deluxe subsidiary, Azamara Cruises, launched in 2007.

Royal Caribbean International: In 1969 a partnership of three Norwegian shipping firms made Wisconsin native Edwin Stephan's dream a reality, and a cruise line composed of modern, purpose-built ships was formed.

STAR CRUISES

Norwegian Cruise Line: Established in 1966 by Norwegian Knut Kloster, the former Norwegian Caribbean Line introduced regularly scheduled Caribbean cruises from Miami. Purchased by Star Cruises in 2000, NCL continues to be an industry innovator.

NIPPON YUSEN KAISHA (NYK)

Crystal Cruises: Founded in 1988 by NYK, one of the world's largest shipping companies, Crystal Cruises strives to offer its passengers the best large, luxury cruise-ship experience in the world.

MEDITERRANEAN SHIPPING COMPANY

MSC Cruises: Established in Naples in 1995, MSC is the family-run cruise division of the world's second-largest container shipping operator. Old hands in the industry, the company began operating the Starlauro line in the 1980s.

CARLSON HOSPITALITY WORLDWIDE

Regent Seven Seas Cruises: RSSC was formed in 1994 when Diamond Cruises merged with Seven Seas Cruises. Previously operating just one ship each, the resulting company has grown to be one of the world's largest luxury cruise lines.

PRIVATELY HELD

Oceania Cruises: Founded by cruise industry veterans Joe Watters and Frank Del Rio in 2003, Oceania's fleet is made up of three mid-size premium vessels. Apollo Management, a private equity fund, made a major investment in 2007.

SeaDream Yacht Club: Seabourn founder Atle Brynestad teamed up with former Seabourn President & CEO Larry Pimentel to establish SeaDream in 2001. The mega-yachts formerly sailed under the Sea Goddess name.

Silversea Cruises: The former owners of Sitmar Cruises, the Lefebvre family of Rome, launched Silversea in 1994 to deliver the most luxurious cruises on the highest-quality ships at sea.

Star Clippers: In 1990, Swedish entrepreneur Mikael Krafft realized his boyhood dream by founding Star Clippers, a modern cruise line that re-creates the golden age of sail with meticulously detailed tall sailing ships.

Windjammer Barefoot Cruises: Over 50 years in the making, the Windjammer line has been inspired by the life of legendary owner Cap'n Mike Burke. The fleet of tall ships is currently operated by Burke's children.

Windstar Cruises: Created in 1984 to offer an alternative to traditional big-ship cruises, Windstar first sailed in 1986. The unique line was sold by Carnival in 2007 to Ambassadors International, Inc., a cruise, marine, travel, and event company.

■ Large spas accompany fully equipped gyms; jogging tracks are common, as are multiple swimming pools and hot tubs.

■ Some lines still offer traditional dining, with two assigned seatings in the main restaurant for dinner. But increasily, most mainstream cruise lines have introduced variations of open seating dining and alternative restaurant options that allow passengers to dine when and with whom they please. Choice is the keyword on these ships, and you can always find something to eat, either from 24-hour room service or a variety of locations. One thing is typical, though; although generous in quantity, food is often likened to banquet-style fare.

■ Service is friendly but not necessarily polished.

■ Ideal for families, these cruise lines offer some of the most extensive programs for children and teens.

What won't you find? As a rule, sodas and bottled water are not complimentary.

Who's on board? First-timers, repeat passengers, young and old alike. Mainstream cruise lines are ideal for anyone who is looking for a fun and exhilarating vacation.

PREMIUM LINES

What you'll find. Premium lines usually offer a more subdued atmosphere and refined style:

■ Ships tend to be newer midsize to large vessels that carry fewer passengers than mainstream ships and have a more spacious feel.

■ Decor is usually more glamorous and subtle, with toned-down colors and extensive original art.

■ Staterooms range from inside cabins for three or four to outside cabins with or without balconies to suites with numerous amenities, including butlers on some lines.

■ In addition to traditional cruise activities, on-board lectures are common. Port talks often include history and cultural topics, in addition to the usual shopping advice.

■ Production shows are somewhat more sophisticated, and gentlemen hosts on some sailings keep single ladies dancing the night away.

■ An exercise or beauty regimen is a pleasure in the fully outfitted gyms and spas. Adults-only retreats and accommodations with spa amenities are a growing trend.

■ Most ships offer both two traditional assigned seatings for dinner as well as variations of open seating dining and alternative restaurant options. High marks are afforded the quality cuisine and presentation. Many ships have upscale bistros or specialty restaurants, which typically require reservations and command an additional charge. But nowadays, there's also usually a more casual dining option available.

■ Attentive service is polished and unobtrusive.

■ Programs for children and teens are well run but not as comprehensive as those found on mainstream ships because there aren't usually as many children on board.

What won't you find? The cruise staff won't bombard you with noise—announcements are kept to a minimum.

Who's on board? First-timers and experienced passengers who enjoy a more upscale experience in lower-key surroundings. Premium lines attract families, singles, and groups; however, expect the passengers to be older on average, particularly on sailings longer than 7 to 10 days.

LUXURY LINES

What you'll find. The air on these deluxe vessels is as rarified as the champagne and caviar:

■ Ships range from megayachts for only a hundred or so privileged guests to midsize vessels, which are considered large for this category. Space is so abundant that you might wonder where the other passengers are hiding.

■ Tasteful and elegant surroundings often include such touches as authentic antiques and priceless art collections.

■ Spacious staterooms are frequently all suites. On the newest ships, all cabins feature an ocean view or balcony, not to mention a high-tech entertainment center with CD or MP3 players and TVs with a VCR (yes, there are still a handful remaining) or DVD. Expect designer bath toiletries, fine linens, and fresh-cut flowers. Some lines include complimentary in-suite bar setups for all categories; butlers attend to the needs of guests in exclusive top-category suites.

■ Enrichment programs with celebrity and scholarly guest speakers and culinary classes taught by famous chefs augment traditional shipboard activities. Libraries are well stocked with books, music, and movies to borrow.

■ Evening entertainment varies by ship size, from cabaret to stylish production shows to none at all. Luxury-minded passengers tend to entertain themselves.

■ Health clubs and spas are fully equipped and staffed with professionals who bring new meaning to indulgence. After jogging or a serious workout, guests can wind down with a swim or savor a relaxing soak in generously sized hot tubs.

■ Open seating is the norm, and guests dine where and with whom they please during dinner hours. Top international chefs are tapped for their culinary expertise in designing menus to please the palate. Meals are prepared to order with the freshest high-quality ingredients and are presented with flair, just like in a top restaurant at home. Complimentary wines accompany meals on most high-end lines.

■ At this level, the service staffs anticipate their guests' desires, and it's rare that a special request goes unfulfilled.

■ Small, adult-oriented luxury cruise ships are usually inappropriate for children and teens. The lack of organized activities makes these ships undesirable for young families.

What won't you find? No one will be groveling for gratuities. If they're not already included in the fare, they are oh-so-discreetly suggested.

Who's on board? Well-off couples and singles accustomed to the best travel accommodations and service. Small groups and families gravitate to the larger vessels in this category. Traveling in style to collect exotic destinations is highly desirable to luxury-minded passengers.

CABINS

In years gone by, cabins were almost an afterthought. The general attitude of both passengers and the cruise lines used to be that a cabin is a cabin and is used only for changing clothes and sleeping. That's why the cabins on most older cruise ships are skimpy in size and short on amenities.

Until you actually get on board you may not realize that nearly every cabin on your ship is identical. How'd they do that? It's simple, really. Cruise ships are built in sections and, except for some luxury suites, the cabins are prefabricated and dropped into place with everything all ready to hook up, even the plumbing. There are some variations in size, but the main difference between cabins in the myriad price categories is location: on a higher or lower deck, forward or aft, inside or outside.

Cabins high on the ship with a commanding view fetch higher fares. But you should also know that they are also more susceptible to side-to-side movement; in rough seas you could find yourself tossed right out of bed. On lower decks, you'll pay less and find more stability, particularly in the middle of the ship.

Forward cabins have a tendency to be oddly shaped, as they follow the contour of the bow, and they may have portholes instead of picture windows. They are also likely to be noisy; when the ship's anchor drops, you won't need a wake-up call. In rough seas, you can feel the ship's pitch (its upward and downward motion) more in the front.

Should you go for the stern location instead? You're more likely to hear engine and machinery noise there, as well as feel the pitch and possibly some vibration. However, many passengers feel the view of the ship's wake (the ripples it leaves behind as its massive engines move it forward) is worth any noise or vibration they might encounter there.

No location is perfect, but midship on a lower deck is almost always preferable to the extremes—either far forward or aft.

Above all, don't be confused by all the categories listed in cruise line brochures—the categories more accurately reflect price levels based on location than any physical differences in the cabins themselves (keep repeating: prefabricated). Shipboard accommodations fall into four basic configurations: inside cabins, outside cabins, balcony cabins, and suites.

INSIDE CABINS

An inside cabin is just that: a stateroom that's located inside the ship with no window or porthole. These are always the least expensive cabins and are ideal for passengers who would rather spend their vacation funds on excursions or other incidentals than on upgraded accommodations. Inside cabins are generally just as spacious as outside cabins, and decor and amenities are similar. On the newest vessels, you may even find small refrigerators and a cozy sitting area.

To give the illusion of more space, inside cabins may have a mock window (complete with curtain) or, in the case of Disney Dream and Disney Fantasy, a monitor with the appearance of a porthole that streams a real-time video view from outside the ship. Many also rely on the generous use of mirrors for an open feeling. On NCL's *Norwegian Epic*, inside single cabins have windows onto the corridor. On *Queen Mary 2* and Royal Caribbean's largest vessels, some inside cabins feature windows overlooking the grand lobby or promenade. Although they don't offer a sea view, these cabins do provide a prime spot for watching Royal Caribbean's nighttime parades on the "street" below.

Many ships locate triple and quad cabins (accommodating three or more passengers) on the inside. Essentially, they look just like a standard double cabin but have bunk beds that either fold down from the wall or disappear into the ceiling. Parents sometimes book an inside cabin for their older children and teens, while their own cabin is an outside across the hall with a window or balcony.

For passengers who want a very dark room for sleeping, an inside cabin is ideal. Use a bit of creativity, and even your inside cabin can have a window on the sea if your ship has a television channel that features a continuous view from the bridge. Tune in that channel before you retire and turn off the sound—it will be dark all night and you will awaken with sunshine and a seascape.

OUTSIDE CABINS
A standard outside cabin has either a picture window or porthole. To give the illusion of more space, these cabins might also rely on the generous use of mirrors for an even airier feeling. In addition to the usual amenities, outside staterooms often have a small refrigerator and a sitting area.

Two twin beds can be joined together to create one large bed, the equivalent of a queen- or king-size bed. Going one step further, standard and larger outside staterooms on modern ships are often outfitted with a small sofa or love seat with a cocktail table or small side table. Some of those tables can be raised for dining. The sofas usually contain fold-out beds and can accommodate a third person. Disney Cruise Line's cabins for five even incorporate a clever Murphy bed that drops down from the wall. Floor-to-ceiling curtains that can be drawn from wall to wall to create a private sleeping space are a nice touch in some outside cabins with sitting areas. Cabins that are termed larger may have a combination bathtub-shower instead of just a shower.

BALCONY CABINS
A balcony—or veranda—cabin is an outside cabin with floor-to-ceiling glass doors that open onto a private deck. Although the cabin may have large expanses of glass, the balcony is sometimes cut out of the cabin's square footage (depending on the ship).

Balconies are usually furnished with two chairs and a table for lounging and casual dining outdoors. However, you should be aware that

CABIN FEVER: Typical Cabin Features

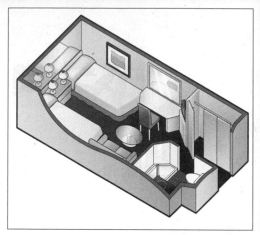

Standard Staterooms

■ There are three standard cabin types: Inside, Outside, and Balcony.

■ The average size of a standard cabin is 175–180 square feet (including the interior space devoted to bathrooms and closets).

■ Strategically placed mirrors as well as clever lighting and furniture placement give the illusion of more space.

■ Beds are usually two twins that can be combined to form a single queen (some also have a sofa bed or fold-down upper berths).

■ Furnishings typically include bedside tables and reading lamps, a combination desk–vanity table and chair or stool, and possibly a small sitting area with either a chair or love seat and coffee table.

■ Hanging closets and drawers and/or shelves are built-in for storage; you may even find unexpected storage beneath the sofa cushions as well as under the beds. Nearly all cabins have a TV and telephone (some with voice mail), an ice bucket and glassware, and many also have a small refrigerator (some are minibars).

■ Bathrooms feature open or enclosed shelves and a shower. Shampoo, lotion, and soaps or shower gel are usually provided, often in dispensers rather than individual packages.

■ A balcony is one of the most popular stateroom amenities and adds an additional dimension to a cruise—personal space with fresh air and sea breezes.

1

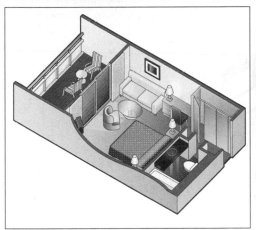

Suites

■ A suite is usually at least 300 square feet.

■ The sleeping area is separated from the living area, but often by a curtain rather than a wall.

■ Some suites have queen- or king-size beds, but often they're two twins that can be combined.

■ Furnishings include everything that's in a standard cabin, but some suites have separate dining alcoves and a butler's pantry. There's often a DVD, VCR, or CD player.

■ Minibars are usually stocked, but the contents are not always complimentary.

■ Storage is generally abundant and many suites have walk-in closets.

■ Bathrooms also contain generous storage and usually a bathtub with shower or a separate shower.

■ Some bathrooms have twin sinks or jetted tubs.

■ A guest powder room is not uncommon in top-of-the-line suites.

■ Toiletries may carry designer labels and include a variety of shampoo,

■ conditioner, shower gel, mouthwash, and soaps.

■ Bathrobes are almost always furnished for use during the cruise.

■ Most suites have balconies; some offer access to a concierge lounge.

balconies are not always completely private. Dividers might be opaque and may not extend all the way from ceiling to floor or from the ship's hull to the railing. On some ships, including those with aft-facing balconies, the balconies are stepped like a layer cake; this means that certain balconies are visible from the decks above.

The furnishings and amenities of balcony cabins are otherwise much like those in standard outside cabins. Like outside staterooms, most balcony staterooms have a separate sitting area outfitted with a small sofa or love seat and small table. Some balcony cabins may even have a combination bathtub-shower instead of just a shower.

> **WORD OF MOUTH**
>
> "A cruise is a way for us to kick back and relax and have some time together without any cell phones, pagers, or radios beeping at us. We book ships that offer an elegant experience rather than casual or high-energy atmosphere. Also, for the Caribbean, we tend to book for the ship and stateroom rather than the ports. We spend much of the time in the cabin and on the veranda so for us booking a suite makes sense."
> —Sue C.

SUITES

Suites are the most lavish accommodations afloat, and although they are always larger than regular cabins, they do not always have separate rooms for sleeping. Some luxury ships designate all accommodations as suites, and they can range in size from about 250 to 1,500 square feet. The most expansive (and expensive) have large living rooms and separate bedrooms and may also have huge private outdoor sundecks equipped with hot tubs, changing rooms, and dining areas.

Even smaller suites (often termed minisuites) and penthouses are generous in size, and the largest villa suites on certain Norwegian Cruise Line ships are more like apartments at sea that measure an extraordinary 5,350 square feet.

Suites almost always have amenities that standard cabins do not have. True suites have separate living and sleeping areas. Depending on the cruise line, you may find a small refrigerator or minibar stocked with complimentary soft drinks, bottled water, and the alcoholic beverages of your choice. A bottle of champagne on ice almost always awaits you upon embarkation. Little extras might include afternoon tea and evening canapés delivered to you and served by a white-gloved butler.

Top-drawer suites on some ships include the luxurious touch of complimentary laundry service, in-cabin Internet connections, and complex entertainment centers with big-screen plasma TVs, DVD players, and CD stereo systems.

Expect roomy closets, abundant storage, and deluxe imported soaps and toiletries in the bathroom. The bathroom may even be outfitted with a jetted tub and separate shower. Butlers' pantries and guest powder rooms are often featured in top-suite categories.

Suite balconies are usually furnished with at least two chairs and a small table for outdoor lounging. Depending on the ship and balcony size, you may also find a table and chairs for alfresco dining and reclining chaise

CLOSE UP

Back-to-Back Sailings

One week at sea might not be enough, so go ahead and book two. Ships with alternating itineraries— Eastern Caribbean one week and Western Caribbean the next—recycle the menus weekly but won't repeat any (or many) ports of call.

Between the time the first cruise ends and the second begins, there are a few things to take into account depending on the cruise line, the port, and customs procedures. Sometimes you're issued a new key–charge card by the purser and invited to relax on board the ship; other times you might have to go into the terminal and check back in. You might even need to get off the ship, go through customs, and then complete the normal boarding process. You'll be informed a day or two before the turnaround, but in any case you do not have to pack up your belongings unless you're changing cabins.

---

longues for sunbathing. These balconies do not always offer 100% privacy. Dividers might be opaque or might not extend all the way from ceiling to floor or from the ship's hull to the railing.

An added bonus to the suite life is the extra level of services many ships offer. At the least you should expect priority boarding and disembarkation, concierge service during the cruise, and top consideration when making restaurant and spa reservations. Even space on sold-out shore excursions may be available to you, or you might be bumped to the top of the waiting list. Some suites come with butler service; the butler can handle tasks from valet services and unpacking your suitcases to daily delivery of tea and hors d'oeuvres. Your butler will make all your reservations for you.

Buyer beware: Most so-called minisuites are usually little more than slightly larger versions of standard balcony cabins and don't often include extra services you can get in regular suites. Sometimes you don't even get more elaborate amenities. They're still generally a good value for the price if space matters.

ITINERARIES

One-week Caribbean cruises come in three distinct flavors: Eastern, Western, and Southern. Longer cruises of 10 and 11 nights are frequently called something like Caribbean Circle or Exotic Caribbean. Short cruises of less than a week generally include ports in the Bahamas and sometimes Key West, Florida.

The Eastern Caribbean is often the choice of first-time cruisers and those veterans who relish more at-sea days. Three, sometimes four, ports of call generally include St. Thomas, St. Maarten, San Juan, and, possibly, a stop at the cruise line's private island for a beach party.

For passengers who consider snorkeling and scuba diving a high priority, the Western Caribbean offers the best options. Typical Western

SHIPS BY ITINERARY AND HOME PORT			
SHIP	HOME PORT	CRUISE LENGTH	ITINERARY
Azamara Cruises			
Azamara Journey	Miami, FL	12 nights	Southern Caribbean
Carnival Cruise Lines			
Carnival Conquest	New Orleans, LA	7 nights	Western Caribbean
Carnival Destiny	Miami, FL	4 or 5 nights	Eastern or Western Caribbean
Carnival Dream	Port Canaveral, FL	7 nights	Eastern or Western Caribbean
Carnival Ecstasy	Port Canaveral, FL	4 or 5 nights	Bahamas and Key West
Carnival Elation	New Orleans, LA	4 or 5 nights	Western Caribbean
Carnival Fantasy	Charleston, SC	5, 6, or 7 nights	Western Caribbean
Carnival Fascination	Jacksonville, FL	4 nights	Bahamas
		5 nights	Bahamas and Key West
Carnival Freedom	Fort Lauderdale, FL	8 nights	Eastern or Western Caribbean
		6 nights	Western Caribbean
Carnival Glory	Miami, FL	7 nights	Eastern or Western Caribbean
Carnival Imagination	Miami, FL	4 nights	Western Caribbean
		3 nights	Bahamas
Carnival Legend	Tampa, FL	7 nights	Western Caribbean
Carnival Liberty	Miami, FL	7 nights	Eastern or Western Caribbean
Carnival Magic	Galveston, TX	7 nights	Western Caribbean
Carnival Miracle	Fort Lauderdale, FL	8 nights	Southern Caribbean
	New York, NY	8 nights	Eastern Caribbean
Carnival Paradise	Tampa, FL	4 or 5 nights	Western Caribbean
Carnival Pride	Baltimore, MD	7 nights	Bahamas or Eastern Caribbean
Carnival Sensation	Port Canaveral, FL	3 or 4 nights	Bahamas
Carnival Triumph	Galveston, TX	4 or 5 nights	Western Caribbean
Carnival Valor	Miami, FL	6 or 8 nights	Eastern, Western, or Southern Caribbean
Carnival Victory	San Juan, PR	7 nights	Southern Caribbean

SHIP	HOME PORT	CRUISE LENGTH	ITINERARY
Celebrity Cruises			
Celebrity Constellation	Miami, FL	14 nights	Southern Caribbean
Celebrity Eclipse	Miami, FL	7 nights	Eastern Caribbean
Celebrity Equinox	Fort Lauderdale, FL	10 or 11 nights	Southern Caribbean
Celebrity Millennium	Miami, FL	4 or 5 nights	Southern Caribbean
Celebrity Silhouette	Cape Liberty, NJ	12	Eastern or Southern Caribbean
Celebrity Solstice	Fort Lauderdale, FL	7 nights	Eastern or Western Caribbean
Celebrity Summit	San Juan, PR	7 nights	Southern Caribbean
Costa Cruises			
Costa Atlantica	Miami, FL	10 nights	Western Caribbean
Crystal Cruises			
Crystal Serenity	Miami, FL	14 nights	Western, Southern Caribbean, and Panama Canal
Crystal Symphony	Miami, FL	10 nights	Eastern Caribbean
Cunard Line			
Queen Mary 2	New York, NY	15 nights	Eastern Caribbean
Queen Victoria	Fort Lauderdale, FL	11 to 15 nights	Eastern, Southern Caribbean, and Panama Canal
Disney Cruise Line			
Disney Dream	Port Canaveral, FL	3, 4, or 5 nights	Bahamas
Disney Fantasy	Port Canaveral, FL	7 nights	Eastern or Western Caribbean
Disney Magic	Port Canaveral, FL	7 nights	Eastern or Western Caribbean
	New York, NY	8 nights	Bahamas
	Galveston, TX	7 nights	Western Caribbean
Holland America Line			
Amsterdam	Fort Lauderdale, FL	7 nights	Eastern Caribbean
		10 nights	Southern Caribbean
Eurodam	Fort Lauderdale, FL	7 nights	Eastern Caribbean
Maasdam	Fort Lauderdale, FL	10 nights	Eastern Caribbean
	Fort Lauderdale, FL	11, 14, or 25 nights	Southern Caribbean
	Fort Lauderdale, FL	21, 24, or 35 nights	Eastern and Southern Caribbean

SHIP	HOME PORT	CRUISE LENGTH	ITINERARY
Nieuw Amsterdam	Fort Lauderdale, FL	7 nights	Eastern or Western Caribbean
Noordam	Fort Lauderdale, FL	10 or 11 nights	Southern Caribbean
Ryndam	Tampa, FL	7 or 14 nights	Western Caribbean
Statendam	Fort Lauderdale, FL	10 to 28 nights	Southern Caribbean and Panama Canal
Westerdam	Fort Lauderdale, FL	7 nights	Eastern or Southern Caribbean
Zuiderdam	Fort Lauderdale, FL	10 or 11 nights	Southern Caribbean and Panama Canal
MSC Cruises			
MSC Poesia	Fort Lauderdale, FL	7 nights	Eastern or Western Caribbean
Norwegian Cruise Line			
Norwegian Dawn	Tampa, FL	7 nights	Western Caribbean
	Miami, FL	10 nights	Southern Caribbean
Norwegian Epic	Miami, FL	7 nights	Eastern or Western Caribbean
Norwegian Gem	New York, NY	7 nights	Bahamas and Florida
	New York, NY	10 nights	Eastern Caribbean
Norwegian Jewel	Miami, FL	7 nights	Eastern and Western Caribbean
	New York, NY	7 nights	Bahamas and Florida
Norwegian Pearl	Miami, FL	7 nights	Western Caribbean
Norwegian Sky	Miami, FL	3 or 4 nights	Bahamas
Norwegian Star	New Orleans, LA	7 nights	Western Caribbean
Norwegian Sun	Port Canaveral, FL	7 nights	Eastern or Western Caribbean
Oceania Cruises			
Marina	Miami, FL	10 or 12 nights	Eastern and Southern Caribbean
Regatta	Miami, FL	10 nights	Eastern Caribbean
Princess Cruises			
Caribbean Princess	San Juan, PR	7 nights	Southern Caribbean
Coral Princess	Fort Lauderdale, FL	14 nights	Panama Canal
Crown Princess	Galveston, TX	7 nights	Western Caribbean
Emerald Princess	Fort Lauderdale, FL	10 nights	Eastern or Southern Caribbean

SHIP	HOME PORT	CRUISE LENGTH	ITINERARY
Grand Princess	Fort Lauderdale, FL	7 nights	Eastern or Southern Caribbean
Island Princess	Fort Lauderdale, FL	10 nights	Southern Caribbean and Panama Canal
Ruby Princess	Fort Lauderdale, FL	7 nights	Eastern Caribbean
Regent Seven Seas Cruises			
Seven Seas Navigator	Fort Lauderdale, FL	10 or 11 nights	Eastern or Western Caribbean
Royal Caribbean International			
Adventure of the Seas	San Juan, PR	7 nights	Southern Caribbean
Allure of the Seas	Fort Lauderdale, FL	7 nights	Eastern or Western Caribbean
Enchantment of the Seas	Baltimore, MD	12 nights	Southern Caribbean
Explorer of the Seas	Cape Liberty, NJ	10 nights	Eastern Caribbean
	Cape Liberty, NJ	11 nights	Southern Caribbean
Freedom of the Seas	Port Canaveral, FL	7 nights	Eastern or Western Caribbean
Grandeur of the Seas	Colón, Panama	7 nights	Southern Caribbean
Jewel of the Seas	Tampa, FL	4 or 5 nights	Western Caribbean
Liberty of the Seas	Fort Lauderdale, FL	4 or 5 nights	Western Caribbean
Majesty of the Seas	Miami, FL	3 nights	Bahamas
	Miami, FL	4 nights	Bahamas and Key West
Mariner of the Seas	Galveston, TX	7 nights	Western Caribbean
Monarch of the Seas	Port Canaveral, FL	3 or 4 nights	Bahamas
Oasis of the Seas	Fort Lauderdale, FL	7 nights	Eastern or Western Caribbean
Serenade of the Seas	San Juan, PR	7 nights	Southern Caribbean
Voyager of the Seas	New Orleans, LA	7 nights	Western Caribbean
Seabourn Cruise Line			
Seabourn Quest	Fort Lauderdale, FL	13 or 14 nights	Southern Caribbean
Seabourn Sojourn	Fort Lauderdale, FL	10 nights	Southern Caribbean
Seabourn Spirit	Fort Lauderdale, FL	7 to 14 nights	Southern Caribbean
	St. Thomas, USVI	5 to 19 nights	Southern Caribbean

SHIP	HOME PORT	CRUISE LENGTH	ITINERARY
SeaDream Yacht Club			
SeaDream I	San Juan, PR	7 nights	Southern Caribbean
	St. Thomas, USVI	7 nights	Southern Caribbean
	Marigot, St. Martin	7 nights	Southern Caribbean
	St. John's, Antigua	7 nights	Southern Caribbean
SeaDream II	San Juan, PR	7 or 8 nights	Southern Caribbean
	St. Thomas, USVI	6, 7, or 8 nights	Southern Caribbean
	Marigot, St. Martin	7 nights	Southern Caribbean
	Bridgetown, Barbados	7 or 9 nights	Southern Caribbean
Silversea Cruise Line			
Silver Cloud	Fort Lauderdale, FL	8, 9, or 10 nights	Southern Caribbean
	Bridgetown, Barbados	9 or 10 nights	Southern Caribbean
	San Juan, PR	7 nights	Southern Caribbean
Silver Spirit	Bridgetown, Barbados	9 nights	Southern Caribbean
	Fort Lauderdale, FL	7 to 14 nights	Southern Caribbean
Silver Whisper	Fort Lauderdale, FL	9 to 15 nights	Southern Caribbean
	Bridgetown, Barbados	7 nights	Southern Caribbean
Star Clippers			
Royal Clipper	Bridgetown, Barbados	7 or 10 nights	Southern Caribbean
Star Clipper	Phillipsburg, St. Maarten	7 nights	Southern Caribbean
Windstar Cruises			
Wind Spirit	Bridgetown, Barbados	7 nights	Southern Caribbean
Wind Surf	Phillipsburg, St. Maarten	7 nights	Southern Caribbean

Caribbean ports include Key West, Jamaica, Grand Cayman, Cozumel, Roatan (Honduras), and sometimes a private island.

Southern Caribbean cruises afford the choice of more island destinations—usually as many as five. Often embarking in San Juan, ships on Southern Caribbean itineraries may call on Antigua, Aruba, Barbados, Tortola, Virgin Gorda, Curaçao, Grenada, Martinique, St. Barths, St. Kitts, St. Lucia, and sometimes St. Thomas or St. Maarten. When sailing from a Florida port of embarkation, a Southern Caribbean cruise is generally longer, often 10 to 12 nights.

Abundant sunny days and balmy nights make the Caribbean an ideal vacation destination any time of year. Even brief late afternoon tropical showers simply sweeten the air without overly dampening spirits. However, experienced cruisers know that storms can crop up at the most inopportune times. Passengers numbering in the hundreds of thousands embark on cruises during the official hurricane season, from June

1 through November 30, without a thought about storms on land or at sea. For some, it's the only time of year they can schedule a family vacation. Others don't give it a second thought. After all, the official hurricane season consumes a full six months of the year.

Although it's something to ponder in terms of comfort and convenience, most travelers do not let hurricane season stand in the way of scheduling a cruise during that time frame. Chances are, you'll never encounter a problem, and a ship at sea is not necessarily the worst place to be when a hurricane is looming over the horizon. Modern cruise ships are equipped with sophisticated communications gear and receive regular weather bulletins and storm advisories. Your ship will have the equipment necessary to ensure your safety.

When a hurricane is imminent, your major concern should be your embarkation port. When a hurricane barrels down on your embarkation city, flights in and out are certain to be delayed or cancelled by airport closures. Assuming you made it to the ship and have sailed, the itinerary will often be modified as necessary to avoid storms. If a hurricane has a tryst with one of your Caribbean port stops, you will alter course to a different (and possibly more interesting) port. In the extreme, you could end up in the Western Caribbean when your planned itinerary is the Eastern Caribbean. The ship will go where the captain and crew feel it is safest. Your very life depends on their judgment, and they take that responsibility seriously. It's a big ocean out there; happily, there's a lot of room for your ship to maneuver safely.

KEEPING IN TOUCH

No longer do passengers have to depend on the Marconi operator in the radio room to send telegraphed ship-to-shore messages. Technology has gone to sea in a big way, and connecting with your family or business from a modern cruise ship is as close as the direct-dial telephone in your cabin. However, since rates vary from a low of $6 to as much as $15 *per minute*, most passengers agree that it's best to reserve their cabin telephone for emergency use only.

The ability to use your own mobile phone from the high seas is a communication alternative that is gaining popularity. It's also cheaper than using a cabin phone if your ship offers the service. Rates from your ship at sea may range from $2.50 to $5 per minute, or more. And this is true even if your own mobile phone company provides the roaming service aboard your ship. When in port, depending on the agreements your home mobile service provider has established, you may be able to connect to local networks.

Email is likely to be the least expensive way to stay in touch, even though charges on board can be expensive. Cruise ship computer systems vary widely, and the speed can be maddeningly slow at times. Most ships have a dedicated Internet center where you can go online using the ship's computers; some ships have in-cabin broadband data ports or wireless systems that allow you to use your own laptop or one you can rent on board in your cabin or in public "hot spots." Packages that

CLOSE UP

Taking Your Toddler to Sea

Cruise ships are wonderful places for family vacations, but you must understand the rules before promising your littlest sailors unlimited playtime, either in the kid's program or the swimming pool. Nothing is sadder than the face of a toddler who isn't allowed in the ship's pool—even the kiddy pool—because he or she isn't potty-trained. Even swim diapers won't pass muster in most cases.

Cruise ships must comply with the Center for Disease Control's (CDC) Vessel Sanitation Program (VSP) regulations. Charged with the prevention of pool contamination and the resulting spread of bacteria that can cause illness after "accidents" in pools and water parks at sea, the VSP provides health and safety requirements to cruise lines, including the ban on *any* diapers in the pools.

The straight poop is that swim diapers are not completely leak-proof. They can prevent solids from escaping,

but cannot contain urine or diarrhea completely, nor do they stop seepage of infection-causing germs.

However, not all cruise ships entirely ban water play for youngsters who are not potty-trained. Special wading pools approved by VSP standards have their own separate water and disinfection systems and heavy-duty filtration units that can be "flushed out" when diaper accidents occur. Such splash zones are found on all Disney Cruise Line *ships* and on Royal Caribbean's *Freedom of the Seas, Liberty of the Seas,* and *Independence of the Seas.*

About those kids' programs: Check the Cruise Line Profiles for age limits—some are as low as two years of age, but most will accept only children three and older. While being toilet trained isn't always a prerequisite for participation, only the counselors on Disney Cruise Line and Carnival Cruise Lines will change diapers.

---

include a flat rate for a block of time are usually available and reduce the per-minute cost.

A few ships still don't have these high-tech communication options, but you won't be cut off totally even then. Some ships offer only a simple email service and charge per email message sent and received. Once on shore, you can find Internet cafés with high-speed connections, often located near the cruise ship pier; almost any crew member can point the way to them.

Planning
Your Cruise

WORD OF MOUTH

"Before booking a cabin guarantee, you should look at the deck plan and find the worst cabin in that category. Would you be okay with that cabin? If so, then go with the guarantee knowing you'd be okay with the worst cabin just in case you get it."

—pet lover

"I am not so crazy about the big ships, but there is a whole industry out there for a reason. Some people LOVE them! You just have to figure out which type you are."

—Tango

With something for everyone and the option to do nothing at all, cruises are truly the best of all vacation styles for travel companions with different interests. Onboard, you may do as much or as little as you please. Off the ship, there's always a new destination over the horizon to tempt you to explore. You only have to unpack once, and the most important item on your list of things to do is getting back to the ship on time after a day in port.

So you know you want to take a cruise, yet the choices you face seem endless. Whether you give it much thought, you probably realize every vacation is about more than money. In addition to spending your hard-earned cash, you're spending your time, and that can be priceless. You could be disappointed if you don't plan wisely. By making informed choices you're less likely to waste your money and precious vacation time.

DOING RESEARCH

Years before the Internet became a savvy traveler's primary information resource, brochures, obtained either from travel agencies or ordered directly from cruise lines, were often the first glimpse of what potential passengers might expect on cruise vacations. In some cases, they still are.

Open any cruise brochure and you're sure to find a dizzying display of information and photographs. What you want are simple facts, organized in an informative manner. What are you likely to find?

First of all, you have to select the right brochure. Although some cruise lines feature their entire fleet and all itineraries in one volume, others publish brochures for specific destinations. Brochures are enticing books, and, fortunately, most contain a table of contents, listing such topics as staterooms, dining options, onboard facilities, activities, entertainment, and children's programs up front.

What more do potential passengers want to know? They want simple facts in language they can follow. Can you bring a bottle of champagne to celebrate a special occasion? Or will one be provided free for the asking? What should you pack to be appropriately dressed? What do the staterooms look like? What is included in the fare (and what is not)? And, most important, what happens if you must cancel in case of an emergency? For answers to those questions and more, begin reading in the *back* of the brochure.

You probably would not start reading a mystery novel on the last page, but if you immediately turn to the last few pages of a cruise brochure you will find the so-called fine print, which everyone needs to know or at least should want to find out. The section may be titled "Things to know before you go," "What you need to know," "Important policies," or even "Terms and conditions." Read it! Read it closely. Also look toward the back of the brochure for details about Air & Sea transportation programs, insurance, and amenity packages to enhance your cruise. Answers to frequently asked questions can be found simply by thumbing through the brochure from back to front.

After absorbing the facts, go back to the front pages of the brochure and take a good look at the illustrations. Would you be happy to share a cruise with the people pictured? Although they are more likely than not models, those people *could* be your shipmates. A brochure that features children in a majority of photos is giving you a solid hint that the cruise line caters to families. Similarly, representations of stylish middle-aged or older couples hint at a particular demographic the line is recruiting.

And here's another thing about those pictures: As a rule, accommodations look exactly like the brochure illustrations and are perfectly adequate for the average passenger; however, most people find their staterooms are somewhat smaller than what they expected. Wide-angle lenses help photographers capture the small space on film, but they also make the cabin appear larger than it is in reality.

Location, location, location. Think of a deck plan as a map of a ship, which, unlike a road map, can give a fairly precise idea of what features the neighborhood will hold, particularly when it's time to select a cabin.

A brief description of ports of call and shore excursions is a practicality covered in most brochures. Ports and itineraries are an important factor in most travelers' cruise selection. The brochures of port-intensive cruise lines tend to provide a tad more insight into the destinations and have more shore-excursion descriptions than their contemporary fun-in-the-sun cousins.

Cruise line Web sites are also excellent resources for decision making and planning. Web sites often display even more current information than brochures, which are printed far in advance. In addition, detailed ports of call and shore excursion information is often more extensive online than in brochures.

Still, for the latest information and answers to your questions, a trusted travel agent is a cruise passenger's best tool.

PLANNING FOR YOUR SPECIAL NEEDS

Who takes cruises these days? Some passengers arrive with more in mind than getting a suntan. Couples not only honeymoon on cruises, but they get married on ships or in ports of call. People with disabilities are drawn to the ease of travel by ship, and singles find the atmosphere conducive to making friends. Same-sex couples can blend into the mix just as easily as large groups and multigeneration families. But if you have a special interest or need, you may want to consider some specific things to make your cruise a satisfying experience.

CRUISE LINES AT A GLANCE

Before you narrow your search to a few specific ships, you want the assurance that you aren't looking at the wrong cruise line. To help you decide which cruise line might be most appropriate for you, we have rated several areas important to most passengers on a scale of 5 (most suitable) to 0 (no options) indicated by the ▲ symbols on the chart at right. A lower number doesn't necessarily indicate an inferior product, however. A cruise line that offers programs for children seasonally will have a lower Family Friendly rating. Although it might have wonderful playrooms with well-planned activities, it will probably be less appealing than a cruise line that caters to families year-round.

Even within a single cruise line's fleet, individual ship facilities can vary widely. The newest vessels often have more dining and entertainment choices and the latest in high-tech gadgetry and gizmos. Look for a general overview here before exploring the details outlined in our Cruise Line Profiles and Cruise Ship Reviews in Chapter 5.

Short cruises are defined as less than seven nights. They are great getaways for busy people as well as a way to sample cruising before committing to a full week, or even longer, at sea.

Although fares are usually quoted per person for an entire cruise, pricing is ultimately based on double occupancy per cabin. For that reason—and also because cruises vary in length—we have simplified our cost ranges to reflect the realistic price of a cabin per night for two passengers. Even fares within a cabin type (inside or outside) vary depending on location, and you may find the category you select is at the high end of a price range even if entry-level fares fall in the lower end.

CRUISE LINE	Cost-Inside Cabin	Cost-Outside Cabin
Azmara Cruises	$$	$$
Carnival Cruise Lines	$	$$
Celebrity Cruises	$$	$$
Costa Cruises	$	$$
Crystal Cruises		$$$$
Cunard Line	$$	$$$
Disney Cruise Line	$$	$$$
Holland America Line	$$	$$$
MSC Cruises	$	$$
Norwegian Cruise Line	$	$$
Oceania Cruises	$$	$$$
Princess Cruises	$	$$
Regent Seven Seas Cruises		$$$$$
Royal Caribbean International	$	$$
Seabourn Cruise Line		$$$$$
SeaDream Yacht Club		$$$$$
Silversea Cruises		$$$$$
Star Clippers	$$$	$$$$
Windstar Cruises		$$$$

Key to Costs:

$$$$$	over $600
$$$$	$450–$600
$$$	$300–$450
$$	$200–$300
$	$125–$200

Short Cruises	Fine Dining	Service	Lectures/Enrichment Programs	Entertainment/ Shows	Family Friendly	Accessible	Spa	Sports Facilities
	▲▲▲▲	▲▲▲▲	▲▲▲▲	▲▲		▲▲▲	▲▲▲▲	▲▲
x	▲▲▲▲	▲▲▲		▲▲▲▲▲	▲▲▲▲▲	▲▲▲	▲▲▲▲	▲▲▲▲▲
x	▲▲▲▲	▲▲▲▲	▲▲▲	▲▲▲	▲▲▲	▲▲▲	▲▲▲▲	▲▲▲
	▲▲	▲▲	▲▲	▲▲▲	▲▲	▲▲▲	▲▲▲	▲▲
	▲▲▲▲▲	▲▲▲▲▲	▲▲▲▲▲	▲▲▲	▲▲	▲▲▲▲	▲▲▲▲	▲▲▲
	▲▲▲▲	▲▲▲▲	▲▲▲▲	▲▲▲	▲▲▲	▲▲▲▲	▲▲▲▲▲	▲▲▲
x	▲▲▲▲	▲▲▲▲	▲▲▲	▲▲▲▲▲	▲▲▲▲▲	▲▲▲▲	▲▲▲▲▲	▲▲▲▲
	▲▲▲▲	▲▲▲▲	▲▲▲▲	▲▲▲	▲▲▲	▲▲▲▲	▲▲▲▲	▲▲▲▲
	▲▲	▲▲▲	▲▲▲	▲▲▲	▲▲	▲▲	▲▲▲	▲▲▲
	▲▲▲	▲▲▲		▲▲▲▲▲	▲▲▲▲▲	▲▲▲	▲▲▲▲	▲▲▲▲▲
	▲▲▲▲	▲▲▲▲	▲▲▲	▲▲		▲▲▲	▲▲▲	▲▲
	▲▲▲▲	▲▲▲	▲▲▲▲	▲▲▲	▲▲▲▲	▲▲▲▲▲	▲▲▲▲	▲▲▲▲
x	▲▲▲▲▲	▲▲▲▲▲	▲▲▲▲	▲▲▲		▲▲▲▲	▲▲▲▲▲	▲▲▲
x	▲▲▲	▲▲▲		▲▲▲▲▲	▲▲▲▲▲	▲▲▲▲	▲▲▲▲	▲▲▲▲▲
	▲▲▲▲▲	▲▲▲▲▲	▲▲▲▲▲	▲▲		▲▲	▲▲▲▲	▲▲▲▲
	▲▲▲▲▲	▲▲▲▲▲	▲▲	▲▲		▲	▲▲▲▲	▲▲▲
x	▲▲▲▲▲	▲▲▲▲▲	▲▲▲▲	▲▲▲		▲▲▲	▲▲▲▲	▲▲▲
	▲▲▲▲	▲▲▲▲					▲▲▲	
	▲▲▲▲	▲▲▲▲▲		▲▲▲			▲▲	▲▲▲

Cruise Line Contacts

You can obtain cruise brochures from your travel agent or directly from the cruise line. Here are the phone numbers and Web sites for all the cruise lines covered in this book:

Azamara Club Cruises (☎ 877/999–9553 ⊕ www.azamaraclubcruises.com)

Carnival Cruise Lines (☎ 800/227–6482 ⊕ www.carnival.com)

Celebrity Cruises (☎ 800/437–3111 ⊕ www.celebrity.com)

Costa Cruises (☎ 800/462–6782 ⊕ www.costacruise.com)

Crystal Cruises (☎ 888/799–4625 ⊕ www.crystalcruises.com)

Cunard Line (☎ 800/728–6273 ⊕ www.cunard.com)

Disney Cruise Line (☎ 888/325–2500 ⊕ www.disneycruise.com)

Holland America Line (☎ 800/577–1728 ⊕ www.hollandamerica.com)

MSC Cruises (☎ 800/666–9333 ⊕ www.msccruises.com)

Norwegian Cruise Line (☎ 800/327–7030 ⊕ www.ncl.com)

Oceania Cruises (☎ 800/531–5658 ⊕ www.oceaniacruises.com)

Princess Cruises (☎ 800/774–6237 ⊕ www.princess.com)

Regent Seven Seas Cruises (☎ 877/505–5370 ⊕ www.rssc.com)

Royal Caribbean International (☎ 800/327–6700 ⊕ www.royalcaribbean.com)

Seabourn Cruise Line (☎ 800/929–9391 ⊕ www.seabourn.com)

SeaDream Yacht Club (☎ 800/707–4911 ⊕ www.seadreamyachtclub.com)

Silversea Cruises (☎ 800/722–9955 ⊕ www.silversea.com)

Star Clippers (☎ 800/442–0551 ⊕ www.starclippers.com)

Windstar Cruises (☎ 877/827–7245 ⊕ www.windstarcruises.com)

HONEYMOONS AND ANNIVERSARIES

With a little careful planning, any cruise can be turned into a special event—a heavenly honeymoon, a renewal of your commitment to each other, or a celebration of a special anniversary.

Cruise lines are certainly aware of the magical effects their vessels have on couples. Nearly all offer options in the way of romance or anniversary packages that can be arranged ahead of time through your travel agent. Packages may include goodies such as a bottle of champagne in your stateroom, logo robes to keep, his-and-hers spa treatments, formal portraits in elegant frames, or breakfast in bed on the morning of your choice. Renewals of vows are sometimes performed privately by the captain upon arrangement or in a festive group setting, followed by a champagne toast to your commitment.

Your very own balcony is the ideal setting for spending time alone together; why not also share a room service meal surrounded by sea sounds? Princess Cruises adds a twist to make the occasion even more memorable—Ultimate Balcony Dining. You choose either a champagne

CLOSE UP

Brochure Speak

Some armchair brochure browsers become enraptured with such descriptions as "crystalline waters" and "historic wonders." These are just some of the buzz words employed to entice you to set sail. But other phrases hint at more practical considerations, and it's helpful to know how to decode the brochure's language:

■ A port of embarkation that is close by—or relatively close to home—means you can drive to your cruise or at least find a convenient, and possibly cheap, airline flight. Look for "homeland cruises" and "convenient departure ports" described in the brochures.

■ The term "all-inclusive" is a misnomer that is rarely, if ever, found in a cruise brochure and only found in practice on some luxury lines. Think *nearly* all-inclusive and be sure to reread the fine print.

■ "Floating resorts" are cruise ships that offer everything from rock-climbing walls and miniature golf courses to facilities and activities that appeal to a wide range of age groups. These are usually the biggest and most modern vessels at sea. Other ships may be a bit older, but that does not mean they are less well equipped to offer the expected amenities, activities, and entertainment.

■ "Choices" are substantially hyped, especially when it comes to dining. It's your vacation, and you should be able to choose where to eat and what to wear, within reason. On days when you have been ashore, are tired, or just do not feel like dressing up, it's nice to have the choice of casual dining versus the more prim-and-proper directive to either dress up for a meal in the restaurant or stay in your room.

■ "Gourmet dining" is a bit too wishful for what you'll normally get on a mainstream cruise. Unless the cruise is on a smaller, extremely exclusive (and expensive) ship, meals are more likely to resemble very good, high-quality banquet food than the made-to-order meals of shoreside gourmet establishments. There's definitely true gourmet dining at sea, but not on every ship.

■ "Fine dining" is something you can often find on a mainstream cruise, but it usually comes with an additional price tag. Some alternative restaurants carry cover charges ranging from nominal to hefty.

■ "Spacious" is in the eye of the beholder. Only the top-category accommodations on many ships afford the spaciousness of an average hotel room. Look for stateroom diagrams and the square footage of your chosen stateroom category, which may or may not be indicated in the brochure.

■ "Elegance" and "luxury" are, again, in the eye of the beholder. A typical Las Vegas resort is not the same as a Miami Beach art deco–era hotel, although each has its own appeal for different tastes. Determine your priorities and make your ship selection carefully.

■ "Fun" is subjective. No one goes on a vacation not to have fun.

■ "Rack rate" fares are never the bottom line. Don't expire from sticker shock—you can expect to pay much less than brochure rate, often as much as half off the published price, depending on when you book your cruise.

2

Planning the Perfect Wedding

Andrea and her fiancé were on a Carnival cruise when she caught a very brief glimpse of a bride and was smitten with the idea of being married on a cruise ship. "Carnival was the first place I called for details," she said. "It was a pleasant surprise to find out they had a whole wedding department. I did no comparison shopping because I knew this was the way I had to do it." Andrea's friends who were also planning weddings spent nearly twice as much on their nuptials as her dream cruise ship ceremony. First she dealt with the cruise line's wedding department: "Carnival assigns you to a wedding coordinator at a company called A Wedding For You. I worked with two women from there. My travel agent did some planning also."

There were 100 wedding guests on board for Andrea's big day, and 57 of them sailed with the newlyweds. Andrea was thrilled: "What a great time!! It was more like a four-day reception! You are allowed as many sailing guests as you want; however,

only 50 people can come aboard to just see the wedding. As soon as the ship was cleared, everyone was allowed to board. We were on the ship by 11:30 and the wedding was at 1. Because the guests boarded so early, we were able to schedule a cocktail hour in the lounge. It worked out nicely. The only drawback was that I wish the actual reception afterward was longer. It was only an hour and a half."

Andrea took advantage of ordering her bouquet and the men's boutonnieres through Carnival and was delighted but said, "It would have cost a fortune to get bouquets for all seven bridesmaids as well, so we did that on our own. You need to keep in mind that you are not allowed to bring fresh flowers on board the ship—they must be silk. Another snag was the ship only had one videographer, and another wedding on the ship that day booked before we did, so they got his services. Your best bet is to book early!"

breakfast ($32 per couple) or a multicourse dinner ($100 per couple) and prepare to be pampered as your own waiter serves it to you on your private balcony.

WEDDINGS

Every couple dreams of a perfect wedding, closely followed by the ideal honeymoon. For many brides and grooms, destination weddings—exchanging vows in an exotic location—are the height of perfection. Tying the knot on a cruise ship offers the best of both worlds: a wedding and honeymoon wrapped into a package that takes the worry out of planning and combines pampering with privacy for newlyweds. Cruise line wedding coordinators take the anxiety out of seemingly insurmountable tasks such as arranging for a marriage license and finding a clergyman—undertakings that assume even more importance in unfamiliar surroundings. Brides-to-be should take note that cruise weddings are increasingly popular. To avoid disappointment, start planning as soon as you've announced your engagement and set a date.

Nearly every cruise line can assist with a ceremony on the ship prior to sailing or while docked in a port of call. Wedding options vary from a simple private ceremony in an intimate ship's chapel to elaborate nuptials and a reception attended by family and friends, who might even sail with the happy couple after sharing their special day. Brides and grooms merely decide what type of wedding they want—aboard ship or ashore in a Caribbean port—and what amenities fit their budgets. The cruise line and wedding coordinator take care of the rest.

Services differ between cruise lines, so you should investigate your options before you book your cruise. Packages can include not only the ceremony but also flowers, photographs, a video recording, champagne, wedding cake, and music. Although a number of newer ships—notably those of Carnival, Costa, Norwegian Cruise Line, Princess, and Royal Caribbean—have dedicated wedding chapels, only Princess Cruises, Azamara Cruises, and Celebrity Cruises can offer the romance of a wedding at sea with the captain officiating on certain ships. Bridal couples marrying on Princess ships can even invite friends and family at home to attend the ceremony virtually by tuning into the line's Wedding Cam on the Internet.

Contacts The Wedding Experience (☎ 877/580-3556 ⊕ www. theweddingexperience.com) is the exclusive wedding service provider for Royal Caribbean International, Celebrity Cruises, Costa Cruises, Princess Cruises, Carnival Cruise Lines, Norwegian Cruise Line, Windstar Cruises, and Azamara Club Cruises.

SOLO TRAVEL

When you're watching your fellow cruisers walking up the gangway two-by-two, you may think you're cruising on Noah's Ark rather than the Love Boat. But it doesn't take long to find other singles on almost any cruise. They may be sailing on their own or in small groups or with family. However, you need not rely solely on singles get-togethers organized by the ship's social staff to meet your fellow cruisers: head to the gym, the hot tub, or the computer center, where striking up a conversation and forming friendships is less forced. Because families generally opt for the early dinner seating, request late seating and ask to be assigned to a large table to increase your opportunity to meet others. You are likely to find the maître d' has arranged tables so that passengers who appear to be traveling by themselves are seated together.

Shipboard hours are easily filled with lectures, shows, and activities where singles are urged to join in and where you can find like-minded fellow passengers. Single women may be delighted to discover the cruise line has arranged to have courtly dance hosts on board to make sure they won't be left out of the dancing and other social activities.

On port days, shore excursions are the most effortless way to see the sights, but don't discount teaming up with newly made friends to explore together independently. If you've been to a port previously, offer to lead a walking tour. Single travelers are eager to share their experiences with one another, and an informal group increases everyone's comfort level when in a new environment.

There are distinct advantages to traveling solo on a cruise ship. The desolation of hotel homesickness is unlikely to strike; plus, there's the luxury of having a stateroom with storage and amenities designed for two. There's also a major drawback: cruising single in a couple's world is pricey. With the exception of Norwegian Cruise Line's *Norwegian Epic*, most modern cruise ships do not have single cabins, and nearly all fares are based on double occupancy. Supplements for sailing solo can range from an additional 25% to 100% of the cost of the basic cruise fare, depending on cabin category and cruise line.

For certain cruises and/or cabin categories, the upscale lines Crystal, Regent Seven Seas, Seabourn, and Silversea charge a relatively low supplement to the solo cruiser's fare for occupying a double cabin. For instance, Seabourn's Run of Ship Single Savings allows guaranteed single occupancy in a Category A or higher suite at 150% or 175% of the double-occupancy fare. If you don't mind relinquishing privacy, some lines, such as Holland America Line, will match you with a roommate. In that case, you pay the lower double-occupancy rate and, if there's no one to pair you up with, you get a cabin to yourself for no additional charge. A singles roommate Match Program is also offered by Princess Cruises for occasional hosted singles cruises. Special offers waiving the single supplement are also available from time to time.

Contacts Cruise Mates (⊕ *www.cruisemates.com/articles/single/*) is an Internet-only cruise magazine and community with feature articles, a singles group cruise calendar, and message board. **SinglesCruise.com** (☎ *800/393–5000* ⊕ *www.singlescruise.com*), a member company of Carlson Travel Group, hosts singles group cruises and will match solo cruise passengers with a roommate of the same sex and smoking preference. **Singles Cruise Resource** (☎ *888/724–5123 or 303/690–8937* ⊟ *303/690–8986* ⊕ *www.singlescruiseresource.com*), an affiliate agency of Cruises, Inc., the world's largest seller of cruises, caters to the needs of singles by finding affordable cruises and reduced single-supplement fares for solo travelers.

FAMILIES

Cruising can be a rewarding family travel experience. Most parents report that their children have such a great time that they barely see them after boarding. Couples who wish to share adult time on their family cruise vacation no longer find it necessary to engage a nanny or bring along a family member to watch over their little ones. Mom can savor some well-earned beauty rest while Dad heads for a solitary jog on the deck, secure in the knowledge that the children are happy and well cared for in the youth center.

Youth programs on today's large cruise ships are staffed by counselors who have been carefully screened and chosen for their ability to relate to children; most have a background in education or early-childhood development. Their function is to provide a safe environment for

CLOSE UP

Baby on Board

Not all moms on board have checked their little ones into cruise camp—some of their babies haven't arrived yet. After baby is born, mothers do the pampering 24/7, so a cruise is the ideal prestork vacation for mothers-to-be to rest up and get pampered themselves.

Expectant moms should be aware of certain time constraints when planning a cruise. Although the stated terms and conditions vary, as a general rule cruise lines will not allow you to sail if you are from 24 to 28 weeks into your pregnancy (or will be before the cruise ends). A statement from your attending physician that establishes your due date might also be required prior to sailing. Also consider, if you're prone to seasickness, combining it with morning sickness might be a mistake.

Even after baby arrives, parents should check with the cruise line for age restrictions—most cruise lines will not allow infants younger than six months old to sail. An exception is Disney Cruise Line, which accepts babies that are at least 12 weeks old and even offers nursery facilities for them (for a fee).

2

age-appropriate play and learning, a day camp at sea. Activities vary by cruise line, but the emphasis is on enjoyable pursuits that can offer an educational bonus. Science and astronomy programs, arts and crafts projects, history and geography of the ports of call, and even training in social graces and dance are only a few of the planned pursuits. The basic complimentary programs usually last all day and, after a late afternoon break, resume in the evening; however, there's usually an hourly charge for late-night babysitting. A notable exception is Cunard Line, which provides complimentary babysitting on their ocean liners.

Not all youth programs are equally comprehensive. Most mainstream and premium cruise lines, including Carnival, Costa, Disney, Holland America, Norwegian, Princess, and Royal Caribbean, operate their programs all day on sea days, but hours may be limited on port days. Upscale lines that feature seasonal children's programs might close entirely on port days, while others offer little more than babysitting for an additional charge. The best programs schedule escorted educational shore excursions for older children and teens; both Carnival and Disney offer kid-oriented excursions in some ports of call. Disney even has regularly scheduled shoreside activities and excursions for all ages at its own private Bahamian Island, Castaway Cay.

Most children's programs are divided by age group, but infants or toddlers who aren't toilet trained generally will not be accepted. Even on ships with nurseries, counselors will rarely change diapers or assist children with their bathroom needs, due to health and legal constraints. The exceptions are Disney Cruise Line and Carnival Cruise Lines. On some ships, parents are issued a beeper to summon them in case of a problem.

Possibly the pickiest passengers on any ship are those in the 13 to 17 age group. Usually the biggest hurdle with teenagers is convincing them that any family vacation can be fun. Teens are not always keen to join group activities. However, there are probably an equal number who enjoy hanging out with others at the teen center. Unlike younger children, teens are generally free to come and go as they please in a less-structured environment. Facilities vary, but most ships have at least a video game area and computers. The newest ships have discreetly chaperoned activity centers and discos designed specifically for teens, yet with an adult flavor; vessels without them usually allow teens to dance in the adult disco until about 11 pm.

Most major cruise lines, including Royal Caribbean, Carnival, Disney, Norwegian, Princess, and Holland America, have invested substantially since the late 1990s in their teen programs. Their facilities and programs give teens a place to go to relieve the boredom that used to result in mischievous pranks (think punching elevator buttons to stop on every floor and mixing up the breakfast order tags hung outside stateroom doors late at night). For teens, there can be a lot of freedom on a ship, but there are also rules. During group activities, they are not allowed to smoke, curse, or consume alcoholic beverages. Security will step in if any vandalism or violent behavior is observed. The same is true for younger children enrolled in the ship's youth programs. Children are subject to disciplinary procedures for unacceptable actions. After a warning, a time-out may be issued, and suspension or dismissal from the program is the ultimate punishment for continued unsuitable behavior. Entire families can be put off the ship at the next port for serious infractions.

In case of an emergency, cruise line counselors are trained to institute YEP, the Youth Evacuation Program. All children under the age of 13 are issued an ID bracelet that must be worn at all times when they register with a shipboard youth program. Upon hearing the ship's emergency signal, parents are instructed to go to their muster stations, stand in the front row, and await the arrival of their children. All children are outfitted with a life jacket, escorted to their assigned muster station, and supervised until they are reunited with their parents.

The number of children on board any cruise depends a lot on the time of year: peak periods for family cruises are during school holidays and summer vacations. Be sure to attend the youth program orientation with your children and enroll them on the first day of the cruise. Prepaid soft-drink cards that allow children to order an unlimited number of fountain drinks anywhere on the ship cost about $5 a day, plus gratuity, and can be real money-savers.

Families can often save money with special discounted fares for young children occupying the same stateroom as their parents. Although infants sail free on some cruise lines, port charges are usually assessed regardless of your child's age. Holland America Line goes the extra distance for young families, providing not only high chairs, booster chairs, and cribs, but even baby food, with at least 30 days' advance notice. Families preparing to sail on Disney or Royal Caribbean with tiny travelers have access to online services that allow them to order baby supplies in advance of their cruise and have them delivered to their stateroom rather than packing them from home. Make sure you or your travel agent requests what you need, and don't forget to reserve a crib for your little one no matter what cruise line you choose.

Disney Cruise Line's staterooms were designed to be particularly family-friendly—nearly all have a split bathroom configuration with one room containing a sink and bathtub with shower and the other a sink and toilet. Norwegian Cruise Line's newest vessels have many interconnecting cabins, often several in a row—a big advantage for large families who want additional bathrooms as well as space.

2

TRAVELERS WITH DISABILITIES

As recently as the early 1990s, accessibility on a cruise ship meant little more than a few inside staterooms set aside for passengers with mobility impairments. Most public restrooms and nearly all en suite bathrooms had a step-over entryway—even passengers without mobility issues often tripped until they became accustomed to them. Even so, the overall conveniences and relative safety associated with a cruise vacation have always appealed to passengers with disabilities.

In the wake of the Americans with Disabilities Act (ADA), the cruise industry began demonstrating voluntary ADA compliance by designing new ships from the keel up with expanded accessibility in mind; now that compliance with the ADA has been declared mandatory, you can expect further measures to make cruising easier for passengers with many kinds of disabilities. Auxiliary aids, such as flashers for the hearing impaired and buzzers for visually impaired passengers, are often available on request. All ship elevators have raised Braille signage, and even some passageway handrails feature directions in Braille at regular intervals.

When evaluating a cruise, passengers with disabilities (ranging from use of a cane or walker to complete dependence on a wheelchair or reliance on a service animal) should pay particular attention not only to the facilities on board their chosen vessel but also to the conditions they are likely to find in ports of call and on shore excursions. More than the usual amount of planning is necessary for smooth sailing. To the extent possible, cruise lines attempt to accommodate guests with a wide range of disabilities. However, they cannot provide personal care and should not be expected to.

Beginning with embarkation, every effort is made to accommodate passengers who require assistance. Even so, certain ship transfer operations may not be fully accessible to wheelchairs or scooters. When a ship is unable to dock, passengers are taken ashore on tenders that are sometimes hard to negotiate even for those without mobility or sensory impairments. Some people with limited mobility may even find it difficult to embark or debark the ship when docked due to the steep angle of gangways caused by high or low tide.

PASSENGERS WHO USE SERVICE ANIMALS

Cruise lines welcome service animals aboard their fleets, and crew members often go the extra distance to provide for their comfort. However, itineraries may include ports of call that have very specific and strict rules about the importation of animals, and it will be your responsibility to find out what special requirements must be met before your service animal will be allowed off the ship.

The Caribbean islands that are the most open to allowing entry to service animals are Aruba, the Bahamas, the Cayman Islands, Curaçao, St. Maarten, Martinique, Guadeloupe, and Puerto Rico, and the Caribbean coastal areas of Venezuela, Colombia, and Mexico. Island nations that have animal quarantine regulations modeled on the British system include Antigua, Barbados, Grenada, Jamaica, St. Lucia, and Trinidad and Tobago. While it does not have a quarantine procedure, the entry policy for the Dominican Republic is in flux at this writing. The best places to obtain specific information on required documentation and immunizations are the U.S. State Department (International Travel Information), local customs offices in the specific ports, personal veterinarians, and The Seeing Eye, Inc. If your service animal does not have the proper proof of vaccinations, or if there are local quarantine requirements, it can be denied the right to leave the ship, and you'll be required to stay on board as well.

Contacts **The Seeing Eye, Inc.** (☎ 973/539–4425 ⊕ www.seeingeye.org). **U.S. Department of State, Bureau of Consular Affairs** (☎ 888/407–4747 ⊕ travel. state.gov/index.html).

PASSENGERS IN WHEELCHAIRS

All cruise lines offer a limited number of staterooms designed to be wheelchair- and/or scooter accessible. Booking a newer vessel will generally assure more choice for passengers with disabilities, including more available cabins in a larger variety of categories, some even with private verandas. Public rooms in these newer ships are more accessible, with ramps and fewer raised thresholds. Nevertheless, physical barriers in both cabins and public rooms remain in many older ships.

For persons incapable of walking, a wheelchair is generally their primary mobility aid for getting on and off the ship. In those instances, crew-member squads may offer assistance that involves carrying passengers. Situations sometimes occur when mobility-impaired passengers may not be able to go ashore at the time they prefer. Or, they may be unable to go ashore at all in certain private islands or ports such as Grand Cayman, where there's no pier and all passengers are tendered ashore. For the safety of all concerned, the ship's captain will make the final determination regarding whether it's possible to carry mobility-impaired passengers and their mobility assistance devices ashore (wheelchair, scooter, walker, etc.). The captain will take into account all appropriate conditions, including weather, the ship's location, weight of the guest, and so on.

Third-party transfer vehicles and shore excursion facilities may not be fully accessible to those with disabilities. Cruise lines attempt to deal only with companies that comply with legal requirements. However,

CLOSE UP

Family Radios

The kids are in the youth center, and you have a beeper in case the counselor feels you're needed. But where's your husband? Don't laugh . . . it happens to me all the time. We're strolling along the Lido Deck, and I ask a question. No response. No surprise. My husband has wandered off. Again. Locating him on a ship with 13 passenger decks can mean a lot of walking.

Enter the solution: a simple pair of two-way radios. By and large, they work beautifully on even the largest ships, although interior steel may stop the signal in a few spots. They're worth their weight in gold for keeping track of older children and teens. Some ships have sets for rent, and they are sold in almost any electron-

ics or computer superstore. When shopping for radios, look for:

■ **Rugged construction:** You want them to be sturdy and capable of standing up to wear and tear and dropping. Water resistance is pretty important on a ship as well.

■ **Subchannels:** These little gems are popular, and the main channels get a lot of use. You want to tune them in to a subchannel to avoid other passengers' chatter.

■ **Rechargeable batteries:** It goes without saying that batteries don't last long, even when they're on standby.

Apply common sense when using your radios. There's no need to shout "Can you hear me?" into your handset or tune the volume to an ear-splitting decibel.

---

they cannot guarantee that all those companies, particularly those contracted in foreign countries, are able to provide accessible facilities to people with disabilities.

If you need a wheelchair for mobility, bring your own; while most ships carry a limited number of wheelchairs, they generally aren't allowed off the ship and are used only during embarkation, debarkation, and in emergencies. If you need a wheelchair or scooter for mobility but aren't able to travel with it, you can rent one for the duration of your cruise.

PASSENGERS WHO REQUIRE OXYGEN

Passengers who need continuous oxygen for chronic conditions must make their own arrangements prior to travel. Cruise lines do permit oxygen to be brought on board ships for personal use, but passengers are required to provide their own oxygen in these circumstances. There are companies that regularly provide supplemental oxygen and/or oxygen equipment for cruise ship passengers. Be sure to bring the service company's address and any local contacts in your ports of call.

Contacts Advanced Aeromedical (☎ 800/346–3556 or 757/481–1590 ⊕ www.aeromedic.com) rents oxygen equipment to cruise ship passengers. **Care Vacations/Cruise Ship Assist** (☎ 877/478–7827 or 780/986–6404 ⊕ www. cruiseshipassist.com) is a Canada-based company that rents mobility equipment, including powered and unpowered wheelchairs and scooters, as well as oxygen and oxygen equipment, and provides airport and hotel transfers to passengers with disabilities. The company services most major ports of embarkation in the United States and Canada and also some ports elsewhere in the world. **Scootaround** (☎ 888/441–7575 or 204/982–0657 ⊕ www.scootaround.com) rents scooters and powered and regular wheelchairs to cruise ship passengers. The company will deliver them to your cruise ship in most North American ports of embarkation.

GAY AND LESBIAN CRUISES

Gay cruises have become a big business over the past few years. Several companies now charter entire ships several times a year for all-gay cruises, featuring such extras as special entertainment, activities, and parties tailored to their clients' unique tastes. Atlantis Events markets primarily to gay men and also owns RSVP Vacations; the cruises are different, especially because RSVP makes more of an effort to appeal to both gay men and lesbians, while Atlantis cruises are really geared solely to gay men. Olivia Cruises specializes in all-lesbian trips. R Family Vacations specializes in family trips for gay parents and their kids. Other companies simply book blocks of cabins for gay and lesbian groups and operate as any other affinity group aboard a cruise ship.

Contacts Atlantis Events (☎ 310/859–8800, 800/628–5268 reservations ⊕ www.atlantisevents.com). **Olivia Cruises & Resorts** (☎ 800/631–6277 or 415/962–5700 ⊕ www.olivia.com). **R Family Vacations** (☎ 866/732–6822 or 845/348–0397 ⊕ www.rfamilyvacations.com). **RSVP Vacations** (☎ 800/328–7787 ⊕ www.rsvpvacations.com).

NUDIST CRUISES

Nudist travel has been growing for several decades. For reasons that are obvious, all-nude cruises aren't permitted unless a group can charter the entire ship. Bare Necessities Tour & Travel is the only company that offers these cruises, usually several times a year on small- to medium-size ships. For those who are curious: yes, nude passengers must have something to sit on in public areas—a towel or, for the more discerning, an elegant silk scarf.

Contacts Bare Necessities Tour & Travel (☎ 800/743–0405 or 512/499–0405 ⊕ www.bare-necessities.com).

GROUP TRAVEL

Enterprising travel agents have long known that organizing a group is a great way to provide a reduced fare to their clients as well as earn enough free tour-conductor berths for themselves to accompany the group. However, anyone who wants to coordinate a family reunion or simply arrange a carefree vacation for friends to travel together can book a group cruise and receive a discounted rate and free berths. To qualify as a group, your party must usually include a minimum of 16 passengers in at least eight cabins (third and fourth passengers in a cabin do not count), although fewer are required on some upscale cruise lines.

As the number of cabins booked increases, the number of free berths rises proportionally. For large groups, there's also the possibility that the cruise line will kick in a few perks, such as a complimentary cocktail party. Before taking on the responsibilities involved in organizing a group cruise, you should be aware that tour conductor berths are not totally free—port charges and taxes are not included. Be sure group members know the arrangement up front and are in agreement. Some groups feel it's more equitable to split the proceeds from the tour conductor berth in order to reduce everyone's cost.

If family and friends are uninterested and your travel agent has no group cruises planned, there are other ways to reap the benefits of a group cruise fare. College alumni organizations sometimes offer group travel opportunities, as do music and sports clubs, museums, civic and church groups, and even cruise-travel Web sites. Look around for like-minded individuals and you're likely to discover that some of them have cruise plans.

Contacts Countryside Travel (☎ 800/603–5755 ⊕ www.cruisemaster.com) specializes in groups and honeymoon cruises. **Cruise Mates** (☎ 602/279–4356 ⊕ www.cruisemates.com/articles/CMcruise/) is an Internet cruise magazine and community that hosts several group cruises a year for online users; bookings are handled by highly qualified independent travel agents. **CruisePlanning.net** (☎ 800/561–0802 or 570/323–0112 ⊕ www.cruiseplanning.net) is a member of the Cruise Planners network that specializes in group cruises. **Jazz Cruises LLC** (☎ 888/852–9987 ⊕ www.jazzcruises-ecp.com) specializes in full-ship charters focused on jazz and popular music. **Sixthman** (☎ 877/749–8462 ⊕ www. sixthman.net) specializes in full-ship charters with an emphasis on celebrating music and fan communities. **Skyscraper Tours, Inc.** (☎ 877/442–5659 ⊕ www. skyscrapertours.com) offers several annual hosted group cruises. **Whet Travel Inc.** (☎ 877/438–9438 ⊕ www.whettravel.com) specializes in large affinity groups interested in music and dance.

PAYING FOR YOUR TRIP

When shopping for a cruise, don't overlook strategies to save money. Watch the travel section of your Sunday newspaper for cruise line promotions, and get quotes from several sources, such as local and Internet travel agencies, for comparison.

Take advantage of your buying power as well. Senior citizens often qualify for discounts, as do airline employees, who are eligible for low rates from interline agents that serve the airline industry. Residents of certain states (particularly those that have cruise ports) are often able to obtain discounted fares during advertised promotions. Some credit card companies reward their users with travel point programs that can be used for substantial fare reductions or even free cruises. If you're on active military duty, retired from military service, a first responder (police officer, firefighter, paramedic), or educator, you may qualify for discounts with some cruise lines. Discounts and promotions have a limited lifetime and might be capacity controlled, but you won't get them if you don't ask. You'll also be required to prove your eligibility.

Many travel agents who specialize in booking cruises belong to consortiums that book blocks of cabins on a number of ships, thus enabling

What Impacts Your Fare

You think airline fares are confusing? Cruise fares rise and fall like waves during a tropical storm and can seem equally contrary. On a single day it's possible to get as many as a half dozen different price quotes directly from many cruise lines because fares fluctuate. You and your shipmates paid for the same cruise, but you may not have paid the same fare.

One thing never changes—do not ever, under any circumstances, pay brochure rate. You can do better, often as much as half off those inflated fares. These factors can enter the mix when pricing cruises:

■ **The date of your cruise:** Fares are seasonal, with the lowest from about the second week of September until the week before Thanksgiving and the highest in summer and during holiday periods.

■ **When you book:** Early booking discounts are nearly always offered; last-minute discounts might be available as well.

■ **Popularity of the ship:** Some ships are stars and fill quickly, while others are wallflowers and just don't book up as fast.

■ **Itinerary:** Certain itineraries hold higher appeal, especially those considered unique or exotic.

■ **Age:** No, not the ship's age. Fare discounts may be available for senior citizens, and children sometimes sail free with their parents.

■ **Where you live:** Regional discounts may be available, particularly if a cruise line is trying to introduce a ship into a port near where you live.

■ **Group pricing:** Even if you're not a member of a group, travel agents may have access to lower group fares.

■ **Who your travel agent is:** Top-performing agencies can pass along lower fares to their clients.

■ **You're a repeat passenger:** Discounts and other goodies are often available to loyal passengers.

■ **The accommodations you choose:** Advertisements for low fares inevitably include the word "from . . ." and the figure that follows is going to get you on board in the lowest category; if you want a better cabin, you'll pay more for the space and location you prefer.

them to pass along group savings to individuals who don't want the hassle of putting together a group of their own but who want the advantage of the lower group fare. Just because a travel agency is small doesn't mean it can't get you the bargains offered by bigger name-brand agencies. Don't be afraid to ask if there are any such deals available.

Timing and flexibility can also save you money. An affordable one-week cruise in May can cost you hundreds of dollars less per person than the same ship and itinerary in travel-heavy June.

Here's one thing that nearly everyone agrees on: It's a great feeling to have the majority of your vacation expenses paid before leaving home. This includes cruises.

The first step in actually booking a cruise is paying a deposit to reserve a cabin. The amount varies by cruise line and the length of the cruise, but it's generally about $250 per person for a one-week sailing. The balance of your fare is usually due from 60 to 75 days prior to the sailing date. Always pay your cruise fare with a credit card. Though it rarely happens, travel agencies can suffer financial difficulties, or unscrupulous travel sellers can prey on unsuspecting victims and disappear with their money. Credit card companies will support you with a refund in the case of fraud or other unforeseen difficulties. Be sure to check your billing statements to ascertain that the charges are credited to the cruise line and not the travel agent.

Many people balk at the idea of putting such large charges on their credit card. However, by saving a set amount every week until your final cruise payment is due, you can pay the entire balance when your next credit card statement arrives.

In the unfortunate event that you must cancel your trip, most cruise deposits are fully refundable before the final payment date. After that, cancellation fees will apply, and these range from the amount of your deposit to 100% of the entire fare, depending on how long you wait before canceling your cruise.

Be aware that many travel agencies now charge a "service fee" for booking your cruise that can range from $15 to $50 or higher and is generally nonrefundable if you cancel at any time. Ask about service fees up front—some agencies tack on additional fees for any changes you make in your booking, such as switching your cabin or dining preference, a name change on the reservation, and even in the event that you request a price reduction if the cruise line lowers the fare for your sailing.

WHEN TO BOOK YOUR CRUISE

You will certainly save money if you can book your cruise far in advance. In addition to having a better choice of desirable staterooms, significantly discounted prices are available to those who place a deposit on a cruise anywhere from six months to a year in advance of sailing. Just as department stores schedule first-of-the-year white sales on linens, the cruise industry has its January through March Wave Season, when it books a large number of passengers for the year. Availability is often the best during this period, and some of the year's choice bargains can be booked during the cruise lines' annual sales push.

Most cruise lines guarantee the lowest advertised fare to all passengers who have booked and paid a deposit. Should the price drop before the final payment is due, cruise lines will extend the reduced fare to early bookings. However, if you book early, it will be up to you to discover the fare reduction and request the lesser amount. Acting on your behalf, a good travel agent will monitor fare fluctuations and do that for you.

A wrinkle in cruise pricing is the last-minute discount offered to new bookings after the final payment is due, usually within 60 days of sailing. Cruise lines do not want to sail with empty cabins and will sometimes offer unsold space at deeply reduced fares in specific geographic regions—often through agencies within driving distance of the port of embarkation. Although these discounts can be substantial, your choice of cabins and locations is limited to whatever is left over. Top suites and the lowest-category inside staterooms almost always sell out early. A last-minute reservation could mean your cabin is in a noisy location over the show lounge or under the galley. Although demand for cruises is high, cruise industry insiders advise that you should never assume the date you want is sold out—always check with a travel agent.

If you booked early and cannot take advantage of the last-minute savings, take heart. Ask your travel agent to check into the lower fare for you anyway: some cruise lines will honor it or may give you an upgraded stateroom or, better still, an onboard credit.

BOOKING YOUR CRUISE

Charting your cruising course doesn't have to be difficult, but it isn't as simple as booking airplane seats or reserving a hotel room. Even after you've settled on a cruise line and cruise ship that's right for you, there will still be many questions to answer and details to get right. First-time cruisers, who may want and need some additional insight and advice, may wish to stick to a traditional travel agent who is close at hand. Of course, if you've taken numerous cruises and are more concerned with the price—and if you're willing to go to bat for yourself if something goes wrong—a Web-based agency might be the way to go.

USING A TRAVEL AGENT

Whether it is your 1st or 50th sailing, your best friend in booking a cruise is a knowledgeable travel agent. The last thing you want when considering a costly cruise vacation is an agent who has never been on a cruise, calls a cruise ship "the boat," or—worse still—quotes brochure rates. The most important steps in cruise travel planning are research, research, and more research; your partner in this process is an experienced travel agent. Booking a cruise is a complex process, and it's seldom wise to try to go it alone, particularly the first time. But how do you find a cruise travel agent you can trust?

First off, look for signs indicating you're dealing with an agency affiliated with Cruise Lines International Association (CLIA). Preferably, your agent should be certified as an Accredited Cruise Counselor (ACC), Master Cruise Counselor (MCC), or Elite Cruise Counselor (ECC) by CLIA. Those agents have completed demanding training programs, including touring or sailing on a specific number of ships. They make it their business to know all they can to serve their clients' needs.

Make sure the travel agency you've chosen belongs to a professional trade organization. In North America, membership in the American Society of Travel Agents (ASTA) indicates an agency has pledged to follow the code of ethics set forth by the world's largest association for travel professionals. In the best of all worlds, your travel agent is affiliated with both ASTA and CLIA. Additionally, many agencies and home-based travel agents belong to such brand-name travel-agent networks as American Express Travel and Uniglobe, which puts the power and support of international corporations in their corner. If you're dealing

2

with a local travel agency, look around the office when you arrive. Racks containing a wide variety of cruise line brochures and the presence of trade magazines and newspapers are good signs. The agent who makes it a point to read industry publications is an informed agent, one who is likely to keep up with the latest trends and who can provide you with up-to-the-minute data.

Some agencies have preferred-supplier relationships with specific cruise lines and prominently display only their products. If you have done your homework and know what cruise line sounds most appealing to you, be alert if an agent tries to change your mind without very specific reasons.

When you've found a jewel of an agent, then what? Ask many questions. Whether you do that in person, over the phone, or by email is up to you. However, it's important that you get to know your agent and that your agent gets to know you. Above all else, be honest about your expectations and budget. Seldom can a travel agent who doesn't know you well guess what your interests are and how much you can afford to spend. Don't be shy. If you have champagne taste and a beer budget, say so. Do not hesitate to interview prospective agents and be wary if they do not interview you right back.

Contrary to what conventional wisdom might suggest, cutting out the travel agent and booking directly with a cruise line won't necessarily get you the lowest price. Nearly three-quarters of all cruise bookings are still handled through travel agents, and many are able to secure group fares or other discounts not offered directly by cruise lines. In fact, cruise line reservation systems simply are not capable of dealing with tens of thousands of direct calls from potential passengers. They will take your reservation and often ask if you would like to assign it to a travel agent. Without an agent working on your behalf, you're on your own. A good travel agent is your advocate.

When you use a travel agent to book a cruise, most cruise line customer service departments are reluctant to respond to your questions over the telephone. Instead, they refer you to your travel agent, who is expected to make queries on your behalf. This is the time a knowledgeable and dedicated travel agent can come in handy. Do not rely on Internet message boards for authoritative responses to your questions—that is a service more accurately provided by your travel agent.

Travel Agent Professional Organizations American Society of Travel Agents (*ASTA* ☎ 703/739-2782, 800/965-2782 24-hr hotline ⊕ www. travelsense.org). **Association of British Travel Agents** (☎ 020/7637-2444 ⊕ www.abta.com). **Association of Canadian Travel Agencies** (☎ 866/725-2282 or 613/237-3657 ⊕ www.acta.ca). **Australian Federation of Travel Agents** (☎ 02/9264-3299 or 1300/363-416 ⊕ www.afta.com.au). **Travel Agents Association of New Zealand** (☎ 04/496-4898 ⊕ www.taanz.org.nz).

Cruise Line Organizations Cruise Lines International Association (*CLIA* ☎ 754/224-2200 ⊕ www.cruising.org).

Recommended Travel Agents AAA (☎ 800/222-6953 ⊕ www.aaa.com) isn't just for car travel. The company has a searchable database to locate member agencies by zip code.

CLOSE UP

10 Questions to Answer Before Visiting a Travel Agent

If you've decided to use a travel agent, congratulations. You'll have someone on your side to make your booking and to intercede if something goes wrong. Ask yourself these 10 simple questions, and you'll be better prepared to help the agent do his or her job:

1. Who will be going on the cruise?

2. What can you afford to spend for the entire trip?

3. Where would you like to go?

4. How much vacation time do you have?

5. When can you get away?

6. What are your interests?

7. Do you prefer a casual or a structured vacation?

8. What kind of accommodations do you want?

9. What are your dining preferences?

10. How will you get to the embarkation port?

American Express Travel (☎ 800/335–3342 ⊕ www.americanexpressvacations. com) offers options for online booking.

America's Vacation Center (☎ 800/490–2921 ⊕ www.americasvacationcenter. com) in business since the 1960s, is a family-owned agency with hundreds of professional Personal Vacation Planners worldwide.

Countryside Travel (☎ 800/603–5755 ⊕ www.cruisemaster.com) specializes in groups and honeymoons.

Cruise Brothers (☎ 800/827–7779 or 401/941–3999 ⊕ www.cruisebrothers. com), in business since the mid-1970s, is one of the largest family-owned, cruises-only agencies in the United States.

Cruise Connections Canada (☎ 800/661–9283 ⊕ www.cruise-connections. com) is Canada's leading cruise retailer and one of the largest cruise retailers in North America.

Cruise One (☎ 800/278–4731 ⊕ www.cruiseone.com) is owned by World Travel Holdings, the world's largest cruise retailer, and offers a satisfaction guarantee. The company has more than 400 member agencies nationwide, and its Web site has a searchable database of member cruise specialists.

Cruise Planners, Inc. (☎ 800/683–0206 ⊕ www.cruiseplanners.com) is a network of home-based agent franchises. The Web site offers a searchable database to locate member agencies.

Cruises Inc. (☎ 888/282–1249 or 800/854–0500 ⊕ www.cruisesinc.com) is owned by World Travel Holdings, the world's largest cruise retailer, and offers a satisfaction guarantee. The company has more than 450 member agencies nationwide, and its Web site has a searchable database of member cruise specialists.

Cruises Only (☎ 800/278–4737 ⊕ www.cruisesonly.com) is owned by World Travel Holdings, the world's largest cruise retailer, and offers a lowest-price

2

guarantee as well as a money-back satisfaction guarantee. Agents are available to assist clients around the clock.

Ensemble Travel (📞 800/442-6871 ⊕ www.ensembletravel.com) is an international network of 1,100 expert travel agencies. Call to be connected to the nearest member agency.

Hartford Holidays (📞 800/828-4813 or 516/746-6670 ⊕ www. hartfordholidays.com) has been family-owned and -operated for 30 years.

Lighthouse Travel (📞 800/719-9917 or 805/566-3905 ⊕ www. lighthousetravel.com) specializes in cruises.

Northstar Cruises (📞 800/249-9360 or 973/228-5005 ⊕ www. northstarcruises.com) is a top producer for most major cruise lines.

Skyscraper Tours, Inc. (📞 877/442-5659 ⊕ www.skyscrapertours.com) offers several annual hosted group cruises.

Uniglobe International (⊕ www.uniglobetravel.com) has more than 700 franchise locations worldwide; the Internet Web site has a searchable database of member cruise agencies.

Vacation.com (📞 800/843-0733 ⊕ www.vacation.com), a subsidiary of Amadeus Global Travel Distribution, is a network of thousands of travel agencies across the United States and Canada.

Virtuoso (📞 866/401-7974 or 817/870-0300) is the world's most exclusive association of upscale travel agencies. Call to locate members specializing in cruises.

BOOKING YOUR CRUISE ONLINE

In addition to local travel agencies, there are many hardworking, dedicated travel professionals working for Web sites. Both big-name travel sellers and mom-and-pop agencies compete for the attention of cyber-savvy clients, and it never hurts to compare prices from a variety of these sources. Some cruise lines even allow you to book directly with them through their Web sites.

As a rule, Web-based and toll-free brokers will do a decent job for you. They often offer discounted fares, though not always the lowest, so it pays to check around. If you know precisely what you want and how much you should pay to get a real bargain—and you don't mind dealing with an anonymous voice on the phone—by all means make your reservations when the price is right. Just don't expect the personal service you get from an agent you know. Also, be prepared to spend a lot of time and effort on the phone if something goes wrong.

Online Agencies Cruise.com (⊕ www.cruise.com 📞 888/333-3116) lays claim to being the largest Web site specializing in discounted cruises on the Internet and offers a lowest-price guarantee.

Cruise Compete (⊕ www.cruisecompete.com 📞 800/764-4410) allows you to get competing bids from top travel agencies, who respond to your request for bids with their best rates for your trip.

Cruise Direct (⊕ *www.cruisedirect.com* ☎ *888/407-2784*) allows customers to book their own travel arrangements through the Web site and a toll-free number.

Cruise411.com (⊕ *www.cruise411.com* ☎ *800/553-7090*) has a booking engine online that allows you to book directly or temporarily hold most cruise reservations without deposit or payment if you prefer to call in your booking.

Expedia (⊕ *www.expedia.com* ☎ *800/397-3342*) is a full-service online travel seller that books cruises, too.

iCruise.com (⊕ *www.icruise.com* ☎ *800/427-8473*) charges a pretty hefty cancellation fee, so be sure you know what you want before using their booking engine.

jetBlue (⊕ *www.jetblue.com* ☎ *800/538-2583*) now allows you to book cruises on its Web site.

Moment's Notice (⊕ *www.moments-notice.com* ☎ *888/241-3366*) offers a searchable database for last-minute deals; call toll-free for reservations.

Orbitz (⊕ *www.orbitz.com* ☎ *888/656-4546*) is a full-service online travel seller that books cruises.

7 Blue Seas (⊕ *www.7blueseas.com* ☎ *800/242-1781*) offers a comprehensive online cruise information Web site; bookings are made through the toll-free call center.

Travelocity (⊕ *www.travelocity.com* ☎ *877/815-5446*) is a full-service online travel seller with a 24-hour help desk for service issues.

CONSUMER PROTECTION

Before you actually book your cruise and make your deposit, it's well worth the effort to check with the Better Business Bureau for complaints against the agent you have decided to use. Always pay by credit card, and make sure the correct amount appears on your statement as a charge by the cruise line, not the travel agency. If you've paid by credit card, you can cancel payment or get reimbursed if there's a problem (and you can provide documentation). Check to see what kind of complaints (if any) have been filed against the agency you've chosen to work with and whether they were resolved. Finally, always consider travel insurance that includes default coverage for your travel agency and cruise line.

Contacts **Canadian Council of Better Business Bureaus** (☎ *416/644-4936* *www.ccbbb.ca/*). **Council of Better Business Bureaus** (☎ *703/276-0100* ⊕ *www.bbb.org*).

INSURANCE

When you book your cruise, your travel agent should ask you if you want to purchase travel insurance. Travel insurance plans cover trip cancellation and interruption, supplier default, and international medi-

2

cal care—or various combinations of these. If the agent doesn't ask you, you should ask for the information.

Comprehensive travel policies typically cover trip cancellation and interruption, letting you cancel or cut your trip short because of a personal emergency, illness, or, in some cases, acts of terrorism in your destination. Such policies also cover evacuation and medical care. Some also cover you for trip delays because of bad weather or mechanical problems, as well as for lost or delayed baggage. Another type of coverage to look for is financial default—that is, when your trip is disrupted because a tour operator, airline, or cruise line goes out of business. Generally you must buy this when you book your trip or shortly thereafter, and it's only available to you if your operator isn't on a list of excluded companies.

If you're going on a cruise (or any trip abroad for that matter), consider buying medical-only coverage at the very least. Neither Medicare nor some private insurers cover medical expenses anywhere outside the United States besides Mexico and Canada (including time aboard a cruise ship, even if it leaves from a U.S. port). Medical-only policies typically reimburse you for medical care (excluding that related to preexisting conditions) and hospitalization abroad and provide for evacuation. You still have to pay the bills and await reimbursement from the insurer, though.

Expect comprehensive travel insurance policies to cost about 4% to 7% of the total price of your trip (it's more like 12% if you're over age 70). A medical-only policy may or may not be cheaper than a comprehensive policy. Always read the fine print of your policy to make sure that you are covered for the risks that are of most concern to you. Compare several policies to make sure you're getting the best price and range of coverage available.

Insurance Comparison Sites **InsureMyTrip.com** (☎ *800/487-4722* ⊕ *www. insuremytrip.com*). **Square Mouth.com** (⊕ *www.quotetravelinsurance.com*).

Comprehensive Travel Insurers **Access America** (☎ *800/284–8300* ⊕ *www. accessamerica.com*). **CSA Travel Protection** (☎ *800/711–1197* ⊕ *www. csatravelprotection.com*). **HTH Worldwide** (☎ *610/254–8700 or 888/243–2358* ⊕ *www.hthworldwide.com*). **Travelex Insurance** (☎ *800/228–9792* ⊕ *www. travelex-insurance.com*). **Travel Guard International** (☎ *715/345–0505 or 800/826–4919* ⊕ *www.travelguard.com*). **Travel Insured International** (☎ *800/243-3174* ⊕ *www.travelinsured.com*).

CRUISE LINE INSURANCE POLICIES

Nearly all cruise lines offer their own line of insurance. Most policies are underwritten by major insurers and typically include trip cancellation–interruption protection, travel delay protection, baggage loss or delay protection, emergency medical and/or dental benefits, emergency medical evacuation and transportation to the nearest medical facility, repatriation of remains in case of death, and other worldwide emergency assistance. All policies contain coverage limitations and terms and conditions that you should read carefully. Policies purchased through the cruise lines are generally based on the total price of the trip booked with them despite age and are often the most cost-effective coverage for senior citizens. However, they may not cover certain add-on elements such as airfare and the cost of a precruise hotel that you paid for independently. Compare the coverage and rates with similar polices from third-party insurers to determine which is best for you.

Some cruise lines, including Holland America Line, Silversea, and Princess Cruises, offer upgraded levels of cruise insurance that include considerably more liberal cancellation policies. They allow you to cancel up to 24 hours prior to departure for any reason whatsoever and receive either a cash refund or cruise credit of 75% to 100% of your fare. Seabourn goes a step further and covers your cruise payment if you must cancel due to a preexisting condition that is denied by insurance—the cruise line will issue a future travel credit equal to the cancellation penalties imposed.

Keep in mind that insurance purchased from an independent carrier is more likely to include coverage if the cruise line goes out of business before or during your cruise. Although it's a rare and unlikely occurrence, you do want to be insured in the event that it happens.

MEDICAL-ONLY PLANS

It's wise to sign up with a medical-assistance company even if you don't purchase other kinds of general travel insurance. Members get doctor referrals, emergency evacuation or repatriation, hotlines for medical consultation, cash for emergencies, and other assistance. Most general travel insurance policies include medical coverage and evacuation.

Medical-Only Insurers **International Medical Group** (☎ 800/628–4664 ⊕ www.imglobal.com). **International SOS** (☎ 215/942–8000 or 713/521–7611 ⊕ www.internationalsos.com). **Wallach & Company** (☎ 800/237–6615 or 504/687–3166 ⊕ www.wallach.com).

MAKING DECISIONS ABOUT YOUR CRUISE

Once you've settled on a specific ship of a particular cruise line, you'll have numerous decisions to make before your travel agent actually completes your booking. You need to settle on your dining arrangements, pick your stateroom, decide how you'll get to the port of embarkation, whether you want to arrive at the port of embarkation early or stay a few days after your cruise, and lay out any special requests or requirements you may have.

MAKING DINING ARRANGEMENTS

Your travel agent will ask you to make a number of decisions before he or she books your cruise. When you're sailing on a traditional cruise with assigned dinner seating, your seating selection can set the tone for your entire trip. Which is best? Early dinner seating is generally scheduled between 6 and 6:30 pm, while late seating can begin from 8:00 to 8:30 pm. The best seating depends on you, your lifestyle, and your personal preferences.

SPECIALTY RESTAURANTS

CRUISE LINE	SHIP	CUISINE TYPE	CHARGE (PER PERSON)
Azamara Club Cruises	Azamara Journey and Quest	Steak house	$15 (comp for suite occupants)
		Mediterranean	$15 (comp for suite occupants)
Carnival	Spirit-class, Conquest-class, and Dream class	Steaks and seafood	$30
	All ships	International with wine pairings	$75
	Carnival Magic	Italian	$10
Celebrity	All ships	Continental	$35
	Solstice-class and Constellation	Italian	$30
	Solstice-class and Constellation, Infinity, and Summit	Creperie	$5
	Solstice-class, except Eclipse and Silhouette	Asian	$25
	Eclipse, Silhouette, Infinity, and Summit	American	$30
Costa	Costa Atlantica	Italian–Tuscan Stakehouse	à la carte (comp dinner for two for suite occupants)
Crystal	All ships	Italian, Asian, Sushi	No charge
	All ships	International with wine pairings	$210
Cunard	Queen Mary 2, Queen Victoria	Mediterranean	$30 dinner, $20 lunch
	Queen Mary 2, Queen Victoria	International	No charge
	Queen Elizabeth	French	à la carte
	Queen Elizabeth	Mexican, Asian, or South American	$10
Disney	All ships	Northern Italian	$20 dinner, $20 Champagne brunch, $10 High Tea
	Disney Dream and Fantasy	French	$75, $174 with wine pairings
Holland America	All ships	Steaks and seafood	$20 dinner, $10 lunch
	All ships	Italian	No charge
	Signature-class	Asian	$15 dinner, lunch no charge
	Nieuw Amsterdam	International with wine pairings	$89

SPECIALTY RESTAURANTS

CRUISE LINE	SHIP	CUISINE TYPE	CHARGE (PER PERSON)
MSC	*Poesia*	Asian	à la carte
Norwegian	All ships	French	$20
	All ships	Steak house	$25
	All ships	Italian	$10
	All ships, except *Sky*	Sushi	$15
	All ships, except *Sky*	Teppanyaki	$25
	All ships, except *Sky* and *Sun*	Asian	$15
	Sky, Sun, Spirit, and *Pride of America*	Tex-Mex	$10
	Norwegian Epic	Chinese	à la carte
	All ships except *Sky, Sun, Spirit,* and *Pride of America* (By Dec. 2011)	Brazilian Churrascaria	$20
Oceania	All ships	Italian	No charge
	All ships	Steak house	No charge
	Marina	French	No charge
	Marina	Asian	No charge
Princess	*Coral* and *Island Princess*	Steak house	$15
	All ships	Italian	$20
	Grand, Caribbean, Crown, Emerald, and *Ruby Princess*	Steaks and seafood	$25
Regent Seven Seas	All ships	Steaks and seafood	No charge
	Mariner, Voyager	French	No charge
Royal Caribbean	Oasis-, Freedom-, Radiance-class and *Enchantment, Mariner,* and *Navigator of the Seas*	Steak house	$30
	Oasis-, Freedom-, Radiance-class, and Voyager-class	Italian	$15 (lunch), $20 (dinner)
	Allure, Splendour, and *Radiance of the Seas*	Brazilian Churrascaria	$25
	All ships	Johnny Rockets diner	$4.95
	Oasis-class	American	$40
	Oasis of the Seas	Spa cuisine	$20 dinner, breakfast and lunch no charge

SPECIALTY RESTAURANTS

CRUISE LINE	SHIP	CUISINE TYPE	CHARGE (PER PERSON)
	Oasis-class, and *Radiance* and *Splendour of the Seas*	Seafood (Oasis), Mexican (Allure, Radiance, Splendour)	à la carte for Seafood, $13 for Mexican
	Oasis-class, and *Radiance* and *Splendour of the Seas*	Asian	à la carte plus $3 (lunch) or $5 (dinner)
	Oasis-class, *Splendour*, and *Radiance of the Seas*	International with wine pairings	$95
Seabourn	All ships	International	No charge
Silversea	All ships	International	$30
	All ships	International with wine pairings	$200
	All ships	Italian	No charge
	Silver Spirit	Asian	$30
Windstar	*Wind Surf*	International and steak house	No charge

You may wish to choose early seating if:

- You have small children accustomed to an early meal and bedtime.
- Your personal routine calls for meals at an earlier hour.
- You retire earlier in the evening and are an early riser.
- You do not want to experience that full feeling at bedtime.
- You want to attend the early shows, enjoy the casino and other activities, and take in the midnight buffet.

Late seating may be better if:

- You're a night owl and do not mind finishing dinner after 10 pm.
- Your itinerary is port intensive, and you don't want to rush to get ready for dinner after a day of touring.
- You like to indulge in a late-afternoon nap.
- You do not care about midnight snacks and like to sleep late.
- Your personal habit is to dine late.
- You enjoy leisurely dining and lingering over coffee at the end of the meal.

Cruise lines understand that strict schedules do not satisfy the desires of all modern cruise passengers. Most cruise lines now include alternatives to the set schedules in the dining room, including casual versions of their dinner menus in their Lido buffets, where more flexibility is allowed in dress- and mealtimes. Specialty à la carte restaurants are showing up on more ships, although a surcharge or gratuity is usually required.

Open seating, an amenity primarily associated with more upscale cruise lines, allows passengers the flexibility of dining any time during restaurant hours and being seated with whomever they please.

Led by Norwegian Cruise Line's Freestyle Cruising concept, other mainstream and premium cruise lines have explored adaptations of open seating to add variety and a more personalized experience for their passengers. Princess Cruises offers Personal Choice dining; Holland America Line's option is called As You Wish dining; Royal Caribbean calls their version of open seating My Time Dining and Celebrity Cruises offers Select Main Dining. Even Carnival Cruise Lines tested the waters with an open seating option and introduced it fleetwide. Some cruise lines will warn you

that, while dining preferences may be requested by your travel agent, no requests are guaranteed. And it's true that table assignments are generally not confirmed until embarkation, but the lines do try to satisfy all their guests. If you are unhappy with your dinner seating, see the maître d' during the first day of your cruise for assistance. Changes after the first evening are generally discouraged; there will even be a designated place to meet with dining room staff and iron out seating problems on embarkation day. Check the daily program for the time and location.

SELECTING YOUR STATEROOM

Your choice of stateroom or cabin is likely to be a major factor in how you enjoy your cruise. If it truly doesn't matter where you sleep, go ahead and book the least-expensive category guarantee you can find. The cheapest cabin on a ship is typically an inside stateroom on a lower deck. Although ship designers do all they can to make these inside cabins feel less claustrophobic, there's no getting around the fact that you won't have any kind of view to the outside world. There's sometimes a curtain where the porthole or window would typically be in an outside cabin, but it will be covering nothing but blank wall space.

There are a few simple ways you can get a bit more for your money. Fares are determined by the type of accommodation reserved, and guarantee bookings—when you reserve a cabin category instead of a specific stateroom—can save you money. The cruise line will assign you a cabin within the fare category you book, or you may even be upgraded to a higher category. Be aware that you could end up at the very front or back of the ship or—much worse—below the disco.

On the other hand, if you view your cabin as your sanctuary, you will want a bit more than standard inside for your home away from home. For an inside cabin with a view of the inside action, Royal Caribbean's Voyager-, Freedom-, and Oasis-class ships and Cunard Line's *Queen*

2

Mary 2 offer accommodations with windows overlooking interior lobbies and, in the case of Royal Caribbean's Oasis-class ships, balconies facing courtyards open to the sky. Obstructed-view outside locations offer natural light, but there might be a lifeboat outside your window instead of an ocean view. Moving up a few categories may cost less than you imagine and result in a more comfortable space with a large window or even a balcony. High-end suites should include perks that justify their cost.

Although cruise ship cabins are not all created equal, they are all designed for comfort, convenience, and practicality. Standard cabins on modern cruise vessels haven't quite achieved parity with land-based resort accommodations in terms of size, but cruise lines recognize that small touches (and more spacious quarters) go a long way toward overall passenger contentment. You're likely to find your cabin equipped with amenities such as a personal safe, robes for use on board, a hair dryer, and bathroom toiletries—the added niceties that hotels have long provided for their guests.

Aside from the little details that vary from cruise line to cruise line, staterooms are furnished for functionality. At the very least, a cabin contains beds (often twin beds that can be combined to form a queen- or king-size bed), a dressing table–writing desk, a chair, drawers or shelf storage, a closet, and a bathroom with shower. There's almost always a television and telephone. Cabins on newer ships often have sitting areas with a sofa or love seat and a coffee table.

The cabin dressing table–writing desk will almost always have two different electric receptacles—one will accept standard U.S.-style plugs (110-volt), and the other is for European-style plugs (220-volt). To plug in more than one gadget at a time, you'll need a power strip, or, for dual voltage appliances, a plug adapter. You'll have to bring along your own adapter—the kind that allows U.S.-style plugs with flat prongs to be inserted into European-style round receptacles. I had always packed a short power strip in order to use more than one appliance until my husband pointed out I could recharge my cell phone while using the computer simply by utilizing the second receptacle with a flat-to-round prong adapter attached. Cabin bathrooms generally feature a dual-voltage plug receptacle suitable for electric shavers only. The hair dryers provided are usually built into the wall or tucked away in a drawer.

GETTING TO THE CRUISE PORT

For the convenience of one-stop shopping, all cruise lines have a so-called Air & Sea program that allows you to purchase your airline ticket to the port of embarkation and your cruise ticket at the same time; you'll also get airport transfers. An added bonus is that by bundling all your air, land, and sea transportation together, you can have a cruise vacation that's much more worry-free. On the other hand, forward-thinking cruisers who buy discounted airline tickets in advance can often save a bundle—or at least enough to cover the cost of a precruise

DECIPHER YOUR DECK PLAN

LIDO DECK

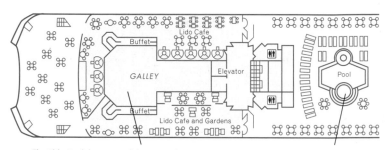

The Lido Deck is a potential source of noise—deck chairs are set out early in the morning and put away late at night; the sound of chairs scraping on the floor of the Lido buffet can be an annoyance.

Music performances by poolside bands can often be heard on upper-deck balconies located immediately below.

UPPER DECK AFT

Take note of where lifeboats are located—views from some outside cabins can be partially, or entirely, obstructed by the boats.

Upper-deck cabins, as well as those far forward and far aft, are usually more susceptible to motion than those in the middle of the ship on a low deck.

Cabins near elevators or stairs are a double-edged sword. Being close by is a convenience; however, although the elevators aren't necessarily noisy, the traffic they attract can be.

Balcony cabins are indicated by a rectangle split into two sections. The small box is the balcony.

2

MAIN PUBLIC DECK

Cabins immediately below restaurants and dining rooms can be noisy. Late sleepers might be bothered by early breakfast noise, early sleepers by late diners.

Theaters and dining rooms are often located on middle or lower decks.

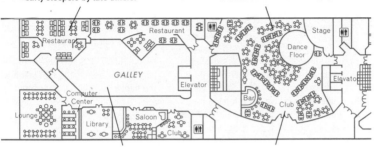

The ship's galley isn't usually labeled on deck plans, but you can figure out where it is by locating a large blank space near the dining room. Cabins beneath it can be very noisy.

Locate the ship's show lounge, disco, children's playroom, and teen center and avoid booking a cabin directly above or below them for obvious reasons.

LOWER DECK AFT

Cabins designated for passengers with disabilities are often situated near elevators.

Interior cabins have no windows and are the least expensive on board.

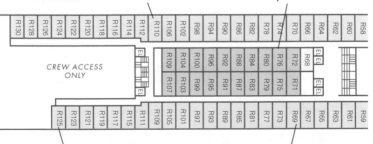

Lower-deck cabins, particularly those far aft, can be plagued by mechanical noises and vibration.

Ocean-view cabins are generally located on lower decks.

CLOSE UP

Missing the Boat

The first port of call on your itinerary might be Key West, but don't hurry there to board the ship if you missed its initial sailing. By trying to do so you'll violate the Passenger Services Act of 1886 (PSA), which was enacted to protect American passenger shipping interests.

The relevant part of the PSA reads as follows: "No foreign vessel shall transport passengers between ports or places in the United States, either directly or by way of a foreign port, under a penalty of $300 for each passenger so transported and landed." An exception was made for cruise ships:

"Foreign-flagged cruise ships may carry passengers from a U.S. port as long as they return them to the same port (a 'cruise to nowhere'). Foreign vessels may also call at intermediate U.S. ports as long as no passenger permanently leaves the vessel at those ports and the vessel makes at least one call at a foreign port."

Even outdated U.S. laws die hard—or hardly ever die—so the PSA still rules the high seas. Yes, a few exceptions exist. And, no, officials won't allow you to pay the fine and board in just any U.S. port.

---

overnight hotel. Comparison shopping makes sense if you have the time and inclination to do it.

The main drawback of an Air & Sea program is an obvious one: you can't choose the time you fly. The cruise lines buy the number of seats they need, but the airlines themselves pick the flights. Although all flights are scheduled to give you enough time to make your embarkation, you might find yourself with an inconvenient flight time, and there's not much you can do about that. Even if your preferred air carrier has nonstop service from your gateway airport directly to your port of embarkation, you might be scheduled with an extremely early departure or with multiple stops along the way.

Flights assigned to cruise passengers aren't always the most desirable since cruise lines pay low contractual fares and because independent travelers tend to book the most desirable flights. Basically, that means you're getting what the airlines have open when the time comes to assign flights. If you want to be assured you'll fly on a particular airline at a particular time, request an "air deviation." For a fee—plus any associated airline charges—the cruise line will attempt to book your preference. There's no guarantee you'll get what you want, but they will try.

Your airline tickets are usually issued 30 days before sailing, and the cruise line cannot confirm specific seat assignments. This is where booking through a travel agent will help you. Most cruise travel specialists are savvy enough to secure flight numbers 30 days out and nail down seat assignments. Make sure yours does.

There are distinct advantages to using a cruise line's Air & Sea program. When major holidays draw near, an Air & Sea program may be the only way to secure any airline reservation, let alone an affordable one. And when you're taking a one-way cruise you'll have to purchase two one-way tickets, which is often more expensive than a round-trip, unless you purchase the cruise line's budget-friendly air add-on.

These programs have perks other than price. For example, there's comfort in knowing someone is looking out for you and your luggage as well as providing ground transportation to the ship. Uniformed cruise line agents meet incoming passengers to smooth their way from airport to pier.

> ### WORD OF MOUTH
>
> "Definitely take a taxi to and from the Miami airport; it is way cheaper per person and much faster than the cruise line bus. Plus you don't have the long waits for other passengers, their bags, and the chaos involved in getting on and off the ship." —George and Eleanor S.

Even with Air & Sea flight arrangements, lengthy airline delays can result in literally missing the boat. However, it's a common misconception that when you use a cruise line's Air & Sea program, the cruise line is responsible for getting you to your ship. On the contrary, the responsibility is with the airline. When cruise lines contract with airlines for tickets, the airline is responsible for getting you to the next port of call if a flight is cancelled; they should even put you on a different airline's flight to ensure that you don't miss the ship if that is possible. However, cruise line personnel will help you make alternate arrangements. You'll be given an emergency telephone number to call in case your flight is delayed, and the line will help you find alternate flights. They can also assist with hotel arrangements and transfers (often the airline will pay for these if they are at fault).

If you must fly to port the same day your ship sails, it's wise to request the first flight of the day from your departure city. Delays in later flights can snowball, creating air-scheduling havoc and scarce seats as flyers scramble to get on board later flights.

You should also consider your flight home as well. Although your itinerary may state that the ship docks back in its home port at 7 am, passengers are unlikely to begin leaving the vessel much earlier than 9 am. Prior to disembarkation, the ship must be cleared by Customs and Immigration. Upon leaving the ship all passengers must be cleared through Customs and Immigration as well. This is normally done in the terminal, either before or after retrieving your luggage. In any event, cruise lines normally warn you not to schedule your flight home before noon or even 1 pm, depending on the port location. In New York City, the suggested time is no earlier than midafternoon.

Suppose you don't want to fly. After 9/11, cruise lines realized that the traveling public wanted more alternatives, and the solution was surprisingly simple. If passengers couldn't get to the ports easily, bring the ports to them. In addition to the busiest embarkation ports of Miami, Fort Lauderdale, Port Canaveral, and New York, other port cities are also capable of handling passenger ships. Some ships cruise from New Orleans, Tampa, Mobile, Jacksonville, Charleston, or Baltimore. By 2005, relative newcomer Galveston, Texas, ranked as the fifth-busiest cruise port in the United States, thanks largely to a substantial drive-to market. Secure parking is always available, either within the port itself or nearby.

ARRIVING EARLY AT THE EMBARKATION PORT

The possibility of flight delays and cancellations is the best reason to pad your vacation with a precruise day of relaxation. Arrive early and unwind—an especially wise move if your home is in the snow-belt and your cruise is in January. The extra expense is well worth the peace of mind.

Pre- and postcruise packages, which can include hotel accommodations and ground transportation, are offered by most cruise lines. Like air-fare, the convenience of a package is often offset by a higher price tag.

With a bit of research, you can make your own independent arrangements at considerable savings. Many hotels near major ports of embarkation have their own packages and offers, which may include transportation to the cruise port. Some hotels offer free or reduced rate parking for the duration of your cruise, a handy addition if you are driving.

Getting Ready

WORD OF MOUTH

"We're taking a 7-day cruise...There are 2 formal nights. Do we still have to have formal dress if we dine in the alternate restaurants?"

—golfette

"I had read somewhere that U.S. citizens would soon be required to have passports to sail the Caribbean. In the past we've only needed certified copies of birth certificates. Does anyone know the status on this?"

—Holdf

Once your ideal cruise is booked, it's time to start getting yourself and your family prepared for the trip. Some of the steps you can take are merely for your convenience while others are really important. But it's critical that you prepare in advance for your cruise; don't wait until the last minute, when even a minor oversight could ruin your vacation. As your sailing date approaches, do not hesitate to ask your travel agent if you have any questions.

Many cruise passengers claim that planning is half the fun, and they really throw themselves into the process. That makes sense when you consider you may be out of touch with your home, family, and business when your cruise ship is at sea. Depending on the itinerary, that could be for many hours, even days, at a time.

You'll sleep better if you think ahead. Some of the things you'll need to do before your cruise take time—for instance, obtaining the proper documents; other details may seem relatively simple but can expand in significance if you leave them all for the last minute. By breaking your preparation down into manageable chunks, you'll have plenty of time to get ready and won't be frazzled in the last week before your cruise. The last thing you want is to leave something important undone because you were in a rush. It's easier to leave your worries behind on the dock when you plan with care.

DOCUMENTS

It's every passenger's responsibility to have proper identification. If you arrive at port without the travel documents you need, you will not be allowed to board your cruise ship and the cruise line will not issue you a refund. Most travel agents know the requirements and can guide you to the proper agencies to obtain the documents you need if you don't already have them.

PASSPORTS

Cruises to the Bahamas, Mexico, and the Caribbean require proof of citizenship for all passengers. As of June 1, 2009, all American citizens are required to present a passport or other approved document denoting citizenship and identity for all land *and* sea travel into the United States. However, the rules can still be confusing:

If you are a U.S. citizen traveling to the Caribbean on a cruise that begins and ends in the same U.S. port, then you will still be permitted to depart from or enter the United States with proof of identity (a government-issued photo ID such as a driver's license), along with proof of citizenship (a certified birth certificate with official seal). A U.S.

issued Enhanced Driver's License (EDL), which denotes identity and citizenship, is also an acceptable alternative to a passport for reentry into the United States.

■ You can also use one of the new U.S. passport cards, which are less expensive than a full passport but aren't good for international air travel (flights to Puerto Rico, St. Thomas, and St. Croix from U.S. airports are *not* considered international travel).

■ You may still be required to present a U.S. passport when you dock in a foreign port, depending on the islands or countries that your cruise ship is visiting. Foreign policies differ.

■ If your cruise begins in one U.S. port and ends in a different port, then you will be required to have a valid passport or passport card.

■ If your cruise begins or ends in Puerto Rico or St. Thomas, then you do not need a valid passport; flights to Puerto Rico are considered regular domestic flights, though flights to St. Thomas are slightly different (no passport is required, but you must show proof of citizenship in the form of a photo ID plus an official birth certificate).

■ If your cruise begins in a foreign port (Barbados, the Dominican Republic, or some other Caribbean island), then you must have a valid passport; a passport card will not do in such a case because you will need the passport to fly back to the United States.

■ Canadian citizens must have a valid passport to enter or leave the United States.

■ Resident aliens of the United States need a valid passport from their home country as well as their Alien Resident Receipt Card (form I-551), commonly known as a green card.

■ Citizens of all other foreign countries—if they aren't permanent residents of the United States—must carry a valid passport and a visa waiver or multiple-entry visa for the United States.

■TIP→ Even if you are taking a cruise that begins and ends in the same U.S. port, you may still want to travel with a valid passport that will enable you to fly from the United States to meet your ship at the first port should you miss the scheduled embarkation; a valid passport will also allow you to leave the ship without significant delays and complications before the cruise ends if you must fly back to the United States due to an emergency.

GETTING OR RENEWING A PASSPORT

Since more people will now require passports to travel, you should apply for a passport as far in advance of your cruise as possible if you don't have one or need to renew your current passport. The process usually takes at least six weeks and can take longer during very busy periods. The best time to apply for a passport or to renew is in fall and winter. Before any trip, check your passport's expiration date, and, if necessary, renew it as soon as possible.

You can expedite your passport application if you're traveling within two weeks by paying a fee of $60 (in addition to the regular passport fee) and appearing in person at a regional passport office. Also, several passport expediting services will handle your application for you (for a hefty fee, of course) and can get you a passport even sooner. For

FODOR'S CRUISE PREPARATION TIME LINE

3 TO 4 MONTHS BEFORE SAILING

■ Check with your travel agent or the State Department for the identification required for your cruise.

■ Gather the necessary identification you need. If you need to replace a lost birth certificate, apply for a new passport, or renew one that's about to expire, start the paperwork now. Doing it at the last minute is stressful and often costly.

60 TO 75 DAYS BEFORE SAILING

■ Make the final payment on your cruise fare. Though the dates vary, your travel agent should remind you when the payment date draws near. Failure to submit the balance on time can result in the cancellation of your reservation.

■ Make a packing list for each person you'll be packing for.

■ Begin your wardrobe planning now. Try things on to make sure they fit and are in good repair (it's amazing how stains can magically appear months after something has been dry cleaned). Set things aside.

■ If you need to shop, get started so you have time to find just the right thing (and perhaps to return or exchange just the right thing). You may also need to allow time for alterations.

■ Make kennel reservations for your pets. (If you're traveling during a holiday period, you may need to do this even earlier.)

■ Arrange for a house sitter.

■ If you're cruising, but your kids are staying home:

■ Make child care arrangements.

■ Go over children's schedules to make sure they'll have everything they need while you're gone (gift for a birthday party, supplies for a school project, permission slip for a field trip).

■ If you have small children, you may want to put together a small bag of treats for them to open while you're gone—make a tape of yourself reading a favorite bedtime story or singing a lullaby (as long as it's you, it will sound fantastic to them).

30 DAYS BEFORE SAILING

■ If you purchased an Air & Sea package, call your travel agent for the details of your airline schedule. Request seat assignments.

■ If your children are sailing with you, check their wardrobes now (do it too early and the really little kids may actually grow out of garments).

■ Make appointments for any personal services you wish to have prior to your cruise. For example, a haircut or manicure.

■ Get out your luggage and check the locks and zippers. Check for anything that might have spilled inside on a previous trip.

■ If you need new luggage or want an extra piece to bring home souvenirs, purchase it now.

2 TO 4 WEEKS BEFORE SAILING

■ Receive your cruise documents through the travel agent, or download them online.

■ Examine the documents for accuracy (correct cabin number, sailing date, and dining arrangements); make sure names are spelled correctly. If there's something you do not understand, ask now.

■ Read all the literature in your document package for suggestions specific to your cruise. Most cruise lines include helpful information.

■ Pay any routine bills that may be due while you're gone.

■ Go over your personalized packing list again. Finish shopping.

3

1 WEEK BEFORE SAILING

■ Finalize your packing list and continue organizing everything in one area.

■ Buy film or digital media and check the batteries in your camera.

■ Refill prescription medications with an adequate supply.

■ Make two photocopies of your passport or ID and credit cards. Leave one copy with a friend and carry the other copy separately from the originals.

■ Get cash and/or traveler's checks at the bank. If you use traveler's checks, keep a separate record of the serial numbers. Get a supply of one-dollar bills for tipping baggage handlers (at the airport, hotel, pier, etc.).

■ You may also want to put valuables and jewelry that you won't be taking with you in the safety deposit box while you're at the bank.

■ Arrange to have your mail held at the post office or ask a neighbor to pick it up.

■ Stop newspaper delivery or ask a neighbor to bring it in for you.

■ Arrange for lawn and houseplant care or snow removal during your absence (if necessary).

■ Leave your itinerary, the ship's telephone number (plus the name of your ship and your stateroom number), and a house key with a relative or friend.

■ If traveling with young children, purchase small games or toys to keep them occupied while en route to your embarkation port.

3 DAYS BEFORE SAILING

■ Confirm your airline flights; departure times are sometimes subject to change.

■ Put a card with your name, address, telephone number, and itinerary inside each suitcase.

■ Fill out the luggage tags that came with your document packet and follow the instructions regarding when and how to attach them.

■ If you haven't already done it online, complete any other paperwork that the cruise line included with your documents (foreign customs and immigration forms, onboard charge application, etc.). Do not wait until you're standing in the pier check-in line to fill them in!

■ Do last-minute laundry and tidy up the house.

■ Pull out the luggage and begin packing.

THE DAY BEFORE SAILING

■ Take pets to the kennel.

■ Water houseplants and lawn (if necessary).

■ Dispose of any perishable food in the refrigerator.

■ Mail any last-minute bills.

■ Set timers for indoor lights.

■ Reorganize your wallet. Remove anything you will not need (department store or gas credit cards, etc.), put them in an envelope.

■ Finish packing and lock your suitcases.

DEPARTURE DAY

■ Adjust the thermostat and double-check the door locks.

■ Turn off the water if there's danger of frozen pipes while you're away.

■ Arrange to be at the airport a minimum of two hours before your departure time (follow the airline's instructions).

■ Have photo ID and/or passport ready for airport check-in.

■ Slip your car keys, parking claim checks, and airline tickets in your carry-on luggage. Never pack these items in checked luggage.

U.S. citizens, a passport costs $135 if you're 16 or older, $105 if you are under 16. It's valid for 10 years if you're 16 or older, 5 years if you are under 16. A cheaper alternative is a passport card, which costs $55 for an adult, $40 for a minor under 16 (though this card is *not* valid for international air travel, only for border crossings by land and sea). You can usually renew a passport by mail as long as you can send in your current passport and are over 16 years old. If you're applying for a passport for the first time, you'll have to appear in person to make your application, but most cities and towns large and small have some office that processes passport applications—usually a post office or courthouse; some public libraries or county or state courthouses even process applications.

> **ONLINE CRUISE PREP**
>
> To expedite your preboarding paperwork, some cruise lines have convenient forms on their Web sites. As long as you have your reservation (or booking) number, you can provide the required immigration information, reserve shore excursions, and even indicate any special requests from the comfort of your home. Be sure to print a copy of the form to present at the pier.

U.S. Passport Information National Passport Information Center (☎ 877/487–2778, 888/874–7793 TDD/TTY ⊕ travel.state.gov).

PERMISSION LETTERS

But you may need even more documentation than that. Often, single parents or grandparents want to take their children or grandchildren on a cruise; it's also not uncommon for parents to invite their teenager's friend to sail along. An often-overlooked requirement is a notarized letter of permission, which is usually required anytime a child under 18 travels to a foreign country with anyone other than both of his or her parents. The absent or noncustodial parent (or parents) must usually give explicit written permission for their children to travel outside the United States.

Airlines, cruise lines, and immigration agents can—and usually will— deny minor children initial boarding or entry to foreign countries without proper proof of identification and citizenship *and* a permission letter from absent or noncustodial parents. This requirement would apply to any single (divorced, widowed, or simply married-but-solo) parents, grandparents, or family friends taking children on a cruise. Many cruises have been spoiled because groups arrived at the dock or the airport with the kids but without a letter of permission. (Or at the very least, there's been a lot of anxiety waiting for faxed letters to arrive at the last minute.)

There's a good reason for why this letter is now a requirement. According to Department of State Publication 10542: "With the number of international child custody cases on the rise, several countries have instituted passport requirements to help prevent child abductions. For example, Mexico has a law that requires a child traveling alone, or with only one parent, or in someone else's custody, to carry written,

SAMPLE PERMISSION LETTER

Here's the text you might use for a typical letter of permission. You should type this up yourself, putting in all the specific details of your trip in place of the blanks.

CONSENT FOR MINOR CHILDREN TO TRAVEL

Date: _____

I (we): _____

authorize my/our minor child(ren): _____

to travel to: _____ on _____

aboard Airline/Flight Number: _____

and/or Cruise Ship: _____

with _____.

Their expected date of return is: _____.

In addition, I (we) authorize:_____ to consent to any necessary routine or emergency medical treatment during the aforementioned trip.

Signed: _____(Parent)

Signed: _____(Parent)

Address: _____

_____

_____

Telephone:_____

Sworn to and signed before me, a Notary Public,

this _____ day of _____, 20_____

_____

Notary Public Signature and Seal

notarized consent from the absent parent or parents. No authorization is needed if the child travels alone and is in possession of a U.S. passport. A child traveling alone with a birth certificate requires written, notarized authorization from both parents."

Proof of identity and citizenship is rather straightforward: you need either a certified copy of a birth certificate or a passport for your child. The permission letter is a bit more vexing since most people aren't aware of the necessity to have it, let alone what it should include. An attorney could prepare a formal affidavit, but a simple letter-style document is adequate as long as it's signed before an authorized notary. To be acceptable, it should include specific details about the trip, the custodial adult(s), and the child(ren). Although no one wants to think about medical emergencies while on vacation, it's also wise to include consent for the custodial adult to authorize emergency treatment for the child in case the need should arise.

> **WORD OF MOUTH**
>
> "Try not to resent the men who wear a navy blue blazer, gray slacks, and the same black shoes for almost every dressy occasion and look just fine. It may be boring, but it's easy to pack!" — Janet N.

Some parents, particularly mothers who do not share the same last name as their children, should take no chances and also carry a copy of their divorce decree or, in the case of widows, a death certificate for their spouse.

After going to all the trouble to secure proper documentation, it could turn out that no one even asks for it. Why did you bother? Because if you had not, the possibility existed that your cruise ship may have sailed without you and your very disappointed family. You may even find that it's easier to enter a port of call than to leave it with your own child.

PICKING A CRUISE WARDROBE

So your closet is not full of designer outfits and matching shoes? Not to worry, neither are the closets of most cruise ship passengers. The reality is that you do not need to overextend a credit card and fill your suitcases with new cruise duds. Despite any fashion anxiety, you probably have almost everything you need.

Cruise wear falls into three categories: casual, informal, and formal. Cruise documents should include information indicating how many evenings fall into each of those categories. You'll know when to wear what by reading your ship's daily newsletter, where each evening's dress code will be prominently announced. Dress codes are primarily directed toward adults, so children's wardrobes can be planned based on what their parents are wearing and the activities they are participating in.

CASUAL WEAR

First and foremost, there's casual wear. This is exactly what it implies: clothing to be comfortable in. Your plans for the day will dictate what you should wear. For warm-weather cruises, you'll typically need swimwear, a cover-up, and sandals for pool and beach. Time spent ashore touring and shopping calls for shorts topped with T-shirts or polo-style shirts and comfy walking shoes. Conservative is the rule to live by, and mix-and-match will save room in your suitcase. If you intend to purchase souvenir T-shirts, plan to make them a part of your cruise wardrobe and pack fewer tops.

Evening casual does not mean shorts. For men it's khaki-type slacks and a nice polo or sport shirt. Ladies' evening-casual outfits might consist of sporty dresses, skirts and tops, or pants outfits. By sticking to two colors and a few accessories, you can mix up tops and bottoms for a different look every night.

The first and last nights on board are always casual for obvious reasons—you may not have your luggage before dinner that first night, and you've already packed for home on the last night. Many people consider denim jeans casual wear. Some cruise lines discourage them in the dining room. Use your own judgment, and keep in mind that denim is hot—you might want to wear lighter fabrics in the Caribbean heat.

INFORMAL WEAR
Informal dress is a little trickier because it applies only to evening wear and can mean different things depending on the cruise line. Informal for women is a dressier dress or pants outfit; for men it almost always includes a sport coat and often a tie. Check your documents carefully for a specific definition of "informal."

FORMAL WEAR
It has been said that Formal Night is fantasyland for women and torture for men—from the sounds of male grumbling, that is. If you like to dress up, this is your night to shine. You'll see women in everything from simple cocktail dresses to elaborate, glittering gowns. Tuxedos (either all black or with a white dinner jacket) or dark suits are required for gentlemen, but a quick review of the dining room will show you that on most mainstream cruises, dark suits prevail. If you have been a mother of the bride lately, chances are your outfit for the wedding is just perfect for formal night. For children, Sunday-best is entirely appropriate.

If a man decides to go all out, then he must decide whether to buy or rent a tuxedo, which is ultimately a point of individual preference. As a rule of thumb, if you're going to wear a tuxedo more than two or three times, it makes economic sense to purchase one. Most cruise lines make it easy to rent the entire outfit, though—and if you do so, it will be waiting for you when you board. Be sure to make these arrangements well before your cruise; your travel agent can get the details from the cruise line.

It has been said that a tuxedo is a rented suit and a dinner jacket is the formal clothing owned by the gentleman wearing it. Whatever the definition or terms of ownership, men look stunning in black tie. If yours is a rental, try it on immediately so alterations can be made if necessary.

Even if you're renting a tuxedo, by all means buy your own studs. You don't have to spend a fortune on them; just get some that look classy. Why? A sure-fire way to spot a rented tuxedo is by the inexpensive studs that come with them. A few words about vests. Many men with a little girth consider them more comfortable than cummerbunds.

Which formal night is most formal? Every woman wants to know the answer to that question because we all have a dress we think is more stylish, or maybe we just feel more beautiful wearing it. Unless you eat like a bird or never gain an ounce, save your roomiest formal outfit for the second formal night.

How glittery can you get without being mistaken for a showgirl? Totally sequined and beaded dresses are not as fashionable as they once were, and you may want to avoid the temptation of borrowing your daughter's frou-frou prom dress as well—neither makes a good fashion statement. When selecting formal outfits, think simple. There's nothing more elegant than a well-cut, simple, black dress. But there's nothing more fun than a flashy or sexy dress that turns heads. It's totally up to you. One of the most practical and useful garments any woman can own is a pair of black, silky cocktail pants. They take up no room at all in the suitcase and don't wrinkle. Best of all, with two dressy tops you have two different formal outfits with a minimum of fuss. Even better, they usually have comfortable elastic waistbands.

If formal is just not a part of your vocabulary or lifestyle, consider booking on one of the cruise lines that have modified it or done away with it altogether. On some cruise lines every night is country-club casual.

OTHER CRUISE WARDROBE TIPS

For versatility and to stretch your options, coordinate your wardrobe by selecting garments in one or two basic colors to mix and match. No one really notices whether you recycle outfits, so don't be afraid to wear the same things more than once. Create different looks with accessories, either from home or purchased in port. To pack small, take only two pairs of shoes; comfortable all-purpose shoes for day and dressier ones for evening. If you must have your big, clunky athletic shoes, wear them on the plane and pack the others.

An absolute essential for women is a shawl or light sweater. Aggressive air-conditioning can make public rooms uncomfortable, particularly if you're sunburned from a day at the beach.

Expenses for cruise ship laundry, pressing, and dry-cleaning services can add up fast, especially laundry, as charges are per item and the rates are similar to those charged in hotels. Happily, some ships have a low-cost or free self-serve laundry room (the room usually has an iron and ironing board in addition to washers and dryers). You can make laundry less important when shopping if you look for clothing made of lightweight microfiber. Besides taking up less suitcase space, microfiber sheds wrinkles and dries quickly. In terms of comfort, these fabrics wick moisture away from the body, keeping you cool in the tropics and necessitating fewer clothing changes. Tuck a small bottle of laundry liquid and clothespins in your suitcase and, in a pinch, you can wash smaller items in your bathroom sink and hang them to dry in the shower. A hair dryer speeds the process along in record time.

After all this obsessing about clothing, consider the unthinkable: What if your luggage is delayed? What if it doesn't show up until the end of the cruise? Unfortunately, this happens. And if it happens to you, do not stress out. Shop here and there and pick up what you need until the next stop—your luggage could appear in the next port. Avoid some of the anxiety lost luggage can cause by carrying on your essentials when you board. Consider using a garment bag or rollaboard containing formal clothing, a bathing suit, and at least one casual outfit just in case.

And here's one last thought about cruise wear: Be considerate by adhering to each evening's dress code and do not rush back to your cabin to change into shorts immediately after dinner.

3

PICKING LUGGAGE

It just so happens that the best luggage for your cruise is also suitable for many other purposes. Airport and pier baggage handlers are notoriously rough with suitcases, so a top consideration is sturdiness. Your suitcase does not have to be top-of-the-line, but it should be built well enough to withstand the rigors of conveyors and sorting machines, not to mention being stacked, dropped, and thrown through the air.

Luggage can be a significant investment, so the right choice in terms of design and durability is important. Brand-name luggage that comes with a good warranty is always desirable, but no-name or private label brands can also stand the test of time.

Hard-sided luggage is usually the longest-wearing of all. In addition to being the most rugged, the built-in locks also make these suitcases the most secure and water-tight. For frequent flyers who want the greatest luggage mileage, it makes sense to look at hard-sided luggage. Improved composition materials have made their shells lighter; however, even when empty they can be heavy.

If casual observations at airport conveyors are any indication, soft-sided suitcases are by far the most popular choice. They're lighter in weight, their zippers can be secured pretty easily, almost all have wheels, and some are expandable for additional packing volume.

What should you look for in a suitcase? Hard-sided suitcases should have metal piano hinges and solid hardware. Combination locks are great, but look for those that also have key locks. Unless a clasp is locked, it could snap open. Wheels (preferably in-line skate type) should turn smoothly and be set wide for stability. Retractable handle assemblies should be strong and adjustable for maximum comfort and ease of maneuverability. Padded interiors with pockets and garment tie-downs are fairly standard.

The soft-sided suitcases you're considering should be covered in a tightly woven ballistic nylon for the greatest durability; other fabrics can snag, pill, and tear more easily. None of these fabrics is indestructible, but ballistic nylon is usually judged to be the best, especially when it's also Teflon® coated. Frame construction is also an important factor in the ultimate stability of the suitcase; it should be strong enough that it does not flex out of shape when the suitcase is fully packed. Corners should be reinforced with rubber bumpers hefty enough to prevent abrasion, which all too often occurs in these vulnerable areas. Wheels and handle assemblies should have the same properties as hard-sided cases; a solid skid plate between the wheels is beneficial to protect the suitcase fabric from damage when inevitable encounters with curbs and escalators occur. Look for self-healing, industrial-grade zippers that move smoothly and have large-enough zipper pulls for ease of use. Interiors can include a variety of wet bags, pockets, and other organizers, particularly in the lid door.

All suitcases should be well balanced with adequate feet so they do not fall over when you're waiting in a check-in line. In addition, many of the newest models include removable garment bags or suiters for wrinkle-free packing.

Even some of the smallest 22-inch suitcases are outfitted with suiters— those fold-up panels that accommodate hanging garments. These are great wrinkle-proof organizers that tuck formal clothing neatly into the suitcase. The handiest are the ones that are removable for times that you don't need them.

Business travelers have long favored garment bags for carry-on ease and quick, wrinkle-free packing. Their bulky favorites are being replaced these days by garment bags on wheels that are virtually rolling closets with multiple pockets and organizers for folded items, shoes, and even toiletries. Look for the same construction qualities as any soft-sided suitcase. These bags hold a lot but are not sized as carry-ons.

You know the days of massive steamer trunks are history, but is there a maximum amount of luggage that you can bring on a cruise ship? Yes, there really is a limit of sorts. Although some cruise lines state that each passenger is allowed 200 pounds of personal luggage, you're unlikely to see anyone's bags actually being weighed. However, it's not the cruise line restrictions that passengers need to worry about. Cruisers arriving at their embarkation port by air should be aware of airline restrictions. Most major airlines enforce suitcase size and weight policies, resulting in a rude (and expensive) surprise to some travelers with large, heavy suitcases.

Unfortunately, many 29- to 30-inch suitcases now exceed the maximum size limitation of 62 linear inches (a combination of length, width, depth) for airline checked luggage and are often subject to additional charges. Then there's the matter of suitcase wheel assemblies and whether they're included in the measurements or not. That depends on who you ask, and responses are all over the map. It seems the ultimate arbiter of oversize dimensions is the agent checking in passengers at the airport.

Those 29- to 30-inch suitcases are likely to incur excess weight charges, as well. As many travelers discover, they hold so much that they are prone to be overly heavy. Depending on their size, rolling garment bags might also fall into the category of too big to be checked free of charge. These days, you'll usually be charged extra for anything over 50 pounds; on a few airlines the limit is still 70 pounds, but on a few it's even as low as 40 pounds.

Don't even think of expanding a suitcase in the 29- to 30-inch size range to accommodate the addition of souvenirs for the trip home—the

Drugs: What You Can't Pack

It goes without saying that you shouldn't purchase Illegal drugs in the islands and try to bring them into the United States at the end of your cruise. In an odd twist, a group of hapless cruisers attempted to actually board a cruise ship in Florida with stashes they planned to consume on board. They were met in the terminal by U.S. Customs, a drug-sniffing dog, and local law enforcement agents who took the unusual step of examining passengers leaving the United States. It seems the excited group shared their packing lists with one another on the Internet and tipped off the authorities. The most common hiding place for their drugs wasn't very original—inside their underwear—and when they realized the search was on it caused quite a melee.

Moral of this story? Other than exercising discretion when sharing your plans openly in a chat room, just say no to buying drugs in foreign ports unless your vacation strategy includes spending time in the brig—or worse, in a Caribbean jail.

additional size and weight just will not fly these days without adding a fee as robust as the bag. Take a folding tote bag for purchases, and carry it on the plane home.

Remember that two suitcases in the 24- to 26-inch size range will hold as much (or more) than a single larger suitcase and are kinder to your back when you have to lift them. Most airlines charge for checked bags these days, so check with your airline and budget for anything you wish to check. The charges are quite high for excess baggage; don't be caught by surprise at the airport check-in counter.

Whether you buy new bags or carry your trusty old ones, take the following steps before you leave for the airport:

■ Ascertain the exact baggage regulations of the airline(s) you're most likely to fly with and strictly adhere to them.

■ For ease of moving through check-in lines, buy luggage pieces that can piggyback on one another.

■ Measure suitcases for size and include the wheels just in case.

■ Weigh packed suitcases on the bathroom scale.

PACKING

You may find that packing less is more if you follow this experienced travelers' adage: "Pack your suitcases and remove half the contents. Then take twice as much money!" I have a confession. I'm a packaholic. I was hopelessly addicted to overburdening my husband with bulging garment bags and suitcases that barely closed. The overflow from my tote bag got stashed in his pockets. Practicality has forced me to change my ways.

I became a confirmed packing list maker following my very first cruise on the SS *Norway*. I overlooked one little grooming essential that I really needed: tweezers. One of my tablemates forgot to pack her hair dryer. And it dawned on us that a cruise is unlike a resort vacation in one important way: there's no local supermarket or drugstore to pop into when you need something. Although many ships stock a variety of sundries, they may not have just what you need and, if they do, the cost can be considerably more than comparable items at home. My tablemate and I were both able to find suitable replacements ashore for our forgotten items, but we spent two days at sea before arriving in our first port of call where we could shop for them.

> **WORD OF MOUTH**
>
> "Packing lists made getting ready for the trip so much easier. I had spreadsheets for packing clothes, toiletries, and our carry-on bag. My husband thought I was insane, but I didn't forget anything!" — Cindy N.

Aha! A light went on in my brain. If I had checklists, I would be less likely to leave something out of my suitcase. What simplicity. Why hadn't anyone thought of it before? While planning my second cruise, I began by creating basic packing lists for my husband and myself. Over the years I've added and deleted items—for instance, I prefer my own brand of shampoo to the products provided by most hotels and cruise lines. On the other hand, it's seldom necessary to pack a hair dryer these days, although some ships' accommodations don't provide them in all categories. I've welcomed suggestions from users of my Web site, CruiseDiva.com, as well. The packing list for babies was compiled entirely from my readers' input.

I begin with personal essentials and a day-by-day schedule of wardrobe requirements. This has worked fine to rein in my packing excesses. Now, mind you, the following checklists contain just about everything anyone would need on a cruise. As a result, there are many items you can just cross off. How much of each clothing item to pack (such as shirts, shorts, and underwear) is determined by the length of your cruise and your planned activities. A good rule of thumb is to pack one daytime outfit for every two days of travel. However, you may need more shirts and shorts if your plans include adventurous excursions. Clothing tends to get soiled and sweaty under some conditions and you'll want to change more frequently.

Instead of strappy sandals, you may need hiking boots and bug spray, or water shoes and no formal wear. Customize these lists to work for you based on where you're going, what you intend to do, and which cruise line you're traveling with.

PACKING FOR CHILDREN AND TEENS

About the only difference between the wardrobes of parents and younger family members is that children's clothing is smaller and takes up less space in a suitcase. Their requirements will mimic the adult versions of the bathing suits, shorts, T-shirts, shoes, etc., which are outlined in the packing lists. If your plans include dining every night as a family, the children should be suitably attired to conform to the cruise line's dress code, although comfort is more important for their happiness than being overly formal, particularly when it comes to younger children.

Make the planning and packing stage of cruise preparation a family affair by enlisting everyone's help. To make things easy, make stacks of clothing for each child for every day of the cruise, including underwear and socks. Put each day's stack in a zipper-top plastic bag and label them Monday, Tuesday, and so on. Once on board the ship, each child can easily unpack his or her own suitcase and slip the plastic bags into drawers. Every morning they will know what to wear.

Teenagers can be quite independent creatures with very definite ideas about what they prefer to wear. They're likely to insist upon making their own clothing selections. Parents, you might want to keep an eye on what they've chosen to oversee the appropriateness of their wardrobes.

A TRAVEL FIRST-AID KIT

In addition to clothing, consider packing some indispensable first-aid and emergency items. Not all scrapes happen within close proximity of the ship's medical center, and some minor accidents or illnesses do not require treatment. Be prepared at all times, both on board and ashore, with basic items for first aid such as a few adhesive bandages and a small bottle of waterless antibacterial hand sanitizer, which can also be used to clean small cuts.

For all around care, these items should be sufficient:

- adhesive bandages
- first-aid antibacterial cream
- waterless antibacterial hand sanitizer
- aspirin or nonaspirin pain reliever
- antinausea medication
- antidiarrheal medication
- antacid tablets
- antihistamine
- seasickness remedy
- zipper-top plastic bags or ice bag
- dental adhesive
- prescription medications

Even people without dentures may have several capped teeth or fillings. It's rare that a shipboard medical center features a resident dentist, so a small container of dental adhesive or special dental repair kit is handy. A temporary repair can mean the difference between discomfort and relief from sensitivity to hot and cold until a dentist is available in port.

A problem to consider when traveling is edema, the accumulation of excess fluid in body tissues. It's a very common condition, particularly after long airplane flights and while cruising in hot, humid climates. Swollen ankles and feet are regular complaints, but you can take some preventative measures. During precruise flights drink plenty of water but avoid caffeine and alcoholic beverages, walk around the plane every hour, and wear special compression stockings. Should swelling still

PACKING LISTS FOR THE FAMILY

CLOTHING FOR WOMEN
- gowns or cocktail dresses
- dress shoes and hosiery
- skirts, blouses, or pant outfits
- accessories (scarves, pins, etc.)
- shawl or sweater
- casual shoes
- T-shirts or polo shirts
- shorts or slacks
- bathing suit
- tennis shoes and socks
- undergarments
- sleepwear

CLOTHING FOR MEN
- tuxedo and accessories (studs, formal shirts, tie, cummerbund, belt), or dark business suit with shirts and ties
- dress shoes and black socks
- sport coat
- slacks and belt
- polo or golf shirts
- khaki pants
- casual shoes
- T-shirts
- shorts
- bathing suit
- tennis shoes and socks
- undergarments
- sleepwear

PACKING FOR BABY
Mothers accustomed to carrying diaper bags chock-full of gear know their babies and toddlers have as many essentials as most infantry divisions in the field. Your own physician should be your guide, but consider these suggestions from a pediatrician and experienced moms when packing for small passengers' general travel needs:

- Children's Benadryl (seasickness or restlessness)
- PediaCare decongestant
- sunblock
- adhesive bandages
- Children's Tylenol
- diaper rash ointment
- hat
- disinfectant ointment
- water shoes
- diapers
- bottles and sippy cups
- disposable bibs
- diaper wipes
- hand and face wipes
- cotton swabs
- nail clippers
- poolside robe
- bathing suit
- sunglasses
- bottled water
- juice boxes
- favorite blanket or toy
- pacifiers
- thermometer

For flights, the pediatrician suggests giving little ones a sippy cup during airplane take-offs and landings. Also consider bringing an umbrella stroller for walks around the ship and in port with your baby. The stroller is especially handy at airports.

ESSENTIALS FOR YOUR CARRY-ON

Your carry-on is your hedge against lost luggage. In addition to the toiletries, valuables, and medicines you can't do without, you should consider putting a basic change of clothing and fresh undergarments in it as well. In case your luggage is delayed, those items should help you make it through the time it takes for your suitcases to catch up with you.

As of this writing, heightened security measures have restricted the amounts of liquids, gels, and aerosols that can be carried onto airplanes. However, solid cosmetics and personal hygiene items such as lipstick, lip balm, and similar solids are permitted in carry-on bags without restriction. For carry-on liquids and gels, each container must be three ounces or smaller, and all the containers must be placed inside a single, quart-size, zippered, clear plastic bag. One, and only one, plastic bag is allowed per passenger. Exceptions to the size restrictions are made for prescription and over-the-counter medicines, as well as baby formula and breast milk, all of which must be declared before inspection. For the latest regulations on what's allowed and what isn't, check with the Transportation Security Administration (www.tsa.gov).

■ passport, money, documents, and keys

■ camera, film or memory cards, and extra batteries

■ extra glasses

■ reading glasses (if you use them)

■ contact lens supplies

■ toothbrush and toothpaste

■ mouthwash and dental floss

■ deodorant

■ shampoo and conditioner (if you want your own brand)

■ sunglasses

■ shaving kit

■ jewelry

■ hat or cap

■ travel clock

■ small flashlight and nightlight

■ perfume

■ body and hand lotions

■ talcum powder

■ sun screen

■ cosmetics

■ brushes, combs, and hair spray

■ hair dryer (if your cruise ship doesn't provide them)

■ curling iron

■ shower cap

■ feminine hygiene products

■ short, multiplug extension cord

■ notebook and pen

■ duct tape

■ cable ties

■ liquid laundry soap

■ folding tote bag or waist pack

■ binoculars

Post-9/11 airline regulations still prohibit sharp objects in carry-on bags, so pack your Swiss Army knife, larger tools (more than 7 inches in length), and razor-type implements (like box cutters, utility knives, and razor blades not in a cartridge) in your checked luggage. Your safety razor, a cigarette lighter, and one book of safety (non-strike anywhere) matches may be taken onto the airplane in carry-on baggage. When in doubt about whether an item is allowed in your carry-on, check the current list on the TSA Web site ⊕ *www.tsa.gov.*

3

CLOSE UP

Tips for Checked Luggage

The following tips apply whether you're checking your luggage at the airport or the cruise terminal:

■ Arrive at the airport in plenty of time, preferably two hours or more before departure. One of the leading causes of lost luggage is late arrivals—baggage handlers just do not have time to scan your bags and then to get them to the plane.

■ Avoid airport curbside check-in. A whopping 87% of lost or stolen luggage originates at those curbside stations.

■ One of the most common causes of misrouted bags is gate agent error. Know the three-letter code of your destination airport and verify it on the luggage tag before your bag is put on the conveyor belt.

■ Avoid connecting flights whenever possible.

■ Make sure the connection times are adequate. Do not accept anything less than an hour between flights. You might make the plane, but your luggage may not.

■ Secure your bags. Check the locking devices when you arrive at your destination, and report any damage or missing items to the airline or cruise line immediately.

■ Label luggage on the inside and outside with your name, phone number, and address (preferably a business address). Include a copy of your itinerary on the inside of your bags so you can be traced more easily.

■ Remove any old claim checks from the bags.

■ When tagging suitcases for check-in on your ship, use all the tags you receive. Put two tags on each checked bag just in case one is damaged or falls off.

develop, raise your feet and apply an ice-filled zipper-top plastic bag for relief. Sleeping with elevated feet can help as well—try putting a folded blanket or life vest under the mattress.

All medications and first-aid supplies should be in their original containers and should be hand carried—do not pack them in checked luggage. Always have enough prescription medicine on hand for a couple of extra days in case of travel delays when returning home. Contact lens and eyeglasses wearers should consider packing an extra pair.

PACKING STRATEGIES

Once your major wardrobe selections are complete and the suitcases are ready, devise a streamlined packing strategy. Here are my suggestions:

■ Personalize the packing list and stick with it. Assemble everything on the list before starting to pack, and check items off when they're folded and placed in the suitcase.

■ Resist the urge to toss in something "just in case"—that's the item you surely won't need.

■ Pack small. When they're compressed, undergarments and knits take only a third of the suitcase space they normally occupy. Simply fill a large zippered storage bag with these articles and force all the air out before zipping it shut. Keep in mind that when you use zippered storage bags to compress clothing, you'll save room and get more in your luggage, but the suitcases could end up heavier because they hold more.

■ Plan ahead and shop for sample- or small-size containers of favorite toiletries.

■ Don't forget that you can carry onto your flight only small containers of liquids and gels (whatever will fit in a single, quart-size zippered storage bag); larger sizes will have to go in your checked bags.

■ To help keep garments wrinkle-free, leave them on their hangers, cover them with dry-cleaning bags, and fold over once before placing them in the suitcase. Unpacking is a snap; just open your suitcase and start hanging things in the closet.

■ Do not bring along a travel iron to touch up wrinkled garments. Irons are a fire hazard, and their use in passenger cabins is strongly discouraged. Instead, pack a clothing steamer.

■ T-shirts can serve as a swimsuit cover-up or a nightshirt. Knit sport shirts can do double duty as well; a shirt worn a short time at dinner can easily be donned the next day for touring or lounging on the ship.

■ If the ship has self-service laundry facilities, you can pack lighter and wash clothes midway through the cruise. Remember, other passengers have the same idea, so you might encounter long lines and surly tempers. Use the ship's laundry service instead. It's pricier, but who wants to spend valuable cruise time washing clothes?

■ Use every bit of luggage space. Women's shoes will often fit inside men's. Stuff socks and other small items inside larger space-wasters. A tote bag that folds into its own zippered pocket is handy as a shopping or beach bag and invaluable when it's time to pack the souvenirs that are preventing your suitcase from closing.

■ Cross-pack your luggage with your travel companion. Chances are if a suitcase is missing, it'll turn up eventually. In the meantime, you'll both have fresh clothing until it does.

■ Valuables should never be packed in your checked luggage. Jewelry, medicine, cameras, travel documents, and a change of underclothes belong in your carry-on. For safety and peace of mind, carry traveler's checks, cash, and copies of your passport and credit cards in a money pouch under your clothing.

■ Tuck copies of your packing lists in with your travel documents. If your luggage is waylaid, you'll have a handy record of the contents.

A caveat: Unfortunately, some garments defy the dry-cleaning-bag packing method. Clothing that is slightly creased or wrinkled can often be freshened up by steaming. If you don't have a clothing steamer, just hang those items in the bathroom while taking a hot, steamy shower, and often the wrinkles will fall right out. If all else fails, many ships have ironing stations in their self-service passenger launderettes or, for maximum convenience, send the offending garments to the ship's laundry for pressing.

CLOSE UP

Duct Tape—the Essential Travel Tool

So, your bags are packed and you're ready to cruise? Not quite yet if you skipped the duct tape. You don't want to leave your home port without one of a traveler's handiest necessities. Duct tape no longer belongs only in the garage. Some of its more mundane uses are luggage repair (fix a broken hinge with ease) and security (baggage handlers won't tamper with duct tape; it's too much trouble). Wrapped in duct tape, your luggage is easy to spot in terminals as well. For individuality, duct tape comes in colors, as well as the traditional silver. For even higher suitcase visibility, there are snazzy neon colors. It's water resistant (an important feature for ocean travelers) and can serve as an indestructible luggage tag as well as a strap—just write your name and address on the tape. Best of all, duct tape is easy to tear by hand, so you don't need scissors to cut it.

There are literally thousands of uses for duct tape. Every homeowner knows that when something is supposed to stick together and it doesn't, nothing holds like duct tape. What about at sea? Is the bottom ready to fall out of your cabin's vanity drawer? Tape it until the carpenter arrives. You're a late sleeper and the drapes don't quite close? Keep the sun at bay by taping them together. Everyone has had the stitching in a hem unravel at the last minute. Duct tape to the rescue! There are bottle lids to secure, rattles to silence, drawers that won't stay shut when the ship is rolling, and other little things that happen when you least expect them.

One of duct tape's most creative uses is as a replacement for an uplifting foundation garment. Under low-cut or backless dresses—or when a brassiere just won't work with a gown—create your own Wonder Duct Bra. Duct tape sticks well for hours and peels off without pain. Best of all, the variety of colors means more coordinating choices and even less chance of a sliver of silver tape peeping from a black décolleté neckline.

Frequent travelers have all noticed that luggage often becomes unzipped for one reason or another during baggage handling, either at the airport or cruise terminal. You want to lock your soft-sided luggage, but with current airport security procedures, you may not be able to until after it has been screened. Ask at check-in if you can use cable ties, which can usually be found with electrical supplies in home improvement centers. If your luggage requires hand-screening, you'll find a note inside the suitcase indicating that the contents were examined. If you use a traditional combination or keyed lock, it will be cut off and discarded. Inspectors in foreign countries can't always open the TSA-approved locks.

Once they're attached, cable ties must be removed with scissors or nail clippers. When flying to your embarkation port, never put scissors in your carry-on. Instead, place them in an unlocked outside suitcase pocket or simply pack nail clippers in your carry-on to cut the plastic ties. To keep sticky-fingered baggage handlers from riffling through your things, always secure luggage before checking in at the cruise terminal, and remember to take extra cable ties for the trip home.

Enjoying Your Cruise

WORD OF MOUTH

"We're considering booking a 5-night Caribbean cruise for next summer. . . . There is only one day at sea with 3 port stops. What is there to do during that day when we're at sea?"

—mrg013

"I sail solo often and have always enjoyed myself. I prefer not to hook up with others for excursions as I like to do what I want, whenever I want, and do not feel a need for company. I travel solo and have never felt compromised."

—Kfusto

www.fodors.com/community

With the planning, packing, and anticipation behind them, veteran cruisers sometimes view embarkation day as anticlimactic. However, for first-time cruise passengers, embarking on your first ship can be more than exhilarating—it can be downright intimidating.

Take a deep breath. You've come this far, and your ship is within sight. That first glimpse could well be an "oh my gosh" moment if you've booked a megaship. They're huge and dwarf nearly everything in their vicinity. Sit back and savor the moment because soon you'll be busy. There will be a lot happening around you, and it will all be new. Procedures may differ slightly from cruise line to cruise line, but don't worry: once you understand the process and know what to expect, you can go with the flow.

Above all, don't stress. There can be advantages to waiting in line when you reach the terminal: your luggage may beat you to your cabin, and you could meet some interesting people. After the check-in and boarding process is behind you, the fun and relaxation begin.

Think of the ship as your first destination, a movable port of call. Plan to enjoy your time on board as much as you can. Repeat after me: "They won't run out of food."

BOARDING

What exactly can you expect? First of all, keep in mind that your embarkation day cannot officially begin until the ship is clear of departing passengers and their luggage. The disembarkation process can seem as drawn-out as a divorce. While the previous weeks' passengers make their way reluctantly down the gangway, the staff and crew are busy readying the ship for the next sailing. By the time the last straggler departs, trucks are already arriving at the dock with provisions, and a lot of heavy work is going on behind the scenes. Staterooms and public lounges are thoroughly cleaned and readied, and a steady stream of supplies and luggage is brought aboard. There can even be an exchange of crew members, with some leaving and others arriving. The vessel's entire turnaround procedure is as carefully choreographed as the most intricate ballet.

WHAT TO EXPECT

CHECKING IN

Whether you take a bus transfer or taxi from the airport or a hotel, the first people you encounter at the cruise terminal are baggage handlers. They're not cruise line employees, and they do expect a tip—$2 per suitcase is sufficient. Be sure your ship's luggage tags are securely fastened to your locked suitcases before you hand them over. If you booked a guarantee and haven't received your cabin assignment, your luggage tags may be marked TBA (to be announced), or there may be a blank space where the cabin number should be written in. The baggage handlers will have a copy of the ship's manifest and can give you the proper cabin number.

Cruise line shoreside staff are milling about to point you in the right direction, and they're easily recognizable in official-looking uniforms with name tags and, often, a clipboard. Once inside the terminal, you might encounter a check-in line. Actual boarding time is often scheduled for noon, but some cruise lines will process early arrivals and then direct them to a holding area. During check-in, you'll be asked to produce your documents and any forms you were sent to complete ahead of time—or a printed copy of those you filled in online—plus proof of citizenship and a credit card (to cover charges on board). You're issued a boarding card that usually also doubles as your stateroom key and shipboard charge card. At some point—either before you enter the check-in area or before you proceed to the ship—you and your hand luggage will pass through a security procedure similar to those at airports.

While the gangway is generally not removed until 30 minutes before sailing, U.S. government security regulations require cruise lines to submit certain passenger information to law enforcement authorities at least 60 minutes prior to departure. To meet that requirement, they must have the necessary information in their computers at least 90 minutes before departure. If you arrive too late and your information is not in the system before the deadline, you run the risk being denied boarding even though the ship won't be sailing for more than an hour.

Everyone is eager to get on board and begin their vacation, but this is not the time to get cranky if you have to wait. Keep in mind that you cannot board until the ship is ready for you. Once boarding begins, you'll inevitably have your first experience with the ship's photographer and will be asked to pose for an embarkation picture. It only takes a second, so smile. You're under no obligation to purchase any photos taken of you during the cruise, but they're a nice souvenir if you do decide to buy them.

PAYING FOR THINGS ON BOARD

Let's step back a moment and take a look at what happened when you checked in at the pier. Because a cashless society prevails on cruise ships, an imprint was made of your credit card or you had to place a cash deposit for use against your onboard charges. Then you were issued a boarding/charge card that often doubles as your stateroom key. An itemized bill is provided at the end of the voyage listing your purchases. Most onboard expenditures are charged to your shipboard account, with the exception of casino gaming (though some machines now accept your ship charge card as well as coins and paper money).

In order to avoid surprises at the end of your cruise, it's a good idea to set aside your charge slips and request an interim printout of your bill from the purser to ensure accuracy. Should you change your mind about charging onboard purchases, you can always inform the purser and pay in cash or traveler's checks instead. If your cash deposit was more than you spent, you'll receive a refund; if you charge more than the deposit, you'll be asked to put more on your account.

SETTLING IN

Congratulations! Once you cross the gangway, your cruise has begun. The actual boarding procedures can vary; however, you'll have to produce your boarding card for the security officer who will take your digital image to enter into the ship's security system. When leaving and

> **CAUTION**
>
> If your luggage doesn't appear when and where it should (either at the airport or cruise terminal), report the problem immediately before leaving the building and insist on a local phone number so you can follow up.

reboarding the ship in port, your boarding pass is scanned and your image will appear on a screen for verification.

After you're greeted by the staff members awaiting your arrival, you'll be directed to your cabin, or, depending on the cruise line, a steward will relieve you of your carry-on luggage and accompany you. Stewards on high-end cruise lines such as Seabourn, Regent Seven Seas, SeaDream, and Silversea not only show you the way but also hand you a glass of champagne as a welcome-aboard gesture. Although a tip isn't necessarily expected by the steward who shows you to your cabin, a couple of dollars is usually appreciated by those on mainstream and premium cruise lines. On some luxury lines, gratuities are included in the fare and not expected. Your offer of a tip will be graciously refused.

Some cruise lines restrict access to cabins until a specified time and will direct you to a buffet or restaurant to enjoy lunch while you wait. Once you're in your cabin, make sure that everything is in order. Try the plumbing and set the air-conditioning—your cabin may feel warm while docked, but will cool off quickly when the ship is under way. You should find a copy of the ship's daily schedule in the cabin. Take a few moments to look it over; you'll want to know what time the muster drill takes place (a placard on the back of your cabin door will indicate directions to your emergency station), as well as meal hours and the schedule for various activities and entertainments.

Rented tuxedos are either hanging in the closet or will be delivered sometime during the afternoon, and bon voyage gifts sent by your friends or travel agent usually appear as well. Be patient if you're expecting deliveries, particularly on megaships. Cabin stewards participate in the ship's turnaround and are extremely busy, although yours will no doubt introduce himself at the first available opportunity. It will also be a while before your checked luggage arrives, so, if you haven't had lunch already, your initial order of business is usually the welcome-aboard buffet. Bring along the daily schedule to read more closely while you eat.

While making your way to the Lido buffet, no doubt you'll notice bar waiters offering trays of colorful tropical drinks, often in souvenir glasses that you can keep. Beware: they are not complimentary! If you choose one, you'll be asked to sign for it. Again, as with the photos, you're under no obligation to purchase; however, the glasses are fun souvenirs.

Do your plans for the cruise include booking shore excursions and indulging in spa treatments and salon services? The most popular tours sometimes sell out, spas can be busy during sea days, and salons are particularly busy before formal nights, so your next stops should be the Shore Excursion Desk to book tours and the spa and salon to make appointments.

Dining room seating arrangements are another matter for consideration. Some people like to check the main dining room to determine the location of their table. If it's not to your liking—or if you requested a large table and find yourself assigned to a small one—you'll want to see the headwaiter. He'll be stationed in a lounge with his charts handy to make changes; the daily schedule will indicate where and when to meet with him. If you plan to dine in the ship's specialty restaurants, you'll want to make those reservations as soon as possible.

Do not get in the habit of referring to your cruise ship as a boat. A boat is often carried on a ship, and if you're in a boat, you're either headed for a day ashore or your ship is sinking! Even more confusing to many passengers are the directional terms *port* and *starboard*. An easy way to associate them is by remembering that *port* and *left* each contain four letters.

By late afternoon or early evening, luggage should arrive outside the cabin door, and you can unpack, settle into your cabin, and prepare for dinner. Just in case your luggage does not arrive before dinner, as sometimes happens when you're dining at the early seating, it's a good idea to have toiletries and appropriate attire in your carry-on so you can freshen up and change. Dress codes are always casual on the first evening of cruises.

For the rest of the afternoon and into the night you may find other introductory activities scheduled, such as tours of the spa and fitness center, port and shopping talks, and casino gaming lessons. Of course, there will be the compulsory muster drill, either held prior to sailing or within the first 24 hours of every cruise. No matter what terminology is used to describe it—Muster Station, Lifeboat Drill, General Emergency Stations, Compulsory Coast Guard Drill—this exercise is mandatory and required by law.

THE LIFEBOAT DRILL

Unpleasant and unlikely as it may seem, emergencies do happen. That's why one of the first things you may notice in your stateroom are the bright orange personal flotation devices (PFD), or life jackets, that are often prominently displayed on the beds. When you're checking your stateroom's features, take a moment to study the emergency card on the back of the door. The cards differ, ship by ship, but usually indicate "you are here"—the location of your cabin—and the direction you should go in case of an emergency. Your muster station will be indicated, usually by number or letter.

Cruise lines take the safety of their guests and vessels very seriously, so shortly before sailing an announcement will be made that the lifeboat drill begins when the alarm bells are sounded. Be prepared with your PFD in hand, if you are required to bring it. and proceed to your muster

CLOSE UP

Common Nautical Terms

Before acquainting yourself with your ship, you should add a few nautical terms to your vocabulary:

Berth. Sleeping space on a ship (literally refers to your bed).

Bow. The pointy end of the ship, also known as *forward*. Yes, it's also the front of the ship.

Bridge. The navigational control center (where the captain drives the ship).

Bulkhead. A wall or upright partition separating a ship's compartments.

Cabin. Your accommodation on a ship (used interchangeably with *stateroom*).

Course. Measured in degrees, the direction in which a ship is headed.

Debark. To leave a ship (also known as *disembarkation*).

Draft. The depth of water needed to float a ship; the measurement from a ship's waterline to the lowest point of its keel.

Embark. To go on board a ship (also known as *embarkation*).

Galley. The ship's kitchen.

Gangway. The stairway or ramp used to access the ship from the dock.

Hatch. An opening or door on a ship, either vertical or horizontal.

Head. A bathroom aboard a ship.

Helm. The apparatus for steering a ship.

Muster. To assemble the passengers and/or crew on a ship.

Pitch. Plunging in a longitudinal direction; the up-and-down motion of a ship (a major cause of seasickness).

Port. The left side of the ship when you're facing forward.

Promenade. Usually outside, a deck that fully or partially encircles the ship, popular for walking and jogging.

Roll. Side-to-side movement of the ship (another seasickness culprit).

Stabilizers. Operated by gyroscopes, these retractable finlike devices below the waterline extend from a ship's hull to reduce roll and provide stability. (They're your best friend if you're prone to motion sickness.)

Starboard. The right side of the ship when you're facing forward.

Stern. The rounded end of the ship, also called *aft*. It's the back end.

Tender. A boat carried on a ship that's used to take passengers ashore when it's not possible to tie up at a dock.

Thrusters. Fanlike propulsion devices under the waterline that move a ship sideways.

Wake. The ripples left on the water's surface by a moving ship.

---

station. Carry the life jacket unless you are instructed to wear it, and be sure the ties don't trail on the floor; it's easy to get tripped up on them as you ascend or descend stairs. Crew members will be stationed at the stairwells on each deck to give directions. Procedures vary—on some cruise lines you'll muster in a public room to receive instructions and then continue to the lifeboat station; on others you'll immediately go to the muster station on an open deck; on some ships you are no longer required to bring your PFD to the drill.

In all cases, crew members will be on hand to check your stateroom number off their list and show you how to properly put on your PFD. You'll notice it has two important features: a light that is activated in water and a whistle. An officer assigned to your boat will instruct the group on the procedures to follow if it becomes necessary to actually lower and enter the lifeboats or to jump into the water. Should you have the urge to blow the whistle attached to the PFD, restrain yourself—you should use the whistle only in a real emergency. Stewards check the cabins to make sure that everyone attends the muster drill, so don't even think about hiding out and not participating. In an emergency situation, your survival could depend on it. Afterward, stow your life jackets back in the cabin and prepare for sail-away festivities on the pool deck.

THE FIRST EVENING

A highlight of embarkation day is the first dinner in the main restaurant, where you'll meet your waitstaff and tablemates. Order whatever you like from the menu of appetizers, salads, soups, and entrées, but save room for dessert! Other than iced tea, coffee, hot tea, and tap water, beverages in the dining room are not complimentary on most mainstream and premium ships.

After dinner you'll find the entire ship alive with action. The casino, shops, and lounges will be open to greet guests, and the cruise director usually introduces his staff at a welcome-aboard show in the main theater (shows are scheduled to coordinate with dinner seatings).

Back in your cabin for the night, you'll find that the steward has left the next day's schedule of activities, straightened things up during your absence, filled the ice bucket, provided fresh linens in the bathroom, turned down the bed, and possibly placed a chocolate on your pillow. On mainstream cruise ships you may even find a towel animal—a whimsical creature fashioned from towels—on the bed. Some stewards demonstrate a creative streak, leaving a different one every night.

TIPPING

You don't have to go overboard with extras, but one area not to skimp on is gratuities. Tipping aboard a cruise ship is possibly one of the most delicate—yet frequently debated—topics of conversation among cruise passengers. Whom should you tip? How much should you tip? What is customary and recommended? Should parents tip the full amount for children or is half adequate? Why do you have to tip at all?

Like their land-bound contemporaries, cruise ship service personnel depend on gratuities for a major portion of their compensation. Educate yourself about gratuities by reading your cruise line brochure, where suggested tipping levels are usually listed in the back with the rest of the fine print. Then read over the small booklet that comes with your cruise documents for up-to-the-minute information.

Recommended Tips by Cruise Line

Each cruise line has a different tipping policy. Some allow you to add tips to your shipboard account; others expect you to dole out the dollars in cash on the last night of the cruise. Here are the suggested tipping amounts for each line covered in this book. Gratuity recommendations are often higher if you're staying in a suite with extra services, such as a butler. *The ship profiles in Chapter 5 give you the details:*

Azamara Club Cruises: No tipping expected

Carnival Cruise Line: $10 per person per day

Celebrity Cruises: $11.50 per person per day

Costa Cruises: $11 per person per day

Crystal Cruises: No tipping expected

Cunard Line: $11–$13 per person per day

Disney Cruise Line: $36 per person for 3-night cruises, $48 per person for 4-night cruises, $84 per person for 7-night cruises

Holland American Line: $11 per person per day

MSC Cruises: $8–$12 per person per day

Norwegian Cruise Line: $12 per person per day

Oceania Cruises: $13.50 per person per day

Princess Cruises: $11.50 per person per day

Regent Seven Seas Cruises: No tipping expected

Royal Caribbean: $11.65–$13.90 per person per day

Seabourn Cruises: No tipping expected

SeaDream Yacht Club: No tipping expected

Silversea Cruises: No tipping expected

Star Clippers: $8 per person per day

Windstar Cruises: $12 per person per day

BEFORE YOU BOARD

The whom-to-tip decision is easy. It's up to your discretion to tip anyone who provides a service you would like to recognize. This begins as early as your airport check-in. Porters carrying your bags in airports expect a tip, as do the agents at curbside check-in (even if they charge a fee). Depending on your city, $1 to $2 a bag will do. The same rule applies when you retrieve your suitcases at the baggage claim area at your destination; if you use the services of a porter or skycap, tip him for taking your bags to your bus or taxi. "Wait a minute!" you say, "I'm shelling out all these dollars and I haven't even reached the ship yet." Well, that's true. And one way to avoid tipping is to do everything yourself. It's perfectly acceptable to carry (or roll) your own luggage into and out of airports, but if you accept assistance you should give a tip.

When transfers to and from your ship are a part of your Air & Sea program, gratuities are generally included for luggage handling. In that case, don't worry about the interim tipping. However, if you take a taxi to the pier and hand over your bags to a stevedore, be sure to tip him. He's the person responsible for getting your suitcases onto a pallet and on their way to the ship, but he's not a cruise line employee. Stiff this guy, and hours later you may be filing a missing baggage report. Better, treat him with respect and pass along at least $5 with a handshake and big smile.

You're on board. Now what? Relax. With a couple of exceptions, which are addressed below, cash tips won't be expected until the last night of your cruise.

ON BOARD YOUR SHIP

TIPPING PROCEDURES

During your last day of cruising there will be a disembarkation talk, which is usually conducted by the cruise director. One member of each family is encouraged to attend and, in addition to customs and immigration procedures, tipping is discussed. (Don't worry if you miss the meeting, it will be replayed on television all day long.)

With the advent of alternative dining venues and options for open seating for dinner on contemporary ships, most cruise lines now either automatically add gratuities to passengers' onboard charge accounts or offer automatic tipping as an option, usually in the amount of $10 to $12 per passenger, per day (or, in the case of some lines such as Crystal and Oceania, the amounts may be a few dollars higher; in other cases a bit lower). If that's your cruise line's policy and the amount suits you, then do nothing. In most cases, you're certainly free to adjust the amounts up or down to more appropriate levels or ask that the charge be removed altogether if you prefer distributing cash gratuities.

If your ship is one of those on which tips are still given in cash, small white tip envelopes will appear in your stateroom during the last day of the cruise, along with luggage tags and written disembarkation instructions. As a general rule of thumb, you can count on the following amounts falling within the tipping guidelines:

- Room Steward: $3.50 per day
- Dining Room Waiter: $3.50 per day
- Dining Room Assistant Waiter: $2 per day

Give the tip envelopes to your dining room waiter and assistant waiter on the last night of the cruise, at dinner. If you see your room steward in the hall, you can deliver the tip envelope personally, or you may leave it in the cabin when you go to dinner on the last night. When your accommodations include the services of a butler, you should also reward his service in a similar manner. Whatever you do, don't skip out on dinner in the dining room on the final night of your cruise just to avoid tipping. If you prefer to dine elsewhere that evening, by all means do so, but stop by the dining room to recognize the service of the waitstaff.

As a rule of thumb, for a seven-day cruise, count on gratuities of at least $70 to $90 per person, or more if you are served by a butler in a suite. In addition, it may be suggested that you tip the headwaiter $5 per person per week. If he's rendered some special service (prepared tableside desserts) or if he's been particularly attentive and kept things moving, by all means give him a tip. If he shows up only that last evening with a smile and his hand out, you needn't feel obliged to tip him.

Some passengers claim that a cash tip offered to their cabin steward at the beginning of a cruise does wonders to produce exceptional service. Although I tried it once, I saw no difference in the level of attention I received.

Of course, some higher-end cruise lines suggest higher gratuity amounts per person, per day, such as Cunard, and Oceania. There are also some truly no-tipping-required cruise lines, which include Azamara, Crystal, SeaDream, Seabourn, Silversea, and Regent Seven Seas Cruises. On these cruises, gratuities are considered prepaid. If you feel the service warrants recognition, ask at the Reception Desk if there's a crew appreciation fund to which you can contribute.

Naturally, it would be gauche to offer a tip to an officer or a member of the cruise line's professional staff. However, if an officer or someone on the cruise staff renders out-of-the-ordinary service or is especially helpful, a letter of praise to the cruise line's home office can do wonders for that employee's career.

Finally, remember to have some dollar bills on hand when you disembark the ship. There will still be palms to cross in the cruise terminal and at the airport.

TIPPING FOR YOUR KIDS

Parents often argue the need to tip the entire recommended amount for their children, especially little ones. I wonder if the messes their children leave in the bathroom, cabin, and dining room are invisible to these parents. Not to mention that some tykes run their waiters ragged replacing plates of food that they don't like. Simply because children are smaller than adults doesn't mean they are less trouble to clean up after. Parents have already gotten a reduced (third or fourth passenger) fare for their children or, in some cases, free passage. Some cruise lines, such as MSC Cruises, suggest you tip the cabin steward half the recommended amount for children under 12 when they are the third or fourth person occupying the stateroom. It is customary to tip the counselors in the children's center, particularly if your children have participated in many activities.

AUTOMATIC GRATUITIES

On virtually all ships, a 15% gratuity will automatically be added to your bar bills. That would include the fruity welcome drink you signed for when the ship pulled away from the dock as well as cappuccinos and lattes from the specialty coffee bar. If you use salon and spa services, a similar percentage might be added to the bill; if it isn't, then a 15% tip is expected.

THE EXCEPTIONS

There are exceptions to every rule. These days there are two major exceptions to the no-extra-tipping rule on most cruise ships. The first exception is for room service. Except for bar items and soft drinks, there's no additional charge for what you order from room service;

CLOSE UP

Past Passengers — an Exclusive Group

Your cruise is over—pat yourself on the back. Your plans and preparation for an out-of-the-ordinary trip have paid off, and you'll now have lasting memories of a great vacation. Before you even have a chance to fill your scrapbook, the cruise line wants you to consider doing it all over again. And why not? You're a seasoned sailor, so take advantage of your experience. To entice you back on a future cruise, you may find you're automatically a member of an exclusive club—Latitudes (Norwegian Cruise Line), Mariner Society (Holland America Line), Captain's Circle (Princess Cruises), Castaway Club (Disney Cruise Line), Venetian Society (Silversea Cruises)—to name but a few. Members receive the cruise line's magazine for past passengers, exclusive offers, shipboard perks such as a repeaters' party hosted by the captain, and even the opportunity to sail on members-only cruises.

4

however, it's customary to tip the steward who delivers it and to tip in cash. In most cases, this will not be your regular steward. Depending on what you have ordered and whether it was delivered in a timely manner, $1 to $3 will suffice. If it's just juice and a pot of coffee, the lesser amount will do; a heavy tray with a full dinner would warrant the larger amount.

The second exception is in the à la carte restaurant. More common on modern cruise ships, these dining venues offer a change from the main dining room—often in a private, more intimate atmosphere, with a special menu and personal service. Although there's sometimes no extra charge for the meal, a one-time gratuity may be suggested. Your ship's daily schedule will contain instructions for making reservations and outline tipping protocol. You can usually add a tip to your bill or, if you prefer, offer it discreetly in cash to your main server.

PLACES YOU SHOULD KNOW

Every cruise ship has a distinct personality, whether it's a one-of-a-kind vessel or one of several identical ships built in a class, whose members are virtually indistinguishable from one another (with the possible exception of interior decor). Despite their differences, nearly all ships have certain common elements and other characteristics that set the cruise experience apart from other kinds of travel.

RECEPTION DESK
Sometimes referred to as the Purser's Desk, Guest Services, or Information Desk, this is the place to ask questions you might have as well as to take care of any financial matters. The Reception Desk is centrally located in the lobby or atrium and is generally open 24 hours a day for passenger convenience. Should you misplace a personal item, check for it at the Reception Desk, which also functions as the ship's Lost & Found.

SHORE EXCURSION DESK

Manned by a knowledgeable staff, the Shore Excursion Desk can offer not only the sale of ship-sponsored tours but may also be the place to learn more about ports of call and gain information to tour independently. Although staff members—and the focus of their positions—vary widely, the least you can expect are basic information and port maps. Happily, some shore excursion staff members possess a wealth of information and share it without reservation. On some ships the port lecturer may emphasize shopping, and the cruise lines' recommended merchants, with little to impart regarding sightseeing or the history and culture of ports.

PHOTO SHOP

Caribbean cruises are a series of photo opportunities, and ship's photographers are on hand to capture boarding, sail-away, port arrivals, and other highlights such as the Captain's Reception. On formal nights there are often several locations where you can have portraits taken in front of your choice of backdrops. Photographers seem to pop up everywhere and take far more pictures than you could ever want; however, they provide a unique remembrance, and there's no obligation to purchase the photos. Prices for the prints, which are put on display, range from $7 to $20, depending on size.

Film, digital media, batteries, single-use cameras, and related merchandise may be available in the photo shop. Some ship's photography staffers are capable of processing your film right on board as well as creating a photo CD or prints from digital media.

THE LIBRARY

Cruise ship libraries run the gamut from a few shelves of relatively uninspiring titles to huge rooms crammed with volumes of travel guides, classic novels, and the latest best sellers. As a rule, the smaller the ship, the more likely you are to find a well-stocked library. The space allotted to the library falls in proportion to the emphasis on glitzy stage shows; on small ships the passengers are more likely to lean toward quiet diversions. On ships with sophisticated entertainment centers in staterooms, you may find videocassette or DVD movies as well as books in the library.

INTERNET CAFÉ–BUSINESS CENTER

Being out to sea doesn't mean you have to be out of touch. Ship-to-shore telephone calls can cost $6 to $15 per *minute,* so it makes economic sense to use email to remain in contact with your home or office. Most ships have at the least basic computer systems, while some newer vessels offer more high-tech connectivity—even in-cabin high-speed hookups and wireless connections (Wi-Fi) for either your own laptop computer or one you can rent on board. Expect these services to cost between 35¢ and $1 per minute. However, on many ships you can purchase blocks of time or even unlimited access for the length of your cruise; in these cases, you pay more up front, but you'll save substantially on the per-minute connection charges.

There really is such a thing as a working vacation, and cruise ships are an ideal venue (a substantial portion of this book was written while I was at sea). Meeting rooms with audiovisual equipment are available for corporate functions on many ships. As with any group business function, these facilities should be reserved well in advance of sailing.

DINING ON BOARD

All food, all the time? Not quite, but it's possible to literally eat away the day and most of the night on a cruise. A popular cruise director's joke is "You came on as passengers, and you will be leaving as cargo." While it's meant in fun, it does contain a ring of truth. Food—tasty and plentiful—is available around the clock on most cruise ships, and the dining experience at sea has reached almost mythical proportions. Perhaps it has something to do with legendary midnight buffets, the absence of menu prices, or the vast selection and availability. Whatever the reason, there's a strong emphasis on food aboard cruise ships.

Nearly every cruise passenger can expect numerous opportunities to satisfy hunger pangs: coffee and Danish for early risers, Lido buffet breakfast, sit-down breakfast in the dining room, Lido buffet lunch, sit-down lunch in the dining room, midafternoon ice cream and snacks, afternoon tea, casual buffet dinner, formal dining room dinner, and a midnight buffet or canapés offered by waiters passing through public rooms. Whew! You may also find a pizzeria or a specialty coffee bar on your ship—increasingly popular favorites cropping up on ships old and new. Although pizza is complimentary, expect an additional charge for specialty coffees; cappuccino, espresso, and latte usually cost extra at the coffee bar and, possibly, in the dining room. There may also be a charge for fancy pastries and premium ice cream.

Every ship has at least one main restaurant and a Lido, or casual, buffet alternative, and specialty restaurants are an increasingly important option. Meals in the primary and buffet restaurants are included in the cruise fare, as are round-the-clock room service, midday tea and snacks, and late-night buffets. Most cruise lines levy a surcharge for dining in alternative restaurants, and the extra charge may or may not include a gratuity (if not, you should leave one), although there generally is no additional charge on upscale ships.

Cruise lines make every possible attempt to ensure dining satisfaction. If you have special dietary considerations, such as low-salt, kosher, or food allergies, be sure to indicate them well ahead of time, and check to be certain your needs are known by your waiter once on board. In addition to the usual menu items, spa, low-calorie, low-carbohydrate, or low-fat selections and vegetarian as well as children's menus, are usually available. Requests for dishes not featured on the menu can often be granted if you ask in advance.

Legend has it that a nouveau riche passenger's response to an invitation to dine with the captain during a round-the-world cruise was, "I didn't shell out all those bucks to eat with the help!" Although some cruise passengers decline invitations to dine at the captain's table, there are far more who covet such an experience. You'll know you have been included in that exclusive coterie when an embossed invitation arrives in your stateroom on the day of a formal dinner. RSVP as soon as possible; if you're unable to attend, someone else will be invited in your place.

The evening begins with cocktails, either in a reserved area of a public lounge or the captain's quarters, where the ship's social hostess greets you and makes introductions to the captain and other high-ranking officers. After getting acquainted, you're escorted to the captain's table and you take your place according to prearranged seating; place cards show the way. Then you just sit back and enjoy a sumptuous dinner with exquisite service and fine wines. A photographer will likely appear to preserve the memory, and the picture will be delivered to you the next day, perhaps with a copy of the menu or a note of thanks from your host.

Who is invited? Unfortunately, although there are hundreds of passengers on every cruise who would no doubt enjoy dining with him, there's just one captain. However, some factors can work in your favor when guest lists are drawn up. For instance, if you're a frequent repeater of the cruise line, the occupants of an expensive suite, or if you hail from the captain's hometown and speak his native language you may be considered, but you can't count on an invitation. Honeymooning couples are sometimes selected at random, as are couples celebrating a golden wedding anniversary. Attractive unattached female passengers often round out an uneven number of guests. Requests made by travel agents on behalf of their clients sometimes do the trick.

ENTERTAINMENT

It's hard to imagine, but in the early years of cruise travel, shipboard entertainment consisted of little more than poetry readings and recitals that exhibited the talents of fellow passengers. Those bygone days of sedate amusements in an intimate setting have been replaced by lavish showrooms where sequined and feathered showgirls strut their stuff on stage amid special effects unimagined in the past.

Seven-night Caribbean cruises usually include two original production shows—one often a Las Vegas–style extravaganza and the other a best-of-Broadway show featuring old and new favorites from the Great White Way.

Other shows highlight the talents of individual singers, dancers, magicians, comedians, and even acrobats. Don't be surprised if you're plucked from the audience to take the brunt of a comedian's jokes or act as the magician's temporary assistant. Sit in the front row if appearing onstage appeals to you.

Whether it's relegated to a late-afternoon interlude between bingo and dinner, or a featured evening highlight, a passenger talent show is often a don't-miss production. From pure camp to stylishly slick, what passes for talent is sometimes surprising but seldom boring. Stand-up comedy is generally discouraged. Passengers who want their performance skills to be considered should answer the call for auditions and plan to rehearse the show at least once.

Smoking on a Cruise Ship

One of the unhappiest groups of cruisers I've ever met were four World War II veterans back in 1999 aboard a ship belonging to the now-defunct Renaissance Cruises, which was the only no-smoking cruise line in existence at the time. The vets were all cigarette smokers whose wives thought a cruise on a nonsmoking ship would prompt them to abandon their habit. They groused about their wives' deception but managed to take matters into their own hands by holding a "smoker" on the fantail of the ship in the wee hours of every morning while everyone else was fast asleep.

While such an action isn't necessary on most ships these days, it is getting harder and harder to find a place to light up during a cruise. Ships are catching up to their land-based counterparts, and the smoking lamp has gone out in virtually all restaurants and showrooms at sea, as well as in many of the bars and lounges. While casinos are one of the last bastions of smokers, some have "smoke-free" nights to clear the air.

Only about 20% of American adults are currently smokers, so it's not necessarily a big deal that smoking areas have shrunk. We applaud the cruise lines for their health and safety concerns but also give them high marks for not ostracizing the smoking minority who want to be comfortable.

Smokers realize there are designated places to smoke and places that are entirely smoke-free nearly everywhere they go now, so most are willing to accept the compromise. The first thing they do is check for ashtrays and make friends with other smokers. "We're outcasts, aren't we?" is a common conversation starter between smokers who gather in smoking-designated areas. Cigar aficionados don't suffer the same indignities when they have their own cigar lounge to retreat to. They are accustomed to being banned from most public areas and are happy to find a lounge that accepts them. Otherwise, they are relegated to an outdoor deck, along with pipe smokers.

As a rule of thumb, look for an ashtray; if one is at hand, you can smoke; if there's food served nearby, you can't. *Never* smoke in an elevator, on a stairway, or in a passageway. Numerous cruise lines restrict smoking in cabins, including Celebrity, Disney, MSC Cruises, SeaDream Yacht Club, Royal Caribbean, Regent Seven Seas, and Windstar. Some of those lines, as well as Crystal, include private balconies among the no-smoking zones. For the most smoke-free environments at sea, consider sailing with Azamara and Oceania—each line limits smoking to a designated outside area of the pool deck.

Children are often invited to perform skits they learned during cruise camp, either in passenger talent productions or shows presented for parents and other family members. Not to be outdone, the ship's crew might stage a show featuring the music and culture of their homelands.

If you find the show-lounge stage a bit intimidating and want to perform in a more intimate venue, look for karaoke. Singing along in a lively piano bar is another shipboard favorite for would-be crooners.

Other lounges might feature easy-listening music, jazz, or combos for pre- and postdinner social dancing. Later in the evening, lounges rock with the beat of the 1950s and '60s, and disco reigns into the late-night hours for the truly energetic.

Dance hosts often address the relative disparity between women and men on a cruise by dancing with unaccompanied female passengers on premium-to-upscale ships. In addition to dancing until the wee hours of the morning, hosts are often called upon to greet embarking passengers, give dance lessons, host singles parties and a table in the dining room, and participate in social games, such as bridge, trivia, shuffleboard, and even chess.

Enrichment programs have become a popular pastime at sea. It may come as a surprise that port lecturers on many large contemporary cruise ships offer more information on shore tours and shopping than real insight into the ports of call. If more cerebral presentations are important to you, consider a cruise on a line that features stimulating enrichment programs and seminars at sea. Speakers can include destination-oriented historians, popular authors, business leaders, distinguished government figures, radio or television personalities, and even movie stars.

For a hands-on learning experience, "edutainment" is a relatively new twist in shipboard pursuits. Pottery and scrapbooking classes are a welcome addition to the old standby napkin-folding and scarf-tying demonstrations. If you never seem to find the time at home, check for the availability of classes for a chance to master new computer software programs, delve into the fine points of digital photography, or take piano lessons. A small fee is usually charged for courses or supplies, but some demonstrations are free.

CASINOS AND GAMBLING

On embarkation day, a sure sign that your ship is in international waters is the opening of the casino. Long gone are the days of brandy, cigars, and shipboard poker in the gentlemen's smoking room. The most notable exceptions are the family-oriented ships of Disney Cruise Line, which shuns gaming in favor of more wholesome pastimes.

On ships that feature them, the rationale for locating casinos where most passengers must pass either through or alongside them is obvious—the unspoken allure of winning. Who can resist the siren song of coins clanging in slot machines or the urge to try one's luck at roulette? Even nongamblers occasionally succumb to the temptation to give it a try. Although most passengers would not qualify for high-roller status in Las Vegas or Atlantic City, dealers often patiently assist first-time players. Novices can have a rewarding session in the casino by attending one of the gambling demonstrations held early on in the cruise where complimentary drinks are sometimes offered and door-prize drawings held.

In addition to slot machines in a variety of denominations, cruise ship casinos might feature roulette, craps, and a variety of card games: Caribbean Stud, Let It Ride, Texas Hold 'Em, and blackjack, to name

Drinking and Gambling Ages

Many underage passengers have learned to their chagrin that the rules that apply on land are also adhered to at sea. On most mainstream cruise ships you must be 21 to imbibe alcoholic beverages. There are exceptions—for instance, on cruises departing from countries where the legal drinking age is typically lower than 21. By and large, if you haven't achieved the magic age of 21, your shipboard charge card will be coded as booze-free, and bartenders won't risk their jobs to sell you alcohol.

Gambling is a bit looser, and 18-year-olds can try their luck on cruise lines such as Carnival, Celebrity, Silversea, Norwegian, and Royal Caribbean; most other cruise lines adhere to the age-21 minimum. Casinos are trickier to patrol than bars, though, and minors who look "old enough" may get away with dropping a few coins in an out-of-the-way slot machine before being spotted on a hidden security camera. If you hit a big jackpot, you may have a lot of explaining to do to your parents.

a few. Cruise lines strive to provide fair and professional gambling entertainment and supply gaming guides that set out the rules of play and betting limits for each game. Slot machine and poker tournaments are sometimes scheduled as fast-paced diversions on sea days.

Most casinos are required to close while ships are in port; others may be able to offer 24-hour slot machines and simply close table games. Every casino has a cashier, and you may be able to charge a cash advance to your shipboard account. If you win big—congratulations!—be prepared to complete a W2G form for the Internal Revenue Service. The U.S. Federal Income Tax Act stipulates that all U.S. citizens and permanent residents are required to pay income tax on gambling winnings, even if they were made overseas.

If you don't care for casinos, bingo games and scratch-off lotteries are usually offered.

SHOPPING ON BOARD

You may consider it your duty to shop. Indeed, duty-free shopping is such a popular cruise ship pastime that it's possibly second only to eating. Since shopping in many U.S. territories and Caribbean countries is duty-free, you'll find affordable prices on many goods in your ports of call. But you can also shop right on the ship itself.

Shops on board your cruise ships will carry merchandise ranging from funky to fashionable. Expect reasonable prices on souvenirs and logo items as well as imported perfumes, cosmetics, jewelry, electronics, designer items, clothing, and toys. Additionally, liquor and tobacco products can often be purchased at a substantial savings. At the very least you will not have to pay sales tax and may find rare or difficult-to-find imported brands. Art auctions are another shopping opportunity on many cruise ships.

If you're planning to make any sizable purchase in the Caribbean—whether in duty-free shops or at an art auction—do your homework. Check prices locally and online before you commit a large chunk of money on something that might not live up to its stated value. Although cruise lines offer a value guarantee when purchases are made from certain recommended stores, going through a refund process can be a headache.

Whatever you do, don't fudge the value of your purchases when completing the U.S. Customs form before disembarkation. If you exceed your personal allowance in the ship's duty-free shop, the customs agents will know. It's a murky little secret that cruise lines notify them of big spenders before docking and, at the very least, agents will bust you for the duty and may even confiscate any items you fail to declare. They have seen it all. *For more specific information on customs regulations, see Customs and Duties in Disembarking, below.*

HEALTH AND FITNESS

THE SPA

With all the usual pampering and service in luxurious surroundings, simply being on a cruise can be a stress-reducing experience. Add to that the menu of spa and salon services at your fingertips and you have a recipe for total sensory pleasure.

Most cruise-ship spas are operated by Steiner Leisure, the largest spa and salon operator at sea (the company operates Mandara and the Greenhouse spas aboard cruise ships), with facilities on more than 100 cruise ships worldwide.

In addition to facials, manicures, pedicures, massages, and sensual body treatments, other hallmarks of Steiner Leisure are salon services and products for hair and skin. Founded in 1901 by Henry Steiner of London, by the mid-1990s Steiner Leisure began taking an active role in creating shipboard spas offering a wide variety of wellness therapies and beauty programs for women and men.

Spa services don't usually come cheap, though they are more or less equivalent to what you might pay in any resort spa. Expect to pay $120 for a one-hour Swedish massage ($195 to $265 for a hot stone or specialty massage), $119 to $169 for a facial, and $100 to $110 for an hour of reflexology (therapeutic foot massage). Salon services are also equivalent to what you'd pay in a big-city salon: $35 to $49 for hair styling, $29 to $50 for a manicure, and $45 to $70 for a pedicure. Recently, other kinds of treatments, including teeth whitening, acupuncture, and cosmetic treatments have been on offer aboard some ships. You can brighten your smile for about $200, manage your aching back for $155 to $175 per session, and remove your frown lines with Botox for $350.

Spa Tips

Spas have grown in popularity. Here are some useful things to keep in mind to help you enjoy your shipboard spa experience:

■ Salon appointments for formal nights fill up quickly; book yours as soon as possible.

■ Arrive on time or a few minutes early for appointments.

■ Prior to your appointment, shower off any sunscreen lotions or oils.

■ Towels, robes, and slippers are usually provided for your use, but you may wish to wear your own pool- or shower flip-flops.

■ Attend the spa orientation — you may win a door prize or be selected for a demonstration (such as a mini-facial).

■ Watch for port day specials, packages of discounted spa services.

■ Don't feel pressured to purchase any of the products used during your treatment; if they're recommended but you don't want to buy them, just say no.

■ Check your charge slip before adding a gratuity; most shipboard spas automatically add a tip (however, you may adjust the amount or remove it altogether).

■ While spa and salon services are extras that sometimes come with a hefty price tag, you can still indulge yourself in the complimentary or low-cost facilities that are available on most ships. Saunas, steam rooms, therapy pools, and thermal chambers are relaxing alternatives to expensive body wraps and massages. Depending on the ship, some are free.

4

THE FITNESS CENTER

Cruise vacations can be hazardous to your waistline if you're not careful. Eating "out" for all meals and sampling different cuisines tends to pile on calories. Maintaining a fitness regimen at sea is no problem with a wide assortment of exercise machines such as stationary bikes, treadmills, and stair steppers. As a bonus, shipboard fitness centers with floor-to-ceiling windows have some of the world's most inspiring sea views.

For guests who prefer a more social atmosphere as they burn off sinful chocolate desserts, there are fitness classes for all levels of ability. High-impact energetic aerobics are not for everyone, but any class that raises the heart rate can be toned down and tailored to individual capabilities. In addition, there are stretching classes to warm up for a light jog or brisk walk on deck, and even sit-for-fitness classes for mature passengers or those with delicate joints. Basic aerobics and group exercise classes are most often complimentary, but there's typically a charge of $10 to $12 for specialty classes, such as Pilates, Spinning, yoga, and kickboxing. Perhaps you're just starting a fitness program and require individualized attention. Ask about the services of fitness experts or personal trainers to get you off on the right foot. Their fee is around $75 to $90 per hour.

Even if you don't want to take time out to hit the gym, you can walk on the ship's promenade deck or turn your back on the elevators and use the stairs—they're the ultimate step machines. And you can always control calories by requesting that any sauces be served on the side. Have no fear; it's actually possible to lose weight on a cruise and return home more buff than buffet.

SPORTS ACTIVITIES AND PROGRAMS

Shipboard sports facilities might include a court for basketball, volleyball, or tennis—or all three—a jogging track, or even an in-line skate track. Innovative and unexpected facilities, such as rock-climbing walls, surfing simulators, and bungee trampolines are challenges introduced at sea by Royal Caribbean International. For the less adventurous, more sedate pursuits include table tennis and shuffleboard.

Naturally you'll find at least one swimming pool and possibly several. Just be aware that cruise ship pools are usually on the small side, more appropriate for cooling off than doing laps, and that the majority contain filtered salt water. Princess Grand-class ships have challenging swim-against-the-current pools filled with freshwater for swimming enthusiasts.

Golf is a perennial seagoing favorite of players who want to log the Caribbean's most beautiful and challenging courses on their scorecards and take their games to the next level. Shipboard programs can include clinics, use of full-motion golf cages, and even individual instruction from resident pros using state-of-the-art computer analysis. Once ashore, escorted excursions include everything needed for a satisfying round of play, including equipment and tips from the pro, and the ability to schedule tee times at exclusive courses.

STAYING HEALTHY

THE MEDICAL CENTER

Accidents can happen to even the most careful people, and an unexpected illness can strike at any time. That's why almost every ship has a medical center staffed by a physician. Savvy travelers carry a first-aid kit that should be adequate for minor scrapes and ailments. For more serious problems, the ship's doctor should be able to treat you as well as any general practitioner or clinic ashore. For really complicated medical conditions, such as a heart attack or appendicitis, the ship's medical team evacuates passengers to the nearest hospital ashore. While at sea, evacuation by helicopter can easily cost thousands of dollars. To cover those expenses, travel insurance is a must.

If you're examined by the ship's doctor, you'll be charged for your office visit. Depending on your illness or injury, fees can run from $75 to several hundred dollars. Any medicines prescribed are extra. Recently, an office visit and medications to treat my simple sinus infection cost me $135. A notable exception is if you're injured in some manner aboard ship or during a shore excursion arranged by the cruise line, in which case your treatment should be free. Unless you carry very comprehensive medical insurance coverage, you may not be covered for treatment aboard a cruise ship, or in any foreign country for that matter. You'll be expected to pay for any treatment you require at the time you visit the medical center; you'll then file your own claim later. If your medical coverage is through Medicare, you certainly will not be covered outside the United States. It's worth noting once again that all ships of foreign registry are considered to be outside the United States by Medicare; however, this point is not explained clearly in Medicare's manual.

A ship's pharmacy is limited in scope, so it may or may not have what you need if you forget or lose the prescription medications that you regularly take. Just be aware that even if a drug you require is in stock, you should not expect the ship's doctor to dispense medication without examining you.

4

COMMON AILMENTS

SEASICKNESS

Many first-time passengers are anxious about whether they'll be stricken by seasickness, but there's no way to tell until you actually sail. Those who are felled by it claim that only dying will relieve their discomfort. If you have a problem with motion sickness in automobiles and airplanes, you may be more prone to seasickness; however, if you get nauseated in a smallish sailboat, that doesn't necessarily mean you'll get seasick on a large cruise ship. Modern vessels are equipped with stabilizers that eliminate much of the motion responsible for seasickness. Unless your cruise includes the open sea and wind-whipped water, you may not even feel the ship's movement, particularly if your ship is a megaliner. For first-time passengers concerned with seasickness, a megaliner is precisely the ship of choice. They're very stable in the calm waters of the Caribbean.

Seasickness is a balance problem generally attributed to overactive nerve fibers in the inner ear. Your sensory perception gets out of sync as these nerve fibers attempt to compensate for the unfamiliar motion of the ship moving through water. This condition often disappears on its own in a few days, once you get your sea legs, but by that time you've seen far too much of the inside of your bathroom and are ready to bolt the ship at any cost. You need not suffer; there are a number of remedies available to help align your gyros. Seasickness medications are usually available at no charge from the Medical Center or at the Reception Desk.

Even hardy sailors who never get seasick have been known to avail themselves of medications on occasion. The most common drugs are Dramamine, Dramamine II, and Bonine. All of these are over-the-counter antihistamines that are available at most pharmacies. Antihistamines make most people drowsy, and Dramamine is almost certain to have that effect. Dramamine II and Bonine are nondrowsy formulas, but they still put some people to sleep for a few hours. Considering the alternative, that's not necessarily a bad side-effect. If you want to beat *mal de mer* before it has the chance to sneak up on you, it's better if you take one of these remedies two hours before sailing.

Worn behind the ear, the Transderm Scop patch is a remedy that dispenses a continuous metered dose of medication that's absorbed into the skin and enters the bloodstream. Apply the patch four hours before sailing and it will continue to be effective for three days. You'll need a prescription from your physician for the patch and, while wearing it, you must be vigilant for possible side-effects that include blurred vision, dry mouth, and drowsiness. Unfortunately, you should neither drink alcohol nor drive as long as you are wearing the patch.

If you have a history of motion sickness, do not book an inside cabin. For the terminally seasick, it will begin to resemble a movable coffin in short order.

CONTAGIOUS ILLNESSES

When hundreds of cruise passengers report to the infirmary with similar symptoms that have nothing in common with the motion of the ocean, does that necessarily mean their ship has been attacked by a mysterious disease? Hardly, but you'd never know that from news reports about nasty cruise ship diseases that attack unsuspecting vacationers. Let's face facts—travel by cruise ship often brings together large numbers of people from different regions of North America, as well as other parts of the world. There's no such thing as a cruise ship disease. In confined quarters, certain respiratory and gastrointestinal diseases can quickly spread through person-to-person contact—just as they do in schools, nursing homes, hospitals, and day-care centers. In addition, when ships dock and passengers go ashore, they might be at risk for diseases prevalent in the ports of call they visit. It's even quite possible that some passengers who become ill during a cruise were infected prior to boarding and were actually sick before their symptoms became apparent.

Because respiratory and gastrointestinal diseases can percolate a few days before their symptoms strike with a vengeance, it's highly likely that some passengers bring their bugs on board with them. Although most people are unaware that they have contracted an illness before embarking, others know they are sick but go aboard anyway, not acknowledging their illness for fear of being denied boarding. They might not seek treatment once on board due to the threat of being confined to their staterooms. These alpha passengers can be the beginning of a shipboard epidemic. Two of the most prevalent diseases that spread through cruise ship populations are influenza and noroviruses.

INFLUENZA

In recent studies, influenza infection among travelers has been found to be quite common and may rank right up there with hepatitis A as one of the most common vaccine-preventable diseases infecting travelers. Seasonal epidemics of influenza generally occur during the winter months on an annual or near-annual basis and can cause disease in all age groups. Although rates of infection are highest among infants, children, and adolescents, rates of serious illness and death are highest among people over 65 years of age and people of any age who have

CLOSE UP

4

Nonmedical Seasickness Remedies

No one wants to be drugged up and drowsy when they should be enjoying a cruise. There are nearly as many remedies for seasickness as there are sufferers, but they aren't all medicinal. If you want to cure seasickness but avoid additional medication, you may wish to explore a few homeopathic and natural cures.

■ **Bitters.** Have the bartender mix up a couple tablespoons of Angostura Bitters in a half glass of water or club soda. Do this right away, and you probably will not need the rest of these remedies.

■ **Food.** You may not have an appetite, but you should try to eat something if you become seasick. The nausea associated with seasickness is magnified by an empty stomach. Crackers, bread sticks, or light broth may help. (Any woman who has lived through morning sickness knows the virtues of Saltine crackers.) Crackers and apples are recommended for those who cannot keep liquids down—the apples replace vital bodily fluids.

■ **Fresh Air.** If nothing else, fresh sea air smells good and is bound to improve your mood. Keeping an eye on the horizon can also help restore your sense of balance.

■ **Ginger.** Ginger ale is a widely used home remedy for an upset stomach, and it cannot hurt if you can keep the liquid down. Ginger capsules and crystallized ginger, available in health food stores and supermarkets, are reportedly even more effective.

■ **Lying Down.** Spending valuable cruise time in bed is not fun, but a horizontal position may alleviate some of your symptoms.

■ **Ice.** A hospital trick to prevent vomiting is an ice bag held against the throat just beneath the chin. It really works.

■ **Sea-Bands.** These wristbands work on the principle of acupressure. Each elastic Sea-Band has a round button on the inside; when positioned to press a particular point on the inside of the wrist, the nausea associated with seasickness disappears. Although they look rather tacky with cocktail dresses, they are effective little gems and can be found in many pharmacies, luggage stores, and even at some travel agencies. Many shipboard sundries shops also have them, but if the ship begins to rock and roll, they'll sell out in a heartbeat.

medical conditions that place them at high risk for complications from influenza (e.g., people with chronic cardiopulmonary disease).

When you're traveling, the risk for exposure to influenza depends on the time of year and destination. In the tropics, influenza can occur throughout the year; in the temperate regions of the Southern Hemisphere most activity occurs from April through September. In temperate climates, travelers can also be exposed to influenza in summer, especially when on board a cruise ship with travelers from areas of the world where influenza viruses are circulating. Influenza might be, at best, an inconvenience; however, it can lead to complications, including life-threatening pneumonia, especially among people at increased risk for complications. Annual influenza vaccination is the primary method for preventing influenza and its complications.

NOROVIRUSES

Noroviruses are a group of related viruses that cause acute gastro-enteritis in humans. The incubation period for norovirus-associated gastroenteritis is usually between 24 and 48 hours, but cases can occur within 12 hours of exposure. Symptoms of norovirus infection include vomiting, diarrhea with abdominal cramps, and nausea. Low-grade fever occasionally occurs, and vomiting is more common in children. Dehydration is the most common complication, especially among the young and elderly, and may require medical attention. Symptoms generally last 24 to 60 hours. Recovery is usually complete, and there's no evidence of any serious long-term effect.

Highly contagious noroviruses are transmitted primarily through the fecal-oral route, either by consumption of contaminated food or water or by direct person-to-person spread. During outbreaks of norovirus gastroenteritis, several modes of transmission have been documented. Passengers may be infected initially by contaminated food in a restaurant; they may pass it along to other people directly.

Norovirus is often termed the cruise ship virus, even though the vast majority—some 60% to 80% of outbreaks—occur on land. According to Princess Cruises, "Statistics have shown that the chance of contracting norovirus on land is 1 in 12, and 1 in 4,000 on a cruise ship." However, the virus is harder to miss on a cruise ship since all the sick passengers and crew members are treated by the same physician, who is required to prepare a special report for the CDC if an outbreak affects 2% or more of the passengers or crew. The CDC may launch an investigation if 3% of passengers or crew members become ill. As of this writing, most ship infirmaries treat passengers who exhibit norovirus symptoms at no charge.

HOW TO AVOID ILLNESS

Outbreaks of diseases on cruise ships initially led to the creation of the CDC-operated Vessel Sanitation Program (VSP) in the 1970s. Since that time, twice a year, unannounced inspections have been conducted on all cruise ships calling at or sailing from U.S. ports on foreign itineraries. Inspectors use a checklist to score ships on a 100-point system. A score of 86 or higher is satisfactory. Anything below 86 is not satisfactory, or failing. While VSP standards are not mandated by law, the cruise lines voluntarily comply.

In addition to water and food, which are inspected for cleanliness, VSP inspectors scrutinize whirlpool spas, hot tubs, children's facilities, and other areas of cruise ships. Inspection scores are made public and compiled on what VSP calls a green sheet, making it easy to compare all ships. The green sheet for each ship is available on the Internet at the CDC's Web site. Current scores can be faxed, or an inspection report on an individual ship can even be mailed to you if you request it.

No one wants to get sick during a highly anticipated vacation. The best way to avoid illness is to wash your hands thoroughly and often. A waterless, sanitizing hand cleaner is also recommended by the CDC in conjunction with hand washing or when water is unavailable (hand sanitizers are effective and come in travel-size bottles). You'll see dispensers for hand sanitizer on most ships. Some passengers even go so far as to pack a small aerosol can of a germ-killing spray or packaged disinfectant wipes to treat their stateroom furnishings, bedding, and bathrooms before using them.

If all fails and you get sick, seek medical treatment and observe quarantine procedures as long as you are symptomatic so you don't infect other passengers.

Ship Inspection Reports Vessel Sanitation Program (☎ 800/232-4636 ⊕ *www.cdc.gov/nceh/vsp*).

> **WORD OF MOUTH**
>
> "My husband and I discovered we are closet pleasure hounds. He got a massage with warm oils and heated stones and used the Alpha Capsule which involved music, aromatherapy, warmth, and vibration. He said the massage was heavenly, and the Alpha Capsule was pleasant, but over-rated. As for me, I got a deluxe manicure and pedicure, a facial, and a deep conditioning scalp treatment complete with scalp and shoulder massage. I have never felt so relaxed and pampered. It added to an already fabulous vacation experience." —Sherry L.

DAYS AT SEA

All days at sea are not identical, but they do follow a certain rhythm. Most ships schedule activities, port talks, lectures, games, and fitness programs on a nonstop basis. This is the time to personalize your cruise experience—you can participate in any or all scheduled activities or do nothing more strenuous than lift an umbrella drink while reading a book poolside.

No doubt you noticed the shops and casino were closed when you boarded your ship. Local regulations preclude them from opening while in port; however, once at sea, all the ship's facilities are available during set hours.

Let your daily schedule be your guide. You may want to pack a highlighter to mark the events you don't want to miss. If you want to be active, you can take exercise and fitness classes. If you want to revive and beautify yourself, consider spa and salon services (but remember the caveat about booking these in advance, because the spa is busy on sea days). If you like to gamble, there will usually be casino gaming tournaments and bingo games. Lectures might include port or shopping talks, health and fitness talks, and lifestyle or language classes. Nonstop activities may include bridge lessons and tournaments, pool games, Ping-Pong or shuffleboard, art auctions, dance classes, computer lessons, or even wine tastings and culinary demonstrations. Most activities are complimentary, but some (wine tasting, for example) may carry a

Safety at Sea

Safety begins with you, the passenger. Once settled into your cabin, locate your life vests and review the posted emergency instructions. Make sure the vests are in good condition and learn to secure them properly. Make certain the ship's purser knows if you have a physical infirmity that may hamper a speedy exit from your cabin so that in an emergency he or she can quickly dispatch a crew member to assist you. If you're traveling with children, be sure that child-size life jackets are placed in your cabin.

Within 24 hours of embarkation, you'll be asked to attend a mandatory lifeboat drill. Do so and listen carefully. If you're unsure about how to use your vest, now is the time to ask. Only in the most extreme circumstances will

you need to abandon ship—but it has happened. The time you spend learning the procedure may serve you well in a mishap.

In actuality, the greatest danger facing cruise ship passengers is fire. All cruise lines must meet international standards for fire safety, which require sprinkler systems, smoke detectors, and other safety features. Fires on cruise ships are not common, but they do happen, and these rules have made ships much safer. You can do your part by *not* using an iron in your cabin and taking care to properly extinguish smoking materials. Never throw a lit cigarette overboard—it could be blown back into an opening in the ship and start a fire.

---

fee. In addition, the library and card room are available for quiet pursuits, as are many of the ship's lounges.

The swimming pool is one of the most popular spots on board during sunny sea days. Towels are provided, but you shouldn't use them to save deck chairs. A lively band usually plays poolside, and the pool bar is a great spot to meet and greet new acquaintances. Even if you're not a sun worshipper, you can enjoy the festivities from a shaded chair.

Sea days, particularly if they're the second and next-to-the last days of the cruise, are usually capped by formal evenings. During the first formal night, the captain hosts a reception for all passengers. Complimentary beverages and hors d'oeuvres are usually served, and the captain takes the stage to introduce his officers and staff.

PORT CALLS

Port calls add an allure to cruise ship travel that cannot be duplicated by any other type of vacation experience. In a given seven-day cruise, you'll usually have the opportunity to visit at least four unique destinations. Each morning you wake up in a new place, and each afternoon you steam off to the next stop. What you do ashore depends entirely on your interests and comfort level when confronted by a new environment and culture. After your ship is cleared by local immigration officials, you'll either have a chance to walk down the gangway or board a tender and be taken ashore.

SHORE EXCURSIONS

Cruise lines offer shore excursions that appeal to a wide variety of tastes: sightseeing, hiking, biking, sailing, swimming, kayaking, snorkeling, and a host of other activities. These excursions are tried and tested and, as a rule, provide a good experience for the money. If you prefer to do your own touring, you're naturally free to book a private guide or taxi, rent a vehicle, or use public transportation, and delve into whatever interests you. A cautionary rule of thumb is that it's often better to take a ship's tour if you want to explore an area some distance from where the ship is berthed. In case of any delay, your ship will wait for you if you've booked a ship-sponsored excursion. On the other hand, if you're on your own, well, you're on your own, and the ship will depart without you if you haven't returned by the announced departure time. Give yourself plenty of time to be back at the ship (not on the dock waiting for a tender): at least a half hour before it's scheduled to sail.

To make the most of your hours ashore, research your options ahead of time. Guidebooks are an excellent resource, as are Internet sites devoted to travel—particularly the official tourism sites developed by the countries you're visiting. Friends and fellow passengers who have been there and done that can offer valuable insights into your ports of call.

With the majority of passengers ashore while the vessel is in port, the number of activities on most cruise ships is somewhat curtailed, but programs do not cease entirely. There are still exercise classes, the spa and fitness center remain open, and games and movies are sometimes planned. You can also enjoy the pools in near solitude.

The two activities you won't be able to take part in are gambling and shopping. Customs regulations dictate that both casino and shops close. Also, check your daily schedule for mealtimes and locations, as they may vary on port days.

DISEMBARKING

All cruises come to an end eventually, and it hardly seems fair that you have to leave when it feels as if your vacation has just begun. The debarkation process actually begins the day before you arrive at your ship's home port. During that day your cabin steward delivers special luggage tags to your stateroom, along with customs forms and instructions.

No matter where you live, keep in mind while packing for home that you need to set aside clothing to wear the next morning when you leave the ship. Many people dress in whatever casual outfits they wear for the final dinner on board, or they change into travel clothes after dinner. Be sure to put your passport or other proof of citizenship, airline tickets, and medications in hand luggage.

After packing, remove all the old tags, except for your personal identification, from your suitcases. Then attach the new debarkation tags (they are color- or number-coded according to postcruise transportation plans and flight schedules). Follow the instructions provided, and place the luggage outside your stateroom door for pickup during the hours indicated. (Some ships now offer disembarkation at will and allow you to carry your own bags off the ship; if your ship offers that service and you wish to partake, then you don't have to worry about placing your luggage outside the door.)

A statement itemizing your shipboard charges is delivered before you arise on the morning of debarkation. Plan to get up early enough to check it over for accuracy, finish packing your personal belongings, and vacate your stateroom by the appointed hour. Any discrepancies in your account should be taken care of before leaving the ship, usually at the Reception Desk.

Room service is not available on most ships on debarkation day; however, breakfast is served in the main restaurant as well as the buffet. After breakfast, there's not much to do but wait comfortably in a lounge or on deck for your tag color or number to be called. Norwegian Cruise Line makes this process more pleasant by allowing passengers to remain in their cabins until it's time to leave the ship. Debarkation procedures can sometimes be drawn out by passengers who are unprepared. This is no time to abandon your patience or sense of humor.

Remember that all passengers must meet with Customs and Immigration officials during the debarkation process, either on the ship or in the terminal. Procedures vary and are outlined in your instructions. In some ports, passengers must meet with the officials at a specified hour (usually very early) in an onboard lounge; in other ports, customs forms are collected in the terminal and passports and identification papers are examined there as well.

Once in the terminal, you'll find the luggage is sorted by color or number. Locate yours and, if desired, flag down a porter for assistance. Then, either proceed to your prearranged transportation, get in the taxi line, or retrieve your vehicle from the parking lot. Your cruise is complete and you're officially a veteran sailor!

CUSTOMS AND DUTIES

You're always allowed to bring goods of a certain value back home without having to pay any duty or import tax. But there's a limit on the amount of tobacco and liquor you can bring back duty-free, and some countries have separate limits for perfumes; for exact figures, check with your customs department. The values of so-called "duty-free" goods are included in these amounts. When you shop abroad, save all your receipts, as customs inspectors may ask to see them as well as the items you purchased. If the total value of your goods is more than the

CLOSE UP

Dressing for Disembarkation

On the last night of your cruise, don't shrug off the reminder to set aside clothing to wear ashore before you place your luggage outside your stateroom door. I laughed it off as a corny cruise director's joke. It isn't. On one cruise, a friend accompanying us awoke just in time to report to Immigration that final morning and couldn't find his trousers. Where were they? Oops. Being efficient, he had tucked them into his suitcase the night before! Fortunately, his wife was able to retrieve them, but not before the mandatory 7 am inspection. Wearing a longish golf shirt and navy blue boxers, he reported as instructed and hoped no one would notice that his shorts weren't a bathing suit. Red-faced, he took a lot of good-natured ribbing during a leisurely breakfast.

4

duty-free limit, you'll have to pay a tax (most often a flat percentage) on the value of everything beyond that limit.

U.S. CUSTOMS

ALLOWANCES
Individuals entering the United States from the Caribbean are allowed to bring in $800 worth of duty-free goods for personal use ($1,600 from the U.S. Virgin Islands), including one liter of alcohol (two liters if one was produced in the Caribbean and five liters from the USVI), one carton of cigarettes (five cartons if four are from the USVI), and 100 non-Cuban cigars. Antiques and original artwork are also duty-free. Remember that any liquids, such as alcohol or perfume, that you buy on your cruise—or anytime before you pass through airport security—will have to be packed into your checked luggage before you board your flight home.

SENDING PACKAGES HOME
Although you probably won't want to spend much of your precious shore time looking for a post office, you can send packages home duty-free, with a limit of one parcel per addressee per day (except alcohol or tobacco products or perfume worth more than $5). You can mail up to $200 worth of goods for personal use; label the package "personal use" and attach a list of the contents and their retail value. If the package contains your used personal belongings, mark it "personal goods returned" to avoid paying duty on your laundry. You may also send up to $100 worth of goods as a gift ($200 from the U.S. Virgin Islands); mark the package "unsolicited gift." Items you mailed do not affect your duty-free allowance on your return.

NONCITIZENS
Non-U.S. citizens who are returning home within hours of docking may be exempt from all U.S. Customs duties. Everything you bring into the United States must leave with you when you return home, though. When you reach your own country, you'll have to pay duties there.

How Safe Is Your Cruise Ship?

The Poseidon Adventure probably wasn't the most comforting movie my husband could have viewed the night before embarking on our first cruise. The film stars an ocean liner that goes bottom-up after being swamped by a monster wave, sending the cast scurrying to reach the keel in an upside-down attempt to be rescued. As we ascended the gangway of SS *Norway* the following morning, my husband grinned wickedly and hummed "There's Got to Be a Morning After."

We encountered no severe weather, no massive wave action, no rocking or swaying that we could even feel. It was almost disappointing to be on a cruise liner and not experience any adventure. Unfortunately, that isn't always the case, as we have subsequently learned. Water is a powerful force, and weather conditions exist that can cause a ship to bob and stagger through thundering waves. The worst are rogue waves that appear out of the depths and smash into ships without warning. Such waves are not uncommon; however, it's rare for a cruise ship to encounter one. Most storms are mildly irritating at best, and their importance only increases in dimension if the weather doesn't clear quickly enough for seasick passengers.

The Cruise Lines International Association (CLIA), whose mission is to promote all measures that foster a safe, secure, and healthy cruise ship environment, reminds us: "According to the U.S. Coast Guard, cruising is one of the safest modes of transportation. [Since the early 1980s], more than 100 million passengers safely enjoyed a cruise vacation. During this period only one passenger death due to a marine incident has been reported on any CLIA member cruise vessel operating from a U.S. port. Cruise ships are built to the highest structural stability standards, as set by the International Maritime Organization (IMO)."

Had *Norwegian Dawn* passengers known how well their ship was constructed, they might have been less anxious when a 70-foot wall of water smacked into the ship in April 2005. The rogue wave reached as high as Deck 10, and windows were broken in two cabins. As frightful as the situation was, only four people received minor injuries, and 62 staterooms were waterlogged (the ship has more than 1,100 cabins). That alone says a lot for the reliability of not only *Norwegian Dawn,* but for all cruise ships at sea that must meet IMO regulations for safety and seaworthiness. CLIA agrees the incident was "an excellent example of the high level of structural integrity found on today's cruise ships."

No one at Norwegian Cruise Line could have foreseen how prophetic one of their past marketing campaigns would become. A 1997 brochure suggested, "Out here, the laws of the land do not apply . . . it's different out here." Passengers should never lose sight of one important difference between a cruise and a resort vacation—a cruise ship is not a hotel. Ships move, and the action of the ocean is as unpredictable as the weather.

Information U.S. Customs and Border Protection (✉ For inquiries and complaints, 1300 Pennsylvania Ave. NW, Washington, DC ☎ 877/227–5511 or 202/354–1000 ⊕ www.cbp.gov).

PROBLEM SOLVING

There's no such thing as a perfect vacation, so it's probably unrealistic to expect that you'll have a flawless cruise. Various things—small and large—can go wrong. The best piece of advice I can give you is to remember that no one—not your travel agent, not the cruise line, not the crew, and most of all not you—wants problems to occur. Every officer and staff member on your ship has the same goal: to meet passenger expectations and provide a safe and satisfying voyage. The more you know as a passenger, the better you'll be prepared for what happens—and what doesn't—during the cruise.

YOUR LUGGAGE IS MISSING

As a rule, the larger the ship, the longer it takes for luggage to be delivered on embarkation day. Being one of the first passengers to board the ship doesn't necessarily mean you'll be the first to get your luggage. Sometimes it will all appear early in the day; however, it may materialize piece by piece during the course of the afternoon or perhaps even later on in the evening. On the largest ships, it's not at all uncommon that you would not receive your checked luggage until after the ship has sailed; this doesn't mean your luggage is not on the ship.

If your luggage hasn't arrived by 8 pm and if it appears that all the luggage has been distributed (i.e., you don't see any more in the passageways or being delivered), check with the Reception Desk. Sometimes the room tag affixed to a suitcase has been damaged. In that case, your bag would be set aside until the name on the luggage identification tag could be matched with the manifest. This illustrates why it's very important to have your name on the outside *and* inside of your suitcases.

In the extreme, luggage has been known to be loaded on the wrong ship or accidentally left behind in the cruise terminal. This very rarely happens, but when it does, the guest services staff will do whatever they can to have misdirected suitcases delivered to the ship in the next port of call. In the meantime, they may offer assistance in the form of a shipboard credit so you can purchase clothing and other personal items in the ship's boutiques.

YOU NEED TO SWITCH STATEROOMS

Congratulations if you received a last-minute complimentary upgrade or were able to purchase an upgrade to better accommodations at the pier. After you board the ship and inspect your superior digs, tell your steward about the change and request that he take care of getting your luggage to the right stateroom. It's a good idea to be proactive as well, so take the time to stop by your original cabin. You might find your luggage there already, as well as anything that was delivered for you (rented tuxedo, bon voyage gifts, messages, etc). If the steward is

CLOSE UP

Cruise Manners

Most passengers want to have a satisfying vacation—to explore new places, relax, spend time with family and friends, and have some carefree fun. Unfortunately, some people can get carried away with the carefree part and forget to pack the good manners practiced every day at home:

■ **Adhere to the dress code.** The ship's daily program will indicate the appropriate attire for every evening of the cruise, generally beginning at 6 pm. It's inconsiderate to ignore the guidelines and do as you please.

■ **Do not hog the lounge chairs.** Every morning an invisible cadre of passengers piles towels and personal belongings on chaise longues by the pool to save them for later. This is extremely selfish behavior.

■ **Do not save seats.** Do save a seat for your spouse or traveling companion, but do not try to save entire rows of seats in the show lounge or complete tables in the casual dining area.

■ **Control your children.** For their safety—and the safety of others—children shouldn't be allowed to roam freely around the ship, run around the swimming pool, splash water on other passengers, cavort in the hot tubs, or play in the elevators. Do not allow your children to intrude in adults-only spaces. Some parents are in total denial when it comes to the unruly actions of their children (the disruptive kids can't be theirs).

■ **Be a considerate smoker.** Those who smoke should light up their cigarettes, cigars, and pipes only in areas clearly approved for that purpose.

■ **Do not jog before daybreak.** It should be obvious that if there are cabins located below the deck where

jogging is permitted, then passengers are probably still asleep in them. Run only during the hours indicated in the daily program.

■ **Be mindful of others in the spa and gym.** Wear appropriate workout attire and wipe down the equipment when you are finished using it. Take your turn in a reasonable amount of time.

■ **Turn down the sound.** Portable electronics are wonderful gadgets, but not everyone has the same musical taste as you. In public areas, music players should be used with headphones. When using two-way radios and cell phones, it's seldom necessary to shout.

■ **Await your turn.** Events and activities are scheduled in a certain way for a purpose, including the orderly filling of shore tenders and the disembarkation procedure at the end of the cruise. Do not be in such a hurry that you compromise safety.

■ **Do not complain while you wait.** No one cares to listen to grumbling and whining. It's a vacation, so lighten up and go with the flow.

■ **Listen and follow instructions.** This is never more important than during the muster drill! Listening can ensure your safety in case of an emergency.

Don't forget that the three Cs at sea—Consideration, Courtesy, and Civility—are your guideposts. And don't forget to bring along a pleasant attitude, your sunniest smile, and good manners.

available, tell him your new cabin number. Then, be patient because stewards are very busy on embarkation day.

What if there's something really wrong with your accommodations? Perhaps the air-conditioning doesn't work or there's a major plumbing problem that can't be fixed after repeated attempts. You may be fortunate enough to be moved to a similar cabin, but when ships sail full there often isn't one available. If you're offered a less-expensive category—for instance, your stateroom is outside, but all that is open is an inside—you

> **WORD OF MOUTH**
>
> "Remember, whenever you are not happy with an order, tell the waiters and they are more than happy to bring you something more to your liking. We do, and thus have never experienced a bad meal aboard. We actually wish we could order half portions, since invariably the portions are so large that we cannot finish them. The waiters may think we don't like the food, but actually we are saving room for dessert!" —Vincent F.

4

should expect compensation for the downgrade. The purser may be able to apply a credit for the difference to your shipboard account or advise you that the cruise line will issue a partial refund after the cruise. Permission must be granted by the company's headquarters, so be patient. And get any promise for compensation in writing.

Don't count on moving if you simply don't like your cabin, though. You may notice a small sign on the Reception Desk informing all passengers that the ship is full and change requests cannot be granted. Whether every cabin is occupied or not (the ship may be full to maximum capacity standards), after sailing, the ship's staff is loath to make changes for any reason other than those above.

YOUR DINING ARRANGEMENTS ARE UNSATISFACTORY
When you booked your cruise, you requested early seating, but once on board you discover a late dinner-seating assignment (or vice versa). Perhaps you requested a romantic table for two but find that you're assigned to a table that seats eight. Despite what anyone tells you, cruise lines make no guarantees up front—after all, the dining rooms have only so much space. However, they do want to please all their passengers. They recognize that dining is a highlight of the overall cruise experience, so they make it relatively painless to correct any glitches. The maître d' will be available on embarkation day at a time and place specified in the ship's bulletin to iron out any problems. You may be asked to dine at your assigned table that first night until a more acceptable arrangement can be worked out, at which time you'll be informed of your new table-seating assignment.

Even if you get the seating time and table size you prefer, you could encounter another problem. Sometimes you just don't hit it off with your assigned dining partners, or you meet other people you'd like to spend more time with. Go to the maître d' as soon as possible—no later than the morning of your first full day on board—to make your request for a change. Be patient. He will do his best to accommodate all requests but often changes aren't made on the spot.

YOU MISS A PORT OF CALL

Sometimes weather conditions or mechanical problems cause a cruise ship to bypass a particular port of call. If you read the Contract of Carriage on your ticket, you'll see that cruise lines reserve the right to change the itinerary for just cause. They don't make itinerary alterations on a whim. Don't take it personally—they're not trying to ruin your vacation plans. In this case, there's not much you can do.

If you booked a shore excursion on board, your account will automatically be credited for the cancelled tour. Be sure to check your balance for accuracy, though. If you've prebooked your own tour with an independent shore operator and you've paid in advance, the situation may be a bit trickier. Whether you receive a refund depends on the tour company with which you're dealing. Make sure you understand their policy for refunds in the case of a missed port call before finalizing your plans. If you reserved a rental car, the same caveat applies; make sure you understand the car-rental company's cancellation policy.

YOU DON'T KNOW WHAT'S GOING ON

A problem with communication might more accurately be termed lack of communication. In the event of an unusual situation or emergency, the officers and crew of your vessel are usually more concerned with problem solving than keeping passengers informed. In these situations, it helps to be patient rather than complain that you're not being apprised. The captain and his officers will give you the information you need as soon as they can do so.

A case in point is my experience on the maiden voyage of a brand-new ship. Mel and I noticed while dressing for dinner that our cabin seemed to be getting warm, and it soon became apparent that the entire ship's interior was growing hotter as the evening progressed. Plus, the ship was dead in the water. We were soon informed that an electrical panel had failed and that engineers had shut down the air-conditioning and stopped the ship while making repairs. We appreciated not being left in the dark—a real possibility considering the electrical problem. However, before the captain's announcement over the public address system, the Reception Desk was literally overwhelmed with concerned (and irate) passengers. If you're truly frightened by a situation you don't understand, check with Reception.

EFFECTIVE COMPLAINING

Minor quibbles can be brought to the attention of your waiter (your soup is cold), cabin steward (you need extra pillows), or the Reception Desk (there's a mysterious charge on your account). For slightly weightier matters, the headwaiter or chief housekeeper should be able to work things out—your dinner partners have atrocious eating habits and you want to switch tables, or your cabin steward isn't cleaning your room satisfactorily. However, for big problems, go to the top. See the hotel director immediately when a situation occurs that you feel should be addressed. His assistance will most assuredly be needed if a pipe breaks and floods your accommodations. The most important thing to remember is that you should deal with problems on the ship when they occur; there's not much that can be done after the cruise is over.

If you have a major problem, you'll usually get more satisfaction if you tell the hotel director what you want in terms of compensation, but it's important to be reasonable. If your cabin is flooded, you should expect to be moved and you should expect to have sodden clothing cleaned at no cost to you, and if any of your belongings are ruined, you should expect them to be replaced; you should not expect a refund of your entire fare.

Klaus Lugmaier, longtime Norwegian Cruise Lines hotel director, confides that the most common passenger gripes are bad weather, delays caused by Immigration clearances, and long check-in lines. Possibly his most unusual request was an incident when a passenger wanted to leave the ship during a day at sea and commanded him to order a helicopter. Obviously, there are some requests that cannot be granted under any circumstances.

Keep your travel agent in the loop if something major goes wrong and you need postcruise assistance. Travel agents have the inside track on solving problems by using channels not available to their clients. Getting better service after your cruise (as well as before it) is just one reason why it's better to use a travel agent.

COMMENT CARDS

Every passenger gets a comment card to complete. Assess your experience honestly, and take the time to make any suggestions you have for improvements. Those comments are taken very seriously. Also, praise crew members by name if you've received particularly good service from them. They could receive a promotion as a result.

Cruise Lines and Cruise Ships

WORD OF MOUTH

"I like all the noises that precede the sail-away. But you have to be in the right places. . . . If you're on an outside deck, you can hear an increase in funnel clatter as the engines . . . are brought back on line, and you can see the exhaust blacken with unburned fuel until the cylinder temperature is right. Soon after that, you hear the boarding doors banging shut or the noise of the gangway being withdrawn. You can hear the squeaks and scrapes of the winches bringing in the lines. Then you hear the horn."

—Steven S.

One person's "dreadful" cruise vacation can be another person's best cruise ever. You may love every meal; another person may hate the food. Your cabin may feel comfortable and cheery, if not large; the identical accommodations may have resembled a "cave" for someone else. In cruising, one size definitely does not fit all. What's appealing to one passenger may be unacceptable to another. Ultimately, most cruise complaints arise from passengers whose expectations were not met. They were on the wrong ship for them.

Make no mistake about it: cruise ships have distinct personalities. Windstar's sails and lack of formality define their relaxed appeal, while an ethereal sense of peace and tranquillity permeates the more formal Crystal ships. Even those belonging to the same class and nearly indistinguishable from one another have certain traits that make them stand out. The most notable examples are vessels in the Carnival fleet, which are built in classes. Although the layouts of the ships in the same class vary little, each has its own distinctive theme—on Conquest-class ships you might find yourself amid a celebration of color (*Carnival Glory*) or unabashed heroics (*Carnival Valor*).

Cruise ships may appear to be floating resorts, but you can't check out and go someplace else if you don't like your ship. Whichever one you choose will be your home for seven days or more in most cases. The ship will determine the type of accommodations you'll have, what kind of food you'll eat, what style of entertainment you'll see, and even the destinations you'll visit. If you don't enjoy your ship, you probably won't enjoy your cruise.

That is why the most important choice you'll make when booking a cruise is the combined selection of cruise line and cruise ship. Cruise lines set the tone for their fleets, which is why we have classified lines loosely as Mainstream, Premium, and Luxury, plus unique sailing ships. Not all cruise lines in those categories are alike, although they will share many basic similarities. The cruise industry is relatively fluid, meaning that new features introduced on one ship may not be found on all the ships owned by the same cruise line. For instance, you'll find ice-skating rinks only on the biggest Royal Caribbean ships. However, most cruise lines attempt to standardize the overall experience throughout their fleets (for example, you'll find a rock-climbing wall on *every* Royal Caribbean ship).

Just as trends and fashions evolve over time, cruise lines embrace the ebb and flow of change. To keep up with today's diverse lifestyles, some cruise lines strive to include something that will appeal to everyone on their ships. Others focus on narrower, more traditional elements. Today's passengers have higher expectations, and they sail on ships that are far superior to their predecessors. Happily, they often do so at a much lower comparable fare than in the past.

So, which ship is best? To be honest and direct: only you can determine which ship is best *for you*. You won't find ratings by Fodor's—either quality stars or value scores. Why? Think of those people described above whose expectations were unmet. They assuredly would rate their experience differently than you did if everything on board was to your liking. Ratings are personal and heavily weighted to the reviewer's opinion. What we've tried to do in these cruise line and cruise ship profiles is to give you the telling details that help distinguish one cruise line and cruise ship from another. Rather than inundate you with facts and bury you with opinions, we've tried to be brief and to the point. Travel guides should be empowering, not overwhelming. Use these profiles as a guide, but also ask your friends for their opinions, use a good travel agent who knows the intimate details of the ships he or she sells, and, perhaps most important, trust your own instincts. Your responsibility is to select not only the right cruise line but the right ship for you, and no one knows your expectations better than you do yourself. It's your precious time and money that are at stake. No matter how knowledgeable your travel agent is, how sincere your friends are, or how clearly any expert lays the cards on the table, you're the only one who really knows what you like. A short wait for a table at dinner might not bother you because you would prefer a casual atmosphere with open seating, whereas some people want the security of a set time at an assigned table, where they're served by a waiter who gets to know their preferences. You know what you're willing to trade in order to get what you want most.

RATE YOUR CRUISE SHIP

One way to narrow down your choices is to rate the cruise ships that interest you the most and see which come out on top. Gather cruise line brochures and take a look at the ship profiles that follow in this chapter. Then rank the ships you wish to compare by making a side-by-side list of each ship's features, assigning each one a ranking, such as:

4 = Gotta have it!

3 = Not essential but good to have

2 = Can take it or leave it

1 = Don't care; just not important to me

You can create your own list of desired features, which can be as long and specific as you feel it needs to be. It might look something like this:

- Itinerary
- Home port
- Ship size
- Dining options
- Dinner seatings
- Dress code
- Cabin amenities

- Entertainment options
- Activities
- Enrichment programs
- Recreation facilities
- Fitness center
- Spa
- Children's facilities/programs

The cruise line profiles that follow offer a general idea of what you can expect in terms of the overall experience, quality, and service; individual cruise ship reviews identify features that apply to particular ships or classes of ships. You'll want to compare the features of several cruise lines and ships to determine which ones come closest to matching your needs. Then narrow them down further to a few that appeal most to you.

Service is one important characteristic that is difficult to grade. The composition of staff and crew members on any particular ship can change from week to week as employees complete their contracts and are replaced by others returning from their vacations. To get an idea of what level of service you might anticipate, you can use the cruise-industry concept of passenger-to-crew ratio. Basically, it illustrates how many passengers each crew member must serve and, in theory, the lower the number, the higher the service level. Cruise-industry standard is about 2.5 to 1. Luxury lines may have 1 to 1 ratios or better (a few ships have more crew members than passengers). To compute the passenger-to-crew ratios of ships you're considering, simply divide the number of passengers (based on double occupancy) by the number of crew members. You'll find these figures in the ship statistics for each cruise ship.

The overall price you pay for your cruise is always a consideration. Don't think of the bottom line in terms of the fare alone: there are shipboard charges to factor in as well. The ultimate cost isn't computed only in dollars spent; it's in what you get for your money. The real bottom line is value. Many cruise passengers don't mind spending a bit more to get the vacation they really want.

TYPES OF CRUISE LINES

MAINSTREAM CRUISE LINES

These are contemporary cruise lines with big, big ships that have all the bells and whistles. More passengers sail on mainstream ships than any others, and mainstream cruises account for the mass appeal of cruise vacations.

The biggest player in the cruise industry is Carnival Cruise Lines. With the most ships and lavish—some would say extraordinary—interiors chock-full of grand public spaces and sports facilities, these ships offer a great deal of choice within the Carnival fleet. Nipping at their heels are Royal Caribbean and Norwegian Cruise Line, whose ships are also big and crammed with features, but neither line is quite as bold as

CLOSE UP

New for 2011 and Beyond

Caribbean-bound ships scheduled for launch between 2011 and 2014 include some of the largest and most feature-rich vessels ever to float. We offer an advance preview here of brand-new ships coming over the horizon.

CARNIVAL BREEZE
The third ship in the Dream-class—set to launch in 2012 at 112,000 tons and with a passenger capacity of 3,006—incorporates the new layout and distinctive profile introduced on *Carnival Dream*. Features include Ocean Plaza, an indoor/outdoor café and live music venue featuring a large circular dance floor, a half-mile, open-air promenade encircling the ship where four "scenic" whirlpools are cantilevered out over the sea, a two-level Serenity adults-only retreat, a huge Carnival Water-Works aqua park, a Caribbean-inspired pub, and new stateroom decor.

CELEBRITY REFLECTION
The fifth and final planned Solstice-class ship is scheduled to enter the Celebrity Cruises fleet in the fall of 2012. At 118,000 tons, *Celebrity Reflection* will be a 2,850-guest vessel. Of the larger than usual standard staterooms, 90% will be outside, and 85% of those will have balconies. Expect an exceptional range of guest-inspired services and amenities, and look for all the trademark elements of Solstice-class ships, with a few surprises as well, including a grill restaurant in the Lawn Club.

NORWEGIAN CRUISE LINE
Details were scarce in NCL's announcement that they plan to build two new 143,500-ton Free-style Cruising ships for delivery in spring 2013 and 2014. Each will have approximately 4,000 passenger berths and a rich mix of cabin categories. Unlike *Norwegian Epic*, these ships will have cabins with a more traditional layout and design.

OCEANIA RIVIERA
Oceania Cruises will christen the second vessel built to its specifications in the spring of 2012. At 66,000 tons—nearly double the size of any of the ships that make up the current fleet—*Riviera* will be a sister-ship to *Marina* and carry 1,256 passengers. Nearly 93% of accommodations will offer an ocean view, and 97% of those will have a private balcony. Expanded dining options will include a French bistro and an Asian restaurant.

PRINCESS CRUISES
Two new Princess ships are scheduled to launch in 2013 and 2014, with the first to be named *Royal Princess*. The design of the largest ships in the fleet—at 141,000 tons, each will carry 3,600 passengers in double occupancy—will be an evolution of the line's style, including some new features and expanded signature spaces. New elements include a top deck over-water glass-bottomed walkway on the ship's starboard side; a similarly cantilevered bar on the port side; and an adults-only pool surrounded by seven private cabanas. Expanded areas include the Piazza and the adults-only Sanctuary. The poolside theater will offer high-definition viewing on a larger screen. All outside staterooms will have balconies.

5

Carnival. Costa Cruises and Disney Cruise Line don't have as many ships in their Caribbean-based fleets, but their mainstream appeal lies in different areas. Can't go to Europe? Let Costa deliver a bit of Italy to you. Plan to bring the family? The Disney ships are universally loved by children of all ages.

Once aboard, you can discover why the mainstream cruise lines are so popular. The furnishings and fittings vary, but all generate their own type of excitement. There's nothing like this in Kansas (or Indiana, Ohio, or Arizona). Glittering and glamorous decor in public areas is the norm. Though it's a bit over-the-top sometimes, the setting is still comfortable and inviting. Accommodations are available in a wide range of sizes and price ranges, from inside cabins with no windows for bargain-basement prices to some of the largest suites at sea that cost a king's ransom.

What you do on a mainstream cruise ship is up to you. Activities are scheduled all day and into the evening. Every evening, the professional entertainment staff goes into high gear, and you can either watch production shows and cabaret or participate in karaoke and passenger games. Try a few hands of blackjack in the casino, even if you're not a gambler (except on Disney ships, which have no casinos).

Lounging in the sun is seemingly the most popular daytime pursuit during Caribbean cruises, but there will be a full-service spa and salon for the pampered set and a fitness center for gym rats. Options ashore are fairly standard—large mainstream ships sail to many of the same Caribbean ports and offer similar, if not exactly the same, excursions.

Food on mainstream ships may be lacking in the gourmet department, but the choices will be vast. You can find something to eat almost 24/7, either in traditional shipboard dining rooms, a casual Lido buffet, or alternative dining restaurants. Norwegian Cruise Line (NCL) and Disney Cruise Line put innovative spins on mainstream ships; NCL offers casual, open seating dining, while Disney has a unique alternating restaurant concept.

Everyone sets sail to have a good time, and the atmosphere on board is exhilarating, even overwhelming to some people. You're sure to find passengers who share your interests among the couples, singles, and families on these popular ships.

PREMIUM CRUISE LINES

Ships in premium fleets have a lot in common with those in mainstream lines. They're just a little more: there's a more refined atmosphere, more gracious surroundings, more attentive service. There are still things like pool games, although not quite the high jinks typical of mainstream ships.

Premium ships are among some of the newest afloat, from medium to very large in size. Holland America Line, Princess Cruises (of *Love Boat* fame), and Celebrity Cruises are among the best-known lines, and they have the largest vessels and fleets. Relative newcomers are Azamara Club Cruises and Oceania Cruises with small, yet growing, fleets.

Accommodations usually are a step up in comfort and have refrigerators and other amenities that make them pleasant havens.

Activities tend to be more lifestyle-oriented; computer classes, foreign-language lessons, and enrichment programs are more prevalent. Dress codes range from country-club casual at all times to more traditional, usually with two formal nights on a one-week cruise. The overall mix of passengers may be a bit older, but many families sail during summer and peak school vacation periods, so most of the ships have facilities for children, and some premium ships are among the most family-friendly afloat. Exceptions are Azamara and Oceania Cruises, which have no children's programs at all.

The social and entertainment staffs on premium vessels are no less busy keeping passengers happy. Although some activities sound similar to those on mainstream ships, including pool games and bingo, everything tends to be a bit more sedate. Afternoon music at the pool might be a jazz quartet instead of a reggae band. Production shows are just as lavish on the larger premium ships; cabaret acts fill in on their off-nights and are the norm on smaller ships.

Spas and salons are elaborate, and fitness buffs won't be disappointed by the gym facilities. The itineraries, ports of call, and excursions aren't very different than those on mainstream cruises, but premium cruise lines frequently schedule lengthier cruises to more-far-flung destinations.

Premium ships can't boast about true gourmet dining, but they do ramp up the quality and presentation of their food. Oceania Cruises is highly regarded in this segment for imaginative menus and upscale alternative restaurants. Attentive service shines with more polish and professionalism.

With rare exceptions, ships categorized as premium don't spend the entire year in the Caribbean. From about April or May through October, they reposition to Europe, Alaska, Bermuda, and even Asia and South America. Nevertheless, while in the sunny Caribbean, they aren't your grandparents' cruise lines. Although it may not last as long into the night, the camaraderie that develops naturally at sea is still there.

LUXURY CRUISE LINES

Step aboard and enter the exclusive realm of foie gras and caviar on ships that run the gamut from megayachts for only a hundred or so guests to one of the largest ships ever built. The deluxe and ultraplush ships that belong to luxury fleets are as good as it gets at sea. You can expect to be welcomed as a valued guest and treated to all the courtesies you would expect at any five-star resort.

At the top end of the top lines, you won't be bothered with signing drink receipts—all beverages (alcoholic or not) are included on the ships of Regent Seven Seas Cruises, Silversea Cruises, Seabourn Cruise Line, Crystal Cruises and SeaDream Yacht Club. Cunard Line and Windstar Cruises aren't as inclusive, but have other attributes that nudge them into the luxury category. Most important, all luxury ships provide a level of personal service and courtesy that is unmatched. It's unlikely you'll get more than a few steps from the buffet line before a server relieves you of your plate and shows you to a seat.

With the exception of Cunard, Crystal, and Windstar, luxury ships have all-suite accommodations. Most of these upscale cabins have an ocean view or a private balcony and enough space to throw an intimate predinner cocktail party. These are very social ships, and most are small enough that passengers mix easily. They are also quite formal; guests really like to dress up in their finest. Only Windstar and SeaDream are always casual chic.

Dining is the main event of the evening on most luxury ships. Meals are served during a single open seating (exceptions are Cunard and Crystal), and full dinners from the restaurant menu can be served in your stateroom (served course by course, of course). On the highest of the high-end ships, wine is poured freely during the meals, and no one is rushed to finish dessert and coffee. Main courses are cooked to order, and the food on some lines approaches the level of that in a fine restaurant in any city.

Classical concerts, lectures on the economy and current events, and scaled-back production shows or cabaret are likely diversions. Passengers tend to entertain themselves and need no more stimulation than interesting conversation to have a pleasant time.

No one will hit you with a volleyball at the pool, but you may have to schedule a tee time to use popular golf simulators. Even on the smallest ships, the libraries are stocked with a wide variety of books, and movies are available to watch in the privacy of your stateroom. A call to room service can bring fresh, hot popcorn to your suite. Luxury ships tend to be adult-oriented; only Cunard and Crystal have dedicated facilities and programs for children.

Elegant and serene, luxury ships are stylish without being stuffy. The well-to-do, sophisticated travelers they attract are collectors of destinations. These ships sail to the Caribbean only part-time, usually during the winter season; otherwise, they are sailing less-charted waters around the world.

SAILING SHIPS

Sun, sky, sea, and sails. Just add a brisk wind, and you have a perfect combination. The tall-ship fleet that sails in the Caribbean is truly maritime magic. One of the most magnificent sights at sea is a tall ship under full sail. Star Clippers are superdeluxe sailing vessels that only look as though they've been around for years. In reality, they are modern sailing ships with many of the same comforts and amenities associated with traditional cruise ships.

ABOUT THESE REVIEWS

For each cruise line described, ships that regularly sail in the Caribbean are grouped by class or similar configuration. Keep in mind that not all ships are deployed in the Caribbean year-round; some head for Alaska and Europe during summer months. Some ships owned by the cruise lines listed do not include regularly scheduled Caribbean cruises on their published itineraries as of this writing and are not reviewed in this book. ⇨ *For a complete listing of the ships and the itineraries they are scheduled to follow in the 2011–2012 cruising season, see the chart Ships by Itinerary and Home Port in Chapter 1.*

Because cruise ships can float off to far-flung (and not always tropical) regions, many are designed with an eye to less than perfect weather. For that reason, you're likely to find indoor swimming pools featured on their deck plans. Except in rare cases, such as NCL's *Norwegian Dawn,* these are usually dual-purpose pools that can be covered when necessary by a sliding roof or magrodome to create an indoor swimming environment. Our reviews indicate the total number of swimming pools found on each ship, with such permanently and/or temporarily covered pools included in the total and also noted as "# indoors" in parentheses.

When ships belong to the same class—or are basically similar—they're listed together in the subhead under the name of the class; the year each was introduced is also given in the same order in the statistics section. Capacity figures are based on double occupancy, but when maximum capacity numbers are available (the number of passengers a ship holds when all possible berths are filled), those are listed in parentheses. Many larger ships have three- and four-berth cabins that can substantially increase the total number of passengers on board when all berths are booked.

Unlike other cruise guides, we describe not only the features but also list the cabin dimensions for each accommodation category available on the ships reviewed. Dimensions should be considered approximate and used for comparison purposes, since they sometimes vary depending on the actual location of the cabin. For instance, while staterooms are largely prefabricated and consistent in size and configuration, those at the front of some ships may be oddly curved to conform to the shape of the bow.

Demand is high, and cruise ships are sailing at full capacity these days, so someone is satisfied by every ship. When you're armed with all the right information, we're sure you'll be able to find one that not only fits your style but that offers you the service and value you expect.

5

AZAMARA CLUB CRUISES

In something of a surprise move, parent company Royal Caribbean International announced the formation of an all-new, deluxe cruise line in 2007. Two vessels originally slated for service in the Celebrity Cruises fleet, which were built for now-defunct Renaissance

Azamara Journey at sea

Cruises and acquired with the purchase of the Spanish cruise line Pullmantur, were the basis for the new line, Azamara Cruises. Designed to offer exotic destination-driven itineraries, Azamara Cruises presents a more intimate onboard experience while allowing access to the less traveled ports of call experienced travelers want to visit.

✉ *1050 Caribbean Way, Miami, FL*
☏ *877/999–9553*
⊕ *www.azamaraclub cruises.com*
☞ *Cruise Style: Premium.*

When a cruise line sets a course to break the mold in an industry where the product falls into traditional categories—mainstream, premium, luxury—it's an exciting opportunity for experienced travelers who may want more than what a traditional cruise can deliver. More interested in traveling than cruising, they may still prefer the comfort and convenience that only a cruise ship can deliver in some exotic locales. Azamara Cruises gives this underserved group of travelers what they want—a cruise experience that's a bit different. Not quite luxury but more than premium, Azamara offers a deluxe cruise with concierge-style amenities for which you'd have to upgrade to a suite on other cruise lines.

In addition, since its launch Azamara Club Cruises has added a number of more inclusive amenities to passengers' fares, with no charge for a specific brand of bottled water, soft drinks, specialty coffees and teas; shuttle bus service to/from port communities, where available; house wine served at lunches and dinners; and complimentary self-service laundry.

Extensive overhauls of two ships that formerly sailed for the now-defunct Renaissance Cruises have resulted in interiors that are brighter with the addition of light, neutral carpeting throughout, and splashes of bold color in the upholstery and drapes. Areas that once appeared stuffy are now welcoming, with contemporary artwork further enhancing the decor. Each vessel weighs in at 30,277 tons and carries only 694 passengers. While the size affords a high level of intimacy and makes the ships easy to navigate, there is no skimping on features normally abundant on larger ships, such as private balconies and alternative dining. Cruisers may feel that they've checked into an upscale boutique hotel that just happens to float.

One distinguishing feature of Azamara is a wide range of enrichment programs to accompany the destination-rich itineraries. Popular programs include guest speakers and experts on a wide variety of topics, including destinations, technology, cultural explorations, art, music, and design. Lectures might include how to get the best photos from your digital camera or the proper way to pair wine and food, as taught by resident sommeliers. An onboard "excursion expert" can not only help you select shore excursions based on your personal interests but also will serve as a destination guide, offering information about the culture and history of each port of call. Entertainment, on the other hand, leans toward cabaret-size production shows and variety entertainers in the main lounge. Diverse musical offerings throughout the ships range from upbeat dance bands to intimate piano bar entertainers.

Food

Expect dinner favorites to have an upscale twist, such as gulf shrimp with cognac and garlic, or a filet mignon with black truffle sauce. Azamara chefs bring a fresh approach in contemporary and lighter cuisine— a reflection of what's happening all over the United States. Even though the menus list some trendier items, there will always be classic dishes available. Prime rib and other favorites will continue to be featured on the menu. Boutique wines are complimentary with lunch and dinner.

Specialty restaurants include the Mediterranean-influenced Aqualina and the stylish steak-and-seafood restaurant Prime C. Passengers in Club Suite accommodations may dine in the specialty restaurants every night of the cruise at no charge; all other passengers pay a cover charge. Guests booked in Club Veranda, Club Oceanview, and Club Interior staterooms will be guaranteed two specialty restaurant dinners per cruise. For the remainder of the voyage, stateroom guests are

NOTEWORTHY

■ Through April of 2011, passengers who sailed on Azamara Club Cruises and Celebrity Cruises earned credits toward memberships in both Le Club Voyage and Captain's Club past-passenger programs, regardless of what brand they sailed on. Effective May 2011, Le Club Voyage credits will be earned separately from the Captain's Club program.

■ You may bring two bottles of wine per stateroom aboard for free, but you must pay a $25 corkage fee if you bring your own wine to one of the dining rooms (none if you drink it in your cabin).

■ Smokers are restricted to a small section on the pool deck; all other public and private areas are no-smoking.

■ Self-service laundry facilities are complimentary

5

AZAMARA CRUISES

Top: Grand Lobby on *Azamara Journey*
Bottom: Chairs grouped on deck allow for quiet conversation

welcome in the specialty restaurants based on availability. Daily in-cabin afternoon tea service and delivery of canapés is available to all passengers. There is no charge for bottled water, soft drinks, and specialty coffees and teas.

Fitness and Recreation

In addition to a well-equipped gym and an outdoor jogging track, features of Azamara's fitness program include yoga at sunset, Pilates, and access to an onboard wellness consultant. Both ships offer a full menu of spa treatments, an outdoor spa relaxation lounge, and an aesthetics suite featuring acupuncture, laser hair removal, and microdermabrasion.

Your Shipmates

Azamara is designed to appeal to discerning travelers, primarily American couples of any age who appreciate a high level of service in a nonstructured atmosphere.

Dress Code

Although passengers who choose to wear formal attire are certainly welcome to do so, there are no scheduled formal nights. The nightly dress code is simply "sophisticated" casual—a jacket and tie are never required, but you may see that many men who are accustomed to wearing them will do so anyway.

Junior Cruisers

Azamara Cruises is adult-oriented and not a good choice for families who depend on the availability of child care. The ships have no facilities or programs for children; older teenagers, however, might appreciate the diverse itineraries and well-stocked library.

Service

Gracious and polished service throughout the ships is extended to every guest. Suite accommodations are served by a butler, who will assist with unpacking/packing; delivery of room service, plus afternoon tea, evening hors d'oeuvres, and complimentary cappuccino and espresso; shoe-shine service; and booking assistance with spa, shore excursions, and specialty dining. Stateroom attendants work in teams, and rou-

---

CHOOSE THIS LINE IF ...

Your taste leans toward luxury, but your budget doesn't.	You prefer leisurely open seating dining in casual attire to the stiffness of assigned tablemates and waiters.	The manner in which you "get there" is as important to you as your destination.

tine stateroom cleaning is done by an assistant steward, much as on other cruise lines.

Tipping

Housekeeping and dining gratuities are included in the fare. A standard 18% is added to beverage charges. It is recommended that a $5 per person gratuity be extended when dining in the specialty restaurants.

Past Passengers

Once you've sailed with Azamara Club Cruises for the first time, you will automatically become a member of Azamara's loyalty program, "Le Club Voyage," and receive benefits commensurate with the number of cruises you've taken, including such things as onboard bookings savings for future cruises and free Internet minutes. Adventurer members have been on at least one Azamara Club Cruises cruise. Explorer members have sailed five to nine cruises and get more perks, including an invitation to a senior officer's cocktail party, and a complimentary bag of laundry washed, dried, and pressed per week. After 10 cruises, you become a Discoverer member and can take advantage of expanded Internet minutes and other perks. Azamara Club Cruises also offers Reunion Cruises that feature exclusive members-only benefits, activities, and a private, complimentary excursion during the sailings.

GOOD TO KNOW

Although there's little glitz, there's a lot of glamour to be found on an Azamara cruise. More upscale than premium lines, Azamara doesn't quite hit the luxury mark, yet the worldwide itineraries and diverse shore experiences reflect those of a high-end product at a more affordable price. Care was taken to repurpose underutilized spaces when the ships were renovated. The addition of the Sunset Bar aft of the buffet restaurant fills a previously bleak space with a congenial gathering spot. Ingenious transformations for other areas include a deluxe boutique tucked into a corner of the lower lobby and the covered patio area near the pool furnished with comfortable, oversize loungers and other seating. Total occupancy was also cut slightly by converting 48 standard staterooms into spacious Sky Suites.

5

AZAMARA CRUISES

DON'T CHOOSE THIS LINE IF ...

You want an all-inclusive cruise; alcoholic beverages and soft drinks are not included.

You require the services of a butler; only suites have them.

You insist on smoking whenever and wherever you want to.

AZAMARA JOURNEY, AZAMARA QUEST

CREW MEMBERS	390
ENTERED SERVICE	2000, 2001
GROSS TONS	30,277
LENGTH	593 feet
NUMBER OF CABINS	347
PASSENGER CAPACITY	694
WIDTH	95 feet

700 ft.

500 ft.

300 ft.

Top: Open seating dining
Bottom: Balcony stateroom

Public Areas and Facilities

At 30,277 tons, *Azamara Quest* and *Azamara Journey* are medium-size ships and well suited to the somewhat more exotic itineraries for which they are deployed, whether· in the Caribbean, Europe, Asia, or South America. The ships initially entered service for Renaissance Cruises and served in Spain under the Pullmantur flag until 2007. With their entry into the Azamara Cruises fleet, a new option is available to passengers who prefer the boutique-hotel atmosphere of a smaller ship without the luxury-class price tag.

After a month in dry dock, the ships emerged with a variety of signature features, including the Martini Bar in Casino Luxe, a casual sidewalk café–style coffee bar, and the distinctive Astral Spa with an acupuncture suite and expansive relaxation deck with therapy pool. Each ship has two specialty restaurants. The exclusive experience includes butler service in suites and concierge-style amenities in all categories of accommodations.

Restaurants

The formal Discoveries restaurant has a single open seating for breakfast, lunch, and dinner. Evening meals feature classic favorites with a twist, such as a filet mignon with black truffle sauce. Supplementing the main restaurant is the casual Windows Café, where you can dine indoors or alfresco with a view over the ship's stern. Two upscale alternative restaurants—Aqualina and Prime C—require reservations and carry a cover charge for most guests. A poolside grill offers hamburgers, salads, pasta, and other favorites for lunch and dinner, a pizzeria dishes up a variety of pies by the slice, and patisseries serve specialty coffee drinks and pastries; 24-hour room service augments dining choices.

Accommodations

Layout: Designed for lengthy cruises, all staterooms have ample closet and storage space, and even standard cabins have at least a small sitting area, although bathrooms in lower categories are somewhat tight. Wood cabinetry adds warmth to the decor. In keeping with the trend for more balconies, 73% of all outside cabins and suites have them.

Amenities: Amenities include plush beds and bedding that were added during the ships' makeovers. Bath toiletries, a hair dryer, TV, refrigerator, personal safe, and robes for use during the cruise are all included, but you must move up to a suite to have a bathtub, as lower-category cabins have showers only.

Suites: Full suites are particularly luxurious, with living–dining rooms, entertainment centers, minibars, two TVs, separate bedrooms, whirlpool bathtubs, guest powder rooms, and very large balconies overlooking either the bow or stern. Thirty-two Sky Suites newly incorporated into each ship have a queen-size bed, minibar, television, whirlpool, personal safe, and hair dryer.

Worth Noting: Six staterooms are designated as wheelchair accessible.

In the Know

Forward-facing Royal Suite balconies offer remarkable views, but depending on the force of the wind when the ship is under way, they can be virtually unusable. Also, it's best to keep the suite balcony doors locked when at sea, as they tend to slide open if the ship rolls from side to side.

Pros and Cons

Pros: One staff member for every two passengers and the attention of a butler for suites ensures unparalleled service at this level of deluxe cruising. Bartenders in the Martini Bar are willing to follow your instructions to mix your favorite variation of the famous cocktail even if it's not on the extensive menu. The quiet sounds of a grand piano and deep, welcoming seating add to the ambience of the Drawing Room for after-dinner cocktails and conversation.

Cons: Despite being more expensive than other similar accommodations, aft-facing Sunset Verandas on decks 6 and 7 are simply standard balcony cabins with larger balconies sandwiched between suites. Although families are not discouraged from sailing, there are no children's programs or facilities. Upscale amenities don't quite make up for the lack of bathroom space in standard staterooms.

Cabin Type	Size (sq. ft.)
Penthouse	560
Royal Suites	440–501
Sky Suites	266
Sunset Veranda	175
Ocean-view Balcony	175
Ocean View	170–175
Inside	158

FAST FACTS

- 9 passenger decks
- 2 specialty restaurants, dining room, buffet, pizzeria
- Wi-Fi, safe, minibar (some), retrigerator, DVD (some)
- 1 pool
- Fitness classes, gym, hair salon, 2 hot tubs, spa, steam room
- 8 bars, casino, dance club, library, showroom
- Dry-cleaning, laundry facilities, laundry service
- Internet terminal
- No-smoking cabins

5

AZAMARA CRUISES

Casual dining

CARNIVAL CRUISE LINES

The world's largest cruise line originated the Fun Ship concept in 1972 with the relaunch of an aging ocean liner, which got stuck on a sandbar during its maiden voyage. In true entrepreneurial spirit, founder Ted Arison shrugged off an inauspicious

Lobby Bar on board *Carnival Fantasy*

beginning to introduce superliners a decade later. Sporting red-white-and-blue flared funnels, which are easily recognized from afar, new ships are continuously added to the fleet and rarely deviate from a successful pattern. If you find something you like on one vessel, you're likely to find something similar on another.

✉ *3655 N.W. 87 Ave., Miami, FL*

☎ *305/599–2600 or 800/227–6482*

⊕ *www.carnival.com*

☞ *Cruise Style: Mainstream.*

Each vessel features themed public rooms, ranging from ancient Egypt to futuristic motifs. More high-energy than cerebral, the entertainment consists of lavish Las Vegas–style revues presented in main show lounges by a company of singers and dancers. Other performers might include magicians, jugglers, acrobats, and even passengers taking part in the talent show or stepping up to the karaoke microphone. Live bands play a wide range of musical styles for dancing and listening in smaller lounges. Each ship has a disco, piano bar, and a comedy club.

Arrive early to get a seat for bingo and karaoke. Adult activities, particularly the competitive ones, tend to be silly and hilarious and play to full houses. Relaxing poolside can be difficult when bands crank up the volume or the cruise director selects volunteers for pool games; fortunately, it's always in fun and mostly entertaining. There's generally a quieter second pool to retreat to.

Carnival is so sure that passengers will be satisfied with their cruise experience that they are the only cruise line to offer a Vacation Guarantee. Just notify them before arriving at the first port of call if you're unhappy for any reason. Should you choose to disembark at the ship's first non-U.S. port, Carnival will refund the unused portion of your cruise fare and pay for your flight back to your embarkation port. It's a generous offer for which they get very few takers.

Food
Carnival ships have both flexible dining options and casual alternative restaurants. Although the tradition of two set mealtimes for dinner prevails on Carnival ships, the line's experiment with an open seating concept—Your Time Dining—proved so successful that it has been implemented fleet-wide.

Choices are numerous, and the skill of Carnival's chefs have elevated the line's menus to an unexpected level. Although the waiters still sing and dance, the good-to-excellent dining room food appeals to American tastes. Upscale supper clubs on certain ships serve cuisine comparable to the best midrange steak houses ashore.

Carnival serves the best food of the mainstream cruise lines. In addition to the regular menu, vegetarian, low-calorie, low-carbohydrate, low-salt, and no-sugar selections are available. A children's menu includes such favorites as macaroni and cheese, chicken fingers, and peanut butter-and-jelly sandwiches. If you don't feel like dressing up for dinner, the Lido buffet serves full meals, including sandwiches, a salad bar, rotisserie chicken, Asian stir-fry, and excellent pizza.

Fitness and Recreation
Manned by staff members trained to keep passengers in shipshape form, Carnival's trademark spas and fitness centers are some of the largest and best equipped at sea. Spas and salons are operated by Steiner Leisure, and treatments include a variety of massages, body wraps, and facials; salons offer hair and nail services. Tooth whitening is a recent addition. Fitness centers have state-of-the-art cardio and strength-training equipment, a jogging track, and basic exercise classes at no charge. There's a fee for personal training, body composition analysis, and specialized classes such as yoga and Pilates.

Your Shipmates
Carnival's passengers are predominantly active Americans, mostly couples in their mid-thirties to mid-fifties. Many families enjoy Carnival cruises in the Caribbean year-round. Holidays and school vacation periods are very popular with families, and you'll see a lot of kids in summer. More than 670,000 children sailed

5

CARNIVAL CRUISE LINES

Top: *Carnival Victory* dining room
Bottom: *Carnival Legend* waterslide

Top: *Carnival Triumph* walking and jogging track
Middle: *Carnival Elation* at sea
Bottom: *Carnival Destiny* penthouse suite.

on Carnival ships in 2011—a sixfold increase in the past decade.

Dress Code

Two "cruise elegant" nights are standard on seven-night cruises; one is the norm on shorter sailings. Although men should feel free to wear tuxedos, dark suits (or sport coats) and ties are more prevalent. All other evenings are "cruise casual," with jeans and dress shorts permitted in the dining rooms. All ships request that no short-shorts or cutoffs be worn after 6 pm, but that policy is often ignored.

Junior Cruisers

Camp Carnival, run year-round by professionals, earns high marks for keeping young cruisers busy and content. Dedicated children's areas include great playrooms with separate splash pools. Toddlers from two to five years are treated to puppet shows, sponge painting, face painting, coloring, drawing, and crafts. As long as diapers and supplies are provided, staff will change toddlers. Activities for ages six to eight include arts and crafts, pizza parties, computer time, T-shirt painting, a talent show, and fitness programs. Nine- to 11-year-olds can play Ping-Pong, take dance lessons, play video games, and participate in swim parties, scavenger hunts, and sports. Tweens ages 12 to 14 appreciate the social events, parties, contests, and sports in Circle C. Every night they have access to the ships' discos, followed by late-night movies, karaoke, or pizza.

Club O2 is geared toward teens from 15 to 17. Program directors play host at the spacious teen clubs, where kicking back is the order of the day between scheduled activities. The fleetwide Y-Spa program for older teens offers a high level of pampering. Staff members also accompany teens on shore excursions designed just for them.

Daytime group babysitting for infants two and under allows parents the freedom to explore ports of call without the kids until noon. Parents can also pursue leisurely adults-only evenings from 10 pm to 3 am, when slumber party–style group babysitting is available for children from ages 6 months to 11 years. Babysitting

CHOOSE THIS LINE IF ...

You want an action-packed casino with a choice of table games and rows upon rows of clanging slot machines.	You don't mind standing in line—these are big ships with a lot of passengers, and lines are not uncommon.	You don't mind hearing announcements over the public-address system reminding you of what's next on the schedule.

fees are $6 an hour for one child and $4 an hour for each additional child.

Service

Service on Carnival ships is friendly but not polished. Stateroom attendants are not only recognized for their attention to cleanliness but also for their expertise in creating towel animals—cute critters fashioned from bath towels that appear during nightly turndown service. They've become so popular that Carnival publishes an instruction book on how to create them yourself.

Tipping

A gratuity of $10 per passenger per day is automatically added to passenger accounts, and gratuities are distributed to stewards and waitstaff. Passengers may adjust the amount based on the level of service experienced. All beverage tabs at bars get an automatic 15% addition.

Past Passengers

After sailing on one Carnival cruise, you'll receive access to your past sailing history on the Carnival Web site. You are recognized on subsequent cruises with color-coded key cards. Gold (starting you're your 2nd cruise), Platinum (starting with your 10th cruise), or Platinum Milestone (starting with your 25th cruise)—which serve as your entrée to a by-invitation-only cocktail reception. You're also eligible for exclusive discounts on future cruises on all the cruise lines owned by Carnival Corporation.

Platinum members are eligible for Concierge Club benefits, including priority embarkation and debarkation, guaranteed dining assignments, supper club and spa reservations, a logo item gift, and complimentary laundry service. Platinum Milestone benefits include shipboard credits when sailing on your 25th, 50th, 75th, or 100th cruise.

5

CARNIVAL CRUISE LINES

DON'T CHOOSE THIS LINE IF ...

You want an intimate, sedate atmosphere. Carnival's ships are big and bold.

You want elaborate accommodations. Carnival suites are spacious but not as feature-filled as the term *suite* may suggest.

You're turned off by men in tank tops. Casual on these ships means casual indeed.

CONQUEST CLASS
Carnival Conquest, Glory, Valor, Liberty, Freedom

CREW MEMBERS	1,160
ENTERED SERVICE	2002, 2003, 2004, 2005, 2007
GROSS TONS	110,000
LENGTH	952 feet
NUMBER OF CABINS	1,487
PASSENGER CAPACITY	2,974 (3,700 max)
WIDTH	116 feet

700 ft.
500 ft.
300 ft.

Top: *Carnival Glory* at sea
Bottom: Conquest-class balcony cabin

Public Areas and Facilities
Taking Fun Ships to new lengths and widths, Conquest-class ships are among the largest in the Carnival fleet. They're basically larger and more feature-filled versions of earlier Destiny-class vessels. More space translates into additional decks, an upscale Supper Club, and even more bars and lounges; however, well-proportioned public areas belie the ships' massive size. You'll hardly notice that there's slightly less space per passenger after you take a thrilling trip down the spiral waterslide.

Public rooms flow forward and aft from stunning central atriums. Just off each ship's main boulevard is an array of specialty bars, dance lounges, discos, piano bars, and show lounges, plus seating areas along the indoor promenades. The promenade can get crowded between dinner seatings and show-lounge performances, but with so many different places to spend time, you're sure to find one with plenty of room and an atmosphere to suit your taste.

Restaurants
Two formal restaurants serve open seating breakfast and lunch, and dinner is served in two traditional assigned seatings or an open seating option. The casual Lido buffet's food stations offer a variety of choices (including a deli, salad bar, dessert station, and different daily regional cuisines). By night it is transformed into the Seaview Bistro for casual dinner. The ship also has an upscale supper club that requires reservations and assesses a cover charge. You'll also find a pizzeria, outdoor poolside grills where burgers and other favorites are prepared, a specialty coffee bar with pastries, a complimentary sushi bar, and 24-hour room service that offers a limited selection of breakfast items, sandwiches, and snacks.

Accommodations
Cabins: As on all Carnival ships, cabins are roomy and generally larger than industry standard. More than 60% have an ocean view and, of those, 60% have balconies. For those suites and ocean-view cabins that have them, private balconies outfitted with chairs and tables add additional living space; extended balconies are 50% larger than standard ones. Every cabin has adequate closet and drawer–shelf storage, as well as

bathroom shelves. High-thread-count linens and plush pillows and duvets are a luxurious touch in all accommodations. Suites have a whirlpool tub and walk-in closet; two spacious Captain's Suites were added to *Carnival Liberty* in 2008, and *Carnival Valor* received them in 2011, along with six extra-large scenic ocean view staterooms.

Decor: Light-wood cabinetry, pastel colors, mirrored accents, a small refrigerator, a personal safe, a hair dryer in the top vanity-desk drawer, and a sitting area with sofa, chair, and table are typical amenities.

Bathrooms: Shampoo and bath gel are provided in shower-mounted dispensers; you also get an array of sample toiletries, as well as fluffy towels and a wall-mounted magnifying mirror. Bathrobes for use during the cruise are provided for all.

Worth Noting: A plus for families are a number of connecting staterooms in a variety of ocean-view and interior categories. Balcony dividers can be unlocked to provide connecting access in upper categories. Twenty-five staterooms are designed for wheelchair accessibility.

In the Know
The children's playroom has the best view on the ship—looking forward from high over the bow.

Pros and Cons

Pros: Lounge chairs in an area of the deck above the aft Lido pool are almost always a quiet place to read or snooze in the sunshine. New York–style supper clubs on these ships are some of the best restaurants—and specialty dining bargains—at sea. *Carnival Conquest* and *Carnival Glory* have been retrofitted with Carnival's Seaside Theatres—the jumbo-size LED screens currently featured poolside on newer ships in the Conquest class.

Cons: Cabins and balconies on deck 8 from mid-ship to aft are beneath the Lido swimming pools, bars, and restaurant and tend to suffer from pool-deck noise overhead. A seat at the wine bar should be serene, but the volume from adjacent lounges creates the sensation of being surrounded by dueling musicians. Ultracomfortable massage loungers are strategically placed along the indoor promenade—unfortunately there's a charge for the massage feature.

Cabin Type	Size (sq. ft.)
Captain's Suite	500/582 (Liberty/ Valor)
Penthouse Suite	345
Suite	230
Scenic Ocean View	230–320 (Valor only)
Ocean View with Balcony	185
Ocean View	185
Interior	185

FAST FACTS

- 13 passenger decks
- Specialty restaurant, 2 dining rooms, buffet, ice cream parlor, pizzeria
- Wi-Fi, safe, refrigerator
- 3 pools (1 indoor), children's pool
- Fitness classes, gym, hair salon, 7 hot tubs, sauna, spa, steam room
- 9 bars, casino, dance club, library, showroom, video game room
- Children's programs (ages 2–17)
- Laundry facilities, laundry service
- Internet terminal
- No-smoking cabins

5

CARNIVAL CRUISE LINES

SPIRIT CLASS
Carnival Spirit, Pride, Legend, Miracle

	CREW MEMBERS
	930
	ENTERED SERVICE
	1, 2001, 2002, 2004
700 ft.	**GROSS TONS**
	88,500
	LENGTH
	960 feet
500 ft.	**NUMBER OF CABINS**
	1,062
	PASSENGER CAPACITY
	2,124 (2,667 max)
300 ft.	**WIDTH**
	105.7 feet

Top: *Carnival Legend* at sea
Bottom: Spirit-class balcony
stateroom

Public Areas and Facilities

Spirit-class vessels may seem to be a throwback in size, but these sleek ships have the advantage of fitting through the Panama Canal and, with their additional length, include all the trademark characteristics of their larger fleet mates. They're also racehorses with the speed to reach far-flung destinations.

A rosy red skylight in the front bulkhead of the funnel—which houses the reservations-only upscale Supper Club—caps a soaring, 11-deck atrium. Lovely chapels are available for weddings, either upon embarkation or while in a port of call, and are also used for shipboard religious services.

The upper and lower interior promenade decks are unhampered by a mid-ship restaurant or galley, which means that passenger flow throughout the ships is much improved over earlier, and even subsequent, designs.

Restaurants

One formal restaurant serves open seating breakfast and lunch; it also serves dinner in two traditional assigned evening seatings or an open seating option. The casual Lido buffet with stations offers a variety of food choices (including a deli, salad bar, dessert station, and different daily regional cuisines); at night it becomes the Seaview Bistro for casual dinners. There's also an upscale supper club that requires reservations and an additional charge, a pizzeria, poolside outdoor grills for burgers, hot dogs, and the trimmings, a specialty coffee bar and patisserie, a complimentary sushi bar, and 24-hour room service with a limited menu of breakfast selections, sandwiches, and snacks.

Accommodations

Cabins: Cabins on Carnival ships are generally more spacious than industry standard, and these are no exception. Nearly 80% have an ocean view and, of those, more than 80% have balconies. Suites and some ocean-view cabins have private balconies outfitted with chairs and tables; some cabins have balconies at least 50% larger than average. Every cabin has adequate closet and drawer–shelf storage, as well as bathroom shelves. High-thread-count linens and plush pillows and duvets are a luxurious touch in all accommodations. Suites also have a whirlpool tub and walk-in closet.

Decor: Light-wood cabinetry, soft pastels, mirrored accents, a small refrigerator, a personal safe, a hair dryer, and a sitting area with sofa, chair, and table are typical for ocean-view cabins and suites. Inside cabins have ample room but no sitting area.

Bathrooms: Extras include shampoo and bath gel provided in shower-mounted dispensers and an array of sample toiletries, as well as fluffy towels and a wall-mounted magnifying mirror. Bathrobes for use during the cruise are provided for all.

Worth Noting: Decks 5, 6, and 7 each have a pair of balcony staterooms that connect to adjoining interior staterooms that are ideal for families because of their close proximity to children and teen areas. Sixteen staterooms are designed for wheelchair accessibility.

In the Know

Take a walk on the wild side. The gently curving staircase to the Supper Club is clear Plexiglas and definitely a challenge to descend if heights make you dizzy. Try it anyway—it's quite a heady experience. Wimps can use the elevator.

Pros and Cons

Pros: A quieter choice for reading than the library, which also houses the Internet center, is the delightful enclosed winter garden space located forward on the exterior promenade deck. For relaxation, a soothing therapy pool sits under a skylight in the fitness center, and his-and-hers saunas and steam rooms have glass walls and sea views. Complimentary self-serve ice-cream dispensers are on the Lido Deck.

Cons: These are long ships—really long ships—and you may want to consider any mobility issues and select a cabin near one of the three banks of well-placed elevators. Connecting staterooms are relatively scarce throughout the ships, but balcony dividers can be unlocked between some higher-category cabins. Avid gamers may have difficulty locating the video arcade, which is tucked away at the forward end of the ship in front of the main show lounge and accessible from the interior promenade.

Cabin Type	Size (sq. ft.)
Penthouse Suites	370 (average)
Suite	275
Ocean View	185
Interior	185

FAST FACTS

- 12 passenger decks
- Specialty restaurant, dining room, buffet, ice cream parlor, pizzeria
- Wi-Fi, safe, refrigerator
- 3 pools (1 indoor), children's pool
- Fitness classes, gym, hair salon, 4 hot tubs, sauna, spa, steam room
- 7 bars, casino, 2 dance clubs, library, showroom, video game room
- Children's programs (ages 2–17)
- Laundry facilities, laundry service
- Internet terminal
- No-smoking cabins

Carnival Miracle Gatsby's Garden

DESTINY CLASS
Carnival Destiny, Triumph, Victory

	CREW MEMBERS
	1,050, 1,100
	ENTERED SERVICE
	1996, 1999, 2000
700 ft.	**GROSS TONS**
	101,353, 102,000
	LENGTH
	893 feet
500 ft.	**NUMBER OF CABINS**
	1,321, 1,379
	PASSENGER CAPACITY
	2,642 (3,400 max), 2,758 (3,470 max)
300 ft.	
	WIDTH
	116 feet

Top: *Carnival Victory* in Miami
Bottom: *Carnival Triumph*
atrium

Public Areas and Facilities

The first of the Carnival megaships, weighing in at more than 100,000 tons, everything on the Destiny-class vessels is in keeping with their size—bold interiors highlighted by nine-deck atriums, 200-foot corkscrew waterslides on the Lido Deck, and public areas that often span multiple decks. Though they're all considered Destiny ships, the *Carnival Triumph* and *Carnival Victory* have an additional passenger deck and are therefore bigger and have more cabins and crew than the original *Carnival Destiny*.

The variety of indoor and outdoor spaces ranges from relatively small lounges with a nightclub atmosphere to huge showrooms where lavish production shows are staged. Most public rooms open off wide indoor promenades that branch fore and aft from the spectacular atrium.

Expansive pools and sport decks have plenty of room to spread out for sunning and more active pursuits; all three ships have been retrofitted with massive poolside 270-square-foot LED screens.

Restaurants

Two restaurants, each spanning two decks, serve open seating breakfast and lunch. Dinner is served in two traditional assigned evening seatings with an open seating option. Formal dining is supplemented by a casual Lido buffet, offering a variety of food choices (including a deli, salad bar, dessert station, and regional cuisines that change daily); the buffet restaurant becomes the Seaview Bistro by night for casual dining in a relaxed atmosphere. There are also a pizzeria, patisserie, poolside outdoor grill for burgers, hot dogs, and the trimmings, a specialty coffee bar/patisserie, a complimentary sushi bar, and 24-hour room service with a limited menu of breakfast selections, sandwiches, and snacks.

Accommodations

Cabins: As on all Carnival ships, cabins are generally larger than cruise-industry standard. More than half have an ocean view, and of those, 60% have balconies. For suites and ocean-view cabins that have them, private balconies are outfitted with chairs and tables, adding living space. Every cabin has adequate closet and drawer–shelf storage, as well as bathroom shelves. High-thread-count linens and plump pillows and duvets are a luxurious touch. Suites also have a whirlpool tub and walk-in closet.

Decor: Light-wood cabinetry, soft pastels, mirrored accents, a small refrigerator, a personal safe, a hair dryer, and a sitting area with sofa, chair, and table are typical for ocean-view cabins and suites. Inside cabins do not have a sitting area.

Bathrooms: Shampoo and bath gel dispensers are mounted on shower walls; an array of toiletry samples is stocked, as well as fluffy towels. Bathrobes for use during the cruise are provided for all.

Worth Noting: Numerous ocean-view and inside stateroom categories have connecting doors and are suitable for families. Twenty-five staterooms are designed for wheelchair accessibility.

In the Know

Six balcony cabins (6336, 6344, 6363, 6371, 7316, and 7319 on *Destiny*; 6424, 6432, 6451, 6459, 7416, and 7419 on *Triumph* and *Victory*) wrap around an aft crew staircase. The configuration—they stretch lengthwise along the hull—creates balconies that are twice as long as the average standard balconies.

Pros and Cons

Pros: The central Lido pools have tiered sunning decks that offer more areas to lounge with less foot traffic, as well as a good view of the jumbo-size LED screens. Few passengers discover the upper-level seating area in the Lido restaurant, so there are almost always tables available. When the dinner-and-a-show crowds clear out, the lobby bar is a surprisingly off-the-beaten-path space with a lot of visual impact.

Cons: The galley is between dining rooms on deck 3, so you won't want to consume too many rum drinks before attempting to find your way to dinner. Private balconies on high decks in the middle of the ship may not be the tranquil havens you expect when the band cranks up the volume on the Lido Deck. Lines at the buffet can be seemingly endless at peak meal times.

Cabin Type	Size (sq. ft.)
Penthouse Suite	345
Suite	275
Ocean View	185
Interior	185

FAST FACTS

- 12/13 passenger decks (*Destiny, Triumph/Victory*)
- 2 dining rooms, buffet, ice cream parlor, pizzeria
- Wi-Fi, safe, refrigerator
- 3 pools (1 indoor), children's pool
- Fitness classes, gym, hair salon, 7 hot tubs, sauna, spa, steam room
- 7 bars, casino, 3 dance clubs, library, showroom, video game room
- Children's programs (ages 2–17)
- Laundry facilities, laundry service
- Internet terminal
- No-smoking cabins

5

CARNIVAL CRUISE LINES

Carnival Destiny Lido pool deck and waterslide

FANTASY CLASS

Carnival Fantasy, Ecstasy, Sensation, Fascination, Imagination, Inspiration, Elation, Paradise

CREW MEMBERS	920
ENTERED SERVICE	1990, 1991, 1993, 1994, 1995, 1996, 1998, 1998
GROSS TONS	70,367
LENGTH	855 feet
NUMBER OF CABINS	1,026
PASSENGER CAPACITY	2,052 (2,606 max)
WIDTH	103 feet

700 ft.

500 ft.

300 ft.

Top: *Imagination* at sea
Bottom: *Inspiration* Lido pool deck

Public Areas and Facilities

Bathed in fiber-optic light, glitzy Fantasy-class interiors added expansive six-deck atriums and a new dimension to the original superliner concept. To keep the fun going, these ships offer an almost wearying assortment of places to have a good time. As times and tastes have changed, the ships have evolved as well, with new lobby bars, dedicated club spaces for teens and tweens, miniature golf, and Internet centers. Even newer are Carnival's WaterWorks water park and the Serenity Adult-Only Retreat, which increase the appeal of the older Fantasy-Class vessels.

Only one level below the Lido Deck, the indoor promenade connects major public rooms on a single deck, with only formal dining rooms, shops, and other small spaces one deck below. Large in size and ideal for a short itinerary, these ships have sprawling outdoor pool and sunning areas, but they can feel cramped when sailing at maximum capacity. Cabins provide calm oases from sensory overload. With the exception of the *Carnival Sensation, Carnival Fascination,* and *Carnival Ecstasy,* to which balconies were added to existing cabins, you'll have to book a suite if you want the solitude of a private balcony.

Restaurants

Two formal restaurants serve open seating breakfast and lunch; dinner is served in two traditional assigned evening seatings or an open seating option. The casual Lido buffet with stations offers a variety of food choices (including a deli, salad bar, dessert station, and different daily regional cuisines); at night it becomes the Seaview Bistro for casual dinners. There's also a pizzeria; rotisserie; poolside outdoor grills for burgers, hot dogs, and the trimmings; a specialty coffee bar and patisserie; a complimentary sushi bar; and 24-hour room service with a limited menu of breakfast selections, sandwiches, and snacks.

Accommodations

Cabins: Fantasy-class ships have a higher percentage of inside cabins than the fleet's newer ships, and with the exception of *Carnival Sensation, Carnival Fascination,* and *Carnival Ecstasy,* only the suite categories offer balconies. Every cabin has adequate closet and drawer–shelf storage, as well as bathroom shelves. Light-wood cabinetry and simple decor are the norm for all cabins, while suite embellishments add the convenience of a sitting area and small refrigerator. In addition to the extra space, a whirlpool tub is a deluxe appointment in Penthouse suites. Inside cabins have ample room, and their curtained faux windows mimic those in the more expensive standard ocean-view accommodations. High-thread-count linens and plush pillows and duvets add a touch of luxury to all accommodations.

Bathrooms: Extras include shower-mounted shampoo and bath gel dispensers and an array of sample toiletries, as well as fluffy towels. Bathrobes for use during the cruise are provided for all.

Worth Noting: Doors have been added to a limited number of adjacent cabins to create connecting accommodations on Fantasy-class ships and lighting in the vanity/desk area has been improved on some. Bring your own hair dryer. Twenty-two staterooms are designed for wheelchair accessibility.

In the Know

Penthouse suites, the most expansive on board, are also in the most desirable area—right in the middle of a lower deck. The lesser suites, however, are high in the sky and all the way forward. To get the best fare, book a suite guarantee; you'll pay less, and the location won't matter that much.

Pros and Cons

Pros: Central atriums are simply stunning when sunlight streams in through skylights overhead—they take on a flashy air only when artificially lighted after dark. The surprisingly large libraries are ideal retreats for reading or playing board games. Freshly made, to-die-for pizza and calzones are available around the clock.

Cons: Despite recent upgrades, there's a lot of glitz throughout Fantasy Class ships, which can be somewhat overpowering until you become accustomed to it. These are ships designed for partying, so unless you want to party, it may be difficult to find a late-night hideaway offering peace and quiet. Sushi bars earn high marks for their complimentary creations, although you'll have to pay if you want a glass of sake to drink.

Cabin Type	Size (sq. ft.)
Penthouse Suite	330
Suite	220
Ocean View	185
Interior	160–185

FAST FACTS

- 10 passenger decks
- 2 dining rooms, buffet, ice cream parlor, pizzeria
- Wi-Fi, safe, refrigerator (some)
- 1 pool, children's pool
- Fitness classes, gym, hair salon, 4 hot tubs, sauna, spa, steam room
- 5 bars, casino, dance club, library, showroom, video game room
- Children's programs (ages 2–17)
- Laundry facilities, laundry service
- Internet terminal
- No-smoking cabins

5

CARNIVAL CRUISE LINES

Elation Tiffany's Lounge

DREAM CLASS
Carnival Dream, Magic, Breeze

CREW MEMBERS	1,367
ENTERED SERVICE	2008, 2011, 2012
GROSS TONS	130,000
LENGTH	1,004 feet
NUMBER OF CABINS	1,823
PASSENGER CAPACITY	3,646 (4,631 max)
WIDTH	122 feet

700 ft.

500 ft.

300 ft.

Top: RedFrog Pub, *Carnival Magic*
Bottom: Cucina del Capitano, *Carnival Magic*

Public Areas and Facilities

Carnival's Dream class, the largest and longest ever constructed for their fleet, ushers in an exciting design concept for the line with a new layout, sleek hull, and distinctive profile. The line has made maximum use of the vessels' added size by creating some truly spectacular on-board facilities and amenities. Unique is the Ocean Plaza, an indoor–outdoor café and live music venue with a large, circular dance floor and comfortable seating areas with ocean views and, in a first for Carnival, a half-mile, open-air promenade encircling the ship.

Four "scenic" whirlpools located on the promenade cantilever out over the sea and offer maximum views while you're soaking. Higher up, the Lido Deck is the most elaborate open-deck area of any Carnival ship, with a tropical, resort-style main pool complete with a Seaside Theatre LED screen; an adults-only retreat (called Serenity) with comfortable seating and full bar service; and a huge Carnival WaterWorks aqua park featuring one of the longest water slides at sea. The family-friendly amenities include separate, purpose-built facilities for the line's three distinct children's programs, along with a full schedule of activities catering to each age group.

Restaurants

Two formal restaurants serve open seating breakfast and lunch, while dinner is served in two traditional assigned seatings with an open seating option. The casual Lido buffet's food stations offer a variety of choices (including a deli, salad bar, dessert station, and different daily regional cuisines). By night, it is transformed into the Seaview Bistro for casual dinner. The ship also has an upscale supper club that requires reservations and has a cover charge. Carnival Magic also has a second Italian specialty restaurant for which there is a cover charge. You'll also find a pizzeria, outdoor poolside grills where burgers and other favorites are prepared, a specialty coffee bar with pastries, a complimentary sushi bar, and 24-hour room service that offers a limited selection of breakfast items, sandwiches, and snacks. Finger food is available for a charge in the pubs.

Accommodations

Cabins: As on all Carnival ships, cabins are roomy and generally larger than industry standard. More than 63% have an ocean view and, of those, 77% have balconies. New "cove" balcony staterooms, located closer to the water line, offer up-close sea views and a bit more interior space. Also new are deluxe ocean-view staterooms featuring a unique design with five berths and a two-bath configuration that includes one full bathroom and a second with a combination tub/shower and sink.

Every cabin has adequate closet and drawer/shelf storage, as well as bathroom shelves. High-quality linens and plush pillows and duvets are a luxurious touch in all accommodations.

Bathrooms: Shampoo and bath gel are provided in shower-mounted dispensers; you also receive an array of sample toiletries, as well as fluffy towels and a wall-mounted magnifying mirror. Bathrobes for use during the cruise are provided for all.

Worth Noting: There are connecting staterooms in both ocean-view and interior categories, as well as the spacious new deluxe ocean-view staterooms. Thirty-five staterooms are designed for wheelchair accessibility.

In the Know

Dream-class spas cover 23,750 square feet on two decks. Included in that space are flotation and mud treatment rooms, a huge thalassotherapy pool, and thermal suite with tepidarium, laconium, Oriental and aroma steam baths, and a relaxation lounge.

Pros and Cons

Pros: Adjacent to the expansive spa are 65 spa staterooms and suites that offer a number of exclusive amenities and spa privileges. Two-bathroom staterooms are a boon for families. The bottom level of the atrium has a cantilevered bandstand atop a massive dance floor perfect for practicing the steps you learned in onboard dance lessons.

Cons: Lines can be a problem issue everywhere, especially in the buffet at popular dining times. If the weather is bad outside, interior spaces can seem overwhelmed. Although the decor is somewhat toned down from past Carnival ships, there's still a lot of glitz.

Cabin Type	Size (sq. ft.)
Grand Suite	430
Suite	310
Ocean View with Cove Balcony	230
Ocean View with Balcony	220
Deluxe Ocean View/Ocean View	230/220
Interior	185

FAST FACTS

- 13 passenger decks
- Specialty restaurant, 2 dining rooms, buffet, café, ice cream parlor, pizzeria
- Wi-Fi, safe, refrigerator, DVD (some)
- 3 pools, children's pool
- Fitness classes, gym, 7 hot tubs, sauna, spa, steam room
- 10 bars, casino, 2 dance clubs, library, 2 showrooms, video game room
- Children's programs (ages 2–17)
- Laundry facilities, laundry service
- Internet terminal
- No-smoking cabins

CELEBRITY CRUISES

The Chandris Group, owners of budget Fantasy Cruises, founded Celebrity in 1989. Initially utilizing an unlovely, refurbished former ocean liner from the Fantasy fleet, Celebrity gained a reputation for professional service and fine food despite the shabby-chic

Celebrity Century at anchor

vessel on which it was elegantly served. The cruise line eventually built premium sophisticated cruise ships. Signature amenities followed, including large standard staterooms with generous storage, fully equipped spas, and butler service. Valuable art collections grace the fleet.

✉ *1050 Caribbean Way, Miami, FL*

☎ *800/647–2251*

⊕ *www.celebritycruises.com*

↪ *Cruise Style: Premium.*

Entertainment has never been a primary focus of Celebrity Cruises, although a lineup of lavish revues is presented in the main show lounges. In addition to shows featuring comedians, magicians, and jugglers, bands play a wide range of musical styles for dancing and listening in smaller lounges. You'll find guest lecturers on every Celebrity cruise. Presentations may range from financial strategies, astronomy, wine appreciation, photography tips, and politics to the food, history, and culture of ports of call. Culinary demonstrations, bingo, and art auctions are additional diversions throughout the fleet. There are plenty of activities, all outlined in the daily program of events. There are no public address announcements for bingo or hawking of gold-by-the-inch sales. You can still play and buy, but you won't be reminded repeatedly.

Although spacious accommodations in every category are a Celebrity standard, ConciergeClass, an upscale element on all ships, makes certain premium ocean-view and balcony staterooms almost the equivalent of suites in terms of service. A ConciergeClass stateroom includes numerous extras, such as chilled champagne, fresh fruit, and flowers upon arrival, exclusive room-service menus, evening canapés, luxury bedding, pillows, and linens, upgraded balcony furnishings, priority boarding and luggage service, and other VIP perks. At the touch of a single telephone button, a ConciergeClass desk representative is at hand to offer assistance. Suites are still the ultimate, though, and include the services of a butler to assist with unpacking, booking spa services and dining reservations, shining shoes, and even replacing a popped button.

Food

Aside from the sophisticated ambience of its restaurants, the cuisine has always been a highlight of a Celebrity cruise. However, in early 2007, Celebrity and longtime chef Michael Roux ended their affiliation. His hands-on involvement—personally creating menus and overseeing all aspects of dining operations—was integral in helping the line achieve the reputation it enjoys today. Happily, every ship in the fleet has a highly experienced team headed by executive chefs and food and beverage managers who have developed their skills in some of the world's finest restaurants and hotels.

Alternative restaurants on the Millennium-class ships, and *Celebrity Century* offer fine dining and tableside food preparation amid classic ocean liner and Venetian splendor. Solstice-class ships offer a variety of international cuisines in their specialty restaurants. A less formal evening alternative is offered fleet-wide in Lido restaurants, where you'll find made-to-order sushi, stir-fry, pasta, pizza, and curry stations, as well as a carving station, an array of vegetables, "loaded" baked potatoes, and desserts. The AquaSpa Cafés serve light and healthy cuisine from breakfast until evening. Cafés serve a variety of coffees, teas, and pastries that carry an additional charge. Late-night treats served by white-gloved waiters in public rooms throughout the ships can include mini–beef Wellingtons and crispy tempura.

To further complement the food, in 2004 Celebrity introduced a proprietary Cellarmaster Selection of wines, formulated specifically for Celebrity passengers.

Fitness and Recreation

Celebrity's AquaSpa by Elemis and fitness centers are some of the most tranquil and nicely equipped at sea, with complimentary access to thalassotherapy pools on Millennium-class ships. Spa services are operated by Steiner Leisure, and treatments include a variety of massages, body wraps, and facials. Trendy and traditional hair and nail services are offered in the salons.

NOTEWORTHY

■ Celebrity's AquaSpa facilities and services are some of the best at sea.

■ The letter X on the ships' funnels is the Greek letter for C and stands for Chandris, the line's founding family.

■ Fresh-baked pizzas can be delivered to your stateroom in an insulated carrier.

■ *Celebrity Century* at anchor

Top: The *Millennium* AquaSpa
Bottom: Millennium-class cinema and conference center

5

CELEBRITY CRUISES

Top: *Century* Rendezvous Lounge
Middle: Lunch on deck
Bottom: Lounging on deck

State-of-the-art exercise equipment, a jogging track, and basic fitness classes are available at no charge. There's a fee for personal training, body composition analysis, and specialized classes such as yoga and Pilates. Golf pros offer hands-on instruction, and game simulators allow passengers to play world-famous courses. Each ship also has an Acupuncture at Sea treatment area staffed by licensed practitioners of Oriental medicine.

Your Shipmates
Celebrity caters to American cruise passengers, primarily couples from their mid-thirties to mid-fifties. Many families enjoy cruising on Celebrity's fleet during summer months and holiday periods, particularly in the Caribbean. Lengthier cruises and exotic itineraries attract passengers in the over-sixty age group.

Dress Code
Two formal nights are standard on seven-night cruises. Men are encouraged to wear tuxedos, but dark suits or sport coats and ties are more prevalent. Other evenings are designated "smart casual and above." Although jeans are discouraged in formal restaurants, they are appropriate for casual dining venues after 6 pm. The line requests that no shorts be worn in public areas after 6 pm, and most people observe the dress code of the evening, unlike on some other cruise lines.

Junior Cruisers
Each Celebrity vessel has a dedicated playroom and offers a four-tier program of age-appropriate games and activities designed for children ages 3 to 5, 6 to 8, and 9 to 11. Younger children must be toilet trained to participate in the programs and use the facilities; however, families are welcome to borrow toys for their non–toilet-trained kids. A fee may be assessed for participation in children's dinner parties, the Late-Night Slumber Party, and Afternoon Get-Togethers while parents are ashore in ports of call. Evening in-cabin babysitting can be arranged for a fee. All ships have teen centers, where tweens (ages 12 to 14) and teenagers (ages 15 to 17) can hang out and attend mock-tail and pizza parties.

CHOOSE THIS LINE IF ...
You want an upscale atmosphere at a really reasonable fare.

You want piping-hot late-night pizza delivered to your cabin in pizzeria fashion.

You want to dine amid elegant surroundings in some of the best restaurants at sea.

Service

Service on Celebrity ships is unobtrusive and polished. ConciergeClass adds an unexpected level of service and amenities that are usually reserved for luxury ships or passengers in top-category suites on other premium cruise lines.

Tipping

Gratuities are automatically added daily to onboard accounts in the following amounts (which may be adjusted at your discretion): $11.50 per person per day for passengers in stateroom categories; $12 per person per day for ConciergeClass and AquaClass staterooms; and $15 per person per day for Suites. An automatic gratuity of 15% is added to all beverage tabs.

Past Passengers

Once you've sailed with Celebrity, you become a member of the Captain's Club and receive benefits commensurate with the number of credits you've earned on the cruises you've taken, including free upgrades, the chance to make dining reservations before sailing, and other benefits. Classic members have one to four credits and are invited to a Captain's Club event. Select members have five to nine credits and get more perks, including discounted Internet and laundry service specials. After earning 10 credits you become an Elite member and can take advantage of complimentary Internet and laundry services and access to the Captain's Club lounge. Multiple credits can be earned during a single cruise by booking premium accommodations or sailings of 12 or more nights.

5

CELEBRITY CRUISES

DON'T CHOOSE THIS LINE IF ...

You need to be reminded of when activities are scheduled. Announcements are kept to a minimum.

You look forward to boisterous pool games and wacky contests. These cruises are fairly quiet and adult-centered.

You think funky avant-garde art is weird. Abstract modernism abounds in the art collections.

SOLSTICE CLASS
Solstice, Equinox, Eclipse, Silhouette, Reflection

CREW MEMBERS	1,253
ENTERED SERVICE	2008, 2009, 2010, 2011, 2012
GROSS TONS	122,000
LENGTH	1,033 feet
NUMBER OF CABINS	1,425
PASSENGER CAPACITY	2,850
WIDTH	121 feet

700 ft.

500 ft.

300 ft.

Public Areas and Facilities

Solstice-class ships are the largest and most sophisticated in the Celebrity fleet. The abundant use of draped fabrics, marble, stainless steel, and punches of rich color accent public areas. While most are contemporary in design—even a bit edgy—Celebrity included enough spaces with old-world ambience to satisfy traditionalists. The atmosphere is not unlike a hip, yet luxurious, South Beach hotel filled with grand spaces, as well as intimate nooks and crannies.

The Lawn Club, a half acre of real grass 15 decks above the sea, is where you can play genteel games of croquet, practice golf putting, indulge in lawn games and picnics, or simply take barefoot strolls. In a nearby open-air "theater" (on *Solstice, Equinox,* and *Eclipse*), artisans from the Corning Museum of Glass demonstrate glassmaking in the Hot Glass Show. Also impressive is a tranquil solarium with a lap pool and solar panels overhead. These ships have a lot to offer for families, with a family pool and the most extensive children's facilities in the Celebrity fleet.

Restaurants

The main restaurant serves open seating breakfast and lunch; dinner is served in two traditional assigned seatings or an open seating option that allows you to be seated any time the main restaurant is open. A second dining room, reserved exclusively for AquaClass passengers, serves "clean" cuisine—similar to main dining room selections, though lighter. Formal dining is supplemented by a casual Lido buffet, pizza, sushi bar, the AquaSpa Café with healthy selections, a luncheon grill, a café that offers crepes and other light items with a cover charge, and an extra-charge specialty coffee and tea bar and gelateria for Italian ice cream. No fewer than three upscale alternative restaurants require dinner reservations and charge extra for contemporary French, Asian fusion, and Italian steak-house cuisine. Eclipse and Silhouette replaced the Asian restaurant with one serving modern American food. Silhouette and Reflection introduce the Lawn Club Grill, an outdoor grill restaurant where you can prepare your meat on a hot lava stone or have it grilled to order. Available 24 hours, room service rounds out the dining choices.

Top: Blu, the AquaClass
specialty restaurant
Bottom: Lawn bowling

Accommodations

Layout: Cabins were designed with the assistance of five well-traveled women to add input from a feminine point of view. Although the cabins are 15% larger than those on other Celebrity ships, closet and drawer storage is barely adequate. On the other hand, bathrooms are generous and feature plentiful storage space. An impressive 85% of all outside accommodations have private balconies.

Amenities: A refrigerator, TV, personal safe, hair dryer, sitting area with sofa and table, bathroom toiletries (shampoo, soaps, and lotion), and bathrobes for use during the cruise are standard.

Suites: Suite luxuries vary, but most include a whirlpool tub, DVD, and walk-in closet, while all have butler service, personalized stationery, and a logo tote bag. Penthouse suites have guest powder rooms; Penthouse and Royal suites have whirlpool tubs on the balconies.

Worth Noting: With sofa–trundle beds, many categories are capable of accommodating third and fourth occupants. Connecting staterooms are available in numerous categories. Family staterooms have a second bedroom with bunk beds. Thirty staterooms are designed for wheelchair accessibility.

In the Know

Seats fill up fast in the open-air theater at the forward area of the Lawn Club, so arrive early if you want to see the Hot Glass Show presented there. Standing on the grass at the edge of the theater is discouraged because heavy traffic is hard on the real turf.

Pros and Cons

Pros: On the interactive TV system, you can book shore excursions and spa services, watch on-demand entertainment, preview menus, purchase photos, and place room service orders. AquaClass spa cabins have their own "secret" staircase leading to the spa, up one deck. A Hospitality Director is in charge of overseeing reservations for all specialty dining, ensuring that all requests are handled efficiently.

Cons: Closet space is skimpy in standard accommodations, and there are no self-service laundries. Although dining choices are plentiful, the specialty options will take a chunk from your wallet. The jury is still out on whether the real grass planted for the Lawn Club will survive saltwater spray and other adverse weather conditions.

Cabin Type	Size (sq. ft.)
Penthouse	1,291
Royal Suites	590
Celebrity Suites	394
Sky Suites	300
Family Ocean-view Balcony	575
Ocean-view Balcony	194
Sunset Veranda	194
Ocean View	177
Inside	183–200

FAST FACTS

- 13 passenger decks
- 4 specialty restaurants, 2 dining rooms, buffet, ice cream parlor, pizzeria
- Wi-Fi, safe, refrigerator, DVD (some)
- 3 pools (1 indoor)
- Fitness classes, gym, hair salon, 6 hot tubs, sauna, spa
- 11 bars, cinema, casino, dance club, library, show-room, video game room
- Children's programs (ages 3–17)
- Dry-cleaning, laundry service
- Internet terminal
- No-smoking cabins

The solarium on *Solstice*

MILLENNIUM CLASS
Millennium, Summit, Infinity, Constellation

CREW MEMBERS	999
ENTERED SERVICE	2000, 2001, 2001, 2002
GROSS TONS	91,000
LENGTH	965 feet
NUMBER OF CABINS	1,079, 1,017, 1,023, 1,017
PASSENGER CAPACITY	2,158, 2,034, 2,046, 2,034
WIDTH	105 feet

700 ft.

500 ft.

300 ft.

Public Areas and Facilities

Millennium-class ships are among the largest and most feature-filled in the Celebrity fleet. Innovations include show lounges reminiscent of splendid opera houses, and an alternative restaurant where diners find themselves in the midst of authentic ocean liner decor and memorabilia. The spas simply have to be seen to be believed—they occupy nearly as much space inside as is devoted to the adjacent outdoor Lido Deck pool area. Although the spas offer just about any treatment you can think of—and some you probably haven't—they also house a complimentary hydrotherapy pool and café. These ships have a lot to offer families, with some of the most expansive children's facilities in the Celebrity fleet.

Rich fabrics in jewel tones mix elegantly with the abundant use of marble and wood accents throughout public areas. The atmosphere is not unlike a luxurious European hotel filled with grand spaces that flow nicely from one to the other.

Restaurants

The formal two-deck restaurant serves open seating breakfast and lunch; evening meals are served in two traditional assigned seatings or an open seating option that allows you to be seated any time the main restaurant is open. The casual Lido buffet offers breakfast and lunch. For dinner, it has made-to-order entrées, a carving station, and an array of side dishes. Each ship features a poolside grill for burgers and other fast-food favorites; the spa café serves lighter fare. A specialty coffee bar also serves teas and pastries for an extra charge. Each ship has an upscale alternative restaurant that specializes in tableside food preparation and houses a demonstration kitchen and wine cellar (requiring reservations and a per-person cover charge). A café that offers crepes and other light bites and a steak house, both with a cover charge, are being introduced on one ship a year, which started with Constellation in 2010 and will be complete on Infinity, Summit, and Millennium by Aril 2012. Also being added is an extra-charge ice-cream bar offering authentic gelato. Pizza delivery and 24-hour room service augment dining choices.

Top: *Millennium* Cova Café
Bottom: *Millennium* Ocean Grill

Accommodations

Cabins: As on all Celebrity ships, cabins are thoughtfully designed, with ample closet and drawer/shelf storage, as well as bathroom shelves in all standard inside and outside categories. Some ocean-view cabins and suites have private balconies. Penthouse suites have guest powder rooms. AquaClass, Celebrity's spa-inspired veranda-category accommodations, which were introduced on Solstice-class ships, are also being added to refurbished Millennium-class ships during 2011 and 2012.

Amenities: Wood cabinetry, mirrored accents, a small refrigerator, a personal safe, a hair dryer, and a sitting area with sofa, chair, and table are typical standard amenities. Extras include bathroom toiletries (shampoo, soaps, and lotion) and bathrobes for use during the cruise. Suite luxuries vary, but most include a whirlpool tub, a DVD or VCR, an Internet-connected computer, and a walk-in closet, while all have butler service, personalized stationery, and a logo tote bag. For pure pleasure, Penthouse and Royal suites have outdoor whirlpool tubs on the balconies.

Worth Noting: Most staterooms and suites have convertible sofa beds, and many categories are capable of accommodating third and fourth occupants. Connecting staterooms are available in numerous categories, including Celebrity suites. Family staterooms feature huge balconies, and some have two sofa beds. Twenty-six staterooms are designed for wheelchair accessibility.

In the Know

Enhance your personal outdoor space by booking cabins 6035, 6030, or any of the seven cabins forward of those two on deck 6. You can't tell from the deck plan, but your balcony will be extra deep, and you won't be looking down into a lifeboat.

Pros and Cons

Pros: Grand Foyers on these ships are stylishly appointed, multideck lobbies, with sweeping staircases crying out for grand entrances. There's no charge for use of the thalassotherapy pool in the huge AquaSpa, a facility that rivals the fanciest ashore. The AquaSpa Café serves light and healthy selections for breakfast, lunch, and dinner.

Cons: Crew members try hard to make everyone feel special, but there are just too many passengers to expect that your every wish will be granted on a ship this size. Although you'd expect to pay far more ashore for a comparable meal in one of the extra-charge specialty restaurants, the suggested wines are pricey. Self-service laundries are not featured on Celebrity ships.

Cabin Type	Size (sq. ft.)
Penthouse Suite	1,432
Royal Suite	538
Celebrity Suite	467
Sky Suite	251
Family Ocean View	271
ConciergeClass	191
Ocean View/ Interior	170

FAST FACTS

- 11 passenger decks
- Specialty restaurant, dining room, buffet, ice cream parlor, pizzeria
- Internet (*Constellation*), Wi-Fi, safe, refrigerator, DVD (some)
- 3 pools (1 indoor), children's pool
- Fitness classes, gym, hair salon, 6 hot tubs, sauna, spa, steam room
- 7 bars, casino, cinema, dance club, library, showroom, video game room
- Children's programs (ages 3–17)
- Dry-cleaning, laundry service
- Internet terminal
- No-smoking cabins

5

CELEBRITY CRUISES

COSTA CRUISES

Europe's number-one cruise line combines a continental experience, enticing itineraries, and Italy's classical design and style with relaxing days and romantic nights at sea. Genoa-based Costa Crociere, parent company of Costa Cruise Lines, had been

Dining alfresco

in the shipping business for more than 100 years and in the passenger business for almost 50 years when it was bought by Airtours and Carnival Corporation in 1997. In 2000 Carnival completed a buyout of the Costa line and began expanding the fleet with larger and more dynamic ships.

✉ *200 S. Park Rd., Suite 200, Hollywood, FL*

☎ *954/266–5600 or 800/462–6782*

⊕ *www.costacruise. com*

☞ *Cruise Style: Mainstream.*

Italian-style cruising is a mixture of Mediterranean flair and American comfort, beginning with a *buon viaggio* celebration and topped off by a signature Roman Bacchanal Parade and zany toga party. The supercharged social staff works overtime to get everyone in the mood and encourages everyone to be a part of the action.

Festive shipboard activities include some of Italy's favorite pastimes, such as playing games of bocce, dancing the tarantella, and tossing pizza dough during the Festa Italiana, an Italian street festival at sea. Other nights are themed as well—a welcome-aboard celebration (*Benvenuto A Bordo*), hosted by the captain on the first formal night, and *Notte Tropical,* a tropical deck party with a Mediterranean twist that culminates with the presentation of an alfresco midnight buffet. When it is time to say goodbye, Costa throws a Roman Bacchanal.

There's also a nod to the traditional cruise ship entertainment expected by North American passengers. Pool games, trivia, bingo, and sophisticated production shows blend nicely with classical concerts in lounges where a wide range of musical styles invite dancing or listening. Italian language, arts and crafts, and cooking classes are extremely popular. Every ship has a small chapel suitable for intimate weddings, and Catholic Mass is celebrated most days.

Acknowledging changing habits (even among Europeans), Costa Cruises has eliminated smoking entirely in dining rooms and show lounges. However, smokers are permitted to light up in designated areas in other public rooms, as well as on the pool deck.

An ongoing ship-building program has brought Costa ships into the 21st century with innovative large-ship designs that reflect their Italian heritage and style without overlooking the amenities expected by modern cruisers.

Food

Costa is noted for themed dinner menus that convey the evening's mood. Dining features regional Italian cuisines: a variety of pastas, chicken, beef, and seafood dishes, as well as authentic pizza. European chefs and culinary school graduates, who are members of Chaîne des Rôtisseurs, provide a dining experience that's notable for a delicious, properly prepared pasta course, if not exactly living up to gourmet standards. Vegetarian and healthy diet choices are also offered, as are selections for children. Alternative dining is by reservation only in the upscale supper clubs, which serve traditional Italian cuisine.

While specialty restaurants usually have a separate à la carte charge for each menu item, suite passengers receive one complimentary dinner for two.

Costa ships also retain the tradition of lavish nightly midnight buffets, a feature that is beginning to disappear on other mainstream lines. Room service is available 24 hours from a limited menu.

Fitness and Recreation

Taking a cue from the ancient Romans, Costa places continuing emphasis on wellness and sensual pleasures. Spas and salons are operated by Steiner Leisure, and treatments include a variety of massages, body wraps, and facials that can be scheduled à la carte or combined in packages to enjoy during one afternoon or throughout the entire cruise. Hair and nail services are available in the salons.

State-of-the-art exercise equipment in the gym, a jogging track, and basic fitness classes for all levels of ability are available. Costa ships offer a Golf Academy at Sea, with PGA clinics on the ship and golf excursions in some ports.

5

COSTA CRUISES

Top: Showtime on Costa
Bottom: Casino action

Top: *Costa* chefs
Middle: Jogging on deck
Bottom: Las Vegas–style
entertainment

Your Shipmates

Couples in the 35- to 55-year-old range are attracted to Costa Cruises; on most itineraries, up to 80% of passengers are European, and many of them are of Italian descent. An international air prevails on board, and announcements are often made in a variety of languages. The vibe on Costa's newest megaships is most likely to appeal to American tastes and expectations.

Dress Code

Two formal nights are standard on seven-night cruises. Men are encouraged to wear tuxedos, but dark suits or sport coats and ties are appropriate and more common than black tie. All other evenings are resort casual, although jeans are discouraged in restaurants. It's requested that no shorts be worn in public areas after 6 pm.

Junior Cruisers

Caribbean sailings feature age-specific youth programs that include such daily activities as costume parties, board games, junior aerobics, and even Italian-language lessons for children in four age groups: 3 (toilet trained) to 6; 7 to 11; junior teens 12 to 14; and teens 15 to 17. The actual age groupings may be influenced by the number of children on board. Special counselors oversee activities, and specific rooms are designed for children and teens, depending on the ship. Children under three years old can use the playroom facilities if accompanied and supervised by their parents.

Organized sessions for all children between the ages of 3 and 17 are available every day, even when in port, from 9 to noon and 3 to 6, as well as from 9 to 11:30 in the evening. Parents can enjoy at least a couple of evenings alone by taking advantage of two complimentary Parents Nights Out while their children dine at a supervised buffet or pizza party and take part in evening and nighttime activities. Nighttime group babysitting for children ages 3 to 11 is complimentary in the children's area until 1:30 am. Unfortunately, no late-night babysitting service is offered for children under three, nor is there in-cabin babysitting.

CHOOSE THIS LINE IF ...

You're a satisfied Carnival past passenger and want a similar experience with an Italian flavor.

You want pizza hot out of the oven whenever you get a craving for it.

You're a joiner: there are many opportunities to be in the center of the action.

Service
Service in dining areas can be spotty and rushed, but is adequate, if not always overly friendly.

Tipping
A standard gratuity of $11 per adult per day is automatically added to shipboard accounts and distributed to cabin stewards and dining-room staff; 50% of that amount is added for teens between the ages of 14 and 17; there is no charge for children under the age of 14. Passengers may adjust the amount based on the level of service experienced. A 15% gratuity is added to all beverage tabs, as well as to checks for spa treatments and salon services.

Past Passengers
The Costa Club has three levels of membership: Aquamarine (2,000 points), Coral (2,001 to 5,000 points), and Pearl (5,001 or more points). Points are assigned for the number of cruising days (100 points per day) and the amount of money spent aboard (40 points for 52 euros).

Membership privileges vary, and can include discounts on selected cruises, fruit baskets, and bottles of Spumante delivered to your cabin, discounts on boutique merchandise and beauty treatments, or a complimentary dinner in a specialty restaurant.

GOOD TO KNOW

Mama Mia! Connoisseurs of classical Italian art and design may feel they've died and gone to Caesars Palace. Costa's newest ships try to convey what Americans think of as Roman: gilt surfaces, marble columns, and all. Overlook the gaudiness and pay particular attention to the best details: the Murano-glass chandeliers and lighting fixtures are simply superb. And when you're packing, don't forget to toss something in the suitcase to wear beneath your toga; while sheets and accessories are provided, it's considered bad form to flash fellow passengers during the revelry.

5

COSTA CRUISES

DON'T CHOOSE THIS LINE IF ...

You find announcements in a variety of languages annoying.

You want an authentic Italian cruise. The crew has grown more international than Italian as the line has expanded.

You prefer sedate splendor in a formal atmosphere. The Caribbean-based ships are almost Fellini-esque in style.

COSTA ATLANTICA/MEDITERRANEA

CREW MEMBERS	920
ENTERED SERVICE	2000, 2003
GROSS TONS	86,000
LENGTH	960 feet
NUMBER OF CABINS	1,057
PASSENGER CAPACITY	2,114 (2,682 max)
WIDTH	106 feet

700 ft.
500 ft.
300 ft.

Top: Romantic dinner
Bottom: Costa Magica Grand
Suite

Public Areas and Facilities

The basic layout of these contemporary ships is nearly identical to parent Carnival Cruise Line's Spirit-class vessels. Interiors were designed by Carnival's ship architect Joe Farcus, whose abundant use of marble reflects Costa's Italian heritage. Artwork commissioned specifically for each ship was created by contemporary artists and includes intricate sculptures in silver and glass. Don't overlook the lighting fixtures, which were created especially for the ship, most of them crafted by the artisans in Venice's Murano-glass factories.

The nice flow between public lounges is broken only by piazzas, where you can practice the Italian custom of *passeggiata* (strolling to see and be seen). And there's plenty to see; these are visually stimulating interiors, with vivid colors and decor elements to arouse a sense of discovery. One of the most elegant spaces on board *Costa Atlantica* is Café Florian—inspired by the original in Venice's St. Mark's Square.

Restaurants

A single two-deck-high formal restaurant serves open seating breakfast and lunch, while the Italian-accented cuisine is served in two traditional assigned dinner seatings. An upscale, reservations-only alternative restaurant features Italian specialties—while there is a charge, it's well worth it for the intimate, candlelit atmosphere and interesting menu selection. Coffee shops serve delightful, authentic Italian specialty coffees and treats. The casual Lido buffet, pizzeria, and 24-hour room service are alternatives to dining room meals. Costa is one of the few cruise lines to continue the seagoing tradition of lavish midnight buffets. Room service is available 24 hours from a limited menu.

Accommodations

Cabins: Cabins generally follow the outline of their Carnival counterparts, with the distinctive addition of a Grand Suite category. Nearly 80% of the suites and staterooms have an ocean view, and of those more than 80% have balconies. Every cabin has adequate closet and drawer/shelf storage, as well as bathroom shelves; suites have a walk-in closet.

Amenities: Light-wood cabinetry, pastel decor, Murano-glass lighting fixtures, mirrored accents, a small refrigerator, a personal safe, a hair dryer, and a sitting area with sofa, chair, and table are typical for ocean-view cabins and suites. Inside cabins have somewhat smaller sitting areas for lounging. Suites have DVD players.

Bathrooms: Extras include shampoo and bath gel in shower-mounted dispensers; suites have a whirlpool bathtub.

Worth Noting: Although connecting staterooms are somewhat scarce throughout the ships, balcony dividers can be unlocked to provide connecting access in upper-category staterooms. Eight staterooms are designed for wheelchair accessibility.

In the Know

Tucked away far forward is a stunning chapel with an altar, wood pews, stained-glass panels, and religious icons. Unlike other ships' generic wedding chapels, this is a tiny house of worship afloat.

Pros and Cons

Pros: As one passenger put it, if earlier Costa ships were Armani (clean, cool, and serene), then these are Versace (glittering, sexy, and slightly outrageous). Duty-free boutiques offer enough Italian designer items to satisfy the most addicted shopaholics. Forward on the outdoor promenade decks are serene retreats in the form of enclosed terraces, which might have been termed winter gardens on ocean liners of yore.

Cons: Italians consider cappuccino a breakfast beverage, so don't order it in the dining room following dinner—instead, follow the Roman custom of going out for coffee and head to the café, where traditional espresso and cappuccino are served. A quirk is the strange double use of the balcony in the specialty restaurant, which becomes a cigar lounge after regular dinner hours—don't linger over coffee if you find that offensive. In a nod to the spirit of *la dolce vita*, much socializing takes place during the Italian Bacchanal, but there's a not-so-subtle current of Americanization underlying the experience.

Cabin Type	Size (sq. ft.)
Grand Suites	650
Suites	360
Ocean View*	185
Interior	160

*Extended balcony cabins have balconies at least 50% larger than average.

FAST FACTS

- 12 passenger decks
- Specialty restaurant, dining room, buffet, pizzeria
- Safe, refrigerator, DVD (some)
- 3 pools (1 indoor), children's pool
- Fitness classes, gym, hair salon, 4 hot tubs, sauna, spa, steam room
- 6 bars, casino, cinema, 2 dance clubs, 2 showrooms, video game room
- Children's programs (ages 3–17)
- Laundry facilities, laundry service
- Internet terminal
- Top: *Costa Mediterranea* at sea
- Bottom: European service
- Workout with a sea view

5

COSTA CRUISES

CRYSTAL CRUISES

Winner of accolades and too many hospitality industry awards to count, Crystal Cruises offers a taste of the grandeur of the past along with all the modern touches discerning passengers demand today. Founded in 1990 and owned by Nippon Yusen Kaisha

Crystal Serenity wraparound promenade

(NYK) in Japan, Crystal ships, unlike other luxury vessels, are large, carrying upward of 900 passengers. What makes them distinctive are superior service, a variety of dining options, spacious accommodations, and some of the highest ratios of space per passenger of any cruise ship.

✉ *2049 Century Park E, Suite 1400, Los Angeles, CA*

☎ *888/799–4625 or 310/785–9300*

⊕ *www.crystalcruises. com*

☞ *Cruise Style: Luxury.*

Beginning with ship designs based on the principles of feng shui, the Eastern art of arranging your surroundings to attract positive energy, no detail is overlooked to provide passengers with the best imaginable experience. Just mention a preference for a certain food or beverage and your waiter will have it available whenever you request it.

The complete roster of entertainment and activities includes Broadway-style production shows and bingo, but where Crystal really shines is in the variety of enrichment and educational programs. Passengers can participate in the hands-on Computer University@ Sea, interactive Creative Learning Institute classes, or attend lectures featuring top experts in their fields: keyboard lessons with Yamaha, language classes by Berlitz, wellness lectures with the Cleveland Clinic, and an introduction to tai chi with the Tai Chi Cultural Center. Professional ACBL Bridge instructors are on every cruise, and dance instructors offer lessons in contemporary and social dance styles.

An added highlight for women traveling solo is the Ambassador Host Program, which brings cultured gentlemen on each cruise to dine, socialize, and dance with unaccompanied ladies.

Somewhat unique among cruise lines, Crystal Cruises' casinos observe Nevada gaming rules and offer complimentary cocktails to players at the tables and slot machines.

A delightful daily ritual is afternoon tea in the Palm Court. You're greeted by staff members in 18th-century Viennese brocade and velvet costumes for Mozart Tea, traditional scones and clotted cream are served during English Colonial Tea, and American Tea is a summertime classic created by Crystal culinary artists.

Food
The food alone is reason enough to book a Crystal cruise. Dining in the main restaurants is an event starring a continental-inspired menu of dishes served by European-trained waiters. Off-menu item requests are honored when possible, and special dietary considerations are handled with ease. Full-course vegetarian menus are among the best at sea. Casual poolside dining beneath the stars is offered on some evenings in a relaxed, no-reservations option. A variety of hot-and-cold hors d'oeuvres are served in bars and lounges every evening before dinner and again during the wee hours.

But the specialty restaurants really shine. Contemporary Asian cuisine is served in Silk Road and the Sushi Bar, featuring the signature dishes of Nobu Matsuhisa. Both ships also have Prego, which serves regional Italian cuisine by Piero Selvaggio, owner of Valentino in Los Angeles and Las Vegas.

Exclusive Wine & Champagne Makers dinners are hosted in the Vintage Room. On select evenings, casual poolside theme dinners are served under the stars.

Crystal has an extensive wine list, including its own proprietary label called C Wines, which are produced in California. Unfortunately, there are no complimentary wines with dinner, as is common on other luxury cruise lines. You won't pay extra for bottled water, soft drinks, and specialty coffees; all are included in your basic fare.

Fitness and Recreation
Large spas offer innovative pampering therapies, body wraps, and exotic Asian-inspired treatments by Steiner Leisure. Feng shui principles were scrupulously adhered to in their creation to assure the spas and salons remain havens of tranquillity.

NOTEWORTHY

■ Before sailing, each passenger receives a personal email address.

■ Ambassador Hosts on Crystal cruises are cultured, well-traveled gentlemen, who are accomplished dancers and interact with female passengers.

■ Complimentary self-service laundry rooms as well as complete laundry, dry-cleaning, and valet services are available.

■ Although smoking is allowed in designated areas and in accommodations, smokers cannot light up on private balconies.

Crystal Serenity wraparound promenade

Crystal Serenity fitness center

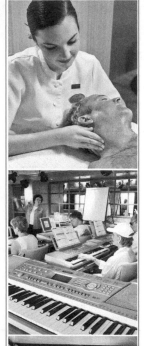

Top: Spa treatment
Middle: Keyboard lessons
Bottom: *Crystal Symphony*
Crystal Penthouse

Fitness centers have a range of exercise and weight-training equipment and workout areas for aerobics classes, plus complimentary yoga and Pilates instruction. In addition, golfers enjoy extensive shipboard facilities, including a driving range practice cage and putting green. Passengers can leave their bags at home and rent top-quality Taylormade clubs for use ashore. The line's resident golf pros offer complimentary lessons and group clinics.

Your Shipmates

Affluent, well-traveled couples, from their late-thirties and up, are attracted to Crystal's destination-rich itineraries, shipboard enrichment programs, and elegant ambience. The average age of passengers is noticeably higher on longer itineraries.

Dress Code

Formal attire is required on at least two designated evenings, depending on the length of the cruise. Men are encouraged to wear tuxedos, and many do, although dark suits are also acceptable. Other evenings are informal or resort casual; the number of each is based on the number of sea days. The line requests that dress codes be observed in public areas after 6 pm, and few, if any, passengers disregard the suggestion. Most, in fact, dress up just a notch from guidelines.

Junior Cruisers

Although these ships are decidedly adult-oriented, Crystal welcomes children but limits the number of children under age three on any given cruise. Children under six months are not allowed without a signed waiver by parents.

Dedicated facilities for children and teens from ages 3 to 17 are staffed by counselors during holiday periods, select summer sailings, and when warranted by the number of children booked. The program is three-tiered for 3- to 7-year-olds, 8- to 12-year-olds, and 13- to 17-year-olds. Activities—including games, computer time, scavenger hunts, and arts and crafts—usually have an eye toward the educational. Teenagers can play complimentary video games to their heart's content in Waves, the arcade dedicated for their use.

CHOOSE THIS LINE IF ...

You crave peace and quiet. Announcements are kept to a bare minimum, and the ambience is sedate.

You prefer to plan ahead. You can make spa, restaurant, shore excursion, and class reservations when you book your cruise.

You love sushi and other Asian delights—Crystal ships serve some of the best at sea.

Babysitting can be arranged with staff members for a fee. Baby food, high chairs, and booster seats are available upon request.

Service
Crystal's European-trained staff members provide gracious service in an unobtrusive manner.

Tipping
Effective in spring 2012, housekeeping and dining gratuities are included in the fare. A 15% gratuity is suggested for spa and salon services.

Past Passengers
You're automatically enrolled in the Crystal Society on completion of your first Crystal cruise and are entitled to special savings and member-only events. Membership benefits increase with each completed Crystal cruise and include such perks as stateroom upgrades, shipboard spending credits, special events, gifts, air upgrades, and even free cruises. Society members also receive Crystal Cruises' complimentary quarterly magazine, which shares up-to-date information on itineraries, destinations, special offers, and society news.

GOOD TO KNOW
Although two assigned dining room seatings are advertised as an advantage that offers flexibility, the reality is that open seating is the true mark of choice and the most preferred option at this level of luxury cruising, and Crystal now offers the choice of Open Dining by Reservation. If you haven't done so in advance, on embarkation day you can reserve a table to dine one night in each specialty restaurant, but don't dawdle until the last minute; if you wait, you may find a line has developed—one of the few lines you'll encounter on board—and all the choice dining times are already booked. You may also be able to reserve additional nights after the cruise is under way, depending on how busy the restaurants are.

Effective in spring 2012, fares include complimentary wines and premium spirits throughout the ships and open bar service in all lounges,

DON'T CHOOSE THIS LINE IF ...

You don't want to follow the dress code. Everyone does, and you'll stand out—and not in a good way—if you rebel.

You want total freedom. Unlike other luxury cruise lines, Crystal assigns you a seating and a table for dinner.

You want a less structured cruise. With set dining times, Crystal is a bit more regimented than other luxury lines.

CRYSTAL SERENITY

CREW MEMBERS	655
ENTERED SERVICE	2003
GROSS TONS	68,000
LENGTH	820 feet
NUMBER OF CABINS	544
PASSENGER CAPACITY	1,070
WIDTH	106 feet

700 ft.

500 ft.

300 ft.

Public Areas and Facilities

Crystal Serenity was Crystal Cruises' long-awaited third ship (introduced in 2003), the first to be added to the line since 1995. Although more than a third larger than Crystal's earlier ships, it's similar in layout and follows the line's successful formula of creating intimate spaces in understated yet sophisticated surroundings.

Stylish public rooms, uncrowded and uncluttered, are clubby in the tradition of elegantly proportioned drawing rooms (even the main show lounge is on a single level). Muted colors and warm woods create a soft atmosphere conducive to socializing in the refined environment. The Palm Court could be mistaken for the kind of British colonial–era lounge you might have seen in Hong Kong or India in the 19th century.

A thoughtful touch is an entirely separate room for scrutinizing the art pieces available for auction. The understatement even continues into the casino, although it contains plenty of slot machines and gaming tables.

Restaurants

The formal restaurant serves open seating breakfast and lunch and offers international cuisine in two traditional early and late assigned dinner seatings or, in a new option, Open Dining by Reservation (available between 6:15 and 9:15 pm). Although there's no additional charge for the intimate Asian- and Italian-specialty restaurants, reservations are required, and a gratuity is suggested for the servers. Exclusive Wine & Champagne Makers dinners are hosted in the Vintage Room. On select evenings, theme dinners are held poolside. Other dining choices include Tastes, a casual café serving breakfast, lunch, and dinner; the Lido buffet for breakfast and lunch; a poolside grill for casual lunch throughout the afternoon; The Bistro, a specialty coffee and wine bar offering morning and afternoon snacks; and an ice-cream bar. Afternoon tea is served in the Palm Court. Room service is available 24 hours, and during dinner hours selections can be delivered from the formal restaurant menu. Suite passengers also have the option of ordering dinner from the specialty restaurants, which is served by their butlers.

Top: *Crystal Serenity* at sea
Bottom: Sushi bar

Accommodations

Cabins: As you'd expect on a luxury vessel, *Crystal Serenity* has no inside cabins. Although suites are generous in size, lesser categories are somewhat smaller than industry standard at this level. All accommodations are designed with ample closet and drawer/shelf storage, as well as bathroom shelves and twin sinks. An impressive 85% of all cabins have private balconies furnished with chairs and tables. Most suites and penthouses have walk-in closets. Crystal Penthouse suites have private workout areas, pantries, and guest powder rooms.

Amenities: Rich wood cabinetry, soft colors, a small refrigerator with complimentary bottled water and soft drinks, a personal safe, two hair dryers, broadband connection for a laptop computer, a flat-screen TV with a DVD player, Aveda bath products, slippers, Frette bathrobes, and an umbrella to use during the cruise are some of the amenities. A sitting area with sofa, chair, and table are typical standard features of all cabins. Most suites and penthouses also have CD players; all have butler service, personalized stationery, and a complimentary fully stocked minibar upon embarkation.

Worth Noting: There are 50 connecting staterooms and 134 staterooms with a third berth for families. Eight staterooms are designed for wheelchair accessibility.

In the Know

A common occurrence on cruise ships is last-night syndrome (when you return to your cabin after that last dinner to find that certain amenities have vanished). On Crystal that is not the case; the last night is just like the first.

Pros and Cons

Pros: A splendid selection of alternative restaurants is yours to enjoy at no additional cost. While most suites and penthouses have whirlpool tub and separate shower, every bathroom has at least a full-size tub. Great for walkers, a wide teak promenade deck encircles the ship.

Cons: This ship offers kid-centric spaces, but fewer than a quarter of the staterooms have a third berth. Anxious moments may pass until dining reservations are secured for specialty restaurants, but those nerves are nothing compared to what you'd experience trying to get a table at the chefs' shoreside counterparts. A West Coast lifestyle prevails, which can be somewhat off-putting to people from flyover country until they relax and go with the flow.

Cabin Type	Size (sq. ft.)
Crystal Penthouse	1,345
Penthouse Suites	538
Regular Penthouses	403
Deluxe Ocean View (w/balcony)	269
Deluxe Ocean View (regular)	226

All dimensions except for regular Deluxe staterooms (the only category that does not have a balcony) include the balcony square footage.

FAST FACTS

■ 9 passenger decks

■ 2 specialty restaurants, dining room, buffet, ice cream parlor

■ Internet, Wi-Fi, safe, minibar (some), refrigerator, DVD

■ 2 pools (1 indoor)

■ Fitness classes, gym, hair salon, 2 hot tubs, sauna, spa, steam room

■ 6 bars, casino, cinema, 2 dance clubs, library, showroom, video game room

■ Children's programs (ages 3–17)

■ Dry-cleaning, laundry facilities, laundry service

■ Internet terminal

■ No kids under 6 months

CRYSTAL SYMPHONY

CREW MEMBERS	545
ENTERED SERVICE	1995
GROSS TONS	51,044
LENGTH	781 feet
NUMBER OF CABINS	470
PASSENGER CAPACITY	922 (1,010 max)
WIDTH	99 feet

700 ft.

500 ft.

300 ft.

Top: Casino gaming
Bottom: University@Sea

Public Areas and Facilities

Although it's a relatively large ship with some big-ship features, *Crystal Symphony* is noteworthy in the luxury market for creating intimate spaces in understated, yet sophisticated surroundings. Generous per-passenger space ratios have become a Crystal trademark, along with forward-facing observation decks, a Palm Court lounge, and a wide teak promenade. A makeover in 2006 refreshed the Bistro Café and shops, reconstructed the casino and Starlite Lounge, and added a new nightclub called Luxe. An even more extensive refurbishment in 2009 transformed the Crystal Penthouses, Lido Café, and Prego Italian restaurant. The most dramatic change was the removal of the indoor swimming pool and hot tub to expand seating for the Trident Grill.

Accented by a lovely waterfall, the focal point of the central two-deck atrium is a sculpture of two ballet dancers created especially for the space. Crystal Cove, the lobby lounge, is the spot to meet for cocktails as you make your way to the nearby dining room. Throughout the ship, public rooms shine with low-key contemporary style and flow easily from one to the next.

Restaurants

The formal restaurant serves open seating breakfast and lunch and offers international cuisine in two traditional assigned dinner seatings or, in a new option, Open Dining by Reservation (available between 6:15 and 9:15 pm). Although there's no additional charge for the intimate Asian- and Italian-specialty restaurants, reservations are required, and a gratuity is suggested for the servers. Exclusive Wine & Champagne Makers dinners are hosted in the Vintage Room. On select evenings, theme dinners are held poolside. Other dining choices include the Lido buffet for breakfast and lunch; a poolside grill for casual lunch throughout the afternoon; The Bistro, a specialty coffee and wine bar offering morning and afternoon snacks; and an ice cream bar. Afternoon tea is served in the Palm Court. Room service is available 24 hours, and during dinner hours selections can be delivered from the formal restaurant menu. Suite passengers also have the option of ordering dinner from the specialty restaurants, which is served by their butlers.

Accommodations

Cabins: There are no inside cabins on *Crystal Symphony*. Still, relatively small stateroom sizes are cozy and chic with boutique-hotel-style decor. All cabins have ample closet and drawer/shelf storage, as well as bathroom shelves. Many have private balconies furnished with chairs and tables. Most suites and penthouses have a walk-in closet. Crystal Penthouse suites have guest powder rooms.

Amenities: Rich wood cabinetry, soft pastel fabrics, a small refrigerator filled with complimentary bottled water and soft drinks, a personal safe, two hair dryers, a flat-screen TV with a DVD player, and a sitting area with sofa, chair, and table are typical standard features in all cabins. Suite and penthouse extras vary, but all have a DVD/CD player, butler service, personalized stationery, and stocked minibars with wine, beer, and choice of liquor.

Bathrooms: Every bathroom has oval glass sinks, granite counters, a full-size tub, Aveda toiletries, plush towels, and bathrobes for use during the cruise. Many suites and penthouses have a whirlpool tub and separate shower.

Worth Noting: Five staterooms are wheelchair accessible.

In the Know

Steam rooms and saunas are completely complimentary, and no spa treatments or other purchases are required before using them. Simply go in anytime you please. In addition, bathrobes and disposable slippers are provided for use in the men's and women's locker rooms.

Pros and Cons

Pros: A refined and gracious atmosphere without a hint of unnecessary glitter is immediately apparent, but it's the professionalism of the staff that adds sparkle. Seating almost as many movie buffs as an average multiplex ashore and serving free popcorn, the large theater screens recent releases as well as classic favorites. Passenger laundries are complimentary, so you can pack light for this ship.

Cons: Although the wine selection is extensive, unlike other top-end luxury cruise lines, wine is not included with dinner. There are only 10 connecting staterooms and 89 staterooms with a third berth available for families. Gratuities are not included in the cost of the fare as they are on most luxury ships, but they can be prepaid or charged to onboard accounts.

Cabin Type	Size (sq. ft.)
Crystal Penthouse	982
Penthouse Suites	491
Regular Penthouses	367
Deluxe Ocean View (w/balcony)	246
Deluxe Ocean View (regular)	202

All dimensions except for regular Deluxe staterooms (the only category that does not have a balcony) include the balcony square footage.

FAST FACTS

- 8 passenger decks
- 2 specialty restaurants, dining room, buffet, ice cream parlor
- Wi-Fi, safe, refrigerator, minibar (some), DVD
- 1 pool
- Fitness classes, gym, hair salon, 1 hot tub, sauna, spa, steam room
- 5 bars, casino, cinema, dance club, library, showroom, video game room
- Children's programs (ages 3–17)
- Dry-cleaning, laundry facilities, laundry service
- Internet terminal
- No kids under 6 months

5

CRYSTAL CRUISES

CUNARD LINE

One of the world's most distinguished names in ocean travel since 1840, the Cunard Line has a long history of deluxe transatlantic crossings and worldwide cruising. The line's ships are legendary for their comfortable accommodations, excellent cuisine, and personal service.

Romantic sunset at sea

After a series of owners tried with little success to revive the company's flagging passenger shipping business, Carnival Corporation offered an infusion of ready cash and the know-how to turn the line around in 1998. Exciting new ships have followed.

✉ *24303 Town Center Dr., Valencia, CA*

☎ *661/753–1000 or 800/728–6273*

⊕ *www.cunard.com*

☞ *Cruise Style: Luxury.*

Entertainment has a decidedly English flavor, with nightly production shows or cabaret-style performances and even plays. An authentic pub gives the liners an even more British air, while music for dancing and listening is played in other bars and lounges. In *Queen Mary 2's* first-ever shipboard planetarium, high-tech presentations and virtual-reality shows offer a virtual ride through space.

Cunard's fine enrichment programs include lectures by experts in their fields, including top designers, master chefs, and artists. Even seamanship and navigation courses are offered to novice mariners. Passengers can plan their activities prior to departure by consulting the syllabus of courses available online at Cunard Line's Web site.

Delightful daily events include afternoon tea and the maritime tradition of sounding the ship's bell at noon. The line offers North Atlantic crossings and seasonal shorter cruises, including some Caribbean itineraries.

Food

Dining aboard a Cunard ship is by class, so dining-room assignments are made according to the accommodation category booked. You can get as much luxury as you are willing to pay for on Cunard liners, where passengers in Junior Suites are assigned to the single-seating Princess Grill; the posh Queen's Grill serves passengers booked in duplex apartments and the most lavish suites. All other passengers are assigned to one of two seatings in the dramatic, multideck-high Britannia Restaurant or Britannia Club Restaurant on *Queen Elizabeth*.

Although fare in Britannia is reasonably traditional and often outstanding, off-menu requests by Grill passengers are commonly granted—provided the galley has the ingredients. Menus also include vegetarian and low-calorie selections.

The most coveted table reservations are those on *Queen Mary 2* and *Queen Victoria* in the restaurants named for Todd English, the celebrity American chef and restaurateur noted for his innovative Mediterranean cuisine and sumptuous desserts. Both dinner ($30 per-person cover charge) and lunch ($20 per person) are offered in the intimate restaurant.

Aboard *Queen Mary 2,* the Chef's Galley is a small reservations-required restaurant, where diners look on as their food is prepared in an open galley setting; the only charge here is for wine. The King's Court buffet is transformed each evening into three no-charge casual alternative dining spots: the Carvery specializes in carved meats; La Piazza is dedicated to pasta, pizza, and Italian dishes; and Lotus offers Asian regional specialties.

Fitness and Recreation

Swimming pools, golf driving ranges, table tennis, paddle tennis court, shuffleboard, and jogging tracks barely scratch the surface of shipboard facilities dedicated to recreation. Top-quality fitness centers offer high-tech workout equipment, a separate weight room, and classes ranging from aerobics to healthy living workshops.

Queen Mary 2's Canyon Ranch Spa Club is a one-of-a-kind facility at sea offering salon services for women and men, including the famous land-based spa's signature 80-minute Canyon Stone Massage. A huge 30- by 15-foot thalassotherapy pool offers a deluge waterfall, air tub, neck fountains, and massage-jet benches and recliner lounges located in the pool. The thermal suite has an herbal sauna, Finnish sauna, aromatic steam room, and reflexology basins. Use of these special features is complimentary with a massage or body treatment; otherwise, there's a per-day charge.

5

CUNARD LINE

Top: Cunard White Star service
Bottom: Illuminations planetarium

Top: Fine dining
Middle: Royal Court Theater
Bottom: Junior suite

The daily SpaClub Passport includes use of the fitness center, thermal suite, aquatherapy center, locker rooms, and a choice of fitness classes. Robes, sandals, and beverages are also available for spa-goers and SpaClub Passport holders in the relaxation lounge. Steiner Leisure operates the more pedestrian spas on the rest of the fleet.

Your Shipmates
Discerning, well-traveled American and British couples from their late-thirties to retirees are drawn to Cunard's traditional style and the notion of a cruise aboard an ocean liner. The availability of spacious accommodations and complimentary self-service laundry facilities makes Cunard liners a good option for families, although there may be fewer children on board than on similarly sized ships.

Dress Code
Glamorous evenings are typical of Cunard cruises, and specified attire includes formal, informal, and casual. Although resort casual clothing prevails throughout the day, Cunard vessels are ocean liners at heart and, as expected, are dressier than most cruise ships at night. To maintain their high standards, the cruise line requests passengers to dress as they would for dining in fine restaurants.

Junior Cruisers
The Kid Zone has a dedicated play area and a splash pool for children ages one to six. Separate programs are reserved for older children ages 7 to 12 and teens up to age 17. Toys and activities range from simple games to more educational computer classes. Children can practice their social graces when they're served their own afternoon teatime goodies. Toddlers are supervised by English nannies. Facilities are operated only until midnight; group babysitting is complimentary. Infants under one year are not allowed; children ages one to two sail free (except for government fees).

Service
Although most crew members are international rather than British, service is formal and sophisticated.

CHOOSE THIS LINE IF ...

You want to boast that you have sailed on the world's largest ocean liner, though larger cruise ships are already plying the waves.

You enjoy a brisk walk. *Queen Mary 2* is massive, and you'll find yourself walking a great deal.

A posh English pub is your ideal of the perfect place to hang out.

Tipping

Suggested gratuities of $13 per person per day (for Grill Restaurant accommodations) or $11 per person per day (all other accommodations) are automatically charged to shipboard accounts for distribution to stewards and waitstaff. An automatic 15% gratuity is added to beverage tabs for bar service. Passengers can still tip individual crew members directly in cash for any special services.

Past Passengers

After one sailing aboard a Cunard liner, passengers are automatically enrolled as members of Cunard World Club; they are accorded Silver status on their second cruise. Silver-level members receive discounts of up to 50% off Early Booking Savings on all sailings, access to the shipboard World Club Representative and World Club Desk, and a quarterly newsletter, *The Cunarder.*

After completing two Cunard cruises or 20 days on board, members are accorded Gold status and are additionally invited to shipboard World Club cocktail receptions, two hours of Internet service, and receive a Gold Cunarder pin. Passengers who complete seven sailings or sail for 48 consecutive days or more, achieve the Platinum status. Additional benefits to Platinum members include a shipboard World Club cocktail reception, priority check-in and boarding in certain embarkation ports, an invitation to the Senior Officers' party, four hours of Internet service, and a Platinum Cunarder pin.

Diamond membership is for guests who have completed 15 voyages or 150 days on board. In addition to the above, they receive priority luggage delivery, complimentary lunch in Todd English, eight hours of Internet service, and a Diamond Cunarder pin.

GOOD TO KNOW

The idea of a multiple-class ship offends some people's sense of democracy, and Cunard ships are ocean liners that adhere in not-so-subtle fashion to the tradition of class distinctions. This is the 21st century, though, so you won't find steerage class, and even regular folks in the cheaper cabins will enjoy the superior surroundings. However, certain areas, including the Queen's Grill Lounge, a private sun terrace, and even a private elevator, are reserved for occupants of privileged accommodations. So luxury on a Cunard ship is a relative experience and certainly more luxurious for some.

5

CUNARD LINE

DON'T CHOOSE THIS LINE IF ...

You prefer informality. Cunard ships are traditional formal liners.

You want real luxury with no add-on costs.

Your sense of direction is really bad. Nearly everyone gets lost on board QM2 at least once.

QUEEN MARY 2

CREW MEMBERS	1,253
ENTERED SERVICE	2004
GROSS TONS	151,400
LENGTH	1,132 feet
NUMBER OF CABINS	1,310
PASSENGER CAPACITY	2,620 (3,090 max)
WIDTH	135 feet

700 ft.

500 ft.

300 ft.

Top: Intimate lounges
Bottom: Grand duplex suite

Public Areas and Facilities

With the clever use of design elements, *Queen Mary 2*, one of the largest passenger liners ever built, bears a striking external resemblance to Cunard's former flagship, the smaller, older *Queen Elizabeth 2*, which was retired from service in 2008. The world's grandest and most expensive liner is something of a transitional ship, incorporating classic ocean-liner features—sweeping staircases, soaring public rooms, a 360-degree promenade deck, and a grand ballroom—all comfortably within a hull that also includes a trendy Canyon Ranch Spa and a full-scale planetarium.

Interior spaces blend the traditional style of early-20th-century liners with all the conveniences 21st-century passengers expect. Public rooms are mainly located on two decks low in the ship—remember, this is a liner designed for North Atlantic crossings. Befitting a queen, the grand lobby is palatial, with broad, curving staircases and stately columns. Wide passageways lead to a variety of lounges, shops, a casino, showroom, and planetarium. The Queen's Room is especially regal.

Restaurants

Different levels of dining assignments correspond to your accommodation category. The Britannia Restaurant serves open seating breakfast and lunch and dinner in two seatings to most passengers; those in AA Britannia Club Balcony Cabins dine in the single-seating Britannia Club Dining Room; those in junior suites and above dine in the single-seating Queens and Princess Grill restaurants. Reservations are required for lunch and dinner in the specialty restaurant named for celebrity chef Todd English. The Chef's Galley is a small reservations-required restaurant, where diners watch as their food is prepared in an open galley; the only charge is for wine. The King's Court buffet serves breakfast and lunch, and is transformed each evening into three no-charge casual alternative dining spots: the Carvery specializes in carved meats; La Piazza is dedicated to pasta, pizza, and Italian dishes; and Lotus offers Asian regional specialties. During the day you can opt for a Pub Lunch, snacks in Sir Samuel's, afternoon tea, and 24-hour room service.

Accommodations

Cabins: Selecting a stateroom or suite on *Queen Mary 2* is complex because of the many variations. As expected on the world's most luxurious liner, an impressive 78% of her accommodations are outside cabins and more than 86% of these feature spacious private balconies. There are fewer than 300 inside cabins; a dozen insides have an atrium view. All accommodations are designed with ample closet, drawer/shelf storage, and bathroom shelves. Private balconies are furnished with chairs, loungers, and tables. Duplex apartment and suite luxuries vary, but most have a whirlpool tub, dressing area, entertainment center, and dining area, and all have private balconies. In addition, duplex apartments and most suites feature guest powder rooms and whirlpool tubs; some have his-and-hers dressing rooms.

Amenities: Warm-wood cabinetry, quality fabrics, a small refrigerator, a personal safe, a hair dryer, broadband computer hookup, interactive television, and a sitting area with sofa or chairs and dual-height table are typical standard amenities. Toiletries, slippers, and bathrobes for use during the cruise are standard.

Worth Noting: Thirty cabins are wheelchair accessible.

In the Know

Yes, you read the deck plan correctly: there's a kennel on *Queen Mary 2*. But, no, sadly you can't bring Fido or Fluffy along on a cruise. Kennel use is restricted to transatlantic crossings, although service animals can avail themselves of the fire hydrant during all sailings.

Pros and Cons

Pros: Proper afternoon tea and great pub-style fare in the Golden Lion suggest that Britannia still rules the waves. Spanning the width of the ship, the Queen's Room is a true ballroom, where you'll want to waltz the night away. Dine in Todd English, named for the celebrity chef who designed the menu—his innovative Mediterranean cuisine is the best thing going on the QM2.

Cons: No one harbors the illusion that booking an inside cabin results in the same level of pampering received by occupants of top suites. There are multiple pools and whirlpools, on the top and aft decks, but no expansive Lido area buffet. The Daily Programme indicates which of the four elevator/stairway lobbies is the closest to each public room, but it's still easy to get lost.

Cabin Type	Size (sq. ft.)
Grand Duplex	2,249
Duplex	1,194
Royal Suite	796
Penthouse	758
Suite	506
Jr. Suite	381
Deluxe	248
Premium Balcony	249
Standard Ocean View/Inside	194

FAST FACTS

- 14 passenger decks
- 2 specialty restaurants, 3 dining rooms, buffet, ice cream parlor, pizzeria
- Internet, Wi-Fi, safe, refrigerator, minibar (some), DVD (some)
- 5 pools (2 indoor), 2 children's pools
- Fitness classes, gym, hair salon, 7 hot tubs, sauna, spa, steam room
- 11 bars, casino, cinema, 2 dance clubs, library, showroom, video game room
- Children's programs (ages 1–17)
- Dry-cleaning, laundry facilities, laundry service
- Internet terminal
- No kids under age 1
- No-smoking cabins

5

CUNARD LINE

QUEEN VICTORIA

CREW MEMBERS	900
ENTERED SERVICE	2007
GROSS TONS	90,000
LENGTH	965 feet
NUMBER OF CABINS	985
PASSENGER CAPACITY	1,970
WIDTH	106 feet

700 ft.
500 ft.
300 ft.

Top: Main pool
Bottom: Queens grill suite

Public Areas and Facilities

Designers drew upon the history of previous Cunard ocean liners to conceive *Queen Victoria's* elegant interiors. From the ship's double- and triple-height spaces—design features of grand liners of the past—to rooms imbued with an elegant yet understated British charm, the overall effect is contemporary and historically classic. The impact of the Grand Lobby's triple-height ceiling, sweeping staircase, and sculpted balconies is immediate and unmistakable.

Queen Victoria herself might well feel at home on entering the double-height Queens Room, a loggia-style venue designed in the manner of the grand ballrooms found in large English country estates, such as Her Majesty's own Osborne House. The ballroom has cantilevered balconies overlooking an inlaid wood dance floor; the staircase is detailed with classically ornate, curved railings.

In addition to the intimate dining spaces and a lounge reserved for occupants of Queens and Princess Grill accommodations, an outdoor terrace is devoted to their exclusive use. All other public rooms are accessible to everyone on board.

Restaurants

The Britannia Restaurant serves dinner in two assigned seatings for most passengers, while those in AA Britannia Club Balcony Cabins dine in the single-seating Britannia Club Dining Room, and those in Princess and Queens Grill-classes also dine in a single seating in their respective restaurants. Todd English, the alternative restaurant, requires reservations and has a fee. The Lido buffet and Golden Lion Pub offer relaxed dining options, while specialty teas, coffees, and pastries are featured in Café Carinthia. A proper English tea is served daily, and room service is always available.

Accommodations

Cabins: Although there are more than two dozen stateroom and suite categories from which to choose, cabins really fall into eight configurations. At the top are the Queens Grill suite categories, which have the most luxurious amenities; next are Princess Grill suites; finally come the standard staterooms (some with a balcony) as well as inside cabins, whose passengers dine in the

Britannia Restaurant. The majority of the cabins fall into the standard categories. More than 86% of the staterooms on the ship are outside and 76% have private balconies. All are designed with ample closet and storage space, and even the least expensive outside categories have a small sitting area. Private balconies are furnished with a table and chairs and some have loungers.

Amenities: All passengers are greeted upon embarkation with sparkling wine or champagne and will find a refrigerator, safe, hair dryer, fresh fruit basket, bath toiletries, slippers, and a bathrobe for use during the cruise. Butlers are on hand to attend to Queens Grill occupants, whose bars are stocked with spirits, wine, and soft drinks.

Worth Noting: Fourteen cabins are wheelchair accessible.

In the Know

Check the deck plan carefully when selecting balcony accommodations—decks 4 through 7 have "jogs" in the interior passageways, where you'll find more than a dozen balcony cabins in various categories that are larger than average. Aft-facing balconies are the most spacious of all.

Pros and Cons

Pros: The promenade deck that encircles the ship is ideal for a casual stroll or serious jogging. Inspired by London's Burlington and Royal Arcades, the well-stocked and enticing shops on board are set amid wood paneling, wrought iron, green marble, and white stone. Highlighted by a glass roof that opens to admit sea breezes, the Winter Garden is a pleasing spot to relax with a cup of tea.

Cons: The first Cunardia museum exhibit at sea (housing Cunard artifacts and memorabilia) is small. Although there is enough storage space in standard accommodations, the one quirk is a lack of drawer space; the desk–vanity contains a shallow drawer and a deeper one holds a built-in hair dryer, leaving limited drawer space for incidentals. Private box seating for shows in the Royal Court Theater requires a reservation and fee.

Cabin Type	Size (sq. ft.)
Grand Suite/Master Suite	1,918–2,131/ 1,100
Penthouse Suite/ Queens Suite/ Princess Suite	520–707/ 508–771/ 335–513
Ocean View with Balcony	242–472
Ocean View/ Interior	180–201/ 152–243

All dimensions include the square footage for balconies.

FAST FACTS

- 12 passenger decks
- Specialty restaurant, 3 dining rooms, buffet, café, ice cream parlor, pizzeria
- Wi-Fi, safe, refrigerator, minibar (some), DVD (some)
- 2 pools
- Fitness classes, gym, hair salon, 4 hot tubs, sauna, spa, steam room
- 10 bars, casino, 2 dance clubs, library, showroom
- Children's programs (ages 1–17)
- Dry-cleaning, laundry facilities, laundry service
- Computer room
- No-smoking cabins

5

CUNARD LINE

Brittania stateroom

DISNEY CRUISE LINE

With the launch of Disney Cruise Line in 1998, families were offered yet another reason to take a cruise. The magic of a Walt Disney resort vacation plus the romance of a sea voyage are a tempting combination, especially for adults who discovered Dis-

Disney ships have a classic style

ney movies and the Mickey Mouse Club as children. Mixed with traditional shipboard activities, who can resist scheduled opportunities for the young and young-at-heart to interact with their favorite Disney characters?

✉ *210 Celebration Pl., Suite 400, Celebration, FL*

☎ *407/566–3500 or 888/325–2500*

⊕ *www.disneycruise. com*

↶ *Cruise Style: Mainstream.*

A Disney cruise begins even before embarkation if you opt to use bus transfers from the Orlando airport or Walt Disney World. A slick orientation video passes the time and gets everyone revved up for their first view of the ship. Passengers who added a precruise stay at Walt Disney World seamlessly complete their cruise check-in before leaving the resort; check-in for the balance of passengers is handled in the efficient Port Canaveral terminal designed especially for Disney. While waiting to board, capture your children's attention by pointing out the cut-away model of a Disney ship and a map of the Bahamas and Caribbean inlaid in the floor. Shipboard entertainment leans heavily on popular Disney themes and characters. Parents are actively involved in the audience with their children at production shows, movies, live character meetings, deck parties, and dancing in the family nightclub. Teens have a supervised, no-adults-allowed club space in the forward fake funnel, where they gather for activities and parties. For adults, there are traditional no-kids-allowed bars and lounges with live music, dancing, theme parties, and late-night comedy as well as daytime wine-tasting sessions, game shows, culinary arts and home entertaining demonstrations, and behind-the-scenes lectures on animation and filmmaking.

For many passengers, the cruise is a three- or four-night extension of a Walt Disney World vacation, while seven-night cruises are more traditional with a Disney twist. All Bahamas and Caribbean cruises call at Castaway Cay, Disney's private island in the Bahamas with its own pier for convenient dockside debarkation.

Food

Don't expect top chefs and gourmet food. This is Disney, and the fare in the two casual restaurants is all-American for the most part, with a third restaurant being a bit fancier, with French-inspired dishes on the menus. Naturally, all have children's menus with an array of favorite sandwiches and entrées. Vegetarian and healthy selections are also available in all restaurants. A bonus is complimentary soft drinks, lemonade, and iced tea throughout the sailing. A beverage station in the buffet area is always open; however, there is a charge for soft drinks ordered from the bars and room service.

Palo, the adults-only restaurant serving northern Italian cuisine on all ships, requires reservations for a romantic evening of fine dining. Although there's a cover charge for dinner, it's a steal and reservations go fast. A champagne brunch and high tea also command a surcharge. More upscale, Remy on Disney Dream and Disney Fantasy serves French cuisine in an elegant atmosphere.

Fitness and Recreation

Three swimming pool areas are designated for different groups: for children (Mickey's Pool, which has a waterslide and requires a parent to be present); for families (Goofy Pool); and adults (Quiet Cove). Young children who aren't potty trained can't swim in the pools but are invited to splash about in the fountain play area near Mickey's Pool. Be sure to bring their swim diapers.

The salon and spa feature a complete menu of hair- and nail-care services as well as facials and massages. The Tropical Rainforest is a soothing coed thermal suite with heated tile lounges. It's complimentary for the day if you book a spa treatment or available on a daily or cruise-long basis for a fee. Introduced on Disney ships are seagoing SpaVillas, indoor–outdoor treatment suites, each of which has a veranda with a hot tub and an open-air shower. In addition to a nicely equipped fitness center and aerobics studio are a jogging track and basketball court.

5

DISNEY CRUISE LINE

Top: Dining in Palo, the adults-only restaurant
Bottom: Family fun at Castaway Cay, Disney's private isle in the Bahamas

Top: A day ashore
Middle: Making a splash in
Mickey's pool
Bottom: *Disney Magic* and *Disney Wonder* at sea

Your Shipmates

Disney Cruises appeal to kids of all ages—the young and not so young, singles, couples, and families. Multigeneration family groups are the core audience for these ships, and the facilities are ideal for family gatherings. What you might not have expected are the numerous newlywed couples celebrating their honeymoons on board.

Dress Code

Three- and four-night cruises are casual; no formal wear is required, and resort casual is the evening dress code for dinner in Animator's Palate and a second casual dining room. A sport coat is appropriate for the third—and fancier—restaurant, as well as Palo, the adults-only restaurant on both ships; however, men won't be turned away and could probably get by without the sport coat. Remy (only on the newest ships) requires a jacket for men, and they won't be seated without one. One-week cruises schedule a semiformal evening and a formal night, during which men are encouraged to wear tuxedos, but dark suits or sport coats and ties are acceptable for both.

Junior Cruisers

As expected, Disney ships have extensive programs for children and teens. Parents are issued a pager for peace of mind and to alert them when their offspring need them. Complimentary age-appropriate activities are scheduled from 9 am to midnight in the Oceaneer Club and Oceaneer Lab for ages 3 (toilet training required) to 10. Activities include arts projects, contests, computer games, pool parties, interactive lab stations, and opportunities for individual and group play. The emphasis is on fun over education, but subtle educational themes are certainly there. Edge is the tweens-exclusive space where kids ages 11 through 13 can play videogames, watch TV, listen to music, and participate in activities with kids their own age. Vibe, the teen club is outfitted with a music system, dance floor, big-screen TV, and Internet café. Scheduled activities include challenging games, photography lessons, sports contests, beach events, and parties, but the club is also a great

You want to cruise with the entire family—mom, dad, the kids, and grandparents.

You enjoy having kids around. (There are adults-only areas to retreat to when the fun wears off.)

Your family enjoys Disney's theme parks and can't get enough wholesome entertainment.

place for teenagers 14 to 17 to just hang out with new friends in an adult-free zone.

An hourly fee is charged for child care in nurseries, which are open during select hours for infants as young as three months through three years. Supply your own diapers, and nursery attendants will change them. Private, in-cabin babysitting is not available on Disney ships.

Service
Friendly service is extended to all passengers, with particular importance placed on treating children with the same courtesy extended to adults.

Tipping
Suggested gratuity amounts are calculated on a per person–per cruise rather than per night basis and can be added to onboard accounts or offered in cash on the last night of the cruise. Guidelines include gratuities for your dining-room server, assistant server, head server, and stateroom host–hostess for the following amounts: $36 for three-night cruises, $48 for four-night cruises, and $84 for seven-night cruises. Tips for room-service delivery, spa services, and the dining manager are at the passenger's discretion. An automatic 15% gratuity is added to all bar tabs.

Past Passengers
Castaway Club membership is automatic after completing a Disney cruise. Benefits include a complimentary gift (such as a tote bag or beach towel), communication about special offers, priority check-in, invitations to shipboard cocktail parties during subsequent cruises, and a special toll-free reservation telephone number (☎ 800/449–3380) for convenience.

GOOD TO KNOW

Silhouettes and abstract images of Mickey Mouse are cleverly hidden by Disney's creative designers throughout the ship, just as they are in the theme parks.

You can buy pins and autograph books on the ships, but the gift shops won't open until after you sail. Drop in at a Disney store before your cruise and purchase them for your kids; they'll appreciate being prepared from the get-go.

Prior to sailing, go online to reserve shore excursions, a table at the adults-only specialty restaurants, and babysitting in the nursery. Children can also be registered for youth programs, and adults can make spa appointments.

If you didn't do it ahead of time, you can register the kids for their age-appropriate programs in the terminal while you wait to board.

5

DISNEY CRUISE LINE

DON'T CHOOSE THIS LINE IF ...

You want to spend a lot of quality time bonding with your kids. Your kids may not want to leave the fun activities.

You want to dine in peace and quiet. The dining rooms and buffet can be boisterous.

You want to gamble. There are no casinos, so you'll have to settle for bingo.

DISNEY MAGIC, DISNEY WONDER

CREW MEMBERS	950
ENTERED SERVICE	1998, 1999
GROSS TONS	83,000
LENGTH	964 feet
NUMBER OF CABINS	877
PASSENGER CAPACITY	1,754 (2,400 max)
WIDTH	106 feet

700 ft.

500 ft.

300 ft.

Top: Friendships are forged on a cruise
Bottom: *Disney Magic* at sea

Public Areas and Facilities

Reminiscent of classic ocean liners, Disney vessels have two funnels (the forward one is nonfunctional) and high-tech interiors behind their art deco and art nouveau styling. Whimsical design accents cleverly incorporate the images of Mickey Mouse and his friends without overpowering the warm and elegant decor. Artwork showcases the creativity of Disney artists and animators. The atmosphere is never stuffy.

More than 15,000 square feet—nearly an entire deck—are devoted to children's activity centers, outdoor activity areas, and swimming pools. Theaters cater to family entertainment with large-scale production shows, movies, dances, lively game shows, and even 3-D movies.

Adults-only hideaways include an avenue of theme bars and lounges tucked into the area just forward of the lobby atrium; the Promenade Lounge, near the aft elevator lobby; and Cove Café, a quiet spot adjacent to the adult pool to relax with coffee or a cocktail, surf the Internet, or read.

Restaurants

In a novel approach to dining, passengers (and their waiters) rotate through the three main dining rooms in assigned seatings—two assigned dinner times on *Disney Wonder* and four on *Disney Magic*. Parrot Cay and Animator's Palate are casual, while Triton's (*Disney Wonder*) and Lumière's (*Disney Magic*) are a bit fancier. Palo is a beautifully appointed northern Italian restaurant for adults only that requires reservations for brunch, dinner, or tea and carries an extra charge. Breakfast and lunch are open seating in dining rooms. Disney characters make an appearance at a character breakfast on seven-night cruises. Breakfast, lunch, and dinner are also offered in the casual pool-deck buffet, while poolside pizzerias, snack bars, grills, and ice-cream bars serve everything from pizza and hot dogs to fresh fruit, wraps, burgers, and frozen treats during the day. Specialty coffees are available in the adults-only Cove Café for an extra charge. Room service is available around the clock.

Accommodations

Cabins: Designed for families, Disney ships have some of the roomiest, most functional staterooms at sea.

Natural woods, imported tiles, and a nautical flavor add to the decor, which even includes the touch of Disney-inspired artwork on the walls. Most cabins can accommodate at least three people and have a sitting area and unique bath-and-a-half arrangement. Three-quarters of all accommodations are outside cabins, and 44% of those include private balconies with kid-proof door handles and higher-than-usual railings for safety. All cabins have adequate closet and drawer/shelf storage, as well as bathroom shelves.

Suites: Suites are truly expansive, with master bedrooms separated from the living areas for privacy. All suites have walk-in closets, a dining table and chairs, a wet bar, a VCR, and a large balcony.

Amenities: Though not luxurious, Disney cabins are comfortably furnished. Each has a flat-screen TV, a small refrigerator, a personal safe, and a hair dryer; bathrobes are provided for use during the cruise in the top-category staterooms. All suites have concierge service.

Worth Noting: Sixteen cabins are wheelchair accessible.

In the Know

Aesthetically pleasing ship design can result in some quirky interior features. Four Navigator Verandah cabins are semiobstructed by slanting superstructure (6134, 6634, 7120, 7620); the rest have nautically furnished verandas with views through large portholes cut into the steel.

Pros and Cons

Pros: There are plenty of connecting cabins that sleep three, four, and five (two-bedroom suites sleep up to seven, one-bedroom suites sleep up to five, and deluxe family balcony staterooms sleep up to five). Soft drinks at meals and beverage stations are included in your cruise fare. Have no fear, adults aren't limited to milk and cookies—each ship has a piano bar/jazz club for easy listening and late-night cocktails.

Cons: Only potty-trained children can enter the swimming pools, so youngsters who wear swim diapers are only allowed to use the Mickey's Pool splash play area; although a Disney cruise isn't all Disney all the time, it can get tiring for passengers who aren't really into it; there's no library on board, but limited reading materials are available in the Cove Café.

Cabin Type	Size (sq. ft.)
Royal Suites	1,029
2-Bedroom Suite	945
1-Bedroom Suite	614
Deluxe Family Balcony	304
Deluxe Balcony	268
Ocean View	226
Deluxe Inside	214
Standard Inside	184
Dimensions include the square footage for balconies	

FAST FACTS

- 11 passenger decks
- Specialty restaurant, 3 dining rooms, buffet, ice cream parlor, pizzeria
- Wi-Fi, safe, refrigerator, DVD (some)
- 2 pools, children's pool
- Fitness classes, gym, hair salon, 4 hot tubs, sauna, spa
- 6 bars, cinema, dance club, 2 showrooms, video game room
- Children's programs (ages 3–17)
- Dry-cleaning, laundry facilities, laundry service
- Internet terminal
- No kids under 12 weeks
- No-smoking cabins

5

DISNEY CRUISE LINE

DISNEY DREAM, DISNEY FANTASY

700 ft.	**CREW MEMBERS**
	1,458
	ENTERED SERVICE
	2011, 2012
	GROSS TONS
	128,000
	LENGTH
	1,115 feet
500 ft.	**NUMBER OF CABINS**
	1,250
	PASSENGER CAPACITY
	2,500 (4,000 max)
300 ft.	**WIDTH**
	125 feet

Public Areas and Facilities

Disney Cruise Line's largest ships are also their most lavish vessels, distinguished for their classic early 20th-century design—which is reminiscent of the golden age of ocean travel—and their state-of-the-art technology. Playful design accents cleverly incorporate the images of Disney characters and themes without overpowering the stylish decor. The atmosphere is never stuffy.

As on their earlier ships, vast areas are devoted to children, outdoor activity areas, and swimming pools. The AquaDuck water coaster propels kids and adults alike on a thrill-filled ride up, down, and around four outside decks, even over the side of the ship. Theaters cater to family entertainment with large-scale production shows, movies, and other events. Adults-only hideaways include an avenue of bars and lounges tucked into deck four aft; Meridian Lounge, located between the specialty restaurants; and Cove Café, a quiet spot adjacent to the adult pool.

Restaurants

In a novel approach to dining, passengers (and their waiters) rotate through the three main dining rooms in assigned seatings, while breakfast and lunch are open seating. Palo is a beautifully appointed northern Italian restaurant for adults that requires reservations for brunch, dinner, or tea and carries an extra charge. Also adults-only and requiring reservations and a surcharge is Remy, the ships' most upscale restaurant that serves French-inspired cuisine for dinner. Breakfast, lunch, and dinner are also offered in the casual pool-deck buffet, which offers table service for dinner. Poolside pizzerias, snack bars, grills, and ice cream bars serve everything from pizza and hot dogs to fresh fruit, wraps, burgers, and frozen treats during the day. Specialty coffees are available in the adults-only Cove Café for an extra charge. Disney characters make an appearance at a character breakfast on seven-night cruises. Room service is available around the clock.

Accommodations

Cabins: Designed specifically for families, Disney's cabins are some of the most functional at sea. A nautical flavor adds to the art deco inspired decor, which even includes a touch of Disney-inspired artwork. Eighty-eight percent

Top: Relaxing in the lounge
Bottom: *A Disney Dream* cabin

of the staterooms have an ocean view and, of those, 90% have a private balcony. Most can accommodate at least three people; categories designated "family" are able to sleep up to five comfortably. All have a sitting area and, with the exception of the standard inside category, feature a unique bath-and-a-half arrangement. Suites have two bathrooms, including one with double sinks and a whirlpool tub. Royal Suites have a second whirlpool tub on the balcony.

Amenities: Though not luxurious, Disney cabins are comfortably furnished and have some useful amenities, including a flat-screen TV, small refrigerator, safe, iPod docking station, and hair dryer. All inside staterooms have a "virtual porthole" with a real-time view of the sea outside of the ship (it can be turned off at night). Shampoo, conditioner, and lotion are provided for all; suites receive upgraded toiletries and bathrobes for use during the cruise. All suites have concierge service and daily deliveries of canapés, fruit, or cookies.

Worth Noting: Thirty-seven staterooms in a variety of categories are equipped for accessibility.

In the Know

To accommodate larger families and groups, there are 500 connecting doors that create adjoining staterooms. Bed frames have been raised to allow more room underneath for luggage storage.

Pros and Cons

Pros: Mickey's Pool (for young kids) and Donald's Pool (for families) are between the forward and aft funnels, allowing parents the opportunity to keep an eye on all their children. The adults-only Quiet Cove has a lounge area in the shallow section of the pool. For privacy, a curtain can be drawn between the sitting and sleeping areas in staterooms.

Cons: Even the largest suites sleep only a maximum of five, although adjoining accommodations will sleep more. Only potty-trained children can enter the swimming pools, so youngsters who wear swim diapers are only allowed to use the Mickey's Pool splash play area. Although a Disney cruise isn't all Disney all the time, it can get tiring for passengers who aren't really into it.

Cabin Type	Size (sq. ft.)
Concierge Royal Suite/1 Bedroom Suite	1,781/622
Concierge Family Balcony/Deluxe Family Balcony/ Deluxe Balcony	306/ 299/ 246
Family Ocean View/Ocean View	306/204
Deluxe Interior/ Standard Interior	200/169

Dimensions include the square footage for balconies

FAST FACTS

- 14 passenger decks
- 2 specialty restaurants, 3 dining rooms, buffet, café, ice cream parlor, pizzeria
- Wi-Fi, safe, refrigerator, DVD (some)
- 3 pools, children's pool
- Fitness classes, gym, hair salon, 8 hot tubs, sauna, spa
- 11 bars, cinema, dance club, show room, video game room
- Children's programs (ages 3–17)
- Dry-cleaning, laundry facilities, laundry service
- Internet terminal
- No kids under 12 weeks
- No-smoking cabins

5

DISNEY CRUISE LINE

HOLLAND AMERICA

Holland America Line has enjoyed a distinguished record of traditional cruises, world exploration, and transatlantic crossings since 1873—all facets of its history that are reflected in the fleet's multimillion-dollar shipboard art and antiques collections. Even the

A day on the Lido Deck

ships' names follow a pattern set long ago: all end in the suffix *dam* and are either derived from the names of various dams that cross Holland's rivers, important Dutch landmarks, or points of the compass. The names are even recycled when vessels are retired, and some are in their fifth and sixth generation of use.

✉ *300 Elliott Ave. W, Seattle, WA*

☎ *206/281–3535 or 800/577–1728*

⊕ *www.hollandamerica. com*

☞ *Cruise Style: Premium Deluxe.*

Noted for focusing on passenger comfort, Holland America Line cruises are classic in design and style, and with an infusion of younger adults and families on board, they remain refined without being stuffy or stodgy. Following a basic design theme, returning passengers feel as at home on the newest Holland America vessels as they do on older ones.

Entertainment tends to be more Broadway-stylish than Las Vegas–brash. Colorful revues are presented in main show lounges by the ships' companies of singers and dancers. Other performances might include a range of cabaret acts: comedians, magicians, jugglers, and acrobats. Live bands play a wide range of musical styles for dancing and listening in smaller lounges and piano bars. Movies are shown daily in cinemas that double as the Culinary Arts Centers.

Holland America Line may never be considered cutting-edge, but the Signature of Excellence concept introduced in 2003 sets it apart from other premium cruise lines. An interactive Culinary Arts Center offers cooking demonstrations and wine-tasting sessions; Explorations Café (powered by the *New York Times*) is a coffeehouse-style library and Internet center; and the Explorations Guest Speakers Series is supported by in-cabin televised programming on flat-screen TVs in all cabins; the traditional Crow's Nest observation lounge has a new nightclub-disco layout, video wall, and sound-and-light systems; and facilities for children and teens have been greatly expanded. Although the initial Signature of Excellence upgrades were completed on the entire Holland America fleet in 2006, additional enhancements are ongoing.

Food

Holland America Line chefs, led by Master Chef Rudi Sodamin, utilize more than 500 different food items on a typical weeklong cruise to create the modern continental cuisine and traditional favorites served to their passengers. Vegetarian options as well as health-conscious cuisine are available, and special dietary requests can be handled with advance notice. Holland America's passengers used to skew older than they do now, so the sometimes bland dishes were no surprise. But the food quality, taste, and selection have greatly improved in recent years. A case in point is the reservations-required Pinnacle Grill alternative restaurants, where fresh seafood and premium cuts of Sterling Silver beef are used to prepare creative specialty dishes. The $20 per person charge for dinner would be worth it for the Dungeness crab cakes starter and dessert alone. Other delicious traditions are afternoon tea, a Dutch Chocolate Extravaganza, and Holland America Line's signature bread pudding.

Flexible scheduling allows for early or late seatings in the two-deck, formal restaurants. An open seating option from 5:15 to 9 has been introduced fleet-wide.

Fitness and Recreation

Well-equipped and fully staffed fitness facilities contain state-of-the-art exercise equipment; basic fitness classes are available at no charge. There's a fee for personal training, body composition analysis, and specialized classes such as yoga and Pilates.

Treatments in the Greenhouse Spa include a variety of massages, body wraps, and facials. Hair styling and nail services are offered in the salons. All ships have a jogging track, multiple swimming pools, and sports courts; some have hydrotherapy pools and soothing thermal suites.

Your Shipmates

No longer just your grandparents' cruise line, today's Holland America sailings attract families and discerning couples, mostly from their late-thirties on up.

NOTEWORTHY

■ Trays of mints, dried fruits, and candied ginger can be found outside the dining rooms.

■ Passengers are presented with a complimentary carryall bag imprinted with the line's logo.

■ Each ship has a wraparound promenade deck for walking, jogging, or stretching out in the shade on a padded steamer chair.

5

HOLLAND AMERICA

Top: Casino action
Bottom: Stay fit or stay loose

Top: Wine tasting
Middle: Production showtime
Bottom: Spa relaxation

Holidays and summer months are peak periods when you'll find more children in the mix. Comfortable retirees are often still in the majority, particularly on longer cruises. Families cruising together who book five or more cabins receive perks such as a fountain-soda package for each family member, a family photo for each stateroom, and complimentary water toys at Half Moon Cay (for Caribbean itineraries that call at the private island). If the group is larger than 10 cabins, the Head-of-Family is recognized with an upgrade from outside stateroom to a veranda cabin. It's the best family deal at sea, and there's no extra charge.

Dress Code

Evenings on Holland America Line cruises fall into two categories: smart casual and formal. For the two formal nights standard on seven-night cruises, men are encouraged to wear tuxedos, but dark suits or sport coats and ties are acceptable, and you'll certainly see them. On smart–casual nights—expect the type of attire you'd see at a country club or upscale resort. It's requested that no T-shirts, jeans, swimsuits, tank tops, or shorts be worn in public areas after 6 pm.

Junior Cruisers

Club HAL is Holland America Line's professionally staffed youth and teen program. Age-appropriate activities planned for children ages 3 to 7 include storytelling, arts and crafts, ice-cream or pizza parties, and games; for children ages 8 to 12 there are arcade games, Sony PlayStations, theme parties, on-deck sports events, and scavenger hunts. Club HAL After Hours offers late-night activities from 10 pm until midnight for an hourly fee. Baby food, diapers, cribs, high chairs, and booster seats may be requested in advance of boarding. Private in-cabin babysitting is sometimes available if a staff member is willing.

Teens aged 13 to 17 have their own lounge, with activities including dance contests, arcade games, sports tournaments, movies, and an exclusive sundeck on some ships. Select itineraries offer water park–type facilities and kid-friendly shore excursions to Half Moon Cay, Holland America Line's private island in the Bahamas.

CHOOSE THIS LINE IF ...

You crave relaxation. Grab a padded steamer chair on the teak promenade deck and watch the sea pass by.

You like to go to the movies, especially when the popcorn is free.

You want to bring the kids. Areas designed exclusively for children and teens are hot new features on all ships.

Service

Professional, unobtrusive service by the Indonesian and Filipino staff is a fleet-wide standard on Holland America Line. It isn't uncommon for a steward or server to remember the names of returning passengers from a cruise taken years before. Crew members are trained in Indonesia at a custom-built facility called the MS *Nieuw Jakarta*, where employees polish their English-language skills and learn housekeeping in mock cabins.

Tipping

Eleven dollars per passenger per day is automatically added to shipboard accounts, and gratuities are distributed to stewards and waitstaff. Passengers may adjust the amount based on the level of service experienced. Room-service tips are usually given in cash (it's at the passenger's discretion here). An automatic 15% gratuity is added to bar-service tabs.

Past Passengers

All passengers who sail with Holland America Line are automatically enrolled in the Mariner Society and receive special offers on upcoming cruises, as well as insider information concerning new ships and product enhancements. Mariner Society benefits also include preferred pricing on many cruises; an invitation to the "Welcome Back" embarkation lunch and Mariner Society champagne reception and awards party hosted by the captain; lapel pins and medallions acknowledging your history of Holland America sailings; a special collectible gift delivered to your cabin; and a subscription to *Mariner*, the full-color magazine featuring news and Mariner Society savings.

GOOD TO KNOW

The sound of delicate chimes still alerts Holland America Line passengers that it's mealtime. Artful flower arrangements never seem to wilt. A bowl of candied ginger is near the dining room entrance if you need a little something to settle your stomach. These simple, but nonetheless meaningful, touches are what make Holland America Line stand out from the crowd.

5

HOLLAND AMERICA

DON'T CHOOSE THIS LINE IF ...

You want to party hard. Most of the action on these ships ends relatively early.

Dressing for dinner isn't your thing. Passengers tend to ramp up the dress code most evenings.

You have an aversion to extending tips. The line's "tipping not required" policy has been dropped.

SIGNATURE CLASS
Eurodam, Nieuw Amsterdam

CREW MEMBERS	929
ENTERED SERVICE	2008, 2010
GROSS TONS	86,273/86,700
LENGTH	936 feet
NUMBER OF CABINS	1,052, 1,053
PASSENGER CAPACITY	2,104, 2,106
WIDTH	106 feet

700 ft.

500 ft.

300 ft.

Top: *Eurodam* at sea
Bottom: The Retreat on
Eurodam, the ultimate getaway

Public Areas and Facilities

Signature-class vessels were so named because they are the first ships in the fleet to be launched with all the so-called Signature of Excellence features fully integrated into them. Larger than the other midsize ships in the fleet, they are pure Holland America, with all the traditional amenities and services plus some added bonuses. You'll find familiar public spaces as well as a second specialty restaurant and adjacent lounge, a new bar that anchors the Explorer's Lounge, and an Italian eatery tucked into a corner of the Lido.

Spa staterooms near the Greenhouse Spa feature Asian-inspired decor and spa amenities. Poolside are private, draped cabanas, and one deck up the tented Retreat cabanas are filled with amenities that include the use of handheld fans, an Evian spray mister, iPods with music preloaded, and chilled water. You can look forward to icy refreshments and afternoon champagne. Cabanas are reserved by the day or by the cruise (for an extra fee).

Restaurants

The formal restaurant offers open seating for breakfast, lunch, and dinner and the option of two traditional assigned dinner seatings or open seating. The Pinnacle Grill alternative restaurant serves lunch and dinner, requires reservations, and has a cover charge. Tamarind offers Pan-Asian fare by reservation; there is a dinner charge, but lunch is complimentary. For casual dining, the Lido restaurant serves buffet breakfast and lunch; for dinner there is waiter service, and a section becomes Canaletto, serving Italian fare (reservation required but no fee). A poolside grill features items ranging from tacos to hamburgers. The extra-charge Explorations Café offers specialty coffees and pastries. Daily afternoon tea service is elevated to Royal Dutch High Tea once per cruise, hors d'oeuvres are served by waiters before dinner, chocolates are offered after dinner, and a chocolate extravaganza buffet is served one night during every cruise. Room service is available 24 hours.

Accommodations

Cabins: Warm wood tones, burnished nickel fixtures, and punches of color complement the drapery, carpeting, and bedspreads in all categories. Eighty-five percent have an ocean view, and 79% of outside state-rooms and suites offer a private veranda with attractive furnishings.

Suites: Penthouse suites are the ultimate in luxury, with separate living-room, dining-room, and bedroom areas. A veranda with hot tub, walk-in closets, bathroom with whirlpool tub, double sinks, separate guest powder room, and butler's pantry complete the features. Offering similar amenities, Deluxe and Superior Verandah Suites have large verandas, dressing areas, and generous sitting areas; the bathrooms also have double sinks, a whirlpool tub, and a separate shower. Suite occupants also enjoy refreshments in the private Neptune Lounge and personal concierge service.

Amenities: All categories are outfitted with plush pillow-top mattresses, bathrobes, Egyptian cotton towels, flat-panel TVs, DVD players, lighted makeup mirrors, hair dryers, massaging showerheads, personal safes, refrigerators, and closets configured for hanging and/or drop-down shelves.

Worth Noting: 30 cabins are designed for wheelchair accessibility.

In the Know

With low lighting, intimate seating areas, and a commanding view from the highest deck on the ship, the Silk Den Lounge is one of the most popular spots on board for cocktails either before or after dinner.

Pros and Cons

Pros: Effective on January 15, 2012, smoking will be prohibited in all cabins. With views of the sea and intimate seating alcoves, the Silk Den Lounge is one of the prettiest and most comfortable in the Holland America fleet. Culinary presentations are offered in a state-of-the-art demonstration kitchen with a bird's-eye view of the chef's dexterity projected on a large screen overhead.

Cons: Oddly, drawers in standard accommodations are sparse, but shelving is adequate. Spa staterooms on deck 10 have Juliet-style balconies that allow fresh sea breezes to enter when the door is open, but there is no room to actually sit outside on the tiny, scalloped balconies. Underutilized, the Lido's poolside rental cabanas restrict the amount of space available to all passengers.

Cabin Type	Size (sq. ft.)
Penthouse Suite	1,318
Deluxe Verandah	510–700
Superior Verandah	398
Deluxe Verandah	254
Ocean View	185
Inside	170–200

Dimensions include the square footage for balconies

FAST FACTS

- 11 passenger decks
- 3 specialty restaurants, dining room, buffet, pizzeria
- Wi-Fi, safe, refrigerator, DVD
- 2 pools
- Fitness classes, gym, hair salon, 5 hot tubs, sauna, spa
- 11 bars, casino, cinema, 2 dance clubs, library, showroom, video game room
- Children's programs (ages 3–17)
- Dry-cleaning, laundry service
- Internet terminal
- No-smoking cabins

5

HOLLAND AMERICA

Eurodam atrium

VISTA CLASS
Zuiderdam, Oosterdam, Westerdam, Noordam

ENTERED SERVICE	2002, 2003, 2004, 2006
PASSENGER CAPACITY	1,916; 1,916; 1,916; 1,918
CREW MEMBERS	817, 817, 817, 820
NUMBER OF CABINS	958, 958, 958, 959
GROSS TONS	82,305
LENGTH	936 feet
WIDTH	106 feet

700 ft.

500 ft.

300 ft.

Top: *Oosterdam* hydro pool
Bottom: Vista-class ocean-
view stateroom

Public Areas and Facilities

Ships for the 21st century, Vista-class vessels integrate new, youthful and family-friendly elements into Holland America Line's classic fleet. Exquisite Waterford crystal sculptures adorn triple-deck atriums and reflect vivid, almost daring color schemes throughout. Although all the public rooms carry the traditional Holland America names (Ocean Bar, Explorer's Lounge, Crow's Nest) and aren't much different in atmosphere, their louder decor (toned down a bit since the introduction of the *Zuiderdam*) may make them unfamiliar to returning passengers.

Veterans of cruises on older Holland America ships will find the layout of public spaces somewhat different; still, everyone's favorite Crow's Nest lounges still offer those commanding views.

Restaurants

The formal dining room offers open seating breakfast and lunch and a choice between two traditional assigned dinner seatings or open seating. The upscale Pinnacle Grill alternative restaurant serves lunch and dinner, requires reservations, and has a cover charge. A casual Lido restaurant serves buffet breakfast and lunch; at dinner the Lido offers waiter service featuring entrées from both the Lido and main dining room menus, and Italian fare is served in the adjacent Canaletto Restaurant. Poolside lunch at the Terrace Grill features a variety of items ranging from nachos, grilled hamburgers, and hot dogs with all the trimmings to sandwiches and gourmet sausages. The extra-charge Explorations Café offers specialty coffees and pastries. Daily afternoon tea service is elevated to Royal Dutch High Tea once per cruise. Complimentary hors d'oeuvres are served by waiters during cocktail hour, hand-dipped chocolates are offered after dinner in the Explorer's Lounge, and a late-night buffet and chocolate extravaganza is served in the Lido Restaurant during every cruise. Room service is available 24 hours.

Accommodations

Cabins: Comfortable and roomy, 85% of all Vista-class accommodations have an ocean view, and almost 80% of those also have the luxury of a private balcony furnished with chairs, loungers, and tables. Every cabin has adequate closet and drawer/shelf storage, as well as bathroom shelves. Some suites have a whirlpool tub, powder room, and walk-in closet.

Suites: Suite luxuries include duvets on beds and a fully stocked minibar; some also have a whirlpool tub, powder room, and walk-in closet. Penthouse Verandah and Deluxe Verandah suites have exclusive use of the private Neptune Lounge, personal concierge service, canapés before dinner, and complimentary laundry, pressing, and dry-cleaning services.

Amenities: All staterooms and suites are appointed with pillow-top mattresses, 250-thread-count cotton bed linens, magnifying halogen-lighted makeup mirrors, hair dryers, a fruit basket, flat-panel TVs, and DVD players. Bathroom extras include Egyptian cotton towels, shampoo, body lotion, and bath gel, plus deluxe bathrobes to use during the cruise.

Worth Noting: Twenty-eight staterooms are wheelchair accessible.

In the Know

If you want complete privacy on your balcony, choose your location carefully. Take a close look at the deck plans for the ones alongside the exterior panoramic elevators. Riders have views of adjacent balconies as well as the seascape.

Pros and Cons

Pros: Adjacent to the Crow's Nest, an outdoor area covered in canvas is a wonderful, quiet hideaway during the day as well as when the interior is transformed into a dance club at night. Exterior panoramic elevators offer an elevated view of the seascape. Half-hour shipboard art tours are available on board the ship, loaded on iPods that you may borrow.

Cons: Missing from the Vista-class ships are self-service laundry rooms, a serious omission for families with youngsters and anyone sailing on back-to-back Caribbean itineraries or cruises of more than a week. Murals in Pinnacle Grill restaurants are strangely chintzy-looking, especially considering the priceless art throughout the rest of the ships' interiors. Traditional appointments stop at the table top in the Pinnacle Grill—some chairs are silvery cast aluminum and so heavy that they don't budge without a great deal of effort.

Cabin Type	Size (sq. ft.)
Penthouse Suites	1,318
Deluxe Verandah Suite	510–700
Superior Verandah Suite	398
Deluxe Ocean View	254
Standard Ocean View	185
Inside	170–200
Dimensions include the square footage for balconies	

FAST FACTS

- 11 passenger decks
- Specialty restaurant, dining room, buffet, pizzeria
- Internet, Wi-Fi, safe, refrigerator, DVD
- 2 pools (1 indoor)
- Fitness classes, gym, hair salon, 5 hot tubs, sauna, spa, steam room
- 9 bars, casino, cinema, 2 dance clubs, library, showroom, video game room
- Children's programs (ages 3–17)
- Dry-cleaning, laundry service
- Internet terminal
- No-smoking cabins

5

HOLLAND AMERICA

ROTTERDAM, AMSTERDAM

CREW MEMBERS	600, 615
ENTERED SERVICE	1997, 2000
GROSS TONS	61,859, 62,735
LENGTH	780 feet
NUMBER OF CABINS	702, 690
PASSENGER CAPACITY	1,404, 1,380
WIDTH	106 feet

700 ft.

500 ft.

300 ft.

Top: Pinnacle Grill dining
Bottom: *Rotterdam* at sea

Public Areas and Facilities

Amsterdam and *Rotterdam* are sister ships, which sail on world cruises and extended voyages. The most traditional ships in the fleet, their interiors display abundant wood appointments in the public areas on promenade and lower promenade decks and priceless works of art throughout.

The Ocean Bar, Explorer's Lounge, Wajang Theater, and Crow's Nest are familiar to longtime Holland American passengers. Newer additions include the spa's thermal suite, a culinary-arts demonstration center in the theater, Explorations Café, and expansive areas for children and teens. In addition to art works commissioned specifically for each ship, Holland America Line celebrates its heritage by featuring antiques and artworks that reflect the theme of worldwide Dutch seafaring history.

Restaurants

The formal dining room offers open seating breakfast and lunch; for dinner, there are two assigned seatings or open seating. The upscale Pinnacle Grill serves lunch and dinner, requires reservations, and has a cover charge. A casual Lido restaurant serves buffet breakfast and lunch; at dinner, the Lido offers waiter service; Italian fare is served in the adjacent Canaletto Restaurant. Poolside lunch at the Terrace Grill features a variety of items ranging from nachos, grilled hamburgers, and hot dogs to sandwiches and gourmet sausages. The extra-charge Explorations Café offers specialty coffees and pastries. Daily afternoon tea service is elevated to Royal Dutch High Tea once per cruise. Complimentary hors d'oeuvres are served by waiters during cocktail hour, hand-dipped chocolates are offered after dinner in the Explorer's Lounge, and a late-night buffet and chocolate extravaganza is served in the Lido Restaurant during every cruise. Room service is available 24 hours.

Accommodations

Cabins: Staterooms are spacious and comfortable, although fewer have private balconies than newer fleet mates. A new cabin category—Lanai cabins, with a door that directly accesses the Promenade Deck—was added during *Rotterdam*'s latest upgrade, as was a spa category that includes spa amenities. Every cabin has adequate closet and drawer/shelf storage, as well as bathroom shelves. Some suites also have a whirlpool tub, powder room, and walk-in closet.

Suites: Extras include duvets on beds, a fully stocked minibar, and personalized stationery. Penthouse Verandah and Deluxe Verandah suites have exclusive use of the private Neptune Lounge, personal concierge service, canapés before dinner on request, binoculars and umbrellas for use during the cruise, an invitation to a VIP party with the captain, and complimentary laundry, pressing, and dry-cleaning services.

Amenities: All staterooms and suites are appointed with pillow-top mattresses, 250-thread-count cotton bed linens, magnifying halo-lighted mirrors, hair dryers, a fruit basket, flat-panel TVs, and DVD players. Bathrooms have Egyptian cotton towels, shampoo, body lotion, and bath gel, plus deluxe bathrobes to use during the cruise.

Worth Noting: Connecting cabins are available in a range of categories. Although there are a number of triple cabins to choose from, there are not as many that accommodate four. Twenty-one staterooms are designed for wheelchair accessibility on *Amsterdam*, 22 on *Rotterdam*.

In the Know
The creation of the expansive floral stained-glass ceiling that provides a focal point for *Amsterdam*'s formal dining room required the use of some state-of-the-art technology that was developed especially for the ship.

Pros and Cons
Pros: Balcony, spa, and Lanai staterooms, as well as The Retreat (a resort-style pool on the aft Lido Deck) were added to *Rotterdam* in 2009. Servers circulate throughout lounges before and after dinner with canapés and other treats. Realistic landscapes with surreal touches accent dining alcoves in the Pinnacle Grill on *Amsterdam*.

Cons: Although outside cabins on the lower promenade deck are ideally situated for easy access to fresh air, the one-way window glass does not offer complete privacy when interior lights are on. Lounges are lively before and after dinner, but many passengers tend to call it a night early. Although you'll find excellent facilities designed for kids and teens, suitable accommodations for families are sparse.

Cabin Type	Size (sq. ft.)
Penthouse Suite	1,159
Deluxe Verandah Suite	556
Verandah Suite	292
Lanai	197 (Rotterdam only)
Ocean View	197
Inside	182

Dimensions include the square footage for balconies

FAST FACTS

- 9 passenger decks
- Specialty restaurant, dining room, buffet
- Wi-Fi, safe, refrigerator, minibar (some), DVD
- 2 pools (1 indoor), 2 children's pools
- Fitness classes, gym, hair salon, 2 hot tubs, sauna, spa
- 6 bars, casino, cinema, dance club, library, showroom, video game room
- Children's programs (ages 3–17)
- Dry-cleaning, laundry facilities, laundry service
- Internet terminal
- No-smoking cabins

5

HOLLAND AMERICA

STATENDAM CLASS
Statendam, Maasdam, Ryndam, Veendam

CREW MEMBERS	580
ENTERED SERVICE	1993, 1993, 1994, 1996
GROSS TONS	55,819/55,575/55,819/57,092
LENGTH	720 feet
NUMBER OF CABINS	630/658/630/675
PASSENGER CAPACITY	1,260/1,258/1260/1,350
WIDTH	101 feet

700 ft.
500 ft.
300 ft.

Public Areas and Facilities
The sister ships included in the S- or Statendam class retain the most classic and traditional characteristics of Holland America Line vessels. Routinely updated with innovative features, including Signature of Excellence upgrades, they combine all the advantages of intimate, midsize vessels with high-tech and stylish details.

At the heart of the ships, triple-deck atriums graced by suspended glass sculptures open onto three so-called promenade decks; the lowest contains staterooms encircled by a wide, teak outdoor deck furnished with padded steamer chairs, while interior, art-filled passageways flow past lounges and public rooms on the two decks above. Either reach the lower dining room floor via the aft elevator, or enter one deck above and make a grand entrance down the sweeping staircase.

Restaurants
The formal dining room offers open seating breakfast and lunch and both assigned and open seating for dinner. The upscale Pinnacle Grill alternative restaurant serves lunch and dinner, requires reservations, and has a cover charge. A casual Lido restaurant serves buffet breakfast and lunch; at dinner the Lido offers waiter service featuring entrées from both the Lido and main dining room menus, and Italian fare is served in the adjacent Canaletto Restaurant. Poolside lunch is served at the Terrace Grill. The extra-charge Explorations Café offers specialty coffees and pastries. Daily afternoon tea service is elevated to Royal Dutch High Tea once per cruise. Complimentary hors d'oeuvres are served by waiters during cocktail hour, hand-dipped chocolates are offered after dinner in the Explorer's Lounge, and a late-night buffet and chocolate extravaganza is served in the Lido Restaurant during every cruise. Room service is available 24 hours.

Accommodations
Cabins: Staterooms are spacious and comfortable, although fewer of them have private balconies than on newer ships. A new cabin category—Lanai cabins, with a door that directly accesses the Promenade Deck—was added to Statendam, Maasdam, and Veendam during the ships' latest upgrades, while a spa category that includes spa amenities was added to Statendam,

Top: Select from an extensive wine list
Bottom: Deluxe veranda suite

Ryndam, and Veendam. Every cabin has adequate closet and drawer/shelf storage, as well as bathroom shelves.

Suites: Suites have duvets on beds, a fully stocked mini-bar, and personalized stationery. Penthouse Verandah and Deluxe Verandah suites have exclusive use of the private Neptune Lounge, personal concierge service, canapés before dinner on request, binoculars and umbrellas for use during the cruise, an invitation to a VIP party with the captain, and complimentary laundry, pressing, and dry-cleaning services.

Amenities: GAll staterooms and suites are now appointed with pillow-top mattresses, 250-thread-count cotton bed linens, magnifying lighted mirrors, hair dryers, a fruit basket, flat-panel TVs, and DVD players. Bathroom extras include Egyptian cotton towels, shampoo, body lotion, and bath gel, plus deluxe bathrobes to use during the cruise.

Worth Noting: Connecting cabins are featured in a range of categories. Six staterooms are wheelchair-accessible on *Statendam* and *Ryndam*; seven on *Maasdam*; and eight on *Veendam*. Nine cabins on each ship are modified with ramps although doors are standard width.

In the Know

In a fleetwide move, Holland American Line will ban smoking in all accommodations categories, though passengers can still light up on balconies.

Pros and Cons

Pros: When the Statendam-class ships emerged from extensive dry docks with more balcony cabins, Spa staterooms, a new Lanai stateroom category with direct access to the walk-around promenade deck, and The Retreat, a resort-style pool area on the aft Lido Deck. Popular with the after-dinner crowd, yet quiet enough for conversation, the Ocean Bar hits just the right balance for late-night socializing.

Cons: Try to make it to the production shows in time to grab seats on the lower level of the main show lounges—railings on the balcony level obstruct the view. Club HAL may not be too kid-friendly if your cruise is primarily booked by older passengers. The popular—and free—Java coffee bars have been eliminated.

Cabin Type	Size (sq. ft.)
Penthouse Suite	1,159
Deluxe Verandah Suite	556
Verandah Suite	292
Lanai	197
Ocean View	197
Inside	182

Dimensions include the square footage for balconies

FAST FACTS

- 10 passenger decks
- Specialty restaurant, dining room, buffet
- Wi-Fi, safe, minibar, refrigerator, DVD
- 2 pools (1 indoor), 2 children's pools
- Fitness classes, gym, hair salon, 2 hot tubs, sauna, spa, steam room
- 9 bars, casino, cinema, dance club, library, showroom, video game room
- Children's programs (ages 3–17)
- Dry-cleaning, laundry facilities, laundry service
- Internet terminal
- No-smoking cabins

5

HOLLAND AMERICA

Share a sunset

MSC CRUISES

More widely known as one of the world's largest cargo shipping companies, MSC has operated cruises with an eclectic fleet since the late 1980s. When the line introduced two graceful, medium-size ships in 2003 and 2004, it ushered in an era of new ship-

Pool deck after dark

building that has seen the fleet grow faster than any other European cruise line. This line is growing into a major player in both Europe and the Caribbean

✉ *6750 N. Andrews Ave., Fort Lauderdale, FL*

☎ *800/666–9333*

⊕ *www.msccruisesusa. com*

☞ *Cruise Style: Premium.*

MSC blankets the Mediterranean nearly year-round with a dizzying selection of cruise itineraries that allow a lot of time in ports of call and include few if any sea days. In summer months, several ships sail off to northern Europe to ply the Baltic. Itineraries planned for repositioning sailings visit some intriguing, off-the-beaten-track ports of call that other cruise lines bypass.

No glitz, no clutter—just elegant simplicity—is the standard of MSC's seaworthy interior decor. Extensive use of marble, brass, and wood reflects the best of Italian styling and design; clean lines and bold colors set their modern sophisticated tone.

MSC adopts some activities that appeal to American passengers without abandoning those preferred by Europeans (you should be prepared for announcements in Italian as well as English while on board). In addition to the guest lecturers, computer classes, and cooking lessons featured in the enrichment programs, Italian-language classes are a popular option. Nightly shows accentuate the cruise line's Mediterranean heritage; there might be a flamenco show in the main showroom and live music for listening and dancing in the smaller lounges, although the disco is a happening late-night spot.

MSC entertainment staff members shine offstage as well as in front of the spotlight. They seek out passengers traveling solo, who might be looking for activity or dance partners, so that they feel fully included in the cruise.

Regardless of the itinerary, be prepared for an Italian-influenced experience. Also expect to hear announcements in several languages.

Food

Dinner on MSC ships is a traditional multiple-course event centered on authentic Italian fare. Menus list Mediterranean regional specialties and classic favorites prepared from scratch. Some favorites include lamb-and-mushroom quiche (a Tuscan dish) and veal scaloppini with tomatoes and mozzarella (a recipe from Sorrento in Campania). Although food is still prepared the Italian way, in a nod to American tastes broiled chicken breast, grilled salmon, and Caesar salad are additions to the dinner menu that are always available. Healthy Choice and vegetarian items are offered as well as tempting sugar-free desserts. A highlight is the bread, freshly baked on board daily. Pizza served in the buffet is some of the best at sea. The nightly midnight buffet is a retro food feast missing from most of today's cruises. Room service is always available, though the options are somewhat limited.

Fitness and Recreation

Up-to-date exercise equipment, a jogging track, and basic fitness classes for all levels are available in the fitness centers.

Spa treatments include a variety of massages, body wraps, and facials that can be scheduled à la carte or combined in packages to encompass an afternoon or the entire cruise. The hottest hair-styling techniques and nail services are offered in the salons. Unlike most cruise lines, MSC Cruises operates its own spas.

Your Shipmates

Most passengers are couples in the 35- to 55-year-old range, as well as some family groups who prefer the international atmosphere prevalent on board. Although more than half the passengers on Caribbean itineraries are North Americans, expect a more international mix on European cruises, with North Americans in the minority.

5

MSC CRUISES

Top: Miniature golf is family fun
Bottom: *MSC Lirica*

Top: Thermal suite
Middle: Expansive pool deck
Bottom: *MSC Lirica* suite with balcony

Dress Code

Two formal nights are standard on seven-night cruises, and three may be scheduled on longer sailings. Men are encouraged to wear dark suits, but sport coats and ties are appropriate. All other evenings are casual, although jeans are discouraged in restaurants. It's requested that no shorts be worn in public areas after 6 pm.

Junior Cruisers

Children from ages 3 to 17 are welcome to participate in age-appropriate youth programs. The Mini Club is for ages 3 to 8, Junior Club for ages 9 to 12, and Teenage Club for youths 13 years and older. Counselors organize daily group activities such as arts and crafts, painting, treasure hunts, games, a mini-Olympics, and shows. Children under age three may use the playroom if accompanied at all times by an adult. Babysitting can be arranged for a fee once you're on board.

Service

Service can be inconsistent, yet it's more than acceptable, even if it's not overly gracious. The mainly Italian staff can seem befuddled by American habits and expectations. Ongoing training and improved English proficiency for staff are top priorities for MSC, and these weaknesses are showing improvement.

Tipping

Customary gratuities are added to your shipboard account in the amount of $12 per person per day for adults and half that amount for children. You can always adjust these amounts at the reception desk or even pay in cash, if you prefer. Automatic 15% gratuities are incorporated into all bar purchases. You may also reward staff in the spa and casino for exceptional service.

CHOOSE THIS LINE IF ...

You appreciate authentic Italian cooking. This is the real thing, not an Olive Garden clone.	You want your ship to look like a ship. MSC's vessels are very nautical in appearance.	You want the continental flair of a premium cruise at a fair price.

Past Passengers

After sailing on MSC Cruises once, you are eligible to join the MSC Club by completing the registration form found in your cabin or by writing to the club through the line's Web site. Membership benefits include discounts on your cruise fare for the best itineraries, travel cancellation insurance, shore excursions, and even onboard purchases. You will also receive *MSC Club News* magazine.

Membership levels are achieved on a point system determined by the number of cruises taken. Classic members have up to 21 points; Silver, between 22 and 42 points; Gold, 43 points and over. Silver and Gold members receive pins to commemorate their status.

GOOD TO KNOW

MSC Cruises has catered almost exclusively to Europeans since the company's founding, and the style and habits favored by North Americans can still seem somewhat foreign to them. For example, Europeans prefer to go out for coffee after dinner; Americans want to be served coffee with their dessert. Unfortunately, this culture clash can cause misunderstandings and some contentiousness. Little things like too-small water glasses and no iced tea can make Americans cranky. To eliminate these issues and broaden their appeal, staff members on board embrace cultural differences, and they try hard to please everyone.

5

MSC CRUISES

DON'T CHOOSE THIS LINE IF ...

Announcements in more than one language get on your nerves.

You aren't able to accept things that are not always done the American way.

You prefer myriad dining choices and casual attire. MSC cruises have assigned seating and observe a dress code.

MUSICA CLASS
MSC Musica, Orchestra, Poesia, Magnifica

CREW MEMBERS	987
ENTERED SERVICE	2006, 2007, 2008, 2010
GROSS TONS	92,400
LENGTH	964 feet
NUMBER OF CABINS	1,275, 1,275, 1,275, 1,259
PASSENGER CAPACITY	2,550, 2,550, 2,550, 2,518
WIDTH	106 feet

700 ft.

500 ft.

300 ft.

Top: *Orchestra* at sea
Bottom: *Musica* Theater

Public Areas and Facilities

MSC Cruises took a giant leap into mainstream cruising with the introduction of this large and entirely new ship class. Highlights of the Musica-class design are a three-deck central foyer, where a piano is suspended on a transparent floor, à la carte restaurants, large-screen outdoor cinemas, and, on *MSC Magnifica*, a covered outdoor pool with retractable roof.

Italian culture prevails throughout, and serves as an important part of the entire cruise experience. Interiors are a blend of art deco and art nouveau themes as well as the authentic Italian designs for which other MSC Cruises ships are known. The extensive use of various colored marbles adds a luxurious quality to public spaces. In addition to its soothing Zen garden and Oriental music, the sushi bar is a bonus to the dining experience.

Restaurants

Two formal restaurants serve Mediterranean- and Italian-accented cuisine in traditional early and late assigned seatings; one restaurant also offers sit-down breakfast and lunch in open seating. Two adjoining buffet restaurants, which during the day seem like a single dining area with long serving counters, are casual dining options for breakfast and lunch. At night, the aft buffet restaurant is reserved for seated dining with a steak-house menu and tables set with linens for an extra charge; the forward buffet restaurant serves pizza. The à la carte Asian and sushi specialty restaurants require reservations and also carry an additional charge. Room service is limited to a menu that includes a continental breakfast and cold sandwiches. Midnight buffets vary nightly, ranging from themed snack-type offerings to a traditional shipboard gala affair.

Accommodations

Cabins: A whopping 80% of staterooms have an ocean view, and 65% have balconies. Superior balcony staterooms are considerably roomier than standard staterooms with a balcony. Beautifully decorated in jewel-tone colors, all are comfortable yet somewhat smaller than the average cabins found on the new ships of other cruise lines. All cabins are furnished with two twin beds that can be combined to create a king, a vanity-desk, TV, adequate closet and storage space, small refrigerator, hair dryer, and have a broadband connection for a laptop.

Suites: Suites, which compare to minisuites on most cruise ships, feature a combination tub–shower in the bathroom, a walk-in closet, plenty of storage, and a sitting area.

Amenities: Bathrooms are supplied with MSC Cruises' own brand of shampoo, bath gel, and soaps, plus a handy sewing repair kit.

Worth Noting: Seventeen cabins that measure 226 square feet are wheelchair-accessible, except on *MSC Magnifica*, which has 16.

In the Know

You might notice an abundance of families and particularly children on your MSC sailing, especially during holiday periods and spring break. Unlike most cruise lines, which might offer seasonal family deals, kids 17 and under sail free on all MSC Cruises' ships.

Pros and Cons

Pros: There's a walking track high atop the ship, but a better bet on windy or wet days is the little-used covered promenade on deck 7. Private gaming rooms for serious gamblers add Las Vegas–style glamour to the casinos. These are "Clean Air" ships, and smoking is allowed only in the casino, the cigar smoking room, one dedicated lounge, and outside on one side of Sun Deck.

Cons: Those who dread announcements in several languages will be pleased to find they are kept to a minimum, except for the boat drill, which can seem endless. After paying extra for specialty coffees and ice cream, you may feel nickel-and-dimed to death. Some in-cabin TV programming might be considered too "adult" for family viewing.

Cabin Type	Size (sq. ft.)
Suites	269
Superior Ocean-View Balcony	191
Ocean-View Balcony	161
Ocean View	183
Inside	151

FAST FACTS

- 12 passenger decks
- Specialty restaurant, 2 dining rooms, 2 buffets, ice cream parlor, pizzeria
- Internet, Wi-Fi, safe, refrigerator
- 2 pools (1 indoor *MSC Magnifica* only), children's pool
- Fitness classes, gym, hair salon, 7 hot tubs, sauna, spa, steam room
- 9 bars, casino, dance club, library, showroom, video game room
- Children's programs (ages 3–17)
- Laundry service
- Internet terminal
- No-smoking cabins

5

MSC CRUISES

NORWEGIAN CRUISE LINE

Norwegian Cruise Line (NCL) set sail in 1966 with an entirely new concept: regularly scheduled Caribbean cruises from the then-obscure port of Miami. Good food and friendly service combined with value fares established NCL as a winner for active adults

Le Cirque–style extravaganza on Norwegian Cruise Line

and families. With the introduction of the now-retired SS *Norway* in 1979, NCL ushered in the era of cruises on megasize ships. Innovative and forward-looking, NCL has been a cruise-industry leader for four decades, and is as much at home in Europe as it is in the Caribbean.

✉ *7665 Corporate Center Dr., Miami, FL*

☎ *305/436–4000 or 800/327–7030*

⊕ *www.ncl.com*

☞ *Cruise Style: Mainstream.*

Noted for top-quality, high-energy entertainment and emphasis on fitness facilities and programs, NCL combines action, activities, and a variety of dining options in a casual, free-flowing atmosphere. Freestyle cruising has meant an end to rigid dining schedules and dress codes. NCL ships now offer a host of flexible dining options that allow passengers to eat in the main dining rooms or any of a number of à la carte and specialty restaurants at any time and with whom they please. Now co-owned by Genting Hong Kong Limited and Apollo Management, a private equity company, NCL continues to be an industry innovator.

More high jinks than high-brow, entertainment after dark features extravagant Las Vegas–style revues presented in main show lounges by lavishly costumed singers and dancers. Other performers might include comedians, magicians, jugglers, and acrobats. Passengers can get into the act by taking part in talent shows or step up to the karaoke microphone. Live bands play for dancing and listening passengers in smaller lounges, and each ship has a lively disco. Some ships include shows by Chicago's world-famous Second City improvisational comedy company. With the launch of

Norwegian Epic in 2010, the Blue Man Group and Cirque Productions (a U.S.-based company somewhat similar in style to Cirque du Soleil) join NCL's talent line-up.

Casinos, bingo sessions, and art auctions are well attended. Adult games, particularly the competitive ones, are fun to participate in and provide laughs for audience members. Goofy pool games are an NCL staple, and the ships' bands crank up the volume during afternoon and evening deck parties.

From a distance, most cruise ships look so similar that it's often difficult to tell them apart, but NCL's largest, modern ships stand out with their distinctive use of hull art. Each new ship is distinguished by murals extending from bow to midship.

When others scoffed at winter cruises to the Caribbean, Bahamas, and Florida from New York City, NCL recognized the demand and has sailed with such success that others have followed in its wake. A Winter Weather Guarantee is offered should foul weather threaten to spoil your vacation plans. If departure from New York is delayed for more than 12 hours due to weather, you will receive an onboard credit of $100 per person on your current departure, or, if you decide to cancel your cruise, you will receive a cruise credit equal to the amount you paid to use on a future NCL cruise within one year and any reasonable incidental expenses you incur in rearranging your travel plans.

Food

Main dining rooms serve what is traditionally deemed continental fare, although it's about what you would expect at a really good hotel banquet. Health-conscious menu selections are nicely prepared, and vegetarian choices are always available. Where NCL really shines is the specialty restaurants, especially the French-Mediterranean Le Bistro (on all ships), the pan-Asian restaurants, and steak houses (on the newer ships). As a rule of thumb, the newer the ship, the wider the variety, because new ships were purpose-built with as many as 10 or more places to eat. You may find Spanish tapas, an Italian trattoria, a steak house, and a pan-Asian restaurant complete with a sushi and sashimi bar and teppanyaki room. Almost all carry a cover charge or are priced à la carte and require reservations. An NCL staple, the late-night Chocoholic Buffet continues to be a favorite event.

5

NORWEGIAN CRUISE LINE

Top: Casual Freestyle dining
Bottom: *Norwegian Jewel* spa relaxation suite

Top: Casino play
Middle: Stay connected to the Internet
Bottom: *Norwegian Dream* superior Ocean View stateroom

Fitness and Recreation

Mandara Spa offers unique and exotic spa treatments fleet-wide on NCL, although facilities vary widely. Spa treatments include a long menu of massages, body wraps, and facials, and current trends in hair and nail services are offered in the salons. The latest addition on board is a medi-spa physician, who can create individualized treatment plans using nonsurgical treatments such as Botox Cosmetic. State-of-the-art exercise equipment, jogging tracks, and basic fitness classes are available at no charge. There's a fee for personal training, body composition analysis, and specialized classes such as yoga and Pilates.

Your Shipmates

NCL's mostly American cruise passengers are active couples ranging from their mid-thirties to mid-fifties. Many families enjoy cruising on NCL ships during holidays and summer months. Longer cruises and more exotic itineraries attract passengers in the over 55 age group.

Dress Code

Resort casual attire is appropriate at all times; the option of one formal evening is available on all cruises of seven nights and longer. Most passengers actually raise the casual dress code a notch to what could be called casual chic attire.

Junior Cruisers

For children and teens, each NCL vessel offers a Kid's Crew program of supervised entertainment for young cruisers ages 2 to 17. Younger children are split into three groups, ages 2 to 5, 6 to 9, and 10 to 12; activities range from storytelling, games, and arts and crafts to dinner with counselors, pajama parties, and treasure hunts.

Group Port Play is available in the children's area to accommodate parents booked on shore excursions. Evening babysitting services are available for a fee. Parents whose children are not toilet trained are issued a beeper to alert them when diaper changing is necessary. Children under two cruise at a reduced fare, and certain itineraries offer specials on third and fourth guests

CHOOSE THIS LINE IF ...

Doing your own thing is your idea of a real vacation. You could almost remove your watch and just go with the flow.

You want to leave your formal dress-up wardrobe at home.

You're competitive. There's always a pickup game in progress on the sports courts.

in the same stateroom. Infants under six months of age cannot travel on NCL ships.

For teens ages 13 to 17, options include sports, pool parties, teen disco, movies, and video games. Some ships have their own cool clubs where teens hang out in adult-free zones.

Service

Somewhat inconsistent, service is nonetheless congenial. Although crew members tended to be outgoing Caribbean islanders in the past; they have largely been replaced by Asians and Eastern Europeans who are well trained yet are inclined to be more reserved.

Tipping

A fixed service charge of $12 per person per day is added to shipboard accounts. An automatic 15% gratuity is added to bar tabs. Staff members may also accept cash gratuities. Passengers in suites who have access to concierge and butler services are asked to offer a cash gratuity at their own discretion.

Past Passengers

Upon completion of your first NCL cruise you're automatically enrolled in Latitudes, the club for repeat passengers. Membership benefits accrue based on the number of cruises completed: Bronze (1 through 4), Silver (5 through 8), Gold (9 through 13), and Platinum (14 or more). Everyone receives *Latitudes*, NCL's online magazine, Latitudes pricing, Latitudes check-in at the pier, a ship pin, access to a special customer service desk and liaison on board, and a members-only cocktail party hosted by the captain. Higher tiers receive a complimentary dinner in Le Bistro, complementary laundry service, priority restaurant reservations, and priority for check-in, tender tickets, and disembarkation.

GOOD TO KNOW

When considering an NCL cruise, keep in mind that the ships weren't cut from a cookie-cutter mold and they differ widely in size and detail. Although all are brightly appointed and attempt to offer a comparable experience, the oldest ships just don't have quite the panache or as many freestyle dining venues as are found on the newer, purpose-built ships. On the plus side, the newest vessels have many options for families, including large numbers of interconnecting staterooms that make them ideal for even supersize clans. NCL has one of the newest fleets at sea.

5

NORWEGIAN CRUISE LINE

DON'T CHOOSE THIS LINE IF ...

You don't like to pay extra for food on a ship. All the best specialty restaurants have extra charges.

You don't want to stand in line. There are lines for nearly everything.

You don't want to hear announcements. They're frequent on these ships—and loud.

NORWEGIAN EPIC

CREW MEMBERS	1,708
ENTERED SERVICE	2010
GROSS TONS	153,000
LENGTH	1,081 feet
NUMBER OF CABINS	2,114
PASSENGER CAPACITY	4,100
WIDTH	133 feet

700 ft.

500 ft.

300 ft.

Public Areas and Facilities

While NCL's largest and newest ship has a unique new cabin design and more than 20 places to dine, the entertainment is a highlight with such celebrated acts as Blue Man Group, Howl at the Moon (a dueling pianos show), the Second City improv ensemble, Legends in Concert, and a one-of-a- kind interactive theatrical dining experience with Cirque-style performers. For the kids, there are Nickelodeon characters onboard and a character breakfast. There's an extra charge for the Cirque dinner show and the character breakfast.

Also epic are the numerous bars and lounges. For the coolest drinks at sea, *Norwegian Epic* has an ice bar—the only one on a cruise ship. The spa features a thermal suites (for which there is a charge), and expansive areas are reserved for children and teens. Pools have three waterslides and a plethora of lounge chairs. For the best view of the sea, there is a rock-climbing wall.

Restaurants

Two main complimentary dining rooms serve breakfast, lunch, and dinner. Specialty restaurants, including French restaurant Le Bistro, Cagney's Steakhouse, a Chinese restaurant, sushi bar, teppanyaki room, a Brazilian churrascaria, and an Italian trattoria–style restaurant carry varying cover charges and require reservations. Screens located throughout the ship show the waiting time you can expect for each restaurant. Casual choices are the Lido Buffet for breakfast, lunch, and dinner; O'Sheehan's Pub for soup, sandwiches, and snacks; and the poolside grill for lunch. The Atrium Bar serves specialty coffees for an additional charge. While the 24-hour room-service menu is limited, made-to-order pizza will be delivered to you anywhere on the ship for a charge.

Accommodations

Cabins: The ship's "New Wave"–style staterooms have curved walls and a unique bathroom with toilet and shower in separate compartments and the sink in the main cabin area. All have a sitting area with sofa and table and exceedingly generous storage. All outside staterooms have a balcony. Several "Spa" accommodations categories have Zen-like appointments and key card access to the spa facilities.

Top: *Epic* Casino
Bottom: *Epic* Courtyard
Penthouse

Courtyard Villas and Penthouses: Courtyard Villas and Penthouses and Owner's Suites have an exclusive concierge lounge and restaurant in addition to a shared private courtyard with pool, hot tub, sundeck, and small gym.

Studios: Originally designed to sleep two on a budget, studios are strictly for solo cruisers. Although the inside cabin is tiny, its occupants have access to the Studio Lounge, a shared lounge for hanging out.

Amenities: A small refrigerator, tea/coffeemaker, safe, broadband Internet connection, duvets on beds, a wall-mounted hair dryer, and bathrobes are standard. Showers have a shampoo/bath-gel dispenser on the wall. Suites have a whirlpool tub, an entertainment center with a CD/DVD player, and concierge and butler service.

Worth Noting: Some staterooms interconnect in most categories. Forty-two staterooms are wheelchair-accessible.

In the Know

You would spend a fortune on tickets alone in Las Vegas or New York City to see the entertainment that is available on *Norwegian Epic* at no additional charge.

Pros and Cons

Pros: Advance reservations can be made online for the restaurants and shows. The ice bar is the coolest lounge at sea, and the admission charge includes two vodka drinks for adults, or juice drinks for the younger set. For thrill seekers, *Norwegian Epic* the first ever rappelling wall at sea and a 33-foot high extreme rock-climbing wall.

Cons: The jury is still out on the bathrooms in the "New Wave" staterooms—with their frosted shower and toilet compartments, privacy can be an issue. The necessity of reservations for dining and reserving seats for the headline shows takes some of the spontaneity out of the "freestyle" concept. Swimming pools are great for splashing about and cooling off, but not adequate for such a large ship.

Cabin Type	Size (sq. ft.)
Owner's Suite/ Courtyard Villa	852/506
Penthouse	322
Deluxe Balcony	245
Ocean View with Balcony	216
Inside	128
Studio	100

Square footage includes balconies

FAST FACTS

- 19 passenger decks

- 8 restaurants, 2 dining rooms, buffet, ice cream parlor, pizzeria

- Internet, WI-FI, safe, refrigerator, DVD (some)

- 3 pools, children's pool

- Fitness classes, gym, hair salon, 5 hot tubs, spa

- 10 bars, casino, dance club, library, 3 showrooms, video game room

- Children's programs (ages 2–17)

- Dry-cleaning, laundry service

- Internet terminal

Epic at sea

5

NORWEGIAN CRUISE LINE

DAWN CLASS
Norwegian Star, Norwegian Dawn

CREW MEMBERS	1,066, 1,065
ENTERED SERVICE	2001, 2002
GROSS TONS	91,740, 92, 250
LENGTH	965 feet
NUMBER OF CABINS	1,174, 1,184
PASSENGER CAPACITY	2,348, 2,368 (2,683 max)
WIDTH	105 feet

700 ft.
500 ft.
300 ft.

Public Areas and Facilities
Purpose-built for NCL's Freestyle cruising concept, *Norwegian Dawn* and *Norwegian Star* each have more than a dozen dining options, a variety of entertainment selections, expansive facilities for children and teens, and enormous spas with indoor lap pools. In what might be termed a supersize "thermal suite" on other ships, the spa areas feature indoor lap pools surrounded by lounge chairs, large whirlpools, saunas, and steam rooms, and, unfortunately, there is an additional charge to use it.

These ships unveiled NCL's superdeluxe Garden Villa accommodations, English pubs, and 24-hour dining in the Blue Lagoon Restaurant. Interior spaces are bright and cheerful, especially the atrium area adjacent to the outdoor promenade, which is flooded with sunlight through expansive windows. A second smaller garden atrium with a prominent waterfall leads the way to the spa lobby. Near the children's splash pool is a hot tub for parents' enjoyment.

Restaurants
Two complimentary dining rooms serve open seating meals for breakfast, lunch, or dinner. Specialty restaurants, including NCL's signature French restaurant Le Bistro, Cagney's Steakhouse, an Asian restaurant, sushi bar, teppanyaki room, Tex-Mex eatery (*Norwegian Star*) or Brazilian churrascaria (*Norwegian Dawn*), and Italian restaurant carry varying cover charges and require reservations. Screens located throughout the ship illustrate the status (full, moderately busy, empty) and waiting time you can expect for each restaurant on board. Casual choices are the Lido Buffet for breakfast, lunch, and dinner; Blue Lagoon for soup, sandwiches, and snacks around the clock; and the poolside grill for lunch. Java Café serves specialty coffees and pastries for an extra charge. Although the 24-hour room service menu is somewhat limited, suite occupants may order from any restaurant on the ship.

Accommodations
Cabins: NCL ships are not noted for large staterooms, but all have a small sitting area with sofa, chair, and table. Most bathrooms are compartmentalized with a sink area, shower, and toilet separated by sliding glass

Top: Cagney's Steakhouse on *Norwegian Dawn*
Bottom: Minisuite

doors. Every cabin has adequate closet and drawer/shelf storage, as well as limited bathroom storage. Suites have walk-in closets.

Amenities: Cherrywood cabinetry, tropical decor, mirrored accents, a small refrigerator, tea/coffeemaker, personal safe, broadband Internet connection, duvets on beds, a wall-mounted hair dryer over the dressing table, and bathrobes for use during the cruise are standard. Bathrooms have a shampoo/bath-gel dispenser mounted on the shower wall as well as a magnifying mirror. Suites have a whirlpool tub, an entertainment center with a CD/DVD player, and concierge and butler service.

Worth Noting: Family-friendly staterooms interconnect in most categories, enabling families of nearly any size to find suitable accommodations. Nearly every stateroom has a third or fourth berth, and some can sleep as many as five and six. Twenty-four staterooms on *Norwegian Dawn* and 20 staterooms on *Norwegian Star* are designed for wheelchair accessibility.

In the Know

Artwork plays a major role in brightening the interiors of both vessels, but *Norwegian Dawn* has a priceless collection of original pop art, featuring original signed works by Andy Warhol, and oil paintings by Impressionists Matisse, Renoir, and Monet.

Pros and Cons

Pros: Reminiscent of European opera houses, the showrooms are grand settings for the lavish production shows and have full proscenium stages. Other ships might have comedy shows, but on these you can look forward to performances by Second City, Chicago's incomparable improvisation artists, with shows in the theater as well as in more intimate nightclub settings. Three-bedroom Garden Villas are among the largest suites at sea, with private whirlpools and outdoor patios for alfresco dining.

Cons: Freestyle dining doesn't mean you can get a table in the main dining rooms at precisely the moment you want, but waiting time can be lessened by timing your arrival at nonpeak periods. Don't stop to smell the banks of flowers in the lobby—they are unabashedly fake. Overcrowding can be a problem in the buffet, popular bars, and around the Lido pools when the ships are booked to their maximum capacity.

Cabin Type	Size (sq. ft.)
Garden Villa	5,350
Owner's Suite	750
Penthouse Suite	366
Romance Suite	288
Family Suite	408–574
Minisuite	229
Ocean View with Balcony	166
Ocean View	158
Inside	142

FAST FACTS

- 11 passenger decks
- 7 restaurants, 2 dining rooms, buffet, ice cream parlor, pizzeria
- Internet, Wi-Fi, safe, refrigerator, DVD (some)
- 2 pools (1 indoor), children's pool
- Fitness classes, gym, hair salon, 6 hot tubs, sauna, spa, steam room
- 9 bars, casino, dance club, library, showroom, video game room
- Children's programs (ages 2–17)
- Dry-cleaning, laundry service
- Internet terminal

Norwegian Dawn at sea

5

NORWEGIAN CRUISE LINE

JEWEL CLASS
Norwegian Jewel, Norwegian Jade, Norwegian Pearl, Norwegian Gem

CREW MEMBERS	1,081, 1,075, 1,084, 1,092
ENTERED SERVICE	2005, 2006, 2006, 2007
GROSS TONS	93,502, 93,558, 93,530, 93,530
LENGTH	965 feet
NUMBER OF CABINS	1,188, 1,201, 1,197, 1,197
PASSENGER CAPACITY	2,376, 2,402, 2,394, 2,394
WIDTH	105 feet

700 ft.

500 ft.

300 ft.

Top: *Norwegian Jewel's* Azura restaurant
Bottom: Hydropool in the spa

Public Areas and Facilities

Jewel-class ships were conceived as the next step in the continuing evolution of Freestyle ship design: the interior location of some public rooms and restaurants has been tweaked since the introduction of Freestyle cruising vessels, and new categories of deluxe accommodations have been added.

These ships have more than a dozen dining alternatives, a variety of entertainment options, enormous spas with thermal suites (for which there is a charge), and expansive areas reserved for children and teens. Pools have waterslides and a plethora of lounge chairs, although when your ship is full it can be difficult to find one in a prime location. *Norwegian Pearl* and *Norwegian Gem* introduced the line's first rock-climbing walls, as well as Bliss Lounge, which has trendy South Beach decor, and the first full-size 10-pin bowling alleys on modern cruise ships.

Restaurants

Two main complimentary dining rooms serve open seating breakfast, lunch, and dinner. Specialty restaurants, including NCL's signature French restaurant Le Bistro, Cagney's Steakhouse, an Asian restaurant, sushi bar, teppanyaki room, tapas and salsa eatery, and an Italian trattoria–style restaurant carry varying cover charges and require reservations. Screens located throughout the ship illustrate the status (full, moderately busy, empty) and waiting time you can expect for each restaurant on board. Casual choices are the Lido Buffet for breakfast, lunch, and dinner; Blue Lagoon for soup, sandwiches, and snacks around the clock; and the poolside grill for lunch. Java Café serves specialty coffees and pastries for an additional charge. Although the 24-hour room service menu is somewhat limited, suite occupants may order from any restaurant on the ship.

Accommodations

Cabins: NCL ships are not noted for large staterooms, but all have a small sitting area with sofa, chair, and table. Every cabin has adequate closet and drawer/shelf storage, as well as limited bathroom storage. Suites have walk-in closets.

Garden and Courtyard Villas: Garden Villas, with three bedrooms, a living-dining room, and private deck garden with a spa tub, are among the largest suites at sea. Courtyard Villas—not as large as Garden Villas—nevertheless have an exclusive concierge lounge and a shared private courtyard with pool, hot tub, sundeck, and small gym.

Amenities: A small refrigerator, tea/coffeemaker, personal safe, broadband Internet connection, duvets on beds, a wall-mounted hair dryer, and bathrobes are standard. Bathrooms have a shampoo/bath-gel dispenser on the shower wall and a magnifying mirror. Suites have a whirlpool tub, an entertainment center with a CD/DVD player, and concierge and butler service.

Worth Noting: Some staterooms interconnect in most categories. Twenty-seven staterooms are wheelchair-accessible.

In the Know
You may feel you've slipped into wonderland when you first encounter some of the fanciful furniture in the lounges aboard each ship and in Bliss Ultra Lounge on *Norwegian Pearl* and *Norwegian Gem*. Some are covered in wildly colorful velvets and are designed as thrones and even lounging beds.

Pros and Cons
Pros: Performances by Second City, Chicago's famous improvisation artists, are scheduled in the theater as well as in more intimate nightclub settings. Escape the crowds in the ship's tranquil library, which is also a good spot to gaze at the sea if your book proves to be less than compelling. With access to a private courtyard pool, hot tub, steam room, exercise area, and sundeck, Courtyard Villa accommodations are like a ship within a ship.

Cons: The thermal suites in the spa have large whirlpools, saunas, steam rooms, and a relaxation area with loungers facing the sea, but there is an additional charge to use the facility. "Freestyle" dining doesn't mean you can get a table in the main dining rooms at precisely the moment you want, but waiting times can be reduced if you time your arrival at nonpeak periods. For such a large ship, the Internet center is tiny.

Cabin Type	Size (sq. ft.)
Garden Villa	4,390
Courtyard Villa	574
Owner's Suites	823
Deluxe Owners Suites*	928*
Penthouse Suite	575
Minisuite	284
Ocean View with Balcony	205–243
Ocean View	161
Inside	143

*Deluxe Owner's Suites on *Norwegian Pearl* and *Norwegian Gem* only.

FAST FACTS

- 15 passenger decks
- 7 restaurants, 2 dining rooms, buffet, ice cream parlor, pizzeria
- Internet, Wi-Fi, safe, refrigerator, DVD (some)
- 2 pools, children's pool
- Fitness classes, gym, hair salon, 6 hot tubs, spa, steam room
- 9 bars, casino, cinema, dance club, library, showroom, video game room
- Children's programs (ages 2–17)
- Dry-cleaning, laundry service
- Internet terminal

The sports deck

NORWEGIAN SKY, NORWEGIAN SUN

CREW MEMBERS	917, 916
ENTERED SERVICE	1999, 2001
GROSS TONS	77,104, 78,309
LENGTH	853 feet
NUMBER OF CABINS	1,001, 968
PASSENGER CAPACITY	2,002, 1,936
WIDTH	105 feet

700 ft.
500 ft.
300 ft.

Public Areas and Facilities

Norwegian Cruise Line hadn't introduced many new ships in awhile at the time *Norwegian Sky* was launched and *Norwegian Sun* was on the drawing board, but it didn't take long before they got the hang of it. With Freestyle cruising growing in popularity, the vessels moved into the forefront of the fleet with multiple restaurant choices, expansive casino, trendy spas, and more family- and kid-friendly facilities.

Rich wood tones and fabric colors prevail throughout. The Observation Lounge is a subdued spot for afternoon tea in a light, tropical setting with nothing to distract attention from the expansive views beyond the floor-to-ceiling windows.

The Internet café is large, and the nearby coffee bar is a delight. Sunshine pours into the atrium through an overhead skylight by day; at night it's the ship's glamorous hub of activity.

Restaurants

Two complimentary dining rooms serve open seating breakfast, lunch, and dinner. Specialty restaurants on both ships that carry varying cover charges and require reservations include NCL's signature French restaurant Le Bistro, steak houses, and Italian eateries; *Norwegian Sun* also has an extra-charge Brazilian Churrascaria, Japanese restaurant, sushi bar, and teppanyaki room, and a complimentary tapas bar. Screens located throughout the ship illustrate the status (full to empty) and waiting time you can expect for each restaurant. Casual choices are the Lido Buffet for breakfast, lunch, and dinner; the poolside grill for lunch; a pizzeria; and an ice cream bar. A coffee bar serves specialty coffees and pastries priced by item. Room service is available 24 hours from a somewhat limited menu.

Accommodations

Cabins: Staterooms are a bit more generous in size than on the previous vessels in the NCL fleet and contain adequate closet and drawer space for a one-week cruise. More than two-thirds have an ocean view, and nearly two-thirds of those have a private balcony. All have a sitting area with sofa, chair, and table. Clever use of primary colors and strategically placed mirrors achieves an open feeling.

Top: Las Ramblas Tapas Bar & Restaurant
Bottom: *Norwegian Sun* at sea

Suites: Suites have walk-in closets as well as whirlpool tubs and entertainment centers. Butlers and a concierge are at the service of suite occupants.

Amenities: Light-wood cabinetry, mirrored accents, a small refrigerator, a tea/coffeemaker, a personal safe, broadband Internet connections, duvets on beds, a wall-mounted hair dryer over the dressing table, and bathrobes for use during the cruise are typical standard amenities. Bathrooms have shampoo and bath gel in shower-mounted dispensers, as well as limited storage.

Worth Noting: Connecting staterooms are available in several categories, including those with balconies. Oddly sandwiched in between decks 6 and 7 forward is deck 6A, which has no direct elevator access. Sixteen cabins are wheelchair accessible.

In the Know

For newlyweds and couples celebrating a second honeymoon, an elegant honeymoon/anniversary romance suite is a luxurious hideaway for two.

Pros and Cons

Pros: Although not the newest ships in the NCL fleet, both have been renovated to add many of the elements found in Dawn- and Jewel-class vessels. For live broadcasts of sporting events and meals and snacks from the nearby buffet, head to the Sports Bar. *Norwegian Sun* has steam rooms and saunas for men and women.

Cons: Plot your course carefully if you plan to dine in the aft main restaurant—a huge galley separates it from the mid-ship restaurant, and you can't get there on a direct route from the atrium. These are sister ships but not twins, and dining facilities vary widely. Standard accommodations are somewhat tight for more than two people on these ships, as is storage space.

Cabin Type	Size (sq. ft.)
Owner's Suite	828
Penthouse and Romance Suite	504
Minisuite	332
Ocean View Balcony	221
Ocean View	145
Deluxe Interior	172
Interior	145

FAST FACTS

- 11 passenger decks
- 4 specialty restaurants, 2 dining rooms, buffet, ice cream parlor, pizzeria
- Wi-Fi, safe, refrigerator (some), DVD (some)
- 2 pools, children's pool
- Fitness classes, gym, hair salon, 5 hot tubs, spa, sauna and steam room (*Norwegian Sun* only)
- 8 bars, casino, dance club, library, showroom, video game room
- Children's programs (ages 2–17)
- Dry-cleaning, laundry service
- Internet terminal

Balcony stateroom

5

NORWEGIAN CRUISE LINE

OCEANIA CRUISES

This distinctive cruise line was founded by Frank Del Rio and Joe Watters, cruise-industry veterans with the know-how to satisfy the wants of inquisitive passengers. By offering itineraries to interesting ports of call and upscale touches—all for fares much lower

Oceania's *Regatta*

than you would expect—they are succeeding quite nicely. Oceania Cruises set sail in 2003 to carve a unique, almost boutique niche in the cruise industry by obtaining midsize R-class ships that formerly made up the popular Renaissance Cruises fleet. The line is now owned by Prestige Cruise Holdings.

✉ *8300 N.W. 33rd St., Suite 308, Miami, FL*

☎ *305/514–2300 or 800/531–5658*

⊕ *www.oceaniacruises. com*

☞ *Cruise Style: Premium.*

Intimate and cozy public spaces reflect the importance of socializing on Oceania ships. Indoor lounges feature numerous conversation areas, and even the pool deck is a social center, where a shaded slice of deck is adjacent to the pool and hot tubs. Defined by billowing drapes and carpeting underfoot, it is furnished with plush sofas and chairs ideal for relaxation. Evening entertainment leans toward light cabaret, solo artists, music for dancing, and conversation with fellow passengers; however, you'll find lively karaoke sessions on the schedule as well. The sophisticated, adult atmosphere on days at sea is enhanced by a combo performing jazz or easy-listening melodies poolside.

Thickly padded single and double loungers are arranged around the pools, but if more privacy appeals to you, private cabanas are available for rent on the smaller ships. Each one has a double chaise longue with a view of the sea; overhead drapery can be drawn back for sunbathing, and the side panels can be left open or closed. Waiters are on standby to offer chilled towels or serve occupants with beverages or snacks. In addition, you can request a spa service in your cabana.

Varied, destination-rich itineraries are an important characteristic of Oceania Cruises, and most sailings are in the 10- to 12-night range. Before arrival in ports of call, lectures are presented on the historical background, culture, and traditions of the islands.

Culinary demonstrations by guest presenters and Oceania's own executive chefs are extremely popular. Lectures on varied topics, computer courses, hands-on arts and crafts classes, and wine or champagne seminars round out the popular enrichment series on board.

Food

Several top cruise-industry chefs were lured away from other cruise lines to ensure that the artistry of world-renowned master chef Jacques Pépin, who crafted five-star menus for Oceania, is properly carried out. The results are sure to please the most discriminating palate. Oceania simply serves some of the best food at sea, particularly impressive for a cruise line that charges far less than luxury rates. The main restaurant offers trendy, French-continental cuisine with an always-on-the-menu steak, seafood, or poultry choice and a vegetarian option.

Intimate specialty restaurants require reservations, but there's no additional charge for Toscana, the Italian restaurant, or Polo Grill, the steak house. On *Marina*, passengers have those and more restaurants from which to choose—Jacques , the first restaurant to bear Jacques Pépin's name, serves French cuisine; Red Ginger features contemporary interpretations of Asian classics; Privée hosts private, seven-course menu degustation dinners for a single party of up to ten; and La Reserve serves exclusive wine and food pairings.

A casual dinner option is Tapas on the Terrace, alfresco dining at the Terrace Café (the daytime Lido Deck buffet). Although service is from the buffet, outdoor seating on the aft deck is transformed into a charming Spanish courtyard with Catalonian-style candleholders and starched linens.

The Terrace Café also serves breakfast and lunch buffet-style, and has a small pizzeria window that operates during the day. At an outdoor poolside grill you can order up burgers, hot dogs, and sandwiches for lunch and then take a seat; waiters are at hand to serve you either at a nearby table or your lounge chair by the pool. Afternoon tea is a decadent spread of finger foods and includes a rolling dessert cart, which has to be seen to be believed.

5

OCEANIA CRUISES

Top: Penthouse Suite
Bottom: Toscana Restaurant

Top: Cocktails before dinner
Middle: Veranda stateroom
Bottom: Martini's Lounge

Fitness and Recreation

Although small on the fleet's original ships, the Canyon Ranch SpaClub spas and salons and well-equipped fitness centers are adequate for the number of passengers on board. Larger and more luxurious spas have been added to the new ships. In addition to individual body-toning machines and complimentary exercise classes, there's a walking-jogging track circling the top of the ship. A personal trainer is available for individual instruction for an additional charge.

Your Shipmates

Oceania Cruises appeal to singles and couples from their late-thirties to well-traveled retirees who have the time for and prefer longer cruises. Most are American couples attracted to the casually sophisticated atmosphere, creative cuisine, and high level of service. Many are past passengers of the now-defunct Renaissance Cruises who are loyal to their favorite ships, which now offer a variety of destination-rich itineraries.

Dress Code

Leave the formal wear at home—attire on Oceania ships is country-club casual every evening, although some guests can't help dressing up to dine in the beautifully appointed restaurants. A jacket and tie are never required for dinner, but many men wear sport jackets, as they would to dine in an upscale restaurant ashore. Jeans, shorts, T-shirts, and tennis shoes are discouraged after 6 pm in public rooms.

Junior Cruisers

Oceania Cruises are adult-oriented and not a good choice for families, particularly those traveling with infants and toddlers. No dedicated children's facilities are available, and parents are completely responsible for their behavior and entertainment. Teenagers with sophisticated tastes (and who don't mind the absence of a video arcade) might enjoy the intriguing ports of call.

Service

Highly personalized service by a mostly European staff is crisp and efficient without being intrusive. Butlers are on hand to fulfill the requests of suite guests and will even assist with packing and unpacking when asked.

CHOOSE THIS LINE IF ...

Socializing plays a more important role in your lifestyle than boogying the night away.

You love to read. These ships have extensive libraries that are ideal for curling up with a good book.

You have a bad back. You're sure to love the Tranquility Beds.

Tipping

Gratuities of $13.50 per person per day are added to shipboard accounts for distribution to stewards and waitstaff; an additional $5 per person per day is added for occupants of suites with butler service. Passengers may adjust the amount based on the level of service experienced. An automatic 18% gratuity is added to all bar tabs for bartenders and drink servers and to all bills for salon and spa services.

Past Passengers

After you take one Oceania cruise, you'll receive several benefits along with a free subscription to the *Oceania Club Journal*. Shipboard Club parties hosted by the captain and senior officers, complimentary amenities or exclusive privileges on select sailings, an Oceania Club membership recognition pin after 5, 10, 15, and 20 cruises, and special pricing and mailings about upcoming promotions are some of the benefits. Members further qualify for elite-level status based on the number of sailings aboard Oceania Cruises. Starting with your fifth cruise, you begin to accrue on every cruise you take, beginning with a $200 shipboard credit per stateroom on cruises five through nine. On your 10th cruise, you will receive a $400 shipboard credit per stateroom plus complimentary gratuities on cruises 10 through 14. On your 15th cruise, you will receive a $500 shipboard credit per stateroom, plus two complimentary spa treatments and complimentary gratuities on cruises 15 through 19. Once you take your 20th cruise, you get a free cruise as well as complimentary spa treatments, a shore excursion, and gratuities on all future cruises.

GOOD TO KNOW

When the three original ships in Oceania's fleet were operated by Renaissance, they were entirely smoke-free, and many people booked cruises because of that. As a concession to smokers, a small area is set aside for them near the pool bar on each ship. Staterooms and balconies continue to be no-smoking zones, and if you light up in either spot, you could find yourself put ashore in the next port.

5

OCEANIA CRUISES

DON'T CHOOSE THIS LINE IF

You like the action in a huge casino. Oceania casinos are small, and seats at a poker table can be difficult to get.

You won't take a cruise without your children. Most passengers book with Oceania anticipating a kid-free atmosphere.

Glitzy production shows are your thing. Oceania's showrooms are decidedly low-key.

MARINA, RIVIERA

CREW MEMBERS	800
ENTERED SERVICE	2011, 2012
GROSS TONS	65,000
LENGTH	774 feet
NUMBER OF CABINS	629
PASSENGER CAPACITY	1,258
WIDTH	105 feet

700 ft.

500 ft.

300 ft.

Top: *Balcony Suite*
Bottom: *Baristas Coffee Bar*

Public Areas and Facilities

Marina is the first brand-new ship built for Oceania Cruises and, although it's an all new design in a larger ship, it includes the basic deluxe features found on the smaller fleet mates—specialty dining in intimate restaurants, country-club casual ambience, and enrichment programs. The emphasis is on destination cruising in style and the decor is classic and comfortable. With a larger ship, designers expanded some of the elements, such as the staircase in the grand foyer, which has a landing with two sweeping sets of steps.

Attention to detail is an Oceania hallmark that can be found in Privée, where a custom-made one-of-a-kind Lalique crystal table is illuminated by a white Venini glass chandelier, and fanciful Murano-glass chandeliers glitter in the buffet restaurant. A classical string quartet plays softly in the background at afternoon tea in Horizons, the observation lounge with dramatic floor-to-ceiling windows.

Restaurants

The Grand Dining Room serves open seating breakfast, lunch, and dinner. Specialty restaurants require reservations, but there's no additional charge for Toscana, the Italian restaurant, Polo Grill, the steak house, the French cuisine served in Jacques, the first restaurant to bear Jacques Pépin's name, or Red Ginger, featuring contemporary interpretations of Asian classics. Also requiring reservations are the exclusive Privée, which hosts private seven-course menu degustation dinners for a single party of up to 10, and La Reserve, where wine and food pairings are featured. The casual buffet restaurant is open for breakfast, lunch, and dinner. In addition, a poolside grill serves hamburgers and a variety of sandwiches and salads at lunchtime, and a pizzeria is in the buffet area. Room service is available 24 hours.

Accommodations

Cabins: All accommodations have a vanity-desk and a sitting area with sofa or chair and a table, generous closet and drawer/shelf storage, marble- and granite-clad bathrooms, hair dryer, robes for use during the cruise, safe, and refrigerator. Inside staterooms have a shower only; all other categories have a separate shower and bathtub. Oceania's Tranquility Beds are dressed in high thread-count linens. Concierge-level stateroom occupants are greeted with a bottle of champagne on ice and have access to a private concierge lounge, a laptop to use during the cruise, complimentary shoe shine and pressing services, priority dining reservations, designer toiletries, and a tote bag.

Suites: In addition to the concierge amenities, suites have an entertainment center with a DVD and CD player, a refrigerator, walk in closet, and marble- and granite-bathrooms with a bathtub and designer toiletries. The top three suite categories have whirlpool tubs and separate showers and a guest powder room. Oceania Suites also have a media room, while Vista and Owner's Suites have private workout rooms. Butlers are on hand to coordinate reservations and serve evening canapés and dinner ordered from the ship's restaurants.

Worth Noting: Six staterooms are designed to be wheelchair-accessible.

In the Know

Oceania's "Tranquility Beds" offer the ultimate in pillow-top, comfort and now they've moved them up a notch in suites by introducing "Prestige Tranquility Beds" with a two-inch thick, pillow top cushion filled with gel and wrapped in Chamomile-infused fiber that are said to aid in inducing relaxation.

Pros and Cons

Pros: Baristas is a delightful coffee bar adjacent to the library with floor-to-ceiling windows. The library is well stocked with more than 2,000 books and periodicals. The Artists Loft is a dedicated enrichment center where artists share their expertise in step-by-step classes.

Cons: There is no self-service laundry. Although there are technically three hot tubs on board, one is a therapy whirlpool adjacent to the spa, and its use incurs a fee. Although there is no charge for the food and service in Le Reserve, the wines are additional.

Cabin Type	Size (sq. ft.)
Owner's Suite/ Vista Suite	2,000/ 1,200–1,500
Oceania Suite/ Penthouse Suite	1,000/420
Ocean View with Balcony	282
Ocean View/ Interior	242/174

FAST FACTS

- 11 passenger decks
- 6 specialty restaurants, 1 dining room, buffet, café, pizzeria
- Wi-Fi, safe, refrigerator, DVD (some)
- 1 pool
- Fitness classes, gym, 2 hot tubs, sauna, spa, steam room
- 7 bars, casino, dance club, library
- Dry-cleaning, laundry facilities, laundry service
- Internet terminal, Wi-Fi
- No-smoking cabins

Martinis, *Marina*

5

OCEANIA CRUISES

REGATTA, INSIGNIA, NAUTICA

CREW MEMBERS	400
ENTERED SERVICE	1998, 1998, 2000
GROSS TONS	30,277
LENGTH	594 feet
NUMBER OF CABINS	342
PASSENGER CAPACITY	684 (824 max)
WIDTH	84 feet

700 ft.

500 ft.

300 ft.

Public Areas and Facilities

Carefully furnished to impart the atmosphere of a private English country manor, these midsize ships are casual yet elegant, with sweeping central staircases and abundant flower arrangements. Brocade and toile fabrics cover the windows, overstuffed sofas, and wing chairs to create a warm and intimate feeling throughout. The entire effect is that of a weekend retreat in the English countryside.

Authentic-looking faux fireplaces are inviting elements adjacent to cozy seating areas in the Grand Bar, near the Martini Bar's grand piano, and in the beautiful libraries—some of the best at sea, with an enormous selection of best sellers, nonfiction, and travel books. The casinos are quite small and can feel cramped, and smoking is prohibited. Though there may be a wait for a seat at a poker table, there are enough slot machines to go around.

Other than decorative trompe-l'oeil paintings in several public areas, the artwork is ordinary.

Restaurants

Oceania passengers enjoy the flexibility of four open seating restaurants. The Grand Dining Room, open for breakfast, lunch, and dinner, serves continental cuisine. Alternative, reservations-required dinner options are Toscana, which serves gourmet Italian dishes, and Polo Grill, the steak house. Terraces, the buffet restaurant, serves breakfast, lunch, and dinner and is transformed into Tapas on the Terrace after dark for a relaxed atmosphere and alfresco dining. All dining venues have nearby bars, and there's no additional cover charge for dining. In addition, a poolside grill serves hamburgers and a variety of sandwiches and salads at lunchtime, and there is a pizzeria in the buffet area. Afternoon tea is an elaborate affair served in Horizons, the observation lounge. Room service is available 24 hours.

Accommodations

Cabins: Private balconies outfitted with chairs and tables add additional living space to nearly 75% of all outside accommodations. All cabins have a vanity-desk and a sitting area with sofa, chair, and table. Every cabin has generous closet and drawer/shelf storage and bath-

Top: Teatime in Horizons
Bottom: Breakfast in bed

room shelves. Owner's and Vista suites have a separate living-dining room, as well as a separate powder room.

Suites: Owner's and Vista suites have an entertainment center with a DVD and CD player, a small refrigerator, and a second TV in the bedroom; the main bathroom has a combination shower-whirlpool tub. Penthouse suites also have refrigerators and bathtubs. Butlers are on hand to coordinate reservations and serve evening canapés and dinner ordered from any of the ship's restaurants.

Amenities: Dark-wood cabinetry, soothing blue decor, mirrored accents, safe, Tranquility Beds, 350-thread-count linens, goose-down pillows, and silk-cut duvets are typical stateroom features. Bathrooms have a hair dryer, shampoo, lotion, and bath gel, plus robes.

Worth Noting: Several cabins accommodate third and fourth passengers, but few have connecting doors. Three staterooms are designed for wheelchair accessibility.

In the Know

Don't plot to take the divine linens home with you—it's been tried with embarrassing consequences.

Pros and Cons

Pros: A relaxed, social atmosphere pervades all areas on board, particularly during sea days when passengers mix easily and create their own entertainment, depending very little on organized activities. Everyone has to have a photograph taken on the lobby staircase—it's practically a twin of the one in the movie *Titanic*. Choose anything chocolate from the dessert cart at teatime—Oceania ships serve some of the most lavish afternoon teas at sea.

Cons: Shipboard charges can add up fast, because drink prices and even Internet services are above the average charged by most cruise lines. The one miniscule self-serve laundry room can get steamy, particularly when there's a wait for the machines. The absence of a sauna in the spa is an unfortunate oversight, although you'll be happy to find a rain shower and nifty tiled steam room in the changing areas.

Cabin Type	Size (sq. ft.)
Owner's	962
Vista Suite	786
Penthouse Suite	322
Concierge/Ocean View with Balcony	216
Deluxe Ocean View	165
Standard Ocean View	150–165
Inside	160

FAST FACTS

- 9 passenger decks
- 2 specialty restaurants, dining room, buffet, pizzeria
- Wi-Fi, safe, refrigerator, DVD (some)
- Pool
- Fitness classes, gym, hair salon, 3 hot tubs, spa, steam room
- 4 bars, casino, dance club, library, showroom
- Dry-cleaning, laundry facilities, laundry service
- Internet terminal
- No-smoking cabins

5

OCEANIA CRUISES

Regatta at sea

PRINCESS CRUISES

Princess Cruises may be best known for introducing cruise travel to millions of viewers, when its flagship became the setting for *The Love Boat* television series in 1977. Since that heady time of small-screen stardom, the Princess fleet has grown both in the num-

Splash around in the family pool

ber and size of ships. Although most are large in scale, Princess vessels manage to create the illusion of intimacy through the use of color and decor in understated yet lovely public rooms graced by multimillion-dollar art collections.

✉ *24305 Town Center Dr., Santa Clarita, CA*
☎ *661/753–0000 or 800/774-6237*
⊕ *www.princess.com*
☞ *Cruise Style: Premium.*

Princess has also become more flexible; Personal Choice Cruising offers open seating dining (when you wish and with whom you please) and entertainment options as diverse as those found in resorts ashore.

The roster of adult activities still includes standbys like bingo and art auctions, but also enrichment programs featuring guest lecturers, cooking classes, wine-tasting seminars, pottery workshops, and computer and digital photography classes. Nighttime production shows tend toward Broadway-style revues presented in the main show lounge, and performers might include comedians, magicians, jugglers, and acrobats. Live bands play a wide range of musical styles for dancing and listening, and each ship has a disco.

At the conclusion of the second formal night, champagne trickles down over a champagne waterfall, painstakingly created by the arrangement of champagne glasses in a pyramid shape. Lovely chapels or the wide-open decks are equally romantic settings for weddings at sea with the captain officiating. Smokers have designated areas inside and on deck to light up, but smoking has been banned in all accommodations and even on private balconies.

Food

Personal choices regarding where and what to eat abound, but because of the number of passengers, unless you opt for traditional assigned seating, you might have to wait for a table in one of the open seating dining rooms. Menus are varied and extensive in the main dining rooms, and the results are good to excellent, considering how much work is going on in the galleys. Vegetarian and healthy lifestyle options are always on the menu, as well as steak, fish, or chicken. A special menu is designed especially for children.

Alternative restaurants are a staple throughout the fleet but vary by ship class. Grand-class ships have upscale Crown Grille steak houses and Sabatini's, an Italian restaurant; both require reservations and carry an extra cover charge. Coral and Island Princess feature a New Orleans–style steak house and Sabatini's. On *Caribbean, Crown, Emerald,* and *Ruby Princess,* a casual evening alternative to the dining rooms and usual buffet is Café Caribe, which serves cuisine with a Caribbean flair. With a few breaks in service, Lido buffets on all ships are almost always open, and a pizzeria and grill offer casual daytime snack choices. The fleet's patisseries and ice-cream bars charge for specialty coffee, some pastries, and premium ice cream. A daily British-style pub lunch is served in the ships' Wheelhouse Bar.

Ultimate Balcony Dining—either a champagne breakfast or full-course dinner—is a full-service meal served on your cabin's balcony. The Chef's Table allows guests (for a fee) to dine on a special menu with wine pairings. After a meeting with the executive chef in the galley, guests sit at a special table in the dining room; the chef joins them for dessert.

Fitness and Recreation

Spa rituals include a variety of treatments; each ship also has a salon. Both the salons and spa are operated by Steiner Leisure, and the menu of spa services includes special pampering treatments designed specifically for men and teens as well as couples. For a half-day fee, escape to the Sanctuary, which offers a relaxing outdoor spa-inspired setting with signature beverages, light meals, massages, attentive service, and relaxing personal entertainment.

Modern exercise equipment, a jogging track, and basic fitness classes are available at no charge. There's a fee for personal training, body composition analysis, and specialized classes such as yoga and Pilates. Grand-class

NOTEWORTHY

■ The traditional gala champagne waterfall on formal night is a not-to-be-missed event.

■ Bathrobes are provided for use during your cruise—all you have to do is ask the room steward to deliver them.

■ Wheelchair-accessible staterooms with 33-inch-wide entry and bathroom doorways, plus bathrooms fitted to ADA standards, are available in an array of categories.

5

PRINCESS CRUISES

Top: Place a bet in the casino
Bottom: Disco into the night

Top: Sunset at sea
Middle: Morning stretch
Bottom: Freshwater Jacuzzi

ships have a resistance pool so you can get your laps in effortlessly.

Your Shipmates

Princess Cruises attract mostly American passengers, ranging from their mid-thirties to mid-fifties. Families enjoy cruising together on the Princess fleet, particularly during holiday seasons and in summer months, when many children are on board. Longer cruises appeal to well-traveled retirees and couples who have the time.

Dress Code

Two formal nights are standard on seven-night cruises; an additional formal night may be scheduled on longer sailings. Men are encouraged to wear tuxedos, but dark suits are appropriate. All other evenings are casual, although jeans are discouraged, and it's requested that no shorts be worn in public areas after 6 pm.

Junior Cruisers

For young passengers ages 3 to 17, each Princess vessel (except *Ocean Princess* and *Pacific Princess*) has a playroom, teen center, and programs of supervised activities designed for different age groups. Activities to engage youngsters include arts and crafts, pool games, scavenger hunts, deck parties, backstage and galley tours, games, and videos. Events such as dance parties in their own disco, theme parties, athletic contests, karaoke, pizza parties, and movie fests occupy teenage passengers. With a nod toward science and educational entertainment, children also participate in learning programs focused on the environment and wildlife in areas where the ships sail.

To allow parents independent time ashore, youth centers operate as usual during port days, including lunch with counselors. For an additional charge, group babysitting is available nightly from 10 pm until 1 am. Self-service laundry facilities and two-way family radios for rent at the Purser's Desk are family conveniences. Infants under six months are not permitted; private in-cabin babysitting is not available on any Princess vessel. Children under age three are welcome in the playrooms if supervised by a parent.

CHOOSE THIS LINE IF ...

You're a traveler with a disability. Princess ships are some of the most accessible at sea.

You like to gamble but hate a smoke-filled casino. Princess casinos are well ventilated and spacious.

You want a balcony. Princess ships feature them in abundance at affordable rates.

Service

Professional service by an international staff is efficient and friendly. It's not uncommon to be greeted in passageways by smiling stewards who know your name.

Tipping

A gratuity of $11.50 per person per day ($12 for passengers in suites and minisuites) is added to shipboard accounts for distribution to stewards and waitstaff. Passengers may adjust the amount based on the level of service experienced. An automatic 15% is added to all bar tabs for bartenders and drink servers; gratuities to other staff members may be extended at passengers' discretion.

Past Passengers

Membership in the Captain's Circle is automatic following your first Princess cruise. All members receive a free subscription to *Captain's Circle*, a quarterly newsletter, as well as discounts on selected cruises.

Perks are determined by the number of cruises completed: Gold (2 through 5), Platinum (6 through 15), and Elite (16 and above). Although Gold members receive only the magazine, an invitation to an onboard event, and the services of the Circle Host on the ship, benefits really begin to accrue once you've completed five cruises. Platinum members receive upgraded insurance (when purchasing the standard policy), expedited check-in, a debarkation lounge to wait in on the ship, and, best of all, limited free Internet access during the cruise. Elite benefits are even more lavish, with many complimentary services, including laundry and dry-cleaning.

GOOD TO KNOW

Some people like the time-honored tradition of assigned seating for dinner, so they can get to know their table companions and their servers; others prefer to choose with whom they dine as well as when. Princess lets you have things your way or both ways.
If you're unsure whether Personal Choice is for you, select Traditional dining when you reserve your cruise. You can easily make the switch to anytime dining once on board; however, it can be impossible to change from Personal Choice to Traditional.

DON'T CHOOSE THIS LINE IF ...

You have a poor sense of direction. Most ships, especially the Grand-class ships, are very large.

You want to meet *The Love Boat* cast. That was just a TV show, and it was more than three decades ago.

You're too impatient to stand in line or wait. Debarkation from the large ships can be lengthy.

CARIBBEAN, CROWN, EMERALD, RUBY PRINCESS

CREW MEMBERS	1,200, 1,200, 1,200, 1,225
ENTERED SERVICE	2004, 2006, 2007, 2008
GROSS TONS	113,000
LENGTH	951 feet
NUMBER OF CABINS	1,557, 1,532, 1,532, 1540
PASSENGER CAPACITY	3,100, 3,080, 3,080, 3,080
WIDTH	118 feet

700 ft.

500 ft.

300 ft.

Top: Movies Under the Stars
Bottom: Broadway-style revue

Public Areas and Facilities

With dramatic atriums and Skywalker's Disco (the spoiler hovering 150 feet above the stern), *Caribbean Princess* is a supersize version of the older Grand-class vessels with an extra deck of passenger accommodations.

Not quite identical to *Caribbean Princess*, *Crown*, *Emerald*, and *Ruby Princess* have introduced more dining options and several signature public spaces have been redesigned or relocated on the ships as well—the atrium on *Crown*, *Emerald*, and *Ruby Princess* resembles an open piazza and sidewalk café; Sabatini's Italian Trattoria is found on a top deck with views on three sides and adjacent space for alfresco dining; and Skywalker's Disco is forward near the funnel (where it's topped with a sports court).

Inside spaces on all three vessels are quietly neutral, with touches of glamour in the sweeping staircases and marble-floor atriums. Surprising intimacy is achieved by the number of public rooms and restaurants that swallow up passengers.

Restaurants

Passengers may choose between two traditional dinner seating times, or an early-bird seating, in an assigned dining room or open seating in the ships' other two formal dining rooms; breakfast and lunch are open seating. Alternative dinner options include reservations-only Sabatini's and Crown Grill (both with an additional charge) and the complimentary Café Caribe, a casual Caribbean buffet with linen-dressed tables and limited waiter service. With a few breaks in service, Lido buffets on all ships are almost always open. A pub lunch is served in the Wheelhouse Bar, and a pizzeria and grill offer casual daytime snack choices. The wine bars, patisseries, and ice-cream bars charge for artisan cheeses, specialty coffee, some pastries, and premium ice cream. Ultimate Balcony Dining and Chef's Table options are available, as are afternoon tea and 24-hour room service.

Accommodations

Cabins: On these ships 80% of the outside staterooms have balconies. The typical stateroom has a sitting area with a chair and table; even the cheapest categories have ample storage. Minisuites have a separate sitting area, a walk-in closet, a combination shower-tub, and a balcony, as well as two TVs. Grand Suites have a separate sitting room and dining room, as well as a walk-in closet. Owner's, Penthouse, Premium, and Vista suites have a separate sitting room with a sofa bed and desk, as well as a walk-in closet.

Amenities: Decorated in attractive pastel hues, all cabins have a refrigerator, a hair dryer, a safe, and bathrobes to use during the cruise. Bathrooms have shampoo, lotion, and bath gel.

Worth Noting: Two family suites are interconnecting staterooms with a balcony that each sleep up to eight people (D105/D101 and D106/D102). Staterooms in a variety of categories will accommodate three and four people, and some adjacent cabins can be interconnected through interior doors or by unlocking doors in the balcony dividers. Twenty-five staterooms are designed for wheelchair accessibility and range in size from 234 to 396 square feet, depending upon the category.

In the Know

These ships are marginally larger than Grand-class with one extra passenger deck, but do they seem crowded? When booked to maximum capacity, lines can form with more frequency than on their smaller fleet mates.

Pros and Cons

Pros: Movies Under the Stars on the huge poolside screen may have seemed like a gimmick, but the clever programming and interactive party atmosphere with free popcorn have proven to be a big hit. The dimly lighted Wheelhouse Bar has oversized comfy chairs and a clubby feel at night and serves complimentary pub lunch. The adults-only Sanctuary is a private, partially shaded deck with posh loungers, waiter service for snacks and drinks, and a fee to keep capacity down.

Cons: Priority dining reservations are extended only to Elite Captain's Circle members. The terrace overlooking the aft swimming pool is a little-used spot after dark, but bring your own refreshments because the nearest bar may close early. Passengers who opt for Personal Choice dining may encounter a short wait for a table unless they're willing to join other diners.

Cabin Type	Size (sq. ft)
Grand Suite	1,279
Other Suites	461–689
Family Suite	607
Minisuite	324
Ocean-View Balcony	233–285
Ocean View	158–182
Inside	163

All dimensions include the square footage for balconies.

FAST FACTS

- 15 passenger decks
- 2 specialty restaurants, 3 dining rooms, buffet, ice cream parlor, pizzeria
- Wi-Fi, safe, refrigerator, DVD (some)
- 4 pools (1 indoor), children's pool
- Fitness classes, gym, hair salon, 7 hot tubs, sauna, spa, steam room
- 9 bars, casino, cinema, 2 dance clubs, library, 2 showrooms, video game room
- Children's programs (ages 3–17)
- Dry-cleaning, laundry facilities, laundry service
- Internet terminal
- No kids under 6 months
- No-smoking cabins

Sailing at sunset

5

CORAL CLASS
Coral Princess, Island Princess

CREW MEMBERS	900
ENTERED SERVICE	2003, 2003
GROSS TONS	92,000
LENGTH	964
NUMBER OF CABINS	987
PASSENGER CAPACITY	1,970
WIDTH	106 feet

700 ft.

500 ft.

300 ft.

Public Areas and Facilities

Princess includes *Coral Princess* and *Island Princess* in their Sun-class category; however, they are larger ships (albeit with a similar capacity to *Sun Princess* and her two sisters), which means much more space per passenger; we feel this necessitates a separate category. All the Personal Choice features attributed to the larger Grand-class ships were incorporated into this design as well as a few unique additions, such as a demonstration kitchen and ceramics lab complete with kiln where ScholarShip@Sea programs are presented. The four-story atrium is similar to that on Sun-class ships, but public rooms are mainly spread fore and aft on two lower decks.

Although signature rooms such as the Wheelhouse Bar are more traditional, the casinos have subtle London- or Paris-like atmospheres with themed slot machines; Crooner's Bar is a retro 1960s Vegas-style martini and piano bar. In addition to the stately Princess Theater showroom, the Universe Lounge has three stages for shows and flexible seating on two levels, making it a multipurpose space.

Restaurants

Passengers may choose between traditional dinner seating times, or an early-bird seating, in one assigned dining room or open seating in the other formal dining room; breakfast and lunch are open seating. Alternative dinner options include reservations-only Sabatini's Italian trattoria and Bayou Café & Steakhouse (both with an extra charge). With a few breaks in service, Lido buffets on all ships are almost always open. A pub lunch is served in the Wheelhouse Bar, and a pizzeria and grill offer casual daytime snack choices. The patisseries and ice cream bars charge for specialty coffee, some pastries, and premium ice cream. Ultimate Balcony Dining and Chef's Table options are available, as is afternoon tea, and 24-hour room service.

Accommodations

Cabins: Stepped out in wedding-cake fashion, more than 83% of ocean-view staterooms include Princess Cruises' trademark private balconies. Even the least expensive inside categories have plentiful storage and a small sitting area with a chair and table. Suites have two

Top: Fast-paced shows
Bottom: Aqua biking

TVs, a sitting area, a wet bar, a large walk-in closet, and a separate bathtub and shower. Minisuites have a separate sitting area, two TVs, a walk-in closet, and a combination bathtub/shower.

Suites: Occupants of 16 suites receive complimentary Internet access, dry cleaning, and shoe polishing, afternoon tea and evening canapés delivered to their suites, and priority embarkation, disembarkation, and tendering privileges. An extended room service menu is also available for them, as are priority reservations for dining and shore excursions.

Amenities: Decorated in pastels and light-wood tones, typical staterooms have a safe, hair dryer, refrigerator, and bathrobes for use during the cruise. Bathrooms have shampoo, lotion, and bath gel.

Worth Noting: Twenty staterooms are designed for wheelchair accessibility and range in size from 217 to 374 square feet, depending on category.

In the Know
Most mid-ship ocean-view cabins on Emerald Deck are designated as obstructed view, and even some balcony staterooms on Emerald and Dolphin decks are considered partially obstructed. And when balconies are arranged in a stepped-out design, the lower ones aren't totally private.

Pros and Cons
Pros: As many as 20 courses in the ScholarShip@Sea Program are offered on each cruise, and you can select from ceramics, cooking fundamentals, computer, and photography classes or attend lectures on a wide range of topics. Cabins that sleep third and fourth passengers are numerous, and the best bet for families are interconnecting balcony staterooms adjacent to facilities dedicated to children and teens on Aloha Deck. The Fine Art Gallery is a dedicated spot for art-auction stock, meaning that displays don't clutter the passageways and distract from the art pieces selected to complement the decor.

Cons: Oddly, the library and card room are situated so they are often used as passageways, which results in a bit more noise than usual in areas that should be quiet. There are only 16 suites on each ship, and none are aft facing with a view of the wake; engine pods on the funnel give the ships a futuristic space-age appearance of jet speed but function mainly as decoration—they can easily make 24 knots, but they don't fly.

Cabin Type	Size (sq. ft.)
Suite	470
Minisuite	285–302
Ocean-View Balcony	217–232
Ocean-View Stand	162
Deluxe	212
Inside	156–166

All dimensions include the square footage for balconies.

FAST FACTS

- 11 passenger decks
- 2 specialty restaurants, 2 dining rooms, buffet, ice cream parlor, pizzeria
- Wi-Fi, safe, refrigerator, DVD (some)
- 3 pools (1 indoor), children's pool
- Fitness classes, gym, hair salon, 5 hot tubs, sauna, spa
- 7 bars, casino, 2 dance clubs, library, 2 showrooms, video game room
- Children's programs (ages 3–17)
- Dry-cleaning, laundry facilities, laundry service
- Internet terminal
- No kids under 6 months
- No-smoking cabins

Lavish buffets in Horizon Court

5

PRINCESS CRUISES

GRAND CLASS
Grand Princess, Golden Princess, Star Princess

CREW MEMBERS	1,100, 1,100, 1,200
ENTERED SERVICE	1998, 2001, 2002
GROSS TONS	109,000
LENGTH	951 feet
NUMBER OF CABINS	1,300
PASSENGER CAPACITY	2,600
WIDTH	118 feet

700 ft.

500 ft.

300 ft.

Top: *Star Princess* at sea
Bottom: *Golden Princess*
grand plaza atrium

Public Areas and Facilities

When *Grand Princess* was introduced as the world's largest cruise ship in 1998, she also boasted one of the most distinctive profiles. Skywalker's Disco appeared futuristic, hovering approximately 150 feet above the waterline, but in a dramatic—and fuel saving—transformation, it was removed from *Grand Princess* in 2011 and replaced with a more conventional nightclub in the heart of the ship. Lighter materials were used in the construction of subsequent ships, and there are no plans on the drawing board to redesign them by removing Skywalker's at this writing.

Grand-class vessels advanced the idea of a floating resort to an entirely new level, with more than 700 staterooms that include private balconies. Like their predecessors, the interiors of Grand-class ships feature soothing pastel tones with splashy glamour in the sweeping staircases and marble-floor atriums. Surprisingly intimate for such large ships, human scale in public lounges is achieved by judicious placement of furniture as unobtrusive room dividers.

The 300-square-foot Times Square–style LED screens that hover over the pools show up to seven movies or events daily.

Restaurants

Passengers may choose between two traditional dinner seating times, or an early-bird seating, in an assigned dining room or open seating in the ships' other two formal dining rooms; breakfast and lunch are open seating. Alternative dinner options include the reservations-only Crown Grill, serving steaks and seafood, and Sabatini's Italian restaurants (both with an extra charge). With a few breaks in service, Lido buffets on all ships are open around the clock. A pub lunch is served in the Wheelhouse Bar, and a pizzeria and grill offer casual daytime snack choices. The patisseries and ice-cream bars charge for specialty coffee, some pastries, and premium ice cream. A wine bar serves extra-charge evening snacks and artisan cheeses. Ultimate Balcony Dining and Chef's Table options are available, as is afternoon tea and 24-hour room service.

Accommodations

Cabins: On these ships, 80% of the outside staterooms have balconies. The typical stateroom has a sitting area with a chair and table; even the cheapest categories have ample storage. Minisuites have a separate sitting area, a walk-in closet, a combination shower-tub, and a balcony, as well as two TVs. Grand Suites have a separate sitting room and dining room, as well as a walk-in closet. Owner's, Penthouse, Premium, and Vista suites have a separate sitting room with a sofa bed and desk, as well as a walk-in closet.

Amenities: Decorated in attractive pastel hues, all cabins have a refrigerator, hair dryer, safe, and bathrobes to use during the cruise. Bathrooms have shampoo, lotion, and bath gel.

Worth Noting: Two family suites are interconnecting staterooms with a balcony that can sleep up to eight people (D105/D101 and D106/D102). Staterooms in a variety of categories will accommodate three and four people, and some adjacent cabins can be interconnected through interior doors or by unlocking doors in the balcony dividers. Twenty-eight staterooms are wheelchair accessible.

In the Know

Port and starboard balconies are stepped out from the ships' hulls in wedding-cake fashion. That means, depending on location, yours will likely be exposed a bit—or a lot—to passengers on higher decks. Exceptions are balconies on Emerald Deck, which are covered.

Pros and Cons

Pros: Skywalker's Disco on *Golden Princess* and *Star Princess* is virtually deserted during the day, when it's the ideal spot to read or just watch the sea. The self-service passenger laundry rooms have ironing stations to touch up garments wrinkled from packing. The Wheelhouse Bar, with soft lighting, comfortable leather chairs, shining brass accents, and nautical decor, has become a Princess tradition for pre- and postdinner cocktails and dancing.

Cons: The popular sports bars have been replaced by smoking lounges. Staterooms and suites located aft and above the Vista lounge can be noisy when bands crank up the volume. Grand Suites on *Grand Princess* aren't as large as those on *Golden Princess* and *Star Princess*, and aren't aft-facing with a view of the ship's wake.

Cabin Type	Size (sq. ft.)
Grand Suite	730/1,314*
Other Suites	468–591
Family Suite	607
Minisuite	323
Ocean View Balcony	232–274
Standard	168
Inside	160

All dimensions include the square footage for balconies. *Grand Princess* dimensions followed by *Golden* and *Star Princess*.

FAST FACTS

- 14 passenger decks
- 2 specialty restaurants, 3 dining rooms, buffet, ice cream parlor, pizzeria
- Wi-Fi, safe, refrigerator
- 4 pools (1 indoor), children's pool
- Fitness classes, gym, hair salon, 9 hot tubs, sauna, spa, steam room
- 9 bars, casino, outdoor cinema, 2 dance clubs, library, 2 showrooms, video game room
- Children's programs (ages 3–17)
- Dry-cleaning, laundry facilities, laundry service
- Internet terminal
- No kids under 6 months
- No-smoking cabins

SUN CLASS
Sun Princess, Dawn Princess, Sea Princess

CREW MEMBERS	900
ENTERED SERVICE	1995, 1997, 1998
GROSS TONS	77,000
LENGTH	856 feet
NUMBER OF CABINS	975
PASSENGER CAPACITY	1,950
WIDTH	106 feet

700 ft.

500 ft.

300 ft.

Top: *Sea Princess* at sea
Bottom: Sun-class ocean-view stateroom

Public Areas and Facilities

Refined and graceful, Sun-class ships offer many of the choices attributed to larger Grand-class ships without sacrificing the smaller-ship atmosphere for which they're noted. The four-story atrium with a circular marble floor, stained-glass dome, and magnificent floating staircase are ideal settings for relaxation, people-watching, and making a grand entrance. Only *Sea Princess* sails Caribbean cruises; *Sun* and *Dawn Princess* are deployed in the South Pacific.

Onboard decor is a combination of neutrals and pastels, which are easy on the eyes after a sunny day ashore. The main public rooms are situated in a vertical arrangement on four lower decks, and, with the exception of promenade deck, cabins are forward and aft. In a nice design twist, the casino is somewhat isolated, and passengers aren't forced to use it as a passageway to reach dining rooms or the art deco main show lounge. *Sea Princess* also has an outdoor Movies Under the Stars LED screen.

Restaurants

Sun-class ships have one dining room with two traditional assigned dinner seatings, or an early-bird seating, and one open seating dining room for Personal Choice cruisers; breakfast and lunch are open seating. Alternative dinner options are the reservations-only Sterling Steakhouse (a section of the buffet that's dressed up for the evening and for which there's a charge) and complimentary traditional Italian dishes in a trattoria-style setting in the pizzeria. With a few breaks in service, Lido buffets on all ships are almost always open. The pizzeria and a grill near the main pool offer casual daytime snack choices. The patisseries and ice cream bars charge for specialty coffee, some pastries, and premium ice cream. Ultimate Balcony Dining is available, as is afternoon tea and 24-hour room service.

Accommodations

Cabins: Princess Cruises' trademark is an abundance of staterooms with private balconies, yet even the least expensive inside categories have ample storage and a small sitting area with a chair and table. Suites have two TVs, a separate sitting area, a dining-height table with chairs, a walk-in closet, double-sink vanities, and a separate shower and whirlpool tub. Minisuites have a separate sitting area, two TVs, a walk-in closet, and a separate shower and whirlpool tub.

Amenities: Decorated in pastel tones, staterooms typically have mirrored accents, a safe, a refrigerator, a hair dryer, and bathrobes for use during the cruise. Bathrooms have shampoo, lotion, and bath gel.

Worth Noting: Cabins that sleep third and fourth passengers aren't as numerous as on other Princess ships, and no staterooms have interconnecting interior doors, although adjacent cabins with balconies can be connected by unlocking balcony divider doors. Nineteen staterooms are designed for wheelchair accessibility and range in size from 213 to 305 square feet, depending on category.

In the Know

Check and double-check your bed configurations when booking an outside quad cabin for your family. There are balcony cabins with three and four berths, but some have two lower twin-size beds that cannot be pushed together to form a queen.

Pros and Cons

Pros: You can always escape the crowds by ducking into to the cozy, wood-paneled reading room, where each oversize chair faces its own bay window. No matter what flavor is on the menu, the dessert soufflés can't be beat. On Riviera Deck a dramatic, partially shaded pool with two hot tubs appears suspended between two decks with its surface between the spa and the Sun Deck above.

Cons: Horizon Court Lido buffet restaurants occupy one of the most prestigious spots on these ships—far forward, with a true view of the horizon—but that means there is no observatory lounge. There's nothing about the interior decor that'll knock your socks off—some areas still have echoes of *The Love Boat* television series sets—but the cool palette enhanced by marble accents showcases impressive original artwork and murals. These are large ships but not large enough to overcome the invasive nature of regularly scheduled art auctions.

Cabin Type	Size (sq. ft.)
Suite	538–695
Minisuite	370–536
Ocean View Balcony	179
Deluxe	173
Ocean View Standard	135–155
Interior	135–148

All dimensions include the square footage for balconies.

FAST FACTS

- 10 passenger decks
- 2 dining rooms, buffet, ice cream parlor, pizzeria
- Wi-Fi, safe, refrigerator
- 3 pools (1 indoor), children's pool
- Fitness classes, gym, hair salon, 5 hot tubs, sauna, spa, steam room
- 7 bars, casino, 2 dance clubs, library, 2 showrooms, video game room
- Children's programs (ages 3–17)
- Dry-cleaning, laundry facilities, laundry service
- Internet terminal
- No kids under 6 months
- No-smoking cabins

Riviera pool

5

PRINCESS CRUISES

REGENT SEVEN SEAS

The 1994 merger of Radisson Diamond Cruises and Seven Seas Cruise Line launched Radisson Seven Seas Cruises with an eclectic fleet of vessels that offered a nearly all-inclusive cruise experience in sumptuous, contemporary surroundings. The line was

The end of a perfect day

rebranded as Regent Seven Seas Cruises in 2006, and ownership passed to Prestige Cruise Holdings (which also owns Oceania Cruises) in 2008. Even shore excursions are included in the fare, and there is no charge for dining in the specialty restaurants.

✉ *1000 Corporate Dr., Suite 500, Fort Lauderdale, FL*
☎ *954/776–6123 or 877/505–5370*
⊕ *www.rssc.com*
☞ *Cruise Style: Luxury.*

Even more inclusive than in the past, the line has maintained its traditional tried-and-true formula—delightful ships offering exquisite service, generous staterooms with abundant amenities, a variety of dining options, and superior lecture and enrichment programs. Guests are greeted with champagne on boarding and find an all-inclusive beverage policy that offers not only soft drinks and bottled water, but also cocktails and select wines at all bars and restaurants throughout the ships.

The cruises are destination focused, and most sailings host guest lecturers—historians, anthropologists, naturalists, and diplomats. Spotlight cruises center around popular pastimes and themes, such as food and wine, photography, history, archaeology, literature, performing arts, design and cultures, active exploration and wellness, antiques, jewelry and shopping, the environment, and marine life. Passengers need no urging to participate in discussions and workshops led by celebrated experts. All passengers have access to these unique experiences on board and on shore.

Activities and entertainment are tailored for each of the line's distinctive ships with the tastes of sophisticated passengers in mind. Don't expect napkin-folding demonstrations or nonstop action. Production revues, cabaret acts, concert-style piano performances, solo performers, and comedians may be featured in show lounges, with combos playing for listening and dancing in lounges and bars throughout the ships. Casinos are more akin to Monaco than Las Vegas. All ships display tasteful and varied art collections, including pieces that are for sale.

Food

Menus may appear to include the usual beef Wellington and Maine lobster, but in the hands of Regent Seven Seas chefs the results are some of the most outstanding meals at sea. Specialty dining varies within the fleet, but the larger ships, *Seven Seas Voyager* and *Seven Seas Mariner*, have the edge with the sophisticated Signatures, featuring the cuisine of Le Cordon Bleu of Paris. Prime 7, on all three ships, is a contemporary adaptation of the classic American steak house offering a fresh, distinctive decor and an innovative menu of the finest prime-aged steak and chops, along with fresh seafood and poultry specialties. In addition, Mediterranean-influenced bistro dinners that need no reservations are served in La Veranda, the venue that is the daytime casual Lido buffet restaurant.

Held in a tranquil setting, Wine Connoisseurs Dinners are offered occasionally on longer cruises to bring together people with an interest in wine and food. Each course on the degustation menu is complemented by a wine pairing. The cost varies according to the special vintage wines that are included.

Room-service menus are fairly extensive, and you can also order directly from the restaurant menus during regular serving hours.

Although special dietary requirements should be relayed to the cruise line before sailing, general considerations such as vegetarian, low-salt, or low-cholesterol food requests can be satisfied on board the ships simply by speaking with the dining room staff. Wines chosen to complement dinner menus are freely poured each evening.

Fitness and Recreation

Although gyms and exercise areas are well equipped, these are not large ships, so the facilities tend to be on the small size. Each ship has a jogging track, and the larger ones feature a variety of sports courts.

The spas and salons aboard Regent Seven Seas ships are operated by Canyon Ranch SpaClub, which offers

5

REGENT SEVEN SEAS

Top: Sunrise jog
Bottom: *Seven Seas Navigator*

Top: Fitness center
Middle: Pool decks are never crowded
Bottom: Pampering in the Carita of Paris spa

an array of treatments and services that can be customized to the individual.

Your Shipmates

Regent Seven Seas Cruises are inviting to active, affluent, well-traveled couples ranging from their late-thirties to retirees who enjoy the ship's chic ambience and destination-rich itineraries. Longer cruises attract veteran passengers in the over-sixty age group.

Dress Code

Suggestions for each evening's dress are listed in your cruise documents. Formal and semi-formal attire is optional on designated evenings only during cruises of 16 nights or more. Men are encouraged to wear tuxedos, and many do so; dark suits are also acceptable. Other evenings are "elegant" or resort casual. It's requested that dress codes be observed in public areas after 6 pm.

Junior Cruisers

Regent Seven Seas' vessels are adult-oriented and do not have dedicated children's facilities. However, a Club Mariner youth program for children ages 5 to 8, 9 to 12, and 13 to 17 is offered on selected sailings, both during summer months and during school holiday periods. Supervised by counselors, the organized, educational activities focus on nature and the heritage of destinations the ship will visit. Activities, including games, craft projects, movies, and food fun, are organized to ensure that every child has a memorable experience. Teens are encouraged to help counselors select the activities they prefer.

Service

The efforts of a polished, unobtrusive staff go almost unnoticed, yet special requests are handled with ease. Butlers provide an additional layer of personal service to guests in the top-category suites.

Tipping

Gratuities are included in the fare, and none are expected. To show their appreciation, passengers may elect to make a contribution to a crew welfare fund that benefits the ship's staff.

CHOOSE THIS LINE IF ...

You want to learn the secrets of cooking like a Cordon Bleu chef (for a charge, of course).

You want to stay connected. Regent Seven Seas Internet packages are reasonably priced by the hour.

A really high-end spa experience is on your agenda.

Past Passengers

Membership in the Seven Seas Society is automatic on completion of a Regent Seven Seas cruise. Members receive discounts on select sailings, exclusive shipboard and shore-side special events on select sailings, a Seven Seas Society recognition cocktail party on every sailing, and *Inspirations* newsletter highlighting special events, sailings, and destination- and travel-related information. The tiered program offers rewards based on the number of nights you have sailed with RSSC. The more you sail, the more you accrue. Bronze benefits are offered to members with 4 to 20 nights. From 21 through 74 nights, Silver members also receive complimentary Internet access on board, free pressing, and an hour of free phone time. From 75 through 199 nights, Gold members are awarded priority disembarkation at some ports, two more hours of complimentary phone time, more complimentary pressing, an exclusive Gold & Platinum activity aboard or ashore on every sailing, and priority reservations at restaurants and spas. From 200 through 399, Platinum members can add complimentary air deviation services (one time per sailing), six additional hours of complimentary phone use, and unlimited free pressing and laundry services; Titanium members who have sailed 400 or more nights get free dry-cleaning and complimentary private-car transfers to and from the airport and pier.

5

REGENT SEVEN SEAS

DON'T CHOOSE THIS LINE IF ...

Connecting cabins are a must. Very few are available, and only the priciest cabins connect.

You can't imagine a Caribbean cruise without the hoopla of pool games and steel bands.

You think dressing up for dinner is too much trouble. Most passengers look forward to the ritual.

SEVEN SEAS NAVIGATOR

CREW MEMBERS	340
ENTERED SERVICE	1999
GROSS TONS	33,000
LENGTH	560 feet
NUMBER OF CABINS	245
PASSENGER CAPACITY	490
WIDTH	81 feet

700 ft.

500 ft.

300 ft.

Top: Casino
Bottom: *Navigator* suite

Public Areas and Facilities

The first ship outfitted uniquely to Regent Seven Seas' specifications, the *Seven Seas Navigator* is a particular favorite of returning passengers for its small-ship intimacy, big-ship features, and comfortable, well-designed accommodations, which are all considered suites.

The generous use of wood and the addition of deep-tone accents to the predominantly neutral color palette give even the larger lounges an inviting feel. Artwork and elaborate flower arrangements add a bit of sparkle and interest to the somewhat angular modern decor.

Due to the aft location of the two-deck-high main showroom, the only lounges that afford sweeping seascapes are Galileo's—typically the most popular public space, with nightly entertainment—and the Vista Lounge. Although views from the Vista Lounge are spectacular, there's no permanent bar, and it's primarily a quiet spot for reading when there are no lectures or activities scheduled there.

Restaurants

Compass Rose restaurant, the main dining room, functions on an open seating basis for breakfast, lunch, and dinner, so there are no set dining assignments. La Veranda, the buffet restaurant, serves breakfast, lunch, and dinner. Prime 7, the specialty steak house, requires reservations for dinner, but there is no charge. At least once during each cruise, dinner is served alfresco on the pool deck. In addition to the buffet, a choice for casual lunch and snacks is the poolside grill. Afternoon tea is served daily, and room service is available 24 hours a day. Dinner can be ordered from the main dining room menu during restaurant hours and served en suite, course by course.

Accommodations

Cabins: Attractive textured fabrics and honeyed wood finishes add a touch of coziness to the larger-than-usual suites in all categories, 90% of which have balconies. All have a vanity-desk, walk-in closet, and sitting area with a sofa, chairs, and table. Marble bathrooms have a separate tub and shower. Master Suites have a separate sitting–dining room, a separate bedroom, and a powder room; only Grand Suites also have a powder room. Master Suites have a second TV in the bedroom, butler service, and whirlpool tub in the master bathroom. Grand and Navigator suites are similarly outfitted. The top three suite categories feature Bose music systems. Penthouse Suites, which include butler service, are only distinguished from Deluxe Suites by location and do not have a whirlpool bathtub.

Amenities: Every suite has an entertainment center with CD/DVD player, stocked refrigerator, stocked bar, safe, hair dryer, and beds dressed with fine linens and duvets. Bath toiletries include shampoo, lotion, and bath gel.

Worth Noting: Few suites have the capacity to accommodate three people, and only 10 far-forward suites adjoin with those adjacent to them. Four suites are wheelchair accessible.

In the Know

From Russia, With Love: Regent Seven Seas took over an unfinished hull that was originally destined to be a Soviet spy ship and redesigned it to create the *Seven Seas Navigator*. They did such a good job completing the interiors that even James Bond would feel at home.

Pros and Cons

Pros: The library contains hundreds of novels, best sellers, and travel books, as well as newspapers, movies for in-suite viewing, and even a selection of board games. Fellow passengers might be as wealthy as Midas, but most are unpretentious. When nothing on the menu appeals to you, don't hesitate to ask for what you'd really like to have for dinner.

Cons: Internet use can be heavy on sea days, and the lines that form in the computer area can add a bit of congestion—and inevitable noise—to the adjacent library, a space that should be a quiet haven. If you book a suite in the far-aft section of the ship, be prepared for an annoying vibration. Unless you prebook a table in Portofino online before your cruise, you could be disappointed to find it unavailable once you board.

Cabin Type	Size (sq. ft.)
Master Suite	1,067
Grand Suite	539
Navigator Suite	448
Penthouse/Balcony Suite	301
Window Suite	301*

*Except for Suite 600, which measures 516

FAST FACTS

- 8 passenger decks
- Specialty restaurant, dining room, buffet
- Wi-Fi, safe, refrigerator, DVD
- Pool
- Fitness classes, gym, hair salon, hot tub, sauna, spa, steam room
- 4 bars, casino, dance club, showroom
- Children's programs (ages 5–17)
- Dry-cleaning, laundry facilities, laundry service
- Internet terminal
- No-smoking cabins

Casual poolside dining

ROYAL CARIBBEAN

Big, bigger, biggest! More than two decades ago, Royal Caribbean launched Sovereign-class ships, the first of the modern megacruise liners, which continue to be an all-around favorite of passengers who enjoy traditional cruising ambience with a touch of

Adventure of the Seas solarium

daring and whimsy tossed in. Plunging into the 21st century, each ship in the current fleet carries more passengers than the entire Royal Caribbean fleet of the 1970s, and has features—such as new surfing pools—that were unheard of in the past.

✉ *1050 Royal Caribbean Way, Miami, FL*

☎ *305/539–6000 or 800/327–6700*

⊕ *www.royalcaribbean. com*

☞ *Cruise Style: Mainstream.*

All Royal Caribbean ships are topped by the company's distinctive signature Viking Crown Lounge, a place to watch the seascape by day and dance away at night. Expansive multideck atriums and the generous use of brass and floor-to-ceiling glass windows give each vessel a sense of spaciousness and style. The action is nonstop in casinos and dance clubs after dark, while daytime hours are filled with poolside games and traditional cruise activities. Port talks tend to lean heavily on shopping recommendations and the sale of shore excursions.

A variety of lounges and high-energy stage shows draws passengers of all ages out to mingle and dance the night away. Production extravaganzas showcase singers and dancers in lavish costumes. Comedians, acrobats, magicians, jugglers, and solo entertainers fill show lounges on nights when the ships' companies aren't performing. Professional ice shows are a highlight of cruises on Voyager-, Freedom-, and Oasis-class ships—the only ships at sea with ice-skating rinks.

Food

Dining is an international experience, with nightly changing themes and cuisines from around the world.

Passenger preference for casual attire and a resortlike atmosphere has prompted the cruise line to add laid-back alternatives to the formal dining rooms in the Windjammer Café and, on certain ships, Johnny Rockets Diner or Park Café; Seaview Café evokes the ambience of an island beachside stand. Royal Caribbean offers you the choice of early or late dinner seating and has introduced an open seating program fleet-wide.

Room service is available 24 hours, but for orders between midnight and 5 am there is a $3.95 service charge. There's a limited menu.

Royal Caribbean doesn't place emphasis on celebrity chefs or specialty alternative restaurants, although they have introduced a more upscale and intimate dinner experience in the form of an Italian specialty restaurant and/or a steak house on all but the Vision-class ships.

Fitness and Recreation

Royal Caribbean has pioneered such new and previously unheard of features as rock-climbing walls, ice-skating rinks, bungee trampolines, and even the first self-leveling pool tables on a cruise ship. Interactive water parks, boxing rings, surfing simulators, and cantilevered whirlpools suspended 112 feet above the ocean made their debuts on the Freedom-class ships.

Facilities vary by ship class, but all Royal Caribbean ships have state-of-the-art exercise equipment, jogging tracks, and rock-climbing walls; passengers can work out independently or in classes guaranteed to sweat off extra calories. Most exercise classes are included in the fare, but there's a fee for specialized spin, yoga, and Pilates classes, as well as the services of a personal trainer. Spas and salons are top-notch, with full menus of day spa–style treatments and services for pampering and relaxation for adults and teens.

Your Shipmates

Royal Caribbean cruises have a broad appeal for active couples and singles, mostly in their thirties to fifties. Families are partial to the newer vessels that have larger staterooms, huge facilities for children and teens, and seemingly endless choices of activities and dining options.

Dress Code

Two formal nights are standard on seven-night cruises; one formal night is the norm on shorter sailings. Men are encouraged to wear tuxedos, but dark suits or sport coats and ties are more prevalent. All other evenings are casual, although jeans are discouraged in

5

ROYAL CARIBBEAN

Top: Adventure Beach for kids
Bottom: Voyager-class interior stateroom

restaurants. It's requested that no shorts be worn in public areas after 6 pm, although there are passengers who can't wait to change into them after dinner.

Junior Cruisers

Supervised age-appropriate activities are designed for children ages 3 through 17; babysitting services are available as well (either group or in-stateroom baby-sitting, but sitters will not change diapers). Children are assigned to the Adventure Ocean youth program by age. They must be at least three years old and toilet trained to participate (children who are in diapers and pull-ups or who are not toilet trained are not allowed in swimming pools or whirlpools). Youngsters who wish to join a different age group must participate in one daytime and one night activity session with their proper age group first; the manager will then make the decision based on their maturity level.

In partnership with toymaker Fisher-Price, Royal Caribbean offers interactive 45-minute Aqua Babies and Aqua Tots play sessions for children ages 6 months to 36 months. The playgroup classes, which are hosted by youth staff members, were designed by early childhood development experts for parents and their babies and toddlers, and teach life skills through playtime activities.

A teen center with a disco is an adult-free gathering spot that will satisfy even the pickiest teenagers.

Service

Service on Royal Caribbean ships is friendly but inconsistent. Assigned meal seatings assure that most passengers get to know the waiters and their assistants, who in turn get to know the passengers' likes and dislikes; however, that can lead to a level of familiarity that is uncomfortable to some people. Some ships have a concierge lounge for the use of suite occupants and top-level past passengers.

Top: Miniature golf
Middle: *Adventure of the Seas*
Bottom: *Serenade of the Seas*
rock-climbing wall

Tipping

Tips can be prepaid when the cruise is booked, added on to shipboard accounts, or given in cash on the last night of the cruise. Suggested gratuities per passenger per day are $5 for the cabin steward ($7.25 for suites),

---

CHOOSE THIS LINE IF ...

You want to see the sea from atop a rock wall—it's one of the few activities on these ships that's free.

You're active and adventurous. Even if your traveling companion isn't, there's an energetic staff on board to cheer you on.

You want your space. There's plenty of room to roam; quiet nooks and crannies are there if you look.

$3.75 for the waiter, $2.15 for the assistant waiter, and $0.75 for the headwaiter. A 15% gratuity is automatically added to all bar tabs.

Past Passengers

After one cruise, you can enroll in the Crown & Anchor Society and earn one Cruise Point for every night you sail with with Royal Caribbean (you get double the points when you book a suite). Member levels and point requirements are: Gold, 3 points; Platinum, 30 points; Emerald, 55 points; Diamond, 80 points; Diamond Plus, 175 points; and Pinnacle Club, 700 points. All members have access to the member section on the Royal Caribbean Web site, and receive an Ultimate Value Booklet and an invitation to a welcome-back party during subsequent cruises. As you move up to higher point levels, benefits include such perks as the use of a private departure lounge and priority check-in (where it is available), the onboard use of robes during the cruise, an invitation to an exclusive onboard event, and complimentary custom air arrangements.

The higher member point levels also receive consideration on a priority wait list for sold-out shore excursions and spa services, concierge service on select ships, priority departure from the ship, complimentary custom air fee, special rates on balcony and suite accommodations, behind-the-scenes tours, and preferred seating in main dining rooms.

GOOD TO KNOW

Royal Caribbean ships are truly resorts afloat, with an emphasis on recreation and family enjoyment. You could spend a week on board the huge Oasis-class, Voyager-class, and Freedom-class ships and never leave. You would also be hard-pressed to try to do everything at hand, so it's important to pace yourself by setting priorities and budgeting your time. A good idea is to try new things that you may not be able to do at home—climb a rock wall and learn to snorkel, for example.

If you're a Crown & Anchor member, your status level is the same whenever you sail on Royal Caribbean's sister cruise line, Celebrity Cruises.

DON'T CHOOSE THIS LINE IF ...

Patience is not one of your virtues. Lines are not uncommon.

You want to do your own laundry. There are no self-service facilities on any Royal Caribbean ships.

You don't want to hear announcements, especially in your cabin. There are a lot on RCI cruises.

OASIS/ALLURE OF THE SEAS

CREW MEMBERS	2,394
ENTERED SERVICE	2009, 2010
GROSS TONS	225,282
LENGTH	1,187 feet
NUMBER OF CABINS	2,706
PASSENGER CAPACITY	5,400
WIDTH	208 feet

700 ft.

500 ft.

300 ft.

Top: *Allure of the Seas* sailing
Bottom: A romantic moment
on a stateroom balcony

Public Areas and Facilities

The world's largest cruise ships are so massive that each is divided into seven neighborhoods—distinguished by purpose (spa and fitness, pool and sports), age (youth zone), design (Central Park and the Boardwalk), or function (entertainment). At the heart of the ships are the indoor Royal Promenade, lined with café-style eateries and lounges. Outdoors, Central Park's pathways meander through the ships' "town square," peaceful by day but more bustling in the evening. Connecting the two is an open-air elevator that doubles as a bar where patrons can order drinks during the ride.

Royal Caribbean hits all the marks with nearly two dozen bars and lounges and a wide variety of restaurants. Outdoor activities include two surfing simulators, two rock-climbing walls, and the first zip-line on a cruise ship that stretches across the Boardwalk. The Boardwalk itself has a carousel in a setting that evokes the nostalgia of seaside piers of yesteryear. The centerpiece of the AquaTheater is the largest and deepest freshwater pool found on a ship where you can swim by day and watch a water show at night.

Restaurants

A single, triple-deck dining room serves open seating breakfast and lunch; dinner is served in either assigned or open seating. Specialty restaurants—Giovanni's Table (Italian), Chops Grille (a steak house), and the gourmet 150 Central Park—charge a supplement and require reservations. Either the casual Windjammer or Wipe Out Café offer buffet service nearly around the clock for breakfast, lunch, dinner, and snacks. Other venues for which there is a charge are Izumi (Asian); Johnny Rockets Diner (burgers); Vintages (tapas); and the self-explanatory Seafood Shack (on Oasis) and Rita's Cantina (on Allure). The Solarium Bistro serves spa cuisine and is complimentary at breakfast and lunch, but there is a charge for dinner. There's also a pizzeria, coffee bar, and doughnut shop. The ice cream parlor and cupcake bakery charge for frozen and sweet treats. Room service is available 24 hours, with a delivery charge after midnight.

Accommodations

Cabins: Three-dozen accommodation categories may seem confusing when making a selection, but they really boil down to variety of suites, outside cabins with balconies that face either the sea or overlook open-air interiors, ocean-view cabins, and interior cabins, some of which overlook the inside promenade. All standard accommodations include a small sitting area, TV, desk-vanity, hair dryer, refrigerator, and safe. Fares and even size are determined more by location in some categories.

Suites: On arrival, suite guests are welcomed with complimentary water, a fruit plate, and their choice of pillow style. Slippers, spa bathrobes, and Vitality bathroom amenities are provided. On the first formal evening, they receive a predinner cheese plate, and on the second formal or final evening of the cruise, a petits fours plate. They also enjoy complimentary 24-hour room service and coffee and tea service, and may order from the main dining room's full menus to dine en suite. A suite attendant is available to fulfill special requests, such as pressing service, which is complimentary on formal evenings.

Worth Noting: Junior suite guests receive complimentary Vitality bathroom amenities, coffee and tea service en suite, bathrobes for use onboard, and a suite attendant to assist with special requests. Forty-six staterooms are wheelchair accessible.

In the Know

Loft suites are two deck high contemporary staterooms with panoramic views. A stairway leads to second level where the master bedroom and bath are located. The main level living area has a convertible sofa bed and a bath with shower. Private balconies have a dining area and, in addition, the Royal Loft Suite has its own hot tub.

Pros and Cons

Pros: Reservations for specialty dining and most shows can be made up to 90 days prior to sailing, something highly recommended. The adults-only solarium has cabanas for rent that afford privacy—something you may be eager to pay for on such a big, busy ship. Two-way radios may not work on the ship; however you can rent a "Wow Phone" that is essentially an iPhone that only works onboard.

Cons: You might want to pack an umbrella—the sprawling Central Park and Boardwalk neighborhoods are open to the elements. On ships this large, lines are inevitable, particularly in the buffets and at disembarkation. Hold onto your wallet—there are extra charges at every turn.

Cabin Type	Size (sq. ft.)
Royal, Sky, Crown Loft Suites	1,524, 722, 545
Royal, Owner's, Grand Suites	1,275, 556, 371
Presidential, Royal Family Suites	1,142, 580
Aqua Theater Suites	673–823
Jr. Suite, Family Balcony	287, 271
Outside, Balcony, Family Outside	179–199, 260
Interior, Balcony, Family Interior	149–194, 260

FAST FACTS

- 16 passenger decks
- 5 specialty restaurants, dining room, 2 buffets, 3 cafés, ice cream parlor, pizzeria
- Wi-Fi, safe, refrigerator, DVD (some)
- 4 pools, children's pool
- Fitness classes, gym, hair salon, 10 hot tubs, spa
- 18 bars, casino, dance club, library
- Children's programs (ages 3–17)
- Dry-cleaning, laundry service
- Internet terminal
- No-smoking cabins

5

ROYAL CARIBBEAN

FREEDOM CLASS
Freedom, Liberty, Independence of the Seas

CREW MEMBERS	1,360
ENTERED SERVICE	2006, 2007, 2008
GROSS TONS	160,000
LENGTH	1,112 feet
NUMBER OF CABINS	1,817
PASSENGER CAPACITY	3,634
WIDTH	185 feet

700 ft.

500 ft.

300 ft.

Top: Johnny Rockets diner
Bottom: Hang 10 on the surf
simulator

Public Areas and Facilities

Although they are no longer the world's largest cruise ships, the Freedom-class vessels live up to Royal Caribbean's reputation for creative thinking that results in features to stir the imagination and provide a resortlike atmosphere at sea. Whether you are hanging 10 in the surf simulator, going a few rounds in the boxing ring, or strolling the Royal Promenade entertainment boulevard, there's almost no reason to go ashore.

The layout is more intuitive than you might expect on such a gigantic ship. Freedom-class vessels have a familiar mall-like promenade lined with shops and bistros, an ice-skating rink/theater, numerous lounges, and dining options, but are not simply enlarged Voyager-class ships. With plenty of room, even the most intimate spaces feel uncrowded. A good fit for extended families, these ships have expansive areas devoted to children and teens and enough adults-only spaces to satisfy everyone.

Restaurants

Triple-deck-high formal dining rooms serve open seating breakfast and lunch; dinner is served in two evening assigned seatings or open seating My Timing Dining. For a more upscale dinner, two specialty restaurants— Portofino, serving Italian fare, and Chops Grille, a steak house—both charge a supplement and require reservations. The casual Lido buffet offers service nearly around the clock for breakfast, lunch, dinner, and snacks. Jade, a section in the buffet, serves Asian food. Johnny Rockets is a popular option for casual meals, though it has a separate charge. In the promenade are a pizzeria, coffee bar, and Ben & Jerry's ice cream, which charges for frozen treats. A complimentary ice-cream bar is poolside, as is a juice bar, which charges by the item. Room service is available 24 hours; however, there is a delivery charge after midnight.

Accommodations

Cabins: As on other Royal Caribbean ships, cabins are bright and cheerful. Although 60% are outside cabins—and a whopping 78% of those have private balconies—bargain inside cabins, including some that are uniquely configured with a bowed window for a view overlooking the action-packed promenade, are plentiful. Cabins in every category have adequate closet and drawer–shelf storage, as well as bathroom shelves. Family ocean-view cabins with a window sleep up to six people with two twin beds (convertible to queen size), bunk beds in a separate area, a sitting room with a sofa bed, a vanity area, and a shower-only bathroom. At 1,215 square feet, the Presidential Suite sleeps 14 people and has an 810-square-foot veranda with a hot tub and bar.

Amenities: Wood cabinetry, a small refrigerator-minibar, broadband Internet connection, a vanity-desk, a flat-panel TV and DVD player, a safe, a hair dryer, and a sitting area with sofa, chair, and table are typical features in all categories. Bathrooms have shampoo and bath gel. Premium beds and bedding complete the comfortable package.

Worth Noting: Thirty-two staterooms are wheelchair accessible.

In the Know

Shipboard personnel expressed concern upon realizing the posteriors of the cows atop Ben & Jerry's marquee were aimed at the bay window of atrium-view stateroom 6305. They suggested the occupants be offered free ice cream during their cruise, so the ships now have a Ben & Jerry's "Sweet."

Pros and Cons

Pros: The FlowRider surfing simulator is so exciting that bleacher seating on three sides of the deck is often full of spectators. Full of bright and whimsical "family" figures, the H2O Zone is a fun place to beat the heat beneath a waterfall, in the fountain sprays, and along a lazy river (where the fountain sculptures mist everyone who floats by). A sports pool accommodates water volleyball, basketball, and golf, and a Solarium contains a tranquil pool for adults, as well as hammocks for relaxation and two huge hot tubs cantilevered 12 feet from the sides of the ship.

Cons: The self-serve frozen-yogurt bar is a cool treat, but its location near the kids' pool means that it often ends up messy. Hang on to your wallet—the burgers, onion rings, and all the trimmings in Johnny Rockets diner are a deal at only $3.95, but the malts are extra. On a ship this large, lines are inevitable, particularly at disembarkation.

Cabin Type	Size (sq. ft.)
Royal Suite	1,406
Presidential Suite	1,215
Owner's Suite	614
Grand Suite	387
Junior Suite	287
Family Stateroom	293
Balcony Stateroom	177–189
Ocean View	161–214
Inside	149–152

FAST FACTS

- 15 passenger decks
- 2 specialty restaurants, dining room, buffet, ice cream parlor, pizzeria
- Internet, Wi-Fi, safe, minibar (some), refrigerator, DVD (some)
- 3 pools, children's pool
- Fitness classes, gym, hair salon, 6 hot tubs, sauna, spa, steam room
- 14 bars, casino, cinema, 2 dance clubs, library, 3 showrooms, video game room
- Children's programs (ages 3–17)
- Dry-cleaning, laundry service
- Internet terminal
- No-smoking cabins

Climb the wall

5

ROYAL CARIBBEAN

VOYAGER CLASS
Voyager, Explorer, Adventure, Navigator, Mariner of the Seas

CREW MEMBERS	1,185
ENTERED SERVICE	1999, 2000, 2001, 2002, 2003
GROSS TONS	142,000
LENGTH	1,020 feet
NUMBER OF CABINS	1,557
PASSENGER CAPACITY	3,114 (3,835 max)
WIDTH	158 feet

700 ft.

500 ft.

300 ft.

Top: Rock-climbing wall
Bottom: Fitness class

Public Areas and Facilities

A truly impressive building program introduced one of these gigantic Voyager-class ships per year over a five-year period. With their rock-climbing walls, ice-skating rinks, in-line skating tracks, miniature golf, and multiple dining venues, they are destinations in their own right. Sports enthusiasts will be thrilled with nonstop daytime action.

The unusual horizontal, multiple-deck promenade-atriums on Voyager-class vessels can stage some of the pageantry for which Royal Caribbean is noted. Fringed with boutiques, bars, and even coffee shops, the mall-like expanses set the stage for evening parades and events, as well as simply spots to kick back for some people-watching.

Other public rooms are equally dramatic. Though it's considered to be three separate dining rooms, the triple-deck height of the single space is stunning. These ships not only carry a lot of people, but carry them well. Space is abundant, and crowding is seldom an issue.

Restaurants

Triple-deck-high formal dining rooms serve open seating breakfast and lunch; dinner is served in two evening assigned seatings or open seating My Timing Dining. For a more upscale dinner, each ship has a specialty restaurant, Portofino, serving Italian fare; *Mariner* and *Navigator* also feature Chops Grille, a steak house. Both specialty restaurants charge a supplement and require reservations. The casual Lido buffet offers service nearly around the clock for meals and snacks. The buffet offers dinner in a casual Island Grill; *Mariner* and *Navigator* also serve Asian fare in their Jade section. Johnny Rockets is a popular option for casual meals, though it also has a separate charge. In the promenade are a pizzeria, coffee bar, and Ben & Jerry's ice cream, which charges for frozen treats. Room service is available 24 hours; however there is a delivery charge after midnight.

Accommodations

Cabins: As on other Royal Caribbean ships, cabins are bright and cheerful. Although more than 60% are outside—and a hefty 75% of those have private verandas—there are still plenty of bargain inside cabins, some with a bowed window for a view overlooking the action-packed promenade. Cabins in every category have adequate closet and drawer–shelf storage and bathroom shelves. Junior Suites have a sitting area, vanity area, and bathroom with bathtub. Family ocean-view cabins with a window sleep up to six people and can accommodate a roll-away bed and/or crib, have two twin beds (convertible to a queen), and additional bunk beds in a separate area, a separate sitting area with a sofa bed, a vanity area, and a private bathroom with shower.

Amenities: Wood cabinetry, a small refrigerator-minibar, broadband Internet connection, a vanity-desk, a TV, a safe, a hair dryer, and a sitting area with sofa, chair, and table are typical Voyager-class features in all categories. Bathrooms have shampoo and bath gel.

Worth Noting: Twenty-six staterooms are designed for wheelchair accessibility.

In the Know

Long queues can form at security and check-in counters before the boarding process begins because many passengers arrive early and clog the terminal before the scheduled boarding time. Avoid the hassle by arriving a bit later to breeze through and start your cruise relaxed.

Pros and Cons

Pros: These ships have many impressive features, but the Royal Promenade, particularly when a parade or other event is center stage, may elicit the biggest "Wow!" Professional ice-skating performances are staged twice during each cruise. Active families will find something—rock climbing, ice-skating, full-size basketball courts, in-line skating, miniature golf—to keep everyone busy, and equipment to participate in all those sports activities is provided at no additional charge.

Cons: With the exception of the gym and some fitness classes, nearly everything else on board—including soft drinks, specialty coffees, meals in the alternative dining venues, spa services, bingo, and alcoholic beverages—carries a price tag. Although there is no charge to attend, you must get tickets for the ice-skating shows. Smokers may be frustrated to find that smoking is prohibited in cabins.

Cabin Type	Size (sq. ft.)
Royal Suite	1,188–1,325
Other Suites*	277–610
Superior/Deluxe/ Family Ocean View**	173–328
Large Ocean View	211
Standard Ocean View	161–180
Interior	153–167

*Owner's (506–618 sq. ft.), Grand (381–390 sq. ft.), Royal Family (512–610 sq. ft.), Jr. (277–299 sq. ft). **Superior (202–206 sq. ft.), Deluxe (173–184 sq. ft.), Family (265–328 sq. ft.).

FAST FACTS

- 14 passenger decks
- Specialty restaurant (2 on *Mariner* and *Navigator*), dining room, buffet, ice cream parlor, pizzeria
- Internet, Wi-Fi, safe, refrigerator, DVD (some)
- 3 pools, children's pool (only *Voyager*, *Explorer*, and *Adventure*)
- Fitness classes, gym, hair salon, 7 hot tubs, sauna, spa, steam room
- 12 bars, casino, cinema, 2 dance clubs, library, 3 showrooms, video game room
- Children's programs (ages 3–17)
- Dry-cleaning, laundry service
- Internet terminal
- No-smoking cabins

5

ROYAL CARIBBEAN

RADIANCE CLASS
Radiance, Brilliance, Serenade, Jewel of the Seas

CREW MEMBERS	857
ENTERED SERVICE	2001, 2002, 2003, 2004
GROSS TONS	90,090
LENGTH	962 feet
NUMBER OF CABINS	1,071/1,056/1,056/1,056
PASSENGER CAPACITY	2,139/2,112/2,112/2,112
WIDTH	106 feet

700 ft.

500 ft.

300 ft.

Top: pool deck
Bottom: Shared moments on your personal balcony

Public Areas and Facilities
Considered by many people to be the most beautiful vessels in the Royal Caribbean fleet, Radiance-class ships are large but sleek and swift, with sun-filled interiors and panoramic elevators that span 10 decks along the ships' exteriors.

High-energy and glamorous spaces are abundant throughout these sister ships. From the rock-climbing wall, children's pool with waterslide, and golf area to the columned dining room, sweeping staircases, and the tropical garden of the solarium, these ships hold appeal for a wide cross section of interests and tastes. The ships are packed with multiple dining venues, including the casual Windjammer, with its indoor and outdoor seating, and the Latte Tudes patisserie, offering specialty coffees, pastries, and ice-cream treats.

Restaurants
The double-deck-high formal dining room serves open seating breakfast and lunch; dinner is served in two assigned seatings or open seating My Timing Dining. For a more upscale dinner, each ship has at least two specialty restaurants—Portofino or Giovanni's Table, serving Italian fare, and Chops Grille, a steak house. Both charge a supplement and require reservations. A revitalization of *Radiance of the Seas* in 2011 added a Brazilian-style churrascaria, Mexican, and Asian restaurants. No word is available on whether the other Radiance-class ships will receive similar upgrades. The casual Lido buffet offers service nearly around the clock for breakfast, lunch, dinner, and snacks. Seaview Café is open for quick lunches and dinners in a laid-back setting (except *Radiance*). A pizzeria in the Solarium serves pizza by the slice; *Radiance* also has a hot dog bar. The coffee bar features specialty coffees and pastries, for which there is a charge. Room service is available 24 hours; however there is a charge after midnight.

Accommodations
Cabins: With the line's highest percentage of outside cabins, standard staterooms are bright and cheery as well as roomy. Nearly three-quarters of the outside cabins have private balconies. Every cabin has adequate closet and drawer/shelf storage, as well as bathroom shelves.

Suites: All full suites and family suites have private balconies and include concierge service. Top-category suites have wet bars, separate living–dining areas, multiple bathrooms, entertainment centers with flat-screen TVs, DVD players, and stereos. Some bathrooms have twin sinks, steam showers, and whirlpool tubs. Junior suites have a sitting area, vanity area, and bathroom with a tub.

Amenities: Light-wood cabinetry, a small refrigerator-minibar, broadband Internet connection, a vanity-desk, a TV, a safe, a hair dryer, and a sitting area with sofa, chair, and table are typical Radiance-class features in all categories. Bathroom extras include shampoo and bath gel.

Worth Noting: Fifteen staterooms are designed for wheelchair accessiblity on *Radiance* and *Brilliance*; 19 on *Serenade* and *Jewel*. *Radiance* also has three single cabins.

In the Know
Other cruise ships may have rollicking sports bars (and these do as well), but Radiance-class vessels also have self-leveling pool tables.

Pros and Cons
Pros: Aft on deck 6, four distinct lounges and a billiard room with self-leveling pool tables form a clubby adult entertainment center furnished in rich colors and accented by warm woods. Not everyone discovers the out-of-the-way Seaview Café, making it a favored casual dining spot for those passengers who take the time to locate it. Spacious family ocean-view cabins sleep up to six people and can accommodate a rollaway bed and/or a crib; the suites also come with two twin beds (convertible into one queen size), additional bunk beds in a separate area, and a separate sitting area with a sofa bed.

Cons: With the traditional and nautical-leaning decor on these otherwise classy ships, the weird free-form atrium sculptures are a jarring throwback to earlier design elements. The location of the pizzeria in the Solarium adds a layer of confusion to an otherwise tranquil retreat. The libraries are tiny and poorly stocked for ships this size.

Cabin Type	Size (sq. ft.)
Royal Suite	1,001
Owner's Suite	512
Grand Suite	358–384
Royal Family Suite	533–586
Junior Suites	293
Superior Ocean View	204
Deluxe Ocean View	179
Large Ocean View	170
Family Ocean View	319
Interior	165

FAST FACTS

- 12 passenger decks
- 2 specialty restaurants (5 on *Radiance*), dining room, buffet, pizzeria
- Internet, Wi-Fi, safe, refrigerator, DVD (some)
- 2 pools (1 indoor), children's pool
- Fitness classes, gym, hair salon, 3 hot tubs, sauna, spa, steam room
- 11 bars, casino, cinema, dance club, library, showroom, video game room
- Children's programs (ages 3–17)
- Dry-cleaning, laundry service
- Internet terminal
- No-smoking cabins

Sports courts

ENCHANTMENT OF THE SEAS

CREW MEMBERS	840
ENTERED SERVICE	1997
GROSS TONS	81,500
LENGTH	989 feet
NUMBER OF CABINS	1,126
PASSENGER CAPACITY	2,252 (2,730 max)
WIDTH	106 feet

700 ft.

500 ft.

300 ft.

Top: Formal dining
Bottom: Ocean-view
stateroom

Public Areas and Facilities

In 2005 *Enchantment of the Seas* (originally a Vision-class ship identical to *Grandeur of the Seas*) was the third Royal Caribbean ship to be lengthened to increase her capacity and facilities. After she was cut in half, a new, 73-foot middle section containing 151 staterooms and suspension bridges that span the pool area and overhang the sea were added. Not only was the pool area expanded by almost 50%, but four bungee trampolines were installed—for real thrills you can soar high above the bow while safely tethered to the trampoline.

For a buzz of a different sort, a pool bar juts out over the water where peekaboo windows set into the deck afford views of the sea below. Nearby floor-mounted water jets create a splash deck for children that transforms into a lighted fountain after dark. Recreational facilities and the spa were also expanded during the renovation. Not to be overlooked, interiors now include the South Beach–style Bolero's lounge as well as a coffee and ice cream bar, a steak house, and an enlarged Windjammer Café.

Restaurants

The double-deck-high formal dining room serves open seating breakfast and lunch; dinner is served in two evening assigned seatings or open seating My Timing Dining. For a more upscale dinner, there is the specialty steak house, Chops Grille, which charges a supplement and requires reservations. The casual Lido buffet offers service nearly around the clock for breakfast, lunch, dinner, and snacks. A pizzeria in the Solarium serves pizza by the slice. The coffee bar features specialty coffees and pastries and Ben & Jerry's ice cream, for which there is a charge. Room service is available 24 hours; however, there is a delivery charge after midnight.

Accommodations

Cabins: Cabins are light and comfortable, although the smallest can be a tight squeeze for more than two adults. Every cabin has adequate closet and drawer/shelf storage, as well as bathroom shelves.

Suites: All full suites and family suites have private balconies, a small refrigerator-minibar; full suites include concierge service. Royal Suites have a living room, wet bar, separate dining area, TV, stereo, and DVD player, separate bedroom, bathroom (with twin sinks, a whirlpool tub, steam shower, and bidet), and separate powder room. Owner's Suites have separate living area, minibar, TV, stereo, and DVD player, dinette area, and bathroom with twin sinks, bathtub, separate shower, and bidet. Grand Suites have a sitting area, stereo and DVD player, bathroom with combination bathtub-shower, and double sink.

Amenities: Light woods, pastel colors, a vanity-desk, a TV, a safe, a hair dryer, and a sitting area with sofa, chair, and table are typical features in all categories. Bathrooms have shampoo and bath gel.

Worth Noting: Fourteen staterooms are designed for wheelchair accessibility.

In the Know

From a seat in Viking Crown Lounge, you could look the Statue of Liberty in the eye. With practice, you might be able to jump that high on a bungee trampoline.

Pros and Cons

Pros: The transformation of an underutilized lounge into Chops Grille and the addition of both a concierge lounge and Bolero's Latin nightclub were brilliant moves during the ship's stretch. With a nod to variety, the jogging track contains a vitality course where fitness stops offer runners the opportunity to jump rope, use sit-up/press-up bars and a step-up station, as well as cool down by performing suggested stretching moves. Four bungee trampolines offer some serious fun for thrill seekers, who must conform to specific height and weight restrictions, making them suitable for most adults and teens.

Cons: With the number of cabins increased to accommodate more passengers, public areas of the ship can suffer overload when sailing fully booked. The tranquil library suffers from an underabundance of books, so bring your own reading material. The poolside Island Bar is only steps away from the splash deck—transformed after dark into a decorative fountain with fiber-optic lights playing off the water—that's pretty boisterous during the day when kids are splashing about.

Cabin Type	Size (sq. ft.)
Royal Suites	1,119
Owner's Suites	511
Grand Suites	349
Royal Family Suites	532
Junior Suites	245
Superior Ocean View	190
Large Ocean View	154
Family Ocean View	449
Family Interior	230
Large Interior	146
Standard Interior	140

FAST FACTS

- 11 passenger decks
- Specialty restaurant, dining room, buffet, ice cream parlor, pizzeria
- Wi-Fi, safe, refrigerator, DVD (some)
- 3 pools (1 indoor), children's pool
- Fitness classes, gym, hair salon, 6 hot tubs, sauna, spa
- 6 bars, casino, dance club, library, showroom, video game room
- Children's programs (ages 3–17)
- Dry-cleaning, laundry service
- Internet terminal
- No-smoking cabins

Enchantment of the Seas at sea

5

ROYAL CARIBBEAN

VISION CLASS
Legend, Splendour, Grandeur, Rhapsody, Vision of the Seas

CREW MEMBERS	720, 720, 760, 765, 765
ENTERED SERVICE	1995, 1996, 1996, 1997, 1998
GROSS TONS	69,130–78,491
LENGTH	867, 867, 916, 915, 915 feet
NUMBER OF CABINS	900, 900, 975, 1,000, 1,000
PASSENGER CAPACITY	1,800–2,000 (2,076–2,435 max)
WIDTH	106 feet

700 ft.

500 ft.

300 ft.

Top: Vision-class Owner's Suite
Bottom: *Splendour of the Seas*

Public Areas and Facilities

The first Royal Caribbean ships to offer balconies in a number of categories, these Vision-class vessels, named for sister ship *Vision of the Seas*, have acres of glass skylights that allow sunlight to flood in and windows that offer wide sea vistas. The soaring central atrium at the heart of each ship is anchored by a champagne bar and fills with music after dark.

Built in pairs, the ships follow the same general layout but are different in overall size and the total number of passengers on board. Cabin sizes also vary somewhat; as the total size of the ships increased from *Legend* and *Splendour* at 69,130 tons (1,800 passengers) to *Grandeur* at 74,140 tons (1,950 passengers), and finally, *Rhapsody* and *Vision* at 78,491 tons (2,000 passengers), so did the size of the accommodations. In some categories, it's only a matter of a few feet, so don't look for huge—or even noticeable—differences.

Restaurants

As was the norm when these ships were built, dining selections on board are pretty basic. The double-deck-high formal dining room serves evening meals in two assigned evening seatings or open seating My Timing Dining; breakfast and lunch in the dining room are always open seating. Windjammer, the casual Lido buffet, serves three meals a day, including a laid-back dinner. Evening meals in the formal dining room and buffet are often regionally themed and feature menus that focus on Italian, French, and American dishes. Room service is available 24 hours a day; however, there is a delivery charge after midnight. A poolside grill serves burgers and snacks in the solarium. A coffee bar offers specialty coffees and pastries for an additional fee. Sadly, there are no specialty restaurants on these ships; however, *Splendour of the Seas* will receive two during a major refurbishment in 2011. No word is available whether the other Vision-class ships will also be upgraded.

Accommodations

Cabins: Cabins are airy and comfortable, but the smaller categories are a tight squeeze for more than two adults. Every cabin has adequate closet and drawer/shelf storage.

Suites: All full suites and family suites have private balconies and a small minibar; full suites also include concierge service. Royal Suites have a living room; wet bar; separate dining area; entertainment center with TV, stereo, and DVD player; separate bedroom; bathroom (twin sinks, whirlpool tub, separate steam shower, bidet); and separate powder room. Owner's Suites have a separate living area; minibar; entertainment center with TV, stereo, and DVD player; dinette area; and one bathroom (twin sinks, bathtub, separate shower, bidet). Grand Suites have similar amenities on a smaller scale.

Amenities: Light woods, pastel colors, a vanity-desk, a TV, a safe, a hair dryer, and a sitting area with sofa, chair, and table are typical Vision-class features in all categories. Bathrooms have shampoo and bath gel.

Worth Noting: On *Legend* and *Splendour*, 17 cabins are wheelchair accessible; on *Grandeur*, *Vision*, and *Rhapsody*, 14 cabins are wheelchair accessible.

In the Know

Not all suites on Vision-class ships are created equal. A Royal Family Suite is a roomy choice for parents with younger children, but goodies that other suites receive—including bathrobes to use on board, welcome-aboard champagne, evening canapés, and concierge service—aren't included.

Pros and Cons

Pros: Open, light-filled public areas offer sea views from almost every angle on these ships. Each vessel features a double-deck-high dining room with sweeping staircases that are a huge improvement over previous ship designs. Tucked into an atrium nook, the Champagne Bar on each ship is not only an elegant spot for predinner cocktails and dancing but also for quiet after-dinner or after-the-show drinks and conversation.

Cons: Some lounges, particularly the popular Schooner Bars, serve as a thoroughfare and suffer from continuous traffic flow before and after performances in the ships' main show lounges. Accommodations lean toward the small side, unless you are willing to pay a premium for a suite. There are no specialty restaurants, and dining options are severely limited as a result.

Cabin Type	Size (sq. ft.)
Royal Suite	1,074
Owner's Suite	523
Grand Suite	355
Royal Family Suite	512
Junior Suite	240
Superior Ocean View	193
Large Ocean View*	154
Interior	135–174

All cabin sizes are averages of the five ships since cabins vary somewhat in size among the Vision-class ships (all *Legend* and *Splendour* cabins are the same size). *Rhapsody* has Family Ocean View cabins at 237 sq. ft.

FAST FACTS

- 11 passenger decks
- 2 specialty restaurants (*Splendour* only), dining room, buffet, ice cream parlor, pizzeria
- Wi-Fi, safe, refrigerator (some), DVD (some)
- 2 pools (1 indoor)
- Fitness classes, gym, hair salon, 4–6 hot tubs, sauna, spa
- 6 bars, casino, dance club, library, showroom, video game room
- Children's programs (ages 3–17)
- Dry-cleaning, laundry service
- Internet terminal
- No-smoking cabins

5

ROYAL CARIBBEAN

SOVEREIGN CLASS
Monarch, Majesty of the Seas

CREW MEMBERS	
856, 912	
ENTERED SERVICE	
1991, 1992	
GROSS TONS	
73,941	
LENGTH	
880 feet	
NUMBER OF CABINS	
1,193, 1,190	
PASSENGER CAPACITY	
2,390, 2,350 (2,774 max)	
WIDTH	
106 feet	

700 ft.
500 ft.
300 ft.

Public Areas and Facilities

Precursor of vessels to come, *Sovereign of the Seas,* which no longer sails in the Royal Caribbean fleet, was the largest cruise ship afloat when it was introduced in 1988. Two sister ships followed and, although they all share the same layout, subtle differences exist in size and the number of passengers they carry. *Majesty* and *Monarch* have received major refurbishments, with the addition of Miami Beach–style Latin clubs, and Johnny Rockets diners. Other improvements include an expanded spa and enlarged areas for children and teens. Balconies were also added to 62 junior suites.

The futuristic atrium, combined with the abundant use of marble and gleaming metal, virtually assured the Sovereign-class ships design longevity. The addition of rock-climbing walls and other features found on subsequent Royal Caribbean vessels, plus sparkling new interior colors, belie the age of these ships.

Restaurants

As was the norm when these ships were built, dining selections on board are pretty basic. Although there are no upscale specialty restaurants, casual dining options are a bit more tempting than on the newer Vision-class ships. Two formal dining rooms serve breakfast and lunch in open seatings and dinner in two assigned seatings or open seating My Timing Dining. The Windjammer casual Lido buffet serves three meals a day, including a casual dinner option. In addition, *Majesty* has Sorrento's Pizza restaurant, Johnny Rockets Diner, and a deli in the Windjammer, while *Monarch* features specialty Asian-fusion cuisine and sushi at Jade and Sorrento's pizzeria. Both ships have Latte-Tudes, a patisserie serving specialty coffees, pastries, and Ben & Jerry's ice cream. All these options carry an extra charge. Room service is available 24 hours; however, there is a delivery charge after midnight.

Accommodations

Cabins: Cabins are comfortable, but standard oceanview and inside categories are a tight squeeze for more than two occupants. When these ships were conceived, staterooms were viewed as primarily for sleeping and changing clothes, so even the suites are on the small size by current standards. Every cabin has adequate closet

Majesty of the Seas: The Centrum

and drawer/shelf storage. The added personal space provided by the balconies in suites and junior suites on both ships is a real plus.

Suites: All suites and junior suites have a minibar, balcony, and bathtub. Royal Family Suites (on *Majesty of the Seas* only) have a sitting area, dining area, two bedrooms (one with two twin beds and an upper bunk, one with queen-size bed), and two bathrooms.

Amenities: Light woods, mirrored accents, a vanity-desk, TV, safe, and hair dryer are typical Sovereign-class features in all categories. Bathrooms have shampoo and bath gel.

Worth Noting: Third and fourth Pullman beds are found in a variety of stateroom categories, as are connecting staterooms—a plus for families that require more room to spread out. Six staterooms are designed for wheelchair accessibility.

In the Know

These ships are ideally suited for short cruises, especially since the addition of more expansive facilities for younger children and teens and a redesigned fitness center and spa.

Pros and Cons

Pros: In addition to an Internet center, Wi-Fi hot spots are in public rooms, and cell phone access at sea is a hot new (albeit very expensive) feature. Each ship has a Schooner Bar, Royal Caribbean's signature piano bar with seagoing flair (models of sailing ships and even a smoky tar scent set the tone). Even at their age, the multideck atriums—cruise ship firsts—are still stunning, and these ships continue to be the best choice for a short getaway cruise.

Cons: Unfortunately, some remnants of late-1980s design are difficult to overcome, including few balconies and low ceilings in the dining rooms. The rock-climbing walls are certainly impressive enough, but they really look like an afterthought, and their awkward position spoils the view overlooking the stern from the Viking Crown Lounge. Standard accommodations are really tight for more than two people, and the lack of passenger laundry facilities is an inconvenience for families.

Cabin Type	Size (sq. ft.)
Royal Suite	670
Owner's Suite	446
Grand Suite	382
Royal Family Suite*	371
Jr. Suite	264
Superior Ocean View	157
Standard Ocean View	122
Inside	119

*Only on *Majesty of the Seas*

FAST FACTS

- 11 passenger decks
- 2 dining rooms, buffet, pizzeria
- Wi-Fi, safe (some), refrigerator (some), DVD (some)
- 2 pools
- Fitness classes, gym, hair salon, 2 hot tubs, sauna (*Majesty* only), spa
- 7 bars, casino, 2 dance clubs, library, showroom, video game room
- Children's programs (ages 3–17)
- Dry-cleaning, laundry service
- Internet terminal
- No-smoking cabins

5

ROYAL CARIBBEAN

Formal dining room

SEABOURN CRUISE LINE

Seabourn was founded on the principle that dedication to personal service in elegant surroundings would appeal to sophisticated, independent-minded passengers whose lifestyles demand the best. Lovingly maintained since their introduction in 1987—and rou-

Make memories to last a lifetime

tinely updated with new features—the original megayachts of Seabourn and their new fleet mates have proved to be a smashing success over the years. They remain favorites with people who can take care of themselves but would rather do so aboard a ship that caters to their individual preferences.

✉ *300 Elliott Ave. West Seattle, WA*
☏ *800/929–9391*
⊕ *www.seabourn.com*
☞ *Cruise Style: Luxury.*

Recognized as a leader in small-ship, luxury cruising, Seabourn delivers all the expected extras—complimentary wines and spirits, a stocked minibar in all suites, and elegant amenities. Expect the unexpected as well—from exclusive travel-document portfolios and luggage tags to the pleasure of a complimentary minimassage while lounging at the pool. If you don't want to lift a finger, Seabourn will even arrange to have your luggage picked up at home and delivered directly to your suite—for a price.

Dining and evening socializing are generally more stimulating to Seabourn passengers than splashy song-and-dance revues. Still, proportionately scaled production shows and cabarets are presented in the main show room and smaller lounge. Movies Under the Stars are shown on the wind-protected Sun Deck at least one evening on virtually all cruises as long as the weather permits. The library stocks not only books but also movies for those who prefer to watch them in the privacy of their suites—popcorn will naturally be delivered with a call to room service.

The Dress Circle Series enrichment program features guest appearances by luminaries in the arts, literature, politics, and world affairs; during Chef's Circle sailings you can learn the secrets of the world's most innovative chefs. Due to the size of Seabourn ships, passengers have the opportunity to mingle with presenters and interact one-on-one.

Peace and tranquillity reign on these ships, so the daily roster of events is somewhat thin. Wine-tastings, lectures, and other quiet pursuits might be scheduled, but most passengers are satisfied to simply do what pleases them.

One don't-miss activity is the daily team trivia contest. Prizes are unimportant: it's the bragging rights that most guests seek.

Although the trio of original Seabourn ships has been upgraded with new features over the years, the line bagan a program to build a new set of larger, even more luxurious triplets that were introduced in 2009 (*Seabourn Odyssey*), 2010 (*Seabourn Sojourn*), and 2011 (*Seabourn Quest*). At this writing there is no word about when (or if) the original megayachts will be retired.

Food

Exceptional cuisine created by celebrity chef Charlie Palmer is prepared *à la minute* and served in open seating dining rooms. Upscale menu offerings include foie gras, quail, fresh seafood, and jasmine crème brûlée. Dishes low in cholesterol, salt, and fat, as well as vegetarian selections, are prepared with the same artful presentation and attention to detail. Wines are chosen to complement each day's luncheon and dinner menus, and caviar is always available. A background of classical music sets the tone for afternoon tea. The weekly Gala Tea features crèpes Suzette.

A casual dinner alternative on the original ships is Restaurant 2, serving innovative cuisine in multiple courses nightly in the Veranda Café, where outdoor tables enhance the romantic atmosphere. Evening attire in the Veranda Café is specified as casual or elegant casual—when men are asked to wear a jacket but no tie. A second and even more laid-back dinner alternative is offered on select occasions in the open-air Sky Bar, where grilled seafood and steaks are served. "Sky Grill" dinners are scheduled on at least a couple of nights during each cruise on all ships, weather permitting. Both Restaurant 2 and Sky Grill require reservations, but happily there is no additional charge for either. Aboard the new ships, Restaurant 2 has a dedicated space, and the Colannade indoor–outdoor restaurant is centered on an open kitchen where you

5

SEABOURN CRUISE LINE

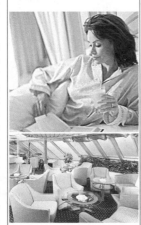

Top: A good book and breakfast in bed
Bottom: The Club

Top: French balcony
Middle: Dining by candlelight in
The Restaurant
Bottom: Relax on deck

can watch chefs prepare your breakfast, lunch, or dinner order. Each evening has a different theme, offering an ever-changing culinary experience.

Room service is always available. Dinner can even be served course by course in your suite during restaurant hours.

Fitness and Recreation
A full array of exercise equipment, free weights, and basic fitness classes is available in the small gym, while some specialized fitness sessions are offered for a fee.

Many passengers are drawn to the pampering spa treatments, including a variety of massages, body wraps, and facials. Hair and nail services are offered in the salon. Both spa and salon are operated by Steiner Leisure.

Your Shipmates
Seabourn's yachtlike vessels appeal to well-traveled, affluent couples of all ages who enjoy destination-intense itineraries, a subdued atmosphere, and exclusive service. Passengers tend to be fifty-plus and retired couples who are accustomed to evening formality.

Dress Code
At least one formal night is standard on seven-night cruises and three to four nights, depending on the itinerary, on two-week cruises. Men are required to wear tuxedos or dark suits after 6 pm, and the majority prefer black tie. All other evenings are elegant casual, and slacks with a jacket over a sweater or shirt for men and a sundress or skirt or pants with a sweater or blouse for women are suggested.

Junior Cruisers
Seabourn Cruise Line is adult-oriented and does not accommodate children under six months (or under one year for trans-ocean sailings and voyages of 15 days or longer). A limited number of suites are available for triple occupancy; anyone two years of age and older traveling as the third passenger in a suite pays 50% of the paid category cruise-only brochure fare. No dedicated children's facilities are present on these

CHOOSE THIS LINE IF ...

You consider fine dining the highlight of your vacation.

You own your own tuxedo. These ships are dressy, and most men wear them on formal evenings.

You feel it's annoying to sign drink tabs; everything is included on these ships.

ships, so parents are responsible for the behavior and entertainment of their children.

Service

Personal service and attention by the professional staff are the orders of the day. Your preferences are noted and fulfilled without the necessity of reminders. It's a mystery how nearly every staff member knows your name within hours, if not minutes, after you board.

Tipping

Tipping is neither required nor expected.

Past Passengers

Once you have completed your first Seabourn cruise, you are automatically enrolled in the Seabourn Club for past guests. Benefits include up to a 50% discount on selected cruises (not combinable with Early Booking Savings); the Seabourn Club newsletters and periodic mailings featuring destinations, special programs, and exclusive savings; and an exclusive online email contact point to the Club Desk through the membership page on the Seabourn Web site.

On the ships, Club members receive a discount on future bookings, special recognition for frequent cruisers, and a Club party hosted by the captain. Passengers who sail 140 days aboard Seabourn are awarded a complimentary cruise of up to 7 days. Those who sail 250 days receive a 14-day cruise reward.

GOOD TO KNOW

Shore excursions often include privileged access to historic and cultural sites when they are not open to the general public. A highlight of Seabourn's warm-weather cruises is a picnic on a private beach when the uniformed captain and crew members wade into the surf to serve champagne and caviar to guests enjoying a refreshing dip in the sea.

5

SEABOURN CRUISE LINE

DON'T CHOOSE THIS LINE IF ...

Dressing down is on your agenda.

You absolutely must have a spacious private balcony. They are limited in number and book fast.

You need to be stimulated by constant activity.

SEABOURN ODYSSEY, SEABOURN SOJOURN, SEABOURN QUEST

CREW MEMBERS	330
ENTERED SERVICE	2009, 2010, 2011
GROSS TONS	32,000
LENGTH	650
NUMBER OF CABINS	225
PASSENGER CAPACITY	450
WIDTH	84

700 ft.

500 ft.

300 ft.

Top: *Seabourn Odyssey* at sea
Bottom: *Seabourn Odyssey* penthouse

Public Areas and Facilities

As the first new class of ultraluxurious ships to be introduced in nearly a decade, *Seabourn Odyssey* and her sister ships promise to continue the line's tradition of understated elegance and signature features in a larger setting. With more space, there are more pools, more hot tubs, and a two-deck spa. The specialty dining room gets its own dedicated space, and there's more room to spread out on deck and in gracious public lounges indoors.

As on the trio of smaller Seabourn vessels, there is a Club bar for predinner cocktails and an observation lounge affording expansive sea views. New for the larger ships is a spacious show lounge with a proper stage for entertainment.

When the water-sports marina is extended, there's even a third swimming option—an enclosed in-sea "pool" with teak deck.

Restaurants

The formal Restaurant serves breakfast, lunch, and dinner in open seating during scheduled hours. The reservations-required dinner option is Restaurant 2, where dishes are prepared individually by the chef in tasting portions. For casual indoor–outdoor dining, The Colonnade serves breakfast, lunch, and dinner from an open kitchen, where your order is individually prepared and each evening's meal has a different theme. Breakfast, lunch, and dinner are also offered poolside at the Patio Grill. Traditional Italian espresso and cappuccino are available at the coffee bar, where sandwiches, sweets, and ice cream are also available. Meals and snacks can be ordered from an extensive room-service menu around the clock. During restaurant hours, dinner can be served course by course en suite.

Accommodations

Cabins: All suites, 90% of which have private verandas, are located midship to forward and none are aft. Eight categories of roomy accommodations are truly of suite proportions, with separate bedrooms in all but the least expensive, which have a curtain that can be drawn between the bed and sitting area for privacy. Even the most modest suites have walk-in closets, a sitting area with a dining-height table for meals, a dressing table, and a granite-topped bathroom with double-sink vanities and a separate shower and tub (with whirlpool jets in Wintergarden and Signature Suites).

Amenities: Amenities also befit true luxury suites: flat-screen interactive TV with DVD player, safe, hair dryer, fully stocked minibar, fresh fruit and flowers, world atlas, personalized stationery, shampoo, conditioner, designer soap and lotion, Egyptian cotton towels and robes, slippers, umbrellas, and beds dressed with silky, high-thread-count linens. Top-category suites have the added benefit of a butler's pantry and guest powder room. Wintergarden and Signature Suites can be configured with two bedrooms by adding a connecting suite to make a Grand Suite.

Worth Noting: Seven suites are designed for wheelchair accessibility.

In the Know

Seabourn Square is the innovative new concierge lounge where you can arrange a tour, check your email in the computer center, get a book from the library, grab a coffee, or ask any questions you might have at the Purser's Desk.

Pros and Cons

Pros: Kayaks, waterskiing, and other complimentary water toys are available at the fold-down Marina during beach parties and when the ships are at anchor. The fully equipped gym has state-of-the-art equipment as well as the Kinesis Wall, a unique pulley-and-cable system that is the newest, most innovative method of exercise available today. There is never a cover charge for specialty dining.

Cons: Choose your suite location carefully—not all balconies are created equally, even those within the same category. Although the spa is opulent and contains two 750-square-foot Spa Villas for private treatments, the thermal suite features differ, and you may not find a therapy pool. Past passengers, particularly those with a long history of sailing with Seabourn, take a proprietary interest in the ships and may seem somewhat cliquish to newcomers.

Cabin Type	Size (sq. ft.)
Grand Wintergarden	1,182
Wintergarden Suites	914
Grand Signature	1,135
Signature Suites	819
Owner's Suites	611–675
Penthouse Suites	436–611
Veranda Suite	269–302
Ocean-View Suite	295

FAST FACTS

- 8 passenger decks
- Specialty restaurant, dining room, buffet
- Wi-Fi, safe, refrigerator, DVD
- 2 pools
- Fitness classes, gym, hair salon, 6 hot tubs, sauna, spa, steam room
- 5 bars, casino, dance club, library, showroom
- Dry-cleaning, laundry facilities, laundry service
- Internet terminal

5

SEABOURN CRUISE LINE

Standard suite

SEABOURN LEGEND, PRIDE, SPIRIT

CREW MEMBERS	160
ENTERED SERVICE	1992, 1988, 1989
GROSS TONS	10,000
LENGTH	439 feet
NUMBER OF CABINS	104
PASSENGER CAPACITY	208
WIDTH	63 feet

700 ft.

500 ft.

300 ft.

Top: Sky Bar
Bottom: Balcony Suite

Public Areas and Facilities

The height of absolute luxury, Seabourn's megayachts surround passengers in comfort and understated style punctuated by polished brass accents and etched-glass panels. Public rooms are intimate but not cramped, although predinner cocktail gatherings tend to strain the available room in the popular Club bar.

The relative amount of ship-wide space devoted to passengers is among the highest in the cruise industry, and the public areas and deck spaces were designed so that no one aboard feels crowded. Fresh flower arrangements add a gracious touch to the classic decor of every public room.

After an ambitious program of extensive refurbishment, which was completed in 2008, each of Seabourn's yachtlike vessels emerged from dry dock ship-shape.

Restaurants

The formal restaurant offers open seating breakfast, lunch, and dinner during scheduled hours. For a more laid-back setting, the Veranda Café has indoor and outdoor seating for breakfast and lunch, plus reservations-required Restaurant 2 serves tasting dinners in a smart-casual atmosphere every evening, including formal nights. The grill serves outdoors when weather permits for lunch and when Sky Grill dinners are scheduled on at least a couple of nights during each cruise. Tea is served every afternoon, and room service is available 24 hours. During scheduled lunch and dinner hours in the formal restaurant, room service is available from the restaurant menu.

Accommodations

Cabins: All suites are on three midlevel decks and none are aft, which can be noisy on a ship with a watersports marina. The roomy accommodations are truly of suite proportions, with large walk-in closets, a spacious sitting area with coffee table that converts to a dining table for meals, a vanity-desk, and a marble bathroom with a separate shower and tub (in most suites). Owner's, Classic, and Double suites have an actual dining table and chairs; Owner's suites have a guest bathroom. Both Owner's and Classic suites have fully furnished balconies.

Amenities: Amenities are also befitting a true luxury suite: a flat-screen TV with DVD player, a Bose Wave CD stereo, a safe, and a hair dryer. Other amenities include a stocked minibar, fresh fruit and flowers, a world atlas, personalized stationery, shampoo, conditioner, designer soap and lotion, Egyptian cotton towels and robes, slippers, umbrellas, and beds dressed with silky, high-thread-count linens. The only apparent difference between the sister ships is that *Seabourn Spirit* and *Seabourn Pride* have twin sinks in the bathrooms, while *Seabourn Legend* bathrooms have but one.

Worth Noting: Four suites are designed for wheelchair accessibility.

In the Know
Brush up on obscure facts before boarding if you plan to participate in Team Trivia: the hotly contested competition can be brutal. Bridge is another serious pastime on Seabourn cruises, so you're sure to find a foursome. Decks and score pads are provided on board, so you can leave your cards at home.

Pros and Cons
Pros: As the high crew member–to–guest ratio suggests, service is nonstop, and if you're the slightest bit indecisive, the staff seems to anticipate your wishes. For pure indulgence, make a selection from the aromatherapy bath menu before a soak in the tub; your cabin attendant will even draw it for you, although you'll have to wash your own back and dry yourself off afterward. Complimentary Massage Moments on deck are soothing tension tamers and an antidote to travel weariness.

Cons: A limited number of mini-balconies are available in standard suites, but they're simply for fresh air, as there's no room to stand outside on them—go this route if you want a taste of the sea air but can't upgrade to a full balcony. A single outdoor swimming pool is deep but not long enough for serious laps. Art, or the absence of it, is noteworthy on a ship of this style; some well-chosen, colorful pieces would add vibrancy to the otherwise predominantly blue and neutral color schemes.

Cabin Type	Size (sq. ft.)
Owner's Suite	530–575
Classic Suite	400
Double Suite	554
Balcony Suite*	277
Ocean View Suite	277

*The balcony isn't functional.

FAST FACTS

- 6 passenger decks
- Specialty restaurant, dining room, buffet
- Wi-Fi, safe, refrigerator, DVD
- Pool
- Fitness classes, gym, hair salon, 3 hot tubs, sauna, spa, steam room
- 3 bars, casino, dance club, library, showroom
- Dry-cleaning, laundry facilities, laundry service
- Internet terminal

5

SEABOURN CRUISE LINE

Water-sports marina

SEADREAM YACHT CLUB

SeaDream yachts began sailing in 1984 beneath the Sea Goddess banner, and after a couple of changes of ownership, total renovation in 2002, and refits in 2007, they have evolved into the ultimate boutique ships. A voyage on one of these sleek megayachts

SeaDream I at sea

is all about personal choice. Passengers enjoy an unstructured holiday at sea doing what they please, making it easy to imagine the diminutive vessel really is a private yacht. The ambience is refined and elegantly casual.

✉ *2601 S. Bayshore Dr., Penthouse 1B, Coconut Grove, FL*

☎ *305/856–5622 or 800/707–4911*

⊕ *www.seadreamyacht club.com*

☞ *Cruise Style: Luxury.*

Fine dining and socializing with fellow passengers and the ships' captains and officers are preferred yachting pastimes. Other than a pianist in the tiny piano bar, a small casino, and movies in the main lounge, there's no roster of activities. The late-night place to be is the Top of the Yacht Bar, where passengers gather to share the day's experiences and kick their shoes off to dance on the teak deck. The captain hosts welcome-aboard and farewell cocktail receptions in the Main Salon each week. Otherwise, you're on your own to do as you please.

A well-stocked library has books and movies for those who prefer quiet pursuits in the privacy of their staterooms. In addition, MP3 players stocked with all types of music—enough to play for a complete sailing without repeating a selection—are available for personal use at no charge.

The weekly picnic on a private beach is considered by many passengers as their most memorable experience ashore during a SeaDream cruise. It begins with refreshing drinks served during a wet landing from Zodiacs and is followed by SeaDream's signature champagne-and-caviar splash served to passengers from a surfboard bar in the crystal-clear water. On voyages where it isn't possible to host the champagne-and-caviar splash ashore, it is celebrated poolside.

SeaDream yachts are often chartered by families, corporations, and other affinity groups, but the company does not charter both ships at the same time. If your chosen sailing is closed to you because of a charter, the other yacht will be available.

Food
Every meal is prepared to order using the freshest seafood and U.S. Prime cuts of beef. Menus include vegetarian alternatives and Asian wellness cuisine for the health-conscious. Cheeses, petits fours, and chocolate truffles are offered after dinner with coffee, and the Grand Marnier soufflé is to die for. A weekly dining event, the Chef's Menu Gustation, features an interesting medley of dishes planned by the executive chef for their variety and flavor; portions are sensibly sized, enabling diners to enjoy each course.

Weather permitting, daily breakfast, lunch, and special dinners are served alfresco in the canopied Topsider Restaurant. Wines are chosen to complement each luncheon and dinner menu from shipboard cellars that stock 3,500 bottles on each ship. Sommeliers are more than happy to discuss the attributes of each vintage and steam off the labels if you want to search for them at home. Snacks, from caviar to popcorn, are always available and delivered wherever you might be when hunger strikes, although there is a charge for caviar.

Room service is always available, and not just in your suite; you can dine anywhere you wish on deck.

Fitness and Recreation
Small gyms on each ship are equipped with treadmills, elliptical machines, recumbent bikes, and free weights. A personal trainer is available for consultation, and tai chi, yoga and aerobics classes are offered on deck as requested by passengers.

The yachts' unique SeaDream Spa facilities are also on the small side, yet offer a full menu of individualized, gentle Asian pampering treatments including massages, facials, and body wraps utilizing Eastern techniques. Hair and nail services are offered in the salon. SeaDream Spa is a member of the Thai Spa Association; products utilized for spa and salon services are among the best available from around the world. Massages are also available in cabanas ashore during the private beach party. Although the spa has regularly

NOTEWORTHY

■ You may use an MP3 player stocked with all types of music at no charge during your cruise.

■ The bar is always open with a wide selection, but an additional fee applies to certain wines and premium liquor brands.

■ Activities directors conduct informal talks prior to each port of call to help you orient yourself ashore.

5

SEADREAM YACHT CLUB

Top: Relax on a Balinese "dream bed"
Bottom: Fitness classes

Top: Dining at Topside
Restaurant
Middle: SeaDream Spa
Bottom: The Top of the
Yacht bar

scheduled hours, treatments can be arranged outside those hours by special request. It's recommended that passengers schedule time for use of the sauna and steam room, as their size limits the number of people who can comfortably use them at once.

Your Shipmates

SeaDream yachts attract energetic, affluent travelers of all ages, as well as groups. Passengers tend to be couples in their mid-forties up to retirees who enjoy the unstructured informality, subdued ambience, and utterly exclusive service.

These ships are not recommended for passengers who use wheelchairs. Although there's one stateroom considered accessible, public facilities have thresholds and the elevator doesn't reach the uppermost deck. Tide conditions can cause the gangway to be steep when docked, and negotiating shore tenders would be impossible.

Dress Code

Leave the formal duds at home—every night is yacht casual on SeaDream. Men wear open-collar shirts and slacks; sport coats are preferred but not required. A tie is never necessary. For women, sundresses, dressy casual skirts and sweaters, or pants and tops are the norm.

Junior Cruisers

SeaDream yachts are adult-oriented. Children under the age of one are not allowed. High chairs and booster seats are available for the youngsters occasionally on board, but no children's facilities or organized activities are available. Parents are responsible for the behavior and entertainment of their children.

Service

Personal service and attention to detail are amazing; everyone will greet you by name within minutes of boarding. Passenger preferences are shared among staff members, who all work hard to assist one another. You seldom, if ever, have to repeat a request. Waiting in line for anything is unthinkable.

CHOOSE THIS LINE IF ...

You enjoy dining as an event, as courses are presented with a flourish and wines flow freely.

You don't like to hear the word "no."

You have good sea legs. In rough seas, the SeaDream yachts tend to bob up and down.

Tipping

Tipping is neither required nor expected.

Past Passengers

The SeaDream Club was designed to extend appreciation to past passengers, who are automatically enrolled in the club upon completion of one sailing. Members receive the *SeaDreamer* newsletter, which is published three times a year and features news and photos from the SeaDream yachts, profiles of the yachts' captains and other onboard personalities, profiles of various ports of call, news of special sailings, and other information of interest.

Other SeaDream Club benefits include advance notice of new itineraries, an annual club-members cruise, perks for introducing new passengers to SeaDream, a priority wait list on sold-out cruises, the ability to reserve spa appointments and shore excursions online, 5%–15% savings when booking a future cruise while on board, an onboard Club member cocktail party, and special savings in the ships' Boutique and Asian Spa.

GOOD TO KNOW

Don't miss cocktails before dinner, when the activities director gives a brief overview of the next day's port of call and other happenings. There's a daily schedule, but you'll miss a lot of fun and camaraderie if you skip the cocktail hour. You may also miss a last-minute decision by the captain to extend a port call or even change the order of ports if there's something interesting going on ashore.

5

SEADREAM YACHT CLUB

DON'T CHOOSE THIS LINE IF ...

You like to dress up. Although you could wear a sport coat to dinner, no one ever wears a tie on these ships.

You must have a balcony. There are none on any of Seadream's yachtlike vessels.

You need structured activities. You'll have to plan your own.

SEADREAM I, SEADREAM II

CREW MEMBERS	95
ENTERED SERVICE	1984, 1985
GROSS TONS	4,300
LENGTH	344 feet
NUMBER OF CABINS	56
PASSENGER CAPACITY	112
WIDTH	47 feet

Top: The Top of the Yacht bar
Bottom: Casino play

Public Areas and Facilities

Although these vessels are not huge, the public rooms are quite spacious; the Main Salon and Dining Salon are large enough to comfortably seat all passengers at once. Decor is elegant in its simplicity and is surprisingly non-nautical. Instead, it's modern and sleek, utilizing the hues of the sea, sky, and sandy beaches. Oriental rugs cover polished teak floors in the reception area and in the large, sun-splashed library, where you'll find more than 1,000 books from which to select, as well as computers to access the Internet. The library also lends movies to watch on the flat-screen TV/DVD player in your suite.

Balinese sun beds are the ideal spot to relax by day, either for sunbathing or reading beneath an umbrella. A telescope mounted at each ship's stern is handy for spotting land and other vessels at sea.

Restaurants

The formal dining room serves open seating breakfast, lunch, and dinner during scheduled hours. For a more casual setting, the Topside restaurant has outdoor seating for breakfast and lunch—either with table service or from a small buffet—plus scheduled dinners alfresco (the indoor restaurant is also open for those who do not wish to dine outside). Snacks are available at the Top of the Yacht Bar, and you only have to ask to receive anything from popcorn to caviar, although the caviar is no longer complimentary. A beach barbecue is scheduled once during every cruise. Room service is always available, and servers will bring your order to you on deck as well as in your suite.

Accommodations

Cabins: Every stateroom is outside with an ocean view; every cabin has a sitting area, and there's plenty of drawer space for storage. A curtain can be drawn between the bed and sitting area for privacy. Bathrooms are marble-clad and have large, glass-enclosed showers with twin showerheads that make up for the tiny bathrooms.

Amenities: All cabins have an entertainment center with a large flat-screen TV, CD, and DVD system; broadband Internet connection; personalized stationery; and a wet bar stocked with complimentary beer, soft drinks, and bottled water. A lighted magnifying mirror and hair dryer are at a vanity table. Beds are dressed with Belgian linens and your choice of synthetic or down pillows and a duvet or woolen blankets. Bathrooms are stocked with deluxe Bulgari shampoo, shower gel, soap, and lotion. Turkish cotton bathrobes and slippers are provided for use during the cruise.

Worth Noting: The single Owner's Suite on each ship has a living room, a dining area, a separate bedroom, a bathroom with a sea view (as well as a separate tub and shower), and a guest bathroom. An Admiral's Suite on each ship features an open-plan living-dining area, a separate master bedroom, three panoramic windows, a marble bathroom with separate tub and shower, and a guest half-bath. Commodore Club staterooms are basically double staterooms with one side configured as a sitting-dining area room and feature two identical bathrooms with showers. One stateroom is designed for wheelchair accessibility.

In the Know

The Balinese sun beds adjacent to the Top of the Yacht Bar have such thick, comfortable pads that passengers occasionally choose to spend the night there after everyone else has gone below deck to their quarters.

Pros and Cons

Pros: The weekly barbecue held on a deserted stretch of beach would be a highlight even if it didn't include champagne and caviar. The Top of the Yacht Bar is the sociable choice. No smoking is allowed indoors, which is either refreshing or an annoyance, depending on your point of view (and habits).

Cons: One stateroom is considered wheelchair accessible, but these ships are not appropriate for anyone confined to a wheelchair, as public facilities have thresholds and the elevator doesn't reach the uppermost deck. Cocktail glasses (and even a corkscrew) are provided in suite cabinets, but there's a charge for wines and spirits ordered for your suite; you might miss schedule changes if you skip cocktails before dinner, when the activities director gives an overview of the next day's happenings.

Cabin Type	Size (sq. ft.)
Owner's Suite	450
Admiral Suite	375
Commodore Club	390
Yacht Club*	195

*Sixteen of the Yacht Club staterooms are convertible to eight Commodore staterooms, giving a variable passenger capacity.

FAST FACTS

- 5 passenger decks
- Dining room, buffet
- Safe, refrigerator, Internet, DVD
- Pool
- Fitness classes, gym, hair salon, hot tub, sauna, spa, steam room
- 3 bars, casino, library, showroom
- Dry-cleaning, laundry service
- Internet terminal
- No-smoking cabins

5

SEADREAM YACHT CLUB

Pool deck

SILVERSEA CRUISES

Silversea Cruises was launched in 1994 by the former owners of Sitmar Cruises, the Lefebvre family of Rome, whose concept for the new cruise line was to build and sail the highest-quality luxury ships at sea. Intimate ships, paired with exclusive amenities and unparal-

The most captivating view on board

leled hospitality are the hallmarks of Silversea cruises. All-inclusive air-and-sea fares can be customized to include not just round-trip airfare but all transfers, porterage, and deluxe precruise accommodations as well.

✉ *110 E. Broward Blvd., Fort Lauderdale, FL*

☎ *954/522–4477 or 800/722–9955*

⊕ *www.silversea.com*

☞ *Cruise Style: Luxury.*

Personalization is a Silversea maxim. Their ships offer more activities than other comparably sized luxury vessels. Take part in those that interest you, or opt instead for a good book and any number of quiet spots to read or snooze in the shade. Silversea's third generation of ships will introduce even more luxurious features when the 36,000-ton *Silver Spirit* launches late in 2009.

Guest lecturers are featured on nearly every cruise; language, dance, and culinary lessons and excellent wine appreciation sessions are always on the schedule of events. Silversea also schedules culinary arts cruises and a series of wine-focused voyages that feature award-winning authors, international wine experts, winemakers, and acclaimed chefs from the world's top restaurants. During afternoon tea, ladies gather for conversation over needlepoint, and the ranks of highly competitive trivia teams increase every successive afternoon.

After dark, the Bar is a predinner gathering spot and the late-night place for dancing to a live band. A multitiered show lounge is the setting for talented singers and musicians, classical concerts, magic shows, big-screen movies, and folkloric entertainers from ashore. A small casino offers slot machines and gaming tables.

Food

Dishes from the galleys of Silversea's master chefs are complemented by those of La Collection du Monde, created by Silversea's culinary partner, the world-class chefs of Relais & Châteaux. Menus include hot and cold appetizers, at least four entrée selections, a vegetarian alternative, and Cruiselite cuisine (low in cholesterol, sodium, and fat). Special off-menu orders are prepared whenever possible, provided that the ingredients are available on board. In the event that they aren't, you may find after a day in port that a trip to the market was made in order to fulfill your request.

Chef Marco Betti, the owner of Antica Pasta restaurants in Florence, Italy, and Atlanta, Georgia, has designed a new menu for La Terrazza that focuses on one of the most luxurious food trends, the "slow food" movement. The goal of the movement is to preserve the gastronomic traditions of Italy through the use of fresh, traditional foods, and it has spread throughout the world. At La Terrazza (by day, a casual buffet) the menu showcases the finest in Italian cooking, from classic favorites to Tuscan fare. The restaurant carries no surcharge. Seating is limited, so reservations are a must to ensure a table—it's one reservation you'll be glad you took the time to book.

An intimate dining experience aboard each vessel is the Wine Restaurant by Relais & Châteaux—Le Champagne. Adding a dimension to dining, the exquisite cuisine is designed to celebrate the wines served—a different celebrated vintage is served with each course. Menus and wines are chosen by Relais & Chateaux sommeliers to reflect regions of the world noted for their rich wine heritage.

An evening poolside barbecue is a weekly dinner event, weather permitting. A highlight of every cruise is the Galley Brunch, when passengers are invited into the galley to select from a feast decorated with imaginative ice and vegetable sculptures. Even when meals are served buffet-style in La Terrazza, you will seldom have to carry your own plate, as waiters are at hand to assist you to your table. Wines are chosen to complement each day's luncheon and dinner menus.

Grilled foods, sandwiches, and an array of fruits and salads are served daily for lunch at the poolside Grill. Always available are extensive selections from the room-service menu. The full restaurant menu may be

Top: Stylish entertainment
Bottom: Terrace Café alfresco dining

5

SILVERSEA CRUISES

Top: Table tennis
Middle: Caring personal service
Bottom: Veranda Suite

ordered from room service and can be served course by course in your suite during regular dining hours.

Fitness and Recreation

The rather small gyms are equipped with cardiovascular and weight-training equipment, and fitness classes on *Silver Whisper* and *Silver Shadow* are held in the mirror-lined, but somewhat confining, exercise room. *Silver Spirit* introduced an expansive, 8,300-square-foot spa and more spacious fitness center.

South Pacific–inspired Mandara Spa offers numerous treatments including exotic-sounding massages, facials, and body wraps. Hair and nail services are available in the busy salon. A plus is that appointments for spa and beauty salon treatments can be made online from 60 days until 48 hours prior to sailing.

Golfers can sign up with the pro on board for individual lessons utilizing a high-tech swing analyzer and attend complimentary golf clinics or participate in a putting contest.

Your Shipmates

Silversea Cruises appeal to sophisticated, affluent couples who enjoy the country-club-like atmosphere, exquisite cuisine, and polished service on board, not to mention the exotic ports and unique experiences ashore.

Dress Code

Two formal nights are standard on seven-night cruises and three to four nights, depending on the itinerary, on longer sailings. Men are required to wear tuxedos or dark suits after 6 pm. All other evenings are either informal, when a jacket is called for (a tie is optional, but most men wear them), or casual, when slacks with a jacket over an open-collar shirt for men and sporty dresses or skirts or pants with a sweater or blouse for women are suggested.

Junior Cruisers

Silversea Cruises is adult-oriented, does not accommodate children less than six months of age, and the cruise line limits the number of children under the age of three on board. The availability of suites for a third passenger is capacity controlled. A youth program staffed by

CHOOSE THIS LINE IF ...

Your taste leans toward learning and exploration.

You enjoy socializing as well as the option of live entertainment, just not too much of it.

You like to plan ahead. You can reserve shore tours, salon services, and spa treatments online.

counselors is available on holiday and select sailings. No dedicated children's facilities are available, so parents are responsible for the behavior and entertainment of their children.

Service

Personalized service is exacting and hospitable yet discreet. The staff strive for perfection and often achieve it. The attitude is decidedly European and begins with a welcome-aboard flute of champagne, then continues throughout as personal preferences are remembered and satisfied. The word *no* doesn't seem to be in the staff vocabulary in any language. Guests in all suites are pampered by butlers.

Tipping

Tipping is neither required nor expected.

Past Passengers

Membership in the Venetian Society is automatic on completion of one Silversea cruise, and members begin accruing benefits: Venetian Society cruise days and eligibility for discounts on select voyages, onboard recognition and private parties, milestone rewards; exclusive gifts, the *Venetian Society Newsletter*, ship visitation privileges, complimentary early embarkation or late debarkation at certain milestones, members-only benefits at select Leading Hotels of the World and Relais & Châteaux hotels and resorts, and select offers through Silversea's preferred partners.

Through the Friends of Society programs, members can double their accumulated cruise days and receive a shipboard spending credit by inviting friends or family members to sail on select Venetian Society sailings. Friends or family will enjoy the same Venetian Society savings as members for those cruises, a really nice perk.

GOOD TO KNOW

You might expect a bit of stodginess to creep in at this level of ultraluxury, but you wouldn't necessarily be correct. Socializing isn't quite as easygoing as on some ships, and some passengers can come off as a bit standoffish. However, you will encounter likeminded fellow passengers if you make the effort to participate in group activities, particularly the highly competitive afternoon trivia sessions. With an increasingly younger crowd on board, you are more likely to encounter partiers at late-night disco sessions than couples waltzing between courses during dinner.

5

SILVERSEA CRUISES

DON'T CHOOSE THIS LINE IF ...

You want to dress informally at all times on your cruise. Passengers on these cruises tend to dress up.

You need highly structured activities and have to be reminded of them.

You prefer the glitter and stimulation of Las Vegas to the understated glamour of Monaco.

SILVER SPIRIT

CREW MEMBERS	376
ENTERED SERVICE	2010
GROSS TONS	36,000
LENGTH	642 feet
NUMBER OF CABINS	270
PASSENGER CAPACITY	540
WIDTH	86 feet

700 ft.

500 ft.

300 ft.

Top: *Silver Spirit* at sea
Bottom: Standard suite

Public Areas and Facilities

The stylish interiors of *Silver Spirit*'s public rooms reflect a 1930s art deco flavor. Although the decor is warmer and more inviting than previous Silversea ships, you'll still find signature spaces like the Humidor, the Bar, and the indoor–outdoor La Terrazza restaurant.

With one of the most generous space-to-guest ratios in the cruise industry, *Silver Spirit* features an expansive 8,300-square-foot spa with a thermal suite and outdoor whirlpool; a state-of-the-art fitness complex with two aerobics studios; up to six places to dine; three high-end, duty-free boutiques; and the largest suites in the Silversea fleet, 95% of which have a private balcony. In addition, deck space is expansive, with plenty of teak chaise longues, two whirlpools, and a bar poolside. The resort-style pool is even heated for cooler weather.

Restaurants

The formal restaurant offers open seating breakfast, lunch, and dinner during scheduled hours. Specialty dining is offered by reservation in Le Champagne, where an extra charge applies for the gourmet meal and wine pairings, and Sieshin Restaurant, which serves Kobe beef, sushi, and Asian seafood specialties (some of which carry a surcharge). Included in your cruise fare, Stars Supper Club offers trendsetting menus and La Terrazza serves Italian cuisines. For casual meals, La Terrazza has indoor and outdoor seating for buffet-style breakfast and lunch. The outdoor Grill offers a laid-back lunch option poolside as well as an alfresco dinner when it is called Black Rock Grill, which allows you to cook meats and seafood to your liking on pre-heated volcanic stones right at your table. Afternoon tea is served daily. Room service arrives with crystal, china, and linens for a complete dining room–style setup in your suite. You may order at any time from the extensive room-service menu or the full restaurant menu during dining hours.

Accommodations

Cabins: Every suite is outside with an ocean view, and 95% have a private teak-floor balcony. Standard suites have a sitting area that can be curtained off from the bed for more privacy. Marble bathrooms have double sinks and a separate glass-enclosed shower as well as a tub. All suites have generous walk-in closets.

Top Suites: In addition to much more space, top-category suites have all the standard amenities plus dining areas, separate bedrooms, and CD players. Silver Suites and above have whirlpool tubs. All categories have butler service.

Amenities: Standard suites have an entertainment center with flat-screen TV and DVD, personalized stationery, cocktail cabinet, safe, and refrigerator stocked with complimentary beer, soft drinks, and bottled water. A hair dryer is provided at a vanity table. Beds are dressed with high-quality linens, duvets, or blankets, and your choice of synthetic or down pillows. Bathrooms have huge towels and terry bathrobes for use during the cruise as well as designer shampoo, soaps, and lotion.

Worth Noting: Sixteen suites have connecting doors; four suites are designed for wheelchair accessibility.

In the Know

When the weather is favorable, you might want to forego stargazing or a walk in the moonlight and settle into a padded deck chair while a movie is screened poolside.

Pros and Cons

Pros: Silversea is one of the industry's most all-inclusive cruise lines, and the onboard atmosphere is sophisticated yet relaxed—and heightened by never having to sign a bar ticket. Champagne on ice welcomes every passenger to his suite. Silver Suites are the most popular accommodations on Silversea ships, and *Silver Spirit* has at least twice as many as her fleet mates.

Cons: One accommodations deck doesn't have a passenger laundry room. The addition of a limited children's program could mean even more youngsters on board than would normally sail on a Silversea cruise, although the supervised activities should keep them busy despite the lack of a dedicated playroom. You could get so spoiled aboard *Silver Spirit* that you'll never want to go home.

Cabin Type	Size (sq. ft.)
Owner's Suite	1,292
Grand Suite	990
Silver Suite	742
Veranda Suite	376
Vista Suite	312

FAST FACTS

- 8 passenger decks
- 4 specialty restaurants, dining room, buffet
- Wi-Fi, safe, refrigerator, DVD
- Pool
- Fitness classes, gym, hair salon, 3 hot tubs, sauna, spa, steam room
- 3 bars, casino, dance club, library, showroom
- Children's program (ages 3–12)
- Dry-cleaning, laundry facilities, laundry service
- Internet terminal

5

SILVERSEA CRUISES

The Spa at Silversea

SILVER SHADOW, SILVER WHISPER

CREW MEMBERS	295
ENTERED SERVICE	2000, 2001
GROSS TONS	28,258
LENGTH	610 feet
NUMBER OF CABINS	191
PASSENGER CAPACITY	382
WIDTH	82 feet

700 ft.

500 ft.

300 ft.

Top: The casino
Bottom: *Silver Shadow* at sea

Public Areas and Facilities

The logical layout of these sister ships, with suites in the forward two-thirds of the ship and public rooms aft, makes orientation simple. The clean, modern decor that defines public areas and lounges might seem almost stark, but it places the main emphasis on large expanses of glass for sunshine and sea views as well as passenger comfort.

Silversea ships boast unbeatable libraries stocked with best sellers, travel books, classics, and movies for in-suite viewing. Extremely wide passageways in public areas are lined with glass-front display cabinets full of interesting and unusual artifacts from the places the ships visit.

The Humidor is a clubby cigar smoking room with overstuffed leather seating and a ventilation system that even nonsmokers can appreciate.

Restaurants

The Restaurant, formal yet simply named, offers open seating breakfast, lunch, and dinner during scheduled hours. Specialty dining is offered by reservation in Le Champagne, where an extra charge applies for the gourmet meal and wine pairings, and La Terrazza, which is complimentary and serves Italian cuisines. For casual meals, La Terrazza has indoor and outdoor seating for buffet-style breakfast and lunch. The outdoor Grill offers a laid-back lunch and dinner option with poolside table service. An al fresco dinner option is the do-it-yourself Black Rock Grill, which allows you to cook meats and seafood to your liking on preheated volcanic stones right at your table. Elaborate afternoon tea is served daily. An evening poolside barbecue is a weekly dinner event as is the Galley Brunch, when passengers are invited into the galley to make their selections. Room service arrives with crystal, china, and a linen tablecloth for a complete dining room–style setup in-suite. You may order at any time from the extensive room-service menu or the full restaurant menu, which can be served course by course in your suite during regular dining hours.

Accommodations

Cabins: Every suite is outside with an ocean view, and more than 80% have a private teak-floor balcony.

Standard suites have a sitting area that can be curtained off from the bed for more privacy. Marble bathrooms have double sinks and a separate glass-enclosed shower as well as a tub. All suites have generous walk-in closets.

Top Suites: In addition to much more space, top-category suites have all the standard amenities plus dining areas, separate bedrooms, and CD players. Silver Suites and above have whirlpool tubs. The top three categories have espresso makers and separate powder rooms.

Amenities: Standard suites have an entertainment center with a TV and DVD, personalized stationery, cocktail cabinet, safe, and refrigerator stocked with complimentary beer, soft drinks, and bottled water. A hair dryer is provided at a vanity table, and you can request a magnifying mirror. Beds are dressed with high-quality linens, duvets, or blankets, and your choice of synthetic or down pillows. Bathrooms have huge towels and terry bathrobes for use during the cruise as well as designer shampoo, soaps, and lotion.

Worth Noting: Two suites are designed for wheelchair accessibility. All suites are served by butlers.

In the Know
Nine Terrace Suites on deck 5 have doors to the outside that access a common, semiprivate veranda area. Even though the area is not furnished, it's like having a balcony without paying a higher fare.

Pros and Cons
Pros: Champagne on ice welcomes you to your suite and continues to flow freely throughout your cruise. Sailing on a Silversea ship is like spending time as a pampered guest at a home in the Hamptons where everything is at your fingertips, and if it isn't, all you have to do is ask. Silversea is so all-inclusive that you'll find your room key–charge card is seldom used for anything but opening your suite door.

Cons: Just about the only line you're likely to encounter on a Silversea ship is the one to use a washing machine in the smallish, yet totally free laundry rooms. In an odd contrast to the contents of display cases and lovely flower arrangements, artwork on the walls is fairly ho-hum and not at all memorable. Although small, the spa's complimentary saunas and steam rooms are adequate and seldom occupied.

Cabin Type	Size (sq. ft.)
Grand Suite	1,286–1,435
Royal Suite	1,312–1,352
Owner's Suite	1,208
Silver Suite	701
Medallion Suite	521
Verandah Suite	345
Terrace Suite	287
Vista Suite	287

FAST FACTS

- 7 passenger decks
- 2 specialty restaurants, dining room, buffet
- Wi-Fi, safe, refrigerator, DVD
- Pool
- Fitness classes, gym, hair salon, 2 hot tubs, sauna, spa, steam room
- 3 bars, casino, dance club, library, showroom
- Dry-cleaning, laundry facilities, laundry service
- Internet terminal

The Poolside Grille serves lunch and light snacks

SILVER CLOUD, SILVER WIND

CREW MEMBERS	
	212
ENTERED SERVICE	
	1994, 1995
GROSS TONS	
	17,400
LENGTH	
	514 feet
NUMBER OF CABINS	
	148
PASSENGER CAPACITY	
	298
WIDTH	
	71 feet

700 ft.
500 ft.
300 ft.

Public Areas and Facilities

Fresh from recent refurbishments, these two yachtlike gems are all about style, understatement, and personal choice, so if you want to snuggle into a book in the well-stocked library, no one will lift an eyebrow. Although there simply isn't enough square footage on these ships for huge rooms, the public spaces are more than adequate and designed to function well. These ships served as the models for their larger sisters, *Silver Shadow* and *Silver Whisper,* which expanded on the smaller ships' concept of locating all passenger accommodations forward and public rooms aft.

The Restaurant is one of the loveliest dining rooms at sea, with a domed ceiling and musicians to provide dance music between courses. Both the Bar or Panorama Lounge are comfortable spots to socialize, dance, or enjoy cocktails before or after the evening entertainment, which might include a classical concert or small-ish production show in the show room or Moonlight Movies, feature films shown outside on the pool deck.

Restaurants

The formal restaurant offers open seating breakfast, lunch, and dinner during scheduled hours. Specialty dining is offered by reservation in Le Champagne, where an extra charge applies for the gourmet meal and wine pairings, and La Terrazza, which is complimentary and serves Italian cuisine. For casual meals, La Terrazza has indoor and outdoor seating for buffet-style breakfast and lunch. The outdoor Grill offers a laid-back lunch and dinner option with poolside table service. Elaborate afternoon tea is served daily. An evening poolside barbecue is a weekly dinner event, as is the Galley Brunch, when passengers are invited into the galley to make their selections. Room service arrives with crystal, china, and a linen tablecloth for a complete dining room–style setup in-suite. You may order at any time from the extensive room-service menu or the full restaurant menu, which can be served course by course in your suite during regular dining hours.

Accommodations

Cabins: All accommodations are considered suites; all are outside and have at least an ocean view; an outstanding 80% also have private balconies. Suite

Top: The bar
Bottom: Royal Suite

interiors are enhanced with appealing artwork, flowers, sitting areas, and bedding topped with plush duvets and choice of pillow style. A writing desk, refrigerator, TV with DVD player, dressing table with lighted mirror and hair dryer, walk-in closet, and safe are all standard. The marble and stone bathrooms have full-size bathtubs.

Amenities: Champagne on ice awaits the arrival of all passengers, and it is replenished as desired; the beverage cabinet is stocked daily on request with individual selections of wines, spirits, and beverages. A fruit basket is replenished daily. Bathrooms are stocked with plush towels and European toiletries, and slippers and bathrobes are provided for use during the cruise.

Worth Noting: Teak-floored balconies have patio furniture and floor-to-ceiling glass doors. Two suites are wheelchair accessible. All suites have butler service.

In the Know
The Medallion Suite on deck 7 onf *Silver Wind* is unique at 678 square feet. Although it has no veranda—large picture windows offer sea views—it is larger than some of the costlier suites and ideal if you require space but not necessarily outdoors.

Pros and Cons
Pros: Silversea is one of the most all-inclusive cruise lines, and the ambience on board is comfortably upscale, heightened by your never having to sign a bar ticket. Wine is poured freely at lunch and dinner, and no one has to cringe when ordering a round of drinks for new friends, which reinforces camaraderie between passengers. Every cruise features regionally specific lectures by noted historians, ambassadors, state leaders, authors and geographers—all experts and each sharing special insights into areas of the world they know intimately.

Cons: Although the minimalist modern decor is accented by beautiful flower arrangements and interesting artwork throughout the ship, livelier splashes of color would be a welcome addition in most public rooms. The sophisticated, all-adult atmosphere is sometimes disrupted by children who are bored by the absence of any activities or facilities for them. The slow pace of evening entertainment isn't satisfying if you prefer splashy production revues and Vegas-type shows.

Cabin Type	Size (sq. ft.)
Grand Suite	1,019–1,314
Royal Suite	736–1,031
Owner's Suite	587–827
Silver Suite	541
Medallion Suite	470–678
Veranda Suite	295
Vista Suite	240

Grand, Royal, and Owner's suites available with one or two bedrooms; Medallion Suite on deck 7 has no balcony.

FAST FACTS

- 6 passenger decks
- 2 specialty restaurants, dining room, buffet
- Wi-Fi, safe, refrigerator, DVD
- 1 pool
- Fitness classes, gym, hair salon, 1 hot tub, sauna, spa, steam room
- 3 bars, casino, dance club, library, showroom
- Dry-cleaning, laundry facilities, laundry service
- Internet terminal

The pool deck

5

SILVERSEA CRUISES

STAR CLIPPERS

In 1991, Star Clippers unveiled a new tall-ship alternative to sophisticated travelers, whose desires included having an adventure at sea but not on board a conventional cruise ship. Star Clippers vessels are four- and five-masted sailing beauties—the world's

Sun yourself on the bow netting

largest barkentine and full-rigged sailing ships. Filled with modern, high-tech equipment as well as the amenities of private yachts, the ships rely on sail power while at sea unless conditions require the assistance of the engines. Minimal heeling, usually less than 6%, is achieved through judicious control of the sails.

✉ *7200 N.W. 19th St., Suite 206, Miami, FL*

☎ *305/442–0550 or 800/442–0551*

⊕ *www.starclippers. com*

☞ *Cruise Style: Sailing Ship.*

A boyhood dream became a cruise-line reality when Swedish entrepreneur Mikael Krafft launched his fleet of authentic re-creations of classic 19th-century clipper ships. The day officially begins when the captain holds an informative daily briefing on deck with a bit of storytelling tossed in. Star Clippers are not cruise ships in the ordinary sense with strict agendas and pages of activities. You're free to do what you please day and night, but many passengers join the crew members topside when the sails are raised or for some of the lighthearted events like crab-racing contests, scavenger hunts, and a talent night. The informality of singing around the piano bar typifies an evening on one of these ships, although in certain ports local performers come aboard to spice up the action with an authentic taste of the local music and arts.

The lack of rigid scheduling is one of Star Clippers' most appealing attractions. The bridge is always open, and passengers are welcome to peer over the captain's shoulder as he plots the ship's course. Crew members are happy to demonstrate how to splice a line, reef a sail, or tie a proper knot.

As attractive as the ships' interiors are, the focal point of Star Clippers cruises is the outdoors. Plan to spend a lot of time on deck soaking in the sun, sea, and sky. It doesn't get any better than that. Consider also that each ship has at least two swimming pools. Granted, they are tiny, but they are a refreshing feature uncommon on true sailing ships and all but the most lavish yachts.

Although the Star Clippers ships are motorized, their engines are shut down whenever crews unfurl the sails (36,000 square feet on *Star Clipper* and *Star Flyer*, and 56,000 square feet on *Royal Clipper*) to capture the wind. On a typical cruise, the ships rely exclusively on sail power any time favorable conditions prevail.

As the haunting strains of Vangelis's symphony "1492: Conquest of Paradise" are piped over the PA system and the first of the sails is unfurled, the only thing you'll hear on deck is the sound of the music and the calls of the line handlers until every sail is in place. While the feeling of the wind powering large ships through the water is spine-tingling, you will miss the wondrous sight of your ship under sail unless the captain can schedule a photo opportunity utilizing one of the tenders. It's one of the most memorable sights you'll see if this opportunity avails itself. However, when necessary, the ships will cruise under motor power to meet the requirements of their itineraries.

Food

Not noted for gourmet fare, the international cuisine is what you would expect from a trendy shoreside bistro, albeit an elegant one. All meals are open seating in the formal dining room during scheduled hours; breakfast and lunch—an impressive spread of seafood, salads, and grilled items—are served buffet-style, while dinners are leisurely affairs served in the European manner. Hint: If you want your salad *before* your main course, just ask; the French style is to serve it after the main course. Menus, created in consultation with chef Jean Marie Meulien (who has been awarded Michelin stars throughout his career), include appetizers, soups, pasta, a sorbet course, at least three choices of entrées, salad, cheese, and, of course, dessert. Mediterranean-inspired entrées, vegetarian, and light dishes are featured. A maître d' is present at the more formal evening meals to seat passengers, but it isn't uncommon on these small ships for them to arrange their own groups of dinner company.

Early risers on each ship find a continental breakfast offered at the Tropical Bar, and coffee and fresh fruit

■ Don't ask for connecting staterooms on Star Clippers ships. There are none.

■ Look for secret hideaways on one of the hidden balconies on either side of *Royal Clipper*'s bow.

■ You are free to dine when and with whomever you wish on Star Clippers ships, including with the officers, who join passengers in the dining room most nights.

5

STAR CLIPPERS

Top: All ships have pools
Bottom: *Royal Clipper* Deluxe Suite

Top: View from the bow
Middle: *Royal Clipper* piano bar
Bottom: *Royal Clipper* spa

are always available in the Piano Bar. Should you want to remain in your swimsuit, casual buffets are set up adjacent to the Tropical Bar at noon (the Deck Snack Buffet) and at 5 pm (the Afternoon Snack). Some of the "snacks" are themed and quite popular—a Neptune seafood luncheon, snacks with waffles or crepes, or a midday taco bar. On select itineraries, an outdoor barbecue is served on shore.

With the exception of occupants of Owner's suites and Deluxe suites on *Royal Clipper*, there is no room service unless you are sick and can't make it to the dining room for meals.

Fitness and Recreation

Formal exercise sessions take a backseat to water sports, although aerobics classes and swimming are featured on all ships. Only *Royal Clipper* has a marina platform that can be lowered in calm waters to access water sports and diving; however, the smaller ships replicate the experience by using motorized launches to reach reefs for snorkeling. A gym-spa with an array of exercise equipment, free weights, spa treatments, and unisex hair services are also found only on *Royal Clipper*. Despite the lack of a formal fitness center on *Star Clipper,* morning aerobics or yoga classes are usually held on deck for active passengers. Massages, manicures, and pedicures can be arranged as well.

Your Shipmates

Star Clippers cruises draw active, upscale American and European couples from their thirties on up, who enjoy sailing but in a casually sophisticated atmosphere with modern conveniences. Many sailings are equally divided between North Americans and Europeans, so announcements are made in several languages accordingly.

This is not a cruise line for the physically challenged; there are no elevators or ramps, nor are staterooms or bathrooms wheelchair accessible. Gangways and shore launches can also be difficult to negotiate.

CHOOSE THIS LINE IF ...

You wouldn't consider a vacation on a traditional cruise ship but are a sailing enthusiast.

You love water sports, particularly snorkeling and scuba diving.

You want to anchor in secluded coves and visit islands that are off the beaten path.

Dress Code

All evenings are elegant casual, so slacks and open-collar shirts are fine for men, and sundresses, skirts, or pants with a sweater or blouse are suggested for women. Coats and ties are never required. Shorts and T-shirts are not allowed in the dining room at dinner.

Junior Cruisers

Star Clippers ships are adult-oriented. Although children are welcome and may participate in shipboard activities suited to their ability, there are no dedicated youth facilities. Parents are responsible for the behavior and entertainment of their children. Mature teens who can live without video games and the company of other teens are the best young sailors.

Service

Service is friendly and gracious, similar to what you would find in a boutique hotel or restaurant. You may find that you have to flag down a waiter for a second cup of coffee, though.

Tipping

Gratuities are not included in the cruise fare and are extended at the sole discretion of passengers. The recommended amount is €8 per person per day. Tips are pooled and shared; individual tipping is discouraged. You can either put cash in the tip envelope that will be provided to you and drop it at the Purser's Office or charge gratuities to your shipboard account. An automatic 15% gratuity is added to each passenger's bar bill.

Past Passengers

Top Gallant is the loyalty club for past passengers. No specific fare discount is offered to members; however, they receive a newsletter and special offers on fare reductions from time to time. Nearly 60% of all passengers choose to make a repeat voyage on Star Clippers ships.

GOOD TO KNOW

Fresh air is prevalent inside as well as on deck. Smoking is restricted to limited public rooms and not permitted in cabins. For the ultimate in fresh air, an unparalleled treat is the climb to a lookout station at the first yardarm on each of *Royal Clipper's* masts, where you can relax on a teak settee and take in the view. Note that although fares are quoted in U.S. dollars, all shipboard charges are in euros. Accounts can be settled with cash, traveler's checks, or credit cards on the final day of your cruise.

5

STAR CLIPPERS

DON'T CHOOSE THIS LINE IF ...

You have a preexisting or potentially serious medical condition. There's no physician on board.

You must have a private balcony—there are a few, but only in top accommodation categories.

You can't live without room service. Only *Royal Clipper* has it, and only in a few high-end suites.

ROYAL CLIPPER

CREW MEMBERS	106
ENTERED SERVICE	2000
GROSS TONS	5,000
LENGTH	439 feet
NUMBER OF CABINS	114
PASSENGER CAPACITY	227
WIDTH	54 feet

700 ft.

500 ft.

300 ft.

Public Areas and Facilities

Royal Clipper is the first five-masted, full-rigged sailing ship built since 1902. As the largest true sailing clipper ship in the world today, she carries 42 sails with a total area of 56,000 square feet.

Unusual for a sailing ship, a three-deck atrium graces the heart of the vessel.

Her interior is decorated in Edwardian-era style with abundant gleaming woods, brass fixtures, and nautical touches. Light filters into the piano bar, three-deck-high atrium, and dining room through the glass bottom and portholes of the main swimming pool located overhead.

The rarely used Observation Lounge is forward of the Deluxe suites and affords great sea views. It is also the location of the computer station for all Internet access.

Restaurants

The multilevel dining room serves a single open seating buffet-style breakfast and lunch. Dinner in the dining room is seated and served European-style. For early risers, a continental breakfast with coffee, fruit, and pastries is set up in the piano bar; specialty coffees are available at the bar for a charge. A buffet lunch is offered most days on deck in the Tropical Bar, as are late-afternoon snacks and predinner canapés. On select itineraries an outdoor luncheon barbecue is prepared one day ashore. Room service is available only to occupants of the Owner's suites and Deluxe suites and passengers who are ill and unable to make it to the dining room.

Accommodations

Cabins: Think yacht, and the cabin sizes make sense. Although efficiently laid out with tasteful, seagoing appointments and prints of clipper ships and sailing yachts on the walls, cabins are small in comparison to most cruise ships. All have a TV, safe, desk-vanity, small settee, hair dryer, and marble bathroom with standard toiletries. Closet space is compact, and bureau drawers are narrow, but an under-the-bed drawer is a useful nautical touch for extra storage.

Top: *Royal Clipper* dining room
Bottom: Sighting land

Suites: Owner's suites, Deluxe suites, and Category 1 cabins have a sitting area, minibar, whirlpool tub-shower combination, and bathrobes to use during the cruise. Deluxe suites also feature a private veranda. Category 1 cabins have doors that open onto a semi-private area on the outside deck. Only the two Owner's suites have connecting doors.

Worth Noting: Cabins have 220-volt electrical outlets and a 110-volt outlet suitable only for electric shavers. For 110-volt appliances, you'll need to bring a transformer; for dual-voltage appliances, pack a plug converter. None of the staterooms is designed for wheelchair accessibility, nor are there any elevators.

In the Know

Most cabin showers have only a 1-inch marble lip, so water tends to spread across the bathroom floor in bumpy seas. Although there's a second drain outside the shower, anything left on the floor will get soaked. A rolled-up beach towel outside the shower will help contain the flood.

Pros and Cons

Pros: The feeling of the wind moving this large vessel through the water is spine-tingling and, fortunately, you won't miss the glorious sight of her under way when the captain schedules a photo op via one of the tenders. The library, with its cushy seating and faux fireplace, is a cozy place to read or play board games, and also offers a surprisingly good selection of books. Massages in the spa are no-nonsense and reasonably priced.

Cons: In Category 3 cabins forward, you'll notice a definite slant to the floor, due to the location near the bow; you may also feel a bit more motion forward than aft, and should also remember that creaking sounds are common on sailing ships; tall passengers will find it difficult to use the treadmills in the low-ceilinged gym.

Cabin Type	Size (sq. ft.)
Owner's Suite	355
Deluxe Suite and Cat. 1 Ocean View	204
Standard Ocean View	150
Cat. 5 Ocean View	118
Inside	107

FAST FACTS

- 5 passenger decks
- Dining room
- Safe, refrigerator, DVD (some)
- 3 pools
- Fitness classes, gym, hair salon, spa, steam room
- 3 bars, library
- Dry-cleaning, laundry service
- Internet terminal
- No-smoking cabins

5

STAR CLIPPERS

Royal Clipper under sail

STAR CLIPPER/STAR FLYER

CREW MEMBERS	72
ENTERED SERVICE	1992
GROSS TONS	3,000
LENGTH	360 feet
NUMBER OF CABINS	85
PASSENGER CAPACITY	170
WIDTH	50 feet

700 ft.

500 ft.

300 ft.

Public Areas and Facilities

With its bright brass fixtures, teak-and-mahogany paneling and rails, and antique prints and paintings of famous sailing vessels, *Star Clipper*'s interior decor reflects the heritage of grand sailing ships.

Porthole-shape skylights create an atriumlike effect in the Piano Bar, which leads to a graceful staircase and the dining room one deck below. The centerpiece of the vaguely Edwardian-style library is a belle époque–period fireplace.

The Piano Bar is noted for being intimate and cozy. The Tropical Bar, one of the most popular areas on board, is the center of social activity for predinner cocktails and late-night socializing and dancing. It's the covered outdoor lounge adjacent to the open deck space, where local entertainers often perform.

Restaurants

The mahogany-panel dining room serves a single open seating buffet-style breakfast and lunch. Dinner in the dining room is seated and served European-style. For early risers, a continental breakfast with coffee, fruit, and pastries is set up in the Piano Bar; specialty coffees are available at the bar for a charge. A buffet lunch is offered most days on deck in the Tropical Bar, as are late-afternoon snacks and predinner canapés. On select itineraries an outdoor luncheon barbecue is prepared one day ashore. Late-night canapés are offered in the Piano Bar. There's no room service unless you're sick and can't make it out to meals.

Accommodations

Cabins: Traditional, yachtlike, and efficiently designed, *Star Clipper*'s cabins are adequate but far from spacious by modern standards. All cabins have a safe, desk-vanity, small settee, hair dryer, TV (except Category 6 inside), and marble bathroom with standard toiletries. As would normally be expected on a sailing vessel, staterooms forward and aft are more susceptible to motion than those amidships. There is also a noticeable slant to the floor in cabins near the bow. Unless you are particularly agile, you will want to avoid the inside cabins on Commodore Deck, where beds are strictly upper and lower berths. Some cabins are outfitted with

Top: Dining on *Star Clipper*
Bottom: Friendly, efficient service

a third pull-down berth, but most passengers will find the space too cramped for three occupants.

Top-Category Cabins: The Owner's Cabin and Category 1 cabins have a minibar, whirlpool tub-shower combination, and the use of bathrobes during the cruise. Category 1 cabin doors open onto the outside deck, and the Owner's Cabin has a sitting room.

Worth Noting: All cabins are equipped with 110-volt electrical outlets and a 110-volt outlet in the bathroom that is suitable for electric shavers only. None of the staterooms is designed for wheelchair accessibility, nor do any staterooms have connecting doors.

In the Know

For tranquillity and ample sunbathing space, head to the stern or the bowsprit net. The sails block less sunlight on the deck around the aft pool, and it tends to be quieter, but crawling onto the netting at the bowsprit is even better.

Pros and Cons

Pros: If the sheer beauty of real sailing silence and harmony with the sea when the engines are turned off and the ship is under sail—isn't enough to satisfy your inner pirate, creature comforts are only as far away as your fingertips. For a jolt of java, stop by the Piano Bar, where you'll find complimentary coffee and tea available around the clock. The best meet-and-mingle spot on board is the dining room, where booths and tables that seat six to eight are designed to maximize socializing.

Cons: There are no tables for two in the dining room. Designed to conserve water, the bathroom taps can be frustrating until you are accustomed to the regulated water flow that shuts off with annoying regularity and must be manually restarted. On a ship this size there aren't too many spots to get away from fellow passengers—fortunately, there aren't that many passengers and there's seldom what anyone would consider a crowd.

Cabin Type	Size (sq. ft.)
Owner's Suite	266
Cat. 1 Ocean View	150
Cat. 2 Ocean View	129
Standard Ocean View	118
Inside	97

FAST FACTS

- 4 passenger decks
- Dining room
- Safe, no TV (some)
- 2 pools
- Fitness classes
- 2 bars, library, laundry service
- Internet terminal
- No-smoking cabins

5

STAR CLIPPERS

Star Clipper under sail

WINDSTAR CRUISES

Are they cruise ships with sails or sailing ships designed for cruises? Since 1986, these masted sailing yachts have filled an upscale niche. They often visit ports of call inaccessible to huge, traditional cruise ships and offer a unique perspective of any cruising

Your Windstar ship at anchor

region. However, Windstar ships seldom depend on wind alone to sail. Nevertheless, if you're fortunate and conditions are perfect, as they sometimes are, the complete silence of pure sailing is heavenly. Stabilizers and computer-controlled ballast systems ensure no more than a mere few degrees of lean.

✉ *2101 4th Ave., Suite 1150, Seattle, WA*
☎ *206/292–9606 or 800/258–7245*
⊕ *www.windstarcruises. com*
☞ *Cruise Style: Luxury.*

When you can tear yourself away from the sight of thousands of yards of Dacron sail overhead, it doesn't take long to read the daily schedule of activities on a typical Windstar cruise. Simply put, there are few scheduled activities. Diversions are for the most part social, laid-back, and impromptu. You can choose to take part in the short list of daily activities; borrow a book, game, or DVD from the library; or do nothing at all. There's never pressure to join in or participate if you simply prefer relaxing with a fully loaded iPod, which you can check out on board.

Evening entertainment is informal, with a small dance combo playing in the main lounges. Compact casinos offer games of chance and slot machines, but don't look for bingo or other organized contests. A weekly show by the crew is delightful; attired in the traditional costumes of their homelands, they present music and dance highlighting their cultures. You may find occasional movies in the main lounges, which are outfitted with state-of-the-art video and sound equipment. Most passengers prefer socializing, either in the main lounge or an outdoor bar where Cigars Under the Stars attracts not only cigar aficionados but stargazers as well.

Welcome-aboard and farewell parties are hosted by the captain, and most passengers attend those as well as the nightly informational sessions regarding ports of call and activities that are presented by the activities staff during predinner cocktails.

A multimillion-dollar Degrees of Difference initiative enhanced each ship from stern to stern in 2006–07. The Yacht Club, which replaced the library on *Wind Surf*, is designed to be the social hub of the ship, with computer stations, a coffee bar, and a more expansive feel than the room it replaced. You will be able to join other passengers in comfortable seating around a large flat-screen TV to cheer on your favorite team during sporting events. In addition, all accommodations and bathrooms have been remodeled with updated materials; new weights and televisions were added to the gym; a couples massage room enhances the *Wind Surf* spa; the casual Veranda was expanded; the decks now have Balinese sun beds; and cooling mist sprayers are near the pools. Subsequent updates to *Wind Spirit* and *Wind Star* are similar but on a smaller scale.

Food

Dining on Windstar ships is as casually elegant as the dress code. There's seldom a wait for a table in open seating dining rooms where tables for two are plentiful. Whether meals are taken in the open and airy top-deck buffet, with its floor-to-ceiling windows and adjacent tables outside, or in the formal dining room, dishes are as creative as the surroundings. Expect traditional entrées but also items that incorporate regional ingredients, such as plantains, for added interest. Save room for petits fours with coffee and a taste of the fine cheeses from the after-dinner cheese cart.

In a nod to healthy dining, low-calorie and low-fat Sail Lite spa cuisine alternatives for breakfast, lunch, and dinner are prepared to American Heart Association guidelines. Additional choices are offered from the vegetarian menu.

Alcoholic beverages and soft drinks are not included in your cruise fare. Neither are the contents of the stocked minibar in your cabin.

A mid-cruise deck barbecue featuring grilled seafood and other favorites is fine dining in an elegantly casual alfresco setting. Desserts are uniformly delightful, and you'll want to try the bread pudding, a Windstar tradition available at the luncheon buffet. With daily tea and hot and cold hors d'oeuvres served several times during the afternoon and evening, no one goes hungry.

NOTEWORTHY

■ The shipboard computers that monitor wind velocity and direction also control heeling of the ships to less than six degrees.

■ Evening entertainment on Windstar usually includes a trio for dancing, a small casino, and stargazing.

■ Windstar ships have hot tubs and saltwater swimming pools in addition to retractable stern-mounted water-sports marinas.

Top: Dining well on board
Bottom: Compass Rose Bar on *Wind Surf*

5

WINDSTAR CRUISES

Top: Backgammon on deck
Middle: Scuba with the dive masters
Bottom: *Wind Surf* stateroom

Room service is always available, and you can place your order for dinner from the restaurant's menu during scheduled dining hours.

Fitness and Recreation

Most of the line's massage and exercise facilities are quite small, as would be expected on a ship that carries fewer than 150 passengers; however, *Wind Surf's* WindSpa and fitness areas are unexpectedly huge. An array of exercise equipment, free weights, and basic fitness classes are available in the gym and Nautilus room. There is an extra charge for Pilates and yoga classes. A wide variety of massages, body wraps, and facial treatments are offered in the spa, while hair and nail services are available for women and men in the salon. Both spa and salon are operated by Steiner Leisure.

Stern-mounted water-sports marinas are popular with active passengers who want to kayak, windsurf, and water-ski. Watery activities are free, including the use of snorkel gear that can be checked out for the entire cruise. The only charge is for diving; PADI-certified instructors offer a two-hour course for noncertified divers who want to try scuba and are also available to lead experienced certified divers on underwater expeditions. The dive teams take care of everything, even prepping and washing down the gear. If you prefer exploring on solid ground, sports coordinators are often at hand to lead an early-morning guided walk in port. Bicycles are available to rent for a half- or full day.

Your Shipmates

Windstar Cruises appeal to upscale professional couples in their late-thirties to sixties and on up to retirees, who enjoy the unpretentious, yet casually sophisticated atmosphere, creative cuisine, and refined service.

Windstar's ships were not designed for accessibility, and are not a good choice for the physically challenged. Although every attempt is made to accommodate passengers with disabilities, *Wind Surf* has only two elevators, and the smaller ships have none. There are no staterooms or bathrooms with wheelchair accessibility, and gangways can be difficult to navigate, depending

CHOOSE THIS LINE IF ...

You want a high-end experience yet prefer to dress casually every night on your vacation.

You love water sports, particularly scuba diving, kayaking, and windsurfing.

You're a romantic: tables for two are plentiful in the dining rooms.

on the tide and angle of ascent. Service animals are permitted to sail if arrangements are made at the time of booking.

Dress Code

All evenings are country-club casual, and slacks with a jacket over a sweater or shirt for men, and sundresses, skirts, or pants with a sweater or blouse for women are suggested. Coats and ties for men are not necessary, but some male passengers prefer to wear a jacket with open-collar shirt to dinner.

Junior Cruisers

Windstar Cruises' unregimented atmosphere is adult-oriented, and children are not encouraged. Children less than two years of age are not allowed at all; older children traveling as the third passenger in a stateroom with their parents incur the applicable third-person fare. No dedicated children's facilities are available, so parents are responsible for the behavior and entertainment of their children.

Service

Personal service and attention by the professional staff is the order of the day. Your preferences are noted and fulfilled without the necessity of reminders. Expect to be addressed by name within a short time of embarking.

Tipping

For many years Windstar sailed under a "tipping not required" policy. Windstar has now changed that policy. A service charge of $12 per guest per day (including children) is now added to each shipboard account. A 15% service charge is added to all bar bills. All these proceeds are paid directly to the crew.

Past Passengers

Windstar guests who cruise once with the line are automatically enrolled in the complimentary Foremast Club. Member benefits include savings on many sailings in addition to the Advance Savings Advantage Program discounts, Internet specials, and a free subscription to the *Foremast Club* magazine.

GOOD TO KNOW

Don't offer to help hoist the sails. They're operated by computer from the bridge and unfurl at the touch of a button in only two minutes. If you're interested in how everything works, take advantage of the open bridge policy and drop in for a chat with the captain.

5

WINDSTAR CRUISES

DON'T CHOOSE THIS LINE IF ...

You must have a spacious private balcony. There are none.

You're bored unless surrounded by constant stimulation. Activities are purposely low-key.

You have mobility problems. These ships are simply not very good for passengers in wheelchairs.

WIND SURF

CREW MEMBERS	190
ENTERED SERVICE	1990
GROSS TONS	14,745
LENGTH	617 feet
NUMBER OF CABINS	156
PASSENGER CAPACITY	312
WIDTH	66 feet

700 ft.

500 ft.

300 ft.

Top: Sea views at the rail
Bottom: *Wind Surf* at sea

Public Areas and Facilities

To make finding your way around simple, remember that all dining and entertainment areas are on the top three decks, with restaurants located forward and indoor-outdoor bars facing aft. The main lounge and casino are midship on Main Deck, as is the Yacht Club, which functions as library/Internet café/coffee bar. The fitness center is one deck higher. Most public areas have expansive sea views, although an exception is the Wind-Spa, which is tucked away aft on deck 2 just forward of the water-sports platform and large sauna. Stairways are rather steep, but forward and aft elevators assure that moving about is relatively easy.

Don't expect nautical kitsch to predominate *Wind Surf*'s decor. Although the main lounge has an understated sailing-flag motif, all other public areas are simply designed for comfort, with deep seats and an abundance of polished teak. Fresh flower arrangements and sailing-related artwork are lovely touches ship-wide.

Restaurants

The formal restaurant serves open seating dinner and is large enough to serve all passengers at once. For a casual setting, the buffet-style Veranda Café has indoor and outdoor seating for breakfast and lunch. An adjacent grill whips up cooked-to-order breakfast items and serves barbecue selections outdoors. A continental breakfast spread is offered in the Compass Rose bar. The Yacht Club Sandwich Bar offers a selection of sandwiches and an espresso bar. Degrees is the reservations-only, casual alternative for dinner that serves steak-house selections and rotating international menus, depending on the night. Other evening choices are Le Marché, an alfresco seafood bar serving fish and shellfish, and Candles, the poolside grill with a steak-and-skewers menu for which there is no charge (although reservations are suggested). Dining service in outdoor areas is subject to weather conditions. Afternoon tea with finger sandwiches and sweets is served daily. Room service is always available, and will serve selections from the dining-room menu during restaurant hours.

Accommodations

Cabins: *Wind Surf*'s ocean-view staterooms are a study in efficiency and clever design. Hanging lockers ("closets" to nonsailors) are generous. A small enclosed cabinet conceals a safe, and an entertainment center includes a flat-screen TV, DVD, and Bose SoundDock speakers for an iPod, which you can borrow from reception fully loaded with music. The combination vanity-desk and bedside table has drawers for ample storage. A few standard cabins have upper fold-down Pullman berths for a third passenger.

Suites: Double the size of standard staterooms, suites were created by reconfiguring two standard cabins to create accommodations with twice as much storage, two bathrooms, and a sitting area with a sofa bed to offer a berth for a third passenger. The bedroom and sitting room can be separated by drawing a curtain for privacy. Two supersize bridge suites have living and dining areas, a bedroom, a walk-in closet, and a bathroom with a whirlpool tub and separate shower.

Worth Noting: Special touches in each stateroom and suite are fresh flowers, terry robes for use during the voyage, and bath toiletries. Teak-floor bathrooms are sensibly laid out and spacious enough for two people to actually share the space. All staterooms and suites are equipped with barware, minibar, and hair dryer. Voltage is 220, so converters are needed for most small appliances. No cabins are wheelchair accessible.

In the Know

Don't be alarmed if you go below deck and find the passageways blocked. Those watertight doors are normally tucked out of sight but must be closed when *Wind Surf* is departing from or arriving in port.

Pros and Cons

Pros: Superb service is delivered with a smile by waiters and stewards who greet you by name from almost the moment you board. All cabins are outside, and none have obstructed views. Teatime at the Compass Rose, where sweets are served in addition to the finger foods and a duo performs easy-listening tunes, is a highlight every afternoon.

Cons: When caviar and all the trimmings are spread out in the Compass Rose one day during the cruise, you might have to fight your fellow passengers to get near it. There are no private balconies associated with any accommodations. There are no tables in the standard staterooms, which makes dining from room service trays inelegant at best.

Cabin Type	Size (sq. ft.)
Suite	376
Ocean View	188
Bridge Suite	500

FAST FACTS

- 6 passenger decks
- Specialty restaurant, dining room, buffet
- Wi-Fi, safe, refrigerator, DVD
- 2 pools
- Fitness classes, gym, hair salon, 2 hot tubs, sauna, spa
- 4 bars, casino, dance club, library
- Laundry service
- Internet terminal
- No-smoking cabins

5

WINDSTAR CRUISES

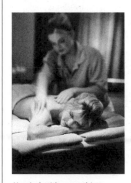

Unwind with a soothing massage

WIND SPIRIT, WIND STAR

	CREW MEMBERS
	90
	ENTERED SERVICE
	1988
700 ft.	**GROSS TONS**
	5,350
	LENGTH
	440 feet
500 ft.	**NUMBER OF CABINS**
	74
	PASSENGER CAPACITY
	148
300 ft.	**WIDTH**
	52 feet

Public Areas and Facilities

Comfort is the element that ties *Wind Spirit*'s interiors together. Blue and cream, echoing hues of the sea and sandy beaches, predominate in the formal restaurant and cozy main lounge, where you'll find a tiny casino tucked into a corner. With its large windows and a skylight, the lounge is flooded with natural light during daytime hours.

Public spaces are proportionately small on such a diminutive vessel and feature yachtlike touches of polished wood, columns wrapped in rope, and nautical artwork ship-wide, as well as abundant fresh flower arrangements. The library contains books, movies to play in your cabin, and a computer center.

Passenger accommodations and public areas are all found in the aft two-thirds of the ship, with dining and entertainment located on the top two decks.

Restaurants

The formal restaurant offers open seating dinner during scheduled hours and is large enough to serve all passengers at once, so there is seldom a wait for a table. In a more casual setting, the buffet-style Veranda Café has indoor and outdoor seating for breakfast and lunch. A grill whips up cooked-to-order breakfast and lunch choices. Dinner under the stars is available at Candles, the poolside grill with a steak-and-skewers menu (no extra charge, but reservations are suggested). The pool bar has a permanent food station for continental breakfast, afternoon tea, desserts, and evening canapés. Afternoon tea with finger sandwiches and sweets is served daily. Room service is always available, and will serve selections from the dining-room menu during restaurant hours.

Accommodations

Cabins: *Wind Spirit*'s ocean-view staterooms are ingeniously designed for efficiency. Hanging lockers (closets) are generous, and contain shoe racks and shelves for gear. A small enclosed cabinet conceals a safe, and an entertainment center includes a flat-screen TV, DVD, and Bose SoundDock speaker for an iPod, which you can borrow from reception fully loaded with music. The combination vanity-desk and bedside table has drawers for ample storage.

Top: Casually elegant dining
Bottom: A sunny day at the pool

Suites: A single Owner's Suite, the only premium accommodation on board, has a sitting area with a sofa bed to offer a berth for a third passenger.

Worth Noting: Special touches in each stateroom are fresh flowers, terry robes for use during the voyage, and bath toiletries. The teak-floor bathrooms are big enough for two. All staterooms and suites are equipped with barware, a minibar, and hair dryer (voltage is standard 110 AC); portholes have deadheads, which can be closed in high seas. Ten staterooms have adjoining doors on *Wind Spirit* and 12 on *Wind Star,* and a limited number of standard cabins have upper fold-down Pullman berths for a third passenger. There are no cabins configured for wheelchair accessibility.

In the Know

Slide out the ingenious hidden table in your stateroom cabinetry, and pull up a chair for relaxed room-service dining.

Pros and Cons

Pros: Movies from an extensive DVD collection can be borrowed to watch in the privacy of your stateroom, and a call to room service is all it takes to get free popcorn. Each evening before dinner, most passengers gather in the lounge for really informative port talks while hot and cold appetizers are served by roaming waiters. Mist sprayers near the pool offer a refreshing way to keep cool.

Cons: With so much time spent outside, the aft pool and hot tub are popular relaxation spots and apt to feel crowded. The water-sports marina can open only when the ship is at anchor, so check the itinerary to determine how often it will be available for use. Ways to entertain yourself are sparse—the gym and library are tiny, and the casino is so small there is only room for a couple of gaming tables and a handful of slot machines.

Cabin Type	Size (sq. ft.)
Suite	220
Ocean View	188

FAST FACTS

- 5 passenger decks
- Dining room, buffet
- Wi-Fi, safe, refrigerator, DVD
- Pool
- Fitness classes, gym, hair salon, hot tub, sauna
- 2 bars, casino, dance club, library
- Laundry service
- Internet terminal
- No-smoking cabins

5

WINDSTAR CRUISES

Wind Spirit at sea

Ports of Embarkation

WORD OF MOUTH

"If you depart from Florida, you may have more days at sea, so more days on the ship and fewer days visiting the islands . . . than if you depart from San Juan."

—Sassafrass

Miami is the world's cruise capital, and more cruise ships are based here year-round than anywhere else. Caribbean cruises depart for their itineraries from several ports on either of Florida's coasts, as well as from cities on the Gulf Coast and East Coast of the United States.

Generally, if your cruise is on an Eastern Caribbean itinerary, you'll likely depart from Miami, Fort Lauderdale, Jacksonville, or Port Canaveral; short three- and four-day cruises to the Bahamas also depart from these ports. Most cruises on Western Caribbean itineraries depart from Tampa, New Orleans, or Galveston, though some depart from Miami as well. Cruises from farther up the East Coast of the United States, including such ports as Baltimore, Maryland; Charleston, South Carolina; and even New York City, usually go to the Bahamas or sometimes Key West and often include a private-island stop or a stop elsewhere in Florida. Cruises to the Southern Caribbean might depart from Miami if they are 10 days or longer, but more likely they will depart from San Juan, Puerto Rico, or some other port deeper in the Caribbean.

Regardless of which port you depart from, air connections may prevent you from leaving home on the morning of your cruise or going home the day you return to port. Or you may wish to arrive early simply to give yourself a bit more peace of mind, or you may just want to spend more time in one of these interesting port cities. Many people choose to depart from New Orleans or Galveston just to have an excuse to spend a couple of days in the city before or after their cruise.

PORT ESSENTIALS

CAR RENTAL
Major Agencies **Alamo** (☎ 800/462-5266 ⊕ www.alamo.com). **Avis** (☎ 800/230-4898 ⊕ www.avis.com). **Budget** (☎ 800/527-0700 ⊕ www. budget.com). **Hertz** (☎ 800/654-3131 ⊕ www.hertz.com). **National Car Rental** (☎ 800/227-7368 ⊕ www.nationalcar.com).

SURCHARGES
To avoid a hefty refueling fee, fill the tank just before you turn in the car, but be aware that gas stations near the rental outlet may charge more than those farther away. If you plan to do a lot of driving (and if you can get a good price), it can be a better deal to buy a full tank of gas when you rent so you can return the car with an empty tank. However, it's never a good deal to pay the huge surcharge for not returning a tank full unless you simply have no other choice. Other surcharges may apply if you are under 25 or over 75, if you want to add an additional driver to the contract, or if you want to drive over state borders or out of a specific radius from your point of rental. You'll also pay extra for child seats, which are compulsory for children under 5, and for a GPS navigation system or electronic toll pass. You can sometimes avoid the

charge for insurance if you have your own, either from your own policy or from a credit card, but know what you are covered for, and read the fine print before making this decision.

DINING

Unless otherwise noted, the restaurants we recommend accept major credit cards and are open for both lunch and dinner. All prices in this guide are given in U.S. dollars, and the following price categories apply.

WHAT IT COSTS IN U.S. DOLLARS					
	¢	$	$$	$$$	$$$$
Restaurants	under $8	$9–$12	$13–$20	$21–$30	over $30
Hotels	under $80	$81–$125	$126–$180	$185–$250	over $250

Restaurant prices are per person for a main course at dinner and do not include any service charges or taxes. Lodging prices are for a double room in high season, excluding service and taxes.

LODGING

Whether you are driving or flying into your port of embarkation, it is often more convenient to arrive the day before or to stay for a day after your cruise. For this reason we offer lodging suggestions for each port of embarkation.

The lodgings we list are convenient to the cruise port and the cream of the crop in each price category. We always list the facilities that are available, but we don't specify whether they cost extra; when pricing accommodations, always ask what's included. Properties are assigned price categories based on the range between their least expensive standard double room in high season (excluding holidays) and the most expensive. But if you find everything sold out or wish to find a more predictable place to stay, there are chain hotels at almost all ports of embarkation.

Assume that hotel rates do not include meals unless they are specified in the review.

BALTIMORE, MARYLAND

Evan Serpick and Roberta Sotonoff

Baltimore's charm lies in its neighborhoods. Although stellar downtown attractions such as the National Aquarium and Camden Yards draw torrents of tourists each year, much of the city's character can be found outside the Inner Harbor. Scores of Baltimore's trademark narrow red-brick row houses with white marble steps line the city's east and west sides. Some neighborhood streets are still made of cobblestone, and grand churches and museums and towering, glassy high-rises fill out the growing skyline. Now the city's blue-collar past mixes with present urban-professional revitalization. Industrial waterfront properties are giving way to high-end condos, and corner bars formerly dominated by National Bohemian beer—once made in the city—are adding micro-brews to their beverage lists. And with more and more retail stores

Security

All cruise lines have instituted stricter security procedures in recent years; however, you may not even be aware of all the changes.

Some of the changes will be more obvious to you. For example, only visitors who have been authorized well in advance are allowed onboard. Proper identification (a government-issued photo ID) is required in all instances to board the ship, whether you are a visitor or passenger. Ship security personnel are stationed at all points of entry to the ship. All hand-carried items are searched by hand in every port (this applies to both crew and passengers).

Some of the changes are more behind the scenes. All luggage is scanned, whether you carry it aboard with you or not, and all packages and provisions brought onboard are scanned.

In addition, every ship has added professionally trained security officers and taken many other measures to ensure the safety of all passengers. Many cruise-line security personnel are former navy or marine officers with extensive maritime experience. Some cruise lines recruit shipboard security personnel from the ranks of former British Gurkha regiments. From Nepal, the Gurkhas are renowned as soldiers of the highest caliber.

replacing old, run-down buildings and parking lots, Baltimore is one of the nation's up-and-coming cities.

ESSENTIALS

HOURS During the summer tourist season, most of Baltimore's stores and attractions usually open around 9 am and close around 9 pm.

INTERNET **Enoch Pratt Free Library** (✉ *400 Cathedral St., Mount Vernon* ☎ *410/396–5500* ⊕ *www.pratt.lib.md.us* ☯ *June–Sept., Mon.–Wed. 10–8, Thurs. 10–5:30, Fri. and Sat. 10–5, Sun. 1–5; Oct.–May, Mon.–Wed. 11–7, Thurs. 10–5:30, Fri. and Sat. 10–5, Sun. 1–5*).

Visitor Information Baltimore Visitor Center (✉ *401 Light St., Inner Harbor* ☎ *877/225–8466* ⊕ *www.baltimore.org*).

THE CRUISE PORT

Well marked and easily accessible by major highways, the South Locust Point Cruise Terminal is about a mile from center city. Several cruise lines offer seasonal cruises from the port, and *Carnival Pride* is based here permanently. Ships dock near the main cruise building, which itself is little more than a hub for arrivals and departures. There are few facilities for passengers in the immediate port area, which is out of walking distance to Baltimore's attractions.

During cruise season, taxis are the best transportation to the downtown area. They cost about $5 one-way and frequent the port. Taxis to Baltimore–Washington International Airport charge a flat rate of $35. Rental cars are generally not necessary; if you fly into Baltimore, you can see the majority of Baltimore by taxi. Guided tours of the city range from $20 to $60.

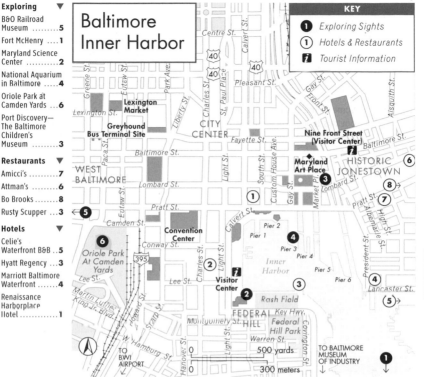

Information Port of Baltimore (✉ *2001 E. McComas St.* ☎ *410/962–8701* ⊕ *www.cruisemaryland.com*).

Airports Baltimore-Washington International Airport (*BWI* ✉ *10 mi south of Baltimore off Rte. 295/Baltimore–Washington Pkwy.* ☎ *410/859–7111 for information and paging* ⊕ *www.bwiairport.com*).

Airport Transfers Airport Taxis (☎ *410/859–1100* ⊕ *www.bwiairporttaxi.com*). **Arrow Taxicab** (☎ *410/358–9696*). **BWI Airport rail station** (☎ *410/672–6167* ⊕ *www.mtamaryland.com*). **BWI SuperShuttle** (☎ *800/258–3826* ⊕ *www. supershuttle.com*). **Carey Limousines** (☎ *888/880–0999* ⊕ *www.carey.com*). **Maryland Area Rail Commuter** (*MARC* ☎ *800/325–7245 or 410/539–5000* ⊕ *www.mtamaryland.com*). **Penn Station** (✉ *Charles St. at Mt. Royal Ave., Mount Vernon* ☎ *800/523–8720*). **Private Car/RMA Worldwide Chauffeured Transportation** (☎ *410/519–0000 or 800/878–7743* ⊕ *www.rmalimo.com*).

PARKING

There's a secure parking lot next to the cruise terminal, where parking costs $15 per day. Drop off your luggage before parking.

EXPLORING BALTIMORE

☺ ★ **B&O Railroad Museum.** The famous Baltimore & Ohio Railroad was founded on the site that now houses this museum, which contains more than 120 full-size locomotives and a great collection of railroad memorabilia, from dining-car china and artwork to lanterns and signals. The 1884 roundhouse (240 feet in diameter and 120 feet high) adjoins one of the nation's first railroad stations. Train rides are available every day but Monday. The Iron Horse Café serves food and drinks. ⊠ *901 W. Pratt St., West Baltimore* ☎ *410/752–2490* ⊕ *www.borail.org* ☜ *$14* ☉ *Mon.–Sat. 10–4, Sun. 11–4.*

☺ **Fodor's Choice** ★ **Fort McHenry.** This star-shaped brick fort is forever associated with Francis Scott Key and "The Star-Spangled Banner," which Key penned while watching the British bombardment of Baltimore during the War of 1812. Key had been detained onboard a truce ship, where he was negotiating the release of one Dr. William Beanes, when the bombardment began; Key knew too much about the attack plan to be released. Through the next day and night, as the battle raged, Key strained to be sure, through the smoke and haze, that the flag still flew above Fort McHenry—indicating that Baltimore's defenders held firm. "By the dawn's early light" of September 14, 1814, he saw the 30- by 42-foot "Star-Spangled Banner" still aloft and was inspired to pen the words to a poem (set to the tune of an old English drinking song). The flag that flew above Fort McHenry that day had 15 stars and 15 stripes, and was hand-sewn for the fort. A visit to the fort includes a 15-minute history film, guided tour, and frequent living-history displays on summer weekends. To see how the formidable fortifications might have appeared to the bombarding British, catch a water taxi from the Inner Harbor to the fort instead of driving. ⊠ *E. Fort Ave., from Light St., take Key Hwy. for 1½ mi and follow signs, Locust Point* ☎ *410/962–4290* ⊕ *www. nps.gov/fomc* ☜ *$7* ☉ *Memorial Day–Labor Day, daily 8–8; Labor Day–Memorial Day, daily 8–5.*

☺ ★ **Maryland Science Center.** Originally known as the Maryland Academy of Sciences, this 200-year-old scientific institution is one of the oldest in the United States. Now housed in a contemporary building, the three floors of exhibits on the Chesapeake Bay, Earth science, physics, the body, dinosaurs, and outer space are an invitation to engage, experiment, and explore. The center has a planetarium, a simulated archaeological dinosaur dig, an IMAX movie theater with a screen five stories high, and a playroom especially designed for young children. ⊠ *601 Light St., Inner Harbor* ☎ *410/685–5225* ⊕ *www.mdsci.org* ☜ *$14.95* ☉ *Me-*

morial Day–Labor Day, Thurs.–Sat. 10–8, Sun.–Wed. 10–6; Labor Day–Memorial Day, Tues.–Fri. 10–5, Sat. 10–6, Sun. 11–5.

ⓒ **National Aquarium in Baltimore.** The most-visited attraction in Maryland
Fodor's Choice has more than 10,000 fish, sharks, dolphins, and amphibians dwell-
★ ing in 2 million gallons of water. The Animal Planet Australia: Wild Extremes exhibit mimics a river running through a gorge. It features lizards, crocodiles, turtles, bats, and a black-headed python, among other animals from Down Under. The aquarium also features reptiles, birds, plants, and mammals in its rain-forest environment, inside a glass pyramid 64 feet high. The rain-forest ecosystem harbors two-toed sloths in calabash trees, parrots in the palms, iguanas on the ground, and red-bellied piranhas in a pool (a sign next to it reads "do not put hands in pool"). Each day in the Marine Mammal Pavilion, Atlantic bottlenose dolphins are part of several entertaining presentations that highlight their agility and intelligence. The aquarium's famed shark tank and Atlantic coral reef exhibits are spectacular; you can wind through an enormous glass enclosure on a spiral ramp while hammerheads and brightly hued tropical fish glide by. Hands-on exhibits include such docile sea creatures as horseshoe crabs and starfish. ■**TIP**→ **Arrive early to ensure admission, which is by timed intervals; by noon, the wait is often two or three hours.** ⊠ *Pier 3, Inner Harbor* ☎ *410/576–3800* ⊕ *www. aqua.org* ⊠ *$24.95* ☉ *Nov.–Feb., Sat.–Thurs. 10–5, Fri. 10–8; Mar.– June, Sept., and Oct., Sat.–Thurs. 9–5, Fri. 9–8; July–Aug. 19, daily 9–8; Aug. 20–31, Sat.–Thurs. 9–6, Fri. 9–8; visitors may tour for up to 1½ hrs after closing. Timed tickets may be required on weekends and holidays; purchase these early in the day.*

ⓒ **Oriole Park at Camden Yards.** Home of the Baltimore Orioles, Camden
★ Yards and the nearby area bustle on game days. Since it opened in 1992, this nostalgically designed baseball stadium has inspired other cities to emulate its neotraditional architecture and amenities. The Eutaw Street promenade, between the warehouse and the field, has a view of the stadium; look for the brass baseballs embedded in the sidewalk that mark where home runs have cleared the fence, or visit the Orioles Hall of Fame display and the monuments to retired Orioles. Daily 90-minute tours to nearly every section of the ballpark, from the massive, JumboTron scoreboard to the dugout to the state-of-the-art beer-delivery system. ⊠ *333 W. Camden St., Downtown* ☎ *410/685–9800 general information, 410/547–6234 tour times, 888/848–2473 tickets to Orioles home games* ⊕ *www.theorioles.com* ⊠ *Eutaw St. promenade free; tour $7* ☉ *Eutaw St. promenade daily 10–3, otherwise during games and tours; tours Mar.–Sept., Mon.–Sat. at 11, noon, 1, and 2; Oct., weekdays at 11:30 and 1:30, Sat. at 11, noon, 1, and 2, Sun. at 12:30, 1, 2, and 3; Nov., Mon.–Sat. at 11:30 and 1:30, Sun. at 12:30 and 2:30.*

ⓒ **Port Discovery—The Baltimore Children's Museum.** At this interactive museum, adults are encouraged to play every bit as much as children. A favorite attraction is the three-story KidWorks, a futuristic jungle gym on which the adventurous can climb, crawl, slide, and swing their way through stairs, slides, ropes, zip lines, and tunnels, and even cross a narrow footbridge three stories up. In Miss Perception's Mystery House, youngsters help solve a mystery surrounding the disappearance of the Baffeld family by sifting through clues; some are written or visual, and others are gleaned by touching and listening. Changing interactive exhibits allow for even more play. ⊠ *35 Market Pl., Inner Harbor* ☎ *410/727–8120* ⊕ *www.portdiscovery.com* ☞ *$12.95* ⊙ *Memorial Day–Labor Day, Mon.–Sat. 10–5, Sun. noon–5; Labor Day–Memorial Day, Tues.–Fri. 9:30–4:30, Sat. 10–5, Sun. noon–5.*

SHOPPING

Baltimore isn't the biggest shopping town, but it does have some malls and good stores here and there. Hampden (the "p" is silent), a neighborhood west of Johns Hopkins University, has funky shops selling everything from housewares to housedresses along its main drag, 36th Street (better known as "The Avenue"). Some interesting shops can be found along Charles Street in Mount Vernon and along Thames Street in Fells Point. Federal Hill has a few fun shops, particularly for furnishings and vintage items. At the Inner Harbor, the Pratt Street and Light Street pavilions of **Harborplace and the Gallery** (☎ *410/332–4191*) contain almost 200 specialty shops that sell everything from business attire to children's toys. The Gallery has J. Crew, Banana Republic, and the Gap, among others.

NIGHTLIFE

Fells Point, just east of the Inner Harbor; Federal Hill, due south; and Canton, due east, have hosts of bars, restaurants, and clubs that draw a rowdy, largely collegiate crowd. If you're seeking quieter surroundings, head for the upscale comforts of downtown or Mount Vernon clubs and watering holes.

BARS AND LOUNGES

Upstairs at **The Brewer's Art** (⊠ *1106 N. Charles St., Mount Vernon* ☎ *410/547–6925* ⊕ *www.belgianbeer.com*) is an elegant bar and lounge with armchairs, marble pillars, and chandeliers, plus a dining room with terrific food; downstairs, the dark basement bar specializes in Belgian-style beers. With its stylized art deco surroundings, the funky **Club Charles** (⊠ *1724 N. Charles St., Station North Arts District* ☎ *410/727–8815*) is a favorite hangout for an artsy crowd, moviegoers coming from the Charles Theater across the street, and, reputation has it, John Waters. **Club Hippo** (⊠ *1 W. Eager St., Mount Vernon* ☎ *410/547–0069* ⊕ *www.clubhippo.com*) is Baltimore's longest-reigning gay bar. A dance club, martini bar, and pub have all helped make **Grand Central** (⊠ *1003 N. Charles St., Mount Vernon* ☎ *410/752–7133*) into a hip gay hot spot. Beer lovers should visit **Max's Taphouse** (⊠ *737 S. Broadway, Fells Point* ☎ *410/675–6297* ⊕ *www.maxs.com*), which has more than 70 brews on tap and about 300 more in bottles. **Red Maple** (⊠ *930 N. Charles St., Mount Vernon* ☎ *410/547–0149* ⊕ *www.930redmaple.com*) is one of the city's most stylish spots for drinks and tapas. At the top of the Belvedere Hotel, the **13th Floor** (⊠ *1 E. Chase St., Mount Vernon* ☎ *410/347–0888*) offers a great view, a long martini list, and live dance music.

COMEDY CLUBS

The Comedy Factory (⊠ *36 Light St., Inner Harbor* ☎ *410/752–4189*) is the best local spot to see live standup.

WHERE TO EAT

Baltimore loves crabs. Soft- or hardshell crabs, crab cakes, crab dip—the city's passion for clawed crustaceans seems to have no end. Flag down a Baltimore native and ask them where the best crab joint is, and you'll get a list of options. In addition to crabs and seafood, Baltimore's restaurant landscape also includes Italian, Afghan, Greek, American, tapas, and other cuisines. The city's dining choices may not compare with those of New York, or even Washington, but it does have some real standouts. Note that places generally stop serving by 10 pm, if not earlier.

For price categories, see ⇨ Dining at the beginning of this chapter.

$-$$
ITALIAN
✕ **Amicci's.** At this self-proclaimed "very casual eatery," you don't have to spend a fortune to get a satisfying taste of Little Italy. Blue jean–clad diners and walls hung with movie posters make for a fun atmosphere. Service is friendly and usually speedy, and the food comes in large portions. Try the chicken Lorenzo: breaded chicken breast covered in a marsala wine sauce, red peppers, prosciutto, and provolone. ⊠ *231 S. High St., Little Italy* ☎ *410/528–1096* ⊕ *www.amiccis.com.*

¢-$
DELI
✕ **Attman's.** Open since 1915, this authentic New York–style deli near the Jewish Museum is the king of Baltimore's "Corned Beef Row." Of the three delis on the row, Attman's has the longest waits and steepest prices, but delivers the highest-quality dishes. Don't be put off by the long lines—they move fairly quickly, and the outstanding corned beef sandwiches are worth the wait, as are the pastrami, homemade chopped liver, and other oversize creations. Attman's closes at 6:30 pm daily. ⊠ *1019 Lombard St., Historic Jonestown* ☎ *410/563–2666* ⊕ *www.attmansdeli.com.*

$$-$$$
SEAFOOD
✕ **Bo Brooks.** Picking steamed crabs on Bo Brooks's waterfront deck as sailboats and tugs ply the harbor is a quintessential Baltimore pleasure. Locals spend hot summer days cracking into warm, spicy crabs and enjoying a refreshing pitcher of beer while a cool breeze blows in from the harbor. Brooks serves its famous crustaceans year-round, along with a menu of Chesapeake seafood classics. Locals know to stick to the Maryland crab soup, crab dip, jumbo lump crab cakes, and fried oysters. ⊠ *2701 Boston St., Canton* ☎ *410/558–0202* ⊕ *www.bobrooks.com.*

$$-$$$
SEAFOOD
✕ **Rusty Scupper.** A tourist favorite, the Rusty Scupper undoubtedly has the best view along the waterfront; sunset here is magical, with the sun sinking slowly into the harbor as lights twinkle on the city's skyscrapers. The interior is decorated with light wood and windows from floor to ceiling; the house specialty is seafood, particularly the jumbo lump crab cake, but the menu also includes beef, chicken, and pasta. Reservations are essential on Friday and Saturday; service can be spotty. ⊠ *402 Key Hwy., Inner Harbor* ☎ *410/727–3678.*

WHERE TO STAY

When booking a hotel or bed-and-breakfast in Baltimore, focus on the Inner Harbor, where you're likely to spend a good deal of time. The downside to staying in hotels near downtown is the noise level, which can rise early in the morning and stay up late into the night—especially if there's a baseball or football game. For quieter options, head to neighborhoods like Fells Point and Canton.

For expanded hotel reviews, visit Fodors.com.

$$
INN/B&B

Celie's Waterfront Bed & Breakfast. Proprietors Nancy and Kevin Kupec oversee every detail of this small inn in the heart of Fells Point. **Pros:** intimate accommodations; situated next to an entertainment district. **Cons:** it can get noisy late at night. *1714 Thames St., Fells Point* *410/522–2323 or 800/432–0184* *www.celieswaterfront.com* *7 rooms, 2 suites In-room: a/c, Wi-Fi. In-hotel: restaurant, parking Breakfast.*

$$$–$$$$
HOTEL

Hyatt Regency. This stretch of Light Street is practically a highway, but the unenclosed skyways allow ready pedestrian access to both Inner Harbor attractions and the convention center. **Pros:** the Inner Harbor is just a skywalk away. **Cons:** service can be slow and unhelpful. *300 Light St., Inner Harbor* *410/528–1234 or 800/233–1234* *baltimore.hyatt.com* *488 rooms, 26 suites In-room: a/c, Wi-Fi. In-hotel: restaurant, bars, tennis courts, pool, gym, parking No meals.*

$$$–$$$$
HOTEL

Marriott Baltimore Waterfront. The city's tallest hotel and the only one directly on the Inner Harbor itself, this upscale 31-story Marriott has a neoclassical interior that uses multihue marbles, rich jewel-tone walls, and photographs of Baltimore architectural landmarks. **Pros:** nice amenities; great location and view. **Cons:** pricey compared to nearby hotels. *700 Aliceanna St., Inner Harbor East* *410/385–3000* *www.marriotthotels.com/bwiwf* *751 rooms In-room: a/c, Internet. In-hotel: restaurant, bar, pool, gym, parking No meals.*

$$$
HOTEL

Renaissance Baltimore Harborplace Hotel. The most conveniently located of the Inner Harbor hotels—across the street from the shopping pavilions—the Renaissance Harborplace meets the needs of tourists, business travelers, and conventioneers. **Pros:** snappy service. **Cons:** some rooms are a bit threadbare. *202 E. Pratt St., Inner Harbor* *410/547–1200 or 800/468–3571* *www.renaissancehotels.com/bwish* *562 rooms, 60 suites In-room: a/c, Internet. In-hotel: restaurant, bar, pool, gym, parking No meals.*

CHARLESTON, SOUTH CAROLINA

Eileen Robinson Smith

Charleston looks like a movie set, an 18th-century etching brought to life. The spires and steeples of more than 180 churches punctuate her low skyline, and tourists ride in horse-drawn carriages that pass grandiose, centuries-old mansions and gardens brimming with heirloom plants. Preserved through the poverty following the Civil War and natural disasters like fires, earthquakes, and hurricanes, much of Charleston's earliest public and private architecture still stands. And thanks to a rigorous preservation movement and strict Board of Architectural

Review, the city's new structures blend with the old ones. If you're boarding your cruise ship here, it's worth coming a few days early to explore the historic downtown and to eat in one of the many superb restaurants. In late spring, plan in advance for the Spoleto U.S.A. Festival. For more than 30 memorable years, arts patrons have gathered to enjoy the international dance, opera, theater, and other performances at venues citywide. Piccolo Spoleto showcases local and regional concerts, dance, theater, and comedy shows.

ESSENTIALS

HOURS Most shops are open from 9 or 10 am to at least 6 pm, but some are open later. A new city ordinance requires bars to close by 2 am.

INTERNET While almost all hotels (and even B&Bs) offer some kind of Internet service, Internet cafés are rare in the Charleston historic district; however, many coffee shops, including all the local Starbucks, offer Wi-Fi.

Visitor Information **Charleston Visitor Center** (⊠ *375 Meeting St., Upper King* ⌖ *423 King St., 29403* ☎ *843/853–8000 or 800/868–8118* ⊕ *www. charlestoncvb.com*).

THE CRUISE PORT

Cruise ships sailing from Charleston depart from the Union Pier Terminal, which is in Charleston's historic district. If you are driving, however, and need to leave your car for the duration of your cruise, take the East Bay Street exit off the new, majestic Arthur Ravenel, Jr. Bridge on I–17 and follow the "Cruise Ship" signs. On ship embarkation days police officers will direct you to the ship terminal from the intersection of East Bay and Chapel streets. Cruise parking is located adjacent to Union Pier.

Information **Port of Charleston** (⊠ *196 Concord St., Market area, at foot of Market St.* ☎ *843/958–8298 for cruise information* ⊕ *www.port-of-charleston.com*).

AIRPORT TRANSFERS

Several cab companies service the airport, including the new Charleston Black Cab Company, which operates a fleet of genuine London cabs with uniformed drivers and costs about $10 more than calling a regular cab—about $50 to downtown. Airport Ground Transportation arranges shuttles, which cost $15 per person to the downtown area, $40 to $45 for a return trip to the airport. CARTA's bus No. 11, a public bus, now goes to the airport for a mere $1.25; it leaves downtown from the Meeting/Mary St. parking garage every 50 minutes, from 5:45 am until 11:09 pm.

PARKING

Parking costs $15 per day ($105 per week) for regular vehicles, $35 per day ($245 per week) for RVs or other vehicles more than 20 feet in length. You pay in advance by cash, check or credit card. A free shuttle bus takes you to the cruise-passenger terminal. Be sure to drop your large luggage off at Union Pier before you park your car; only carry-on size luggage is allowed on the shuttle bus, so if you have any bags larger than 22 inches by 14 inches, they will have to be checked before you

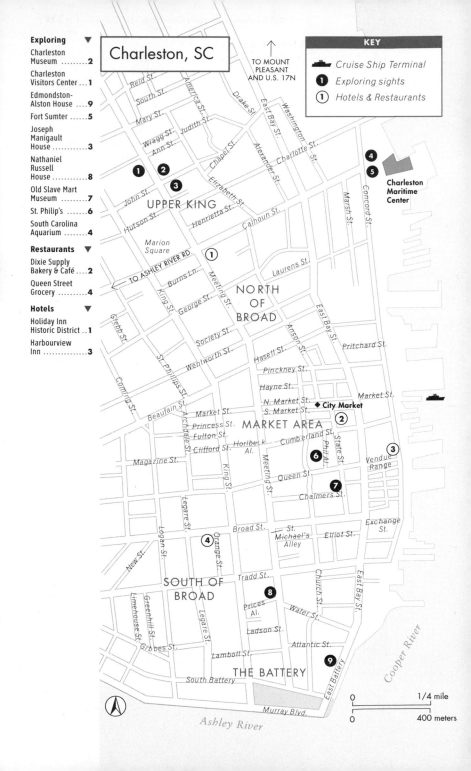

Charleston, SC

TO MOUNT PLEASANT AND U.S. 17N

KEY

🚢 Cruise Ship Terminal

1 Exploring sights

① Hotels & Restaurants

Charleston Maritime Center

Reid St.
South St.
Mary St.
America St.
Drake St.
East Bay St.
Washington St.
Wragg St.
Ann St.
Judith St.
Chapel St.
Alexander St.
Charlotte St.
Elizabeth St.
John St.
UPPER KING
Hutson St.
Henrietta St.
Calhoun St.
Marsh St.
Concord St.
Marion Square
TO ASHLEY RIVER RD.
Burns Ln.
Laurens St.
NORTH OF BROAD
King St.
George St.
Meeting St.
Anson St.
East Bay St.
Pritchard St.
Grebb St.
Society St.
Coming St.
Wentworth St.
Hasell St.
Pinckney St.
St. Philips St.
Hayne St.
Beaufain St.
Market St.
N. Market St.
◆ City Market
Market St.
Arcades
Princess St.
Fulton St.
S. Market St.
MARKET AREA
Horlbeck Al.
Cumberland St.
State St.
Phil Al.
2
Clifford St.
Magazine St.
Vendue Range
3
6
Queen St.
7
Chalmers St.
Legare St.
King St.
Meeting St.
Exchange St.
Broad St.
St. Michael's Alley
Elliot St.
4
Orange St.
Logan St.
New St.
Tradd St.
Church St.
East Bay St.
8
Prices Al.
Water St.
Limehouse St.
Greenhill St.
Ladson St.
Legare St.
Atlantic St.
Gibbes St.
9
Lambott St.
THE BATTERY
East Battery
South Battery
Murray Blvd.

Ashley River

Cooper River

0 ___ 1/4 mile
0 ___ 400 meters

park. Also, you'll need your cruise
tickets to board the shuttle bus

EXPLORING CHARLESTON

The heart of the city is on a peninsula, sometimes just called
"downtown" by the nearly 60,000
residents who populate the area.
Walking Charleston's peninsula is
the best way to get to know the
city. The main downtown historic district is roughly bounded
by Lockwood Boulevard to the
west, Calhoun Street to the north,
the Cooper River to the east, and
the Battery to the south. Nearly
2,000 historic homes and buildings occupy this fairly compact area
divided into South of Broad (Street)
and North of Broad. King Street,
the main shopping street in town,
cuts through Broad Street, and the
most trafficked tourist area ends a

**CHARLESTON
BEST BETS**

■ **Viewing Art.** The city is home
to some 120 galleries, exhibiting
art from Charleston, the South,
and around the world. The Gibbes
Museum of Art and a half-dozen
other museums add to the cultural mix.

■ **The Battery.** The views from
the point—both natural and man-
made—are the loveliest in the
city. Look west to see the harbor;
to the east you'll find elegant
Charleston mansions.

■ **Historic Homes.** Charleston's
preserved, centuries-old, stately
homes, including the Nathaniel
Russell House, are highlights.

few blocks south of the Crosstown, where U.S. 17 cuts across Upper
King. If you don't wish to walk, there are bikes, pedicabs, and trolleys.
Street parking is irksome, as meter readers are among the city's most
efficient public servants. Parking garages, both privately and publicly
owned, charge around $1.50 an hour.

🔄 ★ **Charleston Museum.** While housed in a modern-day brick complex, this
institution was founded in 1773 and is the country's oldest city museum.
To the delight of fans of *Antiques Roadshow,* the collection is especially
strong in South Carolina decorative arts, from silver to snuff boxes.
Kids love the permanent Civil War exhibition, with plenty of Confederate uniforms, and have an interactive good old time on the second
floor in galleries devoted to archaeology and natural history (don't miss
the giant polar bear). Newer exhibits include "The Threads of War,"
which deals with the stripped-down fashions created during the Civil
War shipping blockade (not exactly Scarlett's window drapes, but you
get the picture). ■**TIP→ Combination tickets that give you admission to
the Joseph Manigault House and the Heyward-Washington House are a bargain at $22.** ✉ *360 Meeting St., Upper King* ☎ *843/722–2996* ⊕ *www.
charlestonmuseum.org* ✉ *$10* ☉ *Mon.–Sat. 9–5, Sun. 1–5.*

Charleston Visitor Center. The center's 20-minute film *Forever Charleston*
is a fine introduction to the city. ■**TIP→ The first 30 minutes are free at
the parking lot, making it a real bargain.** ✉ *375 Meeting St., Upper King*
☎ *843/853–8000 or 800/868–8118* ⊕ *www.charlestoncvb.com* ✉ *Free*
☉ *Apr.–Oct., daily 8:30–5:30; Nov.–Mar., daily 8:30–5.*

Edmondston-Alston House. Built in 1825 in late-Federal style, the house
was transformed during the 1840s into the imposing Greek Revival

structure you see today. Tours of the home—furnished with antiques, portraits, silver, and fine china—are informative. ⊠ *21 E. Battery, South of Broad* ☎ *843/722–7171* ⊕ *www.middletonplace.org* ⊠ *$10; $41 with combination ticket for Middleton Place* ☉ *Tues.–Sat. 10–4:30, Sun. 1:30–4:30, Mon. 1–4:30.*

☼ **Fort Sumter National Monument.** Set on a man-made island in Charleston's
★ harbor, this is the hallowed spot where the Civil War began. On April 12, 1861, the first shot of the war was fired at the fort from Fort Johnson (now defunct) across the way. After a 34-hour battle, Union forces surrendered and Confederate troops occupied Sumter, which became a symbol of Southern resistance. The Confederacy managed to hold it, despite almost continual bombardment, from August 1863 to February of 1865. When it was finally evacuated, the fort was a heap of rubble. Today, the National Park Service oversees it, and rangers give interpretive talks and conduct guided tours. To reach the fort, you have to take a ferry; boats depart from Liberty Square Visitor Center, downtown, and from Patriot's Point in Mount Pleasant. There are six crossings daily between mid-March and mid-August. The schedule is abbreviated the rest of the year, so call ahead for details. For those using a GPS to find the boat departure points for Fort Sumter, remember to use the address for Patriots Point and Liberty Square, not the address for the fort itself. ⊠ *1214 Middle St., Sullivan's Island, Charleston Harbor* ☎ *843/577–0242 or 843/883–3123* ⊕ *www.nps.gov/fosu* ⊠ *Fort free; ferry $16* ☉ *Mid-Mar.–early Sept., daily 10–5:30; early Sept.–mid-Mar., daily 10–4 (11:30–4 Jan. and Feb.).* The **Fort Sumter Liberty Square Visitor Center,** next to the South Carolina Aquarium, contains exhibits on the Civil War. This is a departure point for ferries headed to Sullivan's Island, where Fort Sumter itself is located. ⊠ *340 Concord St., Upper King* ☎ *843/577–0242* ⊠ *Free* ☉ *Daily 8:30–5.*

Fodor's Choice **Joseph Manigault House.** Considered by many to be the finest example
★ of Federal-style architecture in the South, this 1803 home was built for rich rice-planting family of Huguenot heritage. Having toured Europe as a gentleman architect, Gabriel Manigault returned to design this house for his brother Joseph as the city's first essay in neoclassicism. The house glows in red brick and is adorned with a two-story piazza balcony. Inside, marvels await: a fantastic "flying" staircase in the central hall; a gigantic Venetian window; elegant plasterwork and mantels; notable Charleston-made furniture; and a bevy of French, English, and American antiques, including some celebrated tricolor Wedgwood pieces. Outside, note the garden "folly." ⊠ *350 Meeting St., Upper King* ☎ *843/722–2996* ⊕ *www.charlestonmuseum.org* ⊠ *$10* ☉ *Mon.–Sat. 10–5, Sun. 1–5.*

Fodor's Choice **Nathaniel Russell House.** One of the nation's finest examples of Adam-
★ style architecture, the Nathaniel Russell House was built in 1808. Russell came to Charleston at age 27 from his native Bristol, Rhode Island, and became one of the city's leading merchants and Federalist fathers in post-Revolutionary times. The ornate interior is distinguished by its Romney portraits, lavish period furnishings, and the famous "free-flying" staircase that spirals up three stories with no visible support. The extensive formal garden is worth a leisurely stroll. ⊠ *51 Meeting St.,*

South of Broad ☎ *843/724–8481* ⊕ *www.historiccharleston.org* ⊠ *$10; $16 with admission to Aiken-Rhett House* ☉ *Mon.–Sat. 10–5, Sun. 2–5.*

★ **Old Slave Mart Museum.** This is likely the only building still in existence that was used for slave auctioning, a practice that ended in 1863. It is part of a complex called Ryan's Mart, which contains the slave jail, the kitchen, and the morgue. It is now a museum that recounts the history of Charleston's role in the slave trade, an unpleasant story but one that is vital to understand. Charleston once served as the center of commercial activity for the South's plantation economy, and slaves were the primary source of labor both within the city and on the surrounding plantations. After a recent renovation, galleries are now outfitted with some interactive exhibits, including push buttons that allow you to hear voices relating stories from the age of slavery. The museum is on one of the few remaining cobblestone streets in town. ⊠ *6 Chalmers St., Market area* ☎ *843/958–6467* ⊕ *www.charlestoncity.info* ⊠ *$7* ☉ *Mon.–Sat. 9–5.*

Fodor's Choice **St. Philip's (Episcopal) Church.** The namesake of Church Street, this graceful
★ late-Georgian building is the second one to rise on its site: the congregation's first building burned down in 1835 and was rebuilt in 1838. During the Civil War, the steeple was a target for shelling; a shell that exploded in the churchyard during services one Sunday didn't deter the minister from finishing his sermon (afterward, the congregation gathered elsewhere for the duration of the war). Notable Charlestonians like John C. Calhoun are buried in the graveyard. ⊠ *146 Church St., Market area* ☎ *843/722–7734* ⊕ *www.stphilipschurchsc.org* ☉ *Church weekdays 9–11 and 1–4; cemetery daily 9–4.*

☾ **South Carolina Aquarium.** The 38,000-gallon Great Ocean Tank houses
★ the tallest aquarium window in North America. Along with sharks, moray eels, and sea turtles, exhibits include more than 5,000 creatures, representing more than 350 species. You travel through the five major regions of the Southeast Appalachian Watershed: the Blue Ridge Mountains, the Piedmont, the Coastal Plain, the Coast, and the Atlantic Ocean. Like the ocean, the aquarium is in constant motion, always adding new exhibits and animals; the latest celebrity creature is an albino alligator. The 4-D theater combines 3-D imagery (with special effects like wind gusts and splashes of water), synchronized to favorite family films. ⊠ *100 Aquarium Wharf, Upper King* ☎ *843/720–1990 or 800/722–6455* ⊕ *www.scaquarium.org* ⊠ *$17.95* ☉ *Apr.–Aug., daily 9–5; Sept.–Mar., daily 9–4.*

6

SHOPPING

The Market area is a cluster of shops and restaurants centered around the **City Market** (⊠ *E. Bay and Market Sts., Market area*). Sweetgrass basket weavers work here, and you can buy the resulting wares, although these artisan-crafts have become expensive. There are T-shirts and souvenir stores here as well as upscale boutiques. In the covered, open-air market, vendors have stalls with everything from jewelry to dresses and purses.

Fodor'sChoice
★ King Street is Charleston's main street and the major shopping corridor downtown. The latest lines of demarcation dividing the street into districts: Lower King (from Broad to Market streets) is the Antiques District, as it is lined with high-end antiques dealers; Middle King (from Market to Calhoun streets) is now called the Fashion District and is a mix of national chains like Banana Republic and Pottery Barn, alternative shops, and locally owned landmark stores and boutiques; Upper King (from Calhoun Street to Spring Street) has been dubbed the Design District. This up-and-coming area has become known for its furniture and interior design stores selling home fashion. Check out the events and stores on ⊕ *www.kingstreetantiquedistrict.com*, ⊕ *www.kingstreetfashiondistrict.com*, and ⊕ *www.kingstreetdesigndistrict.com.*

NIGHTLIFE

★ The elegant **Charleston Grill** (✉ *Charleston Place Hotel, 224 King St., Market area* ☎ *843/577–4522*) has live jazz from 7 to 10 on Friday and 8 to noon on Saturday. Shows range from the internationally acclaimed, Brazilian-influenced Quentin Baxter Ensemble to the Bob Williams Duo, a father and son who play classical guitar and violin. It draws a mature, upscale clientele, hotel guests, well-known locals, and more recently an urbane thirtysomething crowd.

Mercato (✉ *102 N. Market St., Market area* ☎ *843/722–6393* ⊕ *www.mercatocharleston.com*) is a popular restaurant that has become almost as well known for its roster of nightly entertainment Monday through Saturday from 6 to 10. Come early to get a seat at the long, elegant bar; it is best to reserve one of the 12 downstairs tables for dinner, but they do pipe the music into the second-floor dining room.

Southend Brewery (✉ *161 E. Bay St., Market area* ☎ *843/853–4677*) has a lively bar serving beer brewed on the premises. Try the Carolina Blonde with the wood-oven pizzas and the smokehouse barbecue.

Listen to authentic Irish music Thursday through Saturday at **Tommy Condon's** (✉ *15 Beaufain St., Market area* ☎ *843/577–3818* ⊕ *www.tommycondons.com*) rollicking Irish pub. On Wednesday and Sunday a two-piece group plays Irish-influenced music and Americana. Monday there is American music. Have some Irish nachos—cubed potatoes, cheddar cheese, jalapenos, tomatoes, and ranch dressing—with a Guinness or Harp.

WHERE TO EAT

¢ ✕ **Dixie Supply Bakery and Cafe.** It might be a lil' eatery buttressed by
SOUTHERN a Lil' Cricket convenience store, but don't be fooled by appearance. Dixie Supply Bakery and Cafe belongs to an old Charlestonian family (and by old, we mean they arrived here in 1698 or so), that seeks to honor its roots. Dixie dishes up Lowcountry and Southern classics: shrimp and creamy stone-ground grits, fried chicken, and a mighty fine tomato pie. Daily alternating blue-plate specials abound, including fried green tomatoes, shrimp from nearby Wadmalaw Island, summer squash and ricotta cheese ravioli, and a steady assortment of locally plucked

vegetables. ✉ *62 State St., Market area* ☎ *843/722–5650* ⊕ *www. dixiecafecharleston.com.*

¢ ✗ **Queen Street Grocery.** For crepes
AMERICAN and cold-pressed coffee, most folks turn to a venerable Charleston institution: Queen Street Grocery. Established in 1922, the corner shop has endured several guises through the years: butchery, candy shop, and late-night convenience store. Though in 2008, Hank Weed and Mary Wutz returned the store to its roots as a neighborhood grocery store, sourcing much of the produce and other goods from local growers. It's a great preservation act, improved upon by QSG's newest offerings: sweet and savory crepes named for the islands surrounding Charleston. ✉ *133 King St., Market Area* ☎ *843/723–4121* ⊕ *www.qsg29401.com.*

> ### CHARLESTON CRUISE PACKAGES
>
> For a listing of all hotel package discounts you can book along with your cruise, not to mention discounted tours (including the popular plantation tours), attractions, and shopping and dining coupons, visit ⊕ *www. charlestoncruisepackages.com.*

WHERE TO STAY

While the city's best hotels and B&Bs are in the historic district, most of them do not have free parking. If you stay outside of downtown in a chain hotel, you will give up much in charm and convenience but pay significantly less, not to mention park for free. High-season rates are traditionally in effect from March through May and September through November.

For expanded hotel reviews, visit Fodors.com.

$$$–$$$$ 🖼 **HarbourView Inn.** Ask for a room facing the harbor, and you can gaze out onto the kid-friendly fountain and 8 acres of Waterfront Park. **Pros:** continental breakfast can be delivered to room; service is notable; only hotel on the harbor and Waterfront Park. **Cons:** rooms are off long, modern halls; rooms are not particularly spacious. ✉ *2 Vendue Range, Market area* ☎ *843/853–8439 or 888/853–8439* ⊕ *www. harbourviewcharleston.com* ⇆ *52 rooms* ⚐ *In-room: a/c, Wi-Fi. In-hotel: room service, parking* ⦿ *Breakfast.*

$ 🖼 **Holiday Inn Historic District.** Thanks to its staff, this hotel has an outstanding track record for guest satisfaction. **Pros:** well-respected concierge Kevin McQuade offers excellent recommendations; self-parking in attached garage. **Cons:** 50% of rooms (along the back of hotel) have no view due to obstruction by other buildings; a long walk (about six blocks) to the Market. ✉ *125 Calhoun St., Upper King* ☎ *843/805–7900 or 877/805–7900* ⊕ *www.charlestonhotel.com* ⇆ *122 rooms, 4 suites* ⚐ *In-room: a/c, Wi-Fi. In-hotel: restaurant, room service, bar, pool, gym, parking* ⦿ *No meals.*

6

FORT LAUDERDALE, FLORIDA

Paul Rubio

In the 1960s Fort Lauderdale's beachfront was lined with T-shirt shops interspersed with quickie-food outlets, and downtown consisted of a lone office tower, some dilapidated government buildings, and motley other structures waiting to be razed. Today the beach is home to upscale shops and restaurants, while downtown has exploded with new office and luxury residential development. The entertainment and shopping areas—Las Olas Boulevard, Las Olas Riverfront, and Himmarshee Village—are thriving. And Port Everglades is giving Miami a run for its money in passenger cruising, with a dozen cruise-ship terminals, including the world's largest, hosting more than 20 cruise ships with some 3,000 departures annually. A captivating shoreline with wide ribbons of sand for beachcombing and sunbathing makes Fort Lauderdale and Broward County a major draw for visitors, and often tempts cruise-ship passengers to spend an extra day or two in the sun. Fort Lauderdale's 2-mi stretch of unobstructed beachfront has been further enhanced with a sparkling promenade designed more for the pleasure of pedestrians than vehicles.

ESSENTIALS

HOURS   Many museums close on Monday.

INTERNET If you have your own laptop, Broward County has created a fairly extensive Wi-Fi network with numerous hotspots in downtown Fort Lauderdale, providing free Internet access to anyone using suitably equipped laptops. There's also free Wi-Fi in the airport.

BOAT TOURS A water taxi provides service along the intracoastal waterway in Fort Lauderdale between the 17th Street Causeway and Oakland Park Boulevard, and west into downtown along New River daily from 10 am until midnight. A day-pass costs $20.

Water Taxi (☎ 954/467–0008 ⊕ *www.watertaxi.com*).

˜**Visitor Information Greater Fort Lauderdale Convention and Visitors Bureau** (☎ 954/765–4466 ⊕ www.sunny.org).

THE CRUISE PORT

Port Everglades, Fort Lauderdale's cruise port (nowhere near the Everglades, but happily near the beach and less than 2 mi from the airport), is among the world's largest, busiest ports. It's also the straightest, deepest port in the southeastern United States, meaning you'll be out to sea in no time flat once your ship sets sail. At a cost of $75 million, Cruise Terminal 18 has been tripled in size to accommodate Royal Caribbean's Oasis-class ships, the 5,400-passenger Oasis of the Seas and sister Allure of the Seas . The terminal's mega-size (240,000 square feet) accommodates both arriving and departing passengers and their luggage, simultaneously going through processing procedures. The port is south of downtown Fort Lauderdale, spread out over a huge area extending into Dania Beach, Hollywood, and a patch of unincorporated

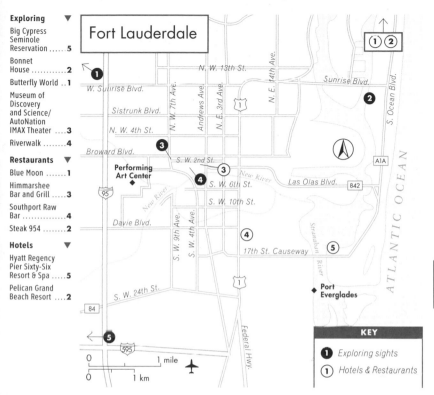

Broward County. A few words of caution: Schedule plenty of time to navigate the short distance from the airport, your hotel, or wherever else you might be staying, especially if you like to be among the first to embark for your sailing. Increased security (sometimes you'll be asked for a driver's license and/or other identification, and on occasion for boarding documentation upon entering the port, other times not) combined with increased traffic, larger parking facilities, construction projects, roadway improvements, and other obstacles mean the old days of popping over to Port Everglades and running up a gangplank in the blink of an eye are history.

If you are driving, there are two entrances to the port. One is from 17th Street, west of the 17th Street Causeway Bridge, turning south at the traffic light onto Eisenhower Boulevard. Or to get to the main entrance, take either State Road 84, running east–west, to the intersection of Federal Highway and cross into the port, or take I–595 east straight into the Port (I–595 becomes Eller Drive once inside the Port). I–595 runs east–west with connections to the Fort Lauderdale–Hollywood International Airport, U.S. 1 (Federal Highway), I–95, State Road 7 (U.S. 441), Florida's Turnpike, Sawgrass Expressway, and I–75.

Contact Port Everglades (✉ *1850 Eller Dr., Fort Lauderdale, FL* ☎ *954/523–3404* ⊕ *www.porteverglades.org*).

AIRPORT TRANSFERS

Fort Lauderdale–Hollywood International Airport is 4 mi south of downtown and 2 mi (about 5 to 10 minutes) from the docks. If you haven't arranged an airport transfer with your cruise line, you can take a taxi to the cruise-ship terminals. The ride in a metered taxi costs about $15 to $18, depending on your departure terminal. Taxi fares for up to four passengers, regulated by the county, are $4.50 for the first mile and $2.40 for each additional mile, 40¢ per minute for waiting time, plus a $2 surcharge for cabs departing from the airport. Yellow Cab is a major presence, and Go Airport Shuttle provides limousine or shared-ride service to and from Port Everglades to all parts of Broward County; fares to most Fort Lauderdale beach hotels are in the $25 to $30 range. Fort Lauderdale Shuttle offers one-way transportation from FLL Airport or surrounding hotels to Port Everglades Cruise Ships. For two people it's total of $22, three people $25, and four people $32.

Contacts Yellow Cab (☎ 954/565–5400). **Go Airport Shuttle** (☎ 954/561–8888 ⊕ goairportshuttle.com). **Fort Lauderdale Shuttle** (☎ 954/525–7796).

PARKING

Two covered parking facilities close to the terminals are Northport (expanded to 4,250 spaces) and Midport (for 2,000 vehicles). Use the Northport garage if your cruise leaves from Terminal 1, 2, or 4; use Midport if your cruise leaves from Terminal 19, 21, 22/24, 25, 26, 27, or 29. The Midport Surface Lot at Terminal 18 has 600 spaces. The cost is $15 per day for either garage or surface lot ($19 for oversized vehicles up to 20 feet). To save a few bucks on your parking tab, two separate companies, Park 'N Fly ($12 per day) and Park 'N Go ($12 per day) provide remote parking just outside Port Everglades, at the exit off I–595, with shuttles to all cruise terminals. Book ahead online for even deeper discounts.

Contacts Park 'N Fly (✉ 2200 N.E. 7th Ave., Dania Beach ✛ at the Port Everglades exit off I–595 ☎ 954/779–1776 ⊕ www.pnf.com). **Park 'N Go** (✉ 1101 Eller Dr., Fort Lauderdale ✛ at the Port Everglades exit off I–595 ☎ 954/760–4525 ⊕ www.bookparkngo.com).

FORT LAUDERDALE BEST BETS

The Beach. With more than 20 mi of ocean shoreline, the scene at Greater Fort Lauderdale's best beaches, especially between Bahia Mar and Sunrise Boulevard, is not to be missed.

The Everglades. Take in the wild reaches in or near the Everglades with an airboat ride. Mosquitoes are friendly, so arm yourself accordingly.

Las Olas Boulevard and the Riverwalk. This is a great place to stroll before and after performances, dinner, libations, and other entertainment.

EXPLORING FORT LAUDERDALE

Like its southeast Florida neighbors, Fort Lauderdale has been busily revitalizing for several years. In a state where gaudy tourist zones often stand aloof from workaday downtowns, Fort Lauderdale is unusual in that the city exhibits consistency at both ends of the 2-mi Las Olas corridor. The sparkling look results from efforts to thoroughly improve both beachfront and downtown. Matching the downtown's innovative arts district, cafés, and boutiques is an equally inventive beach area with its own share of cafés and shops facing an undeveloped shoreline.

> ### IT'S A GIRL
>
> Even as far back as ancient times, mariners have traditionally referred to their ships as "she." To a seaman, a ship is as beautiful and comforting as his mother or sweetheart. You could say a good ship holds a special place in his heart.

☺ **Big Cypress Seminole Reservation.** On the way to the Everglades from Fort Lauderdale is this reservation's two very different attractions.

At the **Billie Swamp Safari,** experience the majesty of the Everglades firsthand. Daily tours of wildlife-filled wetlands and hammocks yield sightings of deer, water buffalo, raccoons, wild hogs, hawks, eagles, and alligators. Sighting of the rare Florida panther are limited to the two captive felines on-site. Animal and reptile shows entertain audiences. Ecotours are conducted aboard motorized swamp buggies, and airboat rides are available, too. The on-site Swamp Water Café serves gator nuggets, frogs' legs, catfish, and Indian fry bread with honey. ✉ *Big Cypress Seminole Indian Reservation, 30000 Gator Tail Trail, Clewiston* ☎ *863/983–6101 or 800/949–6101* ⊕ *www.swampsafari. com* ✍ *Swamp Safari Day Package (ecotour, shows, exhibits, and airboat ride) $49.95* ☉ *Daily 10–5.*

A couple of miles from Billie Swamp Safari is **Ah-Tah-Thi-Ki Museum,** whose name means "a place to learn, a place to remember." This museum documents the traditions and culture of the Seminole Tribe of Florida through artifacts, exhibits, and reenactments of rituals and ceremonies. The 60-acre site includes a living-history Seminole village, nature trails, and a wheelchair-accessible boardwalk through a cypress swamp. ✉ *34725 West Boundary Rd., Clewiston* ☎ *863/902–1113* ⊕ *www.ahtahthiki.com* ✍ *$9* ☉ *Tues.–Sun. 9–5.*

★ **Bonnet House.** A 35-acre oasis in the heart of the beach area, this subtropical estate on the National Register of Historic Places stands as a tribute to the history of Old South Florida. This charming home, built in the roaring '20s, was the winter residence of the late Frederic and Evelyn Bartlett, artists whose personal touches and small surprises are evident throughout. For architecture, artwork, or the natural environment, this place is special. After admiring the fabulous gardens, be on the lookout for playful monkeys swinging from trees. Hours can vary, so call first. ✉ *900 N. Birch Rd.* ☎ *954/563–5393* ⊕ *www.bonnethouse. org* ✍ *$20 for house tours, $10 for grounds only* ☉ *Tues.–Sat. 10–4, Sun. 11–4. Closed Sept.*

6

Butterfly World. As many as 80 butterfly species from South and Central America, the Philippines, Malaysia, Taiwan, and other Asian nations are typically found within the serene 3-acre site inside Tradewinds Park, at the western edge of Pompano Beach, several miles inland. A screened aviary called North American Butterflies is reserved for native species. The Tropical Rain Forest Aviary is a 30-foot-high construction, with observation decks, waterfalls, ponds, and tunnels filled with thousands of colorful butterflies. Kids bug out at the bug zoo with Asian cockroaches as big as your hand. ⊠ *3600 W. Sample Rd., Coconut Creek* ☎ *954/977–4400* ⊕ *www.butterflyworld.com* ⊡ *$24.95* ⊙ *Mon.–Sat. 9–5, Sun. 11–5.*

☾ **Museum of Discovery & Science/AutoNation IMAX Theater.** With more than
★ 200 interactive exhibits, the aim here is to entertain children—*and* adults—with wonders of science. Exhibits include Kidscience, encouraging youngsters to explore the world; and Gizmo City, a look at how gadgets work. Florida Ecoscapes has a living coral reef, plus sharks, rays, and eels. *Runways to Rockets* offers stimulating trips to Mars and the moon while nine different cockpit stimulators let you try out your pilot skills. The AutoNation IMAX theater, part of the complex, shows films, some in 3-D, on an 80 foot by 60 foot screen with 15,000 watts of digital surround sound broadcast from 42 speakers. ⊠ *401 S. W. 2nd St.* ☎ *954/467–6637 museum, 954/463–4629 IMAX* ⊕ *www.mods.org* ⊡ *Museum $11, $16 with one IMAX show (not including full-length feature films)* ⊙ *Mon.–Sat. 10–5, Sun. noon–6.*

★ **Riverwalk.** Lovely views prevail on this paved promenade on the New River's north bank. On the first Sunday of every month a free jazz festival attracts visitors as does an organic, urban farmers' market each Saturday from 9 to 1. From west to east, the Riverwalk begins at the residential New River Sound, passes through the Arts and Science District, then the historic center of Fort Lauderdale, and wraps around the New River until it meets with Las Olas Boulevard's shopping district.

BEACHES

Fort Lauderdale's **beachfront** offers the best of all possible worlds, with easy access not only to a wide band of beige sand but also to restaurants and shops. For 2 mi heading north, beginning at the Bahia Mar yacht basin, along Route A1A you'll have clear views, typically across rows of colorful beach umbrellas, of the sea, and of ships passing into and out of nearby Port Everglades. If you're on the beach, gaze back on an exceptionally graceful promenade.

Pedestrians rank above vehicles in Fort Lauderdale. Broad walkways line both sides of the beach road, and traffic has been trimmed to two gently curving northbound lanes, where in-line skaters skim past slow-moving cars. On the beach side, a low masonry wall doubles as an extended bench, separating sand from the promenade. At night the wall is accented with ribbons of fiber-optic color, quite pretty when working, although outages are frequent. The most crowded portion of beach is between Las Olas and Sunrise boulevards. Tackier aspects of this onetime strip—famous for the springtime madness spawned by the film *Where the Boys Are*—are now but a fading memory, with the possible exception of the icon Elbo Room, an ever-popular bar at the corner of Las Olas and A1A.

North of the redesigned beachfront are another 2 mi of open and natural coastal landscape. Much of the way parallels the **Hugh Taylor Birch State Recreation Area,** preserving a patch of primeval Florida.

SHOPPING

Las Olas Boulevard. The city's best boutiques plus top restaurants and art galleries line a beautifully landscaped street. Window shopping allowed. ⊠ *1 block off New River east of Andrews Ave.* ⊕ *www. lasolasboulevard.com*

Las Olas Riverfront (⊠ *1 block west of Andrews Ave. along New River*), a shopping, dining, and entertainment complex with constantly evolving shops for everything from meals and threads to cigars and tattoos.

The Gallery at Beach Place. Just north of Las Olas Boulevard on Route A1A you can browse touristy beach shops, enjoy lunch or dinner, or carouse at assorted nightspots. ■ **TIP→** Beach Place has covered parking, but you can pinch pennies by using a nearby municipal lot that's metered. ⊠ *17 S. Fort Lauderdale Beach Blvd.*

Galleria Mall. Just west of the Intracoastal Waterway, the split-level emporium entices with Neiman Marcus, Dillard's, and Macy's, plus 150 specialty shops for anything from cookware to exquisite jewelry. Recent upgrades include marble floors and fine dining options. Chow down at Capital Grille, Truluck's, Blue Martini, P.F. Chang's or Seasons 52, or head for the food court, which will defy expectations with its international food-market feel. Galleria is open 10–9 Monday through Saturday, noon–5:30 Sunday. ⊠ *2414 E. Sunrise Blvd.* ☎ *954/564–1015* ⊕ *www.galleriamall-fl.com.*

NIGHTLIFE

Coyote Ugly. Pick up where the film left off with wild girls and wild nights. ⊠ *214 S.W. 2nd St.* ☎ *954/764–8459* ⊕ *www.coyoteuglysaloon.com.*

Living Room. This dance palladium, near the Riverfront, is Fort Lauderdale's hottest Saturday club experience. Friday nights are alternative/gay night. The club is also open on Thursday for ladies night, where ladies drink free and get in free. ⊠ *300 S.W. 1st Ave, Suite 200, 2nd fl.* ☎ *888/992–7555* ⊕ *www.livingroomclub.com.*

O Lounge. This lounge and two adjacent establishments, **Yolo** and **Vibe,** on Las Olas and under the same ownership, cater to Fort Lauderdale's sexy yuppies, businesspeople, desperate housewives, and hungry cougars letting loose during happy hour and on the weekends. Crowds alternate between Yolo's outdoor fire pit, O Lounge's chilled atmosphere and lounge music, and Vibe's more intense beats. Expect flashy cars in the driveway. ⊠ *333 E. Las Olas Blvd.* ☎ *954/523–1000* ⊕ *www. yolorestaurant.com.*

6

Tarpon Bend. Expect casual fun along with a few beers and some great bar food at this consistently busy joint. ⊠ *200 S.W. 2nd St.* ☎ *954/523–3233* ⊕ *www.tarponbend.com.*

Voodoo Lounge. The party gets going late at night. The lounge plays the latest club music and packs the house for ladies night on Wednesday and the gay-straight mixer, "Life's a Drag" on Sunday. ⊠ *111 S.W. 2nd Ave.* ☎ *954/522–0733* ⊕ *www.voodooloungeflorida.com.*

WHERE TO EAT

$$$

AMERICAN

Fodor'sChoice

★

✕ Himmarshee Bar and Grill. There's a reason that Himmarshee Bar and Grill has survived all of downtown Fort Lauderdale's ups and downs— the food is utterly fantastic. While the restaurant is constantly evolving based on customer feedback and the chef's ingenuity, it has perfected a number of dishes in its 15 years while pushing the envelope of flavorful American cuisine with its ever-changing menu. Some items, like the butternut squash purses and the buttermilk blue cheese stuffed dates, have been the talk of the town since the 1990s and remain a fixture with each seasonal menu. Thankfully, so does the amazing herb-seared rare tuna served over a ragout of white bean, wild mushroom, broccolini, shallot, oil poached tomato, and balsamic jus. However, by virtue of using fresh, seasonal products, some good things (or entrées) must come to an end; but on the flip side, it's a great reason to return with each passing season to discover a new favorite dish. ⊠ *210 S.W. 2nd St., Downtown and Las Olas, Fort Lauderdale* ☎ *954/524–1818* ⊕ *www.himmarshee.com.*

$

SEAFOOD

✕ Southport Raw Bar. You can't go wrong at this unpretentious spot where the motto, on bumper stickers for miles around, proclaims, "eat fish, live longer, eat oysters, love longer, eat clams, last longer." Raw or steamed clams, raw oysters, and peel-and-eat shrimp are market priced. Sides range from Bimini bread to key lime pie, with conch fritters, beer-battered onion rings, and corn on the cob in between. Order wine by the bottle or glass, and beer by the pitcher, bottle, or can. Eat outside overlooking a canal, or inside at booths, tables, or in the front or back bars. Limited parking is free, and a grocery-store parking lot is across the street. ⊠ *1536 Cordova Rd.* ☎ *954/525–2526* ⊕ *www.southportrawbar.com.*

$$$$

STEAKHOUSE

Fodor'sChoice

★

✕ Steak 954. Steak 954 has quickly become an institution for Fort Lauderdale's foodies and visitors alike. It's not just the steaks that impress here. The lobster and crab-coconut ceviche and the red snapper tiradito are divine; the butter-poached Maine lobster is perfection; and the raw bar showcases only the best and freshest seafood on the market. Located on the 1st floor of the swanky W Fort Lauderdale, Steak 954 offers spectacular views of the ocean for those choosing outdoor seating; or a sexy, sophisticated ambience for those choosing to dine in the main dining room, with bright tropical colors balanced with dark woods and an enormous jellyfish tank spanning the width of the restaurant. Sunday brunch is very popular, so arrive early for the best views. ⊠ *401 N. Fort Lauderdale Beach Blvd., Along the beach, Fort Lauderdale* ☎ *954/414–8333* ⊕ *www.steak954.com.*

WHERE TO STAY

Fort Lauderdale has a growing and varied roster of lodging options, from beachfront luxury suites to intimate B&Bs to chain hotels along the Intracoastal Waterway. If you want to be on the beach, be sure to mention this when booking your room, since many hotels advertise "waterfront" accommodations that are actually on inland waterways, not the beach.

For expanded hotel reviews, visit Fodors.com.

For price categories, see ⇨ Lodging at the beginning of this chapter.

$$$–$$$$
RESORT
⚟ Hyatt Regency Pier Sixty-Six Resort & Spa. The iconic 17-story tower dominates a lovely 22-acre spread that includes the full-service Spa 66. **Pros:** great views; plenty of activities; free shuttle to beach; easy water taxi access. **Cons:** not on the beach; '70s exterior. ⊠ *2301 S.E. 17th St. Causeway* ☎ *954/525–6666* ⊕ *www.pier66.com* ⇌ *384 rooms and suites* ⇘ *In-room: a/c, Wi-Fi. In-hotel: restaurants, bars, tennis courts, pools, gym, spa, water sports* ⊺⊙⊺ *No meals.*

$$$–$$$$
RESORT
⟳
★
⚟ Pelican Grand Beach Resort. Smack on the beach, this already lovely property has been transformed with a new tower, restaurant and lounge, an old-fashioned ice-cream parlor, and a circulating lazy-river pool that allows guests to float 'round and 'round. **Pros:** you can't get any closer to the beach in Fort Lauderdale. **Cons:** you'll need wheels to access Las Olas's beach-area action. ⊠ *2000 N. Atlantic Blvd.* ☎ *954/568–9431 or 800/525–6232* ⊕ *www.pelicanbeach.com* ⇌ *121 rooms (remainder of 155 total are condos)* ⇘ *In-room: a/c, Internet, Wi-Fi. In-hotel: restaurant, bar, pool* ⊺⊙⊺ *No meals.*

6

GALVESTON, TEXAS

Updated
by Roberta
Sotonoff

A thin strip of an island in the Gulf of Mexico, Galveston is big sister Houston's beach playground—a year-round coastal destination 50 mi away. Many of the first public buildings in Texas, including a post office, bank, and hotel, were built here, but most were destroyed in the Great Storm of 1900. Those that endured have been well preserved, and the Victorian character of the **Historic Downtown Strand Seaport** shopping district and the neighborhood surrounding Broadway is still evident. On the Galveston Bay side of the island (northeast), quaint shops and cafés in old buildings are near the Seaport Museum, harbor-front eateries, and the cruise-ship terminal. On the Gulf of Mexico side (southwest), resorts and restaurants line coastal Seawall Boulevard. The 17-foot-high seawall abuts a long ribbon of sand and provides a place for roller-blading, bicycling, and going on the occasional surrey ride. The city was badly damaged from flooding during Hurricane Ike in 2008, but businesses are now up and running, with few remnants of the storm.

Galveston is a port of embarkation for cruises on Western Caribbean itineraries. It's an especially popular port of embarkation for people living in the southeastern states who don't wish to fly to their cruise. Carnival and Royal Caribbean have ships based in Galveston, offering four-, five-, and seven-day cruises along the Mexican coast and to Jamaica, Grand Cayman, Belize, Bahamas, Key West and Honduras plus a 14-night cruise to the Azores and Spain. Princess Cruises will set sail from Galveston in 2012.

ESSENTIALS

HOURS Shops in the historic district are usually open until at least 7. During peak season some stay open later; the rest of the time they close at 6. This is also the city's nightlife district, and is hopping until late.

INTERNET The best place to check your email is at your hotel. Most of the hotels in Galveston offer some kind of Internet service, though usually for a fee. If you have a laptop, the city has a relatively extensive network of free Wi-Fi zones, including several spots on the Strand.

Visitor Information Galveston Visitors Center (✉ *Ashton Villa, 2328 Broadway* ⊕ *www.galveston.com*).

THE CRUISE PORT

The relatively sheltered waters of Galveston Bay are home to the Texas Cruise Ship Terminal. It's only 30 minutes to open water from here. Driving south from Houston on I–45, you cross a long causeway before reaching the island. Take the first exit, Harborside Drive, left after you've crossed the causeway onto Galveston Island. Follow that for a few miles to the port. Turn left on 22nd Street (also called Kempner Street); there is a security checkpoint before you continue down a driveway. The drop-off point is set up much like an airport terminal, with pull-through lanes and curbside check-in.

Port Contacts Port of Galveston (✉ *Harborside Dr. and 22nd St.* ☎ *409/765–9321* ⊕ *www.portofgalveston.com*).

AIRPORT TRANSFERS

The closest airports are in Houston, 50 mi from Galveston. Houston has two major airports: Hobby Airport, 9 mi southeast of downtown, and George Bush Intercontinental, 15 mi northeast of the city. Traffic into Galveston can be delayed because of ongoing construction.

Unless you have arranged airport transfers through your cruise line, you'll have to make arrangements to navigate the miles between the Houston airport at which you land and the cruise-ship terminal in Galveston. Galveston Limousine Service provides scheduled transportation (return reservations required) between either airport and Galveston hotels or the cruise-ship terminal. Hobby is a shorter ride (1 hour, $45 one-way, $80 round-trip), but Intercontinental (2 hours, $55 one-way, $100 round-trip) is served by more airlines, including international carriers. Taking a taxi allows you to set your own schedule, but can cost twice as much (it's also important to note that there aren't always enough taxis to handle the demands of disembarking passengers, so you might have to wait after you leave your ship). Negotiate the price before you get in.

Contacts Galveston Limousine Service (☎ *800/640–4826* ⊕ *www.galvestonlimousineservice.com*).

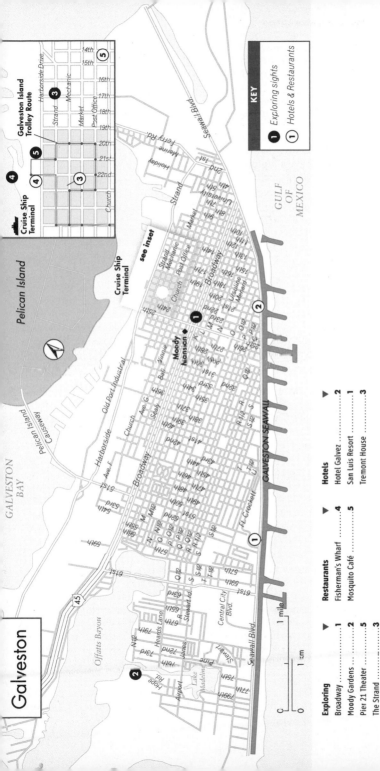

Galveston

KEY

1 Exploring sights

① Hotels & Restaurants

Exploring ▶
Broadway **1**
Moody Gardens **2**
Pier 21 Theater **5**
The Strand **3**
Texas Seaport Museum **4**

Restaurants ▶
Fisherman's Wharf **4**
Mosquito Café **5**

Hotels ▶
Hotel Galvez **2**
San Luis Resort **1**
Tremont House **3**

Pelican Island

Pelican Island Causeway

GALVESTON BAY

Offatts Bayou

GULF OF MEXICO

GALVESTON SEAWALL

Cruise Ship Terminal

see inset

Moody Mansion

Galveston Island Trolley Route

0   1 km
0   1 mile

PARKING

Parking is coordinated by the Port Authority. After you drop off your checked luggage and passengers at the terminal, you receive a color-coded parking pass from the attendant, with directions to a parking lot for your cruise departure. The lots are approximately ½ mi from the terminal. Check-in, parking, and boarding are generally allowed four hours prior to departure. A shuttle bus (carry-on luggage only) runs back and forth between the lots and the terminal every 7 to 12 minutes on cruise arrival and departure days (be sure to drop off your luggage *before* you park the car). The lot is closed other days. Port Authority security checks the well-lighted, fenced-in lots every two hours; there is also a limited amount of covered parking. Parking for a 5-day cruise is $50, 7-day is $70 ($80 covered). Cash, traveler's checks, and credit cards (Visa and MasterCard only) are accepted for payment.

> **GALVESTON BEST BETS**
>
> ■ **The Historic Downtown Strand Seaport.** Galveston's historic district is a great place to stroll, shop, and eat.
>
> ■ **Historic Homes.** The island has some lovely historic homes to explore, particularly during early May, when the Historic Homes Tour lets you into many that aren't usually open to the public.
>
> ■ **Moody Gardens.** There are enough activities at this park to keep any kid happy.

EXPLORING GALVESTON

Broadway. The late 1800s were the heyday of Galveston's port (before Houston's was dug out). Victorian splendor is evident in the meticulously restored homes of this historic district, some of which are now museums. If you're in town the first two weekends of May, don't miss the **Galveston Historic Homes Tour.** In addition to visiting the neighborhood's museums, you can walk through privately owned homes dating from the 1800s. For more information about area house museums or the tour, contact the Heritage Visitors Center. **Moody Mansion** (✉ *2618 Broadway* ☎ *409/762–7668* ⊕ *www.moodymansion.org*), the residence of generations of one of Texas's most powerful families, was completed in 1895. Tour its interiors of exotic woods and gilded trim filled with family heirlooms and personal effects. It's open from 11 to 3 daily, charging $7 admission.

Historic Downtown Strand Seaport. This shopping area is defined by the architecture of its 19th- and early-20th-century buildings, many of which survived the storm of 1900 and are on the National Register of Historic Places. When Galveston was still a powerful port city—before the Houston Ship Channel was dug, diverting most boat traffic inland—this stretch, formerly the site of stores, offices, and warehouses, was known as the Wall Street of the South. As you stroll up the Strand, you'll pass dozens of shops and cafés. ✉ *Church to Harborside and 25th and 19th Sts.*

Moody Gardens is a multifaceted entertainment and educational complex inside pastel-color glass pyramids. Attractions include the 13-story

Aquarium Pyramid, showcasing marine life from four oceans in tanks and touch pools; **Rainforest Pyramid,** a 40,000-square-foot tropical habitat for exotic flora and fauna; **Discovery Museum,** which has changing exhibits; and two **IMAX theaters,** one of which has a space adventure ride. Outside, there is the Colonial Paddleboat ride and **Palm Beach,**a white-sand beach with landscaped grounds, man-made lagoons, a kid-size waterslide and games, and beach chairs. Prices for 1- and 2-day passes are discounted online if you buy them in advance. ⊠ *1 Hope Blvd.* ☎ *409/741–8484 or 800/582–4673* ⊕ *www.moodygardens. com* 🖾 *$8.95–$20.95 per venue, $49.95 (day pass at gate), $64.95 (2-day pass at gate)* ۞ *Daily 10–8.*

Pier 21 Theater. At this theater on the Strand, watch the Great Storm of 1900 come back to life in a multimedia presentation that includes video clips of archival drawings, still photos, and narrated accounts from survivors' diaries. Also playing is a film about the exploits of pirate Jean Lafitte, who used the island as a base. ⊠ *Pier 21, Harborside Dr. and 21st St.* ☎ *409/763–8808* ⊕ *www.galveston.com/pier21theatre* 🖾 *Great Storm $5, Pirate Island $4* ۞ *Memorial Day–Labor Day, Wed.–Mon. 11–6; Labor Day–Memorial Day, Wed.–Mon. 11–5.*

Texas Seaport Museum. Aboard the restored 1877 tall ship *Elissa,* detailed interpretive signs provide information about the shipping trade in the 1800s, including the routes and cargoes this ship carried into Galveston. Inside the museum building is a replica of the historic wharf and information about the ethnic groups that immigrated through this U.S. point of entry after 1837. ⊠ *Pier 21, Number 8* ☎ *409/763–1877* ⊕ *www.tsm-elissa.org* 🖾 *$8* ۞ *Weather permitting 9–5 weekdays and 8–6 weekends.*

BEACHES

The **Seawall** (⊠ *Seawall Blvd. from 61st St. to 25th St.*) on the Gulf-side waterfront attracts runners, cyclists, and rollerbladers. Just below it is a long, free beach near many big hotels and resorts. **Stewart Beach Park** (⊠ *6th St. and Seawall Blvd.* ☎ *409/765–5023* 🖾 *$8 per vehicle*) has a bathhouse, amusement park, bumper boats, miniature-golf course, and a water coaster in addition to saltwater and sand. It's open weekdays 9 to 6, weekends 8 to 6 from March through May; weekdays 8 to 6 and weekends 8 to 7 from June through September; and weekends 9 to 6 during the first two weekends of October. **Galveston Island State Park** (⊠ *13 Mile Rd. and FM 3005, 9.2 mi west of 61st St. on Seawall Blvd.* ☎ *409/737–1222* 🖾 *$5* ۞ *Daily 7 am–10 pm year-round*), on the western, unpopulated end of the island, is a 2,000-acre natural beach habitat ideal for birding, walking, and renewing your spirit.

SHOPPING

The **Strand** (⊠ *Bounded by Strand and Postoffice St. [running east–west] and 25th and 19th Sts. [running north–south]*) is the best place to shop in Galveston. Old storefronts are filled with gift shops, antiques stores, and one-of-a-kind boutiques.

6

More than 50 antiques dealers are represented at the **Emporium at Eibands** (✉ *2201 Postoffice St.* ☎ *409/750–9536*), an upscale showroom filled with custom upholstery, bedding and draperies, antique furniture, and interesting architectural finds.

Head to Footsies (✉ *2211 Strand* ☎ *409/762–2727*) offers footwear for men and women along with trendy women's accessories and fashions from sportswear to eveningwear. .

Old Strand Emporium (✉ *2112 Strand* ☎ *409/515–0715*) is a charming deli and grocery reminiscent of an old-fashioned ice-cream parlor and sandwich shop, with candy bins, packaged nuts, and more.

> **BOARDING PASSES**
>
> Modern ID cards and scanning equipment record passenger comings and goings on the majority of cruise ships these days. With a swipe through a machine (it looks much like a credit-card swipe at the supermarket), security personnel know who is on board the vessel at all times. On most large ships passengers' pictures are recorded digitally at check-in.

NIGHTLIFE

For a relaxing evening, choose any of the harborside restaurant-bars on piers 21 and 22 to sip a glass of wine or a frozen Hurricane as you watch the boats go by. The **Grand 1894 Opera House** (✉ *2020 Postoffice St.* ☎ *409/765–1894 or 800/821–1894* ⊕ *www.thegrand.com*) stages musicals and hosts concerts year-round. It's worth visiting for the ornate architecture alone. Sarah Bernhardt and Anna Pavlova both performed on this storied stage.

WHERE TO EAT

For price categories, see ⇨ Dining at the beginning of this chapter.

$$$–$$$$
SEAFOOD

✗ **Fisherman's Wharf.** Even though Landry's has taken over this harborside institution, locals keep coming here for the reliably fresh seafood and reasonable prices. Dine indoors or watch the boat traffic (and waiting cruise ships) from the patio. Start with a cold combo, like boiled shrimp and grilled rare tuna. For entrées, the fried fish, shrimp, and oysters are hard to beat. ✉ *Pier 22, Harborside Dr. and 22nd St.* ☎ *409/765–5708.*

$$–$$$
AMERICAN

✗ **Mosquito Café.** This homey eatery in Galveston's historic East End serves fresh, contemporary food—including some vegetarian dishes—in a hip, high-ceilinged dining room and on an outdoor patio. Wake up to a fluffy egg frittata or a homemade scone topped with whipped cream, or try a large gourmet salad for lunch. The fish of the day is always a hit. ✉ *628 14th St.* ☎ *409/763–1010* ☾ *No lunch Mon.*

WHERE TO STAY

For price categories, see ⇨ Lodging at the beginning of this chapter.
For expanded hotel reviews, visit Fodors.com.

$$$–$$$$ ⊞ **Hotel Galvez: A Wyndham Historic Hotel.** This renovated six-story Spanish-colonial hotel, built in 1911, was once called "Queen of the Gulf." Teddy Roosevelt and Howard Hughes are just two of the many well-known guests who have stayed here. **ros:** directly on beach; incredible pool area; beautiful grounds. **Cons:** rooms can be small (especially the bathrooms). ⊠ *2024 Seawall Blvd.* ☎ *409/765–7721* ⊕ *www.wyndham. com* ⤏ *231 rooms* ⚐ *In-hotel: Wi-Fi. In-hotel: restaurant, pool, gym* ⎸◯⎹ *No meals.*

$$–$$$ ⊞ **San Luis Resort, Spa and Conference Center.** A long marble staircase alongside a slender fountain with sculpted dolphins welcomes you to the beachfront elegance of this resort. **ros:** great Gulf views; nice pool area. **Cons:** public parking (no valet) is not convenient. ⊠ *5222 Seawall Blvd.* ☎ *409/744–1500 or 800/445–0090* ⊕ *www.sanluisresort. com* ⤏ *244 rooms* ⚐ *In-room: Internet. In-hotel: restaurant, room service, bars, tennis courts, pools, gym, spa, children's programs, parking* ⎸◯⎹ *No meals.*

$$–$$$ ⊞ **Tremont House: A Wyndham Historic Hotel.** A four-story atrium lobby, with ironwork balconies and full-size palm trees, showcases an 1872 hand-carved rosewood bar in what was once a busy dry-goods warehouse. **Pros:** beautiful, historic environment; great location. **Cons:** not a fun scene for young single travelers. ⊠ *2300 Ship's Mechanic Row* ☎ *409/763–0300* ⊕ *www.wyndham.com* ⤏ *119 rooms* ⚐ *In-room: Internet. In-hotel: restaurant, room service, bar, parking* ⎸◯⎹ *No meals.*

JACKSONVILLE, FLORIDA

Sharon Hoffmann and Paul Rubio

One of Florida's oldest cities and at 758 square mi the largest city in the continental United States in terms of land area, Jacksonville is underrated, and makes a worthwhile vacation spot for an extra day or two before or after your cruise. It offers appealing downtown riverside areas, handsome residential neighborhoods, the region's only skyscrapers, a thriving arts scene, and, for football fans, the NFL Jaguars and the NCAA Gator Bowl. Remnants of the Old South flavor the city, especially in the Riverside/Avondale historic district, where moss-draped oak trees frame prairie-style bungalows and Tudor Revival mansions, and palm trees, Spanish bayonet, and azaleas populate Jacksonville's landscape. Northeast of the city, Amelia Island and Fernandina Beach offer some of the nicest coastline in Florida.

ESSENTIALS

HOURS Many museums close on Monday.

INTERNET Most people access the Internet in their hotel, and most hotels offer some kind of Internet access, often Wi-Fi.

Visitor Information Visit Jacksonville (⊠ *208 N. Laura St., Suite 102, Jacksonville* ☎ *904/798–9104 or 800/733–2668* ⊕ *www.visitjacksonville.com*).

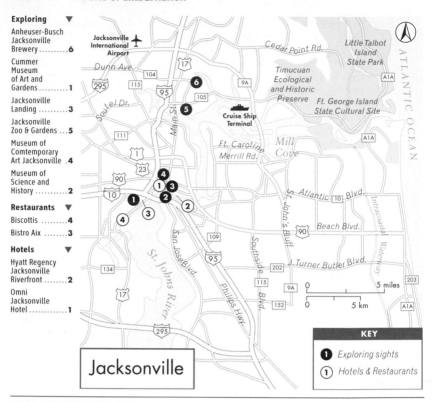

Jacksonville

KEY

❶ *Exploring sights*

① *Hotels & Restaurants*

THE CRUISE PORT

Limited in the sizes of ships it can berth, JAXPORT currently serves as home port to the *Carnival Fascination,* which departs weekly on four- and five-night cruises to Key West and the Bahamas during the fall and winter cruising seasons, with occasional week-long sailings to Grand Turk, Half Moon Cay, and Nassau. The facility is fairly sparse, consisting basically of some vending machines and restrooms, but the embarkation staff receives high marks. The terminal itself is a temporary structure; a permanent cruise terminal has been under consideration for some time, but its fate is uncertain at this writing.

JAXPORT is about 15 minutes from Jacksonville International Airport. Take I–95 South to S.R. 9-A East. Follow 9-A to Heckscher Drive (S.R. 105) west until you reach August Drive. Head south on August Drive, and follow the signs to the cruise terminal.

Port Contacts Jacksonville Port Authority (✉ *9810 August Dr., Jacksonville* ☎ *904/357–3006* ⊕ *www.jaxport.com*).

AIRPORT TRANSFERS

The transfer from Jacksonville airport takes about 15 minutes and costs $30 for up to three passengers by taxi, not including tip. **Yellow Cab–Jacksonville** (☎ *904/355–8294*).

PARKING

There is a fenced and guarded parking lot next to the cruise terminal, within walking distance. Parking costs $15 per day for regular vehicles, $25 for RVs. You must pay in advance by cash or major credit card.

EXPLORING JACKSONVILLE

Because Jacksonville was settled along both sides of the twisting St. Johns River, a number of attractions are on or near a riverbank. Both sides of the river, which is spanned by myriad bridges, have downtown areas and waterfront complexes of shops, restaurants, parks, and museums; some attractions can be reached by water taxi or the Skyway Express monorail system—scenic alternatives to driving back and forth across the bridges—but a car is generally necessary.

Anheuser-Busch Jacksonville Brewery Tour. Guided tours give a behind-the-scenes look at how barley, malt, rice, hops, and water form the "King of Beers." Or you can hightail it through the self-guided tour and head straight to the free beer tastings (if you're 21 years or older, that is). ⊠ *111 Busch Dr.* 🖭 *904/696-8373* ⊕ *www.budweisertours.com* ⊠ *Free* ⊗ *Mon.–Sat. 10–4; guided tours based on availability; call for hrs.*

Cummer Museum of Art & Gardens. The Wark Collection of early-18th-century Meissen porcelain is just one reason to visit this former riverfront estate, which includes 13 permanent galleries with more than 5,500 items spanning more than 8,000 years, and 3 acres of riverfront gardens reflecting northeast Florida's blooming seasons and indigenous varieties. Art Connections allows kids to experience art through hands-on, interactive exhibits. One of the museum's newest additions, the Thomas H. Jacobsen Gallery of American Art, focuses on works by American artists, including Max Weber, N.C. Wyeth, and Paul Manship. ⊠ *829 Riverside Ave.* 🖭 *904/356-6857* ⊕ *www.cummer.org* ⊠ *$10, free Tues. 4–9* ⊗ *Tues. 10–9, Wed.–Sat. 10–5, Sun. noon–5.*

Jacksonville Landing. During the week, this riverfront market caters to locals and tourists alike, with specialty shops, full-service restaurants—including a sushi bar, Italian bistro, and a steak house—and an internationally flavored food court. The Landing hosts more than 250 weekend events each year, ranging from the good clean fun of the Lighted Boat Parade and Christmas Tree Lighting to the just plain obnoxious Florida/Georgia game after-party, as well as live music (usually of the local cover-band variety) in the courtyard. ⊠ *2 W. Independent Dr.* 🖭 *904/353-1188* ⊕ *www.jacksonvillelanding.com* ⊠ *Free* ⊗ *Mon.–Thurs. 10–8, Fri. and Sat. 10–9, Sun. noon–5:30; restaurant hrs vary.*

JACKSONVILLE BEST BETS

■ **Budweiser Brewery Tour.** Behind the scenes on the making of one of the country's most popular beers.

■ **Jacksonville Zoo.** One of the best midsize zoos you'll visit.

■ **Museum of Contemporary Art Jacksonville.** Though small, this is excellent museum is an unexpected treat in northeast Florida.

6

🐧 **Jacksonville Zoo and Gardens.** What's new at the zoo? Plenty. Not only
Fodor's Choice has it seen the births of a rare Amur leopard and a greater kudu calf,
★ it has opened Tuxedo Park, a controlled environment for a group of
Magellanic penguins. Among the other highlights are the rare waterfowl and the Serona Overlook, which showcases some of the world's
most venomous snakes. The Florida Wetlands is a 2½-acre area with
black bears, bald eagles, white-tailed deer, and other animals native to
Florida. The African Veldt has alligators, elephants, and white rhinos,
among other species of African birds and mammals; and the Range of
the Jaguar, winner of the Association of Zoos and Aquarium's Exhibit
of the Year, includes 4 acres of exotic big cats as well as 20 other
species of animals. New additions include Play Park, complete with a
splash park, forest play area, maze, and discovery building; and Stingray
Bay, a 17,000-gallon pool where visitors can pet and feed the mysterious creatures. Parking is free. ⊠ *370 Zoo Pkwy., off Heckscher Dr. E*
☎ *904/757–4463* ⊕ *www.jaxzoo.org* ⊠ *$13.95* ⊙ *Daily 9–5; extended
hrs offered during summer weekends and holidays.*

Fodor's Choice **Museum of Contemporary Art Jacksonville.** In this loftlike downtown
★ building, the former headquarters of the Western Union Telegraph
Company, a permanent collection of 20th-century art shares space
with traveling exhibitions. The museum encompasses five galleries and
ArtExplorium, a highly interactive educational exhibit for kids, as well
as a funky gift shop and Café Nola, open for lunch on weekdays and
for dinner on Thursday and Friday. MOCA Jacksonville also hosts film
series, and workshops throughout the year, and packs a big art-wal-
lop into a relatively small 14,000 square feet. The Art Matters lecture
series is free; Sunday is free for families; a once-a-month Art Walk is
free to all. ⊠ *Hemming Plaza, 333 N. Laura St.* ☎ *904/366–6911*
⊕ *www.mocajacksonville.org* ⊠ *$8* ⊙ *Tues., Wed., Fri., and Sat. 10–4,
Thurs. 10–8, Sun. noon–4; Art Walk 5–9 1st Wed. of month, hrs subject to change.*

🐧 **Museum of Science & History.** MOSH, once known in Jacksonville as
"the children's museum," is for all ages these days, especially with the
installation of the Konica Minolta Super MediaGlobe II. Translation?
It's the next generation of planetarium, one that can project shows of
all kinds on the dome—from blockbuster movies to live NASA feeds to
the 3-D laser shows that accompany the ever-popular, weekend Cosmic
Concerts. The resolution here is four times sharper than that of the most
hi-def TV currently on the market, so whether you're a kid "flying" on
a snowflake or an adult falling into darkness during *Black Holes: The
Other Side of Infinity*, the experience is awesome.

MOSH also has a wide variety of interactive exhibits like the JEA Science Theatre, where you can participate in live experiments related to
electricity and electrical safety; the Florida Naturalist's Center, where
you can explore northeast Florida wildlife; and the Universe of Science, where you'll learn about properties of physical science through
hands-on demonstrations. ⊠ *1025 Museum Circle* ☎ *904/396–6674*
⊕ *www.themosh.org* ⊠ *$10 adult for museum; $15 for museum and
planetarium; except Fri. $5 all admissions, Cosmic Concerts $7–$9; Fri.
$5* ⊙ *Mon.–Thurs. 10–5, Fri. 10–8, Sat. 10–6, Sun. 1–6.*

SHOPPING

Five Points. This small but funky shopping district less than a mile southwest of downtown has new and vintage-clothing boutiques, shoe stores, and antiques shops. It also has a handful of eateries and bars, not to mention some of the city's most colorful characters. ✉ *Intersection of Park, Margaret, and Lomax Sts., Riverside.*

> **BRING GEORGE**
>
> Whenever you leave for a cruise, bring a supply of one-dollar bills. They will come in handy for tipping both airport and port personnel.

San Marco Square. The dozens of interesting apparel, home, and jewelry stores and restaurants are in 1920s Mediterranean-revival–style buildings. ✉ *San Marco and Atlantic Blvds.*

The Shoppes of Avondale. The highlights here include upscale clothing and accessories boutiques, art galleries, home-furnishings shops, a chocolatier, and trendy restaurants. ✉ *St. Johns Ave., between Talbot Ave. and Dancy St.*

WHERE TO EAT

JAXPORT's location on Jacksonville's Westside means there aren't too many nearby restaurants. But by taking a 10- to 15-minute drive south, you'll find a wealth of restaurants for all tastes and price categories.

For price categories, see ⇨ Dining at the beginning of this chapter.

¢   AMERICAN   ✗ **Biscottis.** The local artwork on the redbrick walls is a mild distraction from the jovial yuppies, soccer moms, and metrosexuals—all of whom are among the crowd jockeying for tables in this midsize restaurant. Elbows almost touch, but no one seems to mind. The menu offers the unexpected: wild mushroom ravioli with a broth of corn, leek, and dried apricot; or curry-grilled swordfish with cucumber-fig bordelaise sauce. Be sure to sample from Biscottis's decadent dessert case (we hear the peanut butter ganache is illegal in three states). Brunch, a local favorite, is served until 3 on weekends. ✉ *3556 St. Johns Ave., Avondale* ☎ *904/387–2060* ⊕ *www.biscottis.net* ⚹ *Reservations not accepted.*

$$$ ECLECTIC   ✗ **Bistro Aix.** When a Jacksonville restaurant can make Angelinos feel like they haven't left home, that's saying a lot. With its slick black-leather booths, 1940s brickwork, velvet drapes, and intricate marbled globes, Bistro Aix (pronounced "X") is just that place. Regulars can't get enough of the creamy onion soup, crispy calamari, and house-made potato chips with warm blue-cheese appetizers or entrées like oak-fired fish Aixoise, grilled salmon, and filet mignon. Adventurous diners can sample diverse dishes on a prix-fixe menu for $29. Aix's resident pastry chef ensures no sweet tooth leaves unsatisfied. For the most part, waitstaff are knowledgeable and pleasant, though some patrons find their demeanor snooty, except, of course, the ones from L.A. Call for preferred seating. ✉ *1440 San Marco Blvd., San Marco* ☎ *904/398–1949* ⊕ *www.bistrox.com* ☾ *No lunch weekends.*

WHERE TO STAY

Hotels near the cruise terminals are few and far between, so most cruisers needing a room make the drive to Downtown (15 minutes) or to the Southbank or Riverside (20 minutes).

For price categories, see ⇨ Lodging at the beginning of this chapter.

For expanded hotel reviews, visit Fodors.com.

$$ **Hyatt Regency Jacksonville Riverfront.** It doesn't get much more conve-
HOTEL   nient than this 19-story, downtown, waterfront hotel within walking distance of Jacksonville Landing, Florida Theatre, Times-Union Center, corporate office towers, and the county courthouse. **ros:** riverfront location; rooftop pool and gym; free Wi-Fi in public areas; 24-hour business center; hypoallergenic rooms available. **Cons:** not all rooms are riverfront; slow valet service; no minibars; no in-room Wi-Fi or high-speed Internet. ⊠ *225 Coastline Dr.* ☎ *904/588–1234* ⊕ *www. jacksonville.hyatt.com* ⇨ *963 rooms, 21 suites* ♿ *In-room: Internet. In-hotel: restaurants, bar, pool, gym, laundry facilities, parking, some pets allowed* �‖ *No meals.*

$$ **Omni Jacksonville Hotel.** Spacious guest rooms in Jacksonville's most
HOTEL   luxurious and glamorous hotel are decorated in a chic urban style (think
★   neutral grays and creams, dark wood, stainless steel) and have flat-screen TVs. **ros:** four-diamond on-site restaurant; downtown location; large rooms; rooftop pool; great kids offerings. **Cons:** congested valet area; restaurant pricey; can be chaotic when there's a show at the Times-Union Center across the street. ⊠ *245 Water St.* ☎ *904/355–6664 or 800/843–6664* ⊕ *www.omnijacksonville.com* ⇨ *354 rooms, 4 2-bedroom suites* ♿ *In-room: kitchen (some), Wi-Fi. In-hotel: restaurant, bar, pool, gym, parking, some pets allowed* �‖ *No meals.*

MIAMI, FLORIDA

Paul Rubio   Miami is the busiest of Florida's very busy cruise ports. Because there's so much going on here, you might want to schedule an extra day or two before and/or after your cruise to explore North America's most Latin city. Downtown is a convenient place to stay if you are meeting up with a cruise ship, but South Beach is still the crown jewel of Miami. Miami Beach, particularly the Art Deco District in South Beach—the square-mile section between 6th and 23rd streets—is the heart of Miami's vibrant nightlife and restaurant scene. But you may also want to explore beyond the beach, including the Little Havana, Coral Gables, and Coconut Grove sections of the city.

ESSENTIALS

HOURS   Most of the area's attractions are open every day.

INTERNET   Most people choose to go online at their hotel.

Visitor Information Greater Miami Convention & Visitors Bureau (⊠ *701 Brickell Ave., Suite 2700, Miami* ☎ *305/539–3000, 800/933–8448 in U.S.* ⊕ *www. miamiandbeaches.com).***Miami Beach Visitors Center** (⊠ *1920 Meridian Ave., 1st fl.Miami Beach* ☎ *305/674–1300* ⊕ *www.miamibeachguestservices.com).*

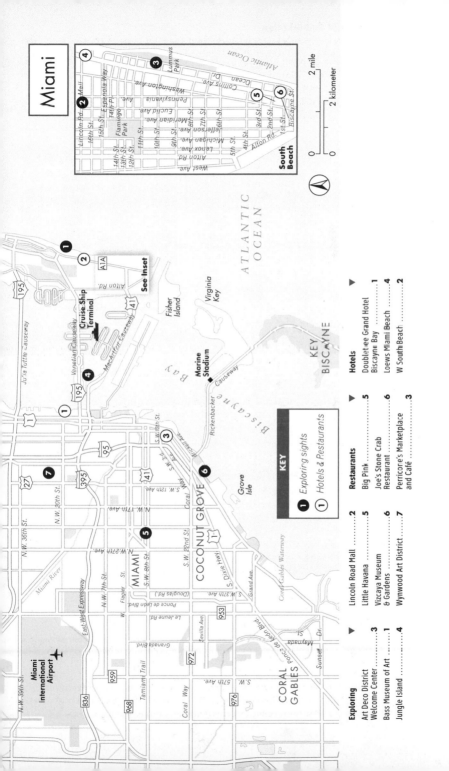

Miami

South Beach

Atlantic Ocean

KEY

| ❶ | Exploring sights |
| ① | Hotels & Restaurants |

Exploring ▶

Art Deco District Welcome Center	3
Bass Museum of Art	1
Jungle Island	4
Lincoln Road Mall	2
Little Havana	5
Vizcaya Museum & Gardens	6
Wynwood Art District	7

Restaurants ▶

Big Pink	5
Joe's Stone Crab Restaurant	6
Perricone's Marketplace and Café	3

Hotels ▶

Doubletree Grand Hotel Biscayne Bay	1
Loews Miami Beach	4
W South Beach	2

ATLANTIC OCEAN

Biscayne Bay

KEY BISCAYNE

Virginia Key

Fisher Island

Marine Stadium

Rickenbacker Causeway

Grove Isle

COCONUT GROVE

CORAL GABLES

MIAMI

Miami International Airport

See Inset

Cruise Ship Terminal

THE CRUISE PORT

The Port of Miami, in downtown Miami near Bayside Marketplace and the MacArthur Causeway, justifiably bills itself as the Cruise Capital of the World. Home to eight cruise lines and the largest year-round cruise fleet in the world, the port accommodates more than 3 million passengers a year for sailings from 3 to 14 days and sometimes longer duration. Air-conditioned terminals include the newer terminals D and E, with dramatic public art installations reflecting sun-drenched waters off the Florida coastline and the Everglades ecosystems. There's duty-free shopping and limousine service. You can get taxis at all the terminals, and car-rental agencies offer shuttles to off-site lots.

MIAMI BEST BETS

■ **Bayside Marketplace.** If you want to stay close to the port, grab some outdoor drinks and eclectic eats at touristy Bayside Marketplace.

■ **Bill Baggs Cape Florida State Park.** Unleash your outdoor enthusiasm at Key Biscayne's Bill Baggs Cape Florida State Park.

■ **South Beach.** Take a 10- to 15-minute cab to South Beach for great people-watching, an art deco tour, or a bit of sun.

■ **Vizcaya Museum.** One of south Florida's largest historic homes is one of the city's best museums.

If you are driving, take I–95 north or south to I–395. Follow the directional signs to the Biscayne Boulevard exit. When you get to Biscayne Boulevard, make a right. Go to 5th Street, which becomes Port Boulevard (look for the American Airlines Arena); then make a left and go over the Port Bridge. Follow the directional signs to your terminal.

Contacts Port of Miami (✉ *1015 North American Way, Miami* ☎ *305/347–4800* ⊕ *www.miamidade.gov/portofmiami).*

AIRPORT TRANSFERS

If you have not arranged an airport transfer through your cruise line, you have a couple of options for getting to the cruise port. The first is a taxi, and fares are regulated by the county, with a flat fare of $24 from Miami International Airport (MIA). This fare is per trip, not per passenger, and includes tolls and $1 airport surcharge but not a tip. SuperShuttle vans transport passengers between MIA and local hotels, as well as the Port of Miami. At MIA the vans pick up at the ground level of each concourse (look for clerks with yellow shirts, who will flag one down). SuperShuttle service from MIA is available on demand; for the return it's best to make reservations 24 hours in advance. The cost from MIA to the cruise port is $16 per person, or $55 if you want the entire van to yourselves.

Information SuperShuttle (☎ *305/871–2000 from MIA, 954/764–1700 from Fort Lauderdale, 800/258–3826 elsewhere* ⊕ *www.supershuttle.com).*

PARKING

Street-level lots are right in front of each of the cruise terminals. In 2010 the $15-million Parking Garage D (with 873 spaces on four levels) opened near two recently constructed terminals serving Carnival Cruise

Lines. Altogether the port's three parking garages (each with an open-air top floor) accommodate 5,871 vehicles, with 56 spaces designated for handicapped guests and another half-dozen or so for passengers with infants. The cost for all, payable in advance, is $20 per day ($40 for RVs) and $7 for short-term parking of less than 4 hours for drop-off/pick-up. You can pay with cash or a credit card, although only with American Express, Master Card, or Visa. There is no valet parking, but a shuttle for cruise passengers (one is wheelchair accessible) can pick you up at the parking garage/lot, take you to the appropriate terminal, and return you to your vehicle after your cruise.

EXPLORING MIAMI

In the 1950s Miami was best known for alligator wrestlers and you-pick strawberry fields or citrus groves. Well, things have changed. Miami on the mainland is South Florida's commercial hub, while its sultry sister Miami Beach (America's Riviera) encompasses 17 islands in Biscayne Bay. Seducing winter refugees with its sunshine, beaches, palms, and nightlife, this is what most people envision when planning a trip to what they think of as Miami. If you want to do any exploring, you'll have to drive.

Art Deco District Welcome Center. Run by the Miami Design Preservation League, the center provides information about the buildings in the district. An improved gift shop sells 1930s–50s art deco memorabilia, posters, and books on Miami's history. Several tours—covering Lincoln Road, Española Way, North Beach, and the entire Art Deco District, among others—start here. You can choose from a self-guided iPod audio tour or join one of the regular morning walking tours at 10:30 am, every day except Thursday when the tour takes place at 6:30 pm. Arrive at the center 15 minutes beforehand. All of the options provide detailed histories of the art deco hotels as well as an introduction to the art deco, Mediterranean revival, and Miami Modern (MiMo) styles found within the Miami Beach Architectural Historic District. Don't miss the special boat tours during Art Deco Weekend, in early January. ✉ *1001 Ocean Dr., at Barbara Capitman Way (10th St.)* ☎ *305/763–8026* ⊕ *www.mdpl.org* 🎫 *Tours $20* ⊙ *Daily 9:30–7.*

Bass Museum of Art. The Bass, in historic Collins Park, is part of the Miami Beach Cultural Park, which includes the Miami City Ballet's Arquitectonica-designed facility and the Miami Beach Regional Library. The original building, constructed of keystone, has unique Maya-inspired carvings. The expansion designed by Japanese architect Arata Isozaki houses another wing and an outdoor sculpture garden. Special exhibitions join a diverse collection of European art. Works on permanent display include *The Holy Family,* a painting by Peter Paul Rubens; *The Tournament,* one of several 16th-century Flemish tapestries; and works by Albrecht Dürer and Henri de Toulouse-Lautrec. Special exhibits often cost a little extra. Docent tours are by appointment. ✉ *2100 Collins Ave.* ☎ *305/673–7530* ⊕ *www.bassmuseum.org* 🎫 *$8* ⊙ *Wed.–Sun. noon–5.*

☾ **Jungle Island.** Originally located deep in south Miami and known as Parrot Jungle, South Florida's original tourist attraction opened in 1936 and moved closer to Miami Beach in 2003. Located on Watson Island, a small stretch of land off of I-395 between Downtown Miami and South Beach, Jungle Island is far more than a park where cockatoos ride tricycles; this interactive zoological park is home to just about every unusual and endangered species you would want to see, including a rare albino alligator, a liger (lion and tiger mix), a 28-foot-long "crocosaur," and a myriad of exotic birds. The most intriguing offerings are the VIP animal tours, including the Lemur Experience ($45 for 45 minutes), in which the highly social primates make themselves at home on your lap or shoulders, and the Penguin Encounter ($30 for 30 minutes), where you can pet and feed warm-weather South African penguins. ✉ *1111 Parrot Jungle Trail, off MacArthur Causeway (I–395)* ☎ *305/400–7000* ⊕ *www.jungleisland.com* ✎ *$32.95, plus $8 parking* ⊙ *Weekdays 10–5, weekends 10–6.*

> **CAUTION**
>
> Airline carry-on restrictions are being updated continuously. Check with your airline before packing, and be aware that large purses will sometimes be counted as a carry-on item!

☾
Fodor's Choice
★
Lincoln Road Mall. A playful 1990s redesign spruced up this open-air pedestrian mall, adding a grove of 20 towering date palms, five linear pools, and colorful broken-tile mosaics to the once-futuristic 1950s vision of Fontainebleau designer Morris Lapidus. Some of the shops are owner-operated boutiques with a delightful variety of clothing, furnishings, jewelry, and decorative design. Others are the typical chain stores of American malls. Remnants of tired old Lincoln Road—beauty supply and discount electronics stores on the Collins end of the strip—somehow fit nicely into the mix. The new Lincoln Road is fun, lively, and friendly for people old, young, gay, and straight—and their dogs. Folks skate, scoot, bike, or jog here. The best times to hit the road are during Sunday morning farmers' markets and on weekend evenings, when cafés bustle, art galleries open shows, street performers make the sidewalk their stage, and stores stay open late.

Two of the landmarks worth checking out at the eastern end of Lincoln Road are the massive 1940s keystone building at 420 Lincoln Road, which has a 1945 Leo Birchanky mural in the lobby, and the 1921 mission-style Miami Beach Community Church, at Drexel Avenue. The Lincoln Theatre (No. 541–545), at Pennsylvania Avenue, is a classical four-story art deco gem with friezes. The New World Symphony, a national advanced-training orchestra led by Michael Tilson Thomas, rehearses and performs here, and concerts are often broadcast via loudspeakers, to the delight of visitors. Just west, facing Pennsylvania, a fabulous Cadillac dealership sign was discovered underneath the facade of the Lincoln Road Millennium Building, on the south side of the mall. At Euclid Avenue there's a monument to Lapidus, who in his 90s watched the renaissance of his whimsical creation. At Lenox Avenue, a black-and-white art deco movie house with a Mediterranean barrel-tile roof is now the Colony Theater (No. 1040), where live theater and experimental films are presented. ⊠ *Lincoln Rd., between Collins Ave. and Alton Rd.* ⊕ *www.lincolnroad.org*

Fodor's Choice **Vizcaya Museum and Gardens.** Of the 10,000 people living in Miami
★ between 1912 and 1916, about 1,000 of them were gainfully employed by Chicago industrialist James Deering to build this European-inspired residence. Once comprising 180 acres, this national historic landmark now occupies a 30-acre tract that includes a native hammock and more than 10 acres of formal gardens with fountains overlooking Biscayne Bay. The house, open to the public, contains 70 rooms, 34 of which are filled with paintings, sculpture, antique furniture, and other fine and decorative arts. The collection spans 2,000 years and represents the Renaissance, baroque, rococo, and neoclassical periods. The 90-minute self-guided Discover Vizcaya Audio Tour is available in both English and Spanish for an additional $5. Guided tours are also available. Moonlight tours, offered on evenings that are nearest the full moon, provide a magical look at the gardens; call for reservations. ⊠ *3251 S. Miami Ave.* ☎ *305/250–9133* ⊕ *www.vizcayamuseum.org* ☞ *$15* ⊗ *Wed.–Mon. 9:30–4:30.*

★ **Wynwood Art District.** Just north of downtown Miami, the funky, urban, and edgy Wynwood Art District is peppered with galleries, art studios, and private collections accessible to the public. Visit during Wynwood's monthly gallery walk on the second Saturday evening of each month when studios and galleries are all open at the same time.

Make sure a visit includes a stop at the **Margulies Collection at the Warehouse** (⊠ *591 N.W. 27th St., between N.W. 5th and 6th Aves., Downtown* ☎ *305/576–1051* ⊕ *www.margulieswarehouse.com*). Martin Margulies's collection of vintage and contemporary photography, videos, and installation art in a 45,000-square-foot space makes for eye-popping viewing. Entrance fee is a $10 donation, which goes to a local homeless shelter for women and children. It's open November to April only, Wednesday to Saturday 11–4.

Fans of edgy art will appreciate the **Rubell Family Collection** (⊠ *95 N.W. 29th St., between N. Miami and N.W. 1st Aves., Downtown* ☎ *305/573–6090* ⊕ *www.rfc.museum*). Mera and Don Rubell have accumulated work by artists from the 1970s to the present, including Jeff Koons, Cindy Sherman, Damien Hirst, and Keith Haring. Admission is $10, and the gallery is open December to August, Wednesday to Saturday 10–6.

BEACHES

Fodor's Choice **Bill Baggs Cape Florida State Park.** Thanks to inviting beaches, sunsets, and
★ a tranquil lighthouse, this park at Key Biscayne's southern tip is worth the drive. In fact, the 1-mi stretch of pure beachfront has been ranked among Florida's best on several occasions. It has 19 picnic shelters, and two cafés that serve light lunches. A stroll or ride along walking and bicycle paths provides wonderful views of Miami's dramatic skyline. From the southern end of the park you can see a handful of houses rising over the bay on wooden stilts, the remnants of Stiltsville, built in the 1940s and now protected by the Stiltsville Trust. The nonprofit group

was established in 2003 to preserve the structures as they showcase the park's rich history. Bill Baggs has bicycle rentals, a playground, fishing piers, and guided tours of the **Cape Florida Lighthouse,** South Florida's oldest structure. The lighthouse was erected in 1845 to replace an earlier one damaged in an 1836 Seminole attack, in which the keeper's helper was killed. The restored cottage and lighthouse offer free tours at 10 am and 1 pm Thursday to Monday. Be there a half hour beforehand. ⊠ *1200 S. Crandon Blvd., Key Biscayne* ☎ *305/361–5811* ⊕ *www. floridastateparks.org/capeflorida* ☜ *$8 per vehicle; $2 per person on bicycle, bus, motorcycle, or foot* ⊗ *Daily 8–dusk.*

Fodor's Choice **South Beach.** A 10-block stretch of white sandy beach hugging the tur-
★ quoise waters along Ocean Drive—from 5th to 15th streets—is one of the most popular in America, known for drawing unabashedly modelesque sunbathers and posers. With the influx of new luxe hotels and hotspots from 16th to 25th streets, the South Beach stand-and-pose scene is now bigger than ever. The beaches crowd quickly on the weekends with a blend of European tourists, young hipsters, and sun-drenched locals offering Latin flavor. Separating the sand from the traffic of Ocean Drive is palm-fringed Lummus Park, with its volleyball nets and chickee huts (huts made of palmetto thatch over a cypress frame) for shade. The beach at 12th Street is popular with gays, in a section often marked with rainbow flags. Locals hang out on 3rd Street beach, in an area called SoFi (South of Fifth) where they watch fit Brazilians play foot volley, a variation of volleyball that uses everything but the hands. Because much of South Beach leans toward skimpy sunning—women are often in G-strings and casually topless—many families prefer the tamer sections of Mid- and North Beach. Metered parking spots next to the ocean are a rare find. Instead, opt for a public garage a few blocks away and enjoy the people-watching as you walk to find your perfect spot on the sand. ⊠ *Ocean Dr. from 5th to 15th Sts., then Collins Ave. to 25th St., Miami Beach* ☎ *305/673–7714.*

SHOPPING

In Greater Miami you're never more than 15 minutes from a major commercial area that serves as both a shopping and entertainment venue for tourists and locals. The shopping is great on a two-block stretch of **Collins Avenue** between 6th and 8th streets. The busy **Lincoln Road Mall** is just a few blocks from the beach and convention center, making it popular with locals and tourists. There's an energy here, especially on weekends, when the pedestrian mall is filled with locals. Creative merchandise, galleries, and a Sunday-morning antiques market can be found among the art galleries and cool cafés. An 18-screen movie theater anchors the west end of the street.

NIGHTLIFE

Miami's pulse pounds with nonstop nightlife that reflects the area's potent cultural mix. On sultry, humid nights with the huge full moon rising out of the ocean and fragrant night-blooming jasmine intoxicating the senses, who can resist Cuban salsa, Jamaican reggae, and Dominican merengue, with some disco and hip-hop thrown in for good measure? When this place throws a party, hips shake, fingers snap, bodies touch. It's no wonder many clubs are still rocking at 5 am.

WHERE TO EAT

> **PACK IT, POST IT**
>
> Pack a pad of Post-It notes when you take a cruise. They come in handy when you need to leave messages for your cabin steward, family, and shipboard friends.

At many of the hottest spots you'll need a reservation to avoid a long wait for a table. And when you get your check, note whether a gratuity is included; most restaurants add 15% (ostensibly for the convenience of—and protection from—Latin-American and European tourists who are used to this practice in their homelands and would not normally tip), but you can reduce or supplement it depending on your opinion of the service. One of Greater Miami's most popular pursuits is bar-hopping. Bars range from intimate enclaves to showy see-and-be-seen lounges to loud, raucous frat parties. There's a New York–style flair to some of the newer lounges, which are increasingly catering to the Manhattan party crowd who escape to South Beach for long weekends. If you're looking for a relatively nonfrenetic evening, your best bet is one of the chic hotel bars on Collins Avenue.

For price categories, see ⇨ Dining at the beginning of this chapter.

$ ✕ **Big Pink.** The decor in this innovative, superpopular diner may remind
AMERICAN you of a roller-skating rink—everything is pink Lucite, stainless steel, and campy (think sports lockers as decorative touches)—and the menu is 3 feet tall, complete with a table of contents. Food is solidly all-American, with dozens of tasty sandwiches, pizzas, turkey or beef burgers, and side dishes, each and every one composed with gourmet flair. Big Pink also makes a great spot for brunch. ⊠ *157 Collins Ave., South Beach* ☎ *305/532–4700* ⊕ *www.mylesrestaurantgroup.com.*

$$$$ ✕ **Joe's Stone Crab Restaurant.** In South Beach's decidedly new-money
SEAFOOD scene, the stately Joe's Stone Crab is an old-school testament to good
Fodor's Choice food and good service. South Beach's most storied restaurant started
★ as a turn-of-the-century eating house when Joseph Weiss discovered succulent stone crabs off the Florida coast. Almost a century later, the restaurant stretches a city block and serves 2,000 dinners a day to local politicians and moneyed patriarchs. Stone crabs, served with legendary mustard sauce, crispy hash browns, and creamed spinach, remain the staple. Though stone crab season runs from October 15 to May 15, Joe's remains open year-round serving other phenomenal seafood dishes. Finish your meal with tart key lime pie, baked fresh daily. ∎TIP➔ Joe's famously refuses reservations, and weekend waits can be three hours long—yes, you read that correctly—so come early or order from Joe's Take Away next door. ⊠ *11 Washington Ave., South Beach* ☎ *305/673–0365, 305/673–4611 for takeout, 800/780–2722 for overnight shipping* ⊕ *www.joesstonecrab.com* ⚫ *Reservations not accepted* ⊙ *No lunch Wed.–Sun. Closed Mon. and Tues. May 15–Oct. 15.*

$$ **✗ Perricone's Marketplace and Café.** Brickell Avenue south of the Miami
ITALIAN   River is burgeoning with Italian restaurants, and this lunch place for
Fodor'sChoice   local bigwigs is the biggest and most popular among them. It's housed
★   partially outdoors and partially indoors in a 125-year-old Vermont
barn. Recipes were handed down from generation to generation, and
the cooking is simple and good. Buy your wine from the on-premises
deli, and enjoy it (for a small corking fee) with homemade minestrone;
a generous antipasto; linguine with a sauté of jumbo shrimp, scallops,
and calamari; or gnocchi with four cheeses. The homemade tiramisu
and cannoli are top-notch. ⊠ *Mary Brickell Village, 15 S.E. 10th St.,
Downtown Miami* ☎ *305/374–9449* ⊕ *www.perricones.com.*

WHERE TO STAY

Staying in downtown Miami will put you close to the cruise terminals,
but there is little to do at night. South Beach is the center of the action
in Miami Beach, but it's fairly distant from the port. Staying in Miami
Beach, but north of South Beach's Art Deco District, will put you on
the beach but nominally closer to the port.

For price categories, see ⇨ Lodging at the beginning of this chapter.

For expanded hotel reviews, visit Fodors.com.

$$ **⊡ Doubletree Grand Hotel Biscayne Bay.** This elegant waterfront option
HOTEL   is at the north end of downtown off a scenic marina, and near many of
Miami's headline attractions: the Port of Miami, Bayside, the Arena,
and the Carnival Center. **Pros:** great bay views; deli and market on-site.
Cons: need a cab to get around. ⊠ *1717 N. Bayshore Dr., Downtown
Miami* ☎ *305/372–0313 or 800/222–8733* ⊕ *www.doubletree.com*
↩ *152 suites* ⚠ *In-room: a/c, kitchen (some), Wi-Fi. In-hotel: restau-
rant, bar, pool, gym, spa, business center, parking* ⎟◎⎟ *No meals.*

$$$–$$$$ **⊡ Loews Miami Beach Hotel.** Loews Miami Beach is marvelous for fami-
HOTEL   lies, businesspeople, groups, and pet-lovers. **Pros:** top-notch amenities
include a beautiful oceanfront pool and immense spa; pets welcome.
Cons: intimacy is lost due to its large size. ⊠ *1601 Collins Ave., South
Beach* ☎ *305/604–1601 or 800/235–6397* ⊕ *www.loewshotels.com/
miamibeach* ↩ *733 rooms, 57 suites* ⚠ *In-room: a/c, Internet, Wi-Fi.
In-hotel: restaurants, bars, pool, gym, spa, beach, business center, park-
ing, some pets allowed* ⎟◎⎟ *No meals.*

$$$ **⊡ W South Beach.** Fun, fresh, and funky, this W is also the flagship for the
HOTEL   brand's evolution toward young sophistication, which means less club
Fodor'sChoice   music in the lobby, more lighting, and more attention to the $40 mil-
★   lion art collection lining the lobby's expansive walls. **Pros:** pool scene;
masterful design; ocean-view balconies in each room. **Cons:** not a classic art deco building. ⊠ *2201 Collins Ave., South Beach, Miami Beach*
☎ *305/938–3000* ⊕ *www.WHotels.com/SouthBeach* ↩ *334 rooms*
⚠ *In-room: a/c, kitchen, Wi-Fi. In-hotel: restaurant, bars, pools, gym,
spa, beach, business center, parking, some pets allowed* ⎟◎⎟ *No meals.*

NEW ORLEANS, LOUISIANA

The spiritual and cultural heart of New Orleans is the French Quarter, where the city was settled by the French in 1718. You could easily spend several days visiting museums, shops, and eateries in this area, but you can get a small sense of the place quickly. If you have time, the rest of the city's neighborhoods, radiating out from this focal point, also make for rewarding rambling. The mansion-lined streets of the Garden District and Uptown, the aboveground cemeteries that dot the city, and the open air along Lake Pontchartrain provide a nice balance to the commercialization of the Quarter. Despite its sprawling size, New Orleans has a small-town vibe, perhaps due to locals' shared cultural habits and history.

ESSENTIALS

HOURS   Shops in the French Quarter tend to be open late, but stores in most of the malls close by 9. Restaurants tend to be open late as well.

INTERNET   **French Quarter Postal Emporium** (⊠ *1000 Bourbon St.* ☎ *504/525–6651* ⊕ *www.frenchquarterpostal.com*) offers Internet service and is also a mailing center.

Visitor Information New Orleans Convention & Visitors Bureau (☎ *800/672–6124 or 504/566–5011* ⊕ *www.neworleanscvb.com*). **New Orleans Multicultural Tourism Network** (⊕ *www.soulofneworleans.com*).

THE CRUISE PORT

The Julia Street Cruise Terminal is at the end of Julia Street on the Mississippi River; the Erato Street Terminal is just to the north. Both terminals are behind the Ernest M. Morial Convention Center. You can walk to the French Quarter from here in about 10 minutes; it's a short taxi ride to the Quarter or nearby hotels. Carnival and Norwegian base ships here at least part of the year.

If you are driving, you'll probably approach New Orleans on I–10. Take the Business 90 West/Westbank exit, locally known as Pontchartrain Expressway, and proceed to the Tchoupitoulas Street/South Peters Street exit. Continue to Convention Center Boulevard, where you will take a right turn. Continue to Henderson Street, where you will turn left, and then continue to Port of New Orleans Place. Take a left on Port of New Orleans Place to Julia Street Terminals 1 and 2, or take a right to get to the Robin Street Wharf.

Port Contacts Port of New Orleans (⊠ *Port of New Orleans Pl. at foot of Julia St.* ☎ *504/522–2551* ⊕ *www.portno.com*).

AIRPORT TRANSFERS

Shuttle-bus service to and from the airport and the cruise port is available through Airport Shuttle New Orleans. Buses leave regularly from the ground level near the baggage claim. Return trips to the airport need to be booked in advance. The cost one-way is $15 per person, and the trip takes about 45 minutes.

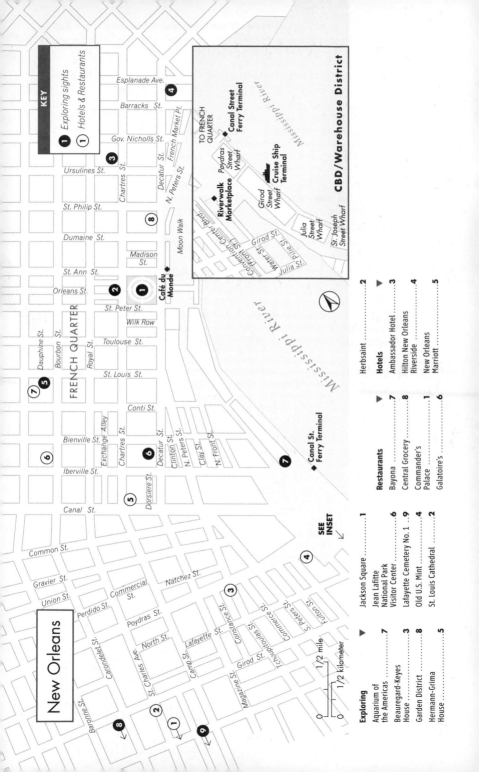

New Orleans

KEY

- Exploring sights
- Hotels & Restaurants

Inset: CBD/Warehouse District

Mississippi River

TO FRENCH QUARTER

Canal Street Ferry Terminal

Poydras Street Wharf

Cruise Ship Terminal

Girod Street Wharf

Riverwalk Marketplace

St. Joseph Street Wharf

Julia Street Wharf

Streets (French Quarter)

Esplanade Ave.
Barracks St.
Gov. Nicholls St.
Ursulines St.
St. Philip St.
Dumaine St.
St. Ann St.
Orleans St.
St. Peter St.
Wilk Row
Toulouse St.
St. Louis St.
Conti St.
Bienville St.
Iberville St.
Canal St.

French Market Pl.
Decatur St.
N. Peters St.
Chartres St.
Moon Walk
Madison St.
Café du Monde
Exchange Alley
Chartres St.
Clinton St.
N. Peters St.
Clay St.
N. Front St.
Dorsiere St.

Dauphine St.
Bourbon St.
Royal St.

FRENCH QUARTER

Mississippi River

Canal St. Ferry Terminal

CBD / Warehouse District streets

Common St.
Gravier St.
Union St.
Perdido St.
Poydras St.
Commercial St.
Natchez St.
Lafayette St.
Girod St.
North St.

Carondelet St.
St. Charles Ave.
Camp St.
Magazine St.
Constance St.
Tchoupitoulas St.
Fulton St.
S. Peters St.
Commerce St.
Baronne St.

SEE INSET

0   1/2 mile
0   1/2 kilometer

A cab ride to or from the airport from uptown or downtown New Orleans costs $28 for the first two passengers and $12 for each additional passenger; there's a fuel surcharge of $1 per trip (not per passenger). At the airport, pick-up is on the lower level, outside the baggage claim area. There may be an additional charge for extra baggage.

Contacts Airport Shuttle New Orleans (☎ 504/522–3500 ⊕ www. airportshuttleneworleans.com).

PARKING

If you are spending some time in the city before or after your cruise, finding a parking space is fairly easy in most of the city, except for the French Quarter, where meter maids are plentiful and tow trucks eager. If in doubt about a space, pass it up and pay to use a parking lot. Avoid parking spaces at corners and curbs: less than 15 feet between your car and the corner will result in a ticket. Watch for temporary "No Parking" signs, which pop up along parade routes and film shoots. Long-term and overnight parking are extremely expensive at hotels and garages. Parking for the duration of your cruise is available for $16 per night and is on Erato Street; if you want, SeaCaps will take your bags directly to the ship so you just have to deal with your hand luggage. RVs can park in a lot on Poydras Street next to Terminal 2 at the Julia Street dock for $32 per night.

NEW ORLEANS BEST BETS

■ **Aquarium of the Americas.** Especially good for families is this fantastic aquarium near the city's convention center.

■ **Eating Well.** A highlight in New Orleans is dining. If you ever wanted to splurge on a great restaurant meal, this is the place to do it. At the very least, have a beignet at Café du Mond.

■ **Hermann-Grima House.** This is one of the best-preserved historic homes in the French Quarter.

EXPLORING NEW ORLEANS

The **French Quarter,** the oldest part of the city, lives up to all you've heard: it's alive with the sights, sounds, odors, and experiences of a major entertainment hub. At some point, ignore your better judgment and take a stroll down **Bourbon Street,** past the bars, restaurants, music clubs, and novelty shops that have given this strip its reputation as the playground of the South. Be sure to find time to stop at Café du Monde for chicory-laced coffee and beignets. With its beautifully landscaped gardens surrounding elegant antebellum homes, the **Garden District** is mostly residential, but most home-owners do not mind your enjoying the sights from outside the cast-iron fences surrounding their magnificent properties.

Aquarium of the Americas Power failures during Katrina resulted in the major loss of the Aquarium's collection of more than 7,000 aquatic creatures. In a dramatic gesture of solidarity, aquariums around the country joined together with the Aquarium of the Americas in an effort to repopulate its stock. The museum, now fully reopened, has four major exhibit areas—the Amazon Rain Forest, the Caribbean Reef, the Mississippi River, and the Gulf Coast—all of which have fish and animals native to that environment. A special treat is the Seahorse Gallery, which showcases seemingly endless varieties of these beautiful creatures. The aquarium's spectacular design allows you to feel part of the watery worlds by providing close-up encounters with the inhabitants. A gift shop and café are on the premises. ⊠ *1 Canal St., French Quarter* ☎ *504/581–4629 or 800/774–7394* ⊕ *www.auduboninstitute. org* ▱ *Aquarium $13.50; combination ticket with IMAX $24; combination ticket for aquarium, zoo, and insectarium $30* ⊙ *Aquarium Tues.–Sun. 10–5.*

Beauregard-Keyes House. This stately 19th-century mansion with period furnishings was the temporary home of Confederate general P.G.T. Beauregard. The house and grounds had severely deteriorated by the 1940s, when the well-known novelist Frances Parkinson Keyes moved in and helped restore it. Her studio at the back of the large courtyard remains intact, complete with family photos, original manuscripts, and her doll, fan, and teapot collections. Keyes wrote 40 novels in this studio, all in longhand, among them the local favorite, *Dinner at Antoine's.* The house suffered some roof damage during Katrina, resulting in water stains along the dining room ceiling. Undaunted, the staff has reopened the site and continues its normal tour schedule. If you do not have time to tour the house, take a peek through the gates at the beautiful walled garden at the corner of Chartres and Ursulines streets. Landscaped in the same sun pattern as Jackson Square, the garden is in bloom throughout the year. ⊠ *1113 Chartres St., French Quarter* ☎ *504/523–7257* ⊕ *www.bkhouse.org* ▱ *$10* ⊙ *Mon.–Sat. 10–3, tours on the hr.*

Garden District. The Garden District is divided into two sections by Jackson Avenue. Upriver from Jackson is the wealthy **Upper Garden District,** where the homes are meticulously kept. Below Jackson, the **Lower Garden District** is considerably rougher. Though the homes here are often just as structurally beautiful, most of them lack the recent restorations of those of the Upper Garden District. The streets are also less well patrolled; wander cautiously. **Magazine Street,** lined with antiques shops and coffeehouses (ritzier along the Upper Garden District, hipper along the Lower Garden District), serves as a southern border to the Garden District, and St. Charles Avenue forms the northern border.

Hermann-Grima House. One of the largest and best-preserved examples of American architecture in the Quarter, this Georgian-style house has the only restored private stable and the only working 1830s Creole kitchen in the Quarter. American architect William Brand built the house in 1831. The house fortunately sustained only minor damage during Katrina and is open for visits and tours. Cooking demonstrations on the open hearth are held here all day Thursday from October through May. You'll want to check the gift shop, which has many local crafts and books. ⊠ *820 St. Louis St., French Quarter* ☎ *504/525–5661* ⊕ *www.hgghh.org* ▱ *$10, combination ticket with Gallier House $18* ⊙ *Tours Mon., Tues., Thurs., Fri. 10, 11, noon, 1, 2. Sat. noon, 1, 2, 3.*

⟳
Fodor's Choice
★

Jackson Square. Surrounded by historic buildings and plenty of the city's atmospheric street life, the heart of the French Quarter is this beautifully landscaped park. Among the notable buildings around the square are **St. Louis Cathedral** and **Faulkner House.** Two Spanish colonial–style buildings, the **Cabildo** and the **Presbytère,** flank the cathedral. The handsome rows of brick apartments on each side of the square are the **Pontalba Buildings.** The park is landscaped in a sun pattern, with walkways set like rays streaming out from the center, a popular garden design in the royal court of King Louis XIV, the Sun King. In the daytime, dozens of artists hang their paintings on the park fence and set up outdoor studios where they work on canvases or offer to draw portraits of passersby. These artists are easy to engage in conversation and are knowledgeable about many aspects of the Quarter and New Orleans. Musicians, mimes, tarot-card readers, and magicians perform on the flagstone pedestrian mall surrounding the square, many of them day and night.

Originally called the Place d'Armes, the square was founded in 1718 as a military parade ground. It was also the site of public executions carried out in various styles, including burning at the stake, beheading, breaking on the wheel, and hanging. A **statue of Andrew Jackson,** victorious leader of the Battle of New Orleans in the War of 1812, commands the center of the square; the park was renamed for him in the 1850s. The words carved in the base on the cathedral side of the statue—"The Union must and shall be preserved"—are a lasting reminder of the federal troops who occupied New Orleans during the Civil War and who inscribed them. ⊠ *French Quarter* ☽ *Park daily 8 am–dusk; flagstone paths on park's periphery open 24 hrs.*

Jean Lafitte National Park Visitor Center. This center has free visual and sound exhibits on the customs of various communities throughout the state, as well as information-rich daily history tours of the French Quarter. The one-hour daily tour leaves at 9:30 am; tickets are handed out one per person (you must be present to get a ticket), beginning at 9 am, for that day's tours only. Arrive at least 15 minutes before tour time to be sure of a spot. The office also supervises and provides information on Jean Lafitte National Park Barataria Unit, a nature preserve (complete with alligators) across the river from New Orleans, and the Chalmette Battlefield, where the Battle of New Orleans was fought in the War of 1812. Each year in January, near the anniversary of the battle, a reenactment is staged at the Chalmette site. ⊠ *419 Decatur St., French Quarter* ☎ *504/589–2636* ☽ *Daily 9–5.*

Fodor's Choice **Lafayette Cemetery No. 1.** Built in 1833, Lafayette Cemetery No. 1 was
★ the first planned cemetery in the city, and remains a testament to the city's history. The cemetery was built during a time that the area was seeing a large influx of Italian, German, Irish, and American immigrants from the North. Many who fought or played a role in the Civil War have plots here, indicated by plaques and headstones that detail the site of their death. Several of the tombs also reflect the toll the Yellow Fever epidemic took on the city during the 19th century, which affected mostly children and newcomers to the city; in 1852, 2,000 yellow-fever victims were buried here. Movies such as *Interview with the Vampire* and *Easy Rider* have used this walled cemetery for its eerie beauty. Open to the public everyday except Sunday, the cemetery is a

6

short walk from the streetcar and a beautiful spot to learn about New Orleans's history. ✉ *1400 block of Washington Ave., Garden District* ☉ *Weekdays 7–2:30, Sat. 7–noon; Save Our Cemeteries tours Mon., Wed., Fri., and Sat. at 10:30.*

Old U.S. Mint. Minting began in 1838 in this ambitious Ionic structure, a project of President Andrew Jackson. The New Orleans mint was to provide currency for the South and the West, which it did until the Confederacy began minting its own currency here in 1861. When supplies ran out, the building served as a barracks, then a prison, for Confederate soldiers; the production of U.S. coins recommenced only in 1879. It stopped again, for good, in 1909. After years of neglect, the federal government handed the Old Mint over to Louisiana in 1966; the state now uses the quarters to exhibit collections of the Louisiana State Museum. At the Barracks Street entrance, notice the one remaining sample of the mint's old walls—it'll give you an idea of the building's deterioration before its restoration. Hurricane Katrina ripped away a large section of the copper roof, and for months, the twisted metal remained on the ground here, one of the most dramatic reminders of the storm in the French Quarter. After years of repairs, the museum reopened to the public in October 2007. At the foot of Esplanade Avenue, notice the memorial to the French rebels against early Spanish rule, the first instance of a New World rebellion against a European power. The rebel leaders were executed on this spot and give nearby Frenchmen Street its name. The principal exhibit here is the **New Orleans Jazz Collection,** a brief but evocative tour through the history of traditional New Orleans jazz. ✉ *400 Esplanade Ave., French Quarter* ☎ *504/568–6993* 🖥 *Free* ☉ *Tues.–Sun. 10–5.*

St. Louis Cathedral. The oldest active cathedral in the United States, this iconic church at the heart of the Old City is named for the 13th-century French king who led two crusades. The current building, which replaced two structures destroyed by fire, dates from 1794 (although it was remodeled and enlarged in 1851). The austere interior is brightened by murals covering the ceiling and stained-glass windows along the first floor. Pope John Paul II held a prayer service for clergy here during his New Orleans visit in 1987; to honor the occasion, the pedestrian mall in front of the cathedral was renamed Place Jean Paul Deux. Nearly every evening in December brings a free concert held inside the cathedral. ✉ *615 Père Antoine Alley, French Quarter* ☎ *504/525–9585* 🖥 *Free.*

SHOPPING

The fun of shopping in New Orleans is in the regional items available throughout the city, in the smallest shops or the biggest department stores. You can take home some of the flavor of the city: its pralines (pecan candies), seafood (packaged to go), Louisiana red beans and rice, coffee (pure or with chicory), and creole and Cajun spices (cayenne pepper, chili, and garlic). There are even packaged mixes of such local favorites as jambalaya, gumbo, beignets, and the sweet red local cocktail called the Hurricane. Cookbooks also share the secrets of preparing distinctive New Orleans dishes. The French Quarter is well known for its fine antiques shops, located mainly on Royal and Chartres streets. The main shopping areas in the city are the French Quarter, with narrow, picturesque streets lined with specialty, gift, fashion, and antiques shops and art galleries; the Central Business District (CBD), populated mostly with jewelry, specialty, and department stores; the Warehouse District, best known for contemporary arts galleries and cultural museums; Magazine Street, home to antiques shops, art galleries, home-furnishing stores, dining venues, fashion boutiques, and specialty shops; and the Riverbend/Maple Street area, filled with clothing stores and some specialty shops.

> ### CALLING CARDS
>
> Print cards with your name, address, phone number, and email address to share with new friends. Stiff, business card–style paper can be purchased at nearly any office supply store, and you can make the cards on your computer at home. Having your cards handy sure beats hunting for pens and scribbling on scraps of paper to swap addresses.

Jax Brewery (⊠ *600 Decatur St., French Quarter* ☎ *504/566–7245* ⊕ *www.jacksonbrewery.com*) was a factory for Jax beer, but now holds a Jax Beer museum and an upscale mall filled with both local shops and national chains. **Riverwalk Marketplace** (⊠ *1 Poydras St., Warehouse* ☎ *504/522–1555* ⊕ *www.riverwalkmarketplace.com*), with 180-some stores, was built in what once was the International Pavilion of the 1984 World's Fair.

6

NIGHTLIFE

No American city places such a premium on pleasure as New Orleans. From swank hotel lounges to sweaty dance clubs, refined jazz clubs and raucous Bourbon Street bars, this city is serious about frivolity. And famous for it. Partying is more than an occasional indulgence in this city—it's a lifestyle. Bars tend to open in the early afternoon and stay open into the morning hours; live music, though, follows a more restrained schedule. Some jazz spots and clubs in the French Quarter stage evening sets around 6 pm or 9 pm; at a few clubs, such as the Palm Court, the bands actually finish by 11 pm. But this is the exception: for the most part, gigs begin between 10 and 11 pm, and locals rarely emerge for an evening out before 10. Keep in mind that the lack of legal closing time means that shows advertised for 11 may not start until after midnight.

Harrah's New Orleans. Commanding the foot of Canal Street, this Beaux Arts–style casino is the largest in the South. Its 100,000 square feet hold 2,900 slots and 120 gaming tables. There's an upscale steak restaurant run by local celebrity-chef John Besh. Valet parking is available. ⊠ *4 Canal St., CBD* ☎ *504/533–6000 or 800/427-7247* ⊕ *www.harrahs.com*.

Mulate's. Across the street from the Convention Center, this large restaurant seats 400, and the dance floor quickly fills with couples twirling and two-stepping to authentic Cajun bands from the countryside. Regulars love to drag first-timers to the floor for impromptu lessons.

The home-style Cajun cuisine is quite good, and the bands play until 10:30 or 11 pm. ⊠ *201 Julia St., Warehouse* ☎ *504/522–1492.*

★ **Pat O'Brien's.** Sure, it's touristy, but there are reasons Pat O's has been a must-stop on the New Orleans cocktail trail for so long. For one thing, there's plenty of room to spread out, from the elegant side bar and piano bar that flank the carriageway entrance to the lush (and in winter, heated) patio. Friendly staff, an easy camaraderie among patrons, and a signature drink—the pink, cloying, and extremely potent Hurricane, which comes with a souvenir glass—make this French Quarter stalwart a pleasant afternoon diversion. ⊠ *718 St. Peter St., French Quarter* ☎ *504/525–4823.*

> **GET MUGGED**
>
> Take along an insulated mug with a lid that you can fill at the beverage station in the buffet area. Your drinks will stay hot or cold, and you won't have to worry about spills. Most bartenders will fill the mug with ice and water or a soft drink. With a straw, your ice will not melt instantly while you lounge at the pool.

★ **Preservation Hall.** The jazz tradition that flowered in the 1920s is enshrined in this cultural landmark by a cadre of distinguished New Orleans musicians, most of whom were schooled by an ever-dwindling group of elder statesmen. There is limited seating on benches—many patrons end up squatting on the floor or standing in back—and no beverages are served or allowed. Nonetheless, the legions of satisfied customers regard an evening here as an essential New Orleans experience. Cover charge is $10, but can run a bit higher for special appearances. Call ahead for performance times; sometimes the show ends before you even begin prepartying. ⊠ *726 St. Peter St., French Quarter* ☎ *504/522–2841 or 504/523–8939.*

Fodor's Choice
★ **The Spotted Cat.** Jazz, old time, and swing bands perform nightly at this rustic club right in the thick of the Frenchmen Street action. Weekends feature afternoon sets as well. Drinks cost a little more at this cash-only destination, but there's never a cover charge, and the entertainment is great—from the popuar bands to the cadres of young, rock-step swing dancers. ⊠ *623 Frenchmen St., Faubourg Marigny* ☎ *504/943–3887.*

★ **Tipitina's.** A bust of legendary New Orleans pianist Professor Longhair, or "Fess," greets visitors at the door of this Uptown landmark, which takes its name from one of his most popular songs. As the concert posters pinned to the walls attest, Tip's hosts a wide variety of touring bands and local acts. The long-running Sunday-afternoon Cajun dance still packs the floor. The Tipitina's Foundation has an office and workshop upstairs, where local musicians affected by Hurricane Katrina can network, gain access to resources, and search for gigs. ⊠ *501 Napoleon Ave., Uptown* ☎ *504/895–8477.*

SIGHTSEEING TOURS

Several local tour companies give two- to four-hour city tours by bus that include the French Quarter, the Garden District, uptown New Orleans, and the lakefront. Prices range from $25 to $125 per person, depending on the kind of experience. Both Gray Line and New Orleans Tours offer a longer tour that combines a two-hour city tour by bus with a two-hour steamboat ride on the Mississippi River. Gray Line and Tours by Isabelle both offer tours of Hurricane Katrina devastation as well.

Tour Contacts Gray Line (☎ 800/535–7786 or 504/569–1401 ⊕ www. graylineneworleans.com). **New Orleans Tours** (☎ 504/592–1991 ⊕ www. notours.com). **Tours by Isabelle** (☎ 877/665–8687 or 504/398–0365 ⊕ www. toursbyisabelle.com).

WHERE TO EAT

For price categories, see ⇨ Dining at the beginning of this chapter.

Don't miss beignets and rich, chicory-laced coffee at **Café du Monde** (⊠ 800 Decatur St., French Quarter ☎ 504/525–4544 ⊟ No credit cards) in the French Quarter, though there's also an outlet in the Riverwalk.

$$$ ✗ **Bayona.** "New World" is the label Louisiana native Susan Spicer
SOUTHERN applies to her cooking style, which results in such special dishes as the
Fodor's Choice Caribbean pumpkin soup with coconut, and Niman Ranch pork chop
★ with a spicy adobo glaze. The lunch omelet of andouille, smoked cheddar, and fried oysters is about as authentic as Louisiana cooking can be. These and other imaginative dishes are served in an early-19th-century Creole cottage that glows with flower arrangements, elegant photographs, and trompe-l'oeil murals suggesting Mediterranean landscapes. Don't skip pastry chef Christy Phebus's sweets, such as a maple semolina cake with golden raisin compote and pomegranate sauce. ⊠430 Dauphine St., French Quarter ☎504/525–4455 ⊕ www.bayona.com ⌘ Reservations essential ⊗ Closed Sun. No lunch Mon. or Tues.

$ ✗ **Central Grocery.** This old-fashioned Italian grocery store produces
CAFÉ authentic muffulettas, one of the gastronomic gifts of the city's Italian immigrants. Good enough to challenge the po'boy as the local sandwich champ, it's made by filling round loaves of seeded bread with ham, salami, mozzarella, and a salad of marinated green olives. Sandwiches, about 10 inches in diameter, are sold in wholes and halves. ■TIP→ The **muffulettas are huge! Unless you're starving, you'll do fine with a half.** You can eat your muffuletta at a counter, or get it to go and dine on a bench on Jackson Square or the Moon Walk along the Mississippi riverfront. The Grocery closes at 5:30 pm. ⊠923 Decatur St., French Quarter ☎504/523–1620 ⊗ No dinner.

$$$ ✗ **Commander's Palace.** No restaurant captures New Orleans's gastro-
CREOLE nomic heritage and celebratory spirit as well as this one, long con-
Fodor's Choice sidered the grande dame of New Orleans's fine dining. The recent
★ renovation has added new life, especially upstairs, where the Garden Room's glass walls have marvelous views of the giant oak trees on the patio below; other rooms promote conviviality with their bright pastels. The menu's classics include sugarcane-grilled pork tenderloin; a spicy and meaty turtle soup; terrific bourbon-lacquered Mississippi quail; and a wonderful griddle-seared gulf fish. Among the addictive desserts is the bread-pudding soufflé. Weekend brunches are a New Orleans

6

tradition. Jackets are preferred at dinner. ✉ *1403 Washington Ave., Garden District* ☎ *504/899–8221* ⊕ *www.commanderspalace.com* ⚓ *Reservations essential.*

$$$
CREOLE
Fodor's Choice
★

✗ **Galatoire's.** Galatoire's has always epitomized the old-style French-Creole bistro. Many of the recipes date to 1905. Fried oysters and bacon en brochette are worth every calorie, and the brick-red rémoulade sauce sets a high standard. Other winners include veal chops in béarnaise sauce, and seafood-stuffed eggplant. The setting downstairs is a single, narrow dining room lighted with glistening brass chandeliers; bentwood chairs and white tablecloths add to its timelessness. You may reserve a table in the renovated upstairs rooms, though the action is on the first floor, where partying regulars inhibit conversation but add good people-watching entertainment value. Friday lunch starts early and continues well into early evening. A jacket is required. ✉ *209 Bourbon St., French Quarter* ☎ *504/525–2021* ⊕ *www.galatoires.com* ☾ *Closed Mon.*

$$
SOUTHERN

✗ **Herbsaint.** Upscale food and moderate prices are among Herbsaint's assets. Chef Donald Link turns out food that sparkles with robust flavors and top-grade ingredients. Small plates and side dishes such as charcuterie, a knock-'em-dead shrimp bisque, house-made pasta, and cheese- or nut-studded salads are mainstays. Don't overlook the rich and flavorful Louisiana cochon with turnips, cabbage, and cracklins. Also irresistible: smoked beef brisket with horseradish potato salad. For dessert, the layered spice cake with figs and pecans will ensure future return trips. The plates provide most of the color in the light-hearted, often noisy, rooms. The wine list is expertly compiled and reasonably priced. ✉ *701 St. Charles Ave., CBD* ☎ *504/524–4114* ⊕ *www. herbsaint.com* ⚓ *Reservations essential* ☾ *Closed Sun. No lunch Sat.*

> **CAUTION**
>
> Items confiscated by airport security will not be returned to you. If you are uncertain whether something will pass the security test, pack it in your checked luggage.

WHERE TO STAY

You can stay in a large hotel near the cruise-ship terminal or in more intimate places in the French Quarter. Hotel rates in New Orleans tend to be on the high end, though deals abound.

For price categories, see ⇨ Lodging at the beginning of this chapter.

For expanded hotel reviews, visit Fodors.com.

$$
▦ **The Ambassador Hotel.** Guest rooms at this hotel bordering the CBD and Warehouse District have real character, with hardwood floors, oversize windows, and high ceilings. **Pros:** distinctive decor; urban-chic atmosphere. **Cons:** some first-floor rooms let in too much noise from street and lobby area. ✉ *535 Tchoupitoulas St., CBD* ☎ *504/527–5271 or 800/455–3417* ⊕ *www.ambassadorneworleans.com* ⟿ *165 rooms* ♿ *In-room: Wi-Fi. In-hotel: restaurant, bar, parking* ⫯❍⫯ *No meals.*

$$$
▦ **Hilton New Orleans Riverside.** The sprawling multilevel Hilton complex sits right on the Mississippi, with superb views. **ros:** well-maintained facilities; hotel runs like a well-oiled machine. **Cons:** the city's biggest

hotel; typical chain service and surroundings; garage needs better lighting and security. ⌧ *Poydras St. at Mississippi River, CBD* ☎ *504/561–0500 or 800/445–8667* ⊕ *www.hilton.com* ⟳ *1,600 rooms, 67 suites* 👍 *In-room: Wi-Fi. In-hotel: restaurants, tennis courts, pools, gym, parking* ⫯⊙⫯ *No meals.*

$$$ ⫯⫯ **New Orleans Marriott Hotel.** The Marriott has a fabulous view of the Quarter, the CBD, and the river. It's an easy walk from the Canal Place mall, the Riverwalk, and the Convention Center. **Pros:** good location; very clean; stunning city and river views. **Cons:** typical chain hotel; inconsistent service. ⌧ *555 Canal St., French Quarter* ☎ *504/581–1000 or 800/228–9290* ⊕ *www.neworleansmarriott.com* ⟳ *1,290 rooms, 54 suites* 👍 *In-room: Internet. In-hotel: restaurant, bar, pool, gym, parking* ⫯⊙⫯ *No meals.*

NEW YORK, NEW YORK

A few cruise lines now base Caribbean-bound ships in New York City year-round; other ships do seasonal cruises to New England and Bermuda or trans-Atlantic crossings. If you're coming to the city from outside the immediate area, you can easily arrive the day before and do a bit of sightseeing and perhaps take in a Broadway show. The cruise port in Manhattan is fairly close to Times Square and Midtown hotels and theaters. But the New York City region now has three major cruise ports. You can also leave from Cape Liberty Terminal in Bayonne, New Jersey, on both Celebrity and Royal Caribbean ships. There's also a cruise terminal in Red Hook, Brooklyn, and this terminal serves Princess ships as well as Cunard's *Queen Mary 2.*

ESSENTIALS

HOURS They say that New York never sleeps, and that's particularly true around Times Square, where some stores are open until 11 pm or later even during the week. But most stores outside of the immediate Times Square area are open from 9 or 10 until 6 or 7. Many museums close on Monday.

INTERNET Internet service is offered by most New York hotels, and there are independent Internet cafés all over town. You might even see cheap Internet service in pizzerias and delis. Starbucks offers wireless service for a fee, but if you have your own laptop you can use the free outdoor Wi-Fi network in Bryant Park (6th Avenue, between 42nd and 41st streets).

Visitor Information NYC & Company Convention & Visitors Bureau (⌧ *810 7th Ave., between W. 52nd and W. 53rd Sts., 3rd fl., Midtown West* ☎ *212/484–1200* ⊕ *www.nycgo.com*). **Times Square Information Center** (⌧ *1560 Broadway, between 46th and 47th Sts., Midtown West* ☎ *212/768–1560* ⊕ *www.timessquarenyc.org* Ⓜ *N, Q, R, S, 1, 2, 3, 7 to 42nd St./Times Square*).

THE CRUISE PORT

The New York Passenger Ship Terminal is on the far west side of Manhattan, five very long blocks from the Times Square area, between 48th and 52nd streets; the vehicle entrance is at 55th Street. Traffic can

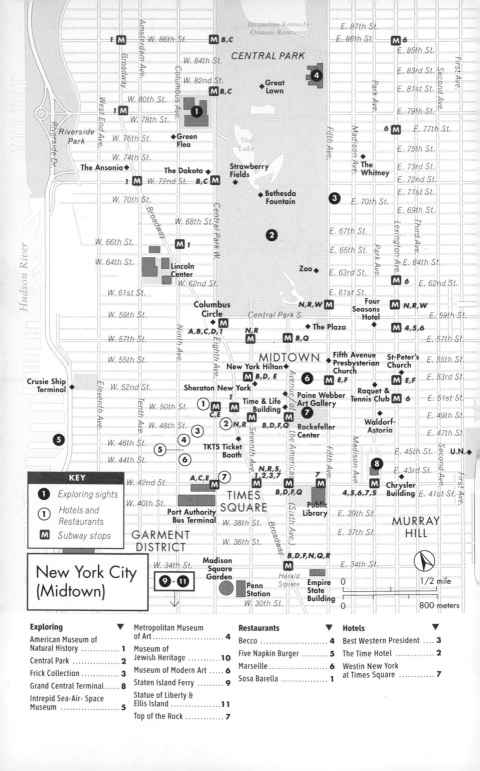

KEY

- **1** Exploring sights
- **(1)** Hotels and Restaurants
- **M** Subway stops

New York City (Midtown)

Exploring ▼

American Museum of Natural History **1**
Central Park **2**
Frick Collection **3**
Grand Central Terminal **8**
Intrepid Sea-Air- Space Museum **5**

Metropolitan Museum of Art **4**
Museum of Jewish Heritage **10**
Museum of Modern Art **6**
Staten Island Ferry **9**
Statue of Liberty & Ellis Island **11**
Top of the Rock **7**

Restaurants ▼

Becco **4**
Five Napkin Burger **5**
Marseille **6**
Sosa Barella **1**

Hotels ▼

Best Western President **3**
The Time Hotel **2**
Westin New York at Times Square **7**

be backed up in the area on days that cruise ships arrive and depart, so allow yourself enough time to check in and go through security. There are no nearby subway stops, though city buses do cross Midtown at 50th and 42nd streets. If you don't have too much luggage, it is usually faster and more convenient to have a taxi drop you off at the intersection of 50th Street and the West Side Highway, directly across the street from the entrance to the lower-level of the terminal; then you can walk right in and take the escalator or elevator up to the embarkation level.

Cape Liberty Terminal in Bayonne is off Route 440. From the New Jersey Turnpike, take Exit 14A, then follow the signs for 440 South, and make a left turn into the Cape Liberty Terminal area (on Port Terminal Boulevard). If you are coming from Long Island, you cross Staten Island, and after crossing the Bayonne Bridge take 440 North, making a right into the terminal area. If you are coming from Manhattan, you can also reach the terminal by public transit. Take the New Jersey Transit light-rail line from the PATH trains in Hoboken; get off at the Bayonne stop, and from there you can take a taxi to the terminal (about 2 mi away); there may be free shuttle bus on cruise sailing dates, but confirm that with your cruise line.

The Brooklyn cruise terminal at Pier 12 in Red Hook, which opened in April 2006, is not convenient to public transportation, so you should plan to take a taxi, drive, or take the bus transfers offered by the cruise lines (the cost for this is about $45 per person from either LaGuardia or JFK). There is a secure, 500-car outdoor parking lot on-site. To reach the terminal from La Guardia Airport, take I–278 W (the Brooklyn-Queens Expressway), Exit 26, Hamilton Avenue; the terminal entrance is actually off Browne Street. From JFK, take I–278 E (again, the Brooklyn-Queens Expressway), and then the same exit. If you arrive early, there's not much in the neighborhood, but there are a few neighborhood delis and restaurants about 15 minutes away on foot; the area is a safe place to walk around during daylight hours, though it's very industrial and unattractive. Red Hook is the home of ships from the Carnival, Princess, and Cunard cruise lines.

Information Cape Liberty Terminal (✉ *14 Port Terminal Blvd., Bayonne, NJ* ☎ *201/823-3737* ⊕ *www.cruiseliberty.com*). **New York Passenger Ship Terminal** (✉ *711 12th Ave., Midtown West, New York, NY* ☎ *212/246-5450* ⊕ *www.nycruiseterminal.com* ✉ *Pier 12, Bldg. 112, Red Hook, Brooklyn, NY* ☎ *718/858-3450*).

NEW YORK BEST BETS

■ **An Art Museum.** Take your pick: the Met, MOMA, or the Frick, but this is a true highlight of New York.

■ **A Broadway Show.** The theater experience in New York is better than almost anywhere else in the world.

■ **Statue of Liberty.** Just the sight of Lady Liberty will melt the coldest heart, though the highlight of the trip is actually the Ellis Island museum, not the statue itself.

6

AIRPORT TRANSFERS

A cab to or from JFK to the passenger-ship terminal in **Manhattan** will cost $45 (a flat fare) plus toll and tip; expect to pay at least $35 on the meter if you are coming from LaGuardia and at least $50 or $60 (not including tolls of about $10 and the tip) from Newark in a regular taxi (from Newark airport, it's usually more cost-effective to call for a car service to pick you up; these services have a flat fare of about $48, not including the tolls and tip).

From Newark Airport it's approximately $30 to **Cape Liberty,** $80 from JFK (plus tolls and tip, so count on at least $110 and be aware that taxis are not obligated to take this route from JFK), and $90 from La Guardia (plus tolls and tip; count on paying more than $110). Royal Caribbean offers bus service from several Mid-Atlantic and Northeast cities on sailing dates, but confirm that with the cruise line.

If your cruise is leaving from **Red Hook,** the taxi fare will be much cheaper if you fly into either La Guardia (about $30) or JFK (about $40); you'll pay at least $80 from Newark Airport (not including tolls and tip). Cruise lines provide bus transfers from all three of the area's airports, but it may be cheaper to take a taxi if you are traveling with more than one other person. Note that all these taxi fares do not include tolls and tips. From Newark, the tolls to Brooklyn can be substantial, adding almost $20 to the fare.

PARKING

You can park at the New York Passenger Ship Terminal for a staggering $30 a day; the fee is payable in advance in cash or traveler's checks (no credit cards).

Parking at Cape Liberty Terminal in Bayonne is $19 per day, payable in cash, traveler's checks, and major credit cards.

Parking at Red Hook, Brooklyn, costs $23 for the first 24 hours and then $20 per day.

TOP ATTRACTIONS

There's no way to do justice to even the most popular tourist stops in New York. Below is information about several top attractions. If you have only a day in the city, choose one or two attractions and buy a Metro card to facilitate easy transfers between the subway and bus (put on as much money as you think you'll use in a day but no less than $4.50). There's a moving series of panels about the World Trade Center at the so-called "Ground Zero" site across from the Millennium Hotel (take the 1 train to Cortlandt Street or the E to World Trade Center); there's another series of memorial panels underneath at the World Trade Center PATH station, which is accessible from the main, streetside memorial area.

American Museum of Natural History. With 45 exhibition halls and more than 32 million artifacts and specimens, the world's largest and most important museum of natural history can easily occupy you for half a day. The dioramas might seem dated, but are fun. The dinosaur exhibits are probably the highlight. Attached to the museum is the **Rose Center**

for Earth and Space, with various exhibits and housing the **Hayden Planetarium** and an **IMAX Theater.** ⊠ *Central Park West at W. 79 St., Upper West Side* ☎ *212/769–5200* ⊕ *www.amnh.org* ⚏ *$20 suggested donation, includes admission to Rose Center for Earth and Space* ☉ *Daily 10–5:45. Rose Center until 8:45 on Fri.*

Central Park. Without Central Park's 843 acres of meandering paths, tranquil lakes, ponds, and open meadows, New Yorkers might be a lot less sane. You can drop by the zoo (near 64th Street, on the east side) or the famous Bethesda Fountain (mid-park, at around 72nd Street), but the main draw is just to wander the lanes. Central Park has one of the lowest crime rates in the city. Still, use common sense and stay within sight of other park visitors, and don't go into the park after dark. Directions, park maps, and events calendars can be obtained from volunteers at two 5th Avenue **information booths,** at East 60th Street and East 72nd Street. ☎ *212/310–6600 for schedule of park events, 212/360–2726 for schedule of walking tours* ⊕ *www.centralparknyc. org* Ⓜ *Subway: A, C, or 1 to Columbus Circle.*

★ **Frick Collection.** Coke-and-steel baron Henry Clay Frick (1849–1919) amassed this superb art collection far from the soot and smoke of Pittsburgh, where he made his fortune. The mansion was designed by Thomas Hastings and built in 1913–14. It opened in 1935, but still resembles a gracious private home, albeit one with bona fide masterpieces in almost every room. This is the best small museum in town by a mile. ⊠ *1 E. 70th St., at 5th Ave., Upper East Side* ☎ *212/288–0700* ⊕ *www.frick.org* ⚏ *$18* ☉ *Tues.–Sat. 10–6, Sun. 11–5* Ⓜ *6 to 68th St./ Hunter College.*

Fodor'sChoice
★ **Grand Central Terminal.** Grand Central is not only the world's largest (76 acres) and the nation's busiest (500,000 commuters and subway riders use it daily) railway station, but also one of the world's greatest public spaces ("justly famous," as critic Tony Hiss noted, "as a crossroads, a noble building . . . and an ingenious piece of engineering"). A massive four year renovation completed in October 1998 restored the 1913 landmark to its original splendor—and then some. There's a nice audio tour for rent for $5 per adult. *Main entrance* ⊠ *E. 42nd St. at Park Ave., Midtown East* ☎ *212/935–3960* ⊕ *www.grandcentralterminal.com* Ⓜ *4, 5, 6, 7, S to 42nd St./Grand Central.*

Ⓒ ***Intrepid* Sea-Air-Space Museum.** Formerly the USS *Intrepid*, this 900-foot aircraft carrier is serving out its retirement as the centerpiece of Manhattan's only floating museum. An A-12 Blackbird spy plane, lunar landing modules, helicopters, seaplanes, and two dozen other aircraft are on deck. Docked alongside, and also part of the museum, are the *Growler,* a strategic-missile submarine; the *Edson,* a Vietnam-era destroyer; and several other battle-scarred naval veterans. Children can explore the ships' skinny hallways and winding staircases, as well as manipulate countless knobs, buttons, and wheels. This museum is within easy walking distance of the main cruise piers in Manhattan. ⊠ *Hudson River, Pier 86, 12th Ave. at W. 46th St., Midtown West* ☎ *212/245–0072 or 877/957–7447* ⊕ *www.intrepidmuseum.org* ⚏ *$24; free to active and retired U.S. military personnel and children under 3* ☉ *Apr.–Sept.,* *weekdays 10–5, weekends 10–6; Oct.–Mar., Tues.–Sun. 10–5; last admission 1 hr before closing* Ⓜ *A, C, E to 42nd St.; M42 bus to pier.*

Fodor's Choice
★ **The Metropolitan Museum of Art.** If the city held no other museum than the colossal Metropolitan Museum of Art, you could still occupy yourself for days roaming its labyrin-

thine corridors. Because the Metropolitan Museum has something approaching 3 million works on display over its more than 7 square mi, you're going to have to make some hard choices. Looking at everything here could take a week. ✉ *5th Ave. at 82nd St., Upper East Side* ☎ *212/535–7710* ⊕ *www.metmuseum.org* 🎫 *$20 suggested donation* ☉ *Tues.–Thurs. and Sun. 9:30–5:30, Fri. and Sat. 9:30–9.*

Museum of Jewish Heritage—A Living Memorial to the Holocaust. In a granite hexagon rising 85 feet above Robert F. Wagner Jr. Park at the southern end of Battery Park City, this museum pays tribute to the 6 million Jews who perished in the Holocaust. It's one of the best such museums in the country. ✉ *36 Battery Pl., Battery Park City, Lower Manhattan* ☎ *646/437–4200* ⊕ *www.mjhnyc.org* 🎫 *$12, free on Wed. 4–10* ☉ *Thurs. and Sun.–Tues. 10–5:45, Wed. 10–8, Fri. and eve of Jewish holidays 10–3* Ⓜ *4, 5 to Bowling Green.*

Museum of Modern Art (MoMA). The masterpieces—Monet's *Water Lilies,* Picasso's *Les Demoiselles d'Avignon,* Van Gogh's *Starry Night*—are still here, but for now the main draw at MoMA is, well, MoMA. A "modernist dream world" is how critics described the museum after its $425 million face-lift. Unfortunately, the museum was an instant success, which means lines are sometimes down the block. For the shortest wait, get here before the museum opens; you can avoid some of the crowding by entering through the 54th Street side. Be prepared for sticker shock when you buy your ticket. ✉ *11 W. 53rd St., between 5th and 6th Aves., Midtown East* ☎ *212/708–9400* ⊕ *www.moma.org* 🎫 *$20* ☉ *Sat.–Mon., Wed., and Thurs. 10:30–5:30, Fri. 10:30–8* Ⓜ *Subway: E, V to 5th Ave./53rd St.; B, D, E to 7th Ave.; B, D, F, V to 47th–50th Sts./Rockefeller Center.*

Staten Island Ferry. The best transit deal in town is the Staten Island Ferry, a free 20- to 30-minute ride across New York Harbor providing great views of the Manhattan skyline, the Statue of Liberty, the Verrazano-Narrows Bridge, and the New Jersey coast. Ferries embark on various schedules: every 15 minutes during rush hours, every 20–30 minutes most other times, and every hour on weekend nights and mornings. If you can manage it, catch one of the older blue-and-orange ferries, which have outside decks. ✉ *State and South Sts., Lower Manhattan* ☎ *718/390–5253* 🎫 *Free* Ⓜ *Subway: 4, 5 to Bowling Green; 1, 9 to South Ferry.*

Statue of Liberty and Ellis Island. Though you must endure a long wait and onerous security, it's worth the trouble to see one of the iconic images of New York. But the truth is that a trip to the statue is time-consuming and laborious; Ellis Island is a much better investment of your time, especially if you have only a day or two in New York. You're allowed access to the statue's museum only as part of one of the free tours of the promenade (which surrounds the base of the pedestal) or the observatory (at the pedestal's top). The tours are limited to 3,000 participants a day; to guarantee a place, particularly on the observatory tour, you must order tickets ahead of time—they can be reserved up to 180 days in advance, by phone or over the Internet. The narrow, double-helix stairs leading to the statue's crown closed after 9/11, but access reopened on July 4, 2009. Approximately 240 people are allowed to visit the crown each day; tickets are available online (they usually sell out at least 2 months in advance). If you can't get tickets to the crown, you get a good look at the statue's inner structure on the observatory tour. Much more interesting—and well worth exploring—is the Ellis Island museum, which traces the story of immigration in New York City with moving exhibits throughout the restored processing building. Go early if you want to see everything, and allow plenty of time for security and lines. The ferry stops first at the statue and then continues to Ellis Island. ⊠ *Liberty Island* ☎ *212/363–3200, 877/523–9849 ticket reservations* ⊕ *www.statuecruises.com* ⌨ *Ferry $13 round-trip; crown tickets $3* ☉ *Daily 9:30–5; extended hrs in summer (current hrs available at* ⊕ *www.nps.gov/stli/planyourvisit/hours.htm).*

Fodor's Choice ★ **Top of the Rock.** Rockefeller Center's multifloor observation deck, first opened in 1933, and closed in the early 1980s, reopened in 2005. Though overpriced, the experience is infinitely better than that at the Empire State Building, where interminable lines spoil most of the fun. Arrive just before sunset for the best views (which include the Empire State Building). ⊠ *Entrance on 50th St., between 5th and 6th Aves., Midtown West* ☎ *877/692–7625 or 212/698–2000* ⊕ *www.topoftherocknyc.com* ⌨ *$22* ☉ *Daily 8–midnight; last elevator at 11 pm* Ⓜ *B, D, F, V to 47th–50th Sts./Rockefeller Center.*

SHOPPING

You can find almost any major store from virtually any designer or chain in Manhattan. High-end designers tend to be along **Madison Avenue**, between 55th and 86th streets. Some are along **57th Street**, between Madison and 7th avenues. **Fifth Avenue**, starting at Saks Fifth Avenue (at 50th Street) and going up to 59th Street, is a hodgepodge of high-end stores and more accessible options, including the high-end department store Bergdorf-Goodman, at 58th Street. More interesting and individual stores can be found in **SoHo** (between Houston and Canal, West Broadway and Lafayette), and the **East Village** (between 14th Street and Houston, Broadway and Avenue A). **Chinatown** is chock-full of designer knockoffs, crowded streets, and dim sum palaces; though frenetic during the day, it's a fun stop. The newest group of stores in Manhattan is at the **Time-Warner Center,** at Columbus Circle (at 8th Avenue and 59th Street); the high-rise mall has upscale stores and some of the city's best-reviewed and most expensive new restaurants.

BROADWAY SHOWS

Scoring tickets to Broadway shows is fairly easy except for the very top draws. For the most part, the top ticket price for Broadway musicals is now over $140; the best seats for Broadway plays can run as high as $120. **Telecharge** (☏ 212/239–6200 ⊕ www.telecharge.com). **Ticketmaster** (☏ 212/307–4100 ⊕ www. ticketmaster.com).

> **CAUTION**
>
> Store any irreplaceable valuables in the ship purser's safe rather than the one in your cabin. Some insurance policies will not cover the loss of items left in your cabin.

For seats at 25%–50% off the usual price, go to one of the **TKTS booths** (✉ Duffy Sq. at W. 47th St. and Broadway, Midtown West Ⓜ 1, 2, 3, 7, N, Q, R, S, W to 42nd St./Times Sq.; N, R, W to 49th St.; 1 to 50th St. ✉ South St. Seaport at Front and John Sts., Lower Manhattan Ⓜ 2, 3, 4, 5, A, C, E, J, M, Z to Fulton St./Broadway-Nassau ✉ Downtown Brooklyn, at the Myrtle St. Promenade and Jay St., Brooklyn Ⓜ A, C, F to Jay St.-Borough Hall; M, R, 2, 3, 4, 5 to Court St.-Borough Hall ⊕ www.tdf.org).

WHERE TO EAT

The restaurants we recommend below are all in Midtown West, near Broadway theaters and hotels. Make reservations at all but the most casual places or face a numbing wait.

For price categories, see ⇨ Dining at the beginning of this chapter.

$$
ITALIAN
✕ **Becco.** An ingenious concept makes Becco a prime Restaurant Row choice for time-constrained theatergoers. There are two pricing scenarios: one includes an all-you-can-eat selection of antipasti and three pastas served hot out of pans that waiters circulate around the dining room; the other adds a generous entrée to the mix. The pasta selection changes daily, but often includes gnocchi, fresh ravioli, and fettuccine in a cream sauce. The entrées include braised veal shank, grilled double-cut pork chop, and rack of lamb, among other selections. ✉ 355 W. 46th St., between 8th and 9th Aves., Midtown West ☏ 212/397–7597 ⊕ www.becco-nyc.com Ⓜ A, C, E to 42nd St.

$
AMERICAN
✕ **Five Napkin Burger.** This perennially packed Hell's Kitchen burger place/brasserie has been a magnet for burger lovers since day one. Bottles of Maker's Mark line the sleek, alluringly lighted bar in the back, a collection of antique butcher's scales hangs on a tile wall near the kitchen, and meat hooks dangle from the ceiling between the light fixtures. Though there are many menu distractions—deep-fried pickles, warm artichoke dip, to name a few—the main attractions are the juicy burgers, like the original 10-ounce chuck with a tangle of onions, Gruyère cheese, and rosemary aioli. There's a patty variety for everyone, including a ground lamb *kofta* and an onion ring–topped ahi tuna burger. For dessert, have an über-thick black-and-white malted milkshake. ✉ 630 9th Ave., between 44th and 45th Sts., Midtown West

☎ *212/757–2277* ⊕ *www.fivenapkinburger.com* Ⓜ *A, C, E to 42nd St./8th Ave.*

$$ ✗ **Marseille.** With great food and a convenient location near several
MEDITERRANEAN Broadway theaters, Marseille is perpetually packed. Executive chef and partner Andy d'Amico's Mediterranean creations are continually impressive. His bouillabaisse, the signature dish of the region for which the restaurant is named, is a mélange of mussels, shrimp, rouget, and bass swimming in a fragrant fish broth, topped with a garlicky crouton and served with rouille on the side. Leave room for the spongy beignets with chocolate and raspberry dipping sauces. ⊠ *630 9th Ave., at W. 44th St., Midtown West* ☎ *212/333–2323* ⊕ *www.marseillenyc. com* ⚱ *Reservations essential* Ⓜ *A, C, E to 42nd St./Port Authority Bus Terminal.*

$$ ✗ **Sosa Borella.** This is one of the Theater District's top spots for reliable
ITALIAN food at a reasonable cost. The bi-level, casual Argentinian-Italian eatery is an inviting and friendly space where diners choose from a wide range of options. The lunch menu features staples like warm sandwiches and entrée-size salads, whereas the dinner menu is slightly gussied up with meat, fish, and pasta dishes (the rich agnolotti with lamb Bolognese sauce, topped with a wedge of grilled pecorino cheese, is a must-try). The freshly baked bread served at the beginning of the meal with pesto dipping sauce is a nice touch as you wait for your meal. The service can be slow at times, so leave yourself plenty of time before the show. ⊠ *832 8th Ave., between 50th and 51st Sts., Midtown West* ☎ *212/262–8282* ⊕ *www.sosaborella.com* Ⓜ *C, E, 1 to 50th St.*

WHERE TO STAY

There are no real bargains in the Manhattan hotel world, and you'll find it difficult to get a decent room for under $250 during much of the year. However, occasional weekend deals can be found. All the hotels we recommend for cruise passengers are on the West Side, in relatively easy proximity to the cruise ship terminal.

For price categories, see ⇨ *Lodging at the beginning of this chapter.*

For expanded hotel reviews, visit Fodors.com.

¢ 🏨 **Best Western President Hotel.** After a $15 million renovation that transformed it from a ho-hum Best Western, the President is the only politically themed hotel in the city. **Pros:** sleek rooms for the price; convenient location; unique theme. **Cons:** cramped lobby; dark bathrooms; poor views. ⊠ *234 W. 48th St., between 8th Ave. and Broadway, Times Square* ☎ *212/246–8800 or 800/828–4667* ⊕ *www.presidenthotelny. com* ⤴ *334 rooms* ⚲ *In-room: a/c, Wi-Fi. In-hotel: restaurants, room service, bar, gym* Ⓜ *C, E to 50th St.* ¶ *No meals.*

$$–$$$ 🏨 **The Time Hotel.** One of the neighborhood's first boutique hotels, this spot half a block from the din of Times Square tempers trendiness with a touch of humor. **Pros:** acclaimed and popular Serafina restaurant downstairs; surprisingly quiet for Times Square location; good turndown service. **Cons:** decor makes the rooms a little dated; service is inconsistent; water pressure is lacking. ⊠ *224 W. 49th St., between Broadway and 8th Ave., Midtown West* ☎ *212/320–2900 or 877/846–3692* ⊕ *www.*

6

thetimeny.com ⤳ *164 rooms, 29 suites ♿ In-room: a/c, Internet. In-hotel: restaurant, room service, bar, gym, parking* Ⓜ *1, C, E to 50th St.* ⌶◎⌶ *No meals.*

$ 🔛 **Westin New York at Times Square.** A $24 million renovation is complete at this giant Midtown hotel; all rooms come with the Heavenly Bed, flat-screen televisions, and Wi-Fi. For even more comfort, spa-floor rooms come with massage chairs, aromatherapy candles, and other pampering pleasures. **Pros:** busy Times Square location; big rooms; great gym. **Cons:** busy Times Square location; small bathroom sinks; some rooms need to be refreshed. ⊠ *270 W. 43rd St., at 8th Ave., Midtown West* ☎ *212/201–2700 or 866/837–4183* ⊕ *www.westinny.com* ⤳ *863 rooms, 126 suites ♿ In-room: a/c, Wi-Fi. In-hotel: restaurant, room service, bars, gym, spa, parking, some pets allowed* Ⓜ *A, C, E to 42nd St./Times Sq.* ⌶◎⌶ *No meals.*

NORFOLK, VIRGINIA

Ramona Settle

Founded in 1680, Norfolk is no newcomer to the cruise business. One famous passenger, Thomas Jefferson, arrived here in November 1789 after a two-month crossing of the Atlantic. More than 200 years later, this historic seaport welcomes more than 300,000 cruise passengers annually. Situated at the heart of nautical Hampton Roads, Norfolk is home to the largest naval base in the world and is also a major commercial port.

ESSENTIALS

HOURS   Most stores are open weekdays from 10 to 9. Some museums close on Monday and/or Tuesday.

INTERNET   Most of the hotels offer free Wi-Fi service if you have your own laptop. If not, you may be able to find an Internet café, but the local Norfolk Public Library has free Internet access, so why pay? **Norfolk Public Library** (⊠ *235 E. Plume St.* ☎ *757/664–7323* ⊕ *www.npl.lib.va.us*).

Visitor Information Norfolk Convention and Visitors Bureau (⊠ *232 E. Main St.* ☎ *757/664–6620 or 800/368–3097* ⊕ *www.visitnorfolktoday.com*).

THE CRUISE PORT

The new Half Moone Cruise and Celebration Center, as Norfolk calls its cruise terminal is in the center of the attractive, downtown waterfront. It's within walking distance of numerous attractions and amenities. From I–264, take the City Hall exit (Exit 10). At the light, turn right on St. Paul's Boulevard, and follow the signs to the Cedar Grove parking lot.

Information Half Moone Cruise and Celebration Center (⊠ *1 Waterside Dr.* ⊕ *www.cruisenorfolk.org*).

AIRPORT TRANSFERS

Norfolk International Airport (ORF) is 9 mi and 20 minutes away from the cruise terminal. One-way, shared shuttle costs range from $7.50 to $22 per person, and a taxi costs about $18 to $25.

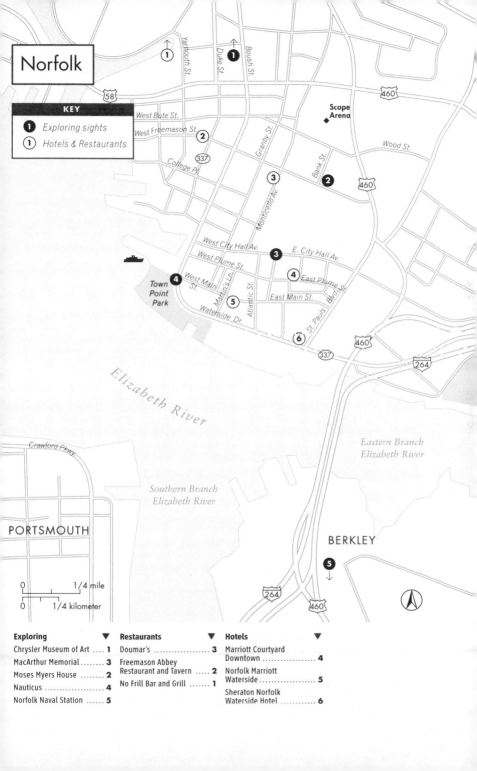

Norfolk

KEY

1 *Exploring sights*
① *Hotels & Restaurants*

Yarmouth St.
Duke St.
Boush St.
West Bute St.
West Freemason St.
College Pl.
Granby St.
Bank St.
Wood St.
Monticello Av.
West City Hall Av.
E. City Hall Av.
West Plume St.
West Main St.
East Plume St.
Malta's Ln.
Atlantic St.
East Main St.
St. Pauls Blvd.
Waterside Dr.

Scope Arena

Town Point Park

Elizabeth River

Crawford Pkwy.

PORTSMOUTH

Southern Branch Elizabeth River

Eastern Branch Elizabeth River

BERKLEY

0   1/4 mile
0   1/4 kilometer

Contacts **Norfolk Airport Express** (☎ 877/455–7462 ⊕ www. norfolkairportexpress.com). **Norfolk International Airport** (ORF ✉ 2200 Norview Ave., Norfolk ☎ 757/857–3351 ⊕ norfolkairport.com).

PARKING

Cedar Grove Parking is the designated facility for cruise passengers. The parking fee ($10 daily) is paid upon entering the lot; Visa, MasterCard, American Express, cash, and traveler's checks are accepted. Less than 1 mi from I–264, this lot is located on Monticello Avenue between Virginia Beach Boulevard and Princess Anne Road in Downtown Norfolk. Shuttles run regularly to the cruise terminal.

NORFOLK BEST BETS

■ **Chrysler Museum of Art.** Though far from New York, Chicago, or Los Angeles, this is one of the major art museums in the U.S.

■ **Nauticus.** The National Maritime Center is one of the region's most popular attractions, and especially good for families.

■ **Norfolk Naval Station.** This giant naval base, the home of the Atlantic Fleet, is an impressive site in itself.

EXPLORING NORFOLK

History meets high-tech in this waterfront city. From 18th-century historic homes and a major art museum to 20th-century battleships and nuclear-powered aircraft carriers, Norfolk has many interesting sites to explore, several of them free and most within walking distance of the cruise terminal.

★ **Chrysler Museum of Art.** By any standard, the Chrysler Museum of Art downtown qualifies as one of America's major art museums. The permanent collection includes works by Rubens, Gainsborough, Renoir, Picasso, Cézanne, Matisse, Warhol, and Pollock, a list that suggests the breadth available here. Classical and pre-Columbian civilizations are also represented. The decorative-arts collection includes exquisite English porcelain and art nouveau furnishings. The Chrysler is home to one of the most important glass collections in America, which includes glass objects from the 6th century BC to the present, with particularly strong holdings in Tiffany, French art glass, and English cameo, as well as artifacts from ancient Rome and the Near and Far East. ✉ 245 W. Olney Rd. ☎ 757/664–6200 ⊕ www.chrysler.org ⛝ Free ☉ Wed. 10–9, Thurs.–Sat. 10–5, Sun. noon–5.

MacArthur Memorial. The MacArthur Memorial is the burial place of one of America's most distinguished military officers. General Douglas MacArthur (1880–1964) agreed to this navy town as the site for his monument because it was his mother's birthplace. In the rotunda of the old City Hall, converted according to MacArthur's design, is the mausoleum; 11 adjoining galleries house mementos of MacArthur's career, including his signature corncob pipe and the Japanese instruments of surrender that concluded World War II. However, this is a monument not only to General MacArthur but to all those who served in wars from the Civil to the Korean War. Its Historical Center holds 2½ million documents and more than 100,000 photographs, and assists scholars, students, and researchers from around the world. The general's staff car is on display in the gift shop, where a 24-minute biography is shown. ✉ *Bank St. at City Hall Ave., MacArthur Square* ☎ *757/441–2965* ⊕ *www.macarthurmemorial.org* 🎫 *Free (donations accepted)* ⊘ *Mon.–Sat. 10–5, Sun. 11–5.*

Moses Myers House. The Federal redbrick Moses Myers House, built by its namesake between 1792 and 1796, is exceptional, and not just for its elegance. The furnishings, 70% of them original, include family portraits by Gilbert Stuart and Thomas Sully. A transplanted New Yorker as well as Norfolk's first Jewish resident, Myers made his fortune in Norfolk in shipping, then served as a diplomat and a customhouse officer. His grandson married James Madison's grandniece; his great-grandson served as mayor; and the family kept the house for five generations. ✉ *323 E. Free Mason St.* ☎ *757/333–1086* ⊕ *www.chrysler.org/houses.asp* 🎫 *Free* ⊘ *Fri.–Sun. noon–5.*

☺ ★ **Nauticus.** A popular attraction on Norfolk's redeveloped downtown waterfront, Nauticus is a maritime science museum featuring hand-on exhibits, interactive theaters, and high-definition films that celebrate the local connection to the seaport. Visitors can touch a shark, learn about weather and underwater archaeology, and explore the mysteries of the Elizabeth River. A NOAA Environmental Resource Center is an invaluable stop for education materials. Temporary exhibits in both the Changing Gallery and Forecastle Gallery keep things fresh. The Hampton Roads Naval Museum on the second floor and the battleship *Wisconsin* adjacent to the building are also popular attractions operated by the U.S. Navy, and are included in the Nauticus admission. ✉ *1 Waterside Dr.* ☎ *757/664–1000* ⊕ *www.nauticus.org* 🎫 *$11.95* ⊘ *Daily 10–5.*

☺ **Norfolk Naval Station.** On the northern edge of the city, the Norfolk Fodor's Choice ★ Naval Station is an impressive sight, home to more than 100 ships of the Atlantic Fleet. The base was built on the site of the Jamestown Exposition of 1907; many of the original buildings survive and are still in use. Several large aircraft carriers, built at nearby Newport News, call Norfolk home port and can be seen from miles away, especially at the bridge-tunnel end of the base. You may see two, each with a crew of up to 6,300, beside slightly smaller amphibious carriers that discharge marines in both helicopters and amphibious assault craft. The submarine piers, floating dry docks, supply center, and air station are all worth seeing. The *Victory Rover* and *Carrie B.* provide boat tours from downtown Norfolk to the naval station, and Hampton Roads Transit operates tour trolleys most of the year, departing from the naval-base tour office. Visitor access is by tour only, and photo ID is required to enter the base. ✉ *9079 Hampton Blvd.* ☎ *757/444–7955* ⊕ *www.navstanorva.navy.mil/tour* 🎫 *Tour $7.50 (cash only and there is no ATM on premises)* ⊘ *Tours: Jan. 1–Mar. 15, Tues.–Sun. at 1:30; Mar. 16–May 17, every ½ hr 11–2; May 18–Aug. 30, every 30 mins 10–2; Aug. 31–Nov. 1, hourly 11–2; Nov. 2–Dec. 31, Tues.–Sun. at 1:30.*

6

SHOPPING

If you forget to pack something for your cruise, you'll find stores galore within walking distance of the cruise terminal at the handsome MacArthur Center Mall.

You can meet painters, sculptors, glassworkers, jewelers, photographers, and other artists at work in their studios at the **d'Art Center** (⊠ *Selden Arcade, 208 E. Main St.* ☏ *757/625–4211* ⊕ *www.d-artcenter.org*); the art is for sale.

> ### BEACH AND BUY
>
> A nylon tote bag that folds compactly into its own pocket can be used as a beach bag during your cruise and as an extra carry-on for your return home.

An eclectic mix of chic shops, including antiques stores, bars, and eateries, lines the streets of **Ghent**, a turn-of-the-20th-century neighborhood that runs from the Elizabeth River to York Street, to West Olney Road and Llewellyn Avenue. The intersection of Colley Avenue and 21st Street is the hub.

In Ghent the upscale clothing and shoe boutiques at the **Palace Shops** (⊠ *21st St. at Llewellyn Ave.*) are a good place to search out some finery.

WHERE TO EAT

In addition to hotel restaurants, downtown Norfolk has many fine-dining restaurants as well as casual eateries in Waterside Festival Marketplace, where there's a versatile food court, and in the MacArthur Center Mall, including Johnny Rockets and Kincaid's—good food values for the price.

For price categories, see ⇨ *Dining at the beginning of this chapter.*

¢ ✕ **Doumar's.** After he introduced the world to its first ice-cream cone at
BARBECUE the 1904 World's Fair in St. Louis, Abe Doumar founded this drive-in institution in 1934. It's still operated by his family. Waitresses carry to your car the specialties of the house: barbecue, limeade, and ice cream in waffle cones made according to an original recipe. For breakfast, try the Egg-O-Doumar, a bargain at $2.70. The Food Network's "Diners, Drive-Ins, and Dives" featured Doumars twice in 2008. ⊠ *20th St. at Monticello Ave.* ☏ *757/627–4163* ⊕ *www.doumars.com* ☉ *Closed Sun.*

$ ✕ **Freemason Abbey Restaurant and Tavern.** This former church near the
AMERICAN historic business district has been drawing customers for a long time, and not without reason. It has 40-foot-high cathedral ceilings and large windows, making for an airy, and dramatic, dining experience. You can sit upstairs, in the large choir loft, or in the main part of the church downstairs. Beside the bar just inside the entrance is an informal sort of "diner" area, but with the whole menu to choose from. Regular appetizers include artichoke dip and Santa Fe shrimp. There's a dinner special every weeknight, such as lobster, prime rib, and wild game (wild boar or alligator, for example). ⊠ *209 W. Freemason St.* ☏ *757/622–3966* ⊕ *www.freemasonabbey.com.*

$ ✕ **No Frill Bar and Grill.** This expansive café is in an antique building in the
CAFÉ heart of Ghent. Beneath a tin ceiling and exposed ductwork, a central bar
★ is surrounded by several dining spaces with cream-and-mustard walls and

wooden tables. Signature items include the ribs; the Funky Chicken Sandwich, a grilled chicken breast with bacon, tomato, melted Swiss cheese, and Parmesan pepper dressing on rye; and the Spotswood Salad of baby spinach, Granny Smith apples, and blue cheese. ⊠ *806 Spotswood Ave., at Colley Ave.* ☎ *757/627–4262* ⊕ *www.nofrillgrill.com.*

WHERE TO STAY

There are hotels within walking distance of the cruise port, or if you have a car, there are numerous chain motels on the outskirts of town where you can save a little money.

For price categories, see ⇨ Lodging at the beginning of this chapter.

For expanded hotel reviews, visit Fodors.com.

$-$$ ⊞ **Marriott Courtyard Downtown.** Built in 2005, this eight-story hotel is near everything visitors want to see and where business travelers need to be. **ros:** convenient downtown location. **Cons:** the hotel has a smoke-free policy. ⊠ *520 Plume St.* ☎ *757/963–6000 or 800/321–2211* ⊕ *www.marriott.com* ⇦ *137 rooms, 3 suites* ⅄ *In-room: a/c, Wi-Fi. In-hotel: restaurant, room service, pool, laundry facilities, parking* ⅋ *No meals.*

$$ ⊞ **Norfolk Marriott Waterside.** Located in the redeveloped downtown area, this hotel is connected to the Waterside Festival Marketplace shopping area by a ramp and it's close to Town Point Park, site of many festivals. **Pros:** great central location; two blocks from the Waterside Festival Marketplace. **Cons:** parking is pricey, and a walk with luggage. ⊠ *235 E. Main St.* ☎ *757/627–4200 or 800/228–9290* ⊕ *www.marriott.com* ⇦ *396 rooms, 8 suites* ⅄ *In-room: a/c, Wi-Fi. In-hotel: restaurants, bar, pool, parking* ⅋ *No meals.*

$$ ⊞ **Sheraton Norfolk Waterside Hotel.** Modern is the word for this hotel's furnishings, from the bright, spacious lobby to the ample rooms and large suites. **Pros:** the only hotel that is truly on the waterfront; nice touches such as snacks and cold water served all day; restaurant has a terrific view of Portsmouth. **Cons:** parking—for Norfolk—is pricey; overcrowded rooms may be hard to maneuver for some. ⊠ *777 Waterside Dr.* ☎ *757/622–6664* ⊕ *www.sheraton.com* ⇦ *426 rooms, 20 suites* ⅄ *In-room: a/c. In-hotel: restaurant, bar, pool, parking* ⅋ *No meals.*

6

PORT CANAVERAL, FLORIDA

Steve Master and Paul Rubio

This once-bustling commercial fishing area is still home to a small shrimping fleet, charter boats, and party fishing boats, but its main business these days is as a cruise-ship port. Cocoa Beach itself isn't the spiffiest place around, but what *is* becoming quite clean and neat is the north end of the port, where the Carnival, Disney, and Royal Caribbean cruise lines set sail, as well as Sun Cruz and Sterling casino boats. Port Canaveral is now Florida's second-busiest cruise port. Because of Port Canaveral's proximity to Orlando theme parks (about an hour away), many cruisers combine a short cruise with a stay in the area. The port is also convenient to popular Space Coast attractions such as the Kennedy Space Center and United States Astronaut Hall of Fame in Titusville.

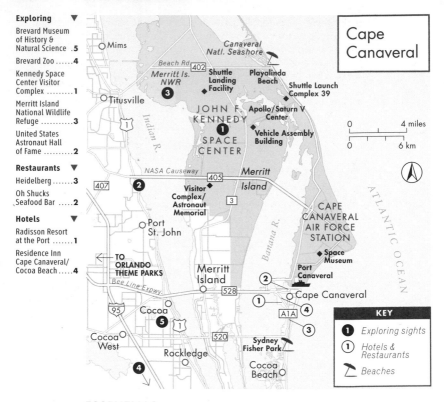

ESSENTIALS

HOURS   Most of the area's attractions are open every day.

INTERNET   Most people choose to go online at their hotel.

Visitor Information Space Coast Office of Tourism (✉ *430 Brevard Ave., Suite 150, Cocoa Village* ☎ *877/572–3224 [877/57–BEACH] or 321/433–4470* ⊕ *www.space-coast.com*).

THE CRUISE PORT

Port Canaveral sees more than 4.6 million passengers passing through its terminals annually. The port expects its business to grow, predicting for instance that it will soon host twice the number of one-day ship visits it did in 2009, for a total of 126.

The port has six cruise terminals and is home to ships from Carnival Cruise Lines, Disney Cruise Line, and Royal Caribbean International. Other cruise lines, such as Holland America and Norwegian Cruise Line, operate seasonally. The port serves as the embarkation point for three-, four-, and seven-day cruises to the Bahamas, Key West, Mexico, Jamaica, and the Virgin Islands.

In Brevard County, Port Canaveral is on State Road (S.R.) 528, also known as the Beeline Expressway, which runs straight to Orlando, which has the nearest airport. To drive to Port Canaveral from there, take the north exit out of the airport, staying to the right, to S.R. 528 (Beeline Expressway) East. Take S.R. 528 directly to Port Canaveral; it's about a 45-minute drive.

Port Contacts Canaveral Port Authority (✉ *445 Challenger Rd., Suite 301, Cape Canaveral* ☎ *321/783–7831 or 888/767–8226* ⊕ *www.portcanaveral.org*).

AIRPORT TRANSFERS

If you are flying into the area, the Orlando airport is 45 minutes away from the docks. If you have not arranged airport transfers with

your cruise line, you will need to make your own arrangements. Taxis are expensive, but many companies offer shared minivan and bus shuttles to Port Canaveral. They are all listed on the Canaveral Port Authority Web site. Some shuttles charge for the entire van, which is a good deal for groups but not for individuals or couples; some will charge a per-person rate. Expect to pay at least $38 per person round-trip, and check the Internet for coupons and special offers.

You will need to make a reservation in advance regardless of which service you use. Some cruisers who want to do some exploring before the cruise rent a car at the airport and drop it off at the port, which houses several major rental-car agencies.

Contacts AAA Cruise Line Connection (☎ *407/908–5566* ⊕ *www.aaasuperride.com*). **Busy Traveler Transport Service** (☎ *321/453–5278 or 800/496–7433* ⊕ *www.abusytraveler.com*).

PARKING

Outdoor, gated lots and a six-story parking garage are near the terminals and cost $15 per day for vehicles up to 20 feet in length and $26 per day for vehicles over 20 feet, which must be paid in advance, either in cash, traveler's checks, or by major credit card (MasterCard and Visa only).

EXPLORING THE CAPE CANAVERAL AREA

With the Kennedy Space Center just 20 minutes away, there is plenty to do in and around Cape Canaveral, though many folks opt to travel the extra hour into Orlando to visit the popular theme parks.

☼ **Brevard Museum of History & Natural Science.** This is the place to come to see what the lay of the local land looked like in other eras. Hands-on activities draw children, who especially migrate toward the Imagination Center, where they can act out history or reenact a space shuttle flight. Not to be missed is the Windover Archaeological Exhibit of 7,000-year-old artifacts indigenous to the region. In 1984, a shallow pond revealed the burial ground of more than 200 American Indians who lived in the area about 7,000 years ago. Preserved in the muck were bones, and, to the archaeologists' surprise, the brains of these ancient people. There's also a butterfly garden and a nature center with 22 acres of trails encompassing three distinct ecosystems—sand pine hills, lake lands, and marshlands. ✉ *2201 Michigan Ave., Cocoa* ☎ *321/632–1830* ⊕ *www.brevardmuseum.org* ⌨ *$6* ⊙ *Thurs.–Sat. 10–3.*

ⓒ **Brevard Zoo.** On a stroll along the shaded boardwalks you get a close-up
Fodor'sChoice look at rhinos, giraffes, cheetahs, alligators, crocodiles, giant anteaters,
★ marmosets, jaguars, eagles, river otters, kangaroos, exotic birds, and kookaburras. Alligator, crocodile, and river-otter feedings are held on alternate afternoons—although the alligators do not dine on the otters. Stop by Paws-On, an interactive learning playground with a petting zone, wildlife detective training academy, and the Indian River Play Lagoon. Hand-feed a giraffe in Expedition Africa or a lorikeet in the Australian Free Flight Aviary, and step up to the Wetlands Outpost, an elevated pavilion that's a gateway to 22 acres of wetlands through which you can paddle kayaks and keep an eye open for the 4,000 species of wildlife that live in these waters and woods. ✉ *8225 N. Wickham Rd., Melbourne* ☎ *321/254–9453* ⊕ *www.brevardzoo.org* ⌨ *$13.75 for general admission; $18.75 for admission, a train ride, and food for the lorikeets* ⊙ *Daily 9:30–5, last admission at 4:15.*

Kennedy Space Center Visitor Complex. This must-see attraction, just southeast of Titusville, is one of Central Florida's most popular sights. Located on a 140,000-acre island 45 minutes outside Orlando, Kennedy Space Center is NASA's launch headquarters. The Visitor Complex gives you a unique opportunity to learn about—and experience—the past, present, and future of America's space program.

ⓒ Interactive programs make for the best experiences here, but if you want
Fodor'sChoice a low-key overview of the facility (and if the weather is foul) take the
★ bus tour, included with admission. Buses depart every 15 minutes, and you can get on and off any bus whenever you like. Stops include the **Launch Complex 39 Observation Gantry,** which has an unparalleled view of the launch pads and the **Apollo/Saturn V Center.** In the Firing Room Theatre, the launch of America's first lunar mission, 1968's *Apollo VIII,* is re-created with a ground-shaking, window-rattling liftoff.

The Saturn V Center also features one of the three remaining Saturn V moon rockets. Other exhibits include **Early Space Exploration,** which highlights the rudimentary yet influential *Mercury* and *Gemini* space programs; **Robot Scouts,** a walk-through exhibit of unmanned planetary probes; and **Exploration Space: Explorers Wanted,** which immerses visitors in exploration beyond Earth. Don't miss the outdoor **Rocket Garden,** with walkways winding beside spare rockets—from early Atlas spacecraft to a *Saturn IB.* The Children's Playdome enables kids to play among the next generation of spacecraft, climb a moon-rock wall, and crawl through rocket tunnels. Astronaut Encounter Theater has two daily programs where retired NASA astronauts share their adventures in space travel and show a short film. The most moving exhibit is the **Astronaut Memorial.** The 70,400-pound black-granite tribute to astronauts who lost their lives in the name of space exploration stands 42½ feet high by 50 feet wide.

More befitting Walt Disney World or Universal Studios (complete with the health warnings), the **Shuttle Launch Experience** is the center's most spectacular attraction. Designed by a team of astronauts, NASA experts, and renowned attraction engineers, the 44,000-square-foot structure uses a sophisticated motion-based platform, special-effects seats, and high-fidelity visual and audio components to simulate the sensations experienced in an actual space-shuttle launch, including MaxQ, Solid Rocker Booster separation, main engine cutoff, and External Tank separation. The journey culminates with a breathtaking view of Earth from space.

The only back-to-back twin **IMAX theater** in the world is in the complex, too. The dream of space flight comes to life on a movie screen five stories tall with dramatic footage shot by NASA astronauts during missions. Realistic 3-D special effects will make you feel like you're in space with them. Films alternate throughout the year. Call for specific shows and times.

Add-on activities include **Lunch with an Astronaut** ($63.99, includes general admission), where astronauts talk about their experiences and engage in a good-natured Q&A; the typical line of questioning from kids: "How do you eat/sleep/relieve yourself in space?" Discover KSC: Today and Tomorrow Tours ($62, general admission included) brings you to sites seldom accessible to the public, such as the Vehicle Assembly Building, the shuttle landing strip, and the 6-million-pound crawler that transports the shuttle to its launch pads. Or see how far the space program has come with the **Cape Canaveral: Then and Now** tour ($62, includes general admission), which visits America's first launch sites from the 1960s and the 21st century's active unmanned-rocket program. ⊠ *Rte. 405, Kennedy Space Center, Titusville* ☎ *877/313-02610* ⊕ *www.kennedyspacecenter.com* ⊠ *General admission includes bus tour, IMAX movies, Visitor Complex shows and exhibits, and the Astronaut Hall of Fame, $41* ☉ *Space Center opens daily at 9; closing times vary according to season (call for details), last regular tour 3 hrs before closing; closed certain launch dates.*

Fodor's Choice **Merritt Island National Wildlife Refuge.** Owned by the National Aeronau-
★ tics and Space Administration (NASA), this 140,000-acre refuge, which adjoins the Canaveral National Seashore, acts as a buffer around Kennedy Space Center while protecting 1,000 species of plants and 500 species of wildlife, including 15 considered federally threatened or endangered. It's an immense area dotted by brackish estuaries and marshes and patches of land consisting of coastal dunes, scrub oaks, pine forests and flatwoods, and palm and oak hammocks. You can borrow field guides and binoculars at the visitor center (5 mi east of U.S. 1 in Titusville on State Road 402) to track down falcons, ospreys, eagles, turkeys, doves, cuckoos, owls, and woodpeckers, as well as loggerhead turtles, alligators, and otters. A 20-minute video about refuge wildlife and accessibility—only 10,000 acres are developed—can help orient you.

You might take a self-guided tour along the 7-mi Black Point Wildlife Drive. The dirt road takes you where there are no traces of encroaching malls or mankind and it's easy to visualize the tribes who made this their home 7,000 years ago. On the Oak Hammock Foot Trail you can see wintering migratory waterfowl and learn about the plants of a hammock community.

If you exit the north end of the refuge, look for the Manatee Observation Area just north of the Haulover Canal (maps are at the visitor center). They usually show up in spring and fall. There are also fishing camps, fishing boat ramps, and six hiking trails scattered throughout the area. Most of the refuge is closed 24 hours prior to a shuttle launch. ⊠ *Rte. 402, across Titusville Causeway, Titusville* ☎ *321/861–0667, 321/861–0669 visitor center* ⊕ *www.fws.gov/merrittisland* ⊠ *Free* ☉ *Daily sunrise–sundown; visitor center weekdays 8–4:30, Sat. 9–5 and Sun. 9–5 (Nov.–Mar.).*

United States Astronaut Hall of Fame. The original *Mercury 7* team and the later *Gemini, Apollo, Skylab,* and shuttle astronauts contributed to make the hall of fame the world's premium archive of astronauts' personal stories. Authentic memorabilia and equipment from their collections tell the story of human space exploration. You'll watch videotapes of historic moments in the space program and see one-of-a-kind items like Wally Schirra's relatively archaic *Sigma 7* Mercury space capsule, Gus Grissom's space suit (colored silver only because NASA thought silver looked more "spacey"), and a flag that made it to the moon. The exhibit **First on the Moon** focuses on crew selection for *Apollo 11* and the Soviet Union's role in the space race. Definitely don't miss Simulation Station, a hands-on discovery center with interactive exhibits that help you learn about space travel. One of the more challenging activities is a space-shuttle simulator that lets you try your hand at landing the craft—and afterward replays a side view of your rolling and pitching descent. ⊠ *6225 Vectorspace Blvd. Titusville* ☎ *877/313–2610* ⊕ *www. kennedyspacecenter.com* ⊠ *$20* ☉ *Opens daily at 9, closing times vary according to season (call for details).*

Astronaut Training Experience (ATX). If you want to live the life of an astronaut, consider enrolling in **ATX ($145).** Held at the United States Astronaut Hall of Fame, it immerses you in an exciting combination of hands-on training and preparation for the rigors of space flight. Veteran NASA astronauts helped design the program, and you'll hear first-hand from them as you progress through an exciting day of mission simulation and exploration at the busiest launch facility on Earth. The cost includes spaceflight simulators, full-scale space shuttle mission simulation, meet and greet with a NASA astronaut and ATX gear. *Age restrictions apply. Space is limited (no pun intended), so call well in advance.*

ORLANDO THEME PARKS

☉ **SeaWorld Orlando.** In the world's largest marine adventure park, every attraction is devoted to demonstrating the ways that humans can protect the mammals, birds, fish, and reptiles that live in the ocean and its tributaries. The presentations are gentle reminders of our responsibility to safeguard the environment, and you'll find that SeaWorld's use of humor plays a major role in this education. The park is small enough that, armed with a map that lists show times, you can plan a chronological approach that flows easily from one attraction to the next. Near the intersection of I–4 and the Beeline Expressway; take I–4 to Exit 71 or 72 and follow signs. ✉ *7007 Sea Harbor Dr., International Drive Area, Orlando* ☎ *888/800–5447* ⊕ *www.seaworld.com* ✏ *$74.95 for a 1-day ticket* ☉ *Daily 9–6 or 7, until as late as 10 summer and holidays; educational programs daily, some beginning as early as 6:30 am.*

☾ **Universal Orlando.** The resort consists of **Universal Studios** (the original movie theme park), **Islands of Adventure** (the second theme park), and **CityWalk** (the dining-shopping-nightclub complex). Although it's bordered by residential neighborhoods and thickly trafficked International Drive, Universal Orlando is surprisingly expansive yet intimate and accessible, with two massive parking complexes, easy walks to all attractions, and a motor launch that cruises to the hotels. Universal Orlando emphasizes "two parks, two days, one great adventure," but you may find the presentation, creativity, and cutting-edge technology bring you back for more. ✉ *1000 Universal Studios Plaza, Orlando* ☎ *407/363–8000* ⊕ *www.universalorlando.com* ✏ *1-day, 1-park ticket $79.99* ☉ *Usually daily 9–7, but hrs vary seasonally; CityWalk restaurants and bars have individual open hrs.*

☾ **Walt Disney World.** Walt Disney World is a huge complex of theme parks and attractions, each of which is worth a visit. Parks include the **Magic Kingdom,** a family favorite and the original here; **Epcot,** Disney's international, educational park; **Disney–MGM Studios,** a movie-oriented theme park; and **Disney's Animal Kingdom,** which is much more than a zoo. Beyond these, there are water parks, elaborate minigolf courses, a sports center, resorts, restaurants, and nightlife. If you have only one day, you'll have to concentrate on a single park; Disney–MGM Studios or Animal Kingdom are easiest to do in a day, but arrive early and expect to stay until park closing, which might be as early as 5 pm for Animal Kingdom or as late as 11 pm during busy seasons at the Magic Kingdom. The most direct route to the Disney Parks from Port Canaveral is S.R. 528 (the Beeline Expressway) to I–4; when you get through Orlando, follow the signs to Disney and expect traffic. ✉ *Lake Buena Vista* ☎ *407/824–4321* ⊕ *disneyworld.disney.go.com* ✏ *1-day, 1-park pass $79* ☉ *Most parks open by 9 am; closing hrs vary, but usually 5 pm for Animal Kingdom and 6–11 pm for other parks, depending on season.*

BEACHES

Alan Shepard Park. Named for the former astronaut, this 5-acre oceanfront park, aptly enough, provides excellent views of shuttle launches. Facilities include 10 picnic pavilions, shower and restroom facilities, and more than 300 parking spaces. Those spaces are in high-demand on launch days, but the park's a nice break any other day, too. Parking is $7 per day, $10 per day on weekends and holidays from early March through Labor Day. Shops and restaurants are within walking distance. ✉ *East end of Rte. 250, Cocoa Beach* ☎ *321/868–3274.*

6

Playalinda Beach. The southern access for the Canaveral National Seashore, remote Playalinda Beach has pristine sands and is the longest stretch of undeveloped coast on Florida's Atlantic seaboard. Its isolation explains why there are limited services (no phones, food service, drinking water, or lifeguards from May 30 to September 1) and why a remote strand of the beach is popular with nude sunbathers. Aside from them, hundreds of giant sea turtles come ashore here from May through August to lay their eggs. Eight parking lots anchor the beach at 1-mi intervals. To get here, take Interstate 95 Exit 220 east and follow the signs. Take bug repellent in case of horseflies. ⊠ *Rte. 402/Beach Rd., New Smyrna Beach* ☎ *321/867–4077* ⊕ *www.nps.gov/cana* ⊠ *$3 per person (admission to National Seashore)* ⊙ *Nov.–Mar., daily 6–6; Apr.–Oct., daily 6–8.*

Sidney Fischer Park. The 10-acre oceanfront has showers, playgrounds, changing areas, picnic areas with grills, snack shops, and plenty of well-maintained, inexpensive surfside parking lots. Beach vendors carry necessities for sunning and swimming. The parking fee is $5 for cars and RVs. ⊠ *2100 block of Rte. A1A, Cocoa Beach* ☎ *321/868–3252.*

SHOPPING

Cocoa Beach Surf Company. The world's largest surf complex has three floors of boards, apparel, sunglasses, and anything else a surfer, wannabe-surfer, or souvenir-seeker could need. Also on-site are a 5,600-gallon fish and shark tank, the Shark Pit Bar & Grill, and the East Coast Surfing Hall of Fame and Museum. Here you can also rent surfboards, bodyboards, and wet suits, as well as umbrellas, chairs, and bikes. And staffers teach grommets (dudes) and gidgets (chicks)—from kids to seniors—how to surf. There are group, semi-private, and private lessons available in one-, two- and three-hour sessions. Prices range from $40 (for a one-hour group lesson) to $120 (three-hour private). All gear is provided. ⊠ *4001 N. Atlantic Ave., Cocoa Beach* ☎ *321/799–9930.*

Fodor's Choice **Ron Jon Surf Shop.** It's impossible to miss Ron Jon: it takes up nearly
★ two blocks along Route A1A and has a giant surfboard and an art deco facade painted orange, blue, yellow, and turquoise. What started in 1963 as a small T-shirt and bathing-suit shop has evolved into a 52,000-square-foot superstore that's open every day 'round the clock. The shop rents water-sports gear as well as chairs and umbrellas, and it sells every kind of beachwear, surf wax, plus the requisite T-shirts and flip-flops. ■ TIP➜ For up-to-the-minute surfing conditions, call the store and press 2 and then 7 for the Ron Jon Surf and Weather Report. ⊠ *4151 N. Atlantic Ave., Rte. A1A* ☎ *321/799–8888* ⊕ *www.ronjonsurfshop.com.*

WHERE TO EAT

The Cove at Port Canaveral has several restaurants if you are looking for a place to eat right at the port.

For price categories, see ⇨ *Dining at the beginning of this chapter.*

$$$ ✕ **Heidelberg.** The cuisine here is definitely German, from the sauerbra-
GERMAN   ten served with potato dumplings and red cabbage to the beef Stroganoff

and spaetzle to the classically prepared Wiener schnitzel. All the
soups and desserts are homemade;
try the Viennese-style apple strudel
and the rum-zapped almond-cream
tortes. Elegant interior touches
include crisp linens and fresh flowers. There's live music Friday and
Saturday evenings. You can also
dine inside the jazz club, Heidi's,
next door. ✉ *7 N. Orlando Ave., opposite City Hall* ☎ *321/783–6806*
⊕ *www.heidisjazzclub.com* ☉ *Closed Mon. No lunch Sun.*

WRITE EASY
Preaddress a page of stick-on labels before you leave home; use them for postcards to the folks back home and you will not have to carry along a bulky address book.

$ **✗Oh Shucks Seafood Bar.** At the only open-air seafood bar on the
SEAFOOD beach, at the entrance of the Cocoa Beach Pier, the main item is oysters, served on the half shell. You can also grab a burger here, crab
legs by the pound, or Oh Shucks's most popular item, coconut fried
shrimp. Some diners complain that the prices don't jibe with the ult-
racasual atmosphere (e.g., plastic chairs), but they're also paying for
the "ex-Pier-ience." There's live entertainment on Wednesday, Friday,
Saturday, and Sunday. ✉ *401 Meade Ave., Cocoa Beach Pier, Cocoa
Beach* ☎ *321/783–7549.*

6

WHERE TO STAY

Many local hotels offer cruise packages that include one night's lodging, parking for the duration of your cruise, and transportation to the
cruise port.

For price categories, see ⇨ *Lodging at the beginning of this chapter.*

For expanded hotel reviews, visit Fodors.com.

$$$ ⊡ **Radisson Resort at the Port.** For cruise-ship passengers who can't wait
RESORT to get under way, this splashy resort, done up in pink and turquoise,
already feels like the Caribbean. **Pros:** cruise-ship convenience; pool
area; free shuttle. **Cons:** rooms around the pool can be noisy; loud
air-conditioning in some rooms; no complimentary breakfast. ✉ *8701
Astronaut Blvd., Cape Canaveral* ☎ *321/784–0000 or 888/201–1718*
⊕ *www.radisson.com/capecanaveralfl* ⇨ *284 rooms, 72 suites* ♿ *In-
room: kitchen (some), Wi-Fi. In-hotel: restaurant, bar, tennis court,
pool, gym, laundry facilities* ⭗ *No meals.*

$$$ ⊡ **Residence Inn Cape Canaveral/Cocoa Beach.** Billing itself as the closest
HOTEL all-suites hotel to the Kennedy Space Center, this four-story Residence
Inn, painted cheery yellow, is also convenient to other area attractions
such as Port Canaveral, the Cocoa Beach Pier, the Brevard Zoo, and
Cocoa Village, and is only an hour from the Magic Kingdom. **Pros:**
helpful staff; free breakfast buffet; pet-friendly. **Cons:** less than picturesque views; street noise in some rooms. ✉ *8959 Astronaut Blvd., Cape
Canaveral* ☎ *321/323–1100 or 800/331–3131* ⊕ *www.marriott.com*
⇨ *150 suites* ♿ *In-room: kitchen, Wi-Fi. In-hotel: pool, gym, laundry
facilities, parking, some pets allowed* ⭗ *Breakfast.*

SAN JUAN, PUERTO RICO

Heather
Rodino

In addition to being a major port of call, San Juan is also a common port of embarkation for cruises on Southern Caribbean itineraries.

For information on dining, shopping, nightlife, and sightseeing see ⇨ *San Juan, Puerto Rico in Chapter 7.*

> ## EXTRA BATTERIES
>
> Even if you don't think you'll need them, bring along extra camera batteries and change them before you think the old ones are dead.

THE CRUISE PORT

Most cruise ships dock within a couple of blocks of Old San Juan. The Paseo de la Princesa, a tree-lined promenade beneath the city wall, is a nice place for a stroll—you can admire the local crafts and stop at the refreshment kiosks. A tourist information center is close to the cruise terminal area. Major sights in Old San Juan are mere blocks from the piers, but be aware that the streets are narrow and steeply inclined in places. Even if you have only a few hours before your cruise, you'll have time to do a little sightseeing. A few ships dock across the bay; if yours does, you'll need to take a taxi everywhere.

AIRPORT TRANSFERS

The ride from the Luis Muñoz Marín International Airport, east of downtown San Juan, to the docks in Old San Juan takes about 20 minutes, depending on traffic. The white "Taxi Turistico" cabs, marked by a logo on the door, have a fixed rate of $19 to the cruise-ship piers; there is a $1 charge for each piece of luggage. Other taxi companies charge by the mile, which can cost a little more. Be sure the driver starts the meter, or agree on a fare beforehand.

Visitor Information Puerto Rico Tourism Company (⊠ *La Princesa Bldg., 2 Paseo de la Princesa, Old San Juan* ☎ *787/721–2400, 787/722–1709, or 800/981–7575* ⊕ *www.seepuertorico.com*).

WHERE TO STAY

If you are planning to spend one night in San Juan before your cruise departs, you'll probably find it easier to stay in Old San Juan, where the cruise-ship terminals are. But if you want to spend a few extra days in the city, there are other possibilities near good beaches a bit farther out. We make some nightlife suggestions in the San Juan port of call section (*see* ⇨ *San Juan in Chapter 4*).

For price categories, see ⇨ *Lodging at the beginning of this chapter.*

For expanded hotel reviews, visit Fodors.com.

$$–$$$

HOTEL

★

🖼 **Gallery Inn.** Nothing like this hotel exists anywhere else in San Juan—or Puerto Rico, for that matter. **Pros:** one-of-a-kind lodging; ocean views; wonderful classical music concerts. **Cons:** no restaurant; an uphill walk from rest of Old San Juan; sometimes raucous pet macaws and cockatoos. ⊠ *204–206 Calle Norzagaray, Old San Juan* ☎ *787/722–*

1808 ⊕ *www.thegalleryinn.com* ⟳ *13 rooms, 10 suites* ⚲ *In-room: no a/c (some), no TV. In-hotel: restaurant* ⦿ *Breakfast.*

$$$$
HOTEL
Fodor's Choice
★

🏨 **Hotel El Convento.** The accommodations here beautifully combine the old and the new. **Pros:** lovely building; atmosphere to spare; plenty of nearby dining options. **Cons:** near some noisy bars. ✉ *100 Calle Cristo, Old San Juan* ⌂ *Box 1048, 00902* ☎ *787/723–9020 or 800/468–2779* ⊕ *www.elconvento.com* ⟳ *63 rooms, 5 suites* ⚲ *In-room: Internet, Wi-Fi. In-hotel: restaurants, bars, pool, gym, parking* ⦿ *No meals.*

$$$$
HOTEL

🏨 **Sheraton Old San Juan Hotel.** This hotel's triangular shape subtly echoes the cruise ships docked nearby. Rooms facing the water have dazzling views of these behemoths as they sail in and out of the harbor. **Pros:** Harbor views; near many dining options; good array of room types. **Cons:** Motel feel to guest rooms; noise from casino overwhelms lobby and restaurants; extra charges for everything from bottled water to Internet access. ✉ *100 Calle Brumbaugh, Old San Juan* ☎ *787/721–5100 or 866/376–7577* ⊕ *www.sheratonoldsanjuan.com* ⟳ *200 rooms, 40 suites* ⚲ *In-room: Internet. In-hotel: restaurant, room service, bar, pool, gym, parking* ⦿ *No meals.*

TAMPA, FLORIDA

6

Kate Bradshaw, Connie Sharpe, Paul Rubio

Although glitzy Miami seems to hold the trendiness trump card and Orlando is the place your kids want to visit annually until they hit middle school, the Tampa Bay area has that elusive quality that many attribute to the "real Florida." The state's second-largest metro area is less fast-lane than its biggest (Miami), or even Orlando, but its strengths are just as varied, from broad cultural diversity to a sun-worshipping beach culture. Florida's third-busiest airport, a vibrant business community, world-class beaches, and superior hotels and resorts—many of them historic—make this an excellent place to spend a week or a lifetime. Several ships are based here year-round and seasonally, most doing Western Caribbean itineraries.

ESSENTIALS

HOURS Some museums are closed on Monday.

INTERNET Most people choose to access the Internet through their hotels. Starbucks has free Wi-Fi.

Visitor Information Tampa Bay & Company (✉ *401 E. Jackson St., Suite 2100, Tampa* ☎ *800/448-2672 or 813/223–1111* ⊕ *www.visittampabay.com*). **Ybor City Chamber Visitor Bureau** (✉ *1600 E. 8th Ave., Suite B104, Tampa* ☎ *813/241–8838* ⊕ *www.ybor.org*).

THE CRUISE PORT

Tampa is the largest shipping port in the state of Florida, and it's becoming ever more important to the cruise industry, now with three passenger terminals. In Tampa's downtown area, the port is linked to nearby Ybor City and the rest of the Tampa Bay Area by the TECO streetcar line.

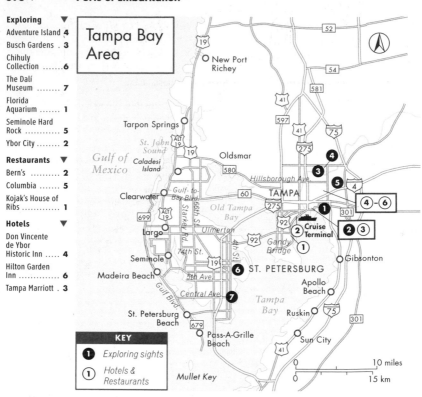

To reach the port by car, take I–4 West to Exit 1 (Ybor City), and go south on 21st Street. To get to terminals 2 and 6, turn right on Adamo Drive (Highway 60), then left on Channelside Drive.

Contacts Tampa Port Authority (✉ *1101 Channelside Dr.* ☎ *813/905–7678 or 800/741–2297* ⊕ *www.tampaport.com*).

AIRPORT TRANSFERS

Both Bay Shuttle and Super Shuttle provide shared van service to and from the airport and the cruise terminal. Expect to pay about $13 to $14 per person.

Information Bay Shuttle (☎ *813/259–9998* ⊕ *www.tampabayshuttle.com*).
Super Shuttle (☎ *727/572–1111 or 800/282–6817* ⊕ *www.supershuttle.com*).

PARKING

Parking is available at the port directly across from the terminals. For terminal 2 (Carnival Cruise Lines)), parking is in a garage across the street. For terminal 3, (Royal Caribbean and Holland America), parking is also in a garage across the street. For Terminal 6, parking is outdoors in a guarded, enclosed lot. The cost is $14 a day, payable by credit card (MasterCard or Visa) or in cash.

EXPLORING THE TAMPA BAY AREA

Florida's west-coast crown jewel as well as its business and commercial hub, Tampa has high-rises and heavy traffic. Amid the bustle is the region's greatest concentration of restaurants, nightlife, stores, and cultural events.

Ⓒ **Adventure Island.** From spring until fall, rides named Splash Attack, Gulf Scream, and Key West Rapids promise heat relief at this Busch Gardens–owned water park. Tampa's most popular "wet" park features waterslides and artificial wave pools in a 30-acre package. One of the attraction's headliners, Riptide, challenges you to race three other riders on a sliding mat through twisting tubes and hairpin turns. Planners of this park also took the younger kids into account, with offerings such as Fabian's Funport, which has a scaled-down pool and interactive water gym. Along with a volleyball complex and a rambling river, there are cafés, snack bars, picnic and sunbathing areas, changing rooms, and, the newest addition, private cabanas. ✉ *4500 Bougainvillea Ave., less than 1 mi north of Busch Gardens, Central Tampa* ☎ *813/987–5660 or 888/800–5447* ⊕ *www.adventureisland. com* 🖼 *$44.95; parking $12* ☉ *Mid-Mar.–late Oct., daily 10–5.*

Ⓒ **Busch Gardens.** The Jungala exhibit at Busch Gardens (added in 2009)
Fodor'sChoice brings Bengal tigers to center stage and puts them at eye level—allowing
★ you to view them from underground caves and underwater windows. The big cats are just one of the reasons the theme park attracts some 4½ million visitors each year. This is a world-class zoo, with more than 2,000 animals, and a live entertainment venue that provides a full day (or more) of fun for the whole family. If you want to beat the crowds, start in the back of the park and work your way around clockwise.

The 335-acre adventure park's habitats offer views of some of the world's most endangered and exotic animals. For the best animal sightings, go to their habitats early, when it's cooler. You can experience up-close animal encounters on the **Serengeti Plain**, a 65-acre free-roaming habitat, home to reticulated giraffes, Grevy's zebras, white rhinos, bongos, impalas, and more. **Myombe Reserve** allows you to view lowland gorillas and chimpanzees in a lush, tropical-rain-forest environment. Down Under–themed Walkabout Way offers those ages five and up an opportunity to hand-feed kangaroos and wallabies (a cup of vittles is $5). ✉ *3000 E. Busch Blvd., 8 mi northeast of downtown Tampa and 2 mi east of I–275 Exit 50, Central Tampa* ☎ *813/987–5000 or*

TAMPA BEST BETS

■ **Busch Gardens.** The area's best theme park is a good family destination.

■ **The Dalí Museum.** One of the finest and most interesting museums in the United States.

■ **Florida Aquarium.** The aquarium is next to the cruise port, so you can just walk, making it a good option even if you have a couple of hours to kill before boarding (they'll even store your luggage if you want to visit after disembarking).

■ **Ybor City.** For nightlife and restaurants, this historic district is Tampa's hot spot.

6

888/800–5447 ⊕ *www.buschgardens.com* 🖃 *$77.99; children $69.99; parking $13* ⊗ *Daily 10–6.*

Fodor's Choice

★

Chihuly Collection. For the uninitiated, those passing this collection's polished exterior may think it's a gallery like any other. Yet what's contained inside is an experience akin to *Alice in Wonderland*. This, the only permanent collection of renowned glass sculptor Dale Chihuly's work, has such impossibly vibrant, larger-than-life pieces as "Float Boat" and "Fire and Ice." You can tour the museum independently or with one of its volunteer docents (no added cost; tours given hourly on an as-needed basis). Each display is lit just so, which adds to the drama of Chihuly's designs. After passing under a hallway with a semi-transparent ceiling through which a brilliant array of smaller glass pieces shine, you'll wind up at the breathtaking finale, "Mille Fiore" ("Million Flowers"), a spectacular glass montage mimicking a wildflower patch, critters and all. Check out the gift shop at the end if you'd like to take some of the magic home with you. A combination ticket gets you a glimpse into the glass-blowing studio. ⊠ *400 Beach Dr., Downtown* ☎ *727/896–4527* ⊕ *www.chihulycollection.com* 🖃 *$15* ⊗ *Mon.– Wed., Fri., and Sat. 10–6, Thurs. 10–8, Sun. noon–6.*

Fodor's Choice

★

The Dalí Museum. Inside and out, the waterfront Dalí Museum, which opened on 1/11/11 (Dalí is said to have been into numerology), is almost as remarkable as the Spanish surrealist's work. The state-of-the-art building has a surreal geodesiclike glass structure called the Dalí Enigma as well as an outdoor labyrinth and a DNA-inspired spiral staircase leading up to the collection. All this, before you've even seen the collection, which is one of the most comprehensive of its kind—courtesy of Ohio magnate A. Reynolds Morse, a friend of Dalí's.

Here, you can scope out his early impressionistic works and see how the painter evolved into the visionary he's now seen to be. The mind-expanding paintings in this downtown headliner include *Eggs on a Plate Without a Plate*, *The Hallucinogenic Toreador*, and more than 90 other oils. You'll also discover more than 2,000 additional works including watercolors, drawings, sculptures, photographs, and objets d'art. Free hour-long tours are led by well-informed docents. ⊠ *1 Dali Blvd.* ☎ *727/823–3767 or 800/442–3254* ⊕ *www.thedali.org* 🖃 *$21* ⊗ *Mon.–Wed., Fri., and Sat. 10–5:30, Thurs. 10–8, Sun. noon–5:30.*

Ⓒ

★

Florida Aquarium. Eels, sharks, and stingrays may be the headliners, but this is much more than a giant fishbowl. It is a dazzling architectural landmark with an 83-foot-high multitier glass dome and 200,000 square feet of air-conditioned exhibit space. It has more than 10,000 aquatic plants, and animals representing species native to Florida and the rest of the world. The major exhibit areas reflect the diversity of Florida's natural habitats—Wetlands, Bays and Beaches, and Coral Reef. Creature-specific exhibits are the No Bone Zone (lovable invertebrates) and Sea Hunt, with predators ranging from sharks to exotic lionfish. The aquarium's most impressive single exhibit is the Coral Reef Gallery, in a 500,000-gallon tank ringed with viewing windows, including an awesome 43-foot-wide panoramic opening. Part of the tank is a walkable tunnel, almost giving the illusion of venturing into underwater depths. There you see a thicket of elkhorn coral teeming with tropical fish. A dark cave reveals sea life you would normally see only on night dives. ⊠ *701 Channelside Dr., Downtown, Tampa* ☎ *813/273–4000* ⊕ *www.flaquarium.org* ⌑ *Aquarium $19.95, Ecotour $21.95; Aquarium/Ecotour combo $35.95; parking $6* ☉ *Daily 9:30–5.*

Seminole Hard Rock Hotel & Casino. In addition to playing one of the hundreds of Vegas-style slot machines, gamers can also get their kicks at the casino's poker and blackjack tables. The lounge serves drinks 24 hours a day. Floyd's restaurant has dinner and nightlife. There is a heavy smell of cigarette smoke here, as with most casinos. ⊠ *5223 N. Orient Rd., off I–4 at N. Orient Rd. Exit* ☎ *813/627–7625 or 866/502–7529* ⊕ *www.seminolehardrock.com* ⌑ *Free* ☉ *Daily 24 hrs.*

Fodor's Choice ★ **Ybor City.** Tampa's lively Latin quarter is one of only a few National Historic Landmark districts in Florida. It has antique-brick streets and wrought-iron balconies. Cubans brought their cigar-making industry to Ybor (pronounced *ee*-bore) City in 1886, and the smell of cigars— hand-rolled by Cuban immigrants—still wafts through the heart of this east Tampa area, along with the strong aroma of roasting coffee. These days the neighborhood is one of Tampa's hot spots, if at times a rowdy one, as empty cigar factories and historic social clubs have been transformed into trendy boutiques, art galleries, restaurants, and nightclubs.

Centennial Park. You can step back into the past at Centennial Park, which re-creates a period streetscape and hosts the Fresh Market every Saturday. ⊠ *8th Ave. and 19th St.*

Ybor City Museum State Park. This park provides a look at the history of the cigar industry. Admission includes a tour of La Casita, one of the shotgun houses occupied by cigar workers and their families in the late 1890s. ⊠ *1818 E. 9th Ave., between Nuccio Pkwy. and 22nd St., from 7th to 9th Ave., Tampa* ☎ *813/247–6323* ⊕ *www.ybormuseum. org* ⌑ *$4, walking tours $6* ☉ *Daily 9–5; walking tours Sat. 10:30.*

BEACHES

☺ **Fort De Soto Park.** Spread over five small islands, 1,136-acre Fort De Soto Park lies at the mouth of Tampa Bay. It has 7 mi of beaches, two fishing piers, a 4-mi hiking–skating trail, picnic-and-camping grounds, and a historic fort that kids of any age can explore. The fort for which it's named was built on the southern end of Mullet Key to protect sealanes in the gulf during the Spanish-American War. Roam the fort or wander the beaches of any of the islands within the park. ⊠ *3500 Pinellas Bayway St., Tierra Verde* ☎ *727/582–2267* ⌑ *Free* ☉ *Beaches, daily sunrise–sunset; fishing and boat ramp, 24 hrs.*

Pass-A-Grille Beach. At the southern tip of St. Pete Beach (past the Don), is the epitome of Old Florida. One of the most popular beaches in the area, it skirts the west end of charming, historic Pass-A-Grille, a neighborhood that draws tourists and locals alike with its stylish yet low-key mom-and-pop motels and restaurants. Best for: families, kiteboarding, sunsets. Amenities: snack bar, showers, restrooms, parking meters. ⊠ *Off Gulf Blvd. (Rte. 699), St. Pete Beach.*

6

SHOPPING

Centro Ybor. Ybor City's destination within a destination is this dining-and-entertainment palace. It has shops, trendy bars and restaurants, and a 20-screen movie theater. ⊠ *1600 E. 8th Ave., Ybor City.*

Channelside. Downtown's Channelside has movie theaters, shops, restaurants, and clubs. ⊠ *615 Channelside Dr., Downtown.*

International Plaza. If you want to grab something at Neiman Marcus or Nordstrom this is the place. You'll also find Betsey Johnson, J.Crew, L'Occitane, Louis Vuitton, Tiffany & Co., and many other upscale shops. ⊠ *2223 N. West Shore Blvd., Airport Area.*

Old Hyde Park Village. It's a typical upscale shopping district in a quiet, shaded neighborhood near the water. Williams-Sonoma and Brooks Brothers are mixed in with bistros and sidewalk cafés. ⊠ *Swann Ave. near Bayshore Blvd., Hyde Park.*

NIGHTLIFE

Although there are more boarded storefronts than in the past, the biggest concentration of nightclubs, as well as the widest variety, is found along 7th Avenue in Ybor City. It becomes a little like Bourbon Street in New Orleans on weekend evenings. **Centro Cantina.** There are lots of draws here: a balcony overlooking the crowds on Seventh Avenue, live music Thursday through Sunday nights, a large selection of margaritas, and more than 30 brands of tequila. Food is served until 2 am. ⊠ *1600 E. 8th Ave., Ybor City* ☎ *813/241–8588.*

Hub. Considered something of a dive—but a lovable one—by a loyal and young local following that ranges from esteemed jurists to nose-ring-wearing night owls, the Hub is known for strong drinks and a jukebox that goes well beyond the usual. ⊠ *719 N. Franklin St., Downtown* ☎ *813/229–1553.*

WHERE TO EAT

For price categories, see ⇨ Dining at the beginning of this chapter.

$$$$ ✕ **Bern's Steak House.** With the air of an exclusive club, this is one of
STEAK Florida's finest steak houses. Rich mahogany paneling and ornate chan-
Fodor's Choice deliers define the legendary Bern's, where the chef ages his own beef,
★ grows his own organic vegetables, and roasts his own coffee. There's also a Cave Du Fromage, housing a discriminating selection of artisanal cheeses from around the world. Cuts of topmost beef are sold by weight and thickness. There's a 60-ounce strip steak that's big enough to feed your pride (of lions), but for most appetites the veal loin chop or 8-ounce chateaubriand is more than enough. The wine list includes approximately 7,000 selections (with 1,000 dessert wines). After dinner, tour the kitchen and wine cellar before having dessert upstairs in a cozy booth. The dessert room is a hit. For a real jolt, try the Turkish coffee with an order of Mississippi mud pie. Casual business attire is recommended. ⊠ *1208 S. Howard Ave., Hyde Park* ☎ *813/251–2421* ⊕ *www.bernssteakhouse.com* ⚔ *Reservations essential.*

$$ ✕ **Columbia.** Make a date for some of the best Latin cuisine in Tampa.
SPANISH A fixture since 1905, this magnificent structure with an old-world air
Fodor'sChoice and spacious dining rooms takes up an entire city block and seems to
★ feed the entire city—locals as well as visitors—throughout the week, but
especially on weekends. The paella, bursting with seafood, chicken, and
pork, arguably is the best in Florida, and the 1905 salad—with ham,
olives, cheese, and garlic—is legendary. The menu has Cuban classics
such as *boliche criollo* (tender eye of round stuffed with chorizo sau-
sage), *ropa vieja* (shredded beef with onions, peppers, and tomatoes),
and *arroz con pollo* (chicken with yellow rice). Don't miss the flamenco
dancing show every night but Sunday. This place is also known for its
sangria. If you can, walk around the building and check out the elabo-
rate, antique decor along every inch of the interior. ⊠ *2117 E. 7th Ave.,
Ybor City* ☎ *813/248–4961* ⊕ *www.columbiarestaurant.com.*

$ ✕ **Kojak's House of Ribs.** Few barbecue joints can boast the staying power
SOUTHERN of this family-owned and -operated pit stop. Located along a shaded
stretch in South Tampa, it debuted in 1978, and has since earned a fol-
lowing of sticky-fingered regulars who have turned it into one of the
most popular barbecue stops in central Florida. It's located in a 1927
house complete with veranda, pillars supporting the overhanging roof,
and brick steps. Day and night, three indoor dining rooms and an out-
door dining porch have a steady stream of hungry patrons digging into
tender pork spareribs that are dry-rubbed and tanned overnight before
visiting the smoker for a couple of hours. Then they're bathed in the
sauce of your choice. Kojak's also has a nice selection of sandwiches,
including sloppy chicken and country-style sausage. This is definitely
not the kind of place you'd want to bring a vegan. ⊠ *2808 Gandy Blvd.,
South Tampa* ☎ *813/837–3774* ⊕ *www.kojaksbbq.com* ☽ *Closed Mon.*

WHERE TO STAY

If you want to be close to the cruise-ship terminal, then you'll have
to stay in Tampa, but if you want to spend more time in the area and
perhaps stay on the beach, St. Petersburg and the beaches are close by.

For price categories, see ⇨ *Lodging at the beginning of this chapter.*

For expanded hotel reviews, visit Fodors.com.

$$$ ▥ **Don Vicente de Ybor Historic Inn.** Built as a home in 1895 by town
B&B/INN founder Don Vicente de Ybor, this inn shows that the working-class
★ cigar city had an elegant side, too. **Pros:** elegant rooms; rich in history;
walking distance to nightlife. **Cons:** rowdy neighborhood on weekend nights. ⊠ *1915 Republica de Cuba, Ybor City* ☎ *813/241–4545 or
866/206–4545* ⊕ *donvicenteinn.com* ⥱ *13 rooms, 3 suites* ⅄ *In-room:
Wi-Fi. In-hotel: restaurant, bar* ❧ *Breakfast.*

$$–$$$ ▥ **Hilton Garden Inn Tampa Ybor Historic District.** Although its modern
HOTEL architecture makes it seem out of place in this historic district, this
★ chain hotel's location across from Centro Ybor is a plus. **Pros:** good
location for business travelers; reasonable rates. **Cons:** chain-hotel feel;
far from downtown. ⊠ *1700 E. 9th Ave., Ybor City* ☎ *813/769–9267*
⊕ *www.hiltongardeninn.com* ⥱ *84 rooms, 11 suites* ⅄ *In-room: Wi-Fi.
In-hotel: restaurant, pool, laundry facilities* ❧ *No meals.*

6

$$$–$$$$ ⊡ **Tampa Marriott Waterside Hotel & Marina.** Across from the Tampa Con-
HOTEL   vention Center, this downtown hotel was built for conventioneers but is
also convenient to tourist spots such as the Florida Aquarium and the
Channelside and Hyde Park shopping districts. **Pros:** great downtown
location; near shopping. **Cons:** gridlock during rush hour; streets tough
to maneuver; area sketchy after dark. ⊠ *700 S. Florida Ave., Down-
town* ☎ *888/268–1616* ⊕ *www.marriott.com* ⇌ *683 rooms, 36 suites*
⅜ *In-room: Wi-Fi. In-hotel: restaurants, bars, pool, gym, spa, laundry
facilities, parking.*

Ports of Call

WORD OF MOUTH

"The islands on [the Southern Caribbean] route are very nice IMHO. Also it's easy to do excursions with a local guide. There will be plenty of them on the dock as you exit the ship. The prices are usually reasonable too."

—jacketwatch

Nowhere in the world are conditions better suited to cruising than in the Caribbean Sea. Tiny island nations, within easy sailing distance of one another, form a chain of tropical enchantment that curves from Cuba in the north all the way down to the coast of Venezuela. There's far more to life here than sand and coconuts, however. The islands are vastly different, with a variety of cultures, topographies, and languages represented. Colonialism has left its mark, and the presence of the Spanish, French, Dutch, Danish, and British is still felt. Slavery, too, has left its cultural legacy, blending African overtones into the colonial/Indian amalgam. The one constant, however, is the weather. Despite the islands' southerly latitude, the climate is surprisingly gentle, due in large part to the cooling influence of the trade winds.

The Caribbean is made up of the Greater Antilles and the Lesser Antilles. The former consist of those islands closest to the United States: Cuba, Jamaica, Hispaniola (Haiti and the Dominican Republic), and Puerto Rico. (The Cayman Islands lie south of Cuba.) The Lesser Antilles, including the Virgin, Windward, and Leeward islands and others, are greater in number but smaller in size, and constitute the southern half of the Caribbean chain.

GOING ASHORE

Traveling by cruise ship presents an opportunity to visit many places in a short time. The flip side is that your stay in each port of call will be brief. For this reason cruise lines offer shore excursions, which maximize passengers' time. There are a number of advantages to shore excursions arranged by your ship: in some destinations, transportation may be unreliable, and a ship-packaged tour is the best way to see distant sights. Also, you don't have to worry about missing the ship. The disadvantage of a shore excursion is the cost—you usually pay more for the convenience of having the ship do the legwork for you, but it's not always a lot more. Of course, you can always book a tour independently, hire a taxi, or use foot power to explore on your own. For each port of call included in this guide we've provided some suggestions for the best ship-sponsored excursions—in terms of both quality of experience and price—as well as some suggestions for what to do if you want to explore on your own.

ARRIVING IN PORT

When your ship arrives in a port, it will tie up alongside a dock or anchor out in a harbor. If the ship is docked, passengers walk down the gangway to go ashore. Docking makes it easy to move between the shore and the ship.

TENDERING

If your ship anchors in the harbor, you will have to take a small boat—called a launch or tender—to get ashore. Tendering is a nuisance; however, participants in shore excursions are given priority. Passengers wishing to disembark independently may be required to gather in a public room, get sequenced boarding passes, and wait until their numbers are called. The ride to shore may take as long as 20 minutes. If you don't like waiting, plan to go ashore an hour or so after the ship drops its anchor. On a very large ship, the wait for a tender can be quite long and frustrating.

Because tenders can be difficult to board, passengers with mobility problems may not be able to visit certain ports. The larger ships are more likely to use tenders. It is usually possible to learn before booking a cruise whether the ship will dock or anchor at its ports of call.

Before anyone is allowed to walk down the gangway or board a tender, the ship must be cleared for landing. Immigration and customs officials board the vessel to examine passports and sort through red tape. It may be more than an hour before you're allowed ashore. You will be issued a boarding pass, which you'll need to get back on board.

7

RETURNING TO THE SHIP

Cruise lines are strict about sailing times, which are posted at the gangway and elsewhere and announced in the daily schedule of activities. Be sure to be back on board (not on the dock waiting to get a tender back to the ship) at least an hour before the announced sailing time or you may be stranded. If you are on a shore excursion that was sold by the cruise line, however, the captain will wait for your group before casting off. That is one reason many passengers prefer ship-packaged tours.

If you're not on one of the ship's tours and the ship sails without you, immediately contact the cruise line's port representative, whose phone number is often listed on the daily schedule of activities. You may be able to hitch a ride on a pilot boat, although that is unlikely. Passengers who miss the boat must pay their own way to the next port.

CARIBBEAN ESSENTIALS

CURRENCY

The U.S. dollar is the official currency on Puerto Rico, the U.S. Virgin Islands, the Turks and Caicos, and the British Virgin Islands. On Grand Cayman you will usually have a choice of Cayman or U.S. dollars when you take money out of an ATM, and you may even be able to get change in U.S. dollars. In Cozumel, Calica, Costa Maya, and Progreso, the Mexican peso is the official currency. The euro is used in a

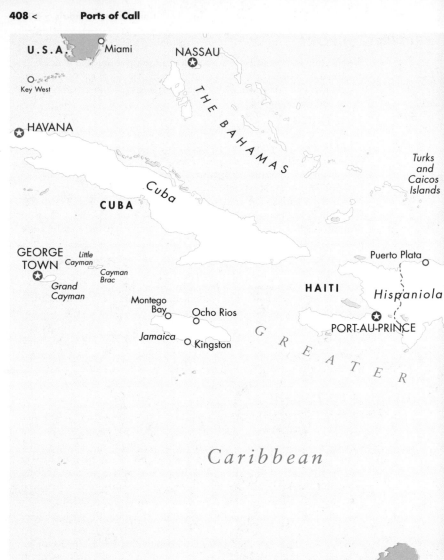

Caribbean

ATLANTIC OCEAN

DOMINICAN REPUBLIC

LEEWARD ISLANDS

St. John Tortola
St. Thomas Virgin Gorda
Anguilla
St. Barthélemy
⊛ SANTO St. Maarten/ Saba
DOMINGO St. Martin Barbuda
SAN JUAN ⊛ St. St. Eustatius
Puerto Croix St. Kitts Antigua
Rico Nevis
Montserrat Marie
Galante
A N T I L L E S Guadeloupe

Dominica
Martinique WINDWARD
Fort-de-France

Sea St. Lucia

Barbados
St. Vincent
Bequia Bridgetown
The
Grenadines
Carriacou
Aruba WILLEMSTAD St. George's
Bonaire Islas Los Grenada
⊛ Curaçao Roques
Tobago
LESSER ANTILLES Port of Spain
Trinidad

La Guaira
⊛
CARACAS

VENEZUELA

| 0 | | 200 miles |
| 0 | | 300 km |

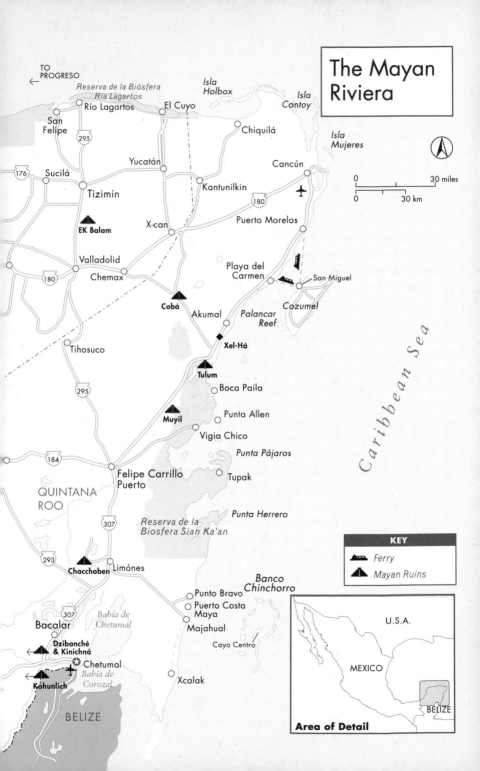

handful of French island (St. Barth, St. Martin, Martinique, Guadeloupe). In most Caribbean ports U.S. paper currency (not coins) is accepted readily. When you pay in dollars you'll almost always get change in local currency, so it's best to carry bills in small denominations. If you need local currency (say, for a trip to one of the French islands that uses the euro), change money at a local bank or use an ATM for the best rate. Most major credit cards are accepted all over the Caribbean, except at local market stalls and small establishments.

> **BUYING LIQUOR AND PERFUME**
>
> If you buy duty-free liquor or perfume while in a Caribbean port, don't forget that you may not bring it aboard your flight home. You will have to put it in your checked bags. Many liquor stores will pack your bottles in bubble wrap and pack them in a good cardboard box. Take advantage of this service.

KEEPING IN TOUCH

Internet cafés are now fairly common on many islands, and you'll sometimes find Internet cafés in the cruise-ship terminal itself—or perhaps in an attached or nearby shopping center. If you want to call home, most cruise ship facilities have phones that accept credit cards or local phone cards (local phone cards are almost always the cheapest option). And on most islands GSM multiband mobile phones will work, though roaming charges may be steep (some plans include Puerto Rico and the U.S. Virgin Islands in their nationwide calling regions).

WHERE TO EAT

Cuisine on the Caribbean's islands is as varied as the islands themselves. The region's history as a colonial battleground and ethnic melting pot creates plenty of variety and adds lots of unusual tropical fruit and spices. In fact, the one quality that defines most Caribbean cooking is its spiciness, acquired from nutmeg, mace, allspice, peppers, saffron, and many other seasonings grown in the islands. Dress is generally casual, although throughout the islands beachwear is inappropriate most anywhere except on the beach. Unless otherwise noted, prices are given in U.S. dollars. The following price categories are used in this book.

WHAT IT COSTS IN U.S. DOLLARS				
	¢	$	$$	$$$	$$$$
At Dinner	under $8	$8–$11	$12–$19	$20–$30	over $30

Prices are per person for a main course at dinner and do not include any service charges.

SHORE EXCURSIONS

Typical excursions include an island or town bus tour, a visit to a beach or rum factory, a boat trip, a snorkeling or diving trip, and charter fishing. In recent years, however, shore excursions have gotten more adventurous, with mild river-rafting, parasailing, jet-skiing, hiking, and biking added to the mix. It's often easier to take a ship-arranged excursion, but it's almost never the cheapest option.

If you prefer to break away from the pack, find a knowledgeable taxi driver or tour operator—they're usually within a stone's throw of the pier—or wander around on your own. A group of four to six people will usually find this option more economical and practical than will a single person or a couple.

Renting a car is also a good option on many islands—again, the more people, the better the deal. But get a good island map before you set off, and be sure to find out how long it will take you to get around.

Conditions are ideal for water sports of all kinds—scuba diving, snorkeling, windsurfing, sailing, waterskiing, and fishing excursions abound. Your shore-excursion director can usually arrange these activities for you if the ship offers no formal excursion.

PRIVATE ISLANDS

Linda Coffman

When evaluating the "best" Caribbean ports of call, many repeat cruise passengers often add the cruise lines' own private islands to their lists of preferred destinations.

The cruise lines established "private" islands to provide a beach break on an island (or part of one) reserved for their exclusive use. While most passengers don't select an itinerary based solely upon calling at a private island, they usually consider them a highlight of their cruise vacation. The very least you can expect of your private island is lush foliage and a wide swath of beach surrounded by azure water. Facilities vary, but a beach barbecue, water-sports equipment rental, lounge chairs, hammocks, and restrooms are standard. Youth counselors come ashore to conduct sand-castle building competitions and lead junior pirates on swashbuckling island treasure hunts.

The use of strollers and wheelchairs equipped with all-terrain wheels may be offered on a complimentary first-come, first-served basis. However, with the exception of some participation sports on the beach, plan to pay for most water toys and activities. Costs associated with private-island fun and recreation can range from $8 for use of a snorkel vest (you may use your own snorkel equipment; however, in the event a floatation vest is required for safety, you must rent one) to $30 for rental of an entire snorkeling outfit for the day (mask, fins, snorkel vest, a mesh bag, fish identification card, and fish food). You can often take a banana-boat ride for $16 to $19 (15-minute ride), sail a small boat or catamaran for $30 to $50 (one hour), paddle a kayak for $18 to $38 (half-hour to hour-and-a-half), ride Jet Skis for $59 to $99 (45 minutes to one hour), parasail for a hefty $79 to $84 (10 minutes or less), or fly through the treetops on a zip line for $85. Floating mats are a relative bargain at $10 to $12 for all-day lounging in the water. You might also find open-air massage cabanas with pricing comparable to the spa charges onboard.

There is generally no charge for food or basic beverages such as those served onboard ship. While soft drinks and tropical cocktails can usually be charged to your shipboard account, you might want to bring a small amount of cash ashore for souvenir shopping, which is usually possible from vendors set up on or near the beach. You will also want to bring beach towels ashore and return them to the ship at the end of the day, because, as Princess Cruises reminds passengers, "Although the locals may offer to do this for you, unfortunately we seldom see the towels again!"

Even if you do nothing more than lie in a shaded hammock and sip fruity tropical concoctions, the day can be one of the most fun and relaxing of your entire cruise.

ISLANDS BY CRUISE LINE

Carnival Cruise Lines is currently the only major cruise line without an extensive private island experience available to the entire fleet. However, select Carnival itineraries include calls at Half Moon Cay, Holland America Line's private paradise, where "Fun Ship" passengers can use all the facilities and participate in organized activities. Similarly, certain Regent Seven Seas cruises include beach days at Princess Cays or Cayo Levantado, located off the Samaná Peninsula on the northeast coast of the Dominican Republic.

Although they do not stop at "private islands" in the strictest sense, the smaller ships of Seabourn and SeaDream offer passengers a day ashore on secluded private beaches where they can enjoy lavish barbecues and take a break from swimming and snorkeling to indulge in champagne and caviar served in the surf.

COSTA CRUISES

An unspoiled island paradise, Costa's **Catalina Island** is just off the coast of the Dominican Republic. Passengers can participate in Costa's "Beach Olympics," schedule a seaside massage, or just kick back on a chaise longue or a complimentary water float. Water-toy rentals, banana-boat rides, and sailing tours are available from independent concessionaires. Local vendors set up souvenir shops offering crafts and T-shirts. The ship provides the food for a lunch barbecue and tropical beverages at the beach bar.

Activities: Snorkeling, sailing, jet-skiing, waterskiing, hiking, volleyball, organized games, massages, shopping.

DISNEY CRUISE LINE

Disney's **Castaway Cay** has a dock, so passengers simply step ashore (rather than tendering, as is required to reach most cruise lines' private islands). Like everything associated with Disney, the line's private island is almost too good to be true. Located in the Abacos, a chain in the Bahamas, only 10% of Castaway Cay is developed, leaving plenty of unspoiled area to explore in Robinson Crusoe fashion. Trams are provided to reach separate beaches designated for children, teens, families, and adults, and areas where Disney offers age-specific activities and extensive, well-planned children's activities. Biking and hiking are so popular that two nature trails—one of them with an observation tower—are mapped out. Passengers can swim to a water platform complete with two slides or cool off in a 2,400-square-foot water-play area equipped with water jets and a splash pad. A 1,200-square-foot soft wet deck area provides freshwater fun for children with an array of pop jets, geysers, and bubblers. There is no charge for the water-play facilities. Excursions range from as passive as a glass-bottom boat tour to the soaring excitement of parasailing. An interactive experience with sting-rays is educational and safe—the gentle creatures' barbs are blunted for safety. In addition to barbecue fare served in two buffet areas with covered seating and several beverage stations, beach games, island-style music, and a shaded game pavilion, there are shops, massage cabanas by the sea, and even a post office. Popular with couples as well as families, 21 private rental cabanas provide the luxury of a deluxe beach retreat with an option to add the personalized service of a cabana host.

Activities: Snorkeling, kayaking, parasailing, sailing, jet-skiing, paddle-boats, water cycles, banana boat rides, fishing, bicycles, basketball, billiards, hiking, Ping-Pong, shuffleboard, soccer, volleyball, organized games, massages, shopping.

HOLLAND AMERICA LINE

Little San Salvador, one of the Bahamian out-islands, was renamed **Half Moon Cay** by Holland America Line to honor Henry Hudson's ship (depicted on the cruise line's logo) as well as to reflect the beach's cres-cent shape. Even after development, the island is still so unspoiled that it has been named a Wild Bird Preserve by the Bahamian National Trust. Passengers, who are welcomed ashore at a West Indies Village complete with shops and straw market, find Half Moon Cay easily accessible—all facilities are connected by hard-surfaced and packed-sand pathways and meet and exceed ADA requirements. An accessible tram also connects the welcome center with the food pavilion and bars; wheelchairs with balloon tires are available. In addition to the beach area for lazing in the sun or in the shade of a rented clamshell, the island has a post office, Bahamian-style chapel, a lagoon where you can interact with stingrays, and the Captain Morgan on the Rocks Island Bar in a "beached" pirate ship For family fun, you'll find a beachfront water park with water-slides and fanciful sea creatures tethered to the sandy bottom of the shallow water. Massage services are available, as are fitness activities. Air-conditioned cabanas can be rented for the day, with or without the services of your own butler.

Activities: Scuba diving, snorkeling, windsurfing, kayaking, parasail-ing, sailing, jet-skiing, Aqua Bikes, fishing, bicycles, basketball, hiking, horseback riding, shuffleboard, volleyball, massages, shopping.

NORWEGIAN CRUISE LINE

Only 120 mi east of Fort Lauderdale in the Berry Island chain of the Bahamas, much of **Great Stirrup Cay** looks as it did when it was acquired by Norwegian Cruise Line in 1977, with bougainvillea, sea grape, and coconut palms as abundant as the colorful tropical fish that inhabit the reef. The first uninhabited island purchased to offer cruise-ship pas-sengers a private beach day, Great Stirrup Cay's white-sand beaches are fringed by coral and ideal for swimming and snorkeling. Permanent facilities have been added to and improved in the intervening years and a seawall was erected to reduce beach erosion and preserve the envi-ronment. A straw market, water-sports centers, bars, volleyball courts, beachside massage stations, a food pavilion, and a 40-feet high and 175-feet long Hippo inflatable waterslide round out the facilities. Sand wheelchairs are available on the island, but the only paved pathway is along the seawall. Extensive island improvements began in 2010 with the excavation of a new entrance channel for tenders and construction of tender docking facilities and a welcome pavilion that is now the site for landings. As a result, the beachfront has been expanded significantly to alleviate crowding. Private beachfront cabanas, two dining facilities, a kid's play area, wave runners, a floating Aqua Park with a variety of water toys, kayak tours through man-made rivers within the island, an eco-cruise, and a stingray encounter experience have been added.

Activities: Snorkeling, kayaking, parasailing, sailing, paddleboats, Ping-Pong, hiking, volleyball, organized games, massages, shopping.

PRINCESS CRUISES

Princess Cays is a 40-acre haven on the southern tip of Eleuthera Island in the Bahamas. Not quite an uninhabited island, it nevertheless offers a wide ribbon of beach, long enough for passengers to splash in the surf, relax in a hammock, or limbo to the beat of local music and never feel crowded. In a similar fashion to booking shore excursions, snorkeling equipment, sea boards, floats, kayaks, paddle wheelers, banana boat rides, aqua chairs, beach clamshells, and bungalows can be pre-reserved on Princess Cruises' Web site. All other equipment and activities must be booked onboard. Nestled in a picturesque palm grove, private bungalows with air-conditioning and ceiling fans and a deck for lounging can be rented for parties of up to six. The Sanctuary at Princess Cays, complete with bungalows for parties of four, is an adults-only haven. A pirate-theme play area for children is supervised. In addition to three tropical bars and the area where a Bahamian barbecue is served, permanent facilities include small shops that sell island crafts and trinkets, but if you head around the back and through the fence, independent vendors sell similar goods for lower prices.

Activities: Snorkeling, kayaking, banana boat rides, sailing, paddleboats, Aqua Bikes, windsurfing, surf fishing, deep sea fishing, hiking, organized games, shopping.

ROYAL CARIBBEAN, CELEBRITY CRUISES, AND AZAMARA CLUB CRUISES

Royal Caribbean, Azamara Club Cruises, and Celebrity Cruises passengers have twice as many opportunities to visit a private island. The lines share two, and many Caribbean itineraries include one or the other.

Coco Cay is a 140-acre island in the Berry Island chain between Nassau and Freeport. Originally known as Little Stirrup Cay, it's within view of Great Stirrup Cay (NCL's private island) and the snorkeling is just as good, especially around a sunken airplane and a replica of Blackbeard's flagship, *Queen Anne's Revenge*. In addition to activities and games ashore, Coco Cay has one of the largest Aqua Parks in the Caribbean, where children and adults alike can jump on an in-water trampoline or climb a floating sand castle before they dig into a beach barbecue or explore a nature trail. Attractions also include an inflatable 40-foot waterslide (fun for adults and kids alike) and a Power Wheels track, where youngsters age 3 to 8 can take a miniature car for a spin at a sedate 3 *mph*. Rounding out the facilities are a Bahamian marketplace, several beach bars, and numerous hammocks for relaxation in the sun or shade.

Activities: Scuba diving, snorkeling, jet-skiing, kayaking, parasailing, hiking, volleyball, organized games, shopping.

Labadee is a 260-acre peninsula approximately 6 mi (10 km) from Cap Haitien on the secluded north coast of Haiti (the port of call is sometimes called "Hispaniola"). Passengers can step ashore on the dock, from which water taxis and five different walking paths, trails, and avenues lead to many areas throughout the peninsula, including the Labadee Town Square and Dragon's Plaza, where a welcome center and central tram station are located. In addition to swimming, water sports, an Aqua Park with floating trampolines and waterslides, and nature trails to explore, bonuses on Labadee are an authentic folkloric show presented by island performers and a market featuring work of local artists and crafters, where you might find an interesting painting or unique wood carving. More adventurous activities include an Alpine Coaster, a thrilling roller coaster experience, and one of the most exciting—and at 2,600 feet in length the longest—zip-line experiences in the Caribbean, which takes place 500 feet above the beaches of Labadee, where riders can reach speeds of 40 to 50 *mph* over the water. Due to the proximity of Labadee to mainland Haiti, in the past it has occasionally been necessary to cancel calls there due to political unrest. In that event, an alternate port is usually scheduled.

Activities: Snorkeling, jet-skiing, kayaking, parasailing, hiking, volleyball, organized games, shopping.

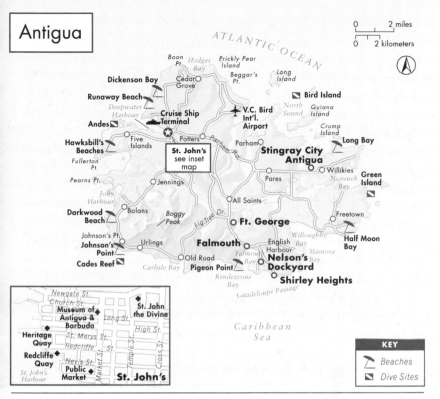

ANTIGUA (ST. JOHN'S)

Jordan Simon

Some say Antigua has so many beaches that you could visit a different one every day for a year. Most have snow-white sand, and many are backed by lavish resorts that offer sailing, diving, windsurfing, and snorkeling. The largest of the British Leeward Islands, Antigua was the headquarters from which Lord Horatio Nelson (then a mere captain) made his forays against the French and pirates in the late 18th century. You may wish to explore English Harbour and its carefully restored Nelson's Dockyard, as well as tour old forts, historic churches, and tiny villages. Appealing aspects of the island's interior include a small tropical rain forest ideal for hiking and ziplining, ancient Native American archaeological digs, and restored sugar mills. Due to time constraints, it's best to make trips this far from port with an experienced tour operator, but you can easily take a taxi to any number of fine beaches on your own and escape from the hordes descending from the ship.

ESSENTIALS

CURRENCY   Eastern Caribbean (EC) dollar (EC$2.67 to US$1). U.S. dollars are generally accepted, but change is given in EC.

INTERNET   There are some small Internet cafés in St. John's and English Harbour; ask at the tourist information booth at the cruise-ship pier.

TELEPHONES A GSM tri-band mobile phone will usually work in Antigua. You can use a LIME (formerly Cable & Wireless) Phone Card (available in $5, $10, and $20 denominations in most hotels and post offices) for local and long-distance calls. To call the United States and Canada, dial 1 + the area code + the seven-digit number, or use the phone card or one of the *CALL USA* phones, which are available at several locations, including the cruise terminal at St. John's and the English Harbour Marina.

COMING ASHORE

Though some ships dock at the deepwater harbor in downtown St. John's, most use Heritage Quay, a multimillion-dollar complex with shops, condominiums, a casino, and a food court. Most St. John's attractions are an easy walk from Heritage Quay; the older part of the city is eight blocks away. A tourist information booth is in the main docking building.

If you intend to explore beyond St. John's, consider hiring a taxi driver–guide. Taxis meet every cruise ship. They're unmetered; fares are fixed, and drivers are required to carry a rate card. Agree on the fare before setting off (make sure you know the price quoted is one-way or round-trip), and plan to tip drivers 10%. Some cabbies may take you from St. John's to English Harbour and wait for a "reasonable" amount of time (about a half-hour) while you look around, for about $50; you can usually arrange an island tour for around $25 per hour. Renting your own car isn't usually practical, since you must purchase a $20 temporary driving permit in addition to the car-rental fee, which is usually about $50 per day in the high season.

EXPLORING ANTIGUA

Falmouth. This town sits on a lovely bay backed by former sugar plantations and sugar mills. The most important historic site here is St. Paul's Church, which was rebuilt on the site of a church once used by troops during the Horatio Nelson period. ⊠ *Antigua.*

Ft. George. East of Liberta—one of the first settlements founded by freed slaves—on Monk's Hill, this fort was built from 1689 to 1720. Among the ruins are the sites for 32 cannons, water cisterns, the base of the old flagstaff, and some of the original buildings. ⊠ *Antigua.*

Fodor'sChoice
★ **Nelson's Dockyard.** Antigua's most famous attraction is the world's only Georgian-era dockyard still in use, a treasure trove for history buffs and nautical nuts alike. In 1671 the governor of the Leeward Islands wrote to the Council for Foreign Plantations in London, pointing out the advantages of this landlocked harbor. By 1704 English Harbour was in regular use as a garrisoned station.

When the Royal Navy abandoned the station at English Harbour in 1889, it fell into a state of decay, though adventuresome yachties still lived there in near-primitive conditions. The Society of the Friends of English Harbour began restoring it in 1951; it reopened with great fanfare as Nelson's Dockyard on November 14, 1961. Within the compound are crafts shops, restaurants, and two splendidly restored

18th-century hotels, the Admiral's Inn and the Copper & Lumber Store Hotel, worth peeking into. The Dockyard is a hub for oceangoing yachts and serves as headquarters for the annual Sailing Week Regatta in late April and early May. Water taxis will ferry you between points for EC$5. The Dockyard National Park also includes serene nature trails accessing beaches, rock pools, and crumbling plantation ruins and hilltop forts.

The **Dockyard Museum,** in the original Naval Officer's House, presents ship models, mock-ups of English Harbour, displays on the people who worked there and typical ships that docked, silver regatta trophies, maps, prints, antique navigational instruments,

ANTIGUA BEST BETS
■ **Dickenson Bay Beach.** One of Antigua's best beaches.
■ **Ecotourism.** Explore the island's forested interior on foot or surrounding coves by kayak.
■ **Jolly Harbour.** A cheap day pass at the Jolly Harbour Resort is a great day at the beach.
■ **Nelson's Dockyard.** This is one of the Caribbean's best historic sights, with many stores, restaurants, and bars.
■ **St. John's.** There's excellent duty-free shopping, especially in Heritage Quay and Redcliffe Quay.

and Nelson's very own telescope and tea caddy. ⊠ *English Harbour, Antigua* ☎ *268/481–5022, 268/463–1060, 268/460–1379 for National Parks Authority* ⊕ *www.antiguamuseums.org* ⊠ *$2 suggested donation* ☉ *Daily 8–5.*

St. John's. Antigua's capital, with some 45,000 inhabitants (approximately half the island's population), lies at sea level at the inland end of a sheltered northwestern bay. Although it has seen better days, a couple of notable historic sights and some good waterfront shopping areas make it worth a visit.

At the far south end of town, where Market Street forks into Valley and All Saints roads, haggling goes on every Friday and Saturday, when locals jam the **Public Market** to buy and sell fruits, vegetables, fish, and spices. Ask before you aim a camera; your subject may expect a tip. This is old-time Caribbean shopping, a jambalaya of sights, sounds, and smells.

Museum of Antigua and Barbuda. Signs at the Museum of Antigua and Barbuda say "Please touch," encouraging you to explore Antigua's past. Exhibits interpret the nation's history, from its geological birth to its political independence in 1981. There are fossil and coral remains from some 34 million years ago; models of a sugar plantation and a wattle-and-daub house; an Arawak canoe; and a wildly eclectic assortment of objects from cannonballs to 1920s telephone exchanges. The museum occupies the former courthouse, which dates from 1750. The superlative museum gift shop carries such unusual items as calabash purses, seed earrings, warri boards (warri being an African game brought over to the Caribbean), and lignum vitae pipes, as well as historic maps and local books. ⊠ *Long and Market Sts., St. John's, Antigua* ☎ *268/462–1469* ⊠ *$2 suggested donation* ☉ *Sun.–Thurs. 8:30–4, Fri. 8:30–3, Sat. 10–2.*

Anglican Cathedral of St. John the Divine. At the south gate of the Anglican Cathedral of St. John the Divine are figures of St. John the Baptist and St. John the Divine, said to have been taken from one of Napoléon's ships and brought to Antigua. The original church was built in 1681, replaced by a stone building in 1745, and destroyed by an earthquake in 1843. The present neo-baroque building dates from 1845; the parishioners had the interior completely encased in pitch pine, hoping to forestall future earthquake damage. Tombstones bear eerily eloquent testament to the colonial days. ✉ *Between Long and Newgate Sts., St. John's, Antigua* ☎ *268/461–0082.*

Heritage Quay. Shopaholics head directly for Heritage Quay, an ugly multimillion-dollar complex. The two-story buildings contain stores that sell duty-free goods, sportswear, down-island imports (paintings, T-shirts, straw baskets), and local crafts. There are also restaurants, a bandstand, and a casino. Cruise-ship passengers disembark here from the 500-foot-long pier. Expect heavy shilling. ✉ *High and Thames Sts., Antigua*

Redcliffe Quay. Redcliffe Quay, at the water's edge just south of Heritage Quay, is the most appealing part of St. John's. Attractively restored (and superbly re-created) buildings in a riot of cotton-candy colors house shops, restaurants, and boutiques and are linked by courtyards and landscaped walkways. ✉ *Antigua.*

Shirley Heights. This bluff affords a spectacular view of English Harbour. The heights are named for Sir Thomas Shirley, the governor who fortified the harbor in 1787. At the top is Shirley Heights Lookout, a restaurant built into the remnants of the 18th-century fortifications. Most notable for its boisterous Sunday barbecues that continue into the night with live music and dancing, it serves dependable burgers, pumpkin soup, grilled meats, and rum punches. ✉ *Antigua.*

Dows Hill Interpretation Centre. Not far from Shirley Heights is the Dows Hill Interpretation Centre, where observation platforms provide still more sensational vistas of the English Harbour area. A multimedia sound-and-light presentation on island history and culture, spotlighting lifelike figures and colorful tableaux accompanied by running commentary and music, results in a cheery, if bland, portrait of Antiguan life from Amerindian times to the present. ✉ *Antigua* ☎ *268/460–1379 for National Parks Authority* 🎟 *EC$15* ⏲ *Daily 9–5.*

Stingray City Antigua. Stingray City Antigua is a carefully reproduced "natural" environment nicknamed by staffers the "retirement home," though the 30-plus stingrays, ranging from infants to seniors, are frisky. You can stroke, feed, even hold the striking gliders, as well as snorkel in deeper, protected waters. The tour guides do a marvelous job of explaining the animals' habits, from feeding to breeding, and their predators (including man). ✉ *Seaton's Village, Antigua* ☎ *268/562–7297* 🌐 *www.stingraycityantigua.com.*

SHOPPING

Redcliffe Quay, on the waterfront at the south edge of St. John's, is by far the most appealing shopping area. Several restaurants and more than 30 boutiques, many with one-of-a-kind wares, are set around landscaped courtyards shaded by colorful trees. **Heritage Quay,** in St. John's, has 35 shops—including many that are duty-free—that cater to the cruise-ship crowd, which docks almost at its doorstep. Outlets here include Benetton, the Body Shop, Sunglass Hut, Dolce & Gabbana, and Osh-kosh B'Gosh. There are also shops along **St. John's, St. Mary's, High,** and **Long streets.** The tangerine-and-lilac-hue four-story **Vendor's Mall** at the intersection of Redcliffe and Thames streets gathers the pushy, pesky vendors that once clogged the narrow streets. It's jammed with stalls; air-conditioned indoor shops sell some higher-price, if not higher-quality, merchandise. On the west coast the Mediterranean-style, arcaded **Jolly Harbour Marina** holds some interesting galleries and shops, as do the marinas and Main Road snaking around English and Falmouth Harbours.

★ **Goldsmitty.** The Goldsmitty is Hans Smit, an expert goldsmith who turns gold, black coral, and precious and semiprecious stones into one-of-a-kind works of art. ⊠ *Redcliffe Quay, St. John's, Antigua* ☎ *268/462–4601.*

Isis. Isis sells island and international bric-a-brac, such as antique jew-elry, hand-carved walking sticks, and glazed pottery. ⊠ *Redcliffe Quay, St. John's, Antigua* ☎ *268/462–4602.*

★ **Noreen Phillips.** Noreen Phillips creates glitzy appliquéd and beaded eve-ning wear—inspired by the colors of the sea and sunset—in sensuous fabrics ranging from chiffon and silk to Italian lace and Indian brocade. ⊠ *Redcliffe Quay, St. John's, Antigua* ☎ *268/462–3127.*

ACTIVITIES

ADVENTURE TOURS

★ **Adventure Antigua.** Adventure Antigua is run by enthusiastic Eli Fuller, who is knowledgeable not only about the ecosystem and geogra-phy of Antigua but also about its history and politics. His thorough seven-hour excursion includes stops at Guiana Island, Pelican Island, Bird Island, and Hell's Gate. The company also offers a fun, shorter "Xtreme amusement park ride" variation on a racing boat catering to adrenaline junkies who "feel the need for speed" that also visits Stingray City, as well as a more sedate Antigua Classic Yacht sail-and-snorkel experience that explains the rich West Indian history of boatbuilding. ⊠ *Antigua* ☎ *268/727–3261 or 268/726–6355* ⊕ *www.adventureantigua.com.*

Antigua Rainforest Canopy Tours. Play Tarzan and Jane at Antigua Rainforest Canopy Tours. You should be in fairly good condition for the ropes chal-lenges, which require upper-body strength and stamina; there are height and weight restrictions. But anyone (vertigo or acrophobia sufferers, beware) can navigate the intentionally rickety "Indiana Jones–inspired" suspension bridges, then fly (in secure harnesses) over a rain-forest-filled valley from one towering turpentine tree to the next on lines with names like "Screamer" and "Leap of Faith." Admission varies slightly, but is usually $85. It's open Monday–Saturday from 8 to 6. ⊠ *Fig Dr., Wallings, Antigua* ☎ *268/562–6363* ⊕ *www.antiguarainforest.com.*

DIVING

Antigua is an unsung diving destination, with plentiful undersea sights to explore, from coral can-

yons to sea caves. Barbuda alone features roughly 200 wrecks on its treacherous reefs. The most accessible wreck is the 1890s bark *Andes,* not far out in Deep Bay, off Five Islands Peninsula. Among the favorite sites are **Green Island, Cades Reef,** and **Bird Island** (a national park). Memorable sightings include turtles, stingrays, and barracuda darting amid basalt walls, hulking boulders, and stray 17th-century anchors and cannon. One advantage is accessibility in many spots for shore divers and snorkelers. Double-tank dives run about $90.

Dockyard Divers (⊠ *Nelson's Dockyard, English Harbour* ☎ *268/460–1178* ⊕ *www.dockyard-divers.com*), owned by British ex-merchant seaman Captain A. G. "Tony" Fincham, is one of the island's most established outfits and offers diving and snorkeling trips, PADI courses, and dive packages with accommodations. They're geared to seasoned divers, but staff work patiently with novices. Tony is a wonderful source of information on the island; ask him about the "Fincham's Follies" musical extravaganza he produces for charity.

KAYAKING

★ **"Paddles" Kayak Eco Adventure.** "Paddles" Kayak Eco Adventure takes you on a 3½-hour tour of serene mangroves and inlets with informative narrative about the fragile ecosystem of the swamp and reefs and the rich diversity of flora and fauna. The tour ends with a hike to sunken caves and snorkeling in the North Sound Marine Park, capped by a rum punch at the fun Creole-style clubhouse. Experienced guides double as kayaking and snorkeling instructors, making this an excellent opportunity for novices. Conrad and Jennie's brainchild is one of Antigua's better bargains. ⊠ *Seaton's Village, Antigua* ☎ *268/463–1944* ⊕ *www. antiguapaddles.com.*

BEACHES

Dickenson Bay. Along a lengthy stretch of powder-soft white sand and exceptionally calm water you can find small and large hotels, water sports, concessions, and beachfront restaurants. There's decent snorkeling at either point. ⊠ *2 mi (3 km) northeast of St. John's, along main coast road, Antigua.*

Half Moon Bay. This ½-mi (1-km) ivory crescent is a prime snorkeling and windsurfing area. On the Atlantic side, the water can be rough at times, attracting intrepid hard-core surfers and wake-boarders. The northeastern end, where a protective reef offers spectacular snorkeling, is much calmer. A tiny bar has restrooms, snacks, and beach chairs. Half Moon is a real trek, but one of Antigua's showcase beaches. ⊠ *On southeast coast, 1.5 mi (2.5 km) from Freetown, Antigua.*

Johnson's Point/Crabbe Hill. This series of connected, deserted beaches on the southwest coast looks out toward Montserrat, Guadeloupe, and St. Kitts. Notable beach bar–restaurants include OJ's, Gibson's, and Turner's. The water is generally placid, though not good for snorkeling. ⊠ *3 mi (5 km) south of Jolly Harbour complex on main west-coast road, Antigua.*

Pigeon Point. Near Falmouth Harbour lie two fine white-sand beaches. The leeward side is calmer, the windward side is rockier, and there are sensational views and snorkeling around the point. Several restaurants and bars are nearby, though Bumpkin's satisfies most on-site needs. ⊠ *Off main south-coast road, southwest of Falmouth, Antigua.*

WHERE TO EAT

$$
ITALIAN
✗ **Big Banana—Pizzas in Paradise.** This tiny, often crowded spot is tucked into one side of a restored 18th-century rum warehouse with broad plank floors, wood-beam ceiling, and stone archways. Cool, Benetton-style photos of locals and musicians jamming adorn the brick walls. Big Banana serves some of the island's best pizza—try the lobster or the seafood variety—as well as such tasty specials as conch salad, fresh fruit crushes, and sub sandwiches bursting at the seams. There's live entertainment some nights, and a large-screen TV for sports fans. ⊠ *Redcliffe Quay, St. John's* 🕾 *268/480–6985* ⊕ *www.bigbanana-antigua.com* ☺ *Closed Sun.*

$$$$
CONTINENTAL
★
✗ **Coconut Grove.** Coconut palms grow through the roof of this open-air thatched restaurant, flickering candlelight illuminates colorful local murals, waves lap the white sand, and the warm waitstaff provides just the right level of service. Jean-François Bellanger's superbly presented dishes fuse French culinary preparations with island ingredients. Top choices include smoked salmon with watermelon-ginger jam, sundried tomatoes, and tapenade; pan-seared snapper medallions served with roasted sweet potato in a saffron white-wine curry; Caribbean bouillabaisse with coconut milk and pumpkin aioli; and chicken stuffed with creole vegetables in mango-kiwi sauce. The kitchen can be uneven, the wine list is unimaginative and overpriced. Nonetheless, Coconut Grove straddles the line between casual beachfront boîte and elegant eatery with aplomb. ⊠ *Siboney Beach Club, Dickenson Bay, Antigua* 🕾 *268/462–1538* ⊕ *www.coconutgroveantigua.net* ⚱ *Reservations essential.*

7

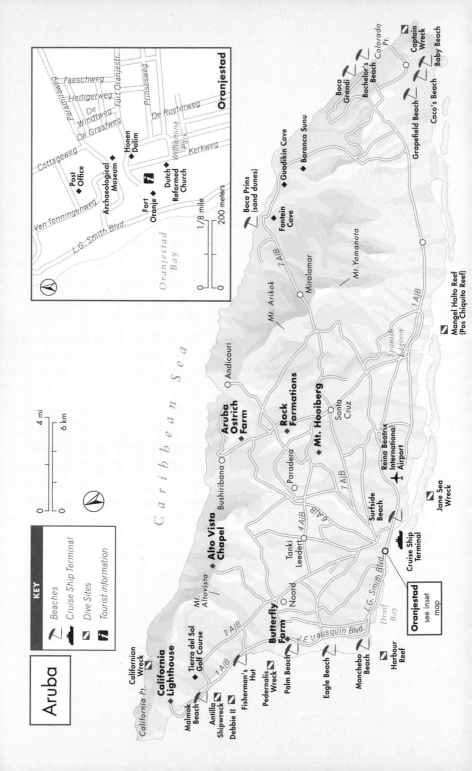

Aruba

KEY

⚘ Beaches
⚓ Cruise Ship Terminal
◰ Dive Sites
ℹ Tourist information

Oranjestad

Faeschweg
Heiligerweg
Baranjawes
Paralonweg
De Windtweg
De Graafweg
Cottageweg
Van Tonningenweg
Fort Oranjestr.
Prinseweg
De Ruyterweg
Kerkweg
Wilhelmina Park
L.G. Smith Blvd.

Post Office
Archeological Museum
Honen Dalim
Fort Oranje
Dutch Reformed Church

Oranjestad Bay

0 — 1/8 mile
0 — 200 meters

Caribbean Sea

0 — 4 mi
0 — 6 km

California Pt.
California Wreck
California Lighthouse
Malmok Beach
Antilla Shipwreck
Debbie II
Fisherman's Hut
Tierra del Sol Golf Course
Mt. Altovista
Pedernalis Wreck
Palm Beach
Eagle Beach
Manchebo Beach
Harbour Reef
Butterfly Farm
J.E. Irausquin Blvd.
Noord
Tanki Leendert
2 A/B
1 A/B
4 A/B
6 A/B
7 A/B
Alto Vista Chapel
Bushiribana
Aruba Ostrich Farm
Andicouri
Rock Formations
Mt. Hooiberg
Paradera
Santa Cruz
Mt. Arikok
Mt. Yamanota
Miralamar
Barranca Sunu
Fontein Cave
Guadikin Cave
Boca Prins (sand dunes)
Reina Beatrix International Airport
Surfside Beach
Cruise Ship Terminal
Oranjestad see inset map
L.G. Smith Blvd.
Druif Bay
Jane Sea Wreck
Spanish Lagoon
7 A/B
1 A/B
Mangel Halto Reef (Pos Chiquito Reef)
Colorado Pt.
Captain Wreck
Baby Beach
Boca Grandi
Bachelor's Beach
Grapefield Beach
Coco's Beach

ARUBA (ORANJESTAD)

Vernon
O'Reilly
Ramesar

Few islands can boast the overt dedication to tourism and the quality of service that Aruba offers. The arid landscape is full of attractions to keep visitors occupied, and the island offers some of the most dazzling beaches in the Caribbean. Casinos and novelty nightclubs abound in Oranjestad, giving the capital an almost Las Vegas appeal. To keep tourists coming back year after year, the island boasts a tremendous variety of restaurants ranging from upscale French eateries to toes-in-the-sand casual dining. Aruba may not be an unexplored paradise, but hundreds of thousands of tourists make it a point to beat a path here every year. Because it's not a very large island, cruise-ship visitors can expect to see a large part of the island on their day ashore. Or they can simply see several of the beautiful beaches. Whether you're planning to be active or to simply relax, this is an ideal cruise port.

ESSENTIALS

CURRENCY The Aruban florin (AFl 1.79 to US$1). The florin is pegged to the U.S. dollar, and Arubans accept U.S. dollars readily, so you need only acquire local currency for pocket change. Note that the Netherlands Antilles florin used on Curaçao is not accepted on Aruba.

INTERNET **Café Internet** ⊠ *8 Royal Plaza Mall, Oranjestad, Aruba* ☎ *297/582–4609.*

TELEPHONE When making calls to anywhere in Aruba, simply dial the seven-digit number. AT&T customers can dial 800–8000 from special phones at the cruise dock and in the airport's arrival and departure halls. Otherwise dial 121 to contact the international operator to place an international call.

7

COMING ASHORE

The Port of Oranjestad is a busy place and is generally full of eager tourists looking for souvenirs or a bite to eat. The port can accommodate up to five ships at a time (and frequently does). The Renaissance Marketplace is right on the port, as are a number of souvenir shops and some decent and inexpensive eating places. The main shopping areas of Oranjestad are all within 10 minutes' walk of the port.

Taxis can be flagged down on the street that runs alongside the port (look for license plates with a "TX" tag). Rates are fixed (i.e., there are no meters; the rates are set by the government and displayed on a chart), though you and the driver should agree on the fare before your ride begins. Rides to Eagle Beach run about $10; to Palm Beach, about $11. If you want to rent a car, you can do so for a reasonable price; driving is on the right, just as in the U.S., and it's pretty easy to get around, though a four-wheel drive vehicle does help in reaching some of the more out-of-the-way places.

EXPLORING ARUBA

Alto Vista Chapel. Alone near the island's northwest corner sits the scenic little Alto Vista Chapel. The wind whistles through the simple mustard-color walls, eerie boulders, and looming cacti. Along the side of the road back to civilization are miniature crosses with depictions of the stations of the cross and hand-lettered signs exhorting "pray for us sinners" and the like—a simple yet powerful evocation of faith. ✛ *To get here, follow the rough, winding dirt road that loops around the island's northern tip, or, from the hotel strip, take Palm Beach Road through three intersections and watch for the asphalt road to the left just past the Alto Vista Rum Shop.*

★ **Aruba Ostrich Farm.** Everything you ever wanted to know about the world's largest living birds can be found at this farm. A large *palapa* (palm-thatched roof) houses a gift shop and restaurant (popular with large bus tours), and tours of the farm are available every half hour. This operation is virtually identical to the facility in Curaçao; it's owned by the same company. ⊠ *Makividiri Rd., Paradera, Aruba* ☎ *297/585–9630* ⊕ *www.arubaostrichfarm.com* ☜ *$12* ⊙ *Daily 9–4.*

Butterfly Farm. Hundreds of butterflies from around the world flutter about this spectacular garden. Guided 20- to 30-minute tours (included in the price of admission) provide an entertaining look into the life cycle of these insects, from egg to caterpillar to chrysalis to butterfly. There's a special deal offered here: after your initial visit, you can return as often as you like for free during your vacation. ⊠ *J. E. Irausquin Blvd., Palm Beach* ☎ *297/586–3656* ⊕ *www.thebutterflyfarm.com* ☜ *$13* ⊙ *Daily 9–4:30; last tour at 4.*

California Lighthouse. The lighthouse, built by a French architect in 1910, stands at the island's far northern end. Although you can't go inside, you can ascend the hill to the lighthouse base for some great views. In this stark landscape, you might feel as though you've just landed on the moon. The lighthouse is surrounded by huge boulders that look like extraterrestrial monsters and sand dunes embroidered with scrub that resembles undulating sea serpents.

Mt. Hooiberg. Named for its shape (*hooiberg* means "haystack" in Dutch), this 541-foot peak lies inland just past the airport. If you have the energy, climb the 562 steps to the top for an impressive view of Oranjestad (and Venezuela on clear days).

Oranjestad. Aruba's charming capital is best explored on foot. L.G. Smith Boulevard, the palm-lined thoroughfare in the center of town, runs between pastel-painted buildings, old and new, of typical Dutch design. You'll find many malls with boutiques and shops here.

Archaeological Museum of Aruba. The Archaeological Museum of Aruba has two rooms chock-full of fascinating artifacts from the indigenous Arawak people, including farm and domestic utensils dating back hundreds of years. ⊠ *J.E. Irausquin Blvd. 2A, Oranjestad, Aruba* ☎ *297/582–8979* ☜ *Free* ⊙ *Tues.–Sun. 10–5.*

Aruba Aloe. Learn all about aloe—its cultivation, processing, and production—at Aruba Aloe, Aruba's own aloe farm and factory. Guided tours lasting about a half hour will show you how the gel—revered for its skin-soothing properties—is extracted from the aloe vera plant and used in a variety of products, including after-sun creams, soaps, and shampoos. Though not the most exciting tour on the island and unlikely to keep kids entertained, it might be a good option in the event of a rainy day. You can purchase the finished goods in the gift shop. ✉ *Pitastraat 115, Oranjestad, Aruba* ☎ *297/588–3222* ✉ *Free* ⊙ *Weekdays 8:30–4, Sat. 9–noon.*

Ft. Zoutman. One of the island's oldest edifices, Ft. Zoutman was built in 1796 and played an important role in skirmishes between British and Curaçao troops in 1803. The Willem III Tower, named for the Dutch monarch of that time, was added in 1868 to serve as a lighthouse. Over time, the fort has been a government office building, a police station, and a prison; now its historical museum displays Aruban artifacts in an 18th-century house. ✉ *Zoutmanstraat, Oranjestad, Aruba* ☎ *297/582–6099* ✉ *Free* ⊙ *Weekdays 8–noon and 1–4.*

ARUBA BEST BETS

■ **Eagle Beach.** One of the most beautiful beaches in the Caribbean, with miles of white sand.

■ **Nightlife.** If your ship stays in port late, take advantage of the island's great bar scene and its many casinos.

■ **Oranjestad.** Aruba's capital is pretty and easy to explore on foot, and it's impossible to get lost.

■ **Snorkeling.** Though you can't dive here, you can snorkel to get a glimpse of what's under the sea.

■ **Windsurfing.** Constant wind allows this adrenaline sport to thrive in Aruba.

Numismatic Museum. The Numismatic Museum displays more than 40,000 historic coins and paper money from around the world. A few pieces were salvaged from shipwrecks in the region. Some of the coins circulated during the Roman Empire, the Byzantine Empire, and the ancient Chinese dynasties; the oldest dates to the 3rd century BC. The museum had its start as the private collection of an Aruban who dug up some old coins in his garden. It's now run by his granddaughter. ✉ *Westraat, Oranjestad, Aruba* ☎ *297/582–8831* ✉ *$5* ⊙ *Weekdays 9–noon and 1:30–4:30* ✉ *Aruba.*

Rock Formations. The massive boulders at Ayo and Casibari are a mystery, as they don't match the island's geological makeup. You can climb to the top for fine views of the arid countryside. On the way you'll doubtless pass Aruba whiptail lizards—the males are cobalt blue, and the females are blue-gray with light-blue dots. The main path to Casibari has steps and handrails, and you must move through tunnels and along narrow steps and ledges to reach the top. At Ayo you can find ancient pictographs in a small cave (the entrance has iron bars to protect the drawings from vandalism). You may also encounter boulder climbers, who are increasingly drawn to Ayo's smooth surfaces. Access to Casibari is via Tanki Highway 4A; you can reach Ayo via Route 6A. Watch carefully for the turnoff signs near the center of the island on the way to the windward side.

SHOPPING

Oranjestad's **Caya G.F. Betico Croes** is Aruba's chief shopping street, lined with several shops advertising "duty-free prices" (again, these are not truly duty-free), boutiques, and jewelry stores noted for the aggressiveness of their vendors on cruise-ship days.

Stores at the **Port of Call Marketplace** (✉ *L.G. Smith Blvd. 17, Oranjestad*) sell fine jewelry, perfumes, low-priced liquor, batiks, crystal, leather goods, and fashionable clothing. **Paseo Herencia** (✉ *L.G. Smith Blvd., Palm Beach* ☎ *297/586–6533*) is the newest mall in Aruba, just min-utes away from the high-rise hotel

> **CAUTION**
>
> Pack and wear a hat to protect your scalp, ears, and face from sun damage and premature aging. Excessive sun exposure contrib-utes to wrinkles and dark spots.

area. It's all about style, and from the great bell tower to the nightly dancing-waters shows and the selection of restaurants, the aim here is to pull in shoppers. Offerings include Cuban cigars, the fine leather goods of Mario Hernandez, Italian denim goods at Moda & Stile, perfumes, cosmetics, and a variety of souvenir shops.

Five minutes from the cruise-ship terminal, the **Renaissance Marketplace** (✉ *L.G. Smith Blvd. 82, Oranjestad*), also known as Seaport Mall, has more than 120 stores selling merchandise to meet every taste and bud-get; the Crystal Casino is also here. The **Royal Plaza Mall** (✉ *L.G. Smith Blvd. 94, Oranjestad*), across from the cruise-ship terminal, has cafés, a post office (open weekdays 8 to 3:30), and such stores as Nautica, Benetton, Tommy Hilfiger, and Gandelman Jewelers. There's also a cybercafé for those who want to send email and get their caffeine fix all in one stop.

ACTIVITIES

BIKING

Pedal pushing is a great way to get around the island; the climate is perfect, and the trade winds help to keep you cool. **Melchor Cycle Rental** (✉ *Bubali 106B, Noord* ☎ *297/587–1787*) rents ATVs and bikes. **Rancho Notorious** (✉ *Boroncana, Noord* ☎ *297/586–0508* ⊕ *www.ranchonotorious.com*) organizes mountain-biking tours.

DIVING AND SNORKELING

With visibility of up to 90 feet, the waters around Aruba are excellent for snorkeling and diving. Advanced and novice divers alike will find plenty to occupy their time, as many of the most popular sites—includ-ing some interesting shipwrecks—are found in shallow waters ranging from 30 to 60 feet.

★ **De Palm Watersports.** De Palm Watersports is one of the best choices for your undersea experience, and the options go beyond basic diving. You can don a helmet and walk along the ocean floor near De Palm Island, home of huge blue parrot fish. You can even do Snuba—which is like scuba diving but without the heavy air tanks—from either a boat or from an island; it costs $65. ✉ *L.G. Smith Blvd. 142, Oranjestad, Aruba* ☎ *297/582–4400 or 800/766–6016* ⊕ *www.depalm.com.*

GOLF

★ **Tierra del Sol.** Tierra del Sol, a stunning course, is on the northwest coast near the California Lighthouse. Designed by Robert Trent Jones Jr., this 18-hole championship course combines Aruba's native beauty—cacti and rock formations—with the lush greens of the world's best courses. The greens fee varies depending on the time of day (from December to March it is $159 in the morning, $124 for early afternoon, and $100 from 3 pm). The fee includes a golf cart equipped with a communications system that allows you to order drinks for your return to the clubhouse. ⊠ *Malmokweg, Aruba* ☎ *297/586–0978.*

KAYAKING

Kayaking is a popular sport on Aruba, especially along the south coast, where the waters are calm. It's a great way to explore the coastline. **Aruba Kayak Adventure** (⊠ *Ponton 90, Oranjestad* ☎ *297/587–7722* ⊕ *www.arubakayak.com*) has excellent half-day kayak trips, which start with a quick lesson before you paddle through caves and mangroves and along the scenic coast. The tour makes a lunch stop at De Palm Island, where snorkeling is included as part of the $110 package.

BEACHES

The beaches on Aruba are beautiful, clean, and easily reached from the cruise-ship terminal in Oranjestad.

Fodor$Choice **Eagle Beach** (⊠ *J. E. Irausquin Blvd., north of Manchebo Beach*), on the
★ southwestern coast, is one of the Caribbean's—if not the world's —best beaches. Not long ago it was a nearly deserted stretch of pristine sand dotted with the occasional thatched picnic hut. Now that the resorts have been completed, this mile-plus-long beach is always hopping. **Manchebo Beach** (⊠ *J. E. Irausquin Blvd., at the Manchebo Beach Resort*) is impressively wide; the shoreline in front of the Manchebo Beach Resort is where officials turn a blind eye to the occasional topless sunbather. This beach merges with Druif Beach, and most locals use the name Manchebo to refer to both. **Palm Beach** (⊠ *J. E. Irausquin Blvd. between the Westin Aruba Resort, Spa & Casino and the Marriott Aruba Ocean Club*) from the Westin Aruba to the Marriott Aruba Ocean Club is the center of Aruban tourism, offering good opportunities for swimming, sailing, and other water sports. In some spots you might find a variety of shells that are great to collect, but not as much fun to step on barefoot—bring sandals just in case.

WHERE TO EAT

$$$ ✕ **Cuba's Cookin'.** This funky little establishment is tucked away on an
CUBAN innocuous street downtown. Nightly entertainment, great authentic
★ Cuban food, and a lively crowd are the draws here. The empanadas are excellent, as is the chicken stuffed with plantains. Don't leave without trying the roast pork, which is pretty close to perfection. The signature dish is the *ropa vieja*, a sautéed flank steak served with a rich sauce (the name literally translates as "old clothes"). Service can be a bit spotty at times, depending on how busy it gets. There's always a crowd, as loyal fans and fun-seekers usually flock to the bar area. ⊠ *Wilhelminastraat 27, Oranjestad, Aruba* ☎ *297/588–0627* ⊕ *www.cubascookin.com* ⊙ *Closed Sun. mid-Apr.–mid-Dec.*

7

$$$ ✕ **Gostoso.** Locals adore the magical mixture of Portuguese, Aruban, and
CARIBBEAN   international dishes on offer at this consistently excellent establishment.
The decor walks a fine line between kitschy and cozy, but the atmosphere
is relaxed and informal and outdoor seating is available. The *bacalhau*
vinaigrette (dressed salted cod) is a delightful Portuguese appetizer and
pairs nicely with most of the Aruban dishes on the menu. Meat lovers
are sure to enjoy the Venezuelan mixed grill, which includes a 14-ounce
steak and chorizo accompanied by local sides like fried plantain. ✉ *Caya
Ing Roland H. Lacle 12, Oranjestad, Aruba* ☎ *297/588–0053* ⊕ *www.
gostosoaruba.com* ⚓ *Reservations essential* ⊘ *Closed Mon.*

BARBADOS (BRIDGETOWN)

Jane E. Zarem   Barbadians (Bajans) are a warm, friendly, and hospitable people, who
are genuinely proud of their country and culture. Although tourism is
the island's number one industry, the island has a sophisticated busi-
ness community and stable government, so life here doesn't skip a beat
after passengers return to the ship. Barbados is the most "British" island
in the Caribbean. Afternoon tea is a ritual, and cricket is the national
sport. The atmosphere, though, is hardly stuffy. This is still the Carib-
bean, after all. Beaches along the island's south and west coasts are
picture-perfect, and all are available to cruise passengers. On the rug-
ged east coast, the Atlantic Ocean attracts world-class surfers. The
northeast is dominated by rolling hills and valleys, while the interior
of the island is covered by acres of sugarcane and dotted with small vil-
lages. Historic plantations, a stalactite-studded cave, a wildlife preserve,
rum distilleries, and tropical gardens are among the island's attractions.
Bridgetown is the capital city, and its downtown shops and historic sites
are a short walk or taxi ride from the pier.

ESSENTIALS

CURRENCY   The Barbados dollar (BDS$) is pegged to the U.S. dollar at the rate of
BDS$1.99 to US$1. U.S. dollars (but not coins) are accepted universally
across the island, but change is given in Barbados currency.

INTERNET   You'll find Internet cafés in and around Bridgetown and at St. Law-
rence Gap on the south coast. Rates range from $2 for 15 minutes to
$8 or $9 per hour.

Connect Internet Cafe ✉ *Shop #9, 27 Broad St., Bridgetown, St. Michael,
Barbados* ☎ *246/228–8648.*

TELEPHONE   Your cell phone should work in Barbados, although roaming charges
can be costly. Alternatively, you can purchase phone cards at the cruise-
ship terminal. Direct-dialing to the United States, Canada, and other
countries is efficient and reasonable. Some toll-free numbers cannot be
accessed in Barbados. To charge your overseas call on a major credit
card or U.S. calling card without incurring a surcharge, dial 800/225–
5872 (1-800/call-usa) from any phone.

COMING ASHORE

Up to eight ships at a time can dock at Bridgetown's Deep Water Harbour, on the northwest side of Carlisle Bay near Bridgetown. The cruiseship terminal has duty-free shops, handicraft vendors, a post office, a telephone station, a tourist information desk, and a taxi stand. To get downtown, follow the shoreline to the Careenage. It's a 15-minute walk or a $3 taxi ride.

Taxis await ships at the pier. Drivers accept U.S. dollars and appreciate a 10% tip. Taxis are unmetered and operate at an hourly rate of $25 to $30 per carload (up to three passengers). Most drivers will cheerfully narrate an island tour. You can rent a car with a valid driver's license, but rates are steep—up to $85 per day during the high season—and some agencies require a two-day rental at that time. Note, too, that driving is on the left, British-style.

EXPLORING BARBADOS

BRIDGETOWN

This bustling capital city is a major duty-free port with a compact shopping area. The principal thoroughfare is Broad Street, which leads west from National Heroes Square.

Nidhe Israel Synagogue. Providing for the spiritual needs of one of the oldest Jewish congregations in the Western Hemisphere, this synagogue was formed by Jews who left Brazil in the 1620s and introduced sugarcane to Barbados. The adjoining cemetery has tombstones dating from the 1630s. The original house of worship, built in 1654, was destroyed in an 1831 hurricane, rebuilt in 1833, and restored with the assistance of the Barbados National Trust in 1987. Friday-night services are held during the winter months, but the building is open to the public year-round. Shorts are not acceptable during services but may be worn at other times. ⊠ *Synagogue La., Bridgetown, St. Michael* ☎ *246/426–5792* ⌨ *Donation requested* ⊗ *Weekdays 9–4.*

CENTRAL AND WEST

⟲ **Gun Hill Signal Station.** The 360-degree view from Gun Hill, 700 feet
Fodor'sChoice above sea level, gave this location strategic importance to the 18th-
★ century British army. Using lanterns and semaphore, soldiers based here could communicate with their counterparts at the Garrison on the south coast and at Grenade Hill in the north. Time moved slowly in 1868, and Captain Henry Wilkinson whiled away his off-duty hours by carving a huge lion from a single rock—which is on the hillside just below the tower. Come for a short history lesson but mainly for the view; it's so gorgeous, military invalids were once sent here to convalesce. ⊠ *Gun Hill, St. George* ☎ *246/429–1358* ⌨ *$5* ⊗ *Weekdays 9–5.*

⟲ **Harrison's Cave.** This limestone cavern, complete with stalactites, stalag
Fodor'sChoice mites, subterranean streams, and a 40-foot waterfall, is a rare find in the
★ Caribbean—and one of Barbados's most popular attractions. The cave reopened in early 2010, after extensive renovations comprising a new visitor center with interpretive displays, life-size models and sculptures, a souvenir shop, improved restaurant facilities, and access for people

7

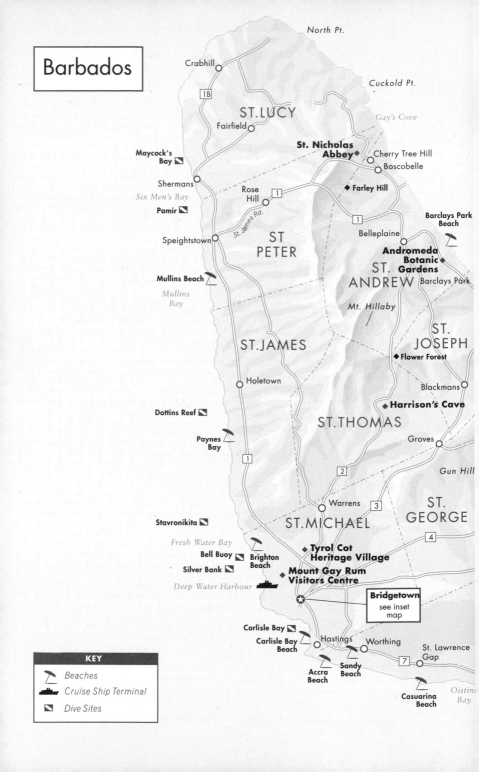

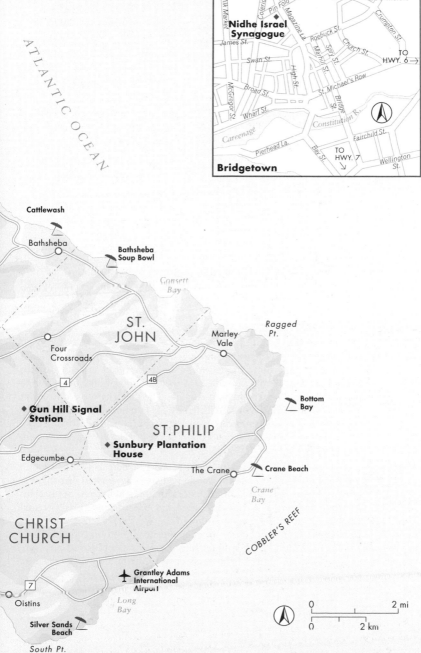
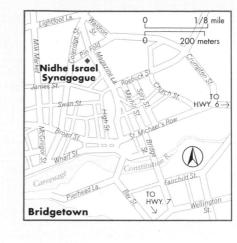

ATLANTIC OCEAN

Bridgetown

Lightfoot La.

Milk Market

Waldron St.

Coleridge St.

Pin Fold

Magazine La.

**Nidhe Israel
Synagogue**

James St.

Roebuck St.

Spry St.

Marhil St.

Church St.

Crumpton St.

TO
HWY. 6 →

Swan St.

High St.

St. Michael's Row

Bridge St.

Constitution R.

Broad St.

McGregor St.

Wharf St.

Careenage

Pierhead La.

Fairchild St.

Wellington St.

Bay St.

TO
HWY. 7
↓

0   1/8 mile

0   200 meters

Cattlewash

Bathsheba

Bathsheba
Soup Bowl

Gonsett
Bay

ST.
JOHN

Marley
Vale

Ragged
Pt.

Four
Crossroads

4

4B

◆ **Gun Hill Signal
Station**

**Bottom
Bay**

ST. PHILIP

◆ **Sunbury Plantation
House**

Edgecumbe

The Crane

Crane Beach

Crane
Bay

CHRIST
CHURCH

COBBLER'S REEF

7

Oistins

✈ **Grantley Adams
International
Airport**

Long
Bay

**Silver Sands
Beach**

South Pt.

0   2 mi

0   2 km

with disabilities. Tours include a nine-minute video presentation and a 40-minute underground journey through the cavern via electric tram. Tours fill up fast, so make a reservation. ⊠ *Hwy. 2, Welchman Hall, St. Thomas* ☎ *246/438–6640* ⊕ *www. harrisonscave.com* ✉ *$30* ⊙ *Wed.– Sun. 8:45–3:45 (last tour).*

Fodor's Choice ★ **Mount Gay Rum Visitors Centre.** On this popular tour, you learn the colorful story behind the world's oldest rum—made in Barbados since 1703. Although the distillery is in the far north, in St. Lucy Parish, tour guides explain the rum-making procedure. Both historic and modern equipment is on display, and rows and rows of barrels are stored in this location. The 45-minute tour runs hourly (last tour begins at 3:30 weekdays; 2:30 on Saturday) and concludes with a tasting and an opportunity to buy bottles of rum and gift items—and even have lunch or cocktails, depending on the time of day. ⊠ *Spring Garden Hwy., Brandons, St. Michael* ☎ *246/425–8757* ⊕ *www.mountgayrum.com* ✉ *$7, $50 with lunch; $35 with cocktails* ⊙ *Weekdays 9–5.*

NORTH AND EAST

Fodor's Choice ★ **Andromeda Botanic Gardens.** More than 600 beautiful and unusual plant specimens from around the world are cultivated in 6 acres of gardens nestled among streams, ponds, and rocky outcroppings overlooking the sea above the Bathsheba coastline. The gardens were created in 1954 with flowering plants collected by the late horticulturist Iris Bannochie. They're now administered by the Barbados National Trust. The Hibiscus Café serves snacks and drinks. ⊠ *Bathsheba, St. Joseph* ☎ *246/433–9384* ✉ *$10* ⊙ *Daily 9–5.*

Fodor's Choice ★ **St. Nicholas Abbey.** There's no religious connection here at all. The island's oldest greathouse (circa 1650) was named after the original British owner's hometown, St. Nicholas Parish near Bristol, and Bath Abbey nearby. Its stone-and-wood architecture makes it one of only three original Jacobean-style houses still standing in the Western Hemisphere. It has Dutch gables, finials of coral stone, and beautiful grounds that include an old sugar mill. The first floor, fully furnished with period furniture and portraits of family members, is open to the public. ⊠ *Cherry Tree Hill, St. Peter* ☎ *246/422–5357* ⊕ *www.stnicholasabbey.com* ✉ *$15* ⊙ *Sun.–Fri. 10–3:30.*

BARBADOS BEST BETS

■ **The East Coast.** The island's windward coast, with its crashing surf, is a "don't miss" sight.

■ **Flower Gardens.** Andromeda Botanic Gardens, Flower Forest, and Orchid World are all scenic and fragrant.

■ **Harrison's Cave.** This extensive limestone cave system is deep beneath Barbados.

■ **Mount Gay Rum Visitors Centre.** Take a tour and a tasting.

■ **St. Nicholas Abbey.** Not an abbey at all, this is one of the oldest Jacobean-style houses in the Western Hemisphere.

SOUTH

Fodor's Choice ★ **Sunbury Plantation House and Museum.** Lovingly rebuilt after a 1995 fire destroyed everything but the thick flint-and-stone walls, Sunbury offers an elegant glimpse of the 18th and 19th centuries on a Barbadian sugar estate. Period furniture, old prints, and a collection of horse-drawn carriages lend an air of authenticity. A buffet luncheon is served daily in the courtyard for $30 per person. ⊠ *Off Hwy. 5, Six Cross Roads, St. Philip* ☎ *246/423–6270* ⊕ *www.barbadosgreathouse. com* ☑ *$7.50* ⊙ *Daily 9:30–4:30.*

> **TIME TIP**
>
> If you don't want to rely on shipboard wake-up calls, be sure to bring your own travel alarm clock; most staterooms do not have clocks.

☾ **Tyrol Cot Heritage Village.** This coral-stone cottage just south of Bridgetown was constructed in 1854 and is preserved as an example of period architecture. In 1929 it became the home of Sir Grantley Adams, the first premier of Barbados and the namesake of its international airport. Part of the Barbados National Trust, the cottage is filled with antiques and memorabilia that belonged to the late Sir Grantley and Lady Adams. It's also the centerpiece of an outdoor "living museum," where artisans and craftsmen have their workshops in a cluster of traditional chattel houses. ⊠ *Rte. 2, Codrington Hill, St. Michael* ☎ *246/424–2074 or 246/436–9033* ☑ *$7* ⊙ *Weekdays 8–4.*

SHOPPING

Duty-free shopping is found in Bridgetown's Broad Street stores and their branches in Holetown and at the cruise-ship terminal. Stores are generally open weekdays 8:30–4:30, Saturday 8:30–1. ■ TIP→ **To purchase items duty-free, you must show your passport and cabin key card.**

Best of Barbados. Best of Barbados was the brainchild of architect Jimmy Walker as a place to showcase the works of his artist wife. Now with five locations, the shops offer products that range from Jill Walker's frameable prints, housewares, and textiles to arts and crafts in both "native" style and modern designs. Everything is made or designed on Barbados. ⊠ *Quayside Centre, Rockley, Christ Church* ☎ *246/421– 6900* ⊕ *www.best-of-barbados.com.*

Fodor's Choice ★ **Earthworks Pottery.** Earthworks is a family-owned and -operated pottery workshop where you can purchase anything from a dish or knickknack to a complete dinner service or one-of-a-kind art piece. You can find the characteristically blue or green pottery decorating hotel rooms for sale in gift shops throughout the island, but the biggest selection (including some "seconds") is at Earthworks, where you also can watch the potters at work. ⊠ *No. 2, Edgehill Heights, St. Thomas* ☎ *246/425–0223* ⊕ *www.earthworks-pottery.com.*

★ **Pelican Craft Centre.** Pelican is made up of a cluster of workshops halfway between the cruise-ship terminal and downtown Bridgetown where craftspeople create and sell locally made leather goods, batik, basketry, carvings, jewelry, glass art, paintings, pottery, and other items. It's open weekdays 9 to 5 and Saturday 9 to 2, with extended hours during

7

holidays or cruise-ship arrivals (when it's also busiest). ⊠ *Princess Alice Hwy., Bridgetown, St. Michael* ☎ 246/427–5350.

ACTIVITIES

FISHING

Billfisher II. *Billfisher II*, a 40-foot Pacemaker, accommodates up to six passengers with three fishing chairs and five rods. Captain Winston ("The Colonel") White has been fishing these waters since 1975. His full-day charters include a full lunch and guaranteed fish (or a 25% refund); all trips include drinks and transportation to and from the boat. ☎ 246/431–0741.

Blue Jay. *Blue Jay* is a spacious, fully equipped, 45-foot Sport Fisherman with a crew that knows the water's denizens—blue marlin, sailfish, barracuda, and kingfish. Four to six people can be accommodated—it's the only charter boat on the island with four chairs. Most fishing is done by trolling. Drinks, snacks, bait, tackle, and transfers are provided. ☎ 246/429–2326 ⊕ *www.bluemarlinbarbados.com.*

GOLF

Barbados Golf Club. Barbados Golf Club, the first public golf course on Barbados, is an 18-hole championship course (6,805 yards, par 72) redesigned in 2000 by golf course architect Ron Kirby. Greens fees with a cart are $125 for 18 holes; $80 for 9 holes. Unlimited three-day and seven-day golf passes are available. Several hotels offer preferential tee-time reservations and reduced rates. Club and shoe rentals are available. ⊠ *Hwy. 7, Durants, Christ Church* ☎ 246/428–8463 ⊕ *www. barbadosgolfclub.com.*

Fodor's Choice
★ **Country Club at Sandy Lane.** At the prestigious Country Club at Sandy Lane, golfers can play on the Old Nine or on either of two 18-hole championship courses: the Tom Fazio–designed Country Club Course or the spectacular Green Monkey Course, reserved for hotel guests and club members only. Golfers have complimentary use of the club's driving range. The Country Club Restaurant and Bar, which overlooks the 18th hole, is open to the public. Greens fees in high season are $155 for 9 holes ($135 for hotel guests) or $240 for 18 holes ($205 for hotel guests). Golf carts, caddies, or trolleys are available for hire, as are clubs and shoes. Carts are equipped with GPS, which alerts you to upcoming traps and hazards, provides tips on how to play the hole, and allows you to order refreshments! ⊠ *Hwy. 1, Paynes Bay, St. James* ☎ 246/444–2500 ⊕ *www.sandylane.com/golf.*

BEACHES

All beaches on Barbados are open to cruise-ship passengers. The west coast has the stunning coves and white-sand beaches dear to the hearts of postcard publishers, plus calm, clear water for snorkeling and swimming. Waterskiing and parasailing are also available on most beaches along the south and west coasts. Windsurfing is best on the south coast.

Accra Beach. This popular beach, also known as Rockley Beach, is next to the Accra Beach Hotel. Look forward to gentle surf and a lifeguard, plenty of nearby restaurants for refreshments, a children's playground, and beach stalls for renting chairs and equipment for snorkeling and other water sports. Parking is available at an on-site lot. ⊠ *Hwy. 7, Rockley, Christ Church.*

Brighton Beach. Calm as a lake, this is where you can find locals taking a quick dip on hot days. Just north of Bridgetown, Brighton Beach is also home to the Cockspur Beach Club. ⊠ *Spring Garden Hwy., Brighton, St. Michael.*

Carlisle Bay. Adjacent to the Hilton Barbados just south of Bridgetown, this broad half circle of white sand is one of the island's best beaches—but it can become crowded on weekends and holidays. Park at Harbour Lights or at the Boatyard Bar and Bayshore Complex, both on Bay Street, where you can also rent umbrellas and beach chairs and buy refreshments. ⊠ *Aquatic Gap, Needham's Point, St. Michael.*

Fodor'sChoice
★
Mullins Beach. This lovely beach just south of Speightstown is a perfect place to spend the day. The water is safe for swimming and snorkeling, there's easy parking on the main road, and Mullins Restaurant serves snacks, meals, and drinks—and rents chairs and umbrellas. ⊠ *Hwy. 1, Mullins Bay, St. Peter.*

Paynes Bay Beach. The stretch of beach just south of Sandy Lane is lined with luxury hotels. It's a very pretty area, with plenty of beach to go around and good snorkeling. Public access is available at several locations along Highway 1; parking is limited. Grab liquid refreshments and a bite to eat at Bomba's Beach Bar. ⊠ *Hwy. 1, Paynes Bay, St. James.*

WHERE TO EAT

$$$
CARIBBEAN
Fodor'sChoice
★
✕ **The Atlantis.** For decades, an alfresco lunch on the Atlantis deck overlooking the ocean has been a favorite of visitors touring the east coast and Bajans alike. Totally renovated and reopened in 2009 by the owners of Little Good Harbour and the Fishpot on the west coast, the revived restaurant effectively combines the atmosphere and good food that have always been the draw with an up-to-date, rather elegant dining room and a top-notch menu that focuses on local produce, seafood, and meats. The Bajan buffet lunch on Wednesday and Sunday is particularly popular; it's also well used for special occasions for local folks. ⊠ *Tent Bay, Bathsheba, St. Joseph* ☎ *246/433–9445* ⊕ *www. atlantishotelbarbados.com* ⌂ *Reservations essential* ☉ *No dinner Sun.*

$$$
CARIBBEAN
✕ **Waterfront Café.** This friendly bistro alongside the Careenage is the perfect place to enjoy a drink, snack, or meal—and to people-watch. Locals and tourists alike gather for all-day alfresco dining on sandwiches, salads, fish, pasta, pepper-pot stew, and tasty Bajan snacks such as buljol, fish cakes, or plantation pork (plantains stuffed with spicy minced pork). The panfried flying-fish sandwich is especially popular. In the evening you can gaze through the arched windows while savoring nouvelle Caribbean cuisine, enjoying cool trade winds, and listening to live jazz. There's a special Caribbean buffet and steel-pan music on Tuesday night from 7 to 9. ⊠ *The Careenage, Bridgetown, St. Michael* ☎ *246/427–0093* ⊕ *www.waterfrontcafe.com.bb* ☉ *Closed Sun.*

7

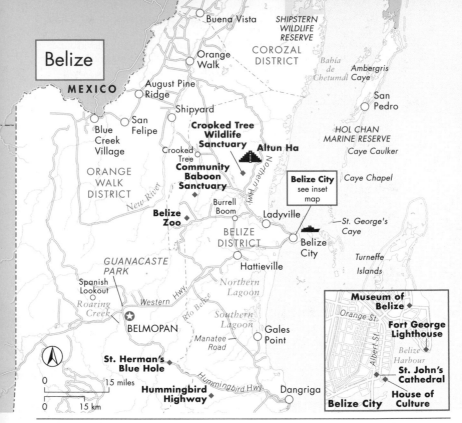

BELIZE CITY, BELIZE

Marlise Kast

Belize probably has the greatest variety of flora and fauna of any country of its size in the world. Here you'll often find more iguanas or howler monkeys than humans. A few miles off the mainland is the Belize Barrier Reef, a great wall of coral stretching the entire 200-mi (333-km) length of the coast. More than 200 cayes (pronounced keys) dot the reef like punctuation marks, and three coral atolls lie farther out to sea. All are superb for diving and snorkeling. Many, like Ambergris Caye (pronounced *Am*-bur-griss Key) and Caye Caulker, are cheery resort islands with ample bars and restaurants, easily reachable on day trips from Belize City. The main choice you'll have to make is whether to stay in Belize City for a little stroll and shopping, and perhaps a dram at one of the Fort George hotels or restaurants, or alternatively to head out by boat, rental car, taxi, or tour on a more active adventure.

ESSENTIALS

CURRENCY Since U.S. currency is universally accepted, there's no need to acquire the Belize dollar (BZ$2 to US$1).

FLIGHTS Especially if you are going to Ambergris Caye, you may prefer to fly, or you can water-taxi over and fly back to maximize your time. There are hourly flights on two airlines. The flight to Caulker takes about

10 minutes and that to San Pedro about 25 minutes. The cost is about BZ$250 round-trip to either island. Be sure you fly out of Belize City's Municipal, not out of the international airport north of the city. **Maya Island Airways** (✉ *Municipal Airstrip, Building #1, 2nd fl., Belize City* ☎ *223–1140* ⊕ *www.mayaregional.com*). **Tropic Air** (✉ *San Pedro* ☎ *226–2012, 800/422–3435 in U.S.* ⊕ *www.tropicair.com*).

INTERNET **Click and Sip Internet Café** (✉ *Fort St., in Fort Street Tourism Village* ☎ *223–1305*).

TELEPHONE Calling locally or internationally is easy, but rates are high; around BZ$1.50 a minute for calls to the U.S. To call the United States, dial 001 or 10–10–199 plus the area code and number. Pay phones, which are located in the Fort Street Tourism Village where you are tendered, and elsewhere downtown, accept only prepaid Belize Telecommunications Ltd. (BTL) phone cards, available in shops in denominations from $5 to $50. Special "USA Connect" prepaid cards, for sale at some stores in Belize City, in denominations of $5 to $20, claim discounts of as much as 57% for calls to the U.S. only. Your U.S.-based GSM phone will probably work on Belize's GSM 1900 system, but you will pay a high surcharge to use it abroad. Foreign calling cards are generally blocked in Belize. Call 113 for local directory assistance, and 115 for an operator.

BELIZE CITY BEST BETS

- **Belize Zoo.** Though small, this collection of native Belize wildlife is excellent.

- **Cave Tubing.** If you are not claustrophobic, this is an unforgettable excursion.

- **Diving.** Belize is becoming known as one of the world's best dive destinations. For the certified, this is a must.

- **Snorkeling in Hol Chan.** The water is teeming with fish, and you don't need to be certified to enjoy the underwater world here.

7

COMING ASHORE

Because Belize City's harbor is shallow, passengers are tendered in. If you're going the independent route, try to get in line early for the tenders, as it sometimes takes 90 minutes or more for all the passengers to be brought ashore. You arrive at the Fort Street Tourism Village complex. It has a collection of gift shops, restaurants, and tour operators nicely situated along the harbor. Bathrooms are spick-and-span, too. At this writing, construction is sputtering on a much-delayed $50-million cruise terminal south of the city center; when it will finally open is anyone's guess.

Taxis, tour guides, and car-rental desks are readily available. Taxi trips—official taxis have green license plates—within Belize City are supposed to be set at BZ$6 to BZ$10 for one person between any two points in the city, plus BZ$1 for each additional person. Taxi fares at night are slightly higher. Outside the city, and from downtown to the suburbs, you're charged by the distance you travel. Hourly rates are negotiable, but expect to pay around $30, or $150 for the day. Drivers are required to display a Taxi Federation rate card. There's no need to tip cab drivers. You can also rent a car at the Tourism Village, but rates can be high (at least $75 per day), and gas is also expensive. Green directional signs point you to nearby destinations such as the Belize Zoo. The Wet Lizard, next to the Tourism Village, also organizes tours for cruise-ship passengers.

EXPLORING BELIZE

Belize Tourism Board. ✉ *64 Regent St., Belize City* ☎ *227–2420* ⊕ *www. travelbelize.org.*

✦ **Altun Ha.** If you've never visited an ancient Maya site, make a trip to Altun Ha, 28 mi (45 km) north of Belize City. Altun Ha, meaning "Rockstone Pond," was a trading center for more than 10,000 Maya that occupied the area as early as 200 BC. ✦ *From Belize City, take the Northern Hwy. north to Mile 18.9. Turn right (east) on the Old Northern Hwy., which is only partly paved, and go 10½ mi (17 km) to the signed entrance road to Altun Ha on the left. Follow this paved road 2 mi (3 km) to the visitor center* ☎ *No phone* ✉ *BZ$10* ☉ *Daily 9–5.*

Belize City. Many Belize hands will tell you that the best way to see Belize City is through a rearview window. But, with an open mind to its peculiarities, and with a little caution (the city has a crime problem, but the tourist police keep a close watch on cruise-ship passengers), you may decide Belize City has a raffish, atmospheric charm rarely found in other Caribbean ports of call. You might even see the ghost of Graham Greene, who visited Belize in 1978 as a guest of General Torrijos. A 5- to 10-minute stroll from the colorful Fort Street Tourism Village brings you into the other worlds of Belize City. On the north side of Haulover Creek is the colonial-style Fort George are, where large old homes, stately but sometimes down at the heels, take the breezes off the sea and share their space with hotels and restaurants. On the south side is bustling Albert Street, the main commercial thoroughfare. But don't stroll too far because parts of Belize City are unsafe. During the daylight hours, as long as you stay within the main commercial district and the Fort George area—and ignore the street hustlers—you should have no problem.

House of Culture, the city's finest colonial structure, is said to have been designed by the illustrious British architect Sir Christopher Wren. Built in 1814, it was once the residence of the governor-general, the queen's representative in Belize. ✉ *Regent St. at Southern Foreshore* ☎ *227–3050* ✉ *BZ$10* ☉ *Mon.–Thurs. 8–5, Fri. 8–4:30* ⊕ *www.nichbelize.org.*

Towering over the entrance to Belize Harbor, the **Fort George Lighthouse and Bliss Memorial** stands guard on the tip of Fort George Point. It was designed and funded by the country's greatest benefactor, Baron Bliss. The English nobleman never actually set foot on the Belizean mainland, but in his will he bequeathed most of his fortune to the people of Belize, and the date of his death, March 9, is celebrated as a national holiday. He is buried here, in a small, low mausoleum perched on the seawall, up a short run of limestone stairs. The lighthouse is for photo ops only—you can't enter it. ✉ *Marine Parade.*

This small but interesting **Museum of Belize** was a Belize City jail from the 1850s to 1993. Displays on Belize history and culture include ancient Mayan artifacts, eclectic memorabilia, colorful Belize postage stamps, and an actual jail cell. Exhibitions change frequently. ⊠ *8 Gabourel La.* ☎ *223–4524* ⊕ *www.nichbelize.org* ☞ *BZ$10* ☺ *Mon.– Thurs. 8–5, Fri. 8–4:30.*

St. John's Cathedral, at the south end of Albert Street, is the oldest Anglican church in Central America, and the only one outside England where kings were crowned. From 1815 to 1845 four kings of the Mosquito Coast (a British protectorate along the coast of Honduras and Nicaragua) were crowned here. ⊠ *Albert St.* ☎ *227–2137* ☺ *Weekdays 6–6.*

☾ **Belize Zoo.** One of the smallest, but arguably one of the best, zoos in the
Fodor's Choice world, this park houses only animals native to Belize. Highlights include
★ spotted and rare black jaguars, pumas, margays, ocelots, jaguarondi, and the Baird's tapir, the national animal of Belize. ⊠ *Western Hwy., 30 mi (49 km) west of Belize City* ☎ *220–8004* ⊕ *www.belizezoo.org* ☞ *BZ$30* ☺ *Daily 8–5.*

☾ **Community Baboon Sanctuary.** This interesting wildlife conservation project is actually a haven for nearly 2,000 black howler monkeys and numerous other species of birds and mammals. ⊠ *Community Baboon Sanctuary, 31 mi (50 km) northwest of Belize City* ☎ *660–3545* ⊕ *www. howlermonkeys.org* ☞ *BZ$14* ☺ *Daily 8–5.*

Crooked Tree Wildlife Sanctuary A paradise for birders and animal lovers, this wildlife sanctuary encompasses a chain of inland waterways around the Northern Lagoon covering about 3,000 acres. Traveling through by canoe, you're likely to see iguanas, crocodiles, coatis, and turtles. The sanctuary's most prestigious visitors, however, are the jabiru storks, several of which usually visit between November and May. ⊠ *Turn west off Northern Hwy. at Mile 30.8, then drive 2 mi (3 km)* ☎ *223–5004 for Belize Audubon Society* ⊕ *www.belizeaudubon.org* ☞ *BZ$8* ☺ *Daily 8–4:30.*

Hummingbird Highway. At Belmopan, the paved Hummingbird Highway is Belize's most scenic road, cutting 54 mi (90 km) southeast through the Maya Mountains to Dangriga, passing Five Blues Lake and Blue Hole national parks. Mile markers on the Hummingbird start in Dangriga.

☾ **St. Herman's Blue Hole Natural Park.** Less than a half-hour south of Belmopan, the 575-acre park has a natural turquoise pool surrounded by mosses and lush vegetation, excellent for a cool dip. ⊠ *Mile 42.5, Hummingbird Hwy.* ☎ *223–5004 for Belize Audubon Society* ⊕ *www. belizeaudubon.org* ☞ *BZ$8* ☺ *Daily 8–4:30*

THE CAYES

Ambergris Caye. Ambergris is the queen of the cayes. With a population of around 9,000, the island's only town, San Pedro, remains a small, friendly, and prosperous village. It has one of the highest literacy rates in the country and an admirable level of awareness about the fragility of the reef. The large number of substantial private houses being built on the edges of town is proof of how much tourism has enriched San Pedro. A water taxi from the Marine Terminal takes about 75 minutes and costs BZ$20 each way. You can also fly.

7

Hol Chan Marine Reserve (Maya for "little channel") is 4 mi (6 km) from San Pedro at the southern tip of Ambergris. Because fishing is forbidden here, snorkelers and divers can see teeming marine life. You can also snorkel with nurse sharks and rays (which gather here to be fed) at Shark-Ray Alley, a sandbar that is part of the reserve. You need above-average swimming skills, as the current is often strong. ⊠ *Southern tip of Ambergris Caye* ⊕ *www.holchanbelize.org* ⊠ *BZ$25 marine reserve fee.*

Caye Caulker. On Caye Caulker, where the one village is home to around 2,000 people, brightly painted houses on stilts line the coral-sand streets. Although the island is being developed more each year, flowers still outnumber cars 10 to 1 (golf carts, bicycles, and bare feet are the preferred means of transportation). The living is easy, as you might guess from all the *no shirt, no shoes, no problem* signs at the bars. This is the kind of place where most of the listings in the telephone directory give addresses like "near football field." A water taxi from the Marine Terminal costs about BZ$20 each way and takes about 45 minutes.

SHOPPING

Belize does not have the crafts tradition of its neighbors, Guatemala and Mexico, and imported goods are expensive due to high duties, but hand-carved items of ziricote or other local woods make good souvenirs. Near the Swing Bridge at Market Square is the **Commercial Center,** which has some food and craft vendors on the first floor and a restaurant and shops on the second. The **Fort Street Tourism Village,** where the ship tenders come in, is a collection of bright and clean gift shops selling T-shirts and Belizean and Guatemalan crafts. Beside the Tourism Village is an informal **Street Vendor Market,** with funkier goods and performances by a "Brukdown" band or a group of Garifuna drummers.

National Handicraft Center (⊠ *2 South Park St., in Fort George section* ☎ *223–3636*) has Belizean souvenir items, including hand-carved figurines, handmade furniture, pottery, and woven baskets. The prices are about as good as you'll find anywhere in Belize, and the sales clerks are friendly. It faces the small Memorial Park, which commemorates the Battle of St. George's Caye and is just a short stroll from the harbor front, the Tourism Village, and many of the hotels in the Fort George area, including the Radisson, Chateau Caribbean, and Great House.

ACTIVITIES

CANOPY TOURS

You may feel a little like Tarzan as you dangle 80 feet above the jungle floor, suspended by a harness, moving from one suspended platform to another. **Jaguar Paw Lodge** (☎ *501/223–4438, 877/424–8552 in U.S.* ⊕ *www.jaguarpaw.com*), off Mile 37 of the Western Highway, has seven platforms set 100 to 250 feet apart. At the last platform you have to rappel to the ground. The cost is BZ$180 to BZ$250, depending on whether lunch and transportation are included. There's a 240-pound weight limit.

CAVE TUBING

Very popular with cruise passengers are river-tubing trips that go through a cave, where you'll turn off your headlamp for a minute of absolute darkness, but these are not for the claustrophobic or those afraid of the dark. **Cave-Tubing in Belize** (☎ *605–1575* ⊕ *www.cave-tubing.com*) specializes in cave-tubing trips. The cost is BZ$100 (not including transportation from the cruise pier); for BZ$150, you can do both the cave-tubing and an ATV trip in the jungle.

DIVING AND SNORKELING

Most companies on Ambergris Caye offer morning and afternoon single-tank dives; snorkel trips begin mid-morning or early afternoon. Dive and snorkeling trips that originate in Caye Caulker are a bit cheaper. **Amigos del Mar** (⊠ *Off Barrier Reef Dr., near Mayan Princess Hotel, Ambergris Caye* ☎ *226–2706* ⊕ *amigosdive.com*) is perhaps the island's most consistently recommended dive operation. It offers a range of local dives as well as trips to Turneffe Atoll and Lighthouse Reef in a fast 48-foot dive boat.

Go out for a snorkel on a sailboat with **Raggamuffin Tours** (⊠ *Front St., Caye Caulker* ☎ *226–0348* ⊕ *www.raggamuffintours.com*), which goes to Hol Chan for BZ$90, including the park entrance fee.

INDEPENDENT TOURS

Several Belize City–based tour guides and operators offer custom trips for ship passengers; companies will usually meet you at the Fort Street Tourism Village. Katie Valk, who owns **Belize Trips** (⌂ *Box 1108, Belize City* ☎ *501/610–1923 in Belize, 561/210–7015 in U.S.* ⊕ *www.belize-trips.com*), is a transplanted New Yorker. Her company can organize a custom trip to just about anywhere in the country. **Ecological Tours & Services.** (⊠ *Fort Street Tourism Village, Belize City* ☎ *223–4874* ⊕ *www.ecotoursbelize.com*), based in Belize City, specializes in organizing independent tours for cruise-ship passengers.

BEACHES

Although the barrier reef limits the wave action and brings seagrass to the shore floor, the wide sandy beaches of Ambergris Caye are among the best in Belize. All beaches in Belize are public. **Mar de Tumbo,** 1½ mi (3 km) south of town near the Tropica Hotel, is the best beach on the south end of the island. **North Ambergris,** accessible by water taxi from San Pedro or by golf cart over the bridge to the north, has miles of narrow beaches and fewer people. **Ramon's Village's beach,** across from the airstrip, is the best in the town area. The beaches on Caulker are not as good as those on Ambergris. Along the front side of the island is a narrow strip of sand, but the water is shallow and swimming conditions are poor. The **Split,** on the north end of the village (turn to your right from the main public pier), is the best place on Caye Caulker for swimming.

WHERE TO EAT

$$-$$$
AMERICAN
Fodor's Choice
★

✗ Riverside Tavern. Owned and managed by Belikin beer baron Sir Barry Bowen's family, Riverside Tavern opened in 2006 and immediately became one of the city's most popular restaurants. The huge signature hamburgers are arguably the best in Belize. (The 6-ounce burger is BZ$16.) The Riverside has added new steak and prime rib dishes, from cattle from Bowen's farm at Gallon Jug. Sit inside in air-conditioned comfort, at tables set around a huge bar, or on the outside covered patio overlooking Haulover Creek. This is one of the few restaurants in Belize with a dress code; shorts aren't allowed at night. The fenced, guarded parking lot right in front of the restaurant makes it easy and safe to park for free. ⊠ *2 Mapp St., off Freetown Rd.* ☎ *223/5640.*

$-$$
SEAFOOD

✗ Wet Lizard. Right next to the Tourism Village, overlooking the boardwalk where cruise-ship tenders drop off passengers, there's no question of the target market of the Wet Lizard. Even so, it's become a popular bar and a place to grab a sandwich or hamburger, even for those not on a cruise ship. An expansion added a gift shop, snack bar, and tour operation. ⊠ *1 Fort St.* ☎ *223/5973* ⊕ *www.thewetlizard.com* ☾ *Closed Sun. and Mon.*

BERMUDA

Sirkka Huish

Basking in the Atlantic, 508 mi (817 km) due east of Cape Hatteras, North Carolina, restrained, polite Bermuda is a departure from other sunny, beach-strewn isles. You won't find laid-back locals wandering around barefoot proffering piña coladas. Bermuda is somewhat formal, and despite the gorgeous weather, residents wearing stockings and heels or jackets, ties, Bermuda shorts, and knee socks are a common sight, whether on the street by day or in restaurants at night. On Bermuda's 22 square mi (57 square km) you will discover that pastel cottages, quaint shops, and manicured gardens betray a more staid, suburban way of life. A self-governing British colony since 1968, Bermuda has maintained some of its English character even as it is increasingly influenced by American culture. Most cruise ships make seven-night loops from U.S. embarkation ports, with four nights at sea and three tied up in port. Increasingly popular are round-trip itineraries originating in northeastern embarkation ports that include a single day or overnight port call in Bermuda before continuing south to the Bahamas or the Caribbean.

ESSENTIALS

CURRENCY

The Bermuda dollar (B$) is on par with the U.S. dollar. You can use American money anywhere, but change is often given in Bermudian currency. ATMs are common.

INTERNET

Expect to pay as much as $10 per hour to check your email on Bermuda. **Logic Communications** ⊠ *The Walkway, 10–12 Burnaby St., Hamilton* ☎ *441/296–9600 and select retail option.*

TELEPHONE

To make a local call, simply dial the seven-digit number. You can find specially marked AT&T USADirect phones at the airport, the cruise-ship dock in Hamilton, and King's Square and Ordnance Island in St. George's. You can also make international calls with a calling card from the main post office. You can make prepaid international calls from the Cable & Wireless Customer Service Centre in Hamilton (Corner of Burnaby and Church St.), which also has international telex, cable, and fax services Monday through Friday from 9 to 4.45.

COMING ASHORE

Three Bermuda harbors serve cruise ships: Hamilton (the capital), St. George's, and King's Wharf at the Royal Naval Dockyard.

In Hamilton, cruise ships tie up right on the city's main street, Front Street. A Visitors Service Bureau is next to the ferry terminal, also on Front Street and nearby; maps and brochures are displayed in the cruise terminal itself.

St. George's actually has two piers that accommodate cruise ships. One is on Ordnance Island, which is in the heart of the city; another pier is nearby at Penno's Wharf. A Visitors Service Bureau is at the World Heritage Centre, 19 Penno's Wharf.

King's Wharf, in the Royal Naval Dockyard at the westernmost end of the island, is the most isolated of the three cruise-ship berthing areas, and it is where the largest vessels dock. But it is well connected to the rest of the island by taxi, bus, and ferry. A Visitors Service Bureau is adjacent to bus stops and the ferry pier.

Taxis are the fastest and easiest way to get around the island, but they are also quite expensive. Four-seaters charge $6.40 for the first mile and $2 for each subsequent mile. You can hire taxis for around $40 per hour for up to four passengers or $55 per hour for up to six passengers (three-hour minimum) if you want to do some exploring, and if you can round up a group of people, this is often cheaper than an island tour offered by your ship. Tip drivers 15%. Rental cars are prohibited, but the island has a good bus and ferry system. You can also rent scooters, but this can be dangerous for the uninitiated and is not recommended.

EXPLORING BERMUDA

HAMILTON

Bermuda's capital since 1815, the city of Hamilton is a small, bustling harbor town. It's the economic and social center of Bermuda, with busy streets lined with shops and offices. International influences, from both business and tourism, have brought a degree of sophistication unusual in so small a city. There are several museums and galleries to explore, but the favorite pastimes are shopping in Hamilton's numerous boutiques and dining in its many upscale restaurants.

Bermuda Underwater Exploration Institute (BUEI). The 40,000-square-foot Ocean Discovery Centre has numerous multimedia and interactive displays designed to acquaint you with the deep sea and its inhabitants. Never heard of a bathysphere? See a replica of this deep-sea diving vehicle, which allowed oceanographer William Beebe and Otis Barton to venture ½ mi down into the deep in 1934. ⊠ *40 Crow La., off E. Broadway* ☎ *441/292-7219* ⊕ *www.buei.org* ⊠ *$12.50* ☉ *Weekdays 9–5, weekends 10–5; last admission at 4.*

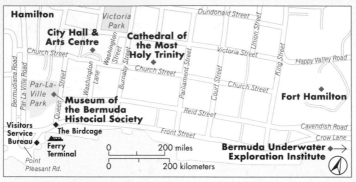

Hamilton

City Hall & Arts Centre

Victoria Park

Cathedral of the Most Holy Trinity

Dundonald Street

Church Street

Washington Street

Washington Lane

Burnaby Street

Church Street

Victoria Street

Union Street

King Street

Happy Valley Road

Bermudiana Road

Par-La-Ville Road

Par-La-Ville Park

Museum of the Bermuda Historical Society

Queen Street

Parliament Street

Court Street

Church Street

Fort Hamilton

Reid Street

Cavendish Road

Crow Lane

Visitors Service Bureau

The Birdcage

Front Street

Ferry Terminal

Point Pleasant Rd.

Bermuda Underwater Exploration Institute

| 0 | | 200 miles |

| 0 | | 200 kilometers |

KEY

Beaches

Cruise Ship Dock

Ferry

Railway Trail

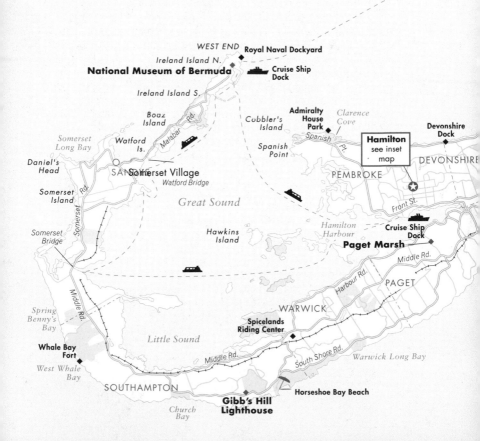

WEST END

Royal Naval Dockyard

Ireland Island N.

National Museum of Bermuda

Cruise Ship Dock

Ireland Island S.

Boaz Island

Malabar Rd.

Cobbler's Island

Clarence Cove

Admiralty House Park

Spanish Point

Devonshire Dock

Watford Is.

Somerset Long Bay

Daniel's Head

Watford Bridge

SANSomerset Village

Spanish Pt.

Hamilton see inset map

DEVONSHIRE

PEMBROKE

Somerset Island

Somerset Rd.

Great Sound

Front St.

Hawkins Island

Hamilton Harbour

Cruise Ship Dock

Somerset Bridge

Paget Marsh

Middle Rd.

PAGET

Middle Rd.

Spring Benny's Bay

Little Sound

Harbour Rd.

WARWICK

Spicelands Riding Center

Whale Bay Fort

Middle Rd.

South Shore Rd.

Warwick Long Bay

West Whale Bay

SOUTHAMPTON

Church Bay

Gibb's Hill Lighthouse

Horseshoe Bay Beach

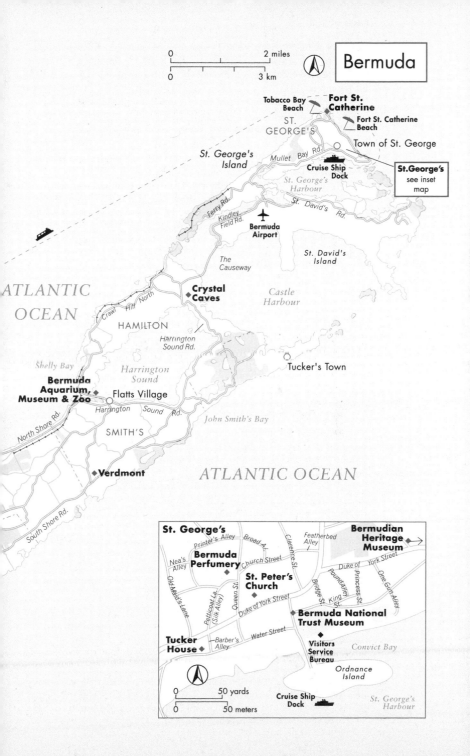

Bermuda

0 ——— 2 miles
0 ——— 3 km

Tobacco Bay Beach — **Fort St. Catherine**
ST. GEORGE'S
Fort St. Catherine Beach
St. George's Island
Town of St. George
Mullet Bay Rd.
Cruise Ship Dock
St. George's Harbour
St.George's see inset map

Ferry Rd.
Kindley Field Rd.
✈ **Bermuda Airport**
St. David's Rd.
St. David's Island

The Causeway

ATLANTIC OCEAN

Crawl Hill North
Crystal Caves
Castle Harbour

HAMILTON
Harrington Sound Rd.
Shelly Bay
Harrington Sound
Bermuda Aquarium, Museum & Zoo ◆ Flatts Village
Harrington Sound Rd.
Tucker's Town

North Shore Rd.
SMITH'S
John Smith's Bay

◆ **Verdmont**
South Shore Rd.

ATLANTIC OCEAN

St. George's

Printer's Alley
Broad Al.
Featherbed Alley
Clarence St.
Bermudian Heritage Museum →
Nea's Alley
Bermuda Perfumery ◆
Church Street
Old Maid's Lane
Petticoat La. (Silk Alley)
Queen St.
Duke of York Street
St. Peter's Church
Bridge St.
Pound Alley
King St.
Duke of York Street
One Gun Alley
Princess St.

Bermuda National Trust Museum ◆

Water Street
Tucker House ◆
Barber's Alley
Visitors Service Bureau ◆
Convict Bay
Ordnance Island

0 ——— 50 yards
0 ——— 50 meters
Cruise Ship Dock
St. George's Harbour

★ **Cathedral of the Most Holy Trinity.** Designed with early Greek Revival flourishes, the cathedral was constructed out of Bermuda limestone and materials imported from France, Nova Scotia, and Scotland. The cathedral was completed in 1911. It has a copper roof, unusual in Bermuda's sea of white-topped buildings. After exploring the interior, you can purchase tickets to climb the 150-odd steps (143 feet) of the tower ⊠ *29 Church St.* ☎ *441/292–4033* ⊕ *www.anglican.bm* ⊡ *Cathedral free; tower $3* ۝ *Cathedral daily 7:30–5 and for Sun. services; tower weekdays 10–4.*

☾ **City Hall and Arts Centre.** Set back from the street behind a fountain and
★ pond, City Hall contains Hamilton's administrative offices as well as two art galleries and a performance hall. Instead of a clock, its tower is topped with a bronze wind vane—a prudent choice in a land where the weather is as important as the time. Massive cedar doors open into a large lobby with beautiful chandeliers and high ceilings. On the first landing, in the East Exhibition Room, is the **Bermuda National Gallery,** the home of Bermuda's national art collection. Farther up the stairs, in the West Wing, the **Bermuda Society of Arts Gallery** displays work by its members. ⊠ *17 Church St.* ☎ *441/292–1234* ⊕ *www.cityhall.bm* ۝ *City Hall weekdays 9–5; National Gallery weekdays 10–4, Sat. 10–2; Society of the Arts weekdays 10–4, Sat. 10–2.*

☾ **Fort Hamilton.** This imposing moat-ringed fortress has underground pas-
★ sageways that were cut through solid rock by Royal Engineers in the 1860s. Built to defend the West End's Royal Naval Dockyard from land attacks, it was outdated even before its completion, but remains a fine example of a polygonal Victorian fort. Even if you're not a big fan of military history, the hilltop site's stellar views and stunning gardens make the trip worthwhile. ⊠ *Happy Valley Rd.* ☎ *441/292–1234* ⊡ *Free* ۝ *Daily 8–sunset.*

★ **Museum of the Bermuda Historical Society/Bermuda Public Library.** This building was once the home of Hamilton's first postmaster, William Bennet Perot, and his family. Mark Twain once lamented that the rubber tree in the front yard didn't bear fruit in the form of hot-water bottles and rubber overshoes. The library was founded in 1839, and its reference section has virtually every book ever written about Bermuda. The museum depicts Bermuda history with household goods and other artifacts, including an 18th-century sedan chair. ⊠ *13 Queen St.* ☎ *441/295–2905 library, 441/295–2487 museum* ⊕ *www.bnl.bm* ⊡ *Library free; museum donations accepted* ۝ *Library Mon.–Thurs. 8:30–7, Fri. 10–5, Sat. 9–5, Sun. 1–5; closed Sun. and at 6 Mon.–Thurs. in July and Aug.; museum weekdays 10–2* ☞ *Tours by appointment.*

ST. GEORGE'S

The settlement of Bermuda began in what is now the town of St. George nearly 400 years ago, when the *Sea Venture* was shipwrecked on Bermuda's treacherous reefs on its way to the colony of Jamestown, Virginia. No trip to Bermuda is complete without a visit to this historic town and UNESCO World Heritage Site.

★ **Bermuda National Trust Museum at the Globe Hotel.** This building was erected in 1700. During the American Civil War, Confederate Major Norman Walker was stationed in the building, where he coordinated the flow of guns, ammunition, and war supplies through Union blockades in American ports. The house saw service as the Globe Hotel during the mid-19th century and became a National Trust property in 1951. ✉ *32 Duke of York St.* ☎ *441/297–1423* ⊕ *www.bnt.bm* 🔖 *$5; $10 combination ticket includes admission to Tucker House and Verdmont* ⊘ *Apr.–Sept., Tues., Wed., Fri., and Sat. 10–4; limited hrs in winter.*

★ **Bermuda Perfumery & Gardens.** In 2005 the perfumery moved from Bailey's Bay in Smith's Parish, where it had been based since 1928, to historic Stewart Hall. Although the location changed, the techniques it uses did not: the perfumery still manufactures and bottles all its island-inspired scents on-site using essential oils extracted from frangipani, jasmine, oleander, and passionflower. Guides are available to explain the entire process, and there's a small museum that outlines the company's history. You can also wander around the gardens and stock up on your favorite fragrances in the showroom. ✉ *Stewart Hall, 5 Queen St.* ☎ *441/293–0627* ⊕ *www.lilibermuda.com* 🔖 *Free* ⊘ *Mon.–Sat. 9–5.*

☺ **Ordnance Island.** A splendid bronze statue of Sir George Somers dominates the island. The dunking stool is a replica of the one used to dunk gossips, nagging wives, and suspected witches. Demonstrations are sometimes given, although volunteers report that getting dunked is no picnic. Also on the island is the *Deliverance II*, a replica of one of two ships—the other was the *Patience*—built by the survivors of the 1609 wreck of the *Sea Venture* to carry them to Jamestown, Virginia, their original destination. ✉ *Across from King's Sq.*

Fodor's Choice **St. Peter's Church.** Because parts of this church date back to 1620, it
★ holds the distinction of being the oldest continuously operating Anglican church in the western hemisphere. It was not the first church to stand on this site, however. It replaced a 1612 structure of posts and palmetto leaves that was destroyed in a storm. The present church was extended in 1713, and the galleries on either side were added in 1833. ✉ *33 Duke of York St.* ☎ *441/297–2459* ⊕ *www.anglican.bm* 🔖 *Donations accepted* ⊘ *Mon.–Sat. 10–4, Sun. service at 11:15.*

★ **Tucker House.** Constructed out of native limestone, Tucker House is typical of many early Bermudian houses. It was built in 1711 for a merchant who used the basement as storage space for his wares, and it was originally close to the shore—landfill has since moved the water back. The house is at the corner of Barber's Alley, named for Joseph Haine Rainey, a freed slave from South Carolina who fled to Bermuda at the outbreak of the American Civil War and made his living here as a barber. After the war, Rainey returned home and, in 1870, became the first black

BERMUDA BEST BETS

■ **Gibbs Hill Lighthouse.** Make the climb to the top, where the reward is an expansive view of the inlets and harbors.

■ **National Museum of Bermuda.** Absorb Bermuda's nautical and military history in this Royal Navy Dockyard museum.

■ **St. George's.** Attend the pierside show hosted by the town crier, where gossips and nagging wives are drenched in a dunking stool.

7

man to be elected to the U.S. House of Representatives. ✉ *5 Water St.* ☏ *441/297–0545* ⊕ *www.bnt.bm* ▣ *$5; $10 combination ticket includes admission to National Trust Museum in Globe Hotel and Verdmont* ⊙ *Nov.–Apr., Wed., Thurs., and Sat. 10–4; May–Oct., weekdays 10–4.*

ELSEWHERE ON THE ISLAND

ⓒ **Bermuda Aquarium, Museum and Zoo.** The aquarium has always been a
Fodor's Choice   pleasant diversion, but thanks to an ambitious expansion project it has
★   become truly great. The 145,000-gallon tank holding the North Rock Exhibit, in the main gallery, gives you a diver's view of Bermuda's famed living coral reefs and colorful marine life. ✉ *40 N. Shore Rd., Flatts Village, Hamilton Parish* ☏ *441/293–2727* ⊕ *www.bamz.org* ▣ *$10* ⊙ *Daily 9–5, last admission at 4; North Rock dive talk at 1:10 daily and seal feeding at 1:30 and 4 daily.*

ⓒ **Crystal Caves.** This fantastic cavern 120 feet underground, which was
Fodor's Choice   discovered in 1907, has spectacular stalactite formations. ✉ *8 Crys-*
★   *tal Caves Rd., off Wilkinson Ave., Bailey's Bay, Hamilton Parish* ☏ *441/293–0640* ⊕ *www.caves.bm* ▣ *One cave $20; combination ticket $27* ⊙ *Daily 9:30–4:30; last combination tour at 4.*

ⓒ **Fort St. Catherine.** This restored fortress is one of the most impressive on
★   the island. The original fort was built around 1613, but it was remodeled and enlarged at least five times. As you travel through the tunnels, you'll come across some startlingly lifelike figures tucked into niches. ✉ *15 Coot Pond Rd., St. George's Parish* ☏ *441/297–1920* ▣ *$7* ⊙ *Weekdays 10–4.*

ⓒ **Gibb's Hill Lighthouse.** The second cast-iron lighthouse ever built soars
★   above Southampton Parish. Designed in London and opened in 1846, the tower stands 117 feet high and 362 feet above the sea. It's a long haul up the 185 spiral stairs, but you can stop to catch your breath at platforms along the way, where photographs and drawings of the lighthouse divert your attention. ✉ *68 St. Anne's Rd., Southampton Parish* ☏ *441/238–8069* ⊕ *www.bermudalighthouse.com* ▣ *$2.50* ⊙ *Daily 9–4:30. Closed mid-Jan.–mid-Feb.*

ⓒ **National Museum of Bermuda.** Inside Bermuda's largest fort, built between
Fodor's Choice   1837 and 1852, the National Museum exhibits its collections in six
★   old stone munitions warehouses, which surround the parade grounds and the Keep Pond. On top of the hill is the Commissioner's House, an unusual cast-iron building constructed from 1823 to 1828 in England and shipped to Bermuda for the chief administrator of the Dockyard.

The National Museum's most popular attraction is **Dolphin Quest** (☏ *441/234–4464* ⊕ *www.dolphinquest.org*) within the fortress's historic keep. Several programs designed for adults and/or children age five and older let you get into the water and touch, play with, and swim alongside dolphins. ✉ *National Museum of Bermuda, Dockyard* ☏ *441/234–1418* ⊕ *www.bmm.bm* ▣ *$10 for museum, $160–$310 for Dolphin Quest* ⊙ *Daily 9:30–4.*

Fodor's Choice   **Paget Marsh.** This small, easily walkable slice of unspoiled native Ber-
★   muda is just minutes from bustling Hamilton. Listen for the cries of the native and migratory birds that visit this natural wetland, jointly owned and preserved by the Bermuda National Trust and the Bermuda

Audubon Society. ⊠ *Lovers La., Paget Parish* ☎ *441/236–6483* ⊕ *www. bnt.bm* ☒ *Free* ☉ *Daily sunrise–sunset.*

☾ **Verdmont.** Though it was used as a home until the mid-20th century,
★ the house has had virtually no structural changes since it was built in about 1710. Verdmont holds a notable collection of historic furnishings. Some are imported from England—such as the early-19th-century piano—but most of the furniture is 18th-century cedar, crafted by Bermudian cabinetmakers. ⊠ *6 Verdmont La., off Collector's Hill, Smith's Parish* ☎ *441/236–7369* ⊕ *www.bnt.bm* ☒ *$5; $10 combination ticket with Bermuda National Trust Museum in Globe Hotel and Tucker House* ☉ *Oct.–Mar., Wed. and Sat. 10–4; Apr.–Sept., Tues., Wed., Fri., and Sat. 10–4.*

SHOPPING

Hamilton has the greatest concentration of shops in Bermuda, and Front Street is its pièce de résistance. Lined with small, pastel-color buildings, this most fashionable of Bermuda's streets houses sedate department stores and snazzy boutiques, with several small arcades and shopping alleys leading off it. A smart canopy shades the entrance to the 55 Front Street Group, which houses Crisson Jewelers. Modern Butterfield Place has galleries and boutiques selling, among other things, Louis Vuitton leather goods. The Emporium, a renovated building with an atrium, has a range of shops, from antiques to souvenirs.

7

St. George's Water Street, Duke of York Street, Hunters Wharf, Penno's Wharf, and Somers Wharf are the sites of numerous renovated buildings that house branches of Front Street stores, as well as artisans' studios. Historic King's Square offers little more than a couple of T-shirt and souvenir shops.

In the West End, **Somerset Village** has a few shops, but they hardly merit a special shopping trip. However, the **Clocktower Mall,** in a historic building at the Royal Naval Dockyard, has a few more shopping opportunities, including branches of Front Street shops and specialty boutiques. The Dockyard is also home to the Craft Market, the Bermuda Arts Centre, and Bermuda Clayworks.

ACTIVITIES

BICYCLING

The best and sometimes only way to explore Bermuda's nooks and crannies—its little hidden coves and 18th-century tribe roads—is by bicycle or motor scooter. A popular option for biking in Bermuda is the **Railway Trail,** a dedicated cycle path blissfully free of cars. Running intermittently the length of the old Bermuda Railway (old "Rattle 'n' Shake"), this trail is scenic and restricted to pedestrian and bicycle traffic. You can ask the staff at any bike-rental shop for advice on where to access the trail.

Eve's Cycle Livery. In three convenient locations around the island, Eve's rents standard-size mountain bikes, as well as motor scooters, including your mandatory helmet. The staff readily supplies advice on where to ride, and there's no charge for a repair waiver. Eve's Cycles on Water Street is convenient if you arrive in Bermuda on a cruise docking in St. George's—the shop is literally a few yards away from the cruise terminal. ⊠ *114 Middle Rd., near S. Shore Rd., Paget Parish* 🖀 *441/236–6247* 🖂 *1 Water St., St. George's* 🖀 *441/236–0839* 🖂 *Maritime La., Dockyard* 🖀 *441/236–6748.*

GOLF

Golf courses make up nearly 17% of the island's 21.6 square mi. The scenery on the courses is usually spectacular, with flowering trees and shrubs decked out in multicolor blossoms against a backdrop of brilliant blue sea and sky. The layouts are remarkably challenging, thanks to capricious ocean breezes, daunting natural terrain, and the clever work of world-class golf architects.

Fairmont Southampton Golf Club is known for its steep terrain. ⊠ *Fairmont Southampton Resort, 101 South Rd., Southampton Parish* 🖀 *441/239–6952* ⊕ *www.fairmont.com/Southampton* 🖾 *Greens fees $86 before 2:30 pm with cart mandatory, $67 after 2:30 pm with cart or $45 walking.*

★ **Mid Ocean Club,** a classic 1921 Charles Blair Macdonald design revamped by Robert Trent Jones Sr. in 1953, is ranked as one of the top 50 courses outside the U.S. by *Golf Digest.* ⊠ *1 Mid Ocean Dr., off S. Shore Rd., Tucker's Town* 🖀 *441/293–1215* ⊕ *www.themidoceanclubbermuda. com* 🖾 *Greens fees $250 ($100 when playing with a member). Nonmembers must be sponsored by a club member (your hotelier can arrange this); nonmember starting times available Mon., Wed., and Fri. except holidays. Caddies $50 for double or $65 for single per bag (tip not included). Cart rental $45 per person. Shoe rentals $10. Club rentals $45. Lessons $55 a ½ hr, $100 per hr.*

SNORKELING

Snorkeling cruises are generally offered from April through September. Smaller boats, which limit capacity to 10 to 16 passengers, offer more personal attention and focus more on the beautiful snorkeling areas themselves. Guides on such tours often relate interesting historical and ecological information about the island. Some larger boats take up to 40 passengers.

Jessie James Cruises. Half-day trips aboard the 31-foot glass-bottomed boat *Pisces*, which holds up to 17 people, cost $65, $45 for children (ages 8–10). The boat takes you to three different sites, including at least two shipwrecks. ⊠ *11 Clarence St., St. George's* 🖀 *441/236–4804* ⊕ *www.jessiejames.bm.*

BEACHES

ℭ **Elbow Beach.** Swimming and bodysurfing are great at this beach, which
★ is bordered by the prime strand of sand reserved for guests of the Elbow Beach Hotel on the left, and the ultraexclusive Coral Beach Club beach area on the right. Protective coral reefs make the waters the safest on the island, and a good choice for families. Mickey's Beach Bar & Bistro (part of the Elbow Beach Hotel) is open for lunch and dinner, though

it may be difficult to get a table. ⊠ *Off South Rd., Paget Parish* Ⓜ *Bus 2 or 7 from Hamilton.*

☺ **Horseshoe Bay.** When locals say they're going to "the beach," they're
Fodor's Choice generally referring to Horseshoe Bay, the island's most popular. With
★ clear water, a crescent of pink sand, a vibrant social scene, and the uncluttered backdrop of South Shore Park, Horseshoe Bay has everything you could ask of a Bermudian beach. A snack bar, changing rooms, beach-rental facilities, and lifeguards add to its appeal. The undertow can be strong, especially on the main beach. ⊠ *Off South Rd., Southampton Parish* ☎ *441/238-2651* Ⓜ *Bus 7 from Hamilton.*

Tobacco Bay Beach. The most popular beach near St. George's—about 15 minutes northwest of the town on foot—this small north-shore strand is huddled in a coral cove. Its beach house has a snack bar, equipment rentals, toilets, showers, changing rooms, and ample parking. It's a 10-minute hike from the bus stop in the town of St. George's, or you can flag down a St. George's Minibus Service van and ask for a lift ($2 per person). In high season the beach is busy, especially midweek, when cruise ships are docked. ⊠ *Coot Pond Rd., St. George's Parish* ☎ *441/297-2756* Ⓜ *Bus 1, 3, 10, or 11 from Hamilton.*

WHERE TO EAT

$ ✕ **Docksider.** Locals come to mingle at this sprawling Front Street sports
BRITISH bar. It's generally more popular as a drinking venue, as it can get quite overcrowded and rowdy. But if you want to catch the game on the big screen with everyone else, an all-day menu of standard pub fare is available, as well as local fish. Go for the English beef pie, fish-and-chips, or a fish sandwich and sip your dessert—a Dark 'n Stormy—out on the porch as you watch Bermuda stroll by. Or if you can't make up your mind, you can always rely on the hearty full English breakfast to fill you up. The pub has a good jukebox, and there's often a DJ or a band on summer weekends. ⊠ *121 Front St., Hamilton* ☎ *441/296-3333* ⊕ *www.dockies.com.*

$ ✕ **Spring Garden Restaurant & Bar.** If you've never had Barbadian, or
CARIBBEAN "Bajan" food, as Barbados natives like to call it, come sit under the indoor palm tree and try panfried flying fish—a delicacy in Barbados. Another good choice is the broiled mahi mahi served in creole sauce, with peas and rice. During lobster season an additional menu appears, featuring steamed, broiled, or curried lobster ($38.50 for the complete dinner). For dessert, try coconut cream pie or raspberry-mango cheesecake. Or eat with the locals at the Friday lunchtime bargain buffet; help yourself to as many starters, mains, and desserts as you can eat for $22. ⊠ *19 Washington La., off Reid St., Hamilton* ☎ *441/295-7416* ⊙ *Closed Sun.*

7

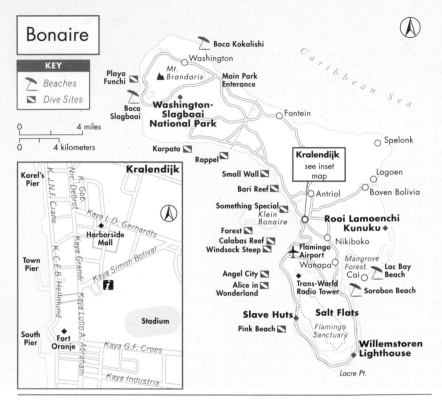

Map Labels

Bonaire

KEY
- Beaches
- Dive Sites

0 — 4 miles
0 — 4 kilometers

Boca Kokalishi
Washington
Mt. Brandaris
Playa Funchi
Main Park Enterance
Boca Slagbaai
Washington-Slagbaai National Park
Caribbean Sea
Fontein
Spelonk
Karpata
Rappel
Kralendijk see inset map
Small Wall
Bari Reef
Lagoen
Boven Bolivia
Antriol
Something Special
Klein Bonaire
Forest
Calabas Reef
Windsock Steep
Rooi Lamoenchi Kunuku
Nikiboko
Flamingo Airport
Wanapa
Mangrove Forest
Cai
Lac Bay Beach
Angel City
Alice in Wonderland
Trans-World Radio Tower
Sorobon Beach
Slave Huts
Pink Beach
Salt Flats
Flamingo Sanctuary
Willemstoren Lighthouse
Lacre Pt.

Kralendijk (inset)
Karel's Pier
K.J.N.E. Crane
Ki. Gob. Nic. Debrot
Kaya Grandi
Kaya L.D. Gerhardts
Harborside Mall
Kaya Simon Bolivar
Town Pier
K.C.E.B. Helmund
Kaya Lullo A. Abraham
Stadium
South Pier
Fort Oranje
Kaya G.F. Croes
Kaya Industria

BONAIRE (KRALENDIJK)

Vernon
O'Reilly
Ramesar

Starkly beautiful Bonaire is the consummate desert island. Surrounded by pristine waters, it is a haven for divers and snorkelers, who flock here from around the world to take advantage of the excellent visibility, easily accessed reefs, and bountiful marine life. Bonaire is the most rustic of the three ABC islands, and despite its dependence on tourism it manages to maintain its identity and simple way of life. There are many good restaurants, most of which are within walking distance of the port. Most of the island's 14,000-some inhabitants live in and around Kralendijk, which must certainly qualify as one of the cutest and most compact capitals in the Caribbean. The best shopping is to be found along the very short stretch of road that constitutes "downtown." Bonaire's beaches tend to be small and rocky, but there is a nice stretch of sandy beach at Lac Bay. It is entirely possible to see almost all of the sights and sounds of the island in one day by taking one of the island tours on offer.

ESSENTIALS

CURRENCY   As of January 2011 the U.S.dollar became the official currency, replacing the NAf guilder, and the island has several ATMs, particularly in Kralendijk.

INTERNET **Bonaire Access** (✉ *Harbourside Mall, Kralendijk, Bonaire* ☎ *No phone.* **Cyber City** (✉ *City Café, Kaya Grandi 7, Kralendijk, Bonaire* ☎ *599/717–8286*).

TELEPHONE You can make international calls from from the Telbo central phone company office (next to the tourism office in Kralendijk), which is open 24 hours a day. The country code for Bonaire is 599; 717 is the exchange for every four-digit telephone number on the island. When making interisland calls, dial 717 plus the local four-digit number.

COMING ASHORE

One of the great benefits of Bonaire to cruise passengers is that the port is right in downtown Kralendijk. Ships usually tender passengers ashore. A four-minute walk takes you to most of the best shopping and restaurants on the island.

Bonaire lives for tourism, so upon the arrival of a cruise ship the locals are ready. Taxis wait right at the port and operate on fixed government rates. All the sights of Kralendijk are within easy walking distance, and a taxi ride to one of the larger resorts on the island will run between $9 and $12. A half-day island tour by taxi costs about $25 per hour for up to two passengers. Fares increase by 50% between midnight and 6 am.

EXPLORING BONAIRE

Two routes, north and south from Kralendijk, the island's small capital, are possible on the 24-mi-long (39-km-long) island; either route will take from a few hours to a full day, depending on whether you stop to snorkel, swim, dive, or lounge. Those pressed for time will find that it's easy to explore the entire island in a day if stops are kept to a minimum.

KRALENDIJK

Bonaire's small, tidy capital city (population 3,000) is five minutes from the airport. The main drag, J. A. Abraham Boulevard, turns into **Kaya Grandi** in the center of town. Along it are most of the island's major stores, boutiques, and restaurants. Across Kaya Grandi, opposite the Littman jewelry store, is Kaya L. D. Gerharts, with several small supermarkets, a handful of snack shops, and some of the better restaurants. Walk down the narrow waterfront avenue called Kaya C.E.B. Hellmund, which leads straight to the **North and South piers.** In the center of town, the Harbourside Mall has chic boutiques. Along this route is **Ft. Oranje**, with its cannons. From December through April, cruise ships dock in the harbor once or twice a week. The diminutive ocher-and-white structure that looks like a tiny Greek temple is the **fish market;** local anglers no longer bring their catches here (they sell out of their homes these days), but you can find plenty of fresh produce brought over from Colombia and Venezuela. Pick up the brochure *Walking and Shopping in Kralendijk* from the tourist office to get a map and full listing of all the monuments and sights in the town.

ELSEWHERE ON BONAIRE

☾ **Rooi Lamoenchi Kunuku.** Owner Ellen Herrera restored her family's home-
★ stead north of Lac Bay, in the Bonairean *kadushi* (cactus) wilderness, to educate tourists and residents about the history and tradition of

authentic kunuku living and show unspoiled terrain in two daily tours. You must make an appointment in advance and expect to spend a couple of hours. ✉ *Kaya Suiza 23, Playa Baribe* ☎ *599/717–8490* 🎫 *$21* ⏲ *By appointment only.*

BONAIRE BEST BETS

■ **Diving.** Bonaire is one of the world's top diving destinations. Shore diving is especially good.

■ **Flamingo spotting.** These shy, graceful birds are one of Bonaire's scenic delights.

■ **Kralendijk.** The accessible town has a nice assortment of restaurants and stores.

■ **Snorkeling.** With reefs close to shore, snorkeling is good right off the beach.

■ **Washington–Slagbaai National Park.** Bonaire's best land-based sight is this well-preserved national park.

Salt Flats. You can't miss the salt flats—voluptuous white drifts that look like mountains of snow. Harvested once a year, the "ponds" are owned by Cargill, which has reactivated the 19th-century salt industry with great success (one reason for that success is that the ocean on this part of the island is higher than the land—which makes irrigation a snap). Look also in the distance across the pans to the abandoned solar saltworks that's now a designated **flamingo sanctuary.** The sanctuary is completely protected, and no entrance is allowed (flamingos are extremely sensitive to disturbances of any kind).

Slave Huts. The salt industry's gritty history is revealed in Rode Pan, the site of two groups of tiny slave huts. The white grouping is on the right side of the road, opposite the salt flats; the second grouping, called the red slave huts (though they appear yellow), stretches across the road toward the island's southern tip. During the 19th century, slaves working the salt pans by day crawled into these huts to rest. Only very small people will be able to enter, but walk around and poke your head in for a look.

Washington–Slagbaai National Park. Once a plantation producing dividivi trees (the pods were used for tanning animal skins), aloe (used for medicinal lotions), charcoal, and goats, the park is now a model of conservation. It's easy to tour the 13,500-acre tropical desert terrain on the dirt roads. As befits a wilderness sanctuary, the well-marked, rugged routes force you to drive slowly enough to appreciate the animal life and the terrain. Goats and donkeys may dart across the road, and if you keep your eyes peeled, you may catch sight of large iguanas camouflaged in the shrubbery.

Bird-watchers are really in their element here. Right inside the park's gate, flamingos roost on the salt pad known as **Salina Mathijs,** and exotic parakeets dot the foot of **Mt. Brandaris,** Bonaire's highest peak, at 784 feet. Some 130 species of birds fly in and out of the shrubbery in the park. Keep your eyes open and your binoculars at hand. Swimming, snorkeling, and scuba diving are permitted, but you're asked not to frighten the animals or remove anything from the grounds. To get here, take the secondary road north from the town of Rincon. The Nature Fee for swimming and snorkeling also grants you free admission to this park—simply present proof of payment and some form of photo ID. ☎ *599/717–8444* ⊕ *www. washingtonparkbonaire.org* ✉ *Free with payment of scuba diving Nature Fee ($25) or $15 without* ☼ *Daily 8–5; you must enter before 3.*

Willemstoren Lighthouse. Bonaire's first lighthouse was built in 1837 and is now automated (but closed to visitors). Take some time to explore the beach and notice how the waves, driven by the trade winds, play a crashing symphony against the rocks. Locals stop here to collect pieces of driftwood in spectacular shapes and to build fanciful pyramids from objects that have washed ashore.

SHOPPING

Although it is a relatively small town, Kralendijk offers a good range of high-end items like watches and jewelry at attractive prices. There are a number of souvenir shops offering T-shirts and trinkets lining the main street of Kaya Grandi.

★ **Atlantis.** Atlantis carries a large range of precious and semiprecious gems. The tanzanite collection is especially beautiful. You will also find Sector, Raymond Weil, and Citizen watches, among others, all at great savings. Since gold jewelry is sold by weight here, it's an especially good buy. ⊠ *Kaya Grandi 32B* ☎ *599/717–7730.*

JanArt Gallery. JanArt Gallery, on the outskirts of town, sells unique paintings, prints, and art supplies; artist Janice Huckaby also hosts art classes. ⊠ *Kaya Gloria 7* ☎ *599/717–5246.*

Littman's. Littman's is an upscale jewelry and gift shop where many items are handpicked by owner Steven Littman on his regular trips to Europe. Look for Rolex, Omega, Cartier, and Tag Heuer watches; fine gold jewelry; antique coins; nautical sculptures; resort clothing; and accessories. ⊠ *Kaya Grandi 33* ☎ *599/717–8160.*

Yenny's Art. Whatever you do, make a point of visiting Yenny's Art. Roam around her house, which is a replica of a traditional Bonaire town complete with her handmade life-size dolls and the skeletons of all her dead pets. Lots of fun (and sometimes kitschy) souvenirs made out of driftwood, clay, and shells are all handmade by Jenny. ⊠ *Kaya Betico Croes 6, near post office* ☎ *599/717–5004.*

ACTIVITIES

BICYCLING

Bonaire is generally flat, so bicycles are an easy way to get around. Because of the heat it's essential to carry water if you're planning to cycle for any distance, and especially if your plans involve exploring the deserted interior. There are more than 180 mi (290 km) of unpaved routes (as well as the many paved roads) on the island.

Cycle Bonaire. Cycle Bonaire rents mountain bikes and gear (trail maps, water bottles, helmets, locks, repair and first-aid kits) for $20 a day or $100 for six days; half-day and full-day guided excursions start at $60, not including bike rental. ⊠ *Kaya Gobernador N. Debrot 77A* ☎ *599/717–2229.*

DIVING AND SNORKELING

Diving and snorkeling are almost a religion on Bonaire, and are by far the most popular activities for cruise passengers. Bonaire has some of the best reef diving this side of Australia's Great Barrier Reef. It takes only 5 to 25 minutes to reach many sites, the current is usually mild, and although some reefs have sudden, steep drops, most begin just offshore and slope gently downward at a 45-degree angle. General visibility runs 60 to 100 feet, except during surges in October and November. You can see several varieties of coral: knobby-brain, giant-brain, elkhorn, staghorn, mountainous star, gorgonian, and black.

Ⓒ
★ **Larry's Shore & Wild Side Diving.** Larry's Shore & Wild Side Diving is run by a former army combat diver and offers a variety of appealing options ranging from the leisurely to downright scary. This company has become an extremely popular choice, so try to book as early as possible. ☎ 599/790–9156 ⊕ *www.larryswildsidediving.com.*

Mushi Mushi. The *Mushi Mushi* is a catamaran offering a variety of two- and three-hour cruises starting at $50 per person. It departs from the Bonaire Nautico Marina in downtown Kralendijk (opposite the restaurant It Rains Fishes). ☎ *599/790–5399.*

BEACHES

Don't expect long stretches of glorious powdery sand. Bonaire's beaches are small, and though the water is blue (several shades of it, in fact), the sand isn't always white. Bonaire's National Parks Foundation requires all non-divers to pay a $10 annual Nature Fee in order to enter the water anywhere around the island (divers pay $25). The fee can be paid at most dive shops.

Klein Bonaire. Just a water-taxi hop across from Kralendijk, this little island offers picture-perfect white-sand beaches. The area is protected, so absolutely no development has been allowed. Make sure to pack everything before heading to the island, including water and an umbrella to hide under, because there are no refreshment stands or changing facilities, and there's almost no shade to be found. Boats leave from the Town Pier, across from the City Café, and the round-trip water-taxi ride costs roughly $20 per person.

Lac Bay Beach. Known for its festive music on Sunday nights, this open bay area with pink-tinted sand is equally dazzling by day. It's a bumpy drive (10 to 15 minutes on a dirt road) to get here, but you'll be glad when you arrive. It's a good spot for diving, snorkeling, and kayaking (as long as you bring your own), and there are public restrooms and a restaurant for your convenience. ⊠ *Off Kaminda Sorobon, Lac Cai.*

Windsock Beach (*aka Mangrove Beach*). Near the airport (just off E.E.G. Boulevard), this pretty little spot looks out toward the north side of the island and has about 200 yards of white sand along a rocky shoreline. It's a popular dive site and swimming conditions are good. ⊠ *Off E.E.G. Blvd. near Flamingo Airport.*

WHERE TO EAT

$$$ ✗ **Appetite.** This recent edition to the downtown dining scene is an oasis
CONTINENTAL of chic. The historic house offers cozy private rooms and a large court-
★ yard, which always seems to be buzzing. The menu encourages diners
to forget the main course and order a series of starters, but such items
as stewed veal cheek with crispy sweetbreads are worth the splurge.
The restaurant is just a few steps away from the Tourism Corporation
Bonaire office. ⊠ *Kaya Grandi 12* ☎ *599/717–3919* ☉ *Closed Sun.*

$$$ ✗ **City Café/City Restaurant.** This busy waterfront eatery is also one of the
ECLECTIC most reliable nightspots on the island, so it's always hopping day or night.
Fodor's Choice Breakfast, lunch, and dinner are served daily at reasonable prices. Seafood
★ is always featured, as are a variety of sandwiches and salads. The pita
sandwich platters are a good lunchtime choice for the budget challenged.
Weekends, there's always live entertainment and dancing. This is the
place to people-watch on Bonaire, as it seems everyone ends up at City
Café eventually. ⊠ *Hotel Rochaline, Kaya Grandi 7* ☎ *599/717–8286*
⊕ *www.citybonaire.com.*

CALICA (PLAYA DEL CARMEN), MEXICO

Marlise Kast Just minutes away from Calica, Playa del Carmen has become one of
Latin America's fastest-growing communities, with a pace almost as
hectic as Cancún's. Hotels, restaurants, and shops multiply here faster
than you can say "Kukulcán." Some are branches of Cancún establishments whose owners have taken up permanent residence in Playa, while
others are owned by American and European expats (predominately
Italians) who came here years ago. It makes for a varied, international
community. Avenida 5, the first street in town parallel to the beach, is a
long pedestrian walkway with shops, cafés, and street performers; small
hotels and stores stretch north from this avenue. Avenida Juárez, running east–west from the highway to the beach, is the main commercial
zone for the Riviera Maya corridor. Here locals visit the food shops,
pharmacies, hardware stores, and banks that line the curbs. People
traveling the coast by car usually stop here to stock up on supplies—its
banks, grocery stores, and gas stations are the last ones until Tulum.

ESSENTIALS

CURRENCY The Mexican peso (MX$12.05 to US$1). U.S. dollars and credit cards
are widely accepted in the area, from the port to Playa del Carmen, but
it's best to have pesos—and small bills—when you visit ruins, where
cashiers often run out of change. There is no advantage to paying in
dollars, but there may be an advantage to paying in cash. However, in
late 2010, Mexican laws regarding U.S. dollar conversions changed.
Foreign travelers and Mexicans can change only $1,500 per month into
pesos, which may begin to have an effect on the willingness of locals to
accept cash payments in U.S. dollars.

INTERNET Playa del Carmen offers free Wi-Fi in all public parks and along Calle
4 between 15 and 10 Avenue. There are also several Internet cafés on
Avenida 5 in Playa del Carmen.

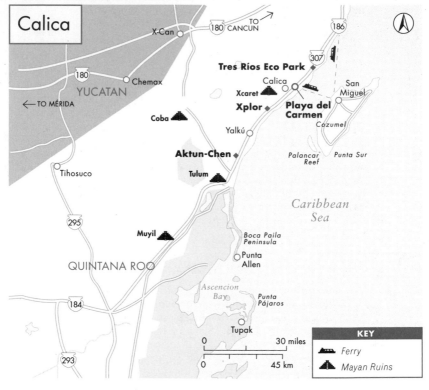

Casa Tucan (⊠ *Calle 4 between Avs. 10 and 15, Playa del Carmen,* ☎ *984/873–0283*).

TELEPHONE Most pay phones accept prepaid Ladatel cards, sold in 30-, 50-, or 100-peso denominations. To use the card, insert it in the pay phone's slot, dial 001 (for calls to the U.S.) or 01 (for calls within Mexico), followed by the area code and number. Credit is deleted from the card as you use it, and the balance is displayed on the small screen on the phone.

COMING ASHORE

The port at Calica, about 3 mi south of the town of Playa del Carmen (between Playa del Carmen and Xcarat), is small. Sometimes ships actually dock, and other times passengers are tendered to shore. There is a makeshift market at the port, where locals sell crafts. Beyond that, there is not much to do, and you'll need to head into Playa del Carmen proper to find restaurants and even tour operators. If you really want to shop, skip the vendors at the port and head to Playa del Carmen's Avenida 5, where you can easily spend an afternoon browsing shops and enjoying restaurants.

Taxis and tour buses are available at the port to take you to Playa del Carmen and other destinations, but lines often form as passengers wait for taxis, so plan accordingly if you really want to pack a lot of activity into your day. Your taxi will have you in Playa del Carmen or in Xcaret in under 10 minutes, but you'll pay a whopping $10 for the short trip.

EXPLORING CALICA

Fodors Choice
★

Aktun-Chen. The name of these amazing underground caves is Mayan for "the cave with cenote inside." These amazing caves, stimated to be about 5 million years old, are the area's largest. You walk through the underground passages, past stalactites and stalagmites, until you reach the cenote with its various shades of deep green. There is also a canopy tour and one cenote where you can swim. You don't want to miss this one. ⊠ *Carretera 307, Km 107* ☎ *984/109–2061* ⊕ *www.aktunchen. com* ⊟ *$26 cave tour, $38 canopy tour, $21 cenote tour* ☉ *Daily 9–4.*

Muyil. This photogenic archaeological site at the northern end of the Reserva de la Biosfera Sian Ka'an is underrated. Once known as Chunyaxché, it's now called by its ancient name, Muyil (pronounced mool-*hill*). It dates from the late preclassic era, when it was connected by road to the sea and served as a port between Cobá and the Mayan centers in Belize and Guatemala. The most notable site at Muyil today is the remains of the 56-foot **Castillo**—one of the tallest on the Quintana Roo coast—at the center of a large acropolis. During excavations of the Castillo, jade figurines representing the moon and fertility goddess Ixchel were found. Recent excavations at Muyil have uncovered some smaller structures. The ruins stand near the edge of a deep-blue lagoon and are surrounded by almost impenetrable jungle—so be sure to bring bug repellent. You can drive down a dirt road on the side of the ruins to swim or fish in the lagoon. The bird-watching is also exceptional here. ⊕ *muyil.smv.org* ⊟ *$3* ☉ *Daily 8–5.*

Playa del Carmen. Once upon a time, Playa del Carmen was a fishing village with a ravishing deserted beach. The villagers fished and raised coconut palms to produce copra, and the only foreigners who ventured here were beach bums and travelers catching ferries to Cozumel. That was a long time ago, however. These days the beach is far from deserted, although it is still delightful, with its alabaster-white sand and turquoise-blue waters. In fact Playa has become one of Latin America's fastest-growing communities, with a population of more than 135,000 and a pace almost as hectic as Cancún's. The ferry pier, where the hourly boats arrive from and depart for Cozumel, is another busy part of town. The streets leading from the dock have shops, restaurants, cafés, a hotel, and food stands. If you take a stroll north from the pier along the beach, you'll find the serious sun worshippers. On the pier's south side is the sprawling Playacar complex. The development is a labyrinth of residences and all-inclusive resorts bordered by an 18-hole championship golf course. ⊹ *3 mi (5 km) north of Calica.*

The excellent 32-acre **Xaman Ha Aviary** (⊠ *Paseo Xaman-Ha, Mza 13-A Lote 1, Playacar* ☎ *984/873–0330* ⊕ *www.aviarioxamanha.com*), in the middle of the Playacar development, is home to more than 30 species

7

of native birds. It's open daily 9 to 5, and admission is $22.

Tulum. Tulum (pronounced tool-*lum*) is a quickly growing town built near the spectacular ruins that draw most visitors here. But its charm extends past the famous ruins: pristine beaches, $10 cabanas, and open-air markets explain the town's increasing popularity with travelers.

The archaeological site itself is the Yucatán Peninsula's most-visited Mayan ruin, attracting more than 2 million people annually. Though most of the architecture is of unremarkable postclassic (1000–1521) style, the amount of attention that Tulum receives is not entirely undeserved. Its location—on a beach known for its sugar-white sand, by the blue-green Caribbean—is breathtaking. ⊠ *Carretera 307, Km 133, Tulum* ☎ *983/837–2411* 🖅 *$5 entrance, $3 parking, $4 video fee, $1.50 shuttle from parking to ruins* ⊙ *Daily 8–5.*

ℭ
Fodor's Choice
★
Xcaret. Among the most popular attractions at this outdoor theme park at the Paradise River Raft, the Butterfly Pavilion, and ocean-fed aquarium, and a replica Maya village. The park has a Wild Bird Breeding Aviary, nurseries for both abandoned flamingo eggs and sea turtles, and a series of underwater cavers that you can explore by snorkel or Snuba (a hybrid of snorkeling and Scuba). The entrance fee covers only access to the grounds and the exhibits; all other activities and equipment— from sea treks and dolphin tours to lockers and swim gear—are extra. The $99 Plus Pass includes park entrance, lockers, snorkel equipment, food, and drinks. ☎ *984/871–5200, 998/883–0470 in Cancún* ⊕ *www. xcaret.com* 🖅 *$69 Basic Pass; $99 Plus Pass* ⊙ *Daily 8:30 am–10 pm.*

Xplor. Designed for thrill-seekers, this 125-acre park features underground rafting in water caves and the cenotes of Riviera Maya. You can also swim in a stalactite river, ride in an amphibian-vehicle, or soar across the park on the longest zip line in Mexico. A buffet lunch is included in the admission price. ⊠ *Carretera 307, Km 282, Xcaret* ☎ *998/849–5275* ⊕ *www.xplor.travel* 🖅 *$99* ⊙ *Mon.–Sat. 9–5.*

SHOPPING

Playa del Carmen's Avenida 5 between calles 4 and 10 is the best place to shop along the coast. Boutiques sell folk art and textiles from around Mexico, and clothing stores carry lots of sarongs and beachwear made from Indonesian batiks. A shopping area called Calle Corazon, between calles 12 and 14, has a pedestrian street, art galleries, restaurants, and boutiques.

CALICA BEST BETS

■ **A Day at Xcaret.** Particularly for families, this ecological theme park is a great way to spend the day.

■ **Beaches.** The beaches in the Riviera Maya are stellar.

■ **Diving.** From Playa del Carmen it's only a short hop to some of the Yucatán's best dive sites.

■ **Shopping.** Playa del Carmen's Avenida 5 can easily keep you occupied for your day in port if you are a shopaholic.

★ **Hacienda Tequila** (✉ *Av. 5 and Calle 14, Playa del Carmen* ☎ *984/803–0821*) sells traditional Mexican crafts and clothing as well as 480 different types of tequila. Free tastings are available, and there is a small museum displaying the various stages of tequila production.

At **La Hierbabuena Artesanía** (✉ *Av. 5 between Calles 8 and 10* ☎ *984/873–1741*), owner Melinda Burns offers a collection of fine Mexican clothing and crafts.

ACTIVITIES

DIVING

The PADI and SSI-affiliated **Abyss** (✉ *Av. 1 between Calles 10 and 12* ☎ *984/873–2164* ⊕ *www.abyssdiveshop.com*) offers introductory courses and dive trips ($50 for one tank, $70 for two tanks). The oldest shop in town, **Tank-Ha Dive Center** (✉ *Calle 10 between Avs. 5 and 10, Playa del Carmen* ☎ *984/873–0302* ⊕ *www.tankha.com*), has PADI-certified teachers and runs diving and snorkeling trips to the reefs and caverns. A one-tank dive costs $45; for a two-tank trip it's $75. Dive packages are also available, as well as trips to Cozumel.

GOLF

Playa del Carmen's golf course is an 18-hole, par-72 championship course designed by Robert von Hagge. The greens fee is $200; there's also a special twilight fee of $120. Information is available from the **Casa Club de Golf** (☎ *984/873–4990*).

7

WHERE TO EAT

$$ ✗**Babe's Noodles & Bar.** Photos and paintings of old Hollywood pinup
THAI models decorate the walls and are even laminated onto the bar of this
★ Swedish-owned Thai restaurant known for its fresh and interesting fare. Everything is cooked to order—no prefab dishes here. Try the spring rolls with peanut sauce, or the sesame noodles, made with chicken or pork, veggies, lime, green curry, and ginger. In the Buddha Garden you can sip a mojito or sit at the bar and watch the crowds on nearby 5th Avenue. The lemonade, blended with ice and mint, is incredibly refreshing. If the place is crowded, head to their second location on Avenida 5 between calles 28 and 30. ✉ *Calle 10 between Avs. 5 and 10* ☎ *984/120–2592* ⊕ *www.babesnoodlesandbar.com* ✉ *Av. 5 between Calles 28 and 30* ☎ *984/803–0056*.

¢–$ ✗**Hot.** This café is a great place to get an early start before a full day of
CAFÉ sightseeing, shopping, or even sunbathing. It opens at 7 am and whips up great egg dishes (the chili-and-cheese omelet is particularly good), baked goods, and hot coffee. Everything, including delicious bagels and bread, is made on the premises. Salads and sandwiches are available at lunch. ✉ *Calle 14 Norte, between Avs. 5 and 10* ☎ *984/879–4520* ⊕ *www.hotbakingcompany.com* ▤ No credit cards.

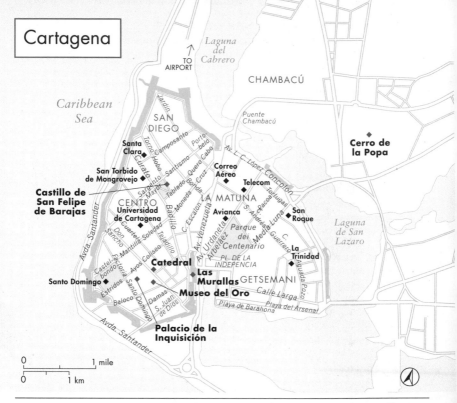

Cartagena

Caribbean Sea

TO AIRPORT

Laguna del Cabrero

CHAMBACÚ

Puente Chambacú

SAN DIEGO

Santa Clara

San Torbido de Mongrovejo

Castillo de San Felipe de Barajas

CENTRO
Universidad de Cartagena

Correo Aéreo
Telecom

LA MATUNA

Avianca

Parque del Centenario

PL. DE LA INDEPENCIA

Catedral

Las Murallas

Museo del Oro

GETSEMANI

Calle Larga

Playa de Barahona

Playa del Arsenal

Santo Domingo

Palacio de la Inquisición

Cerro de la Popa

San Roque

La Trinidad

Laguna de San Lazaro

Avda. Santander

0 | 1 mile
0 | 1 km

CARTAGENA, COLOMBIA

Marlise Kast

Ever wondered what the "Spanish Main" refers to? This is it. Colombia's Caribbean coast invokes ghosts of conquistadors, pirates, and missionaries journeying to the New World in search of wealth, whether material or spiritual. Anchoring this shore is the magnificent colonial city of Cartagena—officially *Cartagena de Indias* (Cartagena of the Indies)—founded in 1533. Gold and silver passed through here en route to Spain, making the city an obvious target for pirates, hence the construction of Cartagena's trademark walls and fortresses. Outside the *Ciudad Amurallada* (walled city) lie less historic beaches and water excursions. If Colombia conjures up images of drug lords and paramilitary guerillas, think again; security is quite visible (without being oppressive) here in the country's top tourist destination. Take the same precautions you'd follow visiting any city of one million people, and you should have a grand time.

ESSENTIALS

CURRENCY The Colombian peso (COP 1,878 to US$1). In Colombia, peso prices are denoted with the "$" sign, too. If they carry a lot of zeros, they likely are not dollar prices, but always ask. ATMs are ubiquitous around town.

INTERNET Upon arrival or before departure, you can check your email at the bank of computers in the Terminal de Cruceros. In town, you can check your email at **Micronet** (✉ *Calle de la Estrella No. 4-47, near university* ☎ *575/664–0328.*

SAFETY Security is tighter in Cartagena than elsewhere in Colombia, so you certainly can navigate the city on your own. (Knowing some Spanish helps.) However, the scarcity of English speakers and English signage at the city's tourist attractions and the persistence of vendors, street touts, and the periodic con artist mean that many cruise passengers opt for the reassurance of an organized shore excursion. If you set out on your own, under no circumstances should you deal with anyone who approaches you on the street offering to change money; rip-offs are guaranteed.

TELEPHONE The Terminal de Cruceros has ample phones for your use. Local numbers in Cartagena have seven digits. For international calls, dial 009 followed by country and area codes and local number. The U.S. mobile carrier AT&T offers roaming options in this region of Colombia for calls back to the United States; if you have a tri-band GSM phone it should work.

CARTAGENA BEST BETS

■ **Cruise the Harbor.** A boat trip around the city's inner bay allows to you appreciate the city's formidable walls and fortresses.

■ **Islas del Rosario.** The beaches of nearby Islas del Rosario are an hour away by boat.

■ **Ride a Coche.** Take the quintessential horse-and-buggy ride through the streets.

■ **Visit Palacio de la Inquisición.** Cartagena's most-visited sight is this historic—and creepy—center for the Spanish Inquisition.

■ **Walk Las Murallas.** Walking the city's massive stone walls is a favorite tourist pastime.

COMING ASHORE

Cruise ships dock at the modern Terminal de Cruceros (cruise terminal) on Isla de Manga, an island connected by a bridge to the historic city center, about 2 mi (3 km) northwest of the docks. You'll find telephones, Internet cafés, and a duty-free shop in the terminal.

A small army of taxis waits in front of the terminal. Expect to pay 14,000 pesos for the 10-minute drive to the walled city; the same fare will get you to the nearby beaches at Bocagrande. Drivers are all too happy to take you on your own do-it-yourself guided tour. Most charge around 18,000 pesos for an hour of waiting time. There's little need to rent a car here. Cartagena, at least the area of tourist interest, is so compact, and walking the labyrinth of cobblestone streets in the Old City is far more enjoyable than driving.

EXPLORING CARTAGENA

Nothing says Cartagena quite like a ride in a horse-drawn carriage, or *coche*, as it is known locally. Drivers are a wealth of information about Cartagena, and many do speak English. The downside for you is that the rides begin near dusk—it's a far cooler time of the day, after all—and your need to be back on ship may not coincide with that schedule. Do check. You can pick up carriages at many places, including the Plaza de los Coches, near the Puerta del Reloj in the walled city, or the Hotel Caribe in Bocagrande. Expect to pay around $200 (in pesos) for a two-hour tour (this kind of excursion is best when the cost is split among a group).

Castillo de San Felipe de Barajas. Designed by Antonio de Arévalo in 1639, the Fort of St. Philip's steep-angled brick and concrete battlements were arranged so that if part of the castle were conquered the rest could still be defended. A maze of tunnels, minimally lit today to allow for spooky exploration, still connects vital points of the fort. Acoustics were perfect in the tunnels, allowing occupants of the fort to hear the footsteps of the approaching enemy. You can walk here from the walled city in about 30 minutes; a 10,000-peso taxi ride is an easier option. ⊠ *Av. Pedro de Heredia at Carrera 17* ☎ *575/666–4790* 🔊 *15,000 pesos* ⊙ *Daily 8–6.*

Catedral. Cartagena's Plaza de Bolívar is a shady place from which to admire the 16th-century cathedral, with its colorful bell tower and 20th-century dome. Inside is a massive gilded altar. A statue of South American liberator Simón Bolívar stands watch over his namesake plaza. ⊠ *Plaza de Bolívar.*

Fodor's Choice   **Cerro de la Popa.** For spectacular views of Cartagena, ascend this hill, the
★   highest ground around. Because of its strategic location, the 17th-century hilltop convent did double duty as a fortress during the colonial era. It now houses a museum and a chapel dedicated to the Virgin de la Candelaria, Cartagena's patron saint. There is no public transport to get you here; taxis charge about 8,000 pesos. ⊠ *2 mi (3 km) southeast of Ciudad Amurallada* ☎ *575/666–2331* 🔊 *7,000 pesos* ⊙ *Daily 8:30–5:30.*

Las Murallas. Cartagena survived only because of its *murallas* (walls), which remain the city's most distinctive feature today. Repeated sacking by pirates and foreign invaders convinced the Spaniards of the need to enclose the region's most important port. Construction began about 1600 and was completed in 1796. Walking along the thick walls remains one of Cartagena's time-honored tourist pastimes. The Puerta del Reloj is the principal gate to the innermost sector of the Ciudad Amurallada. Its four-sided clock tower was a relatively late addition (1888), and has become the best-known symbol of the city. ⊠ *Area bounded by Bahía de las Ánimas, Caribbean Sea, and Laguna de San Lázaro* ⊙ *24 hrs.*

Museo del Oro y Arqueología. The Gold and Archaeological Museum, a project of Colombia's Central Bank, displays an assortment of artifacts culled from the Sinús, an indigenous group that lived in the region 2,000 years ago. ⊠ *Carrera 4 No. 33–26* ☎ *575/660–0778* 🔊 *Free* ⊙ *Tues.– Fri. 10–1 and 3–7, Sat. 10–1 and 2–5.*

Fodor's Choice   **Palacio de la Inquisición.** Arguably Cartagena's most-visited tourist attraction
★   documents the darkest period in the city's history. The 1770 Palace of the Inquisition served as the second headquarters of the repressive arbiters of political and spiritual orthodoxy who once exercised jurisdiction over northern South America. Although the museum also displays benign colonial and pre-Columbian artifacts, everyone heads to the ground floor to "Eeeewww" over the implements of torture—racks and thumbscrews, to name but two. ⊠ *Carrera 4 No. 33–26* ☎ *575/664–7381* 🔊 *14,000 pesos* ⊙ *Daily 9–5.*

SHOPPING

Think "Juan Valdez" if you're looking for something to take the folks back home. Small bags of fine Colombian coffee, the country's signature souvenir, are available in most tourist-oriented shops. Colombia also means emeralds, and you'll find plenty in the jewelry shops on or near Calle Pantaleón, beside the cathedral. Don't forget the duty-free shop in the Terminal de Cruceros for those last-minute purchases. The name of **Las Bóvedas** (✉ *North of Plaza Fernández de Madrid*) translates as "the vaults," and the city's best crafts shops occupy this row of storerooms built in the 18th century to hold gunpowder and other military essentials. Your stockpile here will consist of hats, hammocks, and leather goods.

ACTIVITIES

DIVING

Coral reefs line the coast south of Cartagena, although warm-water currents have begun to erode them in recent years. There is still good diving to be had in the Islas del Rosario, an archipelago of 27 coral islands about 21 mi (35 km) southwest of the city. **Buzos de Barú** (✉ *Bocagrande, Hotel Caribe Local 9* ☎ *575/665–7675* ⊕ *www.buzosdebaru. com*) organizes snorkeling trips to the Islas del Rosario and scuba diving at underwater wrecks, as well as dive instruction.

BEACHES

For white sand and palm trees, your best bet is **Playa Blanca,** about 15 minutes away by boat. Many people opt for a visit to the **Islas del Rosario,** a verdant archipelago surrounded by aquamarine waters and coral reefs. Tour boats leave from the Muelle de los Pegasos, the pier flanked by statues of two flying horses that is just outside the city walls. Plenty of men with boats will also offer to take you on the one-hour journey. A final option is **Bocagrande,** the resort area on a 3-mi-long (5-km-long) peninsula south of the walled city. High-rise hotels and condos front the gray-sand beach. It gets quite crowded and is very lively, but Bocagrande is probably not the Caribbean beach of which you've always dreamed.

WHERE TO EAT

$–$$
CAFÉ
✗ **Café San Pedro.** Although it serves Colombian fare, this restaurant's eclectic menu includes dishes from Thailand, Italy, and Japan. You can also drop by to have a drink and to watch the activity on the plaza from one of the outdoor tables. ✉ *Plaza San Pedro* ☎ *575/664–5121.*

$–$$
LATIN AMERICAN
✗ **Paco's.** Heavy beams, rough terra-cotta walls, wooden benches, and tunes from an aging Cuban band are the hallmarks of this downtown eatery. Drop by for a drink and some tapas, or try the more substantial *langostinos a la sifú* (lobsters fried in batter). You can sit in the dining room or outside on the Plaza Santo Domingo. ✉ *Plaza Santo Domingo* ☎ *575/664–5057.*

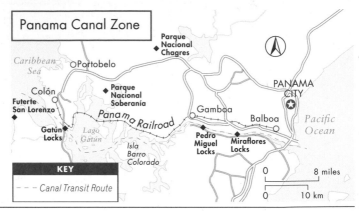

COLÓN, PANAMA

Marlise Kast

When you consider the decades it took to build the canal, not to mention the lives lost and government failures and triumphs involved during its construction, it comes as no surprise that the Panama Canal is often called the Eighth Wonder of the Modern World. Best described as an aquatic bridge, the Panama Canal connects the Caribbean Sea with the Pacific Ocean by raising ships up and over Central America, through artificially created Gatún Lake, the highest point at 85 feet above sea level, and then lowering them back to sea level by using a series of locks, or water steps. A masterful engineering feat, three pairs of locks—Gatún, Pedro Miguel, and Miraflores—utilize gravity to fill and drain as ships pass through chambers 1,000 feet long by 110 feet wide that are "locked" by doors weighing 80 tons apiece, yet actually float into position. Most cruise ships pass through the canal seasonally, when repositioning from one coast to the other; however, partial transits have become an increasingly popular "destination" on regularly scheduled 10- and 11-night Caribbean itineraries. These loop cruises enter the canal from the Caribbean Sea and sail into Gatún Lake, where they remain for a few hours as passengers are tendered ashore for excursions. Ships then pass back through the locks, returning to the Caribbean and stopping at either Cristobal Pier or Colón 2000 Pier to retrieve passengers at the conclusion of their tours.

A day transiting the canal's Gatún Locks begins before dawn as your passenger ship passes through *Bahia Limon* and lines up with dozens of other vessels to await its turn to enter. Before your ship can proceed, two pilots and a narrator will board. The sight of a massive cruise ship being raised dozens of feet into the air by water is so mesmerizing that passengers eagerly crowd all forward decks at the first lock. If you don't find a good viewing spot, head for the rear decks, where there is usually more room and the view is just as intriguing. If you remain aboard, as many passengers do, you'll find plenty of room up front later in the day as your ship retraces its path down to the sea. Due to the tight scheduling of the day's activities—it takes at least 90 minutes for a ship to pass through

Gatún Locks—passengers who wish to go ashore early in the day are advised to sign up for one of the many available shore excursions.

ESSENTIALS

CURRENCY The U.S. dollar, called the balboa, is the currency in Panama; the country does mint its own coins.

INTERNET There's an Internet café at the Colón 2000 Pier.

TELEPHONE You'll find telephones inside Colón's cruise terminal, where you can purchase phone cards, which are a handy and inexpensive way to make calls.

COMING ASHORE

Colón, Panama's second largest city, has little to offer of historic interest, and is simply a jumping-off point to the rain forest and a wide variety of organized tours. Infrequent cruise itineraries may include a day docked in Colón, rather than a partial canal transit. However, no matter how much time your ship spends in Colón, it is usually easier (and recommended) to take an organized shore excursion. If you don't want to go on a ship-sponsored shore excursion, taxi drivers also await ship arrivals, and some can be acceptable private guides for $100 to $120 per day if you just want to explore Portabelo or San Lorenzo. However, as in any foreign port, before setting out with any unofficial car and driver, you should set a firm price and agree upon an itinerary as well as look over the vehicle carefully. It's also possible to rent a car from either Budget or Hertz, both of which have desks at the Colón 2000 terminal.

Although entry time into the canal is always approximate, passenger ships have priority, and most pass through Gatún Locks early in the morning. Passengers booked on shore excursions begin the tendering process soon after the ship sets anchor, which can be as early as 8:30 am. Alternatives to excursions offered by your cruise ship are available from independent tour operators that can be arranged in advance through Web sites or travel agents. You will likely be informed that Panamanian regulations restrict passengers going ashore in Gatún Lake to only those who have booked the cruise line's excursions; however, anyone who has a shore-excursion reservation with a local company should be able to leave the vessel. Before making independent tour arrangements, confirm with your cruise line that you will be allowed to go ashore after presenting your private tour confirmation to the shore-excursion staff on board the ship.

Upon completion of either full or partial canal transits, cruise ships generally dock at either Cristobal Pier or Colón 2000 Pier late in the afternoon, where they may remain for several hours. Passengers who remained on board throughout the canal passage have the opportunity to go ashore, and land tours end at the terminals, where passengers rejoin the ship. A second terminal opened in 2008 and became the homeport for Royal Caribbean's *Enchantment of the Seas*, with the Panamanian government aggressively courting other cruise companies to set up shop here too. All of Colón is considered a high-crime area, and pickpockets have been known to strike even in the seemingly secure areas of the cruise-ship terminals. If you go ashore, you are well advised to leave jewelry and other valuables aboard ship and carry only the cash you need.

7

EXPLORING THE PANAMA CANAL ZONE

The provincial capital of **Colón,** beside the canal's Atlantic entrance, has clearly seen better days, as the architecture of its older buildings attests. Its predominantly Afro-Caribbean population has long had a vibrant musical scene, and in the late 19th and early 20th centuries Colón was a relatively prosperous town. But it spent the second half of the 20th century in steady decay, and things have only gotten worse in the 21st century. For the most part, the city is a giant slum, with unemployment at 30% to 40% and crime on the rise. ⚠ **Travelers who explore Colón on foot are simply asking to be mugged,** and the route between the train station and the bus terminal is especially notorious; do all your traveling in a taxi or rental car. If you do the Panama Railway trip on your own without a tour company, take one of the shuttle vans or hire a taxi to the train station.

Esclusas de Gatún *(Gatún Locks).* Twelve kilometers (7 mi) south of Colón are the Gatún Locks, a triple-lock complex that is nearly a mile long and raises and lowers ships the 85 feet between sea level and Gatún Lake. There's a small viewing platform at the locks and a simple visitor center that's nothing compared to the center at Miraflores Locks. However, the sheer magnitude of the Gatún Locks—they are the canal's largest—is impressive, especially when packed with ships. ✛ *12 km (7 mi) south of Colón* 🔳 *Free* ☉ *Daily 8–4.*

Fuerte San Lorenzo. Perched on a cliff overlooking the mouth of the Chagres River are the ruins of the ancient Spanish *fort* destroyed by pirate Henry Morgan in 1671. The Spaniards built Fort San Lorenzo in 1595, in an effort to protect the South American gold they were shipping down the Chagres River, which was first carried along the Camino de Cruces from Panamá Viejo. The fortress's commanding position and abundant cannons weren't enough of a deterrent for Morgan, whose men managed to shoot flaming arrows into the fort, causing a fire that set off stored gunpowder and forced the Spanish troops to surrender. ✉ *23 km (14 mi) northwest of Gatún Locks* 📷 *No phone* 🔳 *Free* ☉ *Daily 8–4.*

Lago Gatún (Gatún Lake). Covering about 163 square mi, an area about the size of the island nation Barbados, Gatún Lake extends northwest from Parque Nacional Soberanía to the locks of Gatún, just south of Colón. The lake was created when the U.S. government dammed the Chagres River, between 1907 and 1913, so that boats could cross the isthmus at 85 feet above sea level. By creating the lake, the United States saved decades of digging that a sea-level canal would have required. When it was completed, Gatún Lake was the largest man-made lake in the world. The canal route winds through its northern half, past several forest-covered islands (the largest is Barro Colorado, one of the world's first biological reserves). The lake itself is home to crocodiles, manatees, and peacock bass, a species introduced from South America and popular with fishermen. Fishing charters for bass, snook, and tarpon are out of Gamboa.

PORTOBELO

★ Portobelo is an odd mix of colonial fortresses, clear waters, lushly forested hills, and an ugly little town of cement-block houses crowded amid the ancient walls. It holds some of Panama's most interesting colonial ruins, with rusty cannons still lying in wait for an enemy assault, and is a UNESCO World Heritage Site, together with San Lorenzo.

Iglesia de San Felipe. One block east of the Real Aduana is this large white church dating from 1814. It is home to the country's most venerated religious figure: the **Cristo Negro** (Black Christ). The statue spends most of the year to the left of the church's altar, but once a year it's paraded through town in the Festival del Cristo Negro. Each year the Cristo Negro is clothed in a new purple robe, donated by somebody who's earned the honor. Many of the robes that have been created for the statue over the past century are on display in the Museo del Cristo Negro (Black Christ Museum) in the Iglesia de San Juan, a smaller 17th-century church next to the Iglesia de San Felipe. ⊠ *Calle Principal* ☎ *No phone* ☜ *$1* ۞ *Weekdays 8–4, weekends 8:30–3.*

Parque Nacional Portobelo *(Portobelo National Park).* The forested hills that rise behind the bay are part of Portobelo National Park, a vast marine and rain-forest reserve contiguous with Chagres National Park. Though several towns lie within the park, and much of its lowlands were deforested years ago, its inaccessible mountains are covered with dense forest that holds plenty of flora and fauna. While the coastal area is home to everything from ospreys to sea turtles, the mountains serve as refuge for spider monkeys, brocket deer, harpy eagles, and an array of other endangered wildlife. There is no proper park entrance, but you can explore patches of its forested coast and mangrove estuaries on boat trips from Portobelo, when you might see birds such as the ringed kingfisher and fasciated tiger heron.

Portobelo's largest and most impressive fort is **Fuerte San Jerónimo,** at the end of the bay, which is surrounded by the "modern" town. It was built in the 1600s but was destroyed by the pirate Edward Vernon and rebuilt to its current state in 1758. Its large interior courtyard was once a parade ground, but it is now the venue for all annual celebrations involving congo dancers, including New Year's, Carnival, the Festival de Diablos y Congos (shortly after Carnaval), and the town's patron saint's day (March 20).

Fuerte San Fernando, one of three Spanish forts you can visit at Portobelo, is surrounded by forest and is a good place to see birds. This large structure with cannons lies directly across the bay from Batería

---

COLÓN BEST BETS

■ **Explore an Embera Village.** You'll travel by dugout canoe through Chagres National Park.

■ **Kayak on Gatún Lake.** You can paddle among the many islands and mangrove forests.

■ **Panama Railway.** Take a train trip to Panama City for a quick sightseeing tour (you can come back by taxi to save some time).

■ **Portobelo.** Visit historic Panamanian forts.

■ **Rain Forest Aerial Tram.** Travel to Gamboa Rainforest Resort and see the rain forest canopy from above.

7

Santiago. The youngest of Portobelo's forts, Batería Santiago was built in the 1860s, after Vernon's fateful attack. The thick walls are coral, which was cut from the platform reefs that line the coast. Coral was more abundant and easier to cut than the igneous rock found inland, so the Spanish used it for most construction in Portobelo. ■ TIP→ Local boatmen who are usually sitting near the dock next to Batería Santiago can take you across the bay to explore Fuerte San Fernando for $3. They also offer transportation to several local beaches, as well as a trip into the estuary at the end of the bay. ⊠ *Surrounding Portobelo* ☏ *448–2165 or 442–8348* 🖃 *Free* ☉ *24 hrs.*

Real Aduana *(Royal Customs House).* Near the entrance to Fuerte San Jerónimo is the Royal Customs House, where servants of the Spanish crown made sure that the king and queen got their cut from every ingot that rolled through town. Built in 1630, the Real Aduana was damaged during pirate attacks and then destroyed by an earthquake in 1882, only to be rebuilt in 1998. It houses a simple museum with some old coins, cannonballs, and displays on Panamanian folklore. ⊠ *Calle de la Aduana* ☏ *No phone* 🖃 *$1* ☉ *Tues.–Sat. 9–4, weekends 8:30–3.*

SHOPPING

Both Cristobal Pier and Colón 2000 Pier have large shopping malls, where you will find Internet access, telephones, refreshments, and duty-free souvenir shops in relatively secure environments. Stores in both locations feature local crafts such as baskets, wood carvings, and toys, as well as liquor, jewelry, and the ubiquitous souvenir T-shirts. In addition to shops and cafés, Cristobal Pier features an open-air arts and craft market; Colón 2000 Pier has a well-stocked supermarket. Portobelo has a wide-ranging artisan market next to Iglesia de San Felipe.

The most unique locally made souvenirs are colorful appliquéd *molas*, the whimsical textile artwork created by native Kuna women, who come from the San Blas Islands; they are likely to be at hand stitching new designs while they sell the ones they just completed. If you take an excursion to Portobelo, the prices may be better there where several Kuna women are usually selling their molas in the artisan market next to the church.

WHERE TO EAT

$$
SEAFOOD

✕ **Restaurante Los Cañones.** This rambling restaurant with tables among palm trees and Caribbean views is one of Panama's most attractive lunch spots. Unfortunately, the food and service fall short of the setting, but not so far that you'd want to scratch it from your list. In good weather, dine at tables edging the sea surrounded by dark boulders and lush foliage. The other option is the open-air restaurant, decorated with shells, buoys, and driftwood, with a decent view of the bay and forested hills. House specialties include *pescado entero* (whole fried red snapper), *langosta al ajillo* (lobster scampi), and *centolla al jengibre* (king crab in a ginger sauce). ⊠ *2 km (1 mi) before Portobelo on left* ☏ *448–2980* 🖃 *No credit cards* ☉ *Closes at 7 pm.*

COSTA MAYA, MEXICO

Marlise Kast

Puerto Costa Maya is an anomaly. Unlike other tourist attractions in the area (the island of Cozumel being the primary Yucatán cruise port), this port of call near Mahahual has been created exclusively for cruise-ship passengers. The port added a second berth in July 2008. This latest addition known as "New Mahahual" is comprised of theme restaurants like Hard Rock Café and Senior Frogs as well as boutique shops and chain stores such as Lapis Jewelry.

At first glance, the port complex itself may seem to be little more than an outdoor mall. The docking pier (which can accommodate three ships at once) leads to a 70,000-square-foot bazaar-type compound where shops selling local crafts—jewelry, pottery, woven straw hats and bags, and embroidered dresses—are interspersed with duty-free stores and souvenir shops. There are two alfresco restaurants, which serve sea-food, American-friendly Mexican dishes like tacos and quesadillas, and cocktails at shaded tables. An outdoor amphitheater stages eight daily performances of traditional music and dance.

The strip of beach edging the complex has been outfitted with colorful lounge chairs and *hamacas* (hammocks), and may tempt you to linger and sunbathe. If you want to have a truly authentic Mexican experience, though, you'll take advantage of the day tours offered to outlying areas. These give you a chance to see some of the really spectacular sights in this part of Mexico, many of which are rarely visited. This is one port where the shore excursion is the point, and there are no options except to purchase what your ship offers. You can preview what excursions may be offered on the Puerto Costa Maya's own website.

Among the best tours are those that let you explore the gorgeous (and usually deserted) Mayan ruin sites of Kohunlich, Dzibanché, and Chac-choben. The ancient pyramids and temples at these sites, surrounded by jungle that's protected them for centuries, are still dazzling to behold. Since the sites are some distance from the port complex—and require some road travel in one of the port's air-conditioned vans—these tours are all-day affairs. One of the most popular activities with cruise pas-sengers is the three-hour ATV excursion along jungle roads and the Mahahual coastline. Although an adventure, the ATVs tend to be a nuisance to residents and business owners, not to mention wildlife.

Prior to a devastating 2007 hurricane, there was no real reason to go into the small, nearby fishing village of Mahahual (pronounced ma-ha-*wal*). Though there are still about 300 residents, post-hurricane renova-tions have put the village on the map; it now has its own pier as well as a smattering of hotels, restaurants, and shops. Be sure to venture beyond "New Mahahual," which lacks the charm of the nearby beach-front area. Its cement boardwalk along the beach has made Mahahual an ideal spot for a sunset stroll. The crystal-clear waters and unspoiled beaches are delightful for snorkeling, diving, and fishing.

7

ESSENTIALS

CURRENCY The Mexican peso (MX$12.06 to US$1). U.S. dollars and credit cards are accepted by everyone at the port. There is no advantage to paying in dollars, but there may be an advantage to paying in cash.

INFORMATION **Puerto Costa Maya** (⊕ *www.puertocostamaya.com*).

TELEPHONE Most pay phones accept prepaid Ladatel cards, sold in 30-, 50-, or 100-peso denominations. To use the card, insert it in the pay phone's slot, dial 001 (for calls to the U.S.) or 01 (for calls within Mexico), followed by the area code and number. Credit is deleted from the card as you use it, and the balance is displayed on a small screen on the phone.

> ### COSTA MAYA BEST BETS
>
> ■ **Chacchoben.** This archaeological site is near the Belize border.
>
> ■ **Kohunlich.** This ruined city is best known for its great temples with sculpted masks.
>
> ■ **Mahahual.** This small fishing village (pronounced *Ma-ha-wahl*) near the cruise pier has plenty of fine sand and glassy waters for a cushy afternoon in the sun.
>
> ■ **Snorkeling at Banco Chinchorro.** Excellent catamaran snorkeling trips go here.
>
> ■ **Xcalak.** This national reserve offers excellent saltwater fly-fishing and deserted beaches.

WHERE TO EAT

$ ✕ **100% Agave.** This small restaurant-shack is a must for tequila lovers.
MEXICAN Owner Fernando serves up delicious Mexican food and is an expert on tequila and other agave liquors. His margaritas rival any cocktail in Mahahual and his "Micheladas" (beer, lime and hot sauce) are refreshingly punchy. The affordable menu features traditional Mexican, Yucatan, and Tex-Mex specialties. Tequila tasting is part of the experience so be sure to ask Fernando about his barrels of 100% agave blends. The place is easily recognizable by the big tequila bottle out front. ⊠ *Calle Huachinango, 2n road parallel to Malecon, Mahahual* 🕾 *No phone* ⊟ *No credit cards.*

$–$$ ✕ **Nacional Beach Club.** Many travelers stumble on this colorful beach
MEXICAN club and end up staying past sunset. For just $10, you get a beach chair, umbrella and access to the pool, shower and changing facilities. Margaritas can be delivered to you beachside or you can escape the heat by grabbing a bite in the enclosed patio. By day you can munch on tacos, enchiladas and sandwiches and by night enjoy the delicious smoked fish or grilled shrimp. The $2 Coronas make this a popular spot to waste away the day. ⊠ *Mahahual Av. SN Lote 4 Manzana 14, Mahahual* 🕾 *983/110–5354* ⊕ *www.nacionalbeachclub.com* ⊟ *No credit cards.*

COZUMEL, MEXICO

Marlise Kast

Cozumel, with its sun-drenched ivory beaches fringed with coral reefs, fulfills the tourist's vision of a tropical Caribbean island. It's a heady mix of the natural and the commercial. Despite a mini-construction boom in the island's sole city, San Miguel, there are still wild pockets scattered throughout the island where flora and fauna flourish. Smaller than Cancún, Cozumel surpasses its fancier neighbor in many ways. It has more history and ruins, superior diving and snorkeling, more authentic cuisine, and a greater diversity of handicrafts at better prices. The numerous coral reefs, particularly the world-renowned Palancar Reef, attract divers from around the world. On a busy cruise-ship day the island can seem completely overrun, but it's still possible to get away, and some good Mayan sights are within reach on long (and expensive) shore excursions.

ESSENTIALS

CURRENCY The Mexican peso (MX$12.06 to US$1). U.S. dollars and credit cards are widely accepted in the area, from the port to Playa del Carmen, but it's best to have pesos—and small bills—when you visit ruins where cashiers often run out of change. There is no advantage to paying in dollars, but there may be an advantage to paying in cash.

INTERNET **CreWorld Internet** (✉ *Av. Rafael E. Melgar and Calle 11 Sur* ☎ *987/872–6509*). **Coffeenet** (✉ *Av. Rafael E. Melgar at Calle 11* ☎ *987/872–6394*).

TELEPHONE You may be able to find pay phones that accept prepaid Ladatel cards, sold in 30-, 50-, or 100-peso denominations at the cruise pier and at the plaza. To use the card, insert it in the pay phone's slot, dial 001 (for calls to the U.S.) or 01 (for calls within Mexico), followed by the area code and number. Credit is deleted from the card as you use it, and the balance is displayed on a small screen on the phone. Most people use their own cell phones.

COMING ASHORE

As many as six ships call at Cozumel on a busy day, tendering passengers to the downtown pier in the center of San Miguel or docking at the two international piers 4 mi (6 km) away. From the downtown pier you can walk into town or catch the ferry to Playa del Carmen. Taxi tours are also available. A four-hour island tour (4 people maximum), including the ruins and other sights, costs about $70 to $100, but negotiate the price before you get in the cab. The international pier is close to many beaches, but you'll need a taxi to get into town. There's rarely a wait for a taxi, but prices are high, and drivers are often aggressive, asking double or triple the reasonable fare. When in doubt, ask to see the rate card required of all taxi drivers. Expect to pay $10 for the ride into San Miguel from the pier. Tipping is not necessary.

Passenger ferries to Playa del Carmen leave Cozumel's main pier approximately every other hour from 5 am to 10 pm. They also leave Playa del Carmen's dock about every other hour on the hour, from 6 am to 11 pm (but note that service sometimes varies according to demand). The trip takes 45 minutes. Verify the times: bad weather and changing schedules can prompt cancellations.

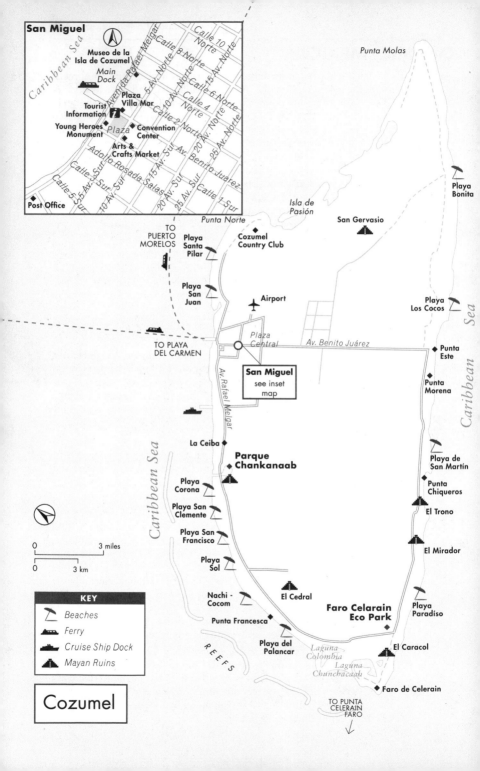

San Miguel

Caribbean Sea

Museo de la
Isla de Cozumel

Main
Dock

Tourist
Information

Young Heroes
Monument

Arts &
Crafts Market

Plaza
Villa Mar

Convention
Center

Plaza

Post Office

Calle 10 Norte
Calle 8 Norte
Calle 6 Norte
Calle 4 Norte
Calle 2 Norte

Avenida Rafael Melgar
5 Av. Norte
10 Av. Norte
15 Av. Norte
20 Av. Norte
25 Av. Norte

Adolfo Rosada Salas
15 Av. Sur
10 Av. Sur
5 Av. Sur
Av. Benito Juárez
20 Av. Sur
25 Av. Sur
Calle 1 Sur

Calle 3 Sur
Calle 5 Sur

Punta Molas

Punta Norte

TO PUERTO
MORELOS

Playa
Santa
Pilar

Cozumel
Country Club

Isla de
Pasión

San Gervasio

Playa
Bonita

Playa
San
Juan

Airport

Plaza
Central

TO PLAYA
DEL CARMEN

Av. Benito Juárez

San Miguel
see inset
map

Av. Rafael Melgar

Playa
Los Cocos

Punta
Este

Punta
Morena

La Ceiba

**Parque
Chankanaab**

Playa
Corona

Playa San
Clemente

Playa San
Francisco

Playa
Sol

Nachi -
Cocom

Punta Francesca

Playa del
Palancar

El Cedral

**Faro Celarain
Eco Park**

Laguna
Colombia

Laguna
Chunchacaab

R E E F S

Playa de
San Martín

Punta
Chiqueros

El Trono

El Mirador

Playa
Paradiso

El Caracol

Faro de Celerain

TO PUNTA
CELERAIN
FARO

Caribbean Sea

Caribbean Sea

*Caribbean
Sea*

0   3 miles

0   3 km

KEY

Beaches

Ferry

Cruise Ship Dock

Mayan Ruins

Cozumel

EXPLORING COZUMEL

San Miguel is not tiny, but you can easily explore the waterfront and plaza area on foot. The main attractions are the small eateries and shops that line the streets and the main square, where the locals congregate in the evening.

El Cedral. Spanish explorers discovered this site, once the hub of Mayan life on Cozumel, in 1518. Later it became the island's first official city, founded in 1847. Today it's a farming community with small well-tended houses and gardens. Conquistadors tore down much of the Mayan temple, and during World War II the U.S. Army Corps of Engineers destroyed the rest to make way for the island's first airport. All that remains of the Mayan ruins is one small structure with an arch. Nearby is a green-and-white cinder-block church, decorated inside with crosses shrouded in embroidered lace; legend has it that Mexico's first Mass was held here. Vendors display embroidered blouses, hammocks, and other souvenirs at stands around the main plaza. ⊠ *Turn at Km 17.5 off Carretera Sur or Av. Rafael E. Melgar, then drive 3 km (2 mi) inland to site* 🕾 *No phone* 🖭 *Free* ☉ *Daily dawn–dusk.*

> **COZUMEL BEST BETS**
>
> ■ **Diving and Snorkeling.** Excellent reefs close to shore make either diving or snorkeling a must-do activity.
>
> ■ **Mayan Ruins.** Some of the most famous and dazzling ruins are reachable from Cozumel, and if you have never seen a Mayan pyramid, this is your chance.
>
> ■ **People-watching.** You can spend hours just sitting in the main plaza (or at a sidewalk café) watching island life pass by.

Faro Celarain Eco Park. This 247-acre national preserve at Cozumel's southernmost tip is a protected habitat for numerous birds and animals, including crocodiles, flamingos, egrets, and herons. Cars aren't allowed, so you'll need to use park transportation (rented bicycles or park shuttles) to get around here. From observation towers you can spot crocodiles and birds in **Laguna Colombia** or **Laguna Chunchacaab.** Another highlight is the ancient Mayan lighthouse, **El Caracol,** designed to whistle when the wind blows in a certain direction. At the park's (and the island's) southernmost point is the **Faro de Celarain,** a lighthouse that is now a museum of navigation. Climb the 134 steps to the top; it's a steamy effort, but the views are incredible. Beaches here are wide and deserted, and there's great snorkeling offshore. Snorkeling equipment is available for rent, as are kayaks, and there are restrooms at the museum and by the beach. Without a rental car, expect to pay about $40 for a round-trip taxi ride from San Miguel. ⊠ *Southernmost point of Carretera Sur and coastal road* 🕾 *987/872–2940* 🖭 *$10 (cash only)* ☉ *Daily 9–4.*

Parque Chankanaab. Chankanaab (which means "small sea") is a national park with a saltwater lagoon, an archaeological park, and a botanical garden. Scattered throughout are reproductions of a Mayan village, and of Olmec, Toltec, Aztec, and Mayan stone carvings. You can enjoy a cool walk along pathways leading to the sea, where parrotfish and sergeant majors swarm around snorkelers.

You can swim, scuba dive, or snorkel at the beach. There's plenty to see: underwater caverns, a sunken ship, crusty old cannons and anchors, and a sculpture of la Virgen del Mar (Virgin of the Sea). To preserve the ecosystem, park rules forbid touching the reef or feeding the fish.

> ### SHIP SALES
>
> If you find prices on board too much to bear, shop the ship's boutiques on the last day of your cruise, when they are likely to run special sales.

Dive shops, restaurants, gift shops, a snack stand, and dressing rooms with lockers and showers are right on the sand. A small museum has exhibits on coral, shells, and the park's history, as well as some sculptures. ⊠ *Carretera Sur, Km 9* ☎ *987/872–2940* ⊒ *$19* ☉ *Daily 8–4.*

San Gervasio. Surrounded by a forest, these temples make up Cozumel's largest remaining Mayan and Toltec site. San Gervasio was the island's capital and ceremonial center, dedicated to the fertility goddess Ixchel. Its classic- and postclassic-style buildings and temples were continuously occupied from AD 300 to 1500. Typical architectural features include limestone plazas and arches atop stepped platforms, as well as stelae and bas-reliefs. Be sure to see the temple "Las Manitas," with red handprints all over its altar. Plaques clearly describe each structure in Mayan, Spanish, and English. ⊠ *From San Miguel, take cross-island road (follow signs to airport) east to San Gervasio access road; turn left and follow road 7 km (4½ mi)* ⊒ *$7* ☉ *Daily 8–4.*

San Miguel. Be sure to stroll along the *malecón* (boardwalk) and take in the ocean breeze. Cozumel's only town feels more traditional the farther you walk away from the water; the waterfront has been taken over by large shops selling jewelry, imported rugs, leather boots, and souvenirs to cruise-ship passengers. Head inland to the pedestrian streets around the plaza, where family-owned restaurants and shops cater to locals and savvy travelers.

☾ Cozumel's **Museo de la Isla de Cozumel** is housed on two floors of a former
★ hotel. It has displays on natural history—with exhibits on the island's origins, endangered species, topography, and coral-reef ecology—as well as the pre-Columbian and colonial periods. The photos of the island's transformation over the 20th and 21st centuries are especially fascinating, as is the exhibit of a typical Mayan home. Guided tours are available. ⊠ *Av. Rafael E. Melgar, between Calles 4 and 6 Norte* ☎ *987/872–1475* ⊒ *$3* ☉ *Daily 9–5.*

SHOPPING

Cozumel's main souvenir-shopping area is downtown along Avenida Rafael E. Melgar and on some side streets around the plaza. There are also clusters of shops at **Plaza del Sol** (east side of the main plaza) and **Vista del Mar** (⊠ *Av. Rafael E. Melgar 45*). As a general rule, the newer, trendier shops line the waterfront, and the better craft shops can be found around Avenida 5a. Malls at the cruise-ship piers aim to please passengers seeking jewelry, perfume, sportswear, and low-end souvenirs at high-end prices.

Most downtown shops accept U.S. dollars; many goods are priced in dollars. To get better prices, pay with cash—some shops tack a hefty surcharge on credit-card purchases. Shops, restaurants, and streets are always crowded between 10 am and 2 pm, but get calmer in the evening. Traditionally, stores are open from 9 to 1 (except Sunday) and 5 to 9, but those nearest the pier tend to stay open all day, particularly during high season. Most shops are closed Sunday morning.

ACTIVITIES

DIVING AND SNORKELING

Cozumel is famous for its reefs. In addition to Chankanaab Nature Park, a great dive site is La Ceiba Reef, in the waters off La Ceiba and Sol Caribe hotels. Here lies the wreckage of a sunken airplane blown up for a Mexican disaster movie. Cozumel has plenty of dive shops to choose from. **Aqua Safari** (⊠ *Av. Rafael E. Melgar 429, between Calles 5 and 7 Sur* ☎ *987/872–0101* ⊕ *www.aquasafari.com*) is among the island's oldest and most professional shops. Owner Bill Horn has long been involved in efforts to protect the reefs and stays on top of local environmental issues. The shop provides PADI certification, classes on night diving, deep diving and other interests, and individualized dives. **Blue Angel** (⊠ *Carretera Sur, Km 2.3* ☎ *987/872 1631 or 866/779–9986* ⊕ *www.blueangel-scuba.com*) offers combo dive and snorkel trips so families who don't all scuba can still stick together. Along with dive trips to local reefs, they offer PADI courses. **Eagle Ray Divers** (⊠ *La Caleta Marina, near Presidente InterContinental hotel* ☎ *987/872–5735 or 866/465–1616* ⊕ *www.eagleraydivers.com*) offers snorkeling trips (the three-reef trip lets nondivers explore beyond the shore) and dive instruction. As befits their name, the company keeps track of the eagle rays that appear off Cozumel from December to February and runs trips for advanced divers to walls where the rays congregate. Beginners can also see rays around some of the reefs.

FISHING

You can charter high-speed fishing boats for about $420 per half-day or $600 per day (with a maximum of six people). Your hotel can help arrange daily charters—some offer special deals, with boats leaving from their own docks. **Albatros Deep Sea Fishing** (☎ *987/872–7904 or 888/333–4643* ⊕ *www.albatroscharters.com*) offers full-day trips that include boat and crew, tackle and bait, and lunch with beer and soda starting at $575 for up to six people. **3 Hermanos** (☎ *987/107–0655, 651/755–4897 in U.S.* ⊕ *www.cozumelfishing.com*) specializes in deep-sea and fly-fishing trips. Their rates for a half day deep-sea fishing trip start at $350; a full day is $450. They also offer scuba-diving trips, and their boats are available for group charters (a great way to snorkel and cruise around at your own pace) for $400 for up to six passengers.

7

BEACHES

Cozumel's beaches vary from sandy treeless stretches to isolated coves to rocky shores. Most of the development is on the leeward (western) side. Beach clubs have sprung up on the southwest coast; admission, however, is usually free, as long as you buy food and drinks. Clubs offer typical tourist fare: souvenir shops, *palapa* (thatch-roofed) restaurants, kayaks, and cold beer. A cab ride from San Miguel to most clubs costs about $15 each way. Reaching beaches on the windward (eastern) side is more difficult, but the solitude is worth it.

★ South of the resorts lies the mostly ignored (and therefore serene) **Playa Palancar**. Offshore is the famous Palancar Reef, easily accessed by the on-site dive shop. There's also a water-sports center, a bar-café, and a long beach with hammocks hanging under coconut palms. The aroma of grilled fish with garlic butter is tantalizing. Playa del Palancar keeps prices low and rarely feels crowded. **Playa San Francisco** is an inviting 3-mi (5-km) stretch of sandy beach, which extends along Carretera Sur, south of Parque Chankanaab at about Km 10. Amenities include two outdoor restaurants, a bar, dressing rooms, gift shops, volleyball nets, beach chairs, and water-sports equipment rentals. Divers use this beach as a jumping-off point for the San Francisco reef and Santa Rosa wall. The abundance of turtle grass in the water, however, makes this a less-than-ideal spot for swimming. **Punta Chiqueros**, a half-moon-shape cove sheltered by an offshore reef, is the first popular swimming area as you drive north on the coastal road (it's about 8 mi [12 km] north of Parque Faro Celarain Eco Park). Part of a longer beach that some locals call Playa Bonita, the beach has fine sand, clear water, and moderate waves. This is a great place to swim, watch the sunset, and eat fresh fish at the restaurant, also called Playa Bonita.

WHERE TO EAT

$$-$$$ ✕ **Guido's.** Chef Yvonne Villiger works wonders with fresh fish—if the
ITALIAN   wahoo with capers and black olives is on the menu, don't miss it. But
★   Guido's is best known for its pizzas baked in a wood-burning oven, which makes sections of the indoor dining room rather warm. Sit in the pleasant, recently expanded courtyard instead, and order a pitcher of sangria to go with the puffy garlic bread. ⊠ *Av. Rafael E. Melgar 23, between Calles 6 and 8 Norte* 🕾 *987/872–0946* ⊕ *www.guidoscozumel. com* ☾ *No lunch Sun.*

$$-$$$ ✕ **Pancho's Backyard.** Marimbas play beside the bubbling fountain in
MEXICAN   this gorgeous courtyard behind one of Cozumel's best folk-art shops.
★   Though Pancho's is always busy, the waitstaff is amazingly patient and helpful. Cruise-ship passengers seeking a taste of Mexico pack the place at lunch; dinner is a bit more serene. The menu is definitely geared toward tourists (written in English with detailed descriptions and prices in dollars), but regional ingredients make even the standard steak stand out when it's flavored with smoky chipotle chiles. Other stellar dishes include the cilantro cream soup and shrimp flambéed with tequila. ⊠ *Av. Rafael Melgar between Calles 8 and 10 Norte* 🕾 *987/872–2141* ⊕ *www. panchosbackyard.com* ☾ *No lunch Sun.*

CURAÇAO (WILLEMSTAD)

Vernon
O'Reilly-
Ramesar

Try to be on deck as your ship sails into Curaçao. The tiny Queen Emma floating bridge swings aside to allow ships to pass through the narrow channel. Pastel gingerbread buildings on shore look like doll-houses, especially from a large cruise ship. Although the gabled roofs and red tiles show a Dutch influence, the gleeful colors of the facades are peculiar to Curaçao. It's said that an early governor of the island suffered from migraines that were aggravated by the color white, so all the houses were painted in hues from magenta to mauve. Thirty-five mi (56 km) north of Venezuela and 42 mi (68 km) east of Aruba, Curaçao is, at 38 mi (61 km) long and 3 to 7.5 mi (5 to 12 km) wide, the largest of the Netherlands Antilles. Although always sunny, it's never stiflingly hot here because of the constant trade winds. Water sports attract enthusiasts from all over the world, and the reef diving is excellent.

ESSENTIALS

CURRENCY

The NAf guilder (NAf 1.79 to US$1); U.S. currency is accepted almost everywhere on the island, and ATMs are plentiful. The currency is expected to be changed to the Caribbean guilder in 2012 (this currency will also be used by Sint Martin).

INTERNET

Café Internet ✉ *Handelskade 3B, Punda, Willemstad, Curaçao* ☏ *5999/465–5088.* **Wireless Internet Café** ✉ *Hanchi Snoa 1, Punda, Willemstad, Curaçao* ☏ *5999/461–0590.*

TELEPHONE

The telephone system is reliable. To place a local call, dial the seven-digit number. A local call costs NAf 0.50 from a pay phone. Direct-dial access is also available at the AT&T calling center at the cruise-ship terminal and at the megapier in Otrobanda. From other public phones, use phones marked "lenso"; many more of these have been added around the island in recent years. You can also call direct from the air-conditioned Digicel center using a prepaid phone card (open 8 am to 5:30 pm, Monday through Saturday; the center also offers Internet access).

COMING ASHORE

Ships dock at the terminal just beyond the Queen Emma Bridge, which leads to the floating market and the shopping district. The walk to downtown takes less than 10 minutes. Easy-to-read maps are posted dockside and in the shopping area. The terminal has a duty-free shop, telephones, and a taxi stand.

Taxis, which meet every ship, now have meters, although rates are still fixed from point to point of your journey. The government-approved rates, which do not include waiting time, can be found in a brochure called "Taxi Tariff Guide," available at the cruise-ship terminal and at the tourist board. Rates are for up to four passengers. There's a 25% surcharge after 11 pm. It's easy to see the sights on Curaçao without going on an organized shore excursion. Downtown can be done on foot, and a taxi for up to four people will cost about $40 an hour. Taxi fares to places in and around the city range from $8 to $20. Car rentals are available but are not cheap (about $40 per day, plus $10 compulsory insurance).

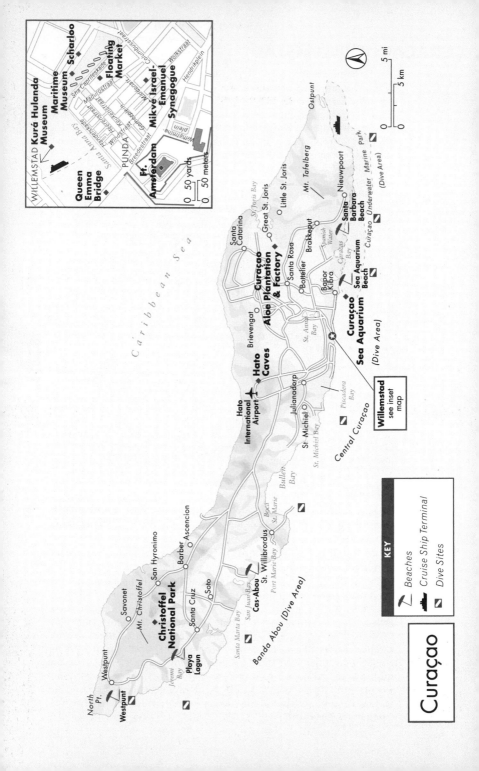

WILLEMSTAD

Kurá Hulanda Museum

Maritime Museum

Scharloo

Floating Market

Mikvé Israel-Emanuel Synagogue

Queen Emma Bridge

Ft. Amsterdam

PUNDA

Sna Caprilestdag

Madurostraat

Keukenstraat

Gomezplein

Breedestraat

Waaigat

Windstraat

Columbusstraat

Werfstraat

Hendrikplein

Wilhelmina plein

Santa Anna Bay

0   50 yards
0   50 meters

Caribbean Sea

Ostpunt

North Pt.

Westpunt

Westpunt

Savonet

Mt. Christoffel

San Hyronimo

Christoffel National Park

Playa Lagun

Jeremi Bay

Santa Cruz

Soto

Ascencion

Barber

San Hyronimo

St. Willibrordus

Cas-Abou

Boca St. Marie

Port Marie Bay

Santa Marta Bay

San Juan Bay

Banda Abou (Dive Area)

Bullen Bay

Boca St. Marie

St. Michiel

St. Michiel Bay

Julianadorp

Piscadera Bay

Central Curaçao

Hato International Airport

Hato Caves

Brievengat

Curaçao Aloe Plantation & Factory

Santa Catarina

Santa Rosa

Bottelier

St. Joris Bay

Great St. Joris

Little St. Joris

Mt. Tafelberg

Nieuwpoort

Santa Barbara Beach

Curaçao Underwater Marine Park

(Dive Area)

Brakkeput

Spanish Water

Caracas Bay

Bapor Kibra

Sea Aquarium Beach

St. Anna Bay

Curaçao Sea Aquarium

(Dive Area)

Willemstad
see inset map

KEY

Beaches

Cruise Ship Terminal

Dive Sites

Curaçao

5 mi

5 km

EXPLORING CURAÇAO

WILLEMSTAD

Willemstad is small and navigable on foot. You needn't spend more than two or three hours wandering around here, although the narrow alleys and various architectural styles are enchanting. English, Spanish, and Dutch are widely spoken. Narrow Santa Anna Bay divides the city into two sides: Punda, where you'll find the main shopping district, and Otrabanda (literally, the "other side"), where the cruise ships dock. Punda is crammed with shops, restaurants, monuments, and markets. Otrabanda has narrow, winding streets full of colonial homes notable for their gables and Dutch-influenced designs.

CURAÇAO BEST BETS

■ **Curaçao Sea Aquarium.** Explore the wonders of the ocean without getting wet.

■ **Diving.** After Bonaire, Curaçao has probably the best diving in the region.

■ **Floating Market.** This unique market is a fun destination, even though it's mostly fruits and vegetables.

■ **Kurá Hulanda Museum.** This is the island's best historical museum.

■ **Punda.** Willemstad's chic and beautiful shopping area is a joy to explore on foot.

You can cross from Otrabanda to Punda in one of three ways: walk over the Queen Emma Bridge; ride the free ferry, which runs when the bridge swings open to let seagoing vessels pass; or take a cab across the Juliana Bridge (about $9). On the Punda side of the city, Handelskade is where you'll find Willemstad's most famous sights—the colorful colonial buildings that line the waterfront. The original red roof tiles came from Europe on trade ships as ballast.

★ **Floating Market.** Each morning dozens of Venezuelan schooners laden with tropical fruits and vegetables arrive at this bustling market on the Punda side of the city. Mangoes, papayas, and exotic vegetables vie for space with freshly caught fish and herbs and spices. The buying is best at 6:30 am—too early for many people on vacation—but there's plenty of action through the afternoon. Any produce bought here should be thoroughly washed or peeled before being eaten. ⊠ *Sha Caprileskade, Punda, Willemstad, Curaçao.*

Ft. Amsterdam. Step through the archway of this fort and enter another century. The entire structure dates from the 1700s, when it was the center of the city and the island's most important fortification. Now it houses the governor's residence, a church (which has a small museum), and government offices. Outside the entrance, a series of majestic gnarled *wayaka* trees are fancifully carved with human forms—the work of local artist Mac Alberto. ⊠ *Foot of Queen Emma Bridge, Punda, Willemstad, Curaçao* ☎ *5999/461–1139* ⊠ *Fort free, church museum $2* ☉ *Weekdays 9:30–1, Sun. service at 10.*

Fodor's Choice **Kura Hulanda Museum.** This fascinating anthropological museum reveals ★ the island's diverse roots. Housed in a restored 18th-century village, the museum is built around a former mercantile square (Kura Hulanda means "Holland courtyard"), where the Dutch once sold slaves. An

7

exhibit on the transatlantic slave trade includes a gut-wrenching replica of a slave-ship hold. Other sections feature relics from West African empires, examples of pre-Columbian gold, and Antillean art. ⊠ *Klipstraat 9, Otrobanda, Willemstad, Curaçao* ☎ *5999/462–1400* ⊕ *www. kurahulanda.com/museum* ☞ *$9* ⊙ *Thurs.–Sat. 10–5.*

Maritime Museum. The museum—designed to resemble the interior of a ship—gives you a sense of Curaçao's maritime history, using model ships, historic maps, nautical charts, navigational equipment, and audiovisual displays. The museum also offers a two-hour guided tour (Wednesday and Saturday, 2 pm) on its "water bus" through Curaçao's harbor—a route familiar to traders, smugglers, and pirates. The museum is wheelchair accessible. ⊠ *Van der Brandhofstraat 7, Scharloo, Willemstad, Curaçao* ☎ *5999/465–2327* ⊕ *www.curacaomaritime.com* ☞ *Museum $10, museum and harbor tour $15* ⊙ *Tues.–Sat. 9–4.*

★ **Mikvé Israel-Emanuel Synagogue.** The temple, the oldest in continuous use in the Western Hemisphere, is one of Curaçao's most important sights and draws thousands of visitors a year. The synagogue was dedicated in 1732 by the Jewish community, which had already grown from the original 12 families who came from Amsterdam in 1651. They were later joined by Jews from Portugal and Spain fleeing persecution from the Inquisition. White sand covers the synagogue floor for two symbolic reasons: a remembrance of the 40 years Jews spent wandering the desert, and a re-creation of the sand used by secret Jews, or *conversos*, to muffle sounds from their houses of worship during the Inquisition. ⊠ *Hanchi Snoa 29, Punda, Willemstad, Curaçao* ☎ *5999/461–1067* ⊕ *www.snoa.com* ☞ *$6; donations also accepted* ⊙ *Weekdays 9–4:30.*

Queen Emma Bridge. Affectionately called the Swinging Old Lady by the locals, this bridge connects the two sides of Willemstad—Punda and Otrobanda—across the Santa Anna Bay. The bridge swings open at least 30 times a day to allow passage of ships to and from the sea. The original bridge, built in 1888, was the brainchild of the American consul Leonard Burlington Smith, who made a mint off the tolls he charged for using it: 2¢ per person for those wearing shoes, free to those crossing barefoot. Today it's free to everyone. The bridge was dismantled and completely repaired and restored in 2005. ⊠ *Willemstad, Curaçao.*

Scharloo. The Wilhelmina Drawbridge connects Punda with the once-flourishing district of Scharloo, where the early Jewish merchants built stately homes. The architecture along Scharlooweg (much of it from the 17th century) is magnificent, and, happily, many of the colonial mansions that had become dilapidated have been meticulously renovated. The area closest to Kleine Werf is a red-light district and fairly run-down, but the rest is well worth a visit. ⊠ *Willemstad, Curaçao.*

ELSEWHERE ON THE ISLAND

★ **Christoffel National Park.** The 1,239-foot Mt. Christoffel, Curaçao's highest peak, is at the center of this 4,450-acre garden and wildlife preserve. The exhilarating climb up—a challenge to anyone who hasn't grown up scaling the Alps—takes about two hours for a reasonably fit person. On a clear day, the panoramic view from the peak stretches to the mountain ranges of Venezuela.

Through the park are eight hiking trails and a 20-mi (32-km) network of driving trails (use heavy-treaded tires if you wish to explore the unpaved stretches). All these routes traverse hilly fields full of prickly pear cacti, divi-divi trees, bushy-haired palms, and exotic flowers. Guided nature walks, horseback rides, and jeep tours can be arranged through the main park office. If you're going without a guide, first study the *Excursion Guide to Christoffel Park*, sold at

SUNGLASSES

When selecting sunglasses, the most important considerations are the amount of UV light that is blocked by the lenses and a proper fit. The lenses should shield your eyes from most angles. Darker lenses do not necessarily offer better UV protection. Look for sunglasses that block 99% of harmful UV rays.

the visitor center. It outlines the various routes and identifies the indigenous flora and fauna. Start out early, as by 10 am the park starts to feel like a sauna.

Horseback tours are conducted from Rancho Alfin, which is in the park. Reservations are required. Additionally, most island sports outfitters offer some kind of activity in the park, such as kayaking, specialized hiking tours, and drive-through tours. ⊠ *Savonet, Curaçao* ☎ *5999/864–0363 for information and tour reservations, 5999/462–6262 for jeep tours, 5999/864–0535 for horseback tours* ⊠ *$10* ⊙ *Mon.–Sat. 8–4, Sun. 6–3; last admission 90 min before closing.*

Curaçao Aloe Plantation and Factory. Drop in for a fascinating tour that takes you through the various stages of production of aloe vera, renowned for its healing powers. You'll get a look at everything from the fields to the final products. At the gift shop, you can buy CurAloe products, including homemade goodies like soap, pure aloe gel, and pure aloe juice, as well as sunscreen and other skin-care products. The plantation is on the way to the Ostrich Farm and run by the same owner. Tours begin throughout the day. ⊠ *Weg Naar Groot St. Joris z/n, Groot St. Joris, Curaçao* ☎ *5999/767–5577* ⊕ *www.aloecuracao.com* ⊠ *$6* ⊙ *Mon.–Sat. 9–4; last tour at 3.*

☺ ★ **Curaçao Sea Aquarium.** You don't have to get your feet wet to see the island's underwater treasures. The aquarium has about 40 saltwater tanks filled with more than 400 varieties of marine life. A restaurant, a snack bar, two photo centers, and souvenir shops are on-site. ⊠ *Seaquarium Beach, Bapor Kibra z/n, Curaçao* ☎ *5999/461–6666* ⊕ *www.curacao-sea-aquarium.com* ⊠ *Aquarium $19; Dolphin Academy $79–$169* ⊙ *Aquarium daily 8:30–5:30, Dolphin Academy daily 8:30–4:30.*

★ **Hato Caves.** Stalactites and stalagmites form striking shapes in these 200,000-year-old caves. Hidden lighting adds to the dramatic effect. Indians who used the caves for shelter left petroglyphs about 1,500 years ago. More recently, slaves who escaped from nearby plantations used the caves as a hideaway. Hour-long guided tours wind down to the pools in various chambers. Keep in mind that there are 49 steps to climb up to the entrance and the occasional bat might not be to everyone's taste. ⊠ *Rooseveltweg z/n, Hato, Curaçao* ☎ *5999/868–0379* ⊠ *$8* ⊙ *Daily 10–4.*

7

SHOPPING

From Dutch classics like embroidered linens, delft earthenware, cheeses, and clogs to local artwork and handicrafts, shopping in Curaçao can turn up some fun finds. But don't expect major bargains on watches, jewelry, or electronics; Willemstad is not a duty-free port (the few establishments that claim to be "duty-free" are simply absorbing the cost of some or all of the tax rather than passing it on to consumers); however, if you come prepared with some comparison prices, you might still dig up some good deals. Hours are usually Monday through Saturday, from 8 to noon and 2 to 6. Most shops are within the six-block area of Willemstad described above. The main shopping streets are Heerenstraat, Breedestraat, and Madurostraat.

Boolchand's. Boolchand's sells electronics, jewelry, Swarovski crystal, Swiss watches, and cameras behind a facade of red-and-white checkered tiles. ✉ *Heerenstraat 4B, Punda, Willemstad, Curaçao* ☎ *5999/461–6233.*

Cigar Emporium. A sweet aroma permeates Cigar Emporium, where you can find the largest selection of Cuban cigars on the island, including H. Upmann, Romeo y Julieta, and Montecristo. Visit the climate-controlled cedar cigar room. However, remember that Cuban cigars cannot be taken back to the United States legally. ✉ *Gomezplein, Punda, Willemstad, Curaçao* ☎ *5999/465–3955.*

New Amsterdam. New Amsterdam is the place to price hand-embroidered tablecloths, napkins, and pillowcases, as well as blue delft. ✉ *Gomezplein 14, Punda, Willemstad, Curaçao* ☎ *5999/461–2437.*

ACTIVITIES

BIKING

Wanna Bike Curaçao. So you wanna bike Curaçao? Wanna Bike Curaçao has the fix: kick into gear and head out for a guided mountain-bike tour through the Caracas Bay peninsula and the salt ponds at the Jan Thiel Lagoon. Although you should be fit to take on the challenge, mountain-bike experience is not required. Tour prices vary, depending on skill level and duration, and cover the bike, helmet, water, refreshments, park entrance fee, and guide—but don't forget to bring a camera. ✉ *Curaçao* ☎ *5999/527–3720* ⊕ *www.wannabike.com.*

DIVING AND SNORKELING

ⓒ **Ocean Encounters.** Ocean Encounters is the largest dive operator on the
★ island. Its operations cover the popular east-coast dive sites, including the *Superior Producer* wreck, where barracudas hang out, and a tugboat wreck. West-end hot spots—including the renowned Mushroom Forest and Watamula dive sites—are accessible from the company's outlet at Westpunt. Ocean Encounters offers a vast menu of scheduled shore and boat dives and packages, as well as certified PADI instruction. In July, the dive center sponsors a kids' sea camp in conjunction with the Sea Aquarium. ✉ *Lions Dive & Beach Resort, Seaquarium Beach, Bapor Kibra z/n, Curaçao* ☎ *5999/461–8131* ⊕ *www.oceanencounters.com.*

BEACHES

☺ **Cas Abao.** This white-sand gem has the brightest blue water in Curaçao, a treat for swimmers, snorkelers, and sunbathers alike. You can take respite beneath the hut-shaded snack bar. The restrooms and showers are immaculate. You can rent beach chairs, paddleboats, and snorkeling and diving gear. The entry fee is $3, and the beach is open from 8 to 6. Turn off Westpunt Highway at the junction onto Weg Naar Santa Cruz; follow until the turnoff for Cas Abao, and then drive along the winding country road for about 10 minutes to the beach. ⊠ *West of St. Willibrordus, about 3 mi (5 km) off Weg Naar Santa Cruz, Curaçao.*

☺ **Playa Knip.** Two protected coves offer crystal-clear turquoise waters. Big (Groot) Knip is an expanse of alluring white sand, perfect for swimming and snorkeling. You can rent beach chairs and hang out under the *palapas* (thatch-roof shelters) or cool off with ice cream at the snack bar. There are restrooms here but no showers. There's no fee. ⊠ *Just east of Westpunt, Banda Abou, Curaçao.*

☺ **Seaquarium Beach.** This 1,600-foot stretch of sandy beach is divided into separate sections, each uniquely defined by a seaside resort or restaurant as its central draw. By day, no matter where you choose to enter the palm-shaded beach, you can find lounge chairs in the sand, thatched shelters, and restrooms. The sections at Mambo and Kontiki beaches also have showers. The island's largest water-sports center (Ocean Encounters at Lions Dive) caters to nearby hotel guests and walk-ins. Mambo Beach is always a hot spot. At Kontiki Beach, you can find a spa, a hair braider, and a restaurant that serves refreshing piña colada ice cream. Unless you're a guest of a resort on the beach, the entrance fee to any section is $3. ⊠ *About 1 mi (1.5 km) east of downtown Willemstad, Bapor Kibra z/n, Curaçao.*

WHERE TO EAT

¢–$
CAFÉ
✕ **Awa di Playa.** Formerly a fisherman's hangout, the ramshackle shed-like structure located on an ocean inlet gives way to an equally ramshackle interior and some of the best local lunches anywhere on the island. There's no menu—the waiter will tell you what's available and you can watch it being cooked in the tiny kitchen. The presentation isn't fancy and the occasional fly makes an appearance, but the food is honest and delicious. ⊠ *Behind Hook's Hut and Hilton, Piscadera Bay, Willemstad* ☎ *5999/462–6939* ▤ *No credit cards* ⊗ *No dinner.*

$$$
ECLECTIC
✕ **Gouverneur de Rouville Restaurant & Café.** Dine on the veranda of a restored 19th-century Dutch mansion overlooking the Santa Anna Bay and the resplendent Punda skyline. Though often busy and popular with tourists, the ambience makes it worth a visit. Intriguing soup options include Cuban banana soup and Curaçao-style fish soup. *Keshi yena* (seasoned meat wrapped in cheese and then baked) and spareribs are among the savory entrées. After dinner, you can stick around for live music at the bar, which stays open until 1 am. The restaurant is also popular for lunch and attracts crowds when cruise ships dock. ⊠ *De Rouvilleweg 9, Otrobanda, Willemstad, Curaçao* ☎ *5999/462–5999* ⊕ *www.de-gouverneur.com.*

7

DOMINICA (ROSEAU)

Roberta
Sotonoff

In the center of the Caribbean archipelago, wedged between the two French islands of Guadeloupe, to the north, and Martinique, to the south, Dominica is a wild place. So unyielding is the terrain that colonists surrendered efforts at colonization, and the last survivors of the Caribbean's original people, the Carib Indians, have made her rugged northeast their home. Dominica—29 mi (47 km) long and 16 mi (26 km) wide—is an English-speaking island, though family and place names are a mélange of French, English, and Carib. The capital is Roseau (pronounced rose-*oh*). If you've had enough of casinos, crowds, and swim-up bars and want to take leave of everyday life—to hike, bike, trek, spot birds and butterflies in the rain forest; explore waterfalls; discover a boiling lake; kayak, dive, snorkel, or sail in marine reserves; or go out in search of the many resident whale and dolphin species—this is the place to do it.

ESSENTIALS

CURRENCY The Eastern Caribbean dollar (EC$2.70 to US$1). U.S. currency is readily accepted, but you will get change in EC dollars. Most major credit cards are accepted, as are traveler's checks.

INTERNET **Cyber Land Internet Café** ⊠ *George St., Roseau* ⊠ *Woodstone Shopping Mall, Roseau* ⊠ *Grandby St., Portsmouth* ☎ *767/440–2605.* **Rituals Coffee** ⊠ *Bayfront, next door to Cocorico, Roseau, Dominica* ☎ *767/440–2233* ⊕ *www.tropicports.com/rituals.*

COMING ASHORE

In Roseau most ships dock along the bay front. Across the street from the pier, in the old post office, is a visitor information center. Taxis, minibuses, and tour operators are available at the berths. If you do decide to tour with one of them, choose one who is certified, and be explicit when discussing where you will go and how much you will pay—don't be afraid to ask questions. The drivers usually quote a fixed fare, which is regulated by the Division of Tourism and the National Taxi Association. Drivers also offer their services for tours anywhere on the island beginning at $25 to $30 an hour for up to four persons; a four- to five-hour island tour for up to four persons will cost approximately $150. You can rent a car in Roseau for about $45–$50, not including insurance and a mandatory EC$30 (US$12) driving permit, but it can be difficult to find things, so you might do better on a guided tour here.

EXPLORING DOMINICA

Most of Dominica's roads are narrow and winding, so you'll need a few hours to take in the sights. Be adventurous, whether you prefer sightseeing or hiking—you'll be amply rewarded.

Ⓒ **Carib Indian Territory.** In 1903, after centuries of conflict, the Carib-
★ bean's first settlers, the Kalinago (more popularly known as the Caribs), were granted approximately 3,700 acres of land on the island's northeast coast. Here a hardened lava formation, **L'Escalier Tête Chien**

Dominica

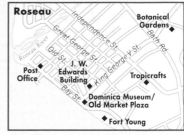

Roseau

Independence St.
Great George St.
Old St.
Roseau River
Bay St.
King George V St.
Beach Rd.

Botanical Gardens ◆

Post Office ◆

J. W. Edwards Building

Tropicrafts ◆

Dominica Museum/ Old Market Plaza ◆

Fort Young ◆

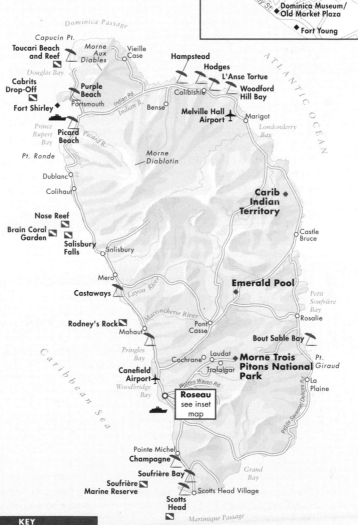

Dominica Passage

Capucin Pt.

Toucari Beach and Reef

Vieille Case

Morne Aux Diables

Hampstead

Hodges

L'Anse Tortue

Douglas Bay

Cabrits Drop-Off

Purple Beach

Calibishie

Woodford Hill Bay

Fort Shirley

Portsmouth

Indian Rd.

Indian R.

Bense

Melville Hall Airport

Marigot

ATLANTIC OCEAN

Prince Rupert Bay

Picard Beach

Picard R.

Londonderry Bay

Pt. Ronde

Morne Diablotin

Dublanc

Carib Indian Territory ◆

Colihaut

Nose Reef

Castle Bruce

Brain Coral Garden

Salisbury Falls

Salisbury

Mero

Emerald Pool ◆

Castaways

Layou River

Petit Soufrière Bay

Macoucherie River

Rosalie

Rodney's Rock

Mahaut

Pont Casse

Bout Sable Bay

Pringles Bay

Cochrane

Laudat

Morne Trois Pitons National Park

Pt. Giraud

Canefield Airport

Trafalgar

La Plaine

Woodbridge Bay

Wotten Waven Rd.

Roseau see inset map

Caribbean Sea

Petite Savanne Delices Rd.

Pointe Michel

Champagne

Soufrière Bay

Grand Bay

Soufrière Marine Reserve

Scotts Head Village

Scotts Head

Martinique Passage

KEY
⛱ *Beaches*
⚓ *Cruise Ship Terminal*
◣ *Dive Sites*

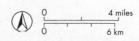

0   4 miles

0   6 km

(Snake's Staircase), runs down into the Atlantic. The name is derived from a snake whose head resembles that of a dog. The ocean alongside Carib Territory is particularly fierce. The shore is full of countless coves and inlets. According to Carib legend, every night the nearby Londonderry Islets transform into grand canoes to take the spirits of the dead out to sea.

Craftspeople have retained their knowledge of basket weaving, wood carving, and canoe building through generations. They fashion long, elegant canoes from the trunk of a single *gommier* tree. You might catch canoe builders at work at **Kalinago Barana Autê** (✉ *Caryfish River, Carib Territory* ☎ *767/445-7979* ⊕ *www.kalinagobaranaaute. com* ✉ *Basic package is about $10* ⊗ *Daily 9–5*), the Carib Territory's place to learn about Kalinago customs, history, and culture. A guided, 45-minute tour explores the village, stopping along the way to see some traditional dances and to learn about plants, dugout canoes, basket weaving, and cassava bread making. The path offers wonderful viewpoints of the Atlantic and a chance to glimpse Isukulati Falls.

DOMINICA BEST BETS

■ **Indian River.** A rowboat ride on the river is relaxing and peaceful.

■ **Kalinago Barana Autê.** This reserve is a great place to learn about the fierce Caribs.

■ **Rain-Forest Trips.** Hiking in Dominica's rain forest is the best way to experience its natural beauty.

■ **Snorkeling in Champagne.** A bubbling volcanic vent makes you feel as if you are snorkeling in champagne.

■ **Whale-Watching.** November through February offers the best whale-watching in the Caribbean.

☾ **Emerald Pool.** Quite possibly the most-visited nature attraction on the island, this emerald-green pool fed by a 50-foot waterfall is an easy trip to make. To reach this spot in the vast Morne Trois Pitons National Park you follow a trail that starts at the side of the road near the reception center (it's an easy 20-minute walk). Along the way, there are lookout points with views of the windward (Atlantic) coast and the forested interior. If you don't want a crowd, check whether there are cruise ships in port before going out, as this spot is popular with cruise-ship tour groups.

Morne Trois Pitons National Park. A UNESCO World Heritage Site, this 17,000-acre swath of lush, mountainous land in the south-central interior (covering 9% of Dominica) is the island's crown jewel. Named after one of the highest (4,600 feet) mountains on the island, it contains the island's famous "boiling lake," majestic waterfalls, and cool mountain lakes.

★ The undisputed highlight of the park is **Boiling Lake.** Reputedly the world's largest such lake, it's a cauldron of gurgling gray-blue water, 70 yards wide and of unknown depth, with water temperatures from 180°F to 197°F. Although generally believed to be a volcanic crater, the lake is actually a flooded fumarole—a crack through which gases escape from the molten lava below. As many visitors discovered in late 2004, the "lake" can sometimes dry up, though it fills again within a few months and, shortly after that, once more starts to boil. The two- to four-hour (one way) hike up to the lake is challenging (on a very rainy day, be prepared to slip and slide the whole way up and back). You'll need attire appropriate for a strenuous hike, and a guide is a must.

On your way to Boiling Lake you pass through the **Valley of Desolation,** a sight that definitely lives up to its name. Harsh sulfuric fumes have destroyed virtually all the vegetation in what must once have

> **BIBS**
>
> With limited and expensive laundry facilities on ships, you may not want to spend your free time cleaning up after your child. It's convenient to bring along a pack of disposable bibs for mealtimes to keep baby's clothing cleaner and stain-free, avoiding messy garments after meals and a lot of laundry time on board the ship.

been a lush forested area. Small hot and cold streams with water of various colors—black, purple, red, orange—web the valley. Stay on the trail to avoid breaking through the crust that covers the hot lava. At the beginning of the Valley of Desolation trail is the **TiTou Gorge,** where you can swim in the pool or relax in the hot-water springs along one side. If you're a strong swimmer, you can head up the gorge to a cave (it's about a five-minute swim) that has a magnificent waterfall; a crack in the cave about 50 feet above permits a stream of sunlight to penetrate the cavern.

Also in the national park are some of the island's most spectacular waterfalls. The 45-minute hike to **Sari Sari Falls,** accessible through the east-coast village of La Plaine, can be hair-raising. But the sight of water cascading some 150 feet into a large pool is awesome. So large are these falls that you feel the spray from hundreds of yards away. Just beyond the village of Trafalgar and up a short hill is the reception facility, where you can purchase passes to the national park and find guides to take you on a rain-forest trek to the twin **Trafalgar Falls;** the 125-foot-high waterfall is called the Father, and the wider, 95-foot-high one, the Mother.

Roseau. Although it's one of the smallest capitals in the Caribbean, Roseau has the highest concentration of inhabitants of any town in the eastern Caribbean. Caribbean vernacular architecture and a bustling marketplace transport visitors back in time. Although you can walk the entire town in about an hour, you'll get a much better feel for the place on a leisurely stroll.

For some years now, the Society for Historical Architectural Preservation and Enhancement (SHAPE) has organized programs and projects to preserve the city's architectural heritage. Several interesting buildings have already been restored. **Lilac House,** on Kennedy Avenue, has three types of gingerbread fretwork, latticed veranda railings, and heavy hurricane shutters. The **J. W. Edwards Building,** at the corner of Old and King George V streets, has a stone base and a wooden second-floor gallery. The **Old Market Plaza** is the center of Roseau's historic district, which was laid out by the French on a radial plan rather than a grid, so streets such as Hanover, King George V, and Old radiate from this area.

7

South of the marketplace is the Fort Young Hotel, built as a British fort in the 18th century; the nearby statehouse, public library, and Anglican cathedral are also worth a visit. New developments at the bay front on Dame M. E. Charles Boulevard have brightened up the waterfront.

☾ The 40-acre **Botanical Gardens,** founded in 1891 as an annex of London's Kew Gardens, is a great place to relax, stroll, or watch a cricket match. In addition to the extensive collection of tropical plants and trees, there's also a parrot aviary. At the Forestry Division office, which is also on the garden grounds, you can find numerous publications on the island's flora, fauna, and national parks. The forestry officers are particularly knowledgeable on these subjects and can also recommend good hiking guides. ⊠ *Between Bath Rd. and Valley Rd.* ☎ *767/448–2401 Ext. 3417* ⊕ *www. da-academy.org/dagardens.html* ⊠ *Free* ☺ *Daily 7–6.*

The old post office now houses the **Dominica Museum.** This labor of love by local writer and historian Dr. Lennox Honychurch contains furnishings, documents, prints, and maps that date back hundreds of years; you can also find an entire Carib hut as well as Carib canoes, baskets, and other artifacts. ⊠ *Dame M. E. Charles Blvd., opposite cruise-ship berth* ☎ *767/448–8923* ⊠ *$3* ☺ *Weekdays 9–4, weekends 9–2 only when a cruise ship is in port.*

SHOPPING

Dominicans produce distinctive handicrafts, with various communities specializing in their specific products. The crafts of the Carib Indians include traditional baskets made of dyed *larouma* reeds and waterproofed with tightly woven *balizier* leaves. These are sold in the Carib Indian Territory and Kalinago Barana Auté as well as in Roseau's shops. Vertivert straw rugs, screw-pine tableware, *fwije* (the trunk of the forest tree fern), and wood carvings are just some examples. Also notable are local herbs, spices, condiments, and herb teas.

One of the easiest places to pick up a souvenir is the Old Market Plaza, just behind the Dominica Museum, in Roseau. Slaves were once sold here, but today handcrafted jewelry, T-shirts, spices, souvenirs, batik, and lacquered and woven bamboo boxes and trays are available from a group of vendors in open-air booths set up on the cobblestones. These are usually busiest when there's a cruise ship berthed across the street. On these days you can also find a vast number of vendors along the bay front.

Baroon International (⊠ *Kennedy Ave. at Old St., Roseau* ☎ *767/449–2888*) sells unusual jewelry from Asia, the United States, and other Caribbean islands. They also feature pieces that are assembled in the store, as well as personal accessories, souvenirs, and special gifts.

Kalinago Barana Auté (⊠ *Salybia, Carib Territory* ☎ *767/445–7979* ⊕ *www.kalinagobaranaaute.com* ☺ *Daily 9–5*) sells handicrafts including carvings, pottery, and lovely handwoven baskets, which you can watch the women weave.

ACTIVITIES

ADVENTURE PARKS

The **Rainforest Adventures Dominica** (✉ *Laudat* ☎ *767/448–8775 or 767/440–3266, 866/759–8726 in U.S.* ⊕ *www.rfat.com*) gives you a bird's-eye view of a pristine forest aboard an open, eight-person gondola. For 90 minutes to two hours, you slowly skim the treetop canopy while a guide provides scientific information about the flora and fauna. At the top there is an optional walking tour that is worth the steps. The cost is $64. Transportation and lunch are extra. This is a popular attraction for cruise-ship passengers, so try to reserve ahead.

Wacky Rollers (✉ *Front St., Roseau* ⌑ *Box 900, Roseau* ☎ *767/440–4386* ⊕ *www.wackyrollers.com*) will make you feel as if you are training for the marines as you swing on a Tarzan-style rope and grab onto a vertical rope ladder, rappel across zip lines, and traverse suspended log bridges, a net bridge, and four monkey bridges (rope loops). It costs $65 for the adult course and should take from 1½ to 3½ hours to conquer the 28 "games." There is also an abbreviated kids' course for $25 with pickup. If you supply your own transport, fees are $5 less. Wacky Rollers also organizes adventure tours around the island. Although the office is in Roseau, the park itself is in Hillsborough Estate, about 20 to 25 minutes north of Roseau.

DIVING AND WHALE-WATCHING

Fodor's Choice ★ Dominica has been voted one of the top 10 dive destinations in the world by *Skin Diver* and *Rodale's Scuba Diving* magazines—and has won many other awards for its underwater sites. They are truly memorable. There are numerous highlights all along the west coast of the island, but the best are those in the southwest—within and around **Soufrière/Scotts Head Marine Reserve.** There is a $2 fee per person to dive, snorkel, or kayak in the reserve. The conditions for underwater photography, particularly macrophotography, are unparalleled. The rates are about $60 for a single tank dive and about $80–$100 for a two-tank dive or from about $95 for a resort course with one open-water dive. All scuba-diving operators also offer snorkeling. Equipment rents for $10 to $25 a day; trips with gear range from $15 to $35. A 10% tax is included.

The **Anchorage Dive & Whale Watch Center** (✉ *Anchorage Hotel, Castle Comfort* ☎ *767/448–2638* ⊕ *www.anchoragehotel.dm*) has two dive boats that can take you out day or night. It also offers PADI instruction (all skill levels), snorkeling and whale-watching trips, and shore diving. It has many of the same trips as Dive Dominica.

Dive Dominica (✉ *Castle Comfort Lodge, Castle Comfort* ☎ *767/448–2188 in U.S.* ⊕ *www.divedominica.com*), one of the island's dive pioneers, conducts NAUI, PADI, and SSI courses as well as Nitrox certification courses. With four boats, it offers diving, snorkeling, and whale-watching trips and packages including accommodation at the Castle Comfort Lodge. Its trips are similar to Anchorage's.

7

HIKING

★ Dominica's majestic mountains, clear rivers, and lush vegetation conspire to create adventurous hiking trails. The island is crisscrossed by ancient footpaths of the Arawak and Carib Indians and the Nègres Maroons, escaped slaves who established camps in the mountains. Existing trails range from easygoing to arduous. To make the most of your excursion, you'll need sturdy hiking boots, insect repellent, a change of clothes (kept dry), and a guide. Hikes and tours run $25 to $50 per person, depending on destinations and duration. Some of the natural attractions within the island's national parks require visitors to purchase a site pass. These are sold for varying numbers of visits. A single-entry site pass costs $5, and a week pass $12.

Local bird and forestry expert **Bertrand Jno Baptiste** (☎ 767/245–4768) leads hikes up Morne Diablotin and along the Syndicate Nature Trail; if he's not available, ask him to recommend another guide. Hiking guides can be arranged through the **Discover Dominica Authority** (✉ *Roseau* ☎ *767/448–2045* ⊕ *www.discoverdominica.com*).

BEACHES

On the west coast, just south of the village of Pointe Michel, **Champagne** is hailed as one of the best spots for swimming, snorkeling, and diving, but not for sunning. It gets its name from volcanic vents that constantly puff steam into the sea, which makes you feel as if you are swimming in warm champagne.

WHERE TO EAT

$–$$　✗ **Cocorico.** It's hard to miss the umbrella-covered chairs and tables at
FRENCH　this Parisian-style café on a prominent bay-front corner in Roseau.
☾　Breakfast crepes, croissants, baguette sandwiches and piping-hot café au lait are available beginning at 8:30 am. Throughout the day you can relax indoors or out and enjoy any of the extensive menu's selections with the perfect glass of wine, and you can even surf the Internet on their computers. ✉ *Bay Front at Kennedy Ave., Roseau* ☎ *767/449–8686* ⊕ *www.natureisle.com/cocorico/* ☾ *Closed Sun. unless ship is in port, then 10–4* ☾ *No dinner.*

¢–$$　✗ **Pearl's Cuisine.** In a creole town house in central Roseau, chef Pearl,
CARIBBEAN　with her robust and infectious character, prepares some of the island's best local cuisine, such as callaloo soup, fresh fish, and rabbit. Her menu changes daily, but she offers such local delicacies as *sousse* (pickled pigs' feet), blood pudding, and rotis. When sitting down, ask for a table on the open-air gallery that overlooks Roseau and prepare for an abundant portion, but make sure you leave space for dessert. ✉ *50 King George V St., Roseau* ☎ *767/448–8707* ☾ *Closed Sun. No dinner.*

FALMOUTH, JAMAICA

By Linda
Coffman

Midway between Ocho Rios and Montego Bay, Falmouth, which was founded in 1769, prospered from Jamaica's status as the world's leading sugar producer. With more than 80 sugar estates nearby, the town was meticulously mapped out in the colonial tradition, with streets named after British royalty and heroes. The richness of the town's historic Georgian structures, many of which are still occupied and maintained, is reflected in its heritage. The city has long been heralded for its forward-thinking hygiene policies (the first piped water supply system in the western hemisphere—established here in 1799—continues to be a source of pride) and progressive politics (Falmouth was the birthplace of Jamaica's abolitionist movement in the early 19th century). The site of many slave revolts, Falmouth's residents turned scores of the town's buildings into safe houses for escaped slaves until the practice of slavery was outlawed in Jamaica in 1838. While Falmouth is seeing a revival with the opening of a purpose-built cruise port in 2011, buildings that may seem unimpressive as they undergo restoration are still rich in history. In 1966 the Jamaican government declared Falmouth a National Monument.

ESSENTIALS

CURRENCY

The Jamaican dollar (J$84 to US$1). Currency-exchange booths are located in the pier area as well as just outside the entrance gate on Sea board Street; however, the U.S. dollar is accepted virtually everywhere, though change may be made in Jamaican dollars.

INTERNET

The entire Falmouth Cruise Port is a Wi-Fi hot spot accessible for a fee by passengers with personal computers. Numerous cafés and bars outside the port area also offer Internet service for a nominal fee.

TELEPHONE

Public telephones are located in the communications center at the Falmouth Cruise Terminal. Travelers also find public phones in the Post Office at the corner of Cornwall and Market Streets. Some U.S. phone companies won't permit credit-card calls to be placed from Jamaica because they've been victims of fraud, so collect calls are often the top option. GSM cell phones equipped with tri-band or world-roaming service will find coverage throughout the Falmouth area.

COMING ASHORE

Cruise ships, including the world's largest, are able to dock at the Falmouth Cruise Port's two berths. A Visitors Information facility is situated in the pier area. The town is located right outside the port gates and places of interest are easily within walking distance. Currency-exchange booths are in the pier area as well as just outside the entrance gate on Seaboard Street. Further, the cruise port area has Wi-Fi service (paid) for passengers with laptops. The Falmouth tourist trolley offers a half-hour tour of the town with regular departures from the Port Transportation Center. Tickets and trolley schedules are available in the Trolley kiosk at the Taxi Shelter building.

For travel out of town, buses and taxis are available. Bus fare to Doctor's Cave Beach in Montego Bay is $20 round-trip, while taxis are priced by the

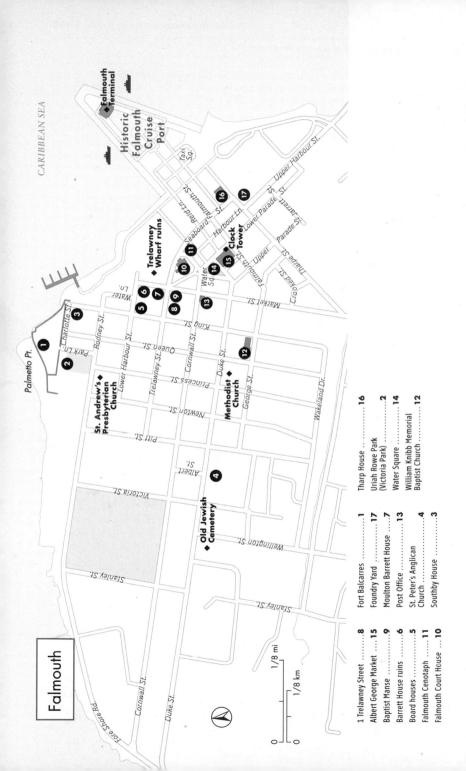

Falmouth

CARIBBEAN SEA

Palmetto Pt.

Historic Falmouth Cruise Port

Falmouth Terminal

Taxi Sq.

Upper Harbour St.

Trelawney Wharf ruins ◆

Clock Tower

Seaboard Ln.

Falmouth St.

Harbour Ln.

Lower Parade St.

Janiar St.

Upper Parade St.

Thorpe St.

Water Sq.

St. Andrew's Presbyterian Church ◆

Water Ln.

Charlotte St.

Park Ln.

Rodney St.

Lower Harbour St.

Queen St.

King St.

Cornwall St.

Duke St.

Trelawney St.

Princess St.

Newton St.

George St.

Methodist Church ◆

Market St.

Crooked St.

Wakeland Dr.

Pitt St.

Albert St.

Victoria St.

Old Jewish Cemetery ◆

Wellington St.

Stanley St.

Cornwall St.

Duke St.

Fort's Shore Rd.

1/8 mi

1/8 km

0

hour at $35 for up to four people for either a guided tour or transportation to a specific destination. Falmouth's location, almost equidistant to both Montego Bay and Ocho Rios makes most tours offered at those ports available from Falmouth as well. In truth, though, it's often difficult to book activities privately in Jamaica, so this is one place in the Caribbean where it's usually to your advantage to take a shore excursion offered by your ship. Many of the most popular and adventurous tours are operated by Chukka Caribbean and can only be booked by cruise passengers directly with the cruise lines as space is presold to ships for their arrival dates. Coaches for prebooked tours pick up passengers inside the Cruise Port, but authorized independent tour operators are also available there to arrange tours on the spot. Car rental isn't recommended in Jamaica due to narrow roads and aggressive drivers.

FALMOUTH BEST BETS

■ **Good Hope Plantation.** The expansive view of the plantation grounds and surrounding countryside from the front garden includes the Martha Brae River.

■ **Historic Falmouth Walking Tour.** Absorb Falmouth's Colonial-era history and discover the town's landmarks and Georgian architectural treasures.

■ **Tharp House.** Located within the Falmouth Cruise Port, the town home of sugar planter John Tharp, is one of Falmouth's most historic building. Once a tax collector's office, it is now expected to become a maritime museum.

EXPLORING FALMOUTH

Falmouth's streets, which were laid out in a grid plan in the mid 1700s, are easily explored on your own. However, even with a map, finding your way around can be confusing due to a lack of street signs. Should you become disoriented or require directions, look for a member of the Falmouth Tourism Courtesy Corps wearing official white shirts and hats. They are on hand to assist visitors and can help with finding a taxi outside the cruise port.

Points of interest include the Falmouth Courthouse and the adjacent Cenotaph War Memorial; Water Square, where Falmouth residents got running water before New York City; Barrett House Ruins, the remains of the town home of planter William Barrett, who owned much of the land upon which the town is built; and Fort Balcarres, built to guard Falmouth Harbor. Other sights include fine examples of Falmouth's Georgian-era architecture, based on classic Greek and Roman designs and adapted to local conditions to create a unique island style, Georgian buildings are recognizable by their double-hung sash windows, keystones, columns, symmetry of facade, and full-length verandas. Constructed of a native limestone over brick and remarkably preserved, most structures are still in use as either private residences or commercial buildings.

WHAT TO SEE OUTSIDE OF FALMOUTH

Good Hope Plantation. Located 20 minutes from Falmouth, the Good Hope estate was the basis of one of the largest sugar fortunes made in 19th-century Jamaica and contains a rare inventory of restored historic buildings.

The Great House was built in 1755 by Thomas Williams for his bride Elizabeth, who died shortly after their marriage and was buried beneath the ground-floor entryway. Subsequently purchased by John Tharp, who also acquired all the adjoining plantations, Good Hope eventually grew to 9,000 acres in its heyday. On today's 2,000-acre estate, with views overlooking the Queen of Spain Valley, the Martha Brae River, and the Cockpit Mountains, all rooms in the Great House are furnished with 18th- and 19th-century Jamaican antiques and, until recently, served as a tourist guest house. Visitors can choose from a variety of activities, including a carriage ride through the grounds, river-tubing on the Martha Brae River, zip-lining through the canopy over the river, ATV exploring, or a more sedate tour of the Great House itself, with or without lunch on the garden patio. Tours are operated by Chukka Caribbean and cannot be purchased independently. So only cruise passengers are able to visit. ⊠ *1 Trelawny St., Falmouth* ☎ *876/469–3444* ⊕ *www.goodhopejamaica. com* ⊠ *Cost of activities varies* ☉ *Daily during cruise ship docking hrs.*

SHOPPING

Coming ashore, you will find more than five-dozen shops along the Cruise Port's pedestrian thoroughfares housing well-known international and established Jamaican merchants. Also in the port is a covered open-air craft market, where some 40 vendors offer their wares and items such as T-shirts, caps, and local seasonings. In town, souvenir vendors set up on Seaboard Street near the Courthouse. Water Square is the location of the Albert George Shopping and Historical Center, where artisans offer local craftwork that showcases the history and culture of the area. The upscale Shops at Rose Hall are within fairly easy reach by taxi between Falmouth and Montego Bay.

ACTIVITIES

Most adventure activities offered to cruise-ship passengers in Montego Bay and Ocho Rios, including water sports, trips to nearby beaches, golf, river-rafting, and sightseeing, are also available to cruise passengers in Falmouth. See both Montego Bay and Ocho Rios for more information.

Historic Falmouth Heritage Walk. This leisurely paced walk takes you through Falmouth's commercial and residential streets while your guide shares the little-known history of the town and what made it a rich and significant port in the late 18th and early 19th centuries. Your guide will also explain how the movement to abolish slavery was essentially founded in Falmouth when you visit the former home and grave of the famous abolitionist William Knibb. ☎ *876/878–7277* ⊕ *www.falmouthheritagewalks. com* ⊠ *$25* ☉ *Times vary throughout the day when ships are in port.*

BEACHES

Doctor's Cave Beach in the heart of Montego Bay, is easily accessible by private taxi from the cruise port for $20 per person round-trip. The beach itself also has an admission fee.

WHERE TO EAT

$–$$ ✕ **Club Nazz and Restaurant.** Conveniently located on Market Street 100
JAMAICAN yards west of Falmouth's major landmark, Water Square, the restaurant
is housed in a restored and brightly painted Georgian-style building that
once served as the town's temporary courthouse. Open seven days a
week, locals and visitors alike dig into Jamaican cuisine, such as curried
goat, jerk chicken or pork, and rice and peas. For the less adventurous,
the chicken sandwich with fries is a safe choice. The full-service bar offers
cold Red Stripe beer, soft drinks, and almost any rum drink you can think
of. Wi-Fi is free for customers. Sadly, most cruise ships set sail before
the evening nightclub scene gets underway with performances by a wide
cross-section of musicians. ⊠ *23 Market St., Falmouth* 🕾 *876/617–5175.*

FREEPORT-LUCAYA, BAHAMAS

Ramona Settle   Grand Bahama Island, the fourth-largest island in the Bahamas, lies
only 52 mi (84 km) off Palm Beach, Florida. In 1492, when Columbus
first set foot in the Bahamas, Grand Bahama was already populated.
Skulls found in caves attest to the existence of the peaceable Lucayans,
who were constantly fleeing the more bellicose Caribs. But it was not
until the 1950s, when the harvesting of Caribbean yellow pine trees
(now protected by Bahamian environmental law) was the island's major
industry, that American financier Wallace Groves envisioned Grand
Bahama's grandiose future as a tax-free port for the shipment of goods
to the United States. It was in that era that the city of Freeport and
later Lucaya evolved. They are separated by a 4-mi (6-km) stretch of
East Sunrise Highway, although few can tell you where one community ends and the other begins. Most of Grand Bahama's commercial
activity is concentrated in Freeport, the Bahamas' second-largest city.
Lucaya, with its sprawling shopping complex and water-sports reputation, stepped up to the role of island tourism capital. Resorts, beaches,
a casino, and golf courses make both cities popular with visitors.

ESSENTIALS

CURRENCY The Bahamian dollar, which trades one-to-one with the U.S. dollar,
which is universally accepted. There's no need to acquire any Bahamian currency.

INTERNET Port Lucaya Marina has free Wi-Fi service if you have your own laptop.

TELEPHONE Calling locally or internationally is easy in the Bahamas. To place a
local call, dial the seven-digit phone number. To call the United States,
dial 1 plus the area code. Pay phones cost 25¢ per call; Bahamian and
U.S. quarters are accepted, as are BATELCO phone cards. To place a
call using a calling card, use your long-distance carrier's access code
or dial 0 for the operator. But beware of using the dedicated long
distance public telephones, which are quite costly. Although most U.S.
cell phones work in the Bahamas, the roaming coast can be very high,
so check with your provider in advance.

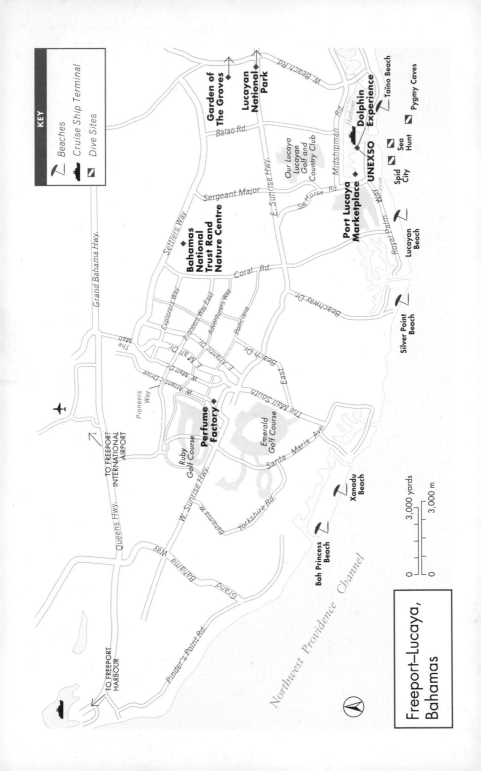

Freeport–Lucaya, Bahamas

KEY

⌐ Beaches
🚢 Cruise Ship Terminal
▨ Dive Sites

Garden of The Groves
Lucayan National Park
Balao Rd.
W. Beach Rd.
Taino Beach
Dolphin Experience
Pygmy Caves
Sea Hunt
Spid City
Our Lucaya Lucaya Golf and Country Club
Midshipman Rd.
Harbour
UNEXSO
Sergeant Major
E. Sunrise Hwy.
Sea Horse Rd.
Port Lucaya Marketplace
Mayan Way
Royal Palm
Lucayan Beach
Bahamas National Trust Rand Nature Centre
Settlers Way
Coral Rd.
Beachway Dr.
Silver Point Beach
Grand Bahama Hwy.
Explorers Way
Pioneers Way East
Adventurers Way
Poinciana
Beach Dr.
East
The Mall
W. Mall Dr.
E Mall Dr.
E Atlantic Dr.
The Mall South
Pioneers Way
W. Atlantic Drive Way
Perfume Factory
Emerald Golf Course
TO FREEPORT INTERNATIONAL AIRPORT
Ruby Golf Course
Santa Maria Ave.
Queens Hwy.
W. Sunrise Hwy.
Bahama
Yorkshire Rd.
Xanadu Beach
Grand Bahama Way
Bah Princess Beach
TO FREEPORT HARBOUR
Pinter's Point Rd.
Northwest Providence Channel

0 — 3,000 yards
0 — 3,000 m

COMING ASHORE

Cruise-ship passengers arrive at Lucayan Harbour, which has a clever Bahamian-style look, extensive cruise-passenger terminal facilities, and an entertainment-shopping village. The harbor lies about 10 minutes west of Freeport. Taxis and limos meet all cruise ships. Two passengers are charged $20 and $27 for trips to Freeport and Lucaya, respectively. Fare to Xanadu Beach is $21; it's $30 to Taïno Beach. The price per person drops $5 for larger groups. It's customary to tip taxi drivers 15%. A three-hour sightseeing tour of the Freeport-Lucaya area costs $25 to $35. Four-hour East or West End trips cost about $40. At this writing, an additional two-berth cruise-ship port in William's Town is undergoing the approval process, but no opening date is set yet.

FREEPORT-LUCAYA BEST BETS

■ **Diving with UNEXSO.** Simply one of the world's most respected diving facilities.

■ **The Dolphin Experience.** Choose your level of involvement.

■ **East End.** Venture beyond the city to the quiet fishing settlements east of Freeport.

■ **Lucayan National Park.** Explore caves, hike to the beach, or kayak its mangrove tidal creek.

■ **Shopping.** Duty-free shopping in the Port Lucaya Marketplace is still good; be sure to haggle if you shop at the straw markets.

Grand Bahama's flat terrain and straight, well-paved roads make for good scooter riding. Rentals run $35 a day (about $15 an hour). Helmets are required and provided. Look for small rental stands in parking lots and along the road in Freeport and Lucaya and at the larger resorts. It's usually cheaper to rent a car than to hire a taxi. Automobiles, jeeps, and vans can be rented at the Grand Bahama International Airport. Some agencies provide free pickup and delivery service to the cruise-ship port and Freeport and Lucaya, but prices are still not cheap; cars begin at $65 per day.

EXPLORING FREEPORT-LUCAYA

Grand Bahama is the only planned island in the Bahamas. Its towns, villages, and sights are well laid out but far apart. Downtown Freeport and Lucaya are both best appreciated on foot. Buses and taxis can transport you the 4-mi (6-km) distance between the two. In Freeport shopping is the main attraction. Bolstered by the Our Lucaya Resort complex, Lucaya has its beautiful beach and water-sports scene, plus more shopping and a big, beautiful new casino. Outside of town, isolated fishing villages, beaches, natural attractions, and the once-rowdy town of West End make it worthwhile to hire a tour or rent a car. The island stretches 96 mi (154 km) from one end to the other.

FREEPORT

★ **Bahamas National Trust Rand Nature Centre.** On 100 acres just minutes from downtown Freeport, a half-mile of self-guided botanical trails shows off 130 types of native plants, including many orchid species. The center is the island's birding hot spot, where you might

HANGERS

Folding or inflatable travel hangers are useful if you need to dry out hand laundry or a bathing suit in your cabin. The ones in your cabin's closet may not be removable.

spy a red-tailed hawk or a Cuban emerald hummingbird. On Tuesday and Thursday free (with admission) guided tours depart at 10:30 am. The visitor center hosts changing local art exhibits. ⊠ *E. Settlers Way* ☎ *242/352–5438* ◖ *$5* ⊙ *Weekdays 9–4; guided nature walk by advance reservation.*

★ **Perfume Factory.** One good reason to visit the International Bazaar, the quiet and elegant Perfume Factory occupies a replica 19th-century Bahamian mansion—the kind built by Loyalists who settled in the Bahamas after the American Revolution. This is the home of Fragrance of the Bahamas, a company that produces perfumes, colognes, and lotions using the scents of jasmine, cinnamon, gardenia, spice, and ginger. Take a free five-minute tour of the mixology laboratory and get a free sample. For $30 an ounce, you can blend your own perfume using any of the 35 scents ($15 for 1½ ounces of blend-it-yourself body lotion). ⊠ *Behind International Bazaar, W. Sunrise Hwy. and Mall Dr., on access road* ☎ *242/352–9391* ⊕ *www.perfumefactory.com* ◖ *Free* ⊙ *Weekdays 9–5.*

LUCAYA

Lucaya, on Grand Bahama's southern coast and just east of Freeport, was developed as the island's resort center. These days it's booming with the megaresort complex called the Our Lucaya Resort, a fine sandy beach, championship golf courses, a casino, a first-class dive operation, and Port Lucaya's shopping and marina facilities. Most cruise ships offer excursions that include a day at Our Lucaya.

♻ **The Dolphin Experience.** Encounter Atlantic bottlenose dolphins in Sanctuary Bay at one of the world's first and largest dolphin facilities, about 2 mi east of Port Lucaya. A ferry takes you from Port Lucaya to the bay to observe and photograph the animals. If you don't mind getting wet, you can sit on a partially submerged dock or stand waist deep in the water and one of these friendly creatures will swim up to you. You can also engage in one of two swim-with-the-dolphins programs, but participants must be 55 inches or taller. ⊠ *Port Lucaya* ☎ *242/373–1244 or 800/992–3483* ⊕ *www.unexso.com* ◖ *2-hr interaction program $75, 2-hr swim program $169, dolphin dive $219, open-ocean experience $199* ⊙ *Mon.–Wed. 8–5, Thurs.–Sun. 8–7.*

Fodor's Choice **Underwater Explorers Society (UNEXSO).** One of the world's most respected
★ diving facilities, UNEXSO welcomes more than 50,000 individuals each year and trains hundreds of them in scuba diving. Facilities include a 17-foot-deep training pool with windows that look out on the harbor, changing rooms and showers, docks, equipment rental, an outdoor café,

and an air-tank filling station. ✉ *On wharf at Port Lucaya Marketplace* ☎ *242/373–1244 or 800/992–3483* ⊕ *www.unexso.com* ✉ *Beginner reef dives $59, dives from $59, night dives $79, dolphin dives $219, shark dives $99* ◷ *Mon.–Wed. 8–5, Thurs.–Sun. 8–7.*

BEYOND FREEPORT-LUCAYA

Grand Bahama Island narrows at picturesque West End, once Grand Bahama's capital and still home to descendants of the island's first settlers. Seaside villages, with concrete-block houses painted in bright blue and pastel yellow, fill in the landscape between Freeport and West End. The East End is Grand Bahama's "back-to-nature" side. The road east from Lucaya is long, flat, and mostly straight. It cuts through a vast pine forest to reach McLean's Town, the end of the road.

Garden of the Groves. This vibrant 12-acre garden, featuring a trademark chapel and waterfalls, is filled with native Bahamian flora, butterflies, and birds. Interpretative signage identifies plant and animal species. First opened in 1973, the park was renovated and reopened in 2008; additions include a labyrinth modeled after the one at France's Cathedral of Chartres, colorful shops and galleries, a playground, and a multideck outdoor café. ✉ *Midshipman Rd. and Churchill Dr., Eastern Grand Bahama* ☎ *242/374–7779* ⊕ *www.thegardenofthegroves.com* ✉ *$15* ◷ *Daily 9–5; guided tours at 11 and 2.*

Fodor's Choice **Lucayan National Park.** In this extraordinary 40-acre seaside land pre-★ serve, trails and elevated walkways wind through a natural forest of wild tamarind and gumbo-limbo trees, past an observation platform, a mangrove swamp, sheltered pools, and one of the largest explored underwater cave systems in the world (more than 6 mi long). You can do independent touring by rental car, entering the caves at two access points; one is closed in June and July, the bat-nursing season. Twenty miles east of Lucaya (allow 45 minutes from the pier each way), the park contains examples of the island's five ecosystems: beach, hardwood forest, mangroves, rocky coppice, and pine forest. Across the road from the caves, two trails form a loop. ✉ *Grand Bahama Hwy.* ☎ *242/352–5438* ⊕ *www.bnt.bs/parks_lucayan.php* ✉ *$3* ◷ *Daily 8:30–4:30.*

SHOPPING

In the stores, shops, and boutiques on Grand Bahama you can find duty-free goods costing up to 40% less than what you might pay back home. At the numerous perfume shops fragrances are often sold at a sweet-smelling 25% below U.S. prices. Be sure to limit your haggling to the straw markets.

★ **Port Lucaya Marketplace** (✉ *Sea Horse Rd.* ☎ *242/373–8446* ⊕ *www.portlucayamarketplace.com*) has more than 100 boutiques and restaurants in 13 pastel-color buildings in a harborside locale, plus an extensive straw market. Local musicians often perform at the bandstand in the afternoons and evenings.

7

ACTIVITIES

FISHING

Private boat charters for up to four people cost $300 and up for a half-day and $350 and up for a full day. Bahamian law limits the catching of game fish to six each of dolphinfish, kingfish, tuna, or wahoo per vessel.

Reef Tours Ltd. (✉ *Port Lucaya Marketplace* ☎ *242/373–5880* ⊕ *www.bahamasvacationguide.com/reeftours*) offers deep-sea fishing for four to six people on custom boats. Equipment and bait are provided free. All vessels are licensed, inspected, and insured. Trips run from 8:30 to 12:15 and from 1 to 4:45, weather permitting ($130 per angler, $60 per spectator). Full-day trips are also available, as are bottom-fishing excursions, glass-bottom-boat tours, snorkeling trips, and sailing–snorkeling cruises. Reservations are essential.

> **PLASTIC BAGS**
>
> Use Zip-loc bags for all toiletries and anything that might spill. Toss a few extras into your suitcase. You may need them later to pack dirty or damp clothes.

GOLF

Fodor's Choice ★ **Our Lucaya Beach and Golf Resort Lucayan Course**, designed by Dick Wilson, is a dramatic 6,824-yard, par-72, 18-hole course featuring a balanced six straight holes, six classic left-turning doglegs, and six right-turning holes. The 18th hole has a double lake, towering limestone structure, and a new clubhouse nearby. Its state-of-the-art instruction facilities include a practice putting green with bunker and chipping areas, covered teaching bays, and a teaching seminar area. A shared electric cart is included in greens fees. Ask about special "twilight" fees that are as low as $55 for 9 holes. ✉ *Our Lucaya Beach and Golf Resort, Lucaya* ☎ *242/373–2002* ⌸ *Resort guests $120, nonguests $130.*

Ruby Golf Course reopened in 2008 with renovated landscaping but basically the same 18-hole, par-72 Jim Fazio design—a lot of sand traps and challenges on holes 7, 9, 10, and 18—especially playing from the blue tees. Hole 10 requires a tee shot onto a dogleg right fairway around a pond. There's a small restaurant-bar and pro shop at the 18th hole. ✉ *West Sunrise Hwy. and Wentworth Ave., Freeport* ☎ *242/352–1851* ⌸ *$65–$90.*

BEACHES

Some 60 mi of magnificent, pristine stretches of sand extend between Freeport-Lucaya and the island's eastern end. Most are used only by people who live in adjacent settlements. The beaches have no public facilities, so beachgoers often headquarter at one of the local beach bars, which often provide free transportation. **Lucayan Beach** is readily accessible from the town's main drag and is always lively and lovely. **Taïno Beach,** near Freeport, is fun for families, water-sports enthusiasts, and partyers. Near Freeport, **Xanadu Beach** provides a mile of white sand. Gold Rock Beach is about 45 minutes from the cruise port, but it's one of the most widely photographed beaches in the Bahamas; at low time, unique sandbars and ridges form.

WHERE TO EAT

$ ✕ **Green Day Cafe.** Now under new management, the former Becky's
BAHAMIAN Bahamian Restaurant is open daily from 7 to 4. Still known for its
breakfast, the restaurant's diner-style booths provide a comfortable
backdrop for the inexpensive menu. The regular menu offers fresh seafood and always a catch of the day. Pancakes, eggs, and special Bahamian breakfasts—stew' fish, boil' fish, or chicken souse (the latter two
are soups flavored with lime), with johnnycake or grits—are served all
day. ✉ *E. Beach Dr. and E. Sunrise Hwy.* ☎ *242/352–5247.*

$$ ✕ **Pier One.** Blown down in the 2004 hurricanes, Pier One is back with
SEAFOOD a sturdier building decorated with the old trademark nautical para-
phernalia. Diners have their choice of picnic tables around the balcony
or inside the spacious dining and bar area. Popular with cruise-ship
passengers because of its location at the port entrance, the restaurant
also hosts shark feedings nightly at 7, 8, and 9. To go with this activity,
order specialties such as smoked shark, blackened lemon shark fillet, or
shark curry with bananas. The extensive menus also offer mussels, pan-
fried mahi, grouper cordon bleu, lobster and mushrooms with cream,
chicken curry, fettuccini with seafood, and steaks. ✉ *Freeport Harbour*
☎ *242/352–6674* ⊕ *www.pieronebahamas.com* ⊘ *No lunch Sun.*

GRAND CAYMAN, CAYMAN ISLANDS

7

Jordan Simon   The largest and most populous of the Cayman Islands, Grand Cay-
man is also one of the most popular cruise destinations in the Western
Caribbean, largely because it doesn't suffer from the ailments afflicting
many larger ports: panhandlers, hasslers, and crime. Instead, the Cay-
man economy is a study in stability, and the environment is healthy and
prosperous. Though the island is rather featureless, Grand Cayman is
a diver's paradise, with pristine waters and a colorful variety of marine
life. Compared with other Caribbean ports, there are fewer things to see
on land here; instead, the island's most impressive sights are underwater.
Snorkeling, diving, and glass-bottom-boat and submarine rides top every
ship's shore-excursion list, and can also be arranged at major aquatic
shops if you don't go on a ship-sponsored excursion. Grand Cayman
is also famous for the nearly 600 offshore banks in George Town; not
surprisingly, the standard of living is high, and nothing is cheap.

ESSENTIALS

CURRENCY   The Cayman Island dollar (CI$ to US$1.25). The U.S. dollar is accepted
everywhere, and ATMs often dispense cash in both currencies, though
you may receive change in Cayman dollars. Prices are often quoted in
Cayman dollars, so make sure you know which currency you're dealing
with so you don't end up paying 25% more than you expected.

INTERNET   **Café del Sol Internet Cafe** ✉ *Marquee Plaza, Seven Mile Beach, Grand
Cayman, Cayman Islands* ☎ *345/946–2233* ⊕ *www.cafedelsol.ky.*

TELEPHONE   To dial the United States, dial 1 followed by the area code and telephone
number. To place a credit-card call, dial 800/744–7777; credit-card and
calling-card calls can be made from any public phone.

Grand Cayman

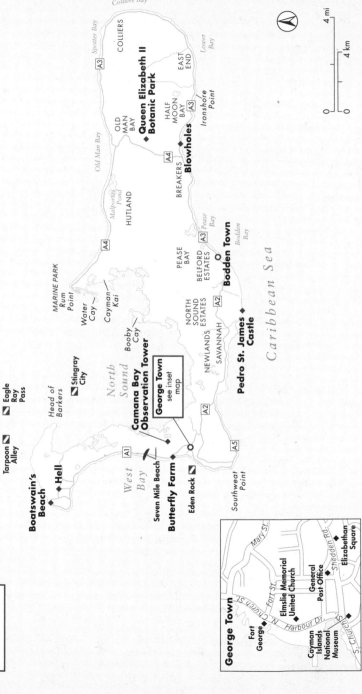

KEY
⬧ Dive Sites

Colliers Bay

Spotter Bay

COLLIERS

A3

Lower Bay

EAST END

Queen Elizabeth II
Botanic Park

OLD MAN BAY

HALF MOON BAY

A3

Ironshore Point

⬧ **Blowholes**

BREAKERS

A4

Old Man Bay

Malportas Pond

HUTLAND

Pease Bay

A3

Bodden Town ○

Boddin Bay

MARINE PARK
Rum Point

PEASE BAY

BELFORD ESTATES

Water Cay

Cayman Kai

Booby Cay

NORTH SOUND ESTATES

A2

⬧ **Pedro St. James Castle**

Caribbean Sea

Stingray City ⬧

North Sound

Camana Bay
Observation Tower

George Town
see inset map

NEWLANDS

SAVANNAH

Head of Barkers

Eagle Ray Pass ⬧

A2

Tarpoon Alley ⬧

A1

West Bay

Hell ⬧

Seven Mile Beach

Butterfly Farm ⬧

Eden Rock ⬧

A5

Southweat Point

Boatswain's Beach ⬧

0 ——— 4 mi
0 ——— 4 km

George Town

Mary St.

Fort St.

N. Church St.

Harbour Dr.

S. Church St.

Shedden Rd.

Fort George ⬧

Elmslie Memorial
United Church

General
Post Office

Elizabethan
Square

Cayman Islands
National Museum ⬧

COMING ASHORE

Ships anchor in George Town Harbour and tender passengers onto Harbour Drive, the center of the shopping district. If you just want to walk around town and shop or visit Seven Mile Beach, you're probably better off on your own, but the Stingray Sandbar snorkeling trip is a highlight of many Caribbean vacations and fills up quickly on cruise-ship days, so it's often better to order that excursion from your ship, even though it will be more crowded and expensive than if you took an independent trip.

A tourist information booth is on the pier, and taxis queue for disembarking passengers. Taxi fares are determined by an elaborate structure set by the government, and although rates may seem high, cabbies rarely try to rip off tourists. Ask to see the chart if you want to check a quoted fare. Taxi drivers won't usually do hourly rates for small-group tours; you must arrange a sightseeing tour with a company. Car rentals range in price from $40 to $95 per day (plus a $7.50 driving permit), so they are a good option if you want to do some independent exploring. You can easily see the entire island and have time to stop at a beach in a single day. ⚠ **Driving in the Cayman Islands is on the left (as in the U.K.), though the steering wheel will be on the left (as in the U.S.).**

EXPLORING GRAND CAYMAN

7

GEORGE TOWN

Begin exploring the capital by strolling along the waterfront Harbour Drive to **Elmslie Memorial United Church,** named after the first Presbyterian missionary to serve in Cayman. Its vaulted ceiling, wooden arches, and sedate nave reflect the religious nature of island residents. In front of the court building, in the center of town, names of influential Caymanians are inscribed on the **Wall of History,** which commemorates the islands' quincentennial in 2003. Across the street is the **Cayman Islands Legislative Assembly Building,** next door to the **1919 Peace Memorial Building**. In the middle of the financial district is the **General Post Office,** built in 1939. Let the kids pet the big blue iguana statues.

🐝 **Cayman Islands National Museum.** Built in 1833, the historically signifi-
Fodor's Choice cant clapboard home of the national museum has had several different
★ incarnations over the years, serving as courthouse, jail, post office, and dance hall. There are also temporary exhibits focusing on aspects of Caymanian culture, a local art collection, and interactive displays for kids. ⊠ *Harbour Dr., George Town, Grand Cayman, Cayman Islands* ☎ *345/949–8368* ⊕ *www.museum.ky* ⊠ *$5* ☉ *Weekdays 9–5, Sat. 10–2.*

ELSEWHERE ON THE ISLAND

🐝 **Blowholes.** When the easterly trade winds blow hard, crashing waves force water into caverns and send impressive geysers shooting up as much as 20 feet through the ironshore. The blowholes were partially filled during Hurricane Ivan in 2004, so the water must be rough to recapture their former elemental drama. ⊠ *Frank Sound Rd., roughly 10 mi (16 km) east of Bodden Town, near East End, Grand Cayman, Cayman Islands.*

☾ **Boatswain's Beach.** Cayman's premier
Fodor's Choice attraction, the Turtle Farm, has
★ been rebranded and transformed
into a marine theme park. The
expanded complex now has several
souvenir shops and restaurants. Still,
the turtles remain a central attraction, and you can tour ponds in the
original research–breeding facility
with thousands in various stages
of growth, some up to 600 pounds
and more than 70 years old. Turtles
can be picked up from the tanks,
a real treat for children and adults
as the little creatures flap their fins
and splash the water. Four areas—
three aquatic and one dry—cover
23 acres; different-color bracelets
determine access (the steep full-
pass admission includes snorkeling
gear). The park helps promote conservation, encouraging interaction
(a Tidal Pool houses invertebrates

such as starfish and crabs) and observation. Animal Program Events
include Keeper Talks, where you might feed birds or iguanas, and biolo-
gists speaking about conservation and their importance to the ecosystem.
✉ *825 Northwest Point Rd., Box 812, West Bay, Grand Cayman, Cayman Islands* ☎ *345/949–3894* ⊕ *www.boatswainsbeach.ky* ✉ *Comprehensive ticket $45, Turtle Farm only $30* ☽ *Daily 8:30–4:30.*

Bodden Town. In the island's original south-shore capital you can find an
old cemetery on the shore side of the road. Graves with A-frame structures are said to contain the remains of pirates. There are also the ruins
of a fort and a wall erected by slaves in the 19th century. The National
Trust runs tours of the restored 1840s Mission House. A curio shop
serves as the entrance to what's called the Pirate's Caves ($8), partially
underground natural formations that are more hokey (decked out with
fake treasure chests and mannequins in pirate garb, with an outdoor
petting zoo) than spooky. ✉ *Grand Cayman, Cayman Islands.*

☾ **Camana Bay Observation Tower.** This 75-foot structure provides striking
★ 360-degree panoramas of otherwise flat Grand Cayman, sweeping from
George Town and Seven Mile Beach to the North Sound. The double-
helix staircase is impressive in its own right. Running alongside the steps
(though an elevator is also available), a floor-to-ceiling mosaic replicates
the look and feel of a dive from seabed to surface. Constructed of countless tiles in 114 different colors, it's one of the world's largest marine-
themed mosaic installations. ✉ *Extending between Seven Mile Beach
and North Sound, 2 mi (3 km) north of George Town, Camana Bay,
Grand Cayman, Cayman Islands* ☎ *345/640–3500* ⊕ *www.camanabay.
com* ✉ *Free* ☽ *Sunrise–10 pm.*

Hell. Quite literally the tourist trap from Hell, especially when overrun by cruise-ship passengers, this attraction does offer free admission, fun photo ops, and sublime surrealism. Its name refers to the quarter-acre of menacing shards of charred brimstone thrusting up like vengeful spirits (actually blackened and "sculpted" by acid-secreting algae and fungi over millennia). The eerie lunarscape is now cordoned off, but you can prove you had a helluva time by taking a photo from

> **STROLLERS**
>
> Parents should bring along an umbrella stroller for walks around the ship as well as the ports of call; people often underestimate how big ships are. It also comes in handy at the airport. Wheel baby right to the departure gate—the stroller is gate checked and will be waiting for you when you arrive at your port of embarkation.

the observation deck. ⊠ *Hell Rd., West Bay, Grand Cayman, Cayman Islands* ☎ *345/949–3358* 🖼 *Free* ☉ *Daily 9–6.*

☾ **Fodor's Choice** ★ **Pedro St. James Castle.** Built in 1780, the greathouse is Cayman's oldest stone structure and the only remaining late-18th-century residence on the island. In its capacity as courthouse and jail, it was the birthplace of Caymanian democracy, where in December 1831 the first elected parliament was organized and in 1835 the Slavery Abolition Act signed.The buildings are surrounded by 8 acres of natural parks and woodlands. You can stroll through landscaping of native Caymanian flora and experience one of the most spectacular views on the island from atop the dramatic Great Pedro Bluff. First watch the impressive multimedia theater show, complete with smoking pots, misting rains, and two film screens where the story of Pedro's Castle is presented on the hour. The poignant Hurricane Ivan Memorial outside uses text, images, and symbols to represent important aspects of that horrific 2004 natural disaster. ⊠ *Pedro Castle Rd., Savannah, Grand Cayman, Cayman Islands* ☎ *345/947–3329* ⊕ *www.pedrostjames.ky* 🖼 *$10* ☉ *Daily 9–5.*

Fodor's Choice ★ **Queen Elizabeth II Botanic Park.** This 65-acre wilderness preserve showcases a wide range of indigenous and nonindigenous tropical vegetation, approximately 2,000 species in total. Splendid sections include numerous water features from limpid lily ponds to cascades; a Heritage Garden with a traditional cottage and "caboose" (outside kitchen) that includes crops that might have been planted on Cayman a century ago; and a Floral Colour Garden arranged by color, the walkway wandering through sections of pink, red, orange, yellow, white, blue, mauve, lavender, and purple. A 2-acre lake and adjacent wetlands includes three islets that provide a habitat and breeding ground for native birds just as showy as the floral displays: green herons, black-necked stilts, American coots, blue-winged teal, cattle egrets, and rare West Indian whistling ducks. The park's star residents are the protected endemic blue iguanas, found only in Grand Cayman. The world's most endangered iguana, they're the focus of the National Trust's Blue Iguana Recovery Program, a captive breeding and reintroduction facility. The Trust conducts 90-minute behind-the-scenes safaris Monday–Saturday at 11 am for $30. ⊠ *367 Botanic Rd., off Frank Sound, Grand Cayman, Cayman Islands* ⊠ *Box 203, Grand Cayman, Grand Cayman, Cayman Islands*

7

☎ *345/947–9462* ⊕ *www.botanic-park.ky* ⬚ *$10* ⊘ *Apr.–Sept., daily 9–6:30; Oct.–Mar., daily 9–5:30; last admission 1 hr before closing.*

SHOPPING

★ **Cathy Church's Underwater Photo Centre and Gallery.** Come see a collection of the acclaimed underwater shutterbug's spectacular color and limited-edition black-and-white underwater photos. Have Cathy autograph her latest coffee-table book and regale you with anecdotes of her globe-trotting adventures. The store also carries the latest marine camera equipment, and she'll schedule private underwater photography instruction. ⊠ *S. Church St., George Town, Grand Cayman, Cayman Islands* ☎ *345/949–7415.*

★ **Guy Harvey's Gallery and Shoppe.** This is where world-renowned marine biologist, conservationist, and artist Guy Harvey showcases his aquatic-inspired action-packed art in nearly every conceivable medium, logo tableware, and sportswear (even logo soccer balls and Zippos). Original paintings, sculpture, and drawings are expensive, but there's something (tile art, prints, lithographs, and photos) in most price ranges. ⊠ *49 S. Church St., George Town, Grand Cayman, Cayman Islands* ☎ *345/943–4891.*

★ **Kirk Freeport Plaza.** This downtown shopping center, home to the Kirk Freeport flagship department store, is ground zero for couture; it's also known for its boutiques selling fine watches and jewelry, china, crystal, leather, perfumes, and cosmetics. ⊠ *Cardinal Ave., George Town, Grand Cayman, Cayman Islands.*

Landmark. Stores in the Landmark sell perfumes, treasure coins, and upscale beachwear; Breezes by the Bay restaurant is upstairs. ⊠ *Harbour Dr., George Town, Grand Cayman, Cayman Islands.*

★ **Pure Art.** About 1½ mi (2½ km) south of George Town, Pure Art purveys wit, warmth, and whimsy right from the wildly colored front steps. Its warren of rooms resembles a garage sale run amok or a quirky grandmother's attic spilling over with unexpected finds, from foodstuffs to functional art. ⊠ *S. Church St., George Town, Grand Cayman, Cayman Islands* ☎ *345/949–9133* ⊕ *www.pureart.ky.*

Tortuga Rum Company. This company bakes, then vacuum-seals, more than 10,000 of its world-famous rum cakes daily, adhering to the original "secret" century-old recipe. There are seven flavors, from banana to Blue Mountain coffee. The 12-year-old rum, blended from private stock though actually distilled in Guyana, is a connoisseur's delight for after-dinner sipping. ⊠ *N. Sound Rd., Industrial Park, George Town, Grand Cayman, Cayman Islands* ☎ *345/949–7701 or 345/949–7867* ⊕ *www.tortugarumcakes.com.*

ACTIVITIES

DIVING AND SNORKELING

Pristine water (visibility often exceeding 100 feet [30 meters]), breathtaking coral formations, and plentiful and exotic marine life mark the **Great Wall**—a world-renowned dive site just off the north side of Grand Cayman. A must-see for adventurous souls is **Stingray City** in the North

Sound, noted as the best 12-foot (3½-meter) dive in the world, where dozens of stingrays congregate, tame enough to suction squid from your outstretched palm. Nondivers gravitate to **Stingray Sandbar,** a shallower part of the North Sound, which has become a popular snorkeling spot; it is also a popular hangout for the stingrays. If someone tells you that the minnows are in at **Eden Rock,** drop everything and dive here (on South Church Street, south of George Town). The schools swarm around you as you glide through the grottoes, forming quivering curtains of liquid silver as shafts of sunlight pierce the sandy bottom.

DiveTech. DiveTech has opportunities for shore diving at its two north-coast locations, which provide loads of interesting creatures, a mini-wall, and the North Wall. With quick access to West Bay, the boats are quite comfortable. Technical training (a specialty of owner Nancy Easterbrook) is unparalleled, and the company offers good, personable service as well as the latest gadgetry such as underwater DPV scooters. Snorkel and diving programs are available year-round for children ages eight and up, SASY (supplied-air snorkeling, which keeps the unit on a personal flotation device) for five and up. ⊠ *Cobalt Coast Resort & Suites, 18-A Sea Fan Dr., West Bay, Grand Cayman, Cayman Islands* ☎ *345/946–5658 or 888/946–5656* ⊕ *www.divetech.com.*

Fodor'sChoice

★

Eden Rock Diving Center. Eden Rock Diving Center, south of George Town, provides easy access to Eden Rock and Devil's Grotto. It features full equipment rental, lockers, shower facilities, and a full range of PADI courses from a helpful, cheerful staff. Costs for guided shore dives and two-tank dives on its Pro 42 jet boat are slightly cheaper than most outfits, without sacrificing quality or comfort. ⊠ *124 S. Church St., George Town, Grand Cayman, Cayman Islands* ☎ *345/949–7243* ⊕ *www.edenrockdive.com.*

Red Sail Sports. Red Sail Sports offers daily trips from most of the major hotels. Dives are often run as guided tours, a perfect option for beginners. If you're experienced and your air lasts a long time, consult the boat captain to see if he requires that you come up with the group (determined by the first person who runs low on air). There is a full range of kids' dive options for ages 5 to 15. The company also operates Stingray City tours, dinner and sunset sails, and just about every major water sport from Wave Runners to windsurfing. ⊠ *Grand Cayman, Cayman Islands* ☎ *345/949– 5965, 877/733–7245, 877/506–6368* ⊕ *www.redsailcayman.com.*

FISHING

Cayman waters are abundant with blue and white marlin, yellowfin tuna, sailfish, dolphinfish, bonefish, and wahoo. Two-dozen boats are available for charter.

★ **Sea Star Charters.** Sea Star Charters, aka Clinton's Watersports, is run by Clinton Ebanks, a fine and very friendly Caymanian who will do whatever it takes to make sure that you have a wonderful time on his two 25- and 31-foot cabin cruisers (and from the 35-foot trimaran used primarily for snorkeling cruises), enjoying light-tackle, bone-, and bottom-fishing. He's a good choice for beginners and offers a nice cultural experience as well as sailing charters and snorkeling with complimentary transportation and equipment. Only cash and traveler's checks are accepted. ⊠ *Grand Cayman, Cayman Islands* ☎ *345/949–1016, 345/916–5234 after 8 am.*

HIKING

★ **Mastic Trail.** The National Trust's internationally significant Mastic Trail, used in the 1800s as the only direct path to and from the North Side, is a rugged 2-mi (3-km) slash through 776 dense acres of woodlands, black mangrove swamps, savannah, agricultural remnants, and ancient rock formations. It embraces more than 700 species, including Cayman's largest remaining contiguous ancient forest (one of the heavily deforested Caribbean's last examples). A comfortable walk depends on weather—winter is better because it's drier, though flowering plants such as the banana orchid set the trail ablaze in summer. Call the National Trust to determine suitability and to book a guide for $30; tours are run daily from 9 to 5 by appointment only, regularly on Wednesday at 9 am (sometimes earlier in summer). The trip takes about three hours. ⊠ *Frank Sound Rd., entrance by fire station at botanic park, Breakers, East End, Grand Cayman, Cayman Islands* ☎ *345/749–1121 for guide reservations, 345/749–1124 for guide reservations* ⊕ *www.nationaltrust.org.ky.*

BEACHES

Fodor's Choice **Seven Mile Beach.** Grand Cayman's west coast is dominated by the famous
★ Seven Mile Beach—actually a 6½-mi-long (10-km-long) expanse of powdery white sand overseeing lapis water stippled with a rainbow of parasails and kayaks. The width of the beach varies with the season; toward the south end it narrows and disappears altogether south of the Marriott, leaving only rock and ironshore. It starts to broaden into its normal silky softness anywhere between Tarquyn Manor and the Reef Grill at Royal Palms. Free of litter and pesky peddlers, it's an unspoiled (though often crowded) environment. At the public beach toward the north end you can find chairs for rent ($10 for the day, including a beverage). The best snorkeling is at either end, by the Marriott and Treasure Island or off the northern section called Cemetery Reef Beach. ⊠ *West Bay Rd., Seven Mile Beach, Grand Cayman, Cayman Islands.*

WHERE TO EAT

$$ ✗ **Breezes by the Bay.** There isn't a bad seat in the house at this nonstop
CARIBBEAN feel-good fiesta festooned with tiny paper lanterns, Christmas lights, ship murals, and Mardi Gras beads (you're "lei'd" upon entering). Wraparound balconies take in a dazzling panorama from South Sound to Seven Mile Beach. It's a joyous nonstop happy hour all day every day, especially at Countdown to Sunset. Signs promise "the good kind of hurricanes," referring to the 23-ounce signature "category 15" cocktails with fresh garnishes; rum aficionados will find 48 varieties (flights available). Equally fresh food at bargain prices, including homemade baked goods and ice creams, isn't an afterthought. ⊠ *Harbor Dr., George Town, Grand Cayman, Cayman Islands* ☎ *345/943–8469* ⊕ *www.breezesbythebay.com.*

$$ ✗ **Sunshine Grill.** This cheerful, cherished locals' secret serves haute com-
CARIBBEAN fort food at bargain-basement prices. Even the chattel-style poolside
☾ building, painted a delectable lemon with lime shutters, whets the appetite. Sunshine ranks high in the island's greatest burger debate, and the jerk chicken egg rolls and fabulous fish tacos elevate pub grub to an art

form. Wash it down with one of the many signature libations, like the Painkiller. ⊠ *Sunshine Suites, West Bay Rd., Seven Mile Beach, Grand Cayman, Cayman Islands* ☎ *345/949–3000.*

GRAND TURK, TURKS AND CAICOS ISLANDS

Ramona Settle

Just 7 mi (11 km) long and a little over 1 mi (1½ km) wide, Grand Turk, the political capital of the Turks and Caicos Islands, has been a longtime favorite destination for divers eager to explore the 7,000-foot-deep pristine coral walls that drop down only 300 yards out to sea. On shore, the tiny, quiet island is home to white-sand beaches, the National Museum, and a small population of wild horses and donkeys, which leisurely meander past the white-walled courtyards, pretty churches, and bougainvillea-covered colonial inns on their daily commute into town. The main settlement on the island is tranquil Cockburn Town, and that's where most of the small hotels, not to mention Pillory Beach, can be found. Although it has the second-largest number of inhabitants of all the Turks and Caicos Island, Grand Turk's permanent population has still not reached 4,000.

ESSENTIALS

CURRENCY The U.S. dollar. You'll find branches of Scotiabank and FirstCaribbean on Grand Turk, with ATMs; all of these are in tiny Cockburn Town.

INTERNET There's no Internet café at the cruise center, but if you have a laptop, you might take it to the restaurant at the Osprey Beach Hotel, where you can take advantage of the hotel's free Wi-Fi.

TELEPHONE To make local calls, dial the seven-digit number. To make calls from the Turks and Caicos, dial 0, then 1, the area code, and the number. All telephone service is provided by LIME (formerly Cable & Wireless), and your U.S. cell phone may work on Grand Turk. Calling cards are available, or you can make a call using AT&T's USADirect by dialing 800/872–2881 to charge the call to your credit card or an AT&T pre-paid calling card.

COMING ASHORE

Cruise ships dock at the southern end of the island, near the former U.S. Air Force base south of the airport. The purpose-built, $40-million cruise center is about 3 mi (5 km) from tranquil Cockburn Town, Pillory Beach, and the Ridge, and far from most of the western shore dive sites. The center has many facilities, including shopping, a large, free-form pool, car-rental booths, and even a dock from which many sea-bound excursions depart. Governor's Beach is adjacent to the cruise-ship complex and one of the island's best beaches, but others are right in and around Cockburn Town.

If you want to come into Cockburn Town, it's reachable by taxi. Taxi rates are per person and by "zone"; you'll find a rate card outside the cruise terminal. You can also rent a car to explore the island on your own terms and schedule.

7

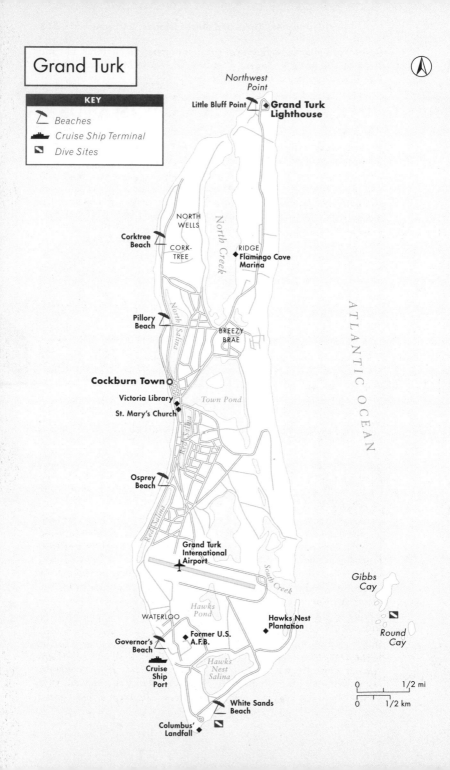

Grand Turk Cruise Terminal (✉ *South Base, Grand Turk Cruise Terminal* ☎ *649/946–1040* ⊕ *www. grandturkcc.com*) has a Web site that shows all the cruise schedules, lists all the shops at the terminal, and completely outlines options for excursions and transportation. A bonus is the live webcam so you can check the actual weather at any given moment.

Grace Bay Car Rentals (✉ *Providenciales* ☎ *649/231–8500* ⊕ *www. gracebaycarrentals.com*) has an office at the port, so you can see the sights on your own time. Remember, driving is on the left.

GRAND TURK BEST BETS

■ **Beaches.** The sand is powdery soft, the water azure blue.

■ **Diving.** If you're certified, there are several world-class dive sights within each reach.

■ **Front Street.** Colorful Front Street will give you the feeling you've stepped back in time.

■ **Gibb's Cay.** To swim with stingrays, take a ship-sponsored trip here; it's an excellent beach.

■ **Turks and Caicos National Museum.** Small but worthy.

EXPLORING GRAND TURK

Pristine beaches with vistas of turquoise waters, small local settlements, historic ruins, and native flora and fauna are among the sights on Grand Turk. Fewer than 4,000 people live on this 7½-square-mi (19-square-km) island, and it's hard to get lost, as there aren't many roads.

COCKBURN TOWN

The buildings in the colony's capital and seat of government reflect a 19th-century Bermudian style. Narrow streets are lined with low stone walls and old street lamps, which are now powered by electricity. The once-vital *salinas* (natural salt pans, where the sea leaves a film of salt) have been restored, and covered benches along the sluices offer shady spots for observing wading birds, including flamingos that frequent the shallows. Be sure to pick up a copy of the tourist board's *Heritage Walk* guide to discover Grand Turk's rich architecture.

Her Majesty's Prison (✉ *Pond St., Cockburn Town* ☎ *No phone*) was built in the 19th century to house runaway slaves and slaves who survived the wreck of the *Trouvadore* in 1841. After the slaves were granted freedom, the prison housed criminals and even modern-day drug runners until it closed in the 1990s. The last hanging here was in 1960. Now you can see the cells, solitary confinement area, and exercise patio. The prison is open only when there is a cruise ship at the port.

☾ **Turks and Caicos National Museum.** In one of the oldest stone buildings on the
★ islands, the national museum houses the Molasses Reef wreck, the earliest shipwreck—dating to the early 1500s—discovered in the Americas. The natural-history exhibits include artifacts left by Taíno, African, North American, Bermudian, French, and Latin American settlers. The most original display is a collection of messages in bottles that have washed ashore from all over the world. ✉ *Duke St., Cockburn Town, Grand*

Turk, Turks and Caicos Islands ☎ 649/946–2160 ⊕ *www.tcmuseum.org* ☞ *$5* ☉ *Mon., Tues., Thurs., and Fri. 9–4, Wed. 9–5, Sat. 9–1.*

ELSEWHERE ON THE ISLAND

Grand Turk Lighthouse. More than 150 years old, the lighthouse, built in the United Kingdom and transported piece by piece to the island, used to protect ships in danger of wrecking on the northern reefs. Use this panoramic landmark as a starting point for a breezy cliff-top walk by following the donkey trails to the deserted eastern beach. ⊠ *Lighthouse Rd., North Ridge.*

SHOPPING

There's not much to buy in Grand Turk, and shopping isn't a major activity here. However, there is a duty-free mall right at the cruise-ship center, where you'll find the usual array of upscale shops, including Ron Jon's Surf Shop, the largest Margaritaville in the world, and Piranha Joe's. There are also shops in Cockburn Town itself.

ACTIVITIES

Most of the activities offered to cruise-ship passengers can be booked only on your ship. These include a horseback ride and swim, dune-buggy safaris, and 4x4 safaris.

BICYCLING

The island's mostly flat terrain isn't very taxing, and most roads have hard surfaces. Take water with you: there are few places to stop for refreshments. Most hotels have bicycles available, but you can also rent them for $10 to $15 a day from **Oasis Divers** (⊠ *Duke St., Cockburn Town* ☎ 649/946–1128 ⊕ *www.oasisdivers.com*).

DIVING AND SNORKELING

★ In these waters you can find undersea cathedrals, coral gardens, and countless tunnels, but note that you must carry and present a valid certificate card before you'll be allowed to dive. As its name suggests, the **Black Forest** offers staggering black-coral formations as well as the occasional black-tip shark. In the **Library** you can study fish galore, including large numbers of yellowtail snapper. At the Columbus Passage separating South Caicos from Grand Turk, each side of a 22-mi-wide (35-km-wide) channel drops more than 7,000 feet. From January through March thousands of Atlantic humpback whales swim through en route to their winter breeding grounds. **Gibb's Cay,** a small cay a couple of miles off Grand Turk, where you can swim with stingrays, makes for a great excursion.

Blue Water Divers (⊠ *Duke St., Cockburn Town, Grand Turk* ☎ 649/946–2432 ⊕ *www.grandturkscuba.com*) has been in operation on Grand Turk since 1983, and is the only PADI Gold Palm five-star dive center on the island. Owner Mitch will undoubtedly put some of your underwater adventures to music in the evening when he plays at the Osprey Beach Hotel or Salt Raker Inn. **Oasis Divers** (⊠ *Duke St., Cockburn Town* ☎ 649/946–1128 ⊕ *www.oasisdivers.com*) specializes in complete gear handling and pampering treatment. It also supplies Nitrox and rebreathers. Besides daily dive trips to the wall, **Sea Eye Diving** (✉ *Duke St., Cockburn Town* ☏☏ *649/946–1407* ⊕ *www.seaeyediving.com*) offers encounters with friendly stingrays on a popular snorkeling trip to nearby Gibbs Cay.

WATER

Tap water on your ship is perfectly safe to drink; purchasing bottled water is only necessary if you prefer the taste.

BEACHES

Grand Turk is spoiled for choices when it comes to beach options: sunset strolls along miles of deserted beaches, picnics in secluded coves, beachcombing on the coralline sands, snorkeling around shallow coral heads close to shore, and admiring the impossibly turquoise-blue waters. **Governor's Beach**, a beautiful crescent of powder-soft sand and shallow, calm turquoise waters that fronts the official British Governor's residence, called Waterloo, is framed by tall casuarina trees that provide plenty of natural shade. On days when ships are in port, the beach is lined with lounge chairs. **Pillory Beach,** with sparkling neon turquoise water, is the prettiest beach on Grand Turk; it also has great off-the-beach snorkeling.

WHERE TO EAT

$

AMERICAN

✕ **Jack's Shack.** For a more local feel, walk 500 meters down the beach from the cruise terminal and you'll find Jack's Shack. This beach bar gets lively with volleyball, and offers chair rentals and tropical drinks. Casual food such as burgers and hot dogs satisfy your hunger. Print a coupon from the Web site for a free shot of T&C's local rum, Bamberra. ✉ *500 meters north of cruise terminal, Grand Turk Cruise Port Terminal* ☏ *649/232–0099* ⊸ *Open when ship is at port* ☉ *Closed anytime a ship is not in port.*

$$

AMERICAN

✕ **Jimmy Buffet's Margaritaville.** The only chain restaurant (so far) in all of the Turks and Caicos is the place to partake in cruise activities even when you're not on a cruise ship. One of the largest Margaritavilles in the world is at the Grand Turk Cruise Terminal and open to all comers (both cruisers and anyone else on the island) when a cruise ship is parked at the dock. Tables are scattered around a large winding pool; there's even a DJ and a FlowRider (a wave pool where you can surf on land—for a fee). You can enjoy 52 flavors of margaritas or the restaurant's own beer, Landshark, while you eat casual bar food such as wings, quesadillas, and burgers. The food is good, the people-watching is great. ✉ *Grand Turk Cruise Terminal* ☏ *649/946–1880* ⊕ *www.margaritavillecaribbean.com* ☉ *Closed when no cruise ship is at pier.*

7

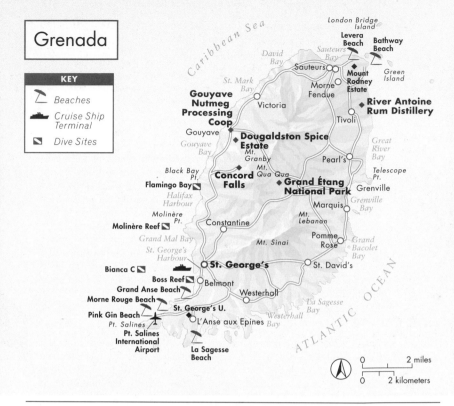

GRENADA (ST. GEORGE'S)

Jane E. Zarem Nutmeg, cinnamon, cloves, cocoa . . . those heady aromas fill the air in Grenada (pronounced gruh-*nay*-da). Only 21 mi (33½ km) long and 12 mi (19½ km) wide, the Isle of Spice is a tropical gem of lush rain forests, white-sand beaches, secluded coves, exotic flowers, and enough locally grown spices to fill anyone's kitchen cabinet. St. George's is one of the most picturesque capital cities in the Caribbean, St. George's Harbour is one of the most picturesque harbors, and Grenada's Grand Anse Beach is one of the region's finest beaches. The island has friendly, hospitable people and enough good shopping, restaurants, historic sites, and natural wonders to make it a popular port of call. About one-third of Grenada's visitors arrive by cruise ship, and that number continues to grow each year.

ESSENTIALS

CURRENCY Eastern Caribbean (E.C.) dollar (EC$2.67 to US$1). U.S. dollars (but not coins) are generally accepted, but change is given in E.C. currency.

INTERNET **Java-Kool Internet Cafe** ⊠ *The Carenage, St. George's, Grenada* ☎ *473/435–3506.*

TELEPHONE Prepaid phone cards, which can be used in special card phones throughout the Caribbean for local or international calls, are sold in various denominations at shops, attractions, transportation centers, and other convenient outlets. For international calls using a major credit card, dial 111; to place a collect call or use a calling card, dial 800/225–5872 from any telephone. Pay phones are available at the Cruise Ship Terminal welcome center, the LIME office on the Carenage in St. George's, shopping centers, and other convenient locations.

COMING ASHORE

The Cruise Ship Terminal near Market Square, on the north side of St. George's, accommodates two large ships; up to four can anchor in the outer harbor. A full range of passenger facilities is available at the terminal, which opens directly into the Esplanade Mall and the minibus terminus; it is also a block from Market Square. You can easily tour the capital on foot, but be prepared to climb up and down steep hills. If you don't want to walk up and down through town, you can find a taxi ($3 or $4 each way) or a water taxi ($4 per person each way) right at the terminal to take you around to the Carenage or to Grand Anse Beach. To explore areas outside St. George's, hiring a taxi or arranging a guided tour is more sensible than renting a car. Taxis are plentiful, and fixed rates to popular island destinations are posted at the terminal's welcome center.

A taxi ride from the terminal to the beach will cost $15, but water taxis are a less expensive and more picturesque way to get there; the one-way fare is about $8 per person to Grand Anse, depending on the number of passengers. Minibuses are the least expensive way to travel between St. George's and Grand Anse; pay EC$1.50 (55¢), but hold on to your hat. They're crowded with local people getting from here to there and often make quick stops and take turns at quite a clip! Still, it's an inexpensive, fun, and safe way to travel around the island. If you want to rent a car and explore on your own, be prepared to pay $12 for a temporary driving permit and about $55 to $75 for a day's car rental.

EXPLORING GRENADA

★ **Concord Falls.** About 8 mi (13 km) north of St. George's, a turnoff from the West Coast Road leads to Concord Falls—actually three separate waterfalls. The first is at the end of the road; when the currents aren't too strong, you can take a dip under the cascade. Reaching the two other waterfalls requires an hour's hike into the forest reserve. It's smart to hire a guide. ⊠ *Off West Coast Rd., St. John's, St. John, Grenada* ⌦ *Changing room $2* ⊙ *Daily 9–5.*

☺ **Dougaldston Spice Estate.** Just south of Gouyave, this historic plantation, now primarily a living museum, still grows and processes spices the old-fashioned way. You can see cocoa, nutmeg, mace, cloves, and other spices laid out on giant racks to dry in the sun. A worker will be glad to explain the process (and will appreciate a small donation). You can buy spices for about $2 a bag. ⊠ *Gouyave, St. John, Grenada* ☎ *No phone* ⌦ *Free* ⊙ *Weekdays 9–4.*

☯ **Gouyave Nutmeg Processing Coopera-**
★ **tive.** Touring the nutmeg-processing co-op, in the center of the west-coast fishing village of Gouyave (pronounced *gwahv*), is a fragrant, fascinating way to spend half an hour. You can learn all about nutmeg and its uses, see the nutmegs laid out in bins, and watch the workers sort them by hand and pack them into burlap bags for shipping worldwide. ⊠ *Gouyave, St. John, Grenada* ☎ *473/444–8337* 🖃 *$1* ⊘ *Weekdays 10–1 and 2–4.*

ID CASES

You can keep track of your boarding pass, shipboard charge/key card, and picture ID when you go ashore by slipping them into a bi-fold business-card carrying case. Cases with a sueded finish are less likely to fall out of your pocket. With security as tight as it is these days, you don't want to lose your ID.

☯ **Grand Étang National Park & Forest Reserve.** Deep in the mountainous inte-
★ rior of Grenada is a bird sanctuary and forest reserve with miles of hiking trails, lookouts, and fishing streams. **Grand Étang Lake** is a 36-acre expanse of cobalt-blue water that fills the crater of an extinct volcano 1,740 feet above sea level. The informative **Grand Étang Forest Center** has displays on the local wildlife and vegetation. ⊠ *Main interior road, between Grenville and St. George's, St. Andrew's, St. Andrew, Grenada* ☎ *473/440–6160* 🖃 *$1* ⊘ *Daily 8:30–4.*

River Antoine Rum Distillery. At this rustic operation, kept open primarily as a museum, a limited quantity of Rivers rum is produced by the same methods used since the distillery opened in 1785. The process begins with the crushing of sugarcane from adjacent fields. The result is a potent overproof rum, sold only in Grenada, that will knock your socks off. ⊠ *River Antoine Estate, St. Patrick's, St. Patrick, Grenada* ☎ *473/442–7109* 🖃 *$2* ⊘ *Guided tours daily 9–4.*

St. George's. Grenada's capital is a bustling West Indian city, most of which remains unchanged from colonial days. Narrow streets lined with shops wind up, down, and across steep hills. Brick warehouses and small shops cling to the waterfront, and pastel-painted homes rise from the waterfront and disappear into steep green hills. ⊠ *Grenada.*

Picturesque **St. George's Harbour,** a submerged volcanic crater, is arguably the prettiest harbor in the Caribbean and the center of town. Schooners, ferries, and tour boats tie up along the seawall or at the small dinghy dock. The **Carenage** (pronounced car-a-*nahzh*), which surrounds horseshoe-shape St. George's Harbour, is the capital's main thoroughfare. Warehouses, shops, and restaurants line the waterfront. The *Christ of the Deep* statue that sits on the pedestrian plaza at the center of the Carenage was presented to Grenada by Costa Cruise Line in remembrance of its ship *Bianca C,* which burned and sank in the harbor in 1961 and is now a favorite dive site.

An engineering feat for its time, the 340-foot-long **Sendall Tunnel** was built in 1895 and named for an early governor. It separates the harbor side of St. George's from the Esplanade on the bay side of town, where you can find the markets (produce, meat, and fish), the Cruise Ship Terminal, the Esplanade Mall, and the public bus station.

Grenada National Museum. The Grenada National Museum, a block from the Carenage, is built on the foundation of a French army barracks and prison that was originally built in 1704. The small museum has exhibitions of news items, photos, and proclamations relating to the 1983 intervention, along with the childhood bathtub of Empress Joséphine (who was born on Martinique), and other memorabilia. ⊠ *Young and Monckton Sts., Grenada* ☎ *473/440–3725* 🖃 *$1* ⊗ *Weekdays 9–4:30, Sat. 10–1.*

Ft. George. Ft. George is high on the hill at the entrance to St. George's Harbour. It's Grenada's oldest fort—built by the French in 1705 to protect the harbor. No shots were ever fired here until October 1983, when Prime Minister Maurice Bishop and some of his followers were assassinated in the courtyard. The fort now houses police headquarters but is open to the public daily; admission is free. The 360-degree view of the capital city, St. George's Harbour, and the open sea is spectacular. ⊠ *Church St., Grenada.*

Market Square. Don't miss St. George's Market Square, a block from the Cruise Ship Terminal. It's open every weekday morning but really comes alive on Saturday from 8 to noon. Vendors sell baskets, spices, brooms, clothing, knickknacks, coconut water, and heaps of fresh produce. A continuing renovation project is increasingly providing permanent cover for the vendors. Historically, Market Square is where parades begin and political rallies take place. ⊠ *Granby St., Grenada.*

St. George's Methodist Church. St. George's Methodist Church was built in 1820 and is the oldest original church in the city. It was damaged in Hurricane Ivan in 2004 but has been completely refurbished. ⊠ *Green St. near Herbert Blaize St., Grenada.*

Ft. Frederick. Overlooking the city of St. George's and the inland side of the harbor, historic Ft. Frederick provides a panoramic view of two-thirds of Grenada. The fort was started by the French and completed in 1791 by the British; it was also the headquarters of the People's Revolutionary Government during the 1983 coup. Today you can get a bird's-eye view of much of Grenada from here. ⊠ *Richmond Hill, Grenada.*

GRENADA BEST BETS

■ **The Beach.** Grand Anse Beach is one of the Caribbean's most beautiful.

■ **Diving and Snorkeling.** Explore dozens of fish-filled sites off Grenada's southwest coast.

■ **Market Square.** Market Square is a bustling produce and spice market.

■ **Nutmeg.** Don't miss a visit to a nutmeg cooperative (and get a pocketful to take home).

■ **Waterfalls.** Concord Falls, just south of Gouyave, and Annandale Falls are among the island's most spectacular.

SHOPPING

Grenada's best souvenirs or gifts for friends back home are spice baskets filled with cinnamon, nutmeg, mace, bay leaves, cloves, turmeric, and ginger. You can buy them for as little as $4 in practically every shop, at the open-air produce market at **Market Square** in St. George's, at the vendor stalls near the pier, and at the **Vendor's Craft and Spice Market** on Grand Anse Beach. Vendors also sell handmade fabric dolls, coral jewelry, seashells, and hats and baskets handwoven from green palm fronds. Bargaining is not appropriate in the shops, and it isn't customary with vendors—although most will offer you "a good price."

★ **Art Fabrik.** At Art Fabrik you'll find batik fabric created by hand in the next-door studio and sold either by the yard or fashioned into dresses, shirts, shorts, hats, and scarves. ⊠ *Young St., St. George's, Carriacou, Grenada* ☎ *473/440–0568* ⊕ *www.artfabrikgrenada.com.*

Tikal. Tikal is known for its regional artwork, jewelry, batik items, and fashions. ⊠ *Young St., St. George's, Carriacou, Grenada* ☎ *473/440–2310.*

ACTIVITIES

DIVING AND SNORKELING

You can see hundreds of varieties of fish and some 40 species of coral at more than a dozen sites off Grenada's southwest coast—only 15 to 20 minutes by boat—and another couple of dozen sites around Carriacou's reefs and neighboring islets. Depths vary from 20 to 120 feet, and visibility varies from 30 to 100 feet.

A spectacular dive is *Bianca C,* a 600-foot cruise ship that caught fire in 1961, sank to 100 feet, and is now encrusted with coral and serves as a habitat for giant turtles, spotted eagle rays, barracuda, and jacks. **Boss Reef** extends 5 mi (8 km) from St. George's Harbour to Point Salines, with a depth ranging from 20 to 90 feet. **Flamingo Bay** has a wall that drops to 90 feet and is teeming with fish, sponges, sea horses, sea fans, and coral. **Molinère Reef** slopes from about 20 feet below the surface to a wall that drops to 65 feet. It's a good dive for beginners, and advanced divers can continue farther out to view the wreck of the *Buccaneer,* a 42-foot sloop.

Aquanauts Grenada. Aquanauts Grenada has a multilingual staff, so instruction is available in English, German, Dutch, French, and Spanish. Two-tank dive trips, accommodating no more than eight divers, are offered each morning to both the Caribbean and Atlantic sides of Grenada. ⊠ *Spice Island Beach Resort, Grand Anse Beach, Grand Anse, St. George, Grenada* ☎ *473/444–1126, 888/446–9235 in U.S.*

EcoDive. EcoDive offers two dive trips daily, both drift and wreck dives, as well as weekly trips to dive Isle de Rhonde. The company also runs Grenada's marine-conservation and education center, which conducts coral-reef monitoring. ⊠ *Coyaba Beach Resort, Grand Anse, St. George, Grenada* ☎ *473/444–7777* ⊕ *www.ecodiveandtrek.com.*

FISHING

Deep sea fishing around Grenada is excellent, with marlin, sailfish, yellowfin tuna, and dolphin fish topping the list of good catches. You can arrange sportfishing trips that accommodate up to five people starting at $475 for a half day and $700 for a full day.

True Blue Sportfishing. True Blue Sportfishing offers big-game charters on its 31-foot *Yes Aye*. It has an enclosed cabin, a fighting chair, and professional tackle. British-born Captain Gary Clifford, who has been fishing since the age of six has run the company since 1998. Refreshments and courtesy transport are included. ⊠ *Grenada* ☎ *473/444–2048* ⊕ *www.yesaye.com.*

BEACHES

Bathway Beach. A broad strip of sand with a natural reef that protects swimmers from the rough Atlantic surf on Grenada's far northern shore, this Levera National Park beach has changing rooms at the park headquarters. ⊠ *Levera, St. Patrick's, St. Patrick, Grenada.*

Grand Anse Beach. In the southwest, about 3 mi (5 km) south of St. George's, Grenada's loveliest and most popular beach is a gleaming 2-mi (3-km) semicircle of white sand lapped by clear, gentle surf. Sea grape trees and coconut palms provide shady escapes from the sun. Brilliant rainbows frequently spill into the sea from the high green mountains that frame St. George's Harbour to the north. The Grand Anse Craft & Spice Market is at the midpoint of the beach. ⊠ *Grand Anse, St. George's, St. George, Grenada.*

WHERE TO EAT

Restaurants add an 8% government tax to your bill and usually add a 10% service charge; if not, tip 10% to 15% for a job well done.

$$
CARIBBEAN
☾
★
✕ **Belmont Estate.** Luncheon is served! If you're visiting the northern reaches of Grenada island, plan to stop for lunch at Belmont Estate, a 400-year-old working nutmeg and cocoa plantation. Settle into the breezy open-air dining room, which overlooks enormous trays of nutmeg, cocoa, and mace drying in the sunshine. A waiter will offer some refreshing local juice and a choice of callaloo or pumpkin soup. Then head to the buffet and help yourself to salad, rice, stewed chicken, beef curry, stewed fish, and vegetables. Dessert may be homemade ice cream, ginger cake, or another delicious confection. ⊠ *Belmont, St. Patrick, St. Patrick, Grenada* ☎ *473/442–9524* ⊕ *www.belmontestate. net* ☾ *Closed Sat. No dinner.*

$$
CARIBBEAN
✕ **The Nutmeg.** West Indian specialties, fresh seafood, great hamburgers, and a waterfront view make the Nutmeg a favorite with locals and visitors alike. It's upstairs on the Carenage (above Sea Change bookstore), with large, open windows from which you can watch the harbor activity as you eat. Try the callaloo soup, curried lambi, fresh seafood, or a steak—or just stop by for a roti and a rum punch. ⊠ *The Carenage, St. George's, St. George, Grenada* ☎ *473/440–2539.*

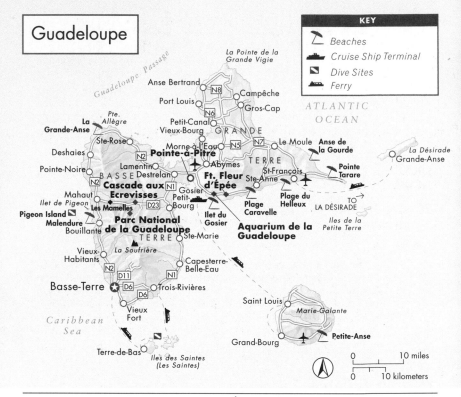

GUADELOUPE (POINTE-À-PITRE)

Eileen Robinson Smith

On a map, Guadeloupe looks like a giant butterfly resting on the sea between Antigua and Dominica. Its two wings—Basse-Terre and Grande-Terre—are the two largest islands in the 659-square-mi (1,054-square-km) Guadeloupe archipelago. The Rivière Salée, a 4-mi (6-km) channel between the Caribbean and the Atlantic, forms the "spine" of the butterfly. A drawbridge near Pointe-à-Pitre, the main city, connects the two islands. Gorgeous scenery awaits, as Guadeloupe is one of the most physically attractive islands in the Caribbean. If you're seeking a resort atmosphere, casinos, and nearly white sandy beaches, your target is Grande-Terre. On the other hand, Basse-Terre's Parc National de la Guadeloupe, laced with trails and washed by waterfalls and rivers, is a 74,100-acre haven for hikers, nature lovers, and anyone brave enough to peer into the steaming crater of an active volcano. The tropical beauty suggests the mythical Garden of Eden.

ESSENTIALS

CURRENCY The euro (€1 to US$1.42). Some of the larger liquor and jewelry stores may accept dollars, but don't count on that. You cannot cash traveler's checks or dollars at the bank, only at a bureau de change, so ATMs are your best bet if you need euros; facing the tourist office, there is one just to the right at the bank.

INTERNET Pointe-à-Pitre has several Internet cafés (there is one right at the new cruise pier); the tourist office can point you in the direction of several more in the immediate vicinity.

TELEPHONE To call the United States from Guadeloupe, dial 001, the area code, and the local number. For calls within Guadeloupe, you now have to put 0590 before the six-digit number. You'll need to purchase a *télécarte* at the post office or at tobacco and grocery shops in order to use the phone booths.

COMING ASHORE

Ships now dock at the new cruise terminal at Pier 5/6, which houses an Internet café, a duty-free shop, and the colorful Karuland Village, where cruisers can browse and buy spices, pareos, and souvenirs or just sit and listen to the local music while having coconut ice cream. In downtown Pointe-à-Pitre, it is about a five-minute walk from the shopping district. Passengers are greeted by local musicians and hostesses, usually dressed in the traditional madras costumes—and often dispensing samplings of local rum and creole specialties. These multilingual staffers operate the information booth and can pair you up with an English-speaking taxi driver for a customized island tour. To get to the main tourist office, walk along the quay to the Place de la Victoire; it is a large white Victorian building with wraparound veranda.

Taxis are metered.and expensive; during rush hour, they can be *very* expensive. Renting a car is a good way to see Guadeloupe, but it is expensive and best booked in advance. Be aware that traffic around Pointe-à-Pitre can be dreadful during rush hour, so allow plenty of time to drop off your car rental and get back to the ship. There are many rental agencies at the airport, but that is a €35 taxi ride from the city at least.

EXPLORING GUADELOUPE

☾ **Aquarium de la Guadeloupe.** Unique in the Antilles, this aquarium in the marina near Pointe-à-Pitre is a good place to spend an hour. The well-planned facility has an assortment of tropical fish, crabs, lobsters, moray eels, coffer fish, and some live coral. It's also a fascinating turtle rescue center and a spectacular shark tank. ⊠ *Pl. Créole off rte. N4, Pointe-à-Pitre, Grande-Terre, Guadeloupe* ☎ *0590/90–92–38* ⊠ *€10* ☾ *Daily 9–7.*

Ft. Fleur d'Épée. The main attraction in Bas-du-Fort is this 18th-century fortress, which hunkers down on a hillside behind a deep moat. It was the scene of hard-fought battles between the French and the English in 1794. You can explore its well-preserved dungeons and battlements and take in a sweeping view of Îles des Saintes and Marie-Galante. ⊠ *Bas-du-Fort, Grande-Terre, Guadeloupe* ☎ *0590/90–94–61* ⊠ *€6* ☾ *Mon. 10–5, Tues.–Sun. 9–5.*

★ **Parc National de la Guadeloupe.** This 74,100-acre park has been recognized by UNESCO as a Biosphere Reserve. The park is bisected by the route de la Traversée, a 16-mi (26-km) paved road lined with masses of tree ferns, shrubs, flowers, tall trees, and green plantains. It's the ideal point of entry. Wear rubber-soled shoes and take along a swimsuit, a sweater, and perhaps food for a picnic. Check on the weather; if Basse-Terre has had a lot of rain, give it up. In the past, after intense rainfall, rockslides have closed the road for months. ⊠ *Administrative Headquarters, rte. de la Traversée, St-Claude, Basse-Terre, Guadeloupe* ☎ *0590/80–86–00* ⊕ *www. guadeloupe-parcnational.com* 🎫 *Free* 🕙 *Weekdays 8–5:30.*

Cascade aux Ecrevisses. Within the Parc National de la Guadeloupe, Crayfish Falls is one of the island's loveliest (and most popular) spots. There's a marked trail (walk care-

---

GUADELOUPE BEST BETS

■ **Beaches.** The southern coast of Grand-Terre has stretches of soft, nearly white sand.

■ **Diving.** Jacques Cousteau called the reef off Pigeon Island one of the world's top dive sites.

■ **Hiking.** The Parc National de la Guadeloupe is one of the Caribbean's most spectacular scenic destinations.

■ **Shopping.** Though Point-à-Pitre itself can be frenetic, it does have a good choice of French goods.

---

fully—the rocks can be slippery) leading to this splendid waterfall, which dashes down into the Corossol River—a good place for a dip. Come early, though; otherwise you definitely won't have it to yourself. ⊠ *Basse-Terre, Guadeloupe.*

Pointe-à-Pitre. Although not the capital, this is the island's largest city, a commercial and industrial hub in the southwest of Grande-Terre. The Isles of Guadeloupe have 450,000 inhabitants, 99.6% of whom live in the cities. Pointe-à-Pitre is bustling, noisy, and hot—a place of honking horns and traffic jams and cars on sidewalks for want of a parking place. By day its pulse is fast, but at night, when its streets are almost deserted, you don't want to be there.

The Centre St-John Perse has transformed old warehouses into a cruise-terminal complex that consists of the spartan Hotel St-John, restaurants, shops, and the port authority headquarters. An impressive terminal serves the ferries that depart for Iles des Saintes, Marie-Galante, Dominica, Martinique, and St. Lucia.

The heart of the old city is Place de la Victoire; surrounded by wooden buildings with balconies and shutters (including the tourism office) and by sidewalk cafés, it was named in honor of Victor Hugues's 1794 victory over the British. During the French Revolution, Hugues ordered the guillotine set up here so that the public could witness the bloody end of 300 recalcitrant royalists.

Even more colorful is the bustling marketplace, between rues St-John Perse, Frébault, Schoelcher, and Peynier. It's a cacophonous place, where housewives bargain for spices, herbs (and herbal remedies), and a bright assortment of papayas, breadfruits, christophenes, and tomatoes. ⊠ *Grande-Terre, Guadeloupe.*

Cathédrale de St-Pierre et St-Paul. For fans of French ecclesiastical architecture, there's the imposing Cathédrale de St-Pierre et St-Paul, built in 1807. Although battered by hurricanes, it has fine stained-glass windows and Creole-style balconies and is reinforced with pillars and ribs that look like leftovers from the Eiffel Tower. ⊠ *Rue Alexandre Isaac at rue de l'Eglise, Grande-Terre, Guadeloupe.*

Musée St-John Perse. Anyone with an interest in French literature and culture (not your average sightseer) won't want to miss the museum dedicated to Guadeloupe's most famous son and one of the giants of world literature, Alexis Léger, better known as St-John Perse, winner of the Nobel Prize for literature in 1960. Some of his finest poems are inspired by the history and landscape—particularly the sea—of his beloved Guadeloupe. Before you go, look for his birthplace at 54 rue Achille René-Boisneuf. ⊠ *At rues Noizières and Achille René-Boisneuf, Grande-Terre, Guadeloupe* ☎ *0590/90–01–92* 🖼 *€2.50* ◷ *Thurs.–Tues. 8:30–12:30 and 2:30–5:30.*

Musée Schoelcher. Musée Schoelcher celebrates Victor Schoelcher, a high-minded abolitionist from Alsace who fought against slavery in the French West Indies in the 19th century. The museum contains many of his personal effects, and exhibits trace his life and work. ⊠ *24 rue Peynier, Grande-Terre, Guadeloupe* ☎ *0590/82–08–04* 🖼 *€3* ◷ *Weekdays 9–5.*

SHOPPING

For serious shopping in Pointe-à-Pitre, browse the boutiques and stores along rue Schoelcher, rue Frébault, and rue Noizières. The multicolored market square and stalls of La Darse are filled mostly with vegetables, fruits, delicious homemade rum liqueurs, and housewares. The air is filled with the fragrance of spices, and they have lovely gift baskets of spices and vanilla lined with madras fabric.

Dody. Across from the market, Dody is the place to go if you want white eyelet (blouses, skirts, dresses, even bustiers). The shop has a high-quality designer line, but you will pay €100 to €300 for a single piece. There's lots of madras, too, which is especially cute in children's clothing. ⊠ *31 rue Frébault, Pointe-à-Pitre, Grande-Terre, Guadeloupe* ☎ *0590/82–18–59.*

Vendôme. Vendôme is Guadeloupe's exclusive purveyor of Stendhal and Germaine Monteil cosmetics. ⊠ *8–10 rue Frébault, Pointe-à-Pitre, Grande-Terre, Guadeloupe* ☎ *0590/83–42–84.*

ACTIVITIES

DIVING

The main diving area at the **Cousteau Underwater Park,** just off Basse-Terre near Pigeon Island, offers routine dives to 60 feet. The numerous glass-bottom boats and other crafts make the site feel like a marine parking lot; however, the underwater sights are spectacular. Guides and instructors are certified under the French CMAS (some also have PADI, but none have NAUI). Most operators offer two-hour dives three times per day for about €45 to €50 per dive; three-dive packages are €120 to €145. Hotels and dive operators usually rent snorkeling gear.

☺ **Les Heures Saines.** Les Heures Saines is the premier operator for dives in the Cousteau Underwater Park. Trips to Les Saintes offer one or two dives for average and advanced divers, with plenty of time for lunch and sightseeing. Wreck, night, and Nitrox diving are also available. The instructors, many of them English speakers, are excellent with children. ⊠ *Le Rocher de Malendure, Plage de Malendure, Bouillante, Basse-Terre, Guadeloupe* ☏ *0590/98–86–63* ⊕ *www.heures-saines.gp.*

HIKING

Fodor's Choice
★ With hundreds of trails and countless rivers and waterfalls, the **Parc National de la Guadeloupe** on Basse-Terre is the main draw for hikers. Some of the trails should be attempted only with an experienced guide. All tend to be muddy, so wear a good pair of boots. Know that even the young and fit can find these outings arduous; the unfit may find them painful.

Vert Intense. Vert Intense organizes fascinating hikes in the national park and to the volcano. You move from steaming hot springs to an icy waterfall in the same hike. Guides are patient and safety-conscious, and can bring you to heights that you never thought you could reach, including the top of Le Soufrière. TThe French-speaking guides, who also know some English and Spanish, can take you to other tropical forests and rivers, where the sport of canyoning can still be practiced. If you are just one or two people, the company can team you up with a group. ⊠ *Rte. de la Soufrière, Mourne Houel, Basse-Terre, Guadeloupe* ☏ *0590/99–34–73 or 0690/55–40–47* ⊕ *www.vert-intense.com.*

BEACHES

★ **Plage Caravelle.** Just southwest of Ste-Anne is one of Grande-Terre's longest and prettiest stretches of sand, the occasional dilapidated shack notwithstanding. Protected by reefs, it's also a fine snorkeling spot. Club med occupies one end of this beach, and nonguests can enjoy its beach and water sports, as well as lunch and drinks, by buying a day pass. You can also have lunch on the terrace of La Toubana Hotel & Spa. ⊠ *Rte. N4, southwest of Ste-Anne, Grande-Terre, Guadeloupe.*

La Grande-Anse. One of Guadeloupe's widest beaches has soft beige sand sheltered by palms. To the west it's a round verdant mountain. It has a large parking area and some food stands, but no other facilities. Right after the parking lot, you can see signage for the creole restaurant Le Karacoli; if you have lunch there (it's not inexpensive), you can *sieste* on the chaise longues. ⊠ *Rte. N6, north of Deshaies, Basse-Terre, Guadeloupe.*

Malendure. Across from Pigeon Island and the Jacques Cousteau Underwater Park, this long, gray, volcanic beach on the Caribbean's calm waters has restrooms, a few beach shacks offering cold drinks and snacks, and a huge parking lot. There might be some litter, but the beach is cleaned regularly. The snorkeling here is good. Le Rocher de Malendure, a fine seafood restaurant, is perched on a cliff over the bay. ⊠ *Rte. N6, Bouillante, Basse-Terre, Guadeloupe.*

WHERE TO EAT

$ ✕ **Caraïbes Café.** This sidewalk café straight out of Paris is the "in"
CAFÉ place for lunch and also a spot for a quick breakfast, a fresh juice
cocktail—try *corossel* (a tropical fruit) and mango juices, a cappuccino,
un coupe (a sundae), or a pastis while you people-watch and listen to
French crooners. The *formule* (fixed-price menu) is always the best
deal. Service is fast and friendly and can even be in English. ✉ *Pl. de la
Victoire, Pointe-à-Pitre, Grande-Terre, Guadeloupe* ☎ *0590/82–92–23*
⊘ *Closed Sun. No dinner.*

$$$ ✕ **Le Rocher de Malendure.** Guests first climb the worn yellow stairs for
FRENCH the panoramic sea views, but return again and again for the food. If
★ you arrive before noon, when the divers pull in, you might snag one of
the primo tables in a gazebo that literally hangs over the Caribbean.
Begin with a perfectly executed mojito. With fish just off the boat, don't
hesitate to try the sushi *antillaise* or grilled crayfish and lobster from the
pool. ✉ *Bord de Mer, Malendure de Pigeon, Bouillante, Basse-Terre,
Guadeloupe* ☎ *0590/98–70–84* ⊘ *Closed Wed. and Sept.–early Oct.*

KEY WEST, FLORIDA

Chelle Koster
Walton and
Paul Rubio

Along with the rest of Florida, Key West—the southernmost city in the
continental United States—became part of American territory in 1821.
In the late 19th century it was Florida's wealthiest city per capita. The
locals made their fortunes from "wrecking"—rescuing people and sal-
vaging cargo from ships that foundered on nearby reefs. Cigar making,
fishing, shrimping, and sponge gathering also became important indus-
tries. Locally dubbed the "Conch Republic," Key West today makes for
a unique port of call. A genuinely American town, it nevertheless exudes
the relaxed atmosphere and pace of a typical Caribbean island. Major
attractions include the home of the Conch Republic's most famous
residents, Ernest Hemingway and Harry Truman; the imposing Key
West Museum of Art and History, a former U.S. Customs House and
site of the military inquest of the USS *Maine*; and the island's renowned
sunset celebrations.

7

ESSENTIALS

CURRENCY The U.S. dollar.

INTERNET Get your morning (or afternoon) buzz at **Coffee Plantation**, and hook
up to the Internet in the comfort of a homelike setting in a circa-1890
Conch house. Munch on sandwiches, wraps, and pastries, and sip a hot
or cold espresso beverage. ✉ *713 Caroline St.* ☎ *305/295–9808* ⊕ *www.
coffeeplantationkeywest.com.*

TELEPHONE You'll be able to find plenty of public phones around Mallory Square.
They're also along the major tourist thoroughfares.

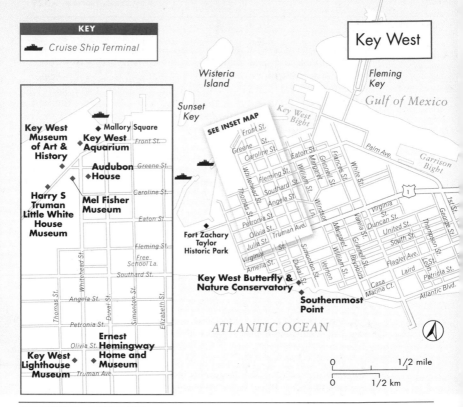

Key West

Wisteria
Island

Sunset
Key

SEE INSET MAP

Key West
Bight

Fleming
Key

Gulf of Mexico

Garrison
Bight

Key West
Museum
of Art &
History

Mallory Square

Key West
Aquarium

Front St.

Audubon
House

Greene St.

Caroline St.

Harry S
Truman
Little White
House
Museum

Mel Fisher
Museum

Eaton St.

Fleming St.

Free
School La.

Southard St.

Thomas St.

Angela St.

Duval St.

Simonton St.

Elizabeth St.

Petronia St.

Whitehead St.

Ernest
Hemingway
Home and
Museum

Olivia St.

Key West
Lighthouse
Museum

Truman Ave.

Front St.

Greene St.

Caroline St.

Eaton St.

Fleming St.

Southard St.

Angela St.

Petronia St.

Olivia St.

Julia St.

Virginia
St.

Amelia St.

Whitehead St.

Thomas St.

Truman Ave.

Duval St.

Margaret St.

Elizabeth St.

William St.

Windsor
Ln.

Simonton St.

Vernon

Eaton St.

Grinnell St.

Francis St.

White St.

Margaret St.

Reynolds

William St.

Grinnell St.

Palm Ave.

Varela St.

Duncan St.

United St.

South St.

Flagler Ave.

Casa
Marina Ct.

Virginia
St.

Thompson St.

Laird

George St.

Leon

St.

Patricia St.

Atlantic Blvd.

Fort Zachary
Taylor
Historic Park

Key West Butterfly &
Nature Conservatory

Southernmost
Point

ATLANTIC OCEAN

0   1/2 mile

0   1/2 km

COMING ASHORE

Cruise ships dock at three different locations. Mallory Square and Pier B are within walking distance of Duval and Whitehead streets, the two main tourist thoroughfares. Passengers on ships that dock at Outer Mole Pier (aka Navy Mole) are shuttled via Conch Train or Old Town Trolley to Mallory Square. Because Key West is so easily explored on foot, there is rarely a need to hire a taxi. If you plan to venture beyond the main tourist district, a fun way to get around is by bicycle or scooter (bike rentals begin at about $12 per day). Key West is a cycling town. In fact, there are so many bikes around that cyclists must watch out for one another as much as for cars. You can get tourist information from the Greater Key West Chamber of Commerce, which is located one block off Duval Street, at 510 Greene Street, in the old "city hall."

The Conch Tour Train can be boarded at Mallory Square or Flagler Station every half-hour; it costs $29 per adult for the 90-minute tour. The Old Town Trolley operates trolley-style buses starting from Mallory Square every 30 minutes for the same price, but the smaller trolleys go places the train won't fit. The Old Town Trolley also has pick up and drop off locations at numerous points around the island.

EXPLORING KEY WEST

Audubon House and Tropical Gardens.
If you've ever seen an engraving by ornithologist John James Audubon, you'll understand why his name is synonymous with birds. See his works in this three-story house, which was built in the 1840s for Captain John Geiger and filled with period furniture. It now commemorates Audubon's 1832 stop in Key West while he was traveling through Florida to study birds. Docents lead a guided tour ($7.50) that points out the rare indigenous plants and trees in the garden. An art gallery sells lithographs of the artist's famed portraits. ✉ *205 Whitehead St.* ☎ *305/294-2116 or 877/294-2470* ⊕ *www.audubonhouse.com* 🎟 *$12; additional $7.50 for tours* ☉ *Daily 9:30–5, last tour starts at 4:30.*

KEY WEST BEST BETS

■ **Boat Cruise.** Being out on the water is what Key West is all about.

■ **Conch Train.** Hop aboard for a narrated tour of the town's tawdry past and rare architectural treasures.

■ **Duval Crawl.** Shop, eat, drink, repeat.

■ **Hemingway.** Visit Ernest Hemingway's historic home for a literary treat.

■ **Sunset in Mallory Square.** The nightly street party is the quintessential Key West experience.

7

★ **Ernest Hemingway Home and Museum.** Amusing anecdotes spice up the guided tours of Ernest Hemingway's home, built in 1801 by the town's most successful wrecker. While living here between 1931 and 1942, Hemingway wrote about 70% of his life's work, including classics like *For Whom the Bell Tolls.* Few of his belongings remain aside from some books, and there's little about his actual work, but photographs help you visualize his day-to-day life. The supposed six-toed descendants of Hemingway's cats—many named for actors, artists, authors, and even a hurricane—have free rein of the property. Tours begin every 10 minutes and take 30 minutes; then you're free to explore on your own. ✉ *907 Whitehead St.* ☎ *305/294-1136* ⊕ *www.hemingwayhome.com* 🎟 *$12* ☉ *Daily 9–5.*

★ **Fort Zachary Taylor Historic State Park.** Construction of the fort began in 1845 but was halted during the Civil War. The fort, finally completed in 1866, was also used in the Spanish-American War. Take a 30-minute guided walking tour of the redbrick fort, a National Historic Landmark, at noon and 2, or self-tour anytime between 8 and 5. One of its most popular features is its man-made beach, a rest stop for migrating birds in the spring and fall; there are also hiking and biking trails and a kayak launch. ✉ *Box 6565; end of Southard St., through Truman Annex* ☎ *305/292-6713* ⊕ *www.floridastateparks.org/forttaylor* 🎟 *$4.50 for 1 person, $7 for 2 people, 50¢ per additional person* ☉ *Daily 8–sunset, tours noon and 2.*

Harry S. Truman Little White House Museum. Recent renovations to this circa-1890 landmark have restored the home and gardens to the Truman era, down to the wallpaper pattern. Engaging 45-minute tours begin every 15 minutes until 4:30. They start with an excellent 10-minute video on the history of the property and Truman's visits. On the grounds of **Truman Annex,** a 103-acre former military parade grounds and barracks, the home served as a winter White House for presidents Truman, Eisenhower, and Kennedy. Visitors can do a self-guided botanical tour of the grounds with a free brochure from the museum store. ⊠ *111 Front St.* ☎ *305/294–9911* ⊕ *www.trumanlittlewhitehouse.com* ⊠ *$15* ⊙ *Daily 9–5, grounds 7–6; last tour at 4:30.*

> **USED BOOKS**
>
> Leave any paperback novels you have finished for the crew library. You will have more room in your suitcase, and crewmembers will have fresh reading material.

☺ ★ **Key West Butterfly & Nature Conservatory.** This air-conditioned refuge for butterflies, birds, and the human spirit gladdens the soul with hundreds of colorful wings—more than 45 species of butterflies alone—in a lovely glass-encased bubble. Waterfalls, artistic benches, paved pathways, birds, and lush, flowering vegetation elevate this above most butterfly attractions. The gift shop and gallery are worth a visit on their own. ⊠ *1316 Duval St.* ☎ *305/296–2988 or 800/839–4647* ⊕ *www.keywestbutterfly.com* ⊠ *$12* ⊙ *Daily 9–5 (last admission 4:30); gallery and shop open until 5:30.*

Key West Lighthouse Museum & Keeper's Quarters Museum. For the best view in town, climb the 88 steps to the top of this 1847 lighthouse. The 92-foot structure has a Fresnel lens, which was installed in the 1860s at a cost of $1 million. The keeper lived in the adjacent 1887 clapboard house, which now exhibits vintage photographs, ship models, nautical charts, and lighthouse artifacts from all along the Key reefs. A kids' room is stocked with books and toys. ⊠ *938 Whitehead St.* ☎ *305/295–6616* ⊕ *www.kwahs.com* ⊠ *$10* ⊙ *Daily 9:30–5; last admission at 4:30.*

Fodor's Choice ★ **Key West Museum of Art and History in the Custom House.** When Key West was designated a U.S. port of entry in the early 1820s, a customhouse was established. Salvaged cargoes from ships wrecked on the reefs were brought here, setting the stage for Key West to become—for a time—the richest city in Florida. The imposing redbrick-and-terra-cotta Richardsonian Romanesque–style building reopened as a museum and art gallery in 1999. ⊠ *281 Front St.* ☎ *305/295–6616* ⊕ *www.kwahs.com* ⊠ *$7* ⊙ *Daily 9:30–5.*

Mel Fisher Maritime Museum. In 1622 two Spanish galleons laden with riches from South America foundered in a hurricane 40 mi west of the Keys. In 1985 diver Mel Fisher recovered the treasures from the lost ships, the *Nuestra Señora de Atocha* and the *Santa Margarita.* Fisher's incredible adventure tracking these fabled hoards and battling the state of Florida for rights is as amazing as the loot you'll see, touch, and learn about in this museum. ⊠ *200 Greene St.* ☎ *305/294–2633* ⊕ *www.melfisher.org* ⊠ *$12* ⊙ *Weekdays 8:30–6, weekends 9:30–6 (last tickets sold at 5:15).*

The Southernmost Point. Possibly the most photographed site in Key West (even though the actual geographic southernmost point in the continental United States lies across the bay on a naval base, where you see a satellite dish), this is a must-see. Who wouldn't want his picture taken next to the big striped buoy that marks the southernmost point in the continental United States? ⊠ *Whitehead and South Sts.* ☎ *No phone.*

SHOPPING

On these streets you'll find colorful local art of widely varying quality, key limes made into everything imaginable, and the raunchiest T-shirts in the civilized world. Browsing the boutiques—with frequent pub stops along the way—makes for an entertaining stroll down Duval Street. Key West is filled with art galleries, and the variety is truly amazing. Much is locally produced by the town's large artist community, but many galleries carry international artists from as close as Haiti and as far away as France. Local artists do a great job of preserving the island's architecture and spirit.

Bahama Village. Where to start your shopping adventure? This cluster of spruced-up shops, restaurants, and vendors is responsible for the restoration of the colorful historic district where Bahamians settled in the 19th century. The village lies roughly between Whitehead and Fort streets and Angela and Catherine streets. Hemingway frequented the bars, restaurants, and boxing rings in this part of town.

★ **Fast Buck Freddie's.** Find a classy, hip selection of gifts, including every flamingo item imaginable here. It also has a whole department called "Tropical Trash," and carries such imaginative items as an electric fan in the shape of a rooster. ✉ *500 Duval St.* ☎ *305/294–2007* ⊕ *www. fastbuckfreddies.com.*

ACTIVITIES

BOAT TOURS

Lazy Dog Kayak Guides (✉ *5114 Overseas Hwy., Key West* ☎ *305/295– 9898* ⊕ *www.lazydog.com*) runs four-hour guided sea kayak–snorkel tours around the mangrove islands just east of Key West. The $60 charge covers transportation, bottled water, a snack, and supplies, including snorkeling gear. A $35 two-hour guided kayak tour is also available.

White Knuckle Thrill Boat Ride. For something with an adrenaline boost, book with this speedboat. It holds up to 10 people and does 360s, fishtails, and other water stunts in the gulf. Cost is $59 each, and includes pickup shuttle. ✉ *Sunset Marina, 555 College Rd., Key West* ☎ *305/797–0459* ⊕ *www.whiteknucklethrillboatride.com.*

DIVING AND SNORKELING

The Florida Keys National Marine Sanctuary extends along Key West and beyond to the Dry Tortugas. Key West National Wildlife Refuge further protects the pristine waters. Most divers don't make it this far out in the Keys, but if you're looking for a day of diving as a break from the nonstop party in Old Town, expect to pay about $45 and upward for a two-tank dive. Serious divers can book dive trips to the Dry Tortugas.

Captain's Corner. This PADI–certified dive shop has classes in several languages and twice-daily snorkel and dive trips ($40–$65) to reefs and wrecks aboard the 60-foot dive boat *Sea Eagle.* Use of weights, belts, masks, and fins is included. ✉ *125 Ann St.* ☎ *305/296–8865* ⊕ *www. captainscorner.com.*

Snuba of Key West. Safely dive the coral reefs without getting a scuba certification. Ride out to the reef on a catamaran, then follow your guide underwater for a one-hour tour of the coral reefs. You wear a regulator with a breathing hose that is attached to a floating air tank on the surface. No prior diving or snorkeling experience is necessary, but you must know how to swim. The $99 price includes beverages. ⊠ *Garrison Bight Marina, Palm Ave. between Eaton St. and N. Roosevelt Blvd.* ☎ *305/292–4616* ⊕ *www.snubakeywest.com.*

FISHING

Any number of local fishing guides can take you to where the big ones are biting, either in the backcountry for snapper and snook or to the deep water for the marlins and shark that brought Hemingway here in the first place.

Key West Bait & Tackle. Prepare to catch a big one with the live bait, frozen bait, and fishing equipment provided here. It also has the Live Bait Lounge, where you can sip ice-cold beer while telling fish tales. ⊠ *241 Margaret St.* ☎ *305/292–1961* ⊕ *www.keywestbaitandtackle.com.*

Key West Pro Guides. Trips include flats and backcountry fishing ($400–$425 for a half day) and reef and offshore fishing (starting at $550 for a half day). ⊠ *G-31 Miriam St.* ☎ *866/259–4205* ⊕ *www.keywestproguides.com.*

BEACHES

ⓒ **Fort Zachary Taylor Historic State Park.** The park's beach is the best and
★ safest place to swim in Key West. There's an adjoining picnic area with barbecue grills and shade trees, a snack bar, and rental equipment, including snorkeling gear. A café serves sandwiches and other munchies. Best for: history-lovers and families. ⊠ *Box 6565; end of Southard St., through Truman Annex* ☎ *305/292–6713* ⊕ *www.floridastateparks.org/forttaylor* ⊑ *$4.50 for 1 person, $7 for 2 people, 50¢ per additional person* ☉ *Daily 8–sunset, tours noon and 2.*

WHERE TO EAT

$$ ✕**El Meson de Pepe.** If you want to get a taste of the island's Cuban
CARIBBEAN heritage, this is the place. Perfect for after watching a Mallory Square sunset, you can dine alfresco or in the dining room on refined versions of Cuban classics. Begin with a megasized mojito while you enjoy the basket of bread and savory sauces. At lunch, the local Cuban population and cruise-ship passengers enjoy Cuban sandwiches and smaller versions of dinner's most popular entrées. A salsa band performs outside at the bar during sunset celebration. ⊠ *Mallory Sq., 410 Wall St.* ☎ *305/295–2620* ⊕ *www.elmesondepepe.com.*

¢ ✕**Lobo's Mixed Grill.** Famous for its selection of wrap sandwiches, Lobo
AMERICAN has a reputation among locals for its 8-ounce, charcoal-grilled ground
ⓒ chuck burger—thick and juicy and served with lettuce, tomato, and pickle on a toasted bun. Mix it up with toppings like Brie, blue cheese, or portobello mushroom. The menu of 30 wraps includes rib eye, oyster, grouper, Cuban, and chicken Caesar. The menu includes salads and quesadillas, as well as a fried-shrimp-and-oyster combo. Beer and wine are served. ⊠ *5 Key Lime Sq., east of intersection of Southard and Duval Sts.* ☎ *305/296–5303* ⊕ *www.loboskeywest.com* ⚐ *Reservations not accepted* ▭ *No credit cards* ☉ *Closed Sun. Apr.–early Dec.*

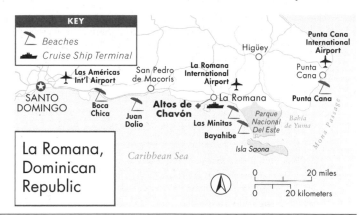

KEY

⚓ Beaches
⛴ Cruise Ship Terminal

Las Américas Int'l Airport
San Pedro de Macorís
La Romana International Airport
Higüey
Punta Cana International Airport
Punta Cana

SANTO DOMINGO
Boca Chica
Juan Dolio
Altos de Chavón
La Romana
Las Minitas
Bayahibe
Parque Nacional Del Este
Bahía de Yuma
Punta Cana
Mona Passage

La Romana, Dominican Republic

Caribbean Sea
Isla Saona

0   20 miles
0   20 kilometers

NIGHTLIFE

Three spots stand out for first-timers among the saloons frequented by Key West denizens. All are within easy walking distance of the cruise-ship piers.

Capt. Tony's Saloon. When it was the original Sloppy Joe's in the mid-1930s Hemingway was a regular. Later, a young Jimmy Buffett sang here and made this watering hole famous in his song "Last Mango in Paris." ✉ *428 Greene St.* ☎ *305/294-1838* ⊕ *www.capttonyssaloon.com.*

Schooner Wharf Bar. An open air waterfront bar and grill in the historic seaport district retains its funky Key West charm. Its margarita ranks among Key West's best. ✉ *202 William St.* ☎ *305/292-3302* ⊕ *www.schoonerwharf.com.*

Sloppy Joe's. There's history and good times at the successor to a famous 1937 speakeasy named for its founder, Captain Joe Russell. Decorated with Hemingway memorabilia and marine flags, the bar is popular with travelers and is full and noisy all the time. ✉ *201 Duval St.* ☎ *305/294-5717* ⊕ *www.sloppyjoes.com.*

LA ROMANA, DOMINICAN REPUBLIC

Eileen Robinson Smith

The Dominican Republic is a beautiful island bathed by the Atlantic Ocean to the north and the Caribbean Sea to the south, and some of its most beautiful beaches are in the area surrounding La Romana, notably Bayahibe Bay. The famed Casa de Campo resort and Marina will be the destination for most cruise passengers who land at La Romana's International Tourist Pier A port call here will allow you to explore the immediate region—even take a day-trip into Santo Domingo—or simply stay and enjoy some nice (but expensive) restaurants and shops. There is also a host of activities cruise passengers can take part in on organized shore excursions.

ESSENTIALS

CURRENCY The coin of the realm is the Dominican peso (approximately RD$36 to US$1 at this writing). The exchange rate fluctuates continuously, but one thing is certain, the Dominican Republic, although still a good value, is not the cheap date it was up until a couple of years ago.

7

TELEPHONE   Telephones are available at the dock, as soon as passengers disembark, and telephone cards can be purchased there as well. Tele-cards can also be bought at the supermarket at Casa de Campo Marina. To call the U.S. or Canada from the D.R., just punch in 1 plus the area code and number. To make calls on the island, you must tap in the area code (809), plus the seven-digit number; if you are calling a Dominican cell phone, you must first punch in 1 then 809 or 829. Unfortunately, there is no Internet café where cruise-ship passengers can access their email, either at the dock or at Casa de Campo.

COMING ASHORE

Ships enter the Casa de Campo International Tourist Port (Muelle Turïstico Internacional Casa de Campo). A group of folkloric dancers and local musicians, playing merengue, greets passengers as they come down the gangway. An information booth with English-speaking staffers is there to assist cruise-ship passengers; the desk is open the entire time the ship is in port.

It is a 15-minute walk into the town of La Romana, or you can jump into a waiting taxi. It's safe to stroll around town, but it's not particularly beautiful, quaint, or even historic; however, it is a real slice of Dominican life. Most people just board the complimentary shuttle and head for the Casa de Campo Marina and/or Altos de Chavón, both of which are at the Casa de Campo resort. Shuttles run all day long.

Taxis line up at the port's docks, and some, but not all, drivers speak English. Staff members from the information kiosk will help to make taxi arrangements. Most rates are fixed and spelled out on a board: $15 to Casa de Campo Marina, $20 to Altos de Chavón. You may be able to negotiate a somewhat lower rate if a group books a taxi for a tour. You can also rent a car at Casa de Campo from National Car Rental; rates are expensive, usually more than $70 a day. Driving into Santo Domingo can be a hair-raising experience, and isn't for the faint of heart, so we don't recommend it.

EXPLORING LA ROMANA

★ **Altos de Chavón.** This re-creation of a 16th-century Mediterranean village sits on a bluff overlooking the Río Chavón, about 3 mi (5 km) east of the main facilities of Casa de Campo. There are cobblestone streets lined with lanterns, wrought-iron balconies, wooden shutters, courtyards swathed with bougainvillea, and **Iglesia St. Stanislaus,** the romantic setting for many a Casa de Campo wedding. More than a museum piece, this village is a place where artists live, work, and play. The village also has a new sports bar, a trendy dance club (Onno's of Cabarete), an amber museum, an archaeological museum, a chic new cigar lounge, a designer jewelry store, boutiques, and restaurants.

Isla Saona. Off the east coast of Hispaniola lies this island, now a national park inhabited by sea turtles, pigeons, and other wildlife. Caves here were once used by Indians. The beaches are beautiful, and legend has it that Columbus once strayed here. Getting here, on catamarans and other excursion boats, is half the fun, but know that it can be a crowd scene.

Santo Domingo. Spanish civilization in the New World began in the 12-block Zona Colonial of Santo Domingo. Strolling its narrow streets, it's easy to imagine this old city as it was when the likes of Columbus, Cortés, and Ponce de León walked the cobblestones, pirates sailed in and out, and colonists were settling themselves. Tourist brochures tout that "history comes alive here"—a surprisingly truthful statement. A fun horse-and-carriage ride throughout the Zone costs $25 for an hour. The steeds are no thoroughbreds, but they clip right along, though any commentary will be in Spanish. The drivers usually hang out in front of the Hostal Nicolas de Ovando. History buffs will want to spend a day exploring the many "firsts" of our continent, which will be included in any cruise-ship excursion. Do wear comfortable shoes.

LA ROMANA BEST BETS

- **Altos de Chavón.** You'll find shopping and dining as well as great views.

- **Golf.** The Teeth of the Dog is one of the Caribbean's best courses despite the cost.

- **Horseback Riding.** Casa de Campo has an excellent equestrian center.

- **Isla Saona.** The powder-soft beach and beautiful water are excellent.

- **Kandela.** The tropical, Las Vegas-style review is a highlight if your ship stays late in port on a night it is performed.

SHOPPING

Altos de Chavón. This re-creation of a 16th-century Mediterranean village is on the grounds of the Casa de Campo resort, where you can find art galleries, boutiques, and souvenir shops grouped around a cobbled square. At the Altos de Chavón Art Studios you can find ceramics, weaving, and screen prints made by local artists. Extra special is Casa Montecristo, a chic cigar lounge, which also offers a tour with cigar history and trivia.

The Casa de Campo Marina. Casa de Campo's top-ranked marina is home to shops and international boutiques, galleries, and jewelers scattered amid restaurants, an ice-cream parlor, bars, banks, beauty salons, and a yacht club. It's a great place to spend some time shopping, sightseeing, and staring at the extravagant yachts. By the way, the Nacional supermercado at the marina has not only groceries but sundries, postcards, and snacks.

ACTIVITIES

Most activities available at Casa de Campo are open to cruise-ship passengers. You'll need to make reservations on the ship, particularly for golf

FISHING

Blue and white marlin, wahoo, sailfish, dorado, and mahimahi are among the most common catches in these waters.

Casa de Campo Marina (✉ *Casa de Campo, Calle Barlovento 3, La Romana* ☎ *809/523–864, Ext. 3165 or 3166* ⊕ *www.casadecampo.com. do*) is the best charter option in the La Romana area. Yachts (22 to 60 footers) are available for deep-sea fishing charters for half or full days. Prices go from $708 to $3,300. Boat excursions for river fishing are available as well. A three-hour excursion takes you down the Chavón River and past the lush vegetation of the bordering tropical forest, and you can go light-tackle angling for championship-size snook (a freshwater fish) as you do so. The price of $110 (minimum two people) includes boat, river guide, tackle, bait, water, and sodas.

> ### CABIN OUTLETS
>
> Most ships' cabins have only one or two electrical outlets located near the desk/vanity table (not counting the shaver-only outlet in the bathroom). A short extension cord allows you to use more than one electrical appliance at once, and gives you a bit more flexibility to move around, particularly if you bring a laptop computer.

GOLF

Fodor's Choice
★
The famed 18-hole Teeth of the Dog course at **Casa de Campo** (✉ *La Romana* ☎ *809/523–3333, 809/523–8115 golf director* ⊕ *www. casadecampo.com.do*), with seven holes on the sea, is often ranked as the number one course in the Caribbean, and is among the top courses in the world. In 2010 it was awarded a gold medal in the resorts category. Greens fees are $225 per round for each nonguest, and $160 for guests, as well as $25 (plus tip) for a mandatory caddy. Pete Dye has designed this and two other globally acclaimed courses here: Dye Fore, with 18 holes close to Altos de Chavón, hugs a cliff that looks over the sea, a river, and the stunning marina ($225 for nonguests, $160 guests); the Links is an 18-hole inland course ($150 and $130).

HORSEBACK RIDING

The 250-acre **Equestrian Center at Casa de Campo** (✉ *La Romana* ☎ *809/523–3333* ⊕ *www.casadecampo.com.do*) has something for both Western and English riders—a dude ranch, a rodeo arena (where Casa's trademark "Donkey Polo" is played), guided trail rides, and jumping and riding lessons. Guided rides run about $56 an hour, $88 for two hours; lessons cost $65 an hour, and jumping lessons are $88 an hour or $55 a half hour. There are early morning and sunset trail rides, too. Handsome, old-fashioned carriages are available for hire as well.

BEACHES

Cruise passengers can buy a day-pass to use the beach and facilities at Casa de Campo ($75 for adults, $45 for children 4–12 years); with that, you get a place in the sun at **Minitas Beach**, towels, nonmotorized water sports, lunch in the Beach Club, and entrance to Altos de Chavón. Otherwise, excursions (sometimes cheaper) are available to several area beaches.

Catalina Island is a diminutive, picture-postcard Caribbean island off the coast of the mainland. Catalina is about a half-hour away by catamaran, and most excursions offer the use of snorkeling equipment as well as a beach barbecue. **Playa Bayahibe** is a beautiful stretch of beach. Shore excursions are organized by the cruise lines to the beach, which is about 30 minutes away from the cruise port by bus. You can also book your own taxi here, and the trip may be cheaper than the cost of a shore excursion if you come with a group. **Saona Island** was once a pristine, idyllic isle. Now, on a busy cruise-ship day there may be as many as 1,000 swimmers there. However, the beach is beautiful. Excursions here usually include a powerboat ride from Casa de Campo Marina; otherwise, you are bused to Bayahibe and board a boat there.

WHERE TO EAT

$$-$$$ ✗ **Peperoni.** Although the name sounds as Italian as *amore,* this restau-
ITALIAN rant's menu is much more eclectic than Italian. It has a classy, contemporary, white-dominated decor; waiters are also dressed in white with long aprons. The marina setting is dreamy—you drink quietly, perhaps dreaming that you have just disembarked from one of the million-dollar yachts. Desserts are worthy here, including a tart key lime paired with mango sorbet. ⊠ *Casa de Campo, Plaza Portafino 16, Casa de Campo Marina, La Romana* ☎ *809/523–2228.*

MARTINIQUE (FORT-DE-FRANCE)

Eileen Robin The largest of the Windward Islands, Martinique is 4,261 mi (6,817 km)
son Smith from Paris, but its spirit and language are decidedly French, with more than a soupçon of West Indian spice. Tangible, edible evidence of the fact is the island's cuisine, a superb blend of French and creole. Martinique is lushly landscaped with tropical flowers. Trees bend under the weight of fruits such as mangoes, papayas, lemons, limes, and bright-red West Indian cherries. Acres of banana plantations, pineapple fields, and waving sugarcane stretch to the horizon. The towering mountains and verdant rain forest in the north lure hikers, while underwater sights and sunken treasures attract snorkelers and scuba divers. Martinique is also wonderful if your idea of exercise is turning over every 10 minutes to get an even tan and your taste in adventure runs to duty-free shopping. A popular excursion goes to St-Pierre, which was buried by ash when Mount Pelée erupted in 1902.

ESSENTIALS

CURRENCY The euro (€1 to US$1.42). You will not be able to use dollars, so plan on getting some euros. You cannot cash traveler's checks or dollars at the bank, only at a bureau de change, so ATMs are your best bet if you need euros. There is a change office at the beginning of Ernest Deproge Street next to the Banque Francaise. Change Caraïbes—is at 14 rue Victor Hugo and Le Bord de Mer. They will still exchange both dollars and traveler's checks and usually offer fair rates.

INTERNET **Cyber Club Caraïbe** (⊠ *16 rue François Arago, Fort-de-France* ☎ *0596/70–31 62* ⊕ *www.cyberclubcaraibe.com*). **Internet Haut Depot** (⊠ *61 rue Victor Hugo, Fort-de-France* ☎ *0596/63–12–20*).

TELEPHONE There are no coin-operated phone booths. Public phones now use a *télécarte,* which you can buy at post offices, café-tabacs, hotels, and *bureaux de change.* To call the United States from Martinique, dial 00 + 1,

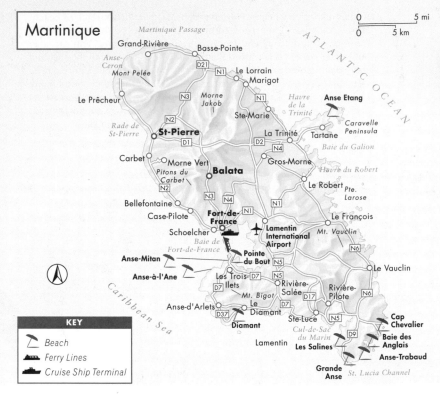

Martinique

Martinique Passage

ATLANTIC OCEAN

Grand-Rivière
Anse-Céron
Basse-Pointe
Mont Pelée
D21
N1
Le Lorrain
Marigot
N1
Le Prêcheur
N3
Morne Jakob
Havre de la Trinité
Anse Etang
Ste-Marie
Caravelle Peninsula
Rade de St-Pierre
N2
St-Pierre
La Trinité
Tartane
D1
D2
N4
Baie du Galion
Carbet
Morne Vert
Gros-Morne
N2
Pitons du Carbet
Balata
Havre du Robert
N3
N4
Le Robert
Pte. Larose
Bellefontaine
N1
Case-Pilote
Fort-de-France
N1
Le François
Schoelcher
Lamentin International Airport
Mt. Vauclin
N6
Baie de Fort-de-France
Anse-Mitan
Pointe du Bout
N5
Le Vauclin
Anse-à-l'Ane
N5
Les Trois-Ilets
D7
Rivière-Salée
Rivière-Pilote
N6
D7
Mt. Bigot
D17
Anse-d'Arlets
D7
Le Diamant
Ste-Luce
N5
Cap Chevalier
D37
Diamant
Cul-de-Sac du Marin
D9
Baie des Anglais
Lamentin
Les Salines
Anse-Trabaud
Grande Anse
St. Lucia Channel
Caribbean Sea

KEY
- Beach
- Ferry Lines
- Cruise Ship Terminal

0   5 mi
0   5 km

the area code, and the local seven-digit number. To call locally, you now have to dial 0596 before the six-digit number. You can make collect calls to Canada through the Bell operator; you can get the AT&T or MCI operators from blue, special-service phones at the cruise ports and in town (try Super Sumo snack bar, on rue de la Liberté, near the library).

COMING ASHORE

Most cruise ships call either at Tourelles (in the old port, about 1½ mi [2 km] from Fort-de-France) or at Pointe Simon, right in downtown Fort-de-France. (It is rare to have a ship anchor in the Baie des Flamands and tender passengers ashore.) Tourist information offices are at each cruise terminal. Uniformed dispatchers assist passengers in finding English-speaking taxi drivers. Passengers who do not wish to walk 20 minutes into Fort-de-France from Tourelles can take a taxi (set rate of €8 for up to four passengers in a van, or €2 for each additional passenger). Expect to pay about €40 per hour for touring; in larger vans the price is usually €10 per person per hour. Independent cruisers can explore the capital and the nearby open-air market on their own. Beaming and knowledge-able hostesses in creole dress greet cruise passengers. Civilian auxiliary police (in blue and orange uniforms) supplement the regular police.

Know that traffic in Fort-de-France can be nightmarish. If you want to go to the beach, a much cheaper option is to take a ferry from Fort-de-France. *Vedettes* (ferries) operate daily between the waterfront pier next to the public land transport terminal and the marina in Pointe du Bout, Anse-Mitan, and Anse-à-l'Ane. Any of the three trips takes about 15 minutes, and the ferries operate about every 30 minutes on weekdays. Renting a car in Fort-de-France is possible, but the heavy traffic can be forbidding. Rates are about €70 per day (high season) for a car with manual transmission; automatics are substantially more expensive and seldom available without reservations.

MARTINIQUE BEST BETS

■ **Beaches.** If you want to relax, the most beautiful beach is Les Salines.

■ **French culture.** Excellent French food and music make this a *paradis* for Francophiles.

■ **La Route des Rhums.** Visit a distillery and become a rum connoisseur.

■ **Shopping.** Browse Fort-de-France's many upscale boutiques and department stores for French wares.

■ **St-Pierre.** Wander the narrow, winding streets of this hill town.

EXPLORING MARTINIQUE

If you want to see the lush island interior and St-Pierre on your own, take the N3, which snakes through dense rain forests, north through the mountains to Le Morne Rouge, then take the coastal N2 back to Fort-de-France via St-Pierre. You can do the 40-mi (64-km) round-trip in half a day, but your best option is to hire an English-speaking driver.

FORT DE FRANCE

With its historic fort and superb location beneath the towering Pitons du Carbet on the Baie des Flamands, Martinique's capital—home to about one-quarter of the island's 400,000 inhabitants—should be a grand place. It hasn't been for decades but it's now coming up fast. An ambitious redevelopment project, still under way, hopes to make it one of the most attractive cities in the Caribbean. The most pleasant districts, such as Didier, Bellevue, and Schoelcher, are on the hillside, reachable only by car or taxi; there are some good shops with Parisian wares and lively street markets. Near the harbor is a marketplace where local crafts and souvenirs are sold. The urban beach between the waterfront and the fort, La Française, has been cleaned up; white sand was brought in, and many cruise-ship passengers frequent it. The new Stewards Urbaine, easily recognized by their red caps and uniforms, are able to answer most visitor questions and give directions.

Bibliothèque Schoelcher. This wildly elaborate Romanesque public library was named after Victor Schoelcher, who led the fight to free the slaves in the French West Indies in the 19th century. The eye-popping structure was built for the 1889 Paris Exposition, after which it was dismantled, shipped to Martinique, and reassembled piece by ornate piece. ⊠ *At rue de la Liberté, which runs along west side of La Savane* ☎ *0596/70–26–67* 🖾 *Free* ⊙ *Mon. 1–5:30, Tues.–Fri. 8:30–5:30, Sat. 8:30–noon.*

La Savane. The heart of Fort-de-France, La Savane is a 12½-acre park filled with trees, fountains, and benches. This urban park has undergone a massive revitalization, completed in late 2010. It is a focal point of the city again, with entertainment and shopping and a pedestrian mall.

> **PRE-PACK**
>
> Set aside a few moments every day to pack up your dirty clothes, then spend the last afternoon of your cruise doing fun things instead of packing.

Attractive wooden stands have been constructed along the edge of the park that house a tourism information office, public restrooms, arts and crafts vendors, a crepe stand, and an ice-cream parlor. Diagonally across from La Savane, you can catch the ferries for the 20-minute run across the bay to Pointe du Bout and the beaches at Anse-Mitan and Anse-à-l'Ane. It's relatively cheap as well as stress-free—much safer, more pleasant, and faster than by car.

★ **Le Musée Régional d'Histoire et d'Ethnographie.** Housed in an elaborate former residence (circa 1888) with balconies and fretwork, the museum has everything from displays of the garish gold jewelry that prostitutes wore after emancipation to reconstructed rooms of a home of proper, middle-class Martinicans. There's even a display of Creole headdresses with details of how they were tied to indicate if a woman was single, married, or otherwise occupied. ⊠ *10 bd. Général de Gaulle* ☎ *0596/72–81–87* 🖭 *€3* ⊗ *Mon. and Wed.–Fri. 8:30–5, Tues. 2–5, Sat. 8:30–noon.*

Rue Victor Schoelcher. Stores sell Paris fashions and French perfume, china, crystal, and liqueurs, as well as local handicrafts along this street running through the center of the capital's primary shopping district, a six-block area bounded by rue de la République, rue de la Liberté, rue Victor Severe, and rue Victor Hugo.

St-Louis Cathedral. The Romanesque cathedral with its lovely stained-glass windows was built in 1878, the sixth church on this site (the others were destroyed by fires, hurricanes, and earthquakes). ⊠ *Rue Victor Schoelcher, Schoelcher, Martinique.*

ELSEWHERE ON MARTINIQUE

Balata. This quiet little town has two sights worth visiting. Built in 1923 to commemorate those Martinicans who fought and died in World War I, **Balata Church** is an exact replica of Paris's Sacré-Coeur Basilica. **Jardin de Balata** (*Balata Gardens*). The Jardin de Balata has thousands of varieties of tropical flowers and plants. This worthy site explains why Martinique is called the Island of Flowers. ⊠ *Rte. de Balata, Balata, Martinique* ☎ *0596/64–48–73* ⊕ *www.jardindebalata.com* 🖭 *€12.50* ⊗ *Daily 9–5* ⊠ *Schoelcher, Martinique.*

St-Pierre. The rise and fall of St-Pierre is one of the most remarkable stories in the Caribbean. Martinique's modern history began here in 1635. By the turn of the 20th century St-Pierre was a flourishing city of 30,000, known as the Paris of the West Indies. As many as 30 ships at a time stood at anchor. By 1902 it was the most modern town in the Caribbean, with electricity, phones, and a tram. On May 8, 1902, two thunderous explosions rent the air. As the nearby volcano erupted, Mont Pelée split in half, belching forth a cloud of burning ash, poisonous gas, and lava that raced down the mountain at 250 mph. At 3,600°F, it instantly vaporized everything in its path; 30,000 people were killed in two minutes.

The **Cyparis Express,** a small tourist train, will take you around to the main sights with running narrative (in French) for a half hour on Saturday, an hour on weekdays, for €10 (€5 for children).

An Office du Tourisme is on the *moderne* seafront promenade. Stroll the main streets and check the blackboards at the sidewalk cafés before deciding where to lunch. Like stage sets for a dramatic opera, there are the ruins of the island's first church (built in 1640), the imposing theater, and the toppled statues. This city, situated on its naturally beautiful harbor and with its narrow, winding streets, has the feel of a European seaside hill town.

Musée Vulcanologique Frank Perret. For those interested in the eruption of 1902, the Musée Vulcanologique Frank Perret is a must. Established in 1933 by a noted American volcanologist, the museum houses photographs of the old town, documents, and a number of relics—some gruesome—excavated from the ruins, including molten glass, melted iron, and contorted clocks stopped at 8 am. An English-speaking guide is often available. ⊠ *Rue Victor Hugo* ☎ *0596/78–15–16* ☜ *€3* ⊘ *Daily 9–5.*

Le Centre de Découverte des Sciences de la Terre. Housed in a sleek building that looks like a dramatic white box, this earth-science museum has high-tech exhibits and interesting films. Watch the documentary on the volcanoes in the Antilles, highlighting the eruption of the nearby Mont Pelée. This site has fascinating summer programs on Wednesday on dance, cuisine, and ecotourism. ⊠ *Habitation Perinelle* ☎ *0596/52–82–42* ⊕ *www.cdst.cg972.fr* ☜ *€5* ⊘ *Tues.–Sun. 9–4:30, 9–5:30 in July and Aug.*

Depaz Distillery. An excursion to Depaz Distillery is one of the island's nicest treats. Established in 1651, for four centuries it has sat at the foot of the volcano. Following a devastating eruption in 1902, the fields of blue cane were replanted and in time, the rum making began all over again. A self-guided tour includes the workers' gingerbread cottages, and sometimes there will be an exhibit of art and sculpture made from wooden casks and parts of distillery machinery. The tasting room sells its rums, including golden and aged rum and distinctive liqueurs made from orange, ginger, and basil, among others, that can add creativity to your cooking. The plantation's greathouse, or chateau, has also opened for public tours. A recommendable restaurant, Le Moulin a Canne, serves creole specialties and—you guessed it—Depaz rum to wash it down. ⊠ *Mont Pelée Plantation* ☎ *0596/78–13–14* ⊕ *www.depazrhum. com* ☜ *Free (for the distillery)* ⊘ *Weekdays 10–5, Sat. 9–4*

SHOPPING

French fragrances, designer scarves and sunglasses, fine china and crystal, leather goods, wine (amazingly inexpensive at supermarkets), and liquor are all good buys in Fort-de-France. Purchases are further sweetened by the 20% discount on luxury items when paid for with certain credit cards.

Among the items produced on the island, look for *bijoux creole* (local jewelry, such as hoop earrings and heavy bead necklaces), white and dark rum, and handcrafted straw goods, pottery, and tapestries.

The area around the cathedral in Fort-de-France has a number of small shops that carry luxury goods. Of particular note are the shops on rue Victor Hugo, rue Moreau de Jones, rue Antoine Siger, and rue Lamartine. The **Galleries Lafayette** department store on rue Schoelcher in downtown Fort-de-France sells everything from perfume to pâté.

ACTIVITIES

FISHING

Deep-sea fishing expeditions in these waters hunt down tuna, barracuda, dolphin fish, kingfish, and bonito, and the big ones—white and blue marlins. You can hire boats from the bigger marinas, particularly in Pointe du Bout, Le Marin, and Le François; most hotels arrange these Hemingway-esque trysts, but will often charge a premium. If you call several days in advance, companies can also put you together with other anglers to keep costs down.

The **Centre de Peche** (✉ *Port de Plaisance, bd. Allègre, Le Marin* ☎ *0596/76–24–20 or 0696/28–80–58*), a fully loaded Davis 47-foot fishing boat, is a sportfisherman's dream. It goes out with a minimum of five anglers for €195 per person for a half-day, or €390 per person for a full day, including lunch. Nonanglers can come for the ride for €95 and €190, respectively. Captain Yves speaks English fluently and is a fun guy.

GOLF

Golf de l'Impératrice Josephine. The 18-hole Le Golf de l'Impératrice Josephine has been renamed in honor of Empress Joséphine Napoléon, whose birthplace, La Pagerie, adjoins this 150-acre track of rolling hills. However, the course is 100% American in design. It is a par-71 Robert Trent Jones course with an English-speaking pro, pro shop, bar, and restaurant. The club offers special greens fees to cruise-ship passengers. There are no caddies. ✉ *Les Trois-Ilets* ☎ *0596/68–32–81.*

HIKING

Parc Naturel Régional de la Martinique. Two-thirds of Martinique is designated as protected land. Trails, all 31 of them, are well marked and maintained. At the beginning of each, a notice is posted advising on the level of difficulty, the duration of a hike, and any interesting facts. The Parc Naturel Régional de la Martinique organizes inexpensive guided excursions year-round. If there have been heavy rains, though, give it up. The tangle of ferns, bamboo trees, and vines is dramatic, but during rainy season, the wet, muddy trails will temper your enthusiasm. ✉ *9 bd. Général de Gaulle, Fort-de-France* ☎ *0596/73–19–30.*

HORSEBACK RIDING

Horseback-riding excursions can traverse scenic beaches, palm-shaded forests, sugarcane fields, and a variety of other tropical landscapes. Trained guides often include running commentaries on the history, flora, and fauna of the island.

Black Horse Ranch. At Black Horse Ranch, one-hour trail rides (€35) go into the countryside and across waving cane fields; two hours on the trail (€40) bring riders near a river. Only Western saddles are used for adults; children can ride English. Semiprivate lessons in French or English are €40 a person, less for kids if they can join a group. ⊠ *Les Trois-Ilets* ☎ *0596/68–37–80.*

BEACHES

Anse-Mitan. Small, family-owned seaside restaurants are half hidden among palm trees and are footsteps from the lapping waves. Inexpensive waterfront hotels line the clean, golden beach, which has excellent snorkeling just offshore. Chaise longues are available for rent from hotels for about €6. ⊠ *Pointe du Bout, Les Trois-Ilets.*

Les Salines. A short drive south of Ste-Anne brings you to a mile-long (1.5-km-long) cove lined with soft white sand and coconut palms. The beach is awash with families and children during holidays and on weekends but quiet during the week. The far end—away from the makeshift souvenir shops—is most appealing. The calm waters are safe for swimming, even for the kids. You can't rent chaise longues, but there are showers. Food vendors roam the sand. ⊠ *Ste-Anne, Schoelcher.*

☺ **Pointe du Bout.** The beaches here are small, man-made, and lined with resorts, including the Hotel Bakoua. Each little strip is associated with its resident hotel, and security guards and closed gates make access difficult. However, if you take a left across from the main pedestrian entrance to the marina—after the taxi stand—then go left again, you will reach the beach for Hotel Bakoua, which has especially nice facilities and several options for lunch and drinks. If things are quiet— particularly during the week—one of the beach boys may rent you a chaise; otherwise, just plop your beach towel down, face forward, and enjoy the delightful view of the Fort-de-France skyline. ⊠ *Pointe du Bout, Les Trois-Ilets.*

WHERE TO EAT

$$ ✗ **Mille & Une Brindilles.** At this trendy salon you can order anything
CAFÉ   from a glass of wine to an aromatic pot of tea in flavors like vanilla or
★   mango. You'll find a litany of tapenades, olive cakes, and flans on the prix-fixe menu. Fred, the bubbly Parisian who is both chef and proprietress, is the queen of terrines, and she makes a delicious tart (like Roquefort and pear) or pâté out of any vegetable or fish. The Saturday brunch (€22) is a very social occasion. The best-ever desserts, such as the Amadéus—as appealing as the classical music that plays—and *moelleux au chocolat,* are what you would want served at your last meal on Earth. Look for the sign on the left side, for the place is easy to miss. ⊠ *27 rte. de Didier, Didier, Fort-de-France* ☎ *0596/71–75–61* ▭ *No credit cards* ☉ *Closed Sun. and Wed. No dinner.*

MONTEGO BAY, JAMAICA

John Bigley and Paris Permenter

Today many explorations of MoBay are conducted from a reclining chair—frothy drink in hand—on Doctor's Cave Beach. As home of Jamaica's busiest cruise pier and the north-shore airport, Montego Bay—or MoBay—is the first taste most visitors have of the island. Travelers from around the world come and go in this bustling community, which ranks as Jamaica's second-largest city. The name Montego is derived from *manteca* (lard in Spanish). The Spanish first named this Bahía de Manteca, or Lard Bay. Why? The Spanish once shipped hogs from this port city. Jamaican tourism began here in 1924, when the first resort opened at Doctor's Cave Beach so that health-seekers could "take the waters." If you can pull yourself away from the water's edge and brush the sand off your toes, you can find some very interesting colonial sights in the surrounding area.

ESSENTIALS

CURRENCY The Jamaican dollar (J$85 to US$1). Currency-exchange booths are set up on the docks at Montego Bay whenever a ship is in port; however, the U.S. dollar is accepted virtually everywhere, though the change you receive back may be made in Jamaican dollars.

INTERNET A growing number of Internet cafés have sprung up in recent years in Montego Bay hotels and cafés. A popular option for many cruise passengers is the Internet café at Doctor's Cave Bathing Club (⊠ *Montego Bay* ☎ 876/952-2566).

TELEPHONE Public telephones (and faxes) are located at the communications center at the Montego Bay Cruise Terminal. Travelers also find public phones in major Montego Bay malls, such as the City Centre Shopping Mall. Some U.S. phone companies won't permit credit-card calls to be placed from Jamaica because they've been victims of fraud, so collect calls are often the top option. GSM cell phones equipped with tri-band or world-roaming service will find coverage throughout the Montego Bay region.

COMING ASHORE

Ships dock at the Montego Cruise Terminal, operated by the Port Authority of Jamaica. West of Montego Bay, the cruise terminal has five berths and accommodates both cruise and cargo shipping. The terminal has shops, a communications center, a visitor information booth, and a taxi stand supervised by the Port Authority of Jamaica. The cruise port in Montego Bay is not within walking distance of the heart of town; however, there's one shopping center (the Freeport Shopping Centre) within walking distance of the docks. If you just want to visit a beach, then Doctor's Cave or the Cornwall Bathing Beach, both public beaches, are very good nearby alternatives, and they are right in town.

From the Montego Cruise Terminal both taxis and shuttle buses take passengers downtown. Taxi service is about US$5 each way to downtown. Expect to pay US$5 per person each way by shuttle bus to the two craft markets, the City Centre Shopping Mall, Margaritaville, or Doctor's Cave Beach. A day pass for the shuttle bus is US$15 and allows passengers to get on and off as they wish. Jamaica is one place in the

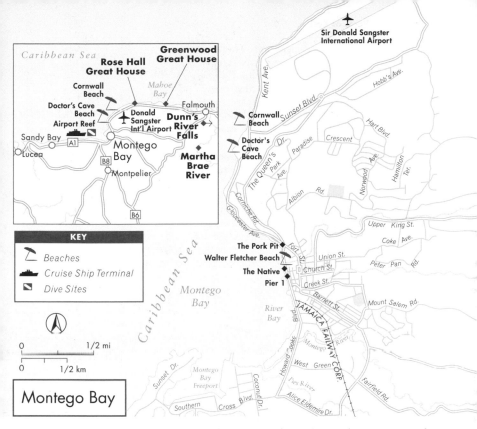

Montego Bay

Caribbean where it's usually to your advantage to take an organized shore excursion offered by your ship unless you just want to do a bit of shopping in town. Private taxis and other transportation providers aren't particularly cheap, and a full-day tour for a small group will run $150 to $180; however, road conditions and travel time have improved significantly with the completion of the North Coast Highway.

If you take a private taxi, you should know that rates are per car, not per passenger. You can flag cabs on the street. All licensed and properly insured taxis display red Public Passenger (PP) license plates. Licensed minivans also bear the red PP plates. If you hire a taxi driver as a tour guide, be sure to agree on a price before the vehicle is put into gear. Car rental fees in Jamaica include the cost of insurance. It is not difficult to rent a car, but driving in Jamaica is done on the left side of the road and it can take a little getting used to.

EXPLORING MONTEGO BAY

Fodor'sChoice **Dunn's River Falls.** One of Jamaica's most popular attractions is an eye-
★ catching sight: 600 feet of cold, clear mountain water splashing over a series of stone steps to the warm Caribbean. The best way to enjoy the falls is to climb the slippery steps: don a swimsuit, take the hand of the person ahead of you, and trust that the chain of hands and bodies leads

to an experienced guide. The leaders of the climbs are personable fellows who reel off bits of local lore while telling you where to step; you can hire a guide's service for a tip of a few dollars. After the climb, you exit through a crowded market, another reminder that this is one of Jamaica's top tourist attractions. If you can, try to schedule a visit on a day when no cruise ships are in port. ⚠ **Always climb with a licensed guide at Dunn's River Falls. Freelance guides might be a little cheaper, but the experienced guides can tell you just where to plant each footstep—helping you prevent a fall.** ⊠ *Off Rte. A1, between St. Ann's Bay and Ocho Rios, Ocho Rios* ☎ *876/974–4767* ⊕ *www. dunnsriverfallsja.com* 🖾 *$15* ☉ *Daily 8:30–5 (last entry 4 pm).*

★ **Greenwood Great House.** Unlike Rose Hall, Greenwood has no spooky legend to titillate, but it's much better than Rose Hall at evoking life on a sugar plantation. The Barrett family, from whom the English poet Elizabeth Barrett Browning descended, once owned all the land from Rose Hall to Falmouth; on their vast holdings they built this and several other greathouses. (The poet's father, Edward Moulton Barrett, "the Tyrant of Wimpole Street," was born at nearby Cinnamon Hill, later the estate of country singer Johnny Cash.) Highlights of Greenwood include oil paintings of the Barretts, china made for the family by Wedgwood, a library filled with rare books from as early as 1697, fine antique furniture, and a collection of exotic musical instruments. There's a pub on-site as well. It's 15 mi (24 km) east of Montego Bay. ⊠ *Greenwood* ☎ *876/953–1077* ⊕ *www.greenwoodgreathouse.com* 🖾 *$14* ☉ *Daily 9–6 (last tour at 5).*

Martha Brae River. This gentle waterway about 25 mi (40 km) southeast of Montego Bay takes its name from an Arawak woman who killed herself because she refused to reveal the whereabouts of a local gold mine. According to legend, she agreed to take her Spanish inquisitors there and, on reaching the river, used magic to change its course, drowning herself and the greedy Spaniards with her. Her *duppy* (ghost) is said to guard the mine's entrance. Rafting on this river is a very popular activity.

Fodor's Choice **Rose Hall.** In the 1700s it may well have been the greatest of greathouses
★ in the West Indies. Today it's popular less for its architecture than for the legend surrounding its second mistress, Annie Palmer. As the story goes, Annie was born in 1802 in England to an English mother and Irish father. When she was 10, her family moved to Haiti, and soon her parents died of yellow fever. Annie was adopted by a Haitian voodoo

priestess and soon became skilled in the practice of voodoo. Annie moved to Jamaica, married, and built Rose Hall, an enormous plantation spanning 6,600 acres with more than 2,000 slaves. There's a pub on-site. It's across the highway from the Hilton Rose Hall Resort & Country Club, A Hilton Resort. ✉ *North Coast Hwy., St. James* ✛ *15 mi (24 km) east of Montego Bay* ☎ *876/953–2323* ✉ *$20* ◷ *Daily 9:15–5:15.*

BINOCULARS

Binoculars are as useful indoors as they are outside. You might think they are only for bringing far-off wildlife and sights within view, but take them into museums, churches, and other buildings to examine the details of artwork, sculptures, and architectural elements.

SHOPPING

Jamaican artisans express themselves in silk-screening, wood carvings, resort wear, hand-loomed fabrics, and paintings. Jamaican rum makes a great gift, as do Tia Maria (the famous coffee liqueur) and Blue Mountain coffee. Wood carvings are one of the top purchases; the finest carvings are made from the Jamaican national tree, lignum vitae, or tree of life, a dense wood that talented carvers transform into dolphins, heads, or fish. Bargaining is expected with crafts vendors.

Gallery of West Indian Art. This is the place to find Jamaican, Cuban, and Haitian paintings. A corner of the gallery is devoted to hand-turned pottery (some painted) and beautifully carved and painted birds and animals. ✉ *11 Fairfield Rd., Montego Bay* ☎ *876/952–4547.*

ACTIVITIES

DIVING AND SNORKELING

Jamaica isn't a major dive destination, but you can find a few rich underwater regions, especially off the north coast. MoBay, known for its wall dives, has **Airport Reef** at its southwestern edge. The site is known for its coral caves, tunnels, and canyons. The first marine park in Jamaica, the **Montego Bay Marine Park,** was established to protect the natural resources of the bay; a quick look at the area lets you see the treasures that lie beneath the surface. The north coast is on the edge of the Cayman Trench, so it boasts a wide array of marine life.

Scuba Jamaica. This company offers serious scuba facilities for dedicated divers. The PADI and NAUI operation also offers Nitrox diving and instruction as well as instruction in underwater photography, night diving, and open-water diving. There's a pickup service for the Montego Bay, Runaway Bay, Discovery Bay, and Ocho Rios areas. Along with the Falmouth location, Scuba Jamaica is also found at the Franklyn D Resort in Runaway Bay and at Travellers Resort in Negril. ✉ *N-Resort, North Coast Hwy., Falmouth* ☎ *876/617–2500, 876/973–4591 in Runaway Bay, 876/957–3039 in Negril* ⊕ *www.scuba-jamaica.com.*

7

GOLF

Golfers appreciate both the beauty and the challenges offered by Jamaica's courses. Caddies are almost always mandatory throughout the island, and rates are $15 to $45 per round of golf. Cart rentals are available at most courses; costs are $20 to $40. Some of the best courses in the country are found near MoBay.

★ **Golf at Half Moon.** This Robert Trent Jones–designed 18-hole course is the home of the Red Stripe Pro Am. Green fees are $105 for guests, $150 for nonguests with twilight packages ranging from $75 to $90. In 2005 the course received an upgrade from Jones protégé Roger Rulewich and once again draws international attention. The course is also home of the Half Moon Golf Academy, which offers one-day sessions, multiday retreats, and hour-long private sessions. ⊠ *Half Moon Resort, North Coast Hwy., 7 mi (11 km) east of Montego Bay* ☎ *876/953–2560* ⊕ *halfmoon.rockresorts.com/activities/golf.asp.*

Hilton Rose Hall Resort and Spa. This course 4 mi (6 km) east of the airport hosts several invitational tournaments. Greens fees run $149 7–10 am, $119 10 am–1:30 pm, and $99 for a twilight round at the 18-hole championship **Cinnamon Hill Ocean Course.** The course was designed by Robert von Hagge and Rick Baril and is adjacent to historic Cinnamon Hill estate. Rates include green fees, cart, caddie, and tax, and apply to both guests and nonguests. ⊠ *North Coast Hwy., St. James* ✛ *15 mi (24 km) east of Montego Bay* ☎ *876/953–2650.*

★ **Ritz-Carlton Golf and Spa Resort, Rose Hall.** One of the nicest courses in Montego Bay, if not Jamaica, is the **White Witch** course at the Ritz-Carlton. The green fees at this 18-hole championship course are $175 for resort guests, $185 for nonguests, and $109 for a twilight round. Designed by Robert von Hagge and Rick Baril, it is literally on the grounds of historic Rose Hall Great House. ⊠ *1 Ritz Carlton Dr., Rose Hall, St. James* ☎ *876/518–0174 or 876/684–5174.*

RIVER RAFTING

Jamaica's many rivers mean a multitude of freshwater experiences, from mild to wild. Jamaica's first tourist activity off the beaches was relaxing rafting trips aboard bamboo rafts poled by local boatmen. Recently, soft-adventure enthusiasts have also been able to opt for white-water action as well with guided tours through several operators.

Fodor's Choice
★ Bamboo rafting in Jamaica originated on the **Rio Grande,** a river in the Port Antonio area. Jamaicans had long used the bamboo rafts to transport bananas downriver; decades ago actor and Port Antonio resident Errol Flynn saw the rafts and thought they'd make a good tourist attraction, and local entrepreneurs quickly rose to the occasion. Today the slow rides are a favorite with romantic travelers and anyone looking to get off the beach for a few hours. The popularity of the Rio Grande's trips spawned similar trips down the **Martha Brae River,** about 25 mi (40 km) from MoBay. Near Ocho Rios, the **Great River** has lazy river rafting as well as energetic kayaking.

Jamaica Tours Limited. This big tour company conducts raft trips down the River Lethe, approximately 12 mi (19 km) southwest of MoBay (a 50-minute trip); the four-hour excursion costs about $54 per person, includes lunch, and takes you through unspoiled hill country. Bookings can also be made through hotel tour desks. ✉ *Providence Dr., Montego Bay* ☎ *876/953–3700* ⊕ *www.jamaicatoursltd.com.*

River Raft Ltd. This company leads trips down the Martha Brae River, about 25 mi (40 km) from MoBay. The cost is $45 per person for the 1½-hour river run, including transportation. ✉ *66 Claude Clarke Ave., Montego Bay* ☎ *876/952–0889* ⊕ *www.jamaicarafting.com.*

BEACHES

★ **Doctor's Cave Beach.** Montego Bay's tourist scene has its roots right on the Hip Strip, the bustling entertainment district along Gloucester Avenue. It's the best beach in Jamaica outside one of the more developed resorts, thanks to its plantation-style clubhouse with changing rooms, showers, gift shops, a bar, a grill, and even a cybercafé. There's a $5 fee for admission; beach chairs and umbrellas are also for rent. More active travelers can opt for parasailing, glass-bottom boat rides, or jet skiing. ✉ *Gloucester Ave., Montego Bay* ☎ *876/952–2566.*

Walter Fletcher Beach. Though not as pretty as Doctor's Cave Beach, or as tidy, Walter Fletcher Beach is home to Aquasol Theme Park, which offers a large beach (with lifeguards and security), water trampolines, Jet Skis, Wave Runners, glass-bottom boats, snorkeling, tennis, go-kart racing, a disco at night, a bar, and a grill. The park is open daily from 10 to 10; admission is $5, with à la carte pricing for most activities. ✉ *Gloucester Ave., Montego Bay* ☎ *876/979–9447.*

WHERE TO EAT

$–$$
CARIBBEAN

✗ **The Native.** Shaded by a large poinciana tree and overlooking Gloucester Avenue, this open-air stone terrace serves Jamaican and international dishes. To go native, start with smoked marlin, move on to the *boonoonoonoos* platter (a sampler of local dishes), and round out with coconut pie or *duckanoo* (a sweet dumpling of cornmeal, coconut, and banana wrapped in a banana leaf and steamed). Live entertainment and candlelit tables make this a romantic choice for dinner on weekends. ✉ *29 Gloucester Ave.* ☎ *876/979–2769.*

¢
JAMAICAN
Fodor's Choice
★

✗ **Pork Pit.** A favorite with many MoBay locals, this no-frills eatery serves Jamaican specialties including some fiery jerk—note that it's spiced to local tastes, not watered down for tourist palates. Many get their food to go, but you can also find picnic tables just outside. ✉ *27 Gloucester Ave.* ☎ *876/940–3008.*

NASSAU, BAHAMAS

Ramona Settle Nassau, the capital of the Bahamas, has witnessed Spanish invasions and hosted pirates, who made it their headquarters for raids along the Spanish Main. The heritage of old Nassau blends the Southern charm of British loyalists from the Carolinas, the African tribal traditions of freed slaves, and a bawdy history of blockade-running during the Civil War and rum-running in the Roaring 1920s. The sheltered harbor bustles with cruise-ship hubbub, while a block away, broad, shop-lined Bay Street is alive with commercial activity. Over it all is a subtle layer of civility and sophistication, derived from three centuries of British rule. Nassau's charm, however, is often lost in its commercialism. There's excellent shopping, but if you look past the duty-free shops you'll also find sights of historical significance that are worth seeing.

ESSENTIALS

CURRENCY The Bahamian dollar trades one-to-one with the U.S. dollar, which is universally accepted. There's no need to acquire any Bahamian currency.

INTERNET You'll find Internet kiosks at Prince George Wharf.

TELEPHONE Calling locally or internationally is easy in the Bahamas. To place a local call, dial the seven-digit phone number. To call the United States, dial 1 plus the area code. Pay phones cost 25¢ per call; Bahamian and U.S. quarters are accepted, as are BATELCO and Indigo phone cards. To place a call using a calling card, use your long-distance carrier's access code or dial 0 for the operator. Be aware that when placing a toll-free call from your hotel you are charged as if for a regular long-distance call.

COMING ASHORE

Cruise ships dock at one of three piers on Prince George Wharf. Taxi drivers who meet the ships may offer you a $2 "ride into town," but the historic government buildings and duty-free shops lie just steps from the dock area. As you leave the pier, look for a tall pink tower—diagonally across from here is the tourist information office. Stop in for maps of the island and downtown Nassau. On most days you can join a one-hour walking tour ($10 per person) conducted by a well-trained guide. Tours generally start every hour on the hour from 10 am to 4 pm; confirm the day's schedule in the office. Just outside, an ATM dispenses U.S. dollars.

As you disembark from your ship, you will find a row of taxis and air-conditioned limousines. Fares are fixed by the government by zones. The fare is $6 for trips within downtown Nassau and on Paradise Island, $9 (plus $1 toll) from downtown to Paradise Island, and $18 from downtown to Cable Beach. Fares are for two passengers; each additional passenger is $3, regardless of the destination. It's customary to tip taxi drivers 15%. You also can hire a car or small van for about $50 per hour. These are fixed costs for two passengers; each additional passenger is $3.

The cheapest way to get to Paradise Island on your own is to take the ferry from the dock area ($3 each way).

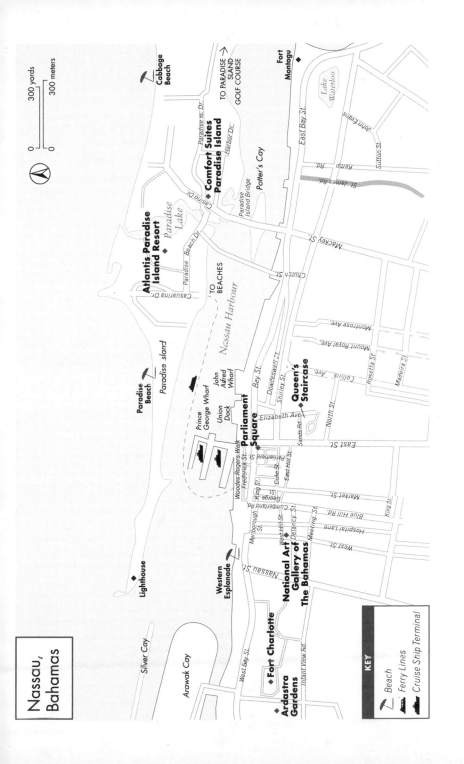

Nassau, Bahamas

300 yards
300 meters

Silver Cay

Arawak Cay

Lighthouse

Paradise Island

Paradise Beach

Cabbage Beach

Atlantis Paradise Island Resort

Paradise Lake

Paradise Is. Dr.

Comfort Suites Paradise Island

Harbor Dr.

Casino Dr.

Paradise Beach Dr.

Casuarina Dr.

Paradise Island Bridge

Potter's Cay

TO PARADISE ISLAND GOLF COURSE

Fort Montagu

Lake Waterloo

East Bay St.

John Evans

Sutton St.

Kemp Rd.

St. James Rd.

Mackey St.

Church St.

Montrose Ave.

Mount Royal Ave.

Collins Ave.

Rosetta St.

Madeira St.

TO BEACHES

Nassau Harbour

Prince George Wharf

John Alfred Wharf

Union Dock

Parliament Square

Bay St.

Dowdeswell St.

Shirley St.

Queen's Staircase

Elizabeth Ave.

Sands Rd.

North St.

East St.

Market St.

King St.

Blue Hill Rd.

Meeting St.

Woodes Rogers Walk

Frederick St.

Parliament St.

Duke St.

East Hill St.

King St.

George St.

Cumberland Rd.

Delancy St.

Hospital Lane

West St.

Marlborough St.

West Hill St.

National Art Gallery of The Bahamas

Western Esplanade

Nassau St.

Fort Charlotte

Ardastra Gardens

Infant View Rd.

West Hill St.

West Bay St.

KEY

Beach

Ferry Lines

Cruise Ship Terminal

EXPLORING NASSAU

Nassau's sheltered harbor bustles with cruise-ship hubbub, while a block away, broad, palm-lined Bay Street is alive with commercial activity. Shops angle for tourist dollars with fine imported goods at duty-free prices, yet you will find a handful of stores overflowing with authentic Bahamian crafts, foods, and other delights. Most of Nassau's historic sites are centered around downtown.

With its thoroughly revitalized downtown—the revamped British Colonial Hilton lead the way—Nassau is recapturing some of its glamour. Nevertheless, modern influence is apparent: fancy restaurants, suave clubs, and trendy coffeehouses have popped up everywhere. This trend comes partly in response to the burgeoning upper-crust crowds that now supplement the spring-breakers and cruise passengers who have traditionally flocked to Nassau.

> ## NASSAU BEST BETS
>
> ■ **Ardastra Gardens.** Flocks of flamingos, the country's national bird, "march" in three daily shows (you can mingle with the flamboyant pink stars afterward).
>
> ■ **Atlantis.** Though very costly, the water park here is a must for families.
>
> ■ **Junkanoo Beach.** Head to this beach (aka Long Wharf Beach) and sit in the shade of a coconut palm (it's a 10-minute walk from the duty-free shops on Bay Street). **Shopping.** To many, shopping is one of Nassau's great delights.

Today the seedy air of the town's not-so-distant past is almost unrecognizable. Petty crime is no greater than in other towns of this size, and the streets not only look cleaner but feel safer. You can still find a wild club or a rowdy bar, but you can also sip cappuccino while viewing contemporary Bahamian art or dine by candlelight beneath prints of old Nassau, serenaded by soft, island-inspired calypso music.

Arawak Cay. Known to Nassau residents as "The Fish Fry," Arawak Cay is one of the best places to knock back a Kalik beer, chat with locals, watch or join in a fast-paced game of dominoes, or sample traditional Bahamian fare. The two-story Twin Brothers and Goldie's Enterprises are two of the most popular places. Try their fried "cracked conch" and Goldie's famous Sky Juice (a sweet but potent gin, coconut-water, and sweet-milk concoction sprinkled with nutmeg). There's usually a live band on the outdoor stage Friday and Saturday nights. ⊠ *W. Bay St. and Chippingham Rd.*

♻ **Ardastra Gardens, Zoo, and Conservation Centre.** Marching flamingos? These national birds give a parading performance at Ardastra daily at 10:30, 2:10, and 4:10. The brilliant pink birds are a delight—especially for children, who can walk among the flamingos after the show. The zoo, with more than 5 acres of tropical greenery and ponds, also has an aviary of rare tropical birds including the bright green Bahama parrot, native Bahamian creatures such as rock iguanas and the little (and harmless) Bahamian boa constrictors, and a global collection of small animals. ⊠ *Chippingham Rd. south of W. Bay St.* ☎ *242/323–5806* ⊕ *www. ardastra.com* ⊠ *$15* ⊙ *Daily 9–5.*

Saving on Atlantis

Frugal cruisers have long known about **Comfort Suites Paradise Island** (⊕ *www.comfortsuites.com*), which is right across the street from the Atlantis Resort. They use it to avoid paying for expensive and limited ship-sponsored day-passes to the resort, which cost well over $150 per person. Book a room here, and everyone in the room (up to four people, regardless of age) is entitled to a free day-pass to the Atlantis Resort's water park. In addition to the base rate (usually about $300 for two people depending on the season), you will also have to pay (at check-in) an additional energy surcharge of $12.95 per *adult* and a housekeeper gratuity of $5 per *adult* on top of the quoted rate, even if you prepay; the third and fourth person cost $10 each

plus all the service charges. Frankly, this isn't as good a deal as it used to be, but families or groups of four can still save a little money by going this route, and then you will have a room in which to shower and change before returning to the ship. Of course, it's a better deal if you can get a discounted rate. (Be aware that you may not have more than four people on a single reservation regardless of their age, and you may not get access to the room in the morning, but it will be ready when you get back from your day of fun at the water park.) When it's time for lunch, you'll find cheaper restaurants within walking distance of Atlantis. You can also book your room and daypass through the Barbados-based travel agency that operates ⊕ *Caribbean Daypass.com*.

7

⊘ **Fort Charlotte.** Built in 1788, this imposing fort comes complete with a waterless moat, drawbridge, ramparts, and a dungeon, where children love to see the torture device where prisoners were "stretched." Young local guides bring the fort to life. (Tips are expected.) Lord Dunmore, who built it, named the massive structure in honor of George III's wife. At the time, some called it Dunmore's Folly because of the staggering expense of its construction. It cost eight times more than was originally planned. (Dunmore's superiors in London were less than ecstatic with the high costs, but he managed to survive unscathed.) Ironically, no shots were ever fired in battle from the fort. ⊠ *W. Bay St. at Chippingham Rd.* ⊠ *$5* ⊗ *Tours daily 8–4.*

Fodor's Choice ★ **National Art Gallery of the Bahamas.** Opened in July 2003, the museum houses the works of esteemed Bahamian artists such as Max Taylor, Amos Ferguson, Brent Malone, John Cox, and Antonius Roberts. The glorious Italianate-colonial mansion, built in 1860 and restored in the 1990s, has double-tiered verandas with elegant columns. It was the residence of Sir William Doyle, the first chief justice of the Bahamas. Join locals on the lawn for movie night under the stars; call for schedule. Don't miss the museum's gift shop, where you'll find books about the Bahamas and Bahamian quilts, prints, and crafts. ⊠ *West and W. Hill Sts., across from St. Francis Xavier Cathedral* ☎ *242/328–5800* ⊕ *www.nagb.org.bs* ⊠ *$5* ⊗ *Tues.–Sat. 10–4.*

Parliament Square. Nassau is the seat of the national government. The Bahamian Parliament comprises two houses—a 16-member Senate (Upper House) and a 41-member House of Assembly (Lower House)—and a ministerial cabinet headed by a prime minister. If the House is in session, sit in to watch lawmakers debate. Parliament Square's pink, colonnaded government buildings were constructed in the late 1700s and early 1800s by Loyalists who came to the Bahamas from North Carolina. The square is dominated by a statue of a slim young Queen Victoria that was erected on her birthday, May 24, in 1905. In the immediate area are a handful of magistrates' courts. Behind the House of Assembly is the **Supreme Court.** Its four-times-a-year opening ceremonies (held the first weeks of January, April, July, and October) recall the wigs and mace-bearing pageantry of the Houses of Parliament in London. The Royal Bahamas Police Force Band is usually on hand for the event. ⊠ *Bay St.* ☎ *242/322–2041* ▣ *Free* ☉ *Weekdays 10–4.*

Queen's Staircase. A popular early-morning exercise regime for locals, the "66 Steps" (as Bahamians call them) are thought to have been carved out of a solid limestone cliff by slaves in the 1790s. The staircase was later named to honor Queen Victoria's reign. Pick up some souvenirs at the ad hoc straw market along the narrow road that leads to the site. ⊠ *Top of Elizabeth Ave. hill, south of Shirley St.*

SHOPPING

Most of Nassau's shops are on Bay Street between Rawson Square and the British Colonial Hotel, and on the side streets leading off Bay Street. Some stores are popping up on the main shopping thoroughfare's eastern end and just west of the Cable Beach strip. Bargains abound between Bay Street and the waterfront. Upscale stores can also be found in Marina Village and the Crystal Court at Atlantis and in the arcade joining the Sheraton Nassau Beach and the Wyndham on Cable Beach. You'll find duty-free prices—generally 25%–50% less than U.S. prices—on imported items such as crystal, linens, watches, cameras, jewelry, leather goods, and perfumes.

ACTIVITIES

FISHING

The waters here are generally smooth and alive with many species of game fish, which is one of the reasons why the Bahamas has more than 20 fishing tournaments open to visitors every year. A favorite spot just west of Nassau is the Tongue of the Ocean, so called because it looks like that part of the body when viewed from the air. The channel stretches for 100 mi. For boat rental, parties of two to six will pay $600 or so for a half-day, $1,600 for a full day.

Born Free Charters (☎ *242/393–4144* ⊕ *www.bornfreefishing.com*) has three boats and guarantees a catch on full-day charters—if you don't get a fish, you don't pay. The **Charter Boat Association** (☎ *242/393–3739*) has 15 boats available for fishing charters.

GOLF

Cable Beach Golf Club (7,040 yards, par 72), the oldest golf course in the Bahamas, will be completely overhauled when Baha Mar gets on with its Cable Beach transformation. For now it remains a well-kept, competitive course that's a favorite with locals and visitors not staying on Paradise Island. ⊠ *W. Bay St., S.E. end of Cable Beach strip* ☎ *242/327–6000 Ext.*

6189 ⛳18 holes $95, 9 holes $70; carts included. Clubs $25 ⊙ Daily 7–5:30; last tee off at 5:15.

One & Only Ocean Club Golf Course (6,805 yards, par 72), designed by Tom Weiskopf, is a championship course surrounded by the ocean on three sides, which means that winds can get stiff. Call to check on cur-

<table>
<tr><td>

CAUTION

Mail overflowing your mailbox is a neon sign to thieves that you aren't home. Have someone pick it up, or better yet, have the post office hold all your mail for you.

</td></tr>
</table>

rent availability and up-to-date prices (those not staying at Atlantis or the One & Only Ocean Club may find themselves shut out completely). ⊠ *Paradise Island Dr. next to airport, Paradise Island* ☎ *242/363–3925, 800/321–3000 in U.S.* ⊕ *www.oneandonlyresorts.com* ⛳*18 holes $260. Clubs $70* ⊙ *Daily 6 am–sundown.*

BEACHES

New Providence is blessed with stretches of white sand studded with palm and sea grape trees. Some of the beaches are small and crescent-shaped; others stretch for miles. Paradise Island's real showpiece is 3-mi-long **Cabbage Beach,** which rims the north coast from the Atlantis lagoon to Snorkeler's Cove. At the west end you can rent Jet Skis and nonmotorized pedal boats, and go parasailing. **Cable Beach** is on New Providence's north shore, about 3 mi (5 km) west of downtown Nassau. Resorts line much of this beautiful, broad swath of white sand, but there is public access. Jet-skiers and beach vendors abound, so don't expect quiet isolation. Just west of Cable Beach is a rambling pink house on the Rock Point promontory, where much of the 1965 Bond film *Thunderball* was filmed. Right in downtown Nassau, **Junkanoo Beach** is spring-break central from late February through April. The man-made beach isn't the prettiest on the island, but it's conveniently located if you only have a few quick hours to catch a tan. Music is provided by bands and DJs to guys with boom boxes; a few bars keep the drinks flowing.

WHERE TO EAT

$ ✕**Double D's.** Don't let the dark-tinted windows and green lighting over BAHAMIAN the doorway put you off. Inside you'll find a simply decorated bar offering friendly service and good native food. This is a popular spot with locals for its Bahamian cuisine and 23-hour service in a town where most kitchens are closed at 10 pm. Try boil' fish—a peppery lime-based broth filled with chunks of boiled potatoes, onions, and grouper—or be adventurous and order a bowl of pigs' feet or sheep-tongue souse. Although souplike, these Bahamian delicacies are typically served only for breakfast. All come with a chunk of johnnycake or a bowl of steaming white grits. ⊠ *E. Bay St. at foot of bridges from Paradise Island* ☎ *242/393–2771.*

$ ✕**Green Parrot.** Sip a green-color Parrot Crush while tackling the large AMERICAN Works Burger as you sit and enjoy the cool breeze and lovely Nassau Harbour scenery. This casual, all-outdoor restaurant and bar is popular with locals. The menu includes burgers, wraps, quesadillas, and other simple but tasty dishes. An extended all-night happy hour on Friday means the huge bar is lively and packed. There is live music on Thursday and Saturday nights and a DJ on Friday. ⊠ *E. Bay St. west of bridges to Paradise Island* ☎ *242/322–9248* ⊕ *www.greenparrotbar.com.*

NEVIS (CHARLESTOWN)

Jordan Simon   In 1493, when Columbus spied a cloud-crowned volcanic isle during his second voyage to the New World, he named it Nieves—the Spanish word for "snows"—because it reminded him of the peaks of the Pyrenees. Nevis rises from the water in an almost perfect cone, the tip of its 3,232-foot central mountain hidden by clouds. Even less developed than sister island St. Kitts—just 2 mi (3 km) away at their closest point, Nevis is known for its long beaches with white and black sand, its lush greenery, the charming if slightly dilapidated Georgian capital of Charlestown, mountain hikes, and its restored sugar plantations that now house charming inns. Even on a day trip Nevis feels relaxed and quietly upscale. You might run into celebrities at the Four Seasons or lunching at the beach bars on Pinney's, the showcase strand. Yet Nevisians (not to mention the significant expat American and British presence) never put on airs, offering warm hospitality to all visitors.

ESSENTIALS

CURRENCY   The Eastern Caribbean dollar (EC$2.67 to US$1). U.S. dollars, major credit cards, and traveler's checks are readily accepted, although large U.S. bills may be difficult to change in small shops—and you'll receive change in the local currency.

INTERNET   Charlestown usually has an operational Internet café, but they rarely last in one location. The tourist office will have the latest information.

TELEPHONE   Phone cards, which you can buy in denominations of $5, $10, and $20, are handy for making local phone calls, calling other islands, and accessing U.S. direct lines. To make a local call, dial the seven-digit number. To call Nevis from the United States, dial the area code 869, then access code 465, 466, 468, or 469 and the local four-digit number.

COMING ASHORE

Cruise ships dock in Charlestown harbor; all but the smallest ships bring passengers in by tender to the central downtown ferry dock. The pier leads smack onto Main Street, with shops and restaurants steps away. Taxi drivers often greet tenders, and there's also a stand a block away. Fares are fairly expensive, but a three-hour driving tour of Nevis costs about $80 for up to four people. Several restored greathouse plantation inns are known for their lunches; your driver can provide information and arrange drop-off and pickup. Before setting off in a taxi, be sure to clarify whether the rate quoted is in E.C. or U.S. dollars.

If your ship docks in St. Kitts, Nevis is a 30- to 45-minute ferry ride from Basseterre. You can tour Charlestown, the capital, in a half hour or so, but you'll need three to four hours to explore the entire island. Most cruise ships arrive in port at around 8 am, and the ferry schedule (figure $18 round-trip) can be irregular, so many passengers sign up for

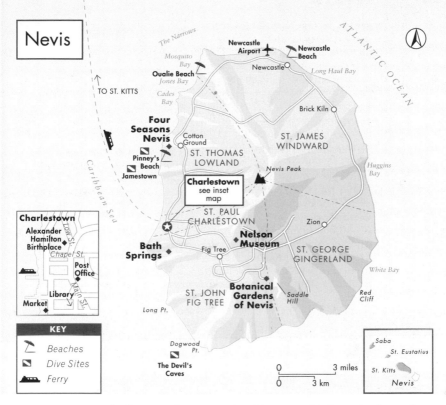

Nevis

The Narrows

Mosquito Bay

Oualie Beach
Jones Bay

Cades Bay

TO ST. KITTS

Four Seasons Nevis

Pinney's Beach

Jamestown

Caribbean Sea

Newcastle Airport

Newcastle Beach

Newcastle

Long Haul Bay

Brick Kiln

Cotton Ground

ST. THOMAS LOWLAND

ST. JAMES WINDWARD

Nevis Peak

Huggins Bay

Charlestown
see inset map

ST. PAUL CHARLESTOWN

Zion

Bath Springs

Fig Tree

Nelson Museum

ST. GEORGE GINGERLAND

White Bay

ST. JOHN FIG TREE

Botanical Gardens of Nevis

Saddle Hill

Red Cliff

Long Pt.

Charlestown
Alexander Hamilton Birthplace
Low St.
Chapel St.
Post Office
Library
Market
Main St.

Dogwood Pt.

The Devil's Caves

ATLANTIC OCEAN

Saba
St. Eustatius
St. Kitts
Nevis

0 _____ 3 miles
0 _____ 3 km

KEY

⌒ Beaches
◼ Dive Sites
⛴ Ferry

a cruise line–run shore excursion. If you travel independently, confirm departure times with the tourist office to be sure you'll make it back to your ship on time.

EXPLORING NEVIS

Bath Springs. The Caribbean's first hotel, the Bath Hotel, built by businessman John Huggins in 1778, was so popular in the 19th century that visitors, including such dignitaries as Samuel Taylor Coleridge and Prince William Henry, traveled two months by ship to "take the waters" in the property's hot thermal springs. It suffered extensive hurricane and probably earthquake damage over the years and languished in disrepair until recently. Local volunteers have cleaned up the spring and built a stone pool and steps to enter the waters; now residents and visitors enjoy the springs, which range from 104°F to 108°F, though signs still caution that you bathe at your own risk, especially if you have heart problems. ✉ *Charlestown outskirts, Nevis, St. Kitts and Nevis* ☎ *No phone.*

★ **Botanical Gardens of Nevis.** In addition to terraced gardens and arbors, this remarkable 7.8-acre site in the glowering shadow of Mt. Nevis has natural lagoons, streams, and waterfalls, superlative bronze mermaids, egrets and herons, and extravagant fountains. You can find a proper rose garden, sections devoted to orchids and bromeliads, cacti, and flowering trees and shrubs—even a bamboo garden. A splendid re-creation of a plantation-style greathouse contains a café with sweeping sea views, and the upscale Galleria shop selling art, textiles, jewelry, and Indonesian teak furnishings sourced during the owners' world travels. ✉ *Montpelier Estate, Nevis, St. Kitts and Nevis* ☎ *869/469–3509* ⊕ *www. botanicalgardennevis.com* 💷 *$10, children 6–12 $7* ☼ *Mon.–Sat. 9–5.*

★ **Charlestown.** About 1,200 of Nevis's 10,000 inhabitants live in the capital. You'll walk smack onto Main Street from the pier. It's easy to imagine how tiny Charlestown, founded in 1660, must have looked in its heyday. The weathered buildings still have fanciful galleries, elaborate gingerbread fretwork, wooden shutters, and hanging plants. The stone building with the clock tower (1825, but mostly rebuilt after a devastating 1873 fire) houses the courthouse and second-floor **library** (a cool respite on sultry days). The little park next to the library is Memorial Square, dedicated to the fallen of World Wars I and II. ✉ *Nevis, St. Kitts and Nevis.*

Alexander Hamilton Birthplace. The Alexander Hamilton Birthplace, which contains the Hamilton **Museum**, sits on the waterfront. This bougainvillea-draped Georgian-style house is a reconstruction of what is believed to have been the American patriot's original home, built in 1680 and likely destroyed during a mid-19th earthquake. Born here in 1755, Hamilton moved to St. Croix when he was about 12. He moved to the American colonies to continue his education at 17; he became George Washington's Secretary of the Treasury and died in a duel with political rival Aaron Burr in 1804. The Nevis House of Assembly occupies the second floor; the museum downstairs contains Hamilton memorabilia, documents pertaining to the island's history, and displays on island geology, politics, architecture, culture, and cuisine. The gift shop is a wonderful source for historic maps, crafts, and books on Nevis. ✉ *Low St., Charlestown, Nevis, St. Kitts and Nevis* ☎ *869/469–5786* ⊕ *www.nevis-nhcs.org* 💷 *$5, with admission to Nelson Museum $7* ☼ *Weekdays 9–4, Sat. 9–noon.*

Nelson Museum. Purportedly this is the Western Hemisphere's largest collection of Lord Horatio Nelson memorabilia, including letters, documents, paintings, and even furniture from his flagship. Nelson was based in Antigua but came on military patrol to Nevis, where he met and eventually married Frances Nisbet, who lived on a 64-acre plantation here. Half the space is devoted to often-provocative displays on island life, from leading families to vernacular architecture to the adaptation of traditional African customs, from cuisine to Carnival.

NEVIS BEST BETS

■ **Charlestown.** The well-preserved little capital is worth a quick stroll.

■ **Golf.** The stunner at the Four Seasons provides challenge aplenty.

■ **Hiking.** Getting out in the countryside on foot is one of the best ways to experience Nevis.

■ **Pinney's Beach.** This long sensuous strand has several beach bars where you can "lime" with locals.

The shop is an excellent source for gifts, from homemade soaps to historical guides. ⊠ *Bath Rd. outside, Charlestown, Nevis, St. Kitts and Nevis* ☏ *869/469–0408* ⊕ *www.nevis-nhcs.org* ⊠ *$5, with Museum of Nevis History $7* ☉ *Weekdays 9–4, Sat. 9–noon.*

SHOPPING

Nevis is certainly not the place for a shopping spree, but there are some wonderful surprises, notably the island's stamps, fragrant honey, ceramics, and batik and hand-embroidered clothing. Other than a few hotel boutiques and isolated galleries, virtually all shopping is concentrated on or just off Main Street in Charlestown. The lovely old stonework and wood floors of the waterfront Cotton Ginnery Complex make an appropriate setting for shops of local artisans.

CraftHouse. The CraftHouse is a marvelous source for local specialties from vetiver mats to leather moccasins; there's a smaller branch in the Cotton Ginnery. ⊠ *Pinney's Rd., Charlestown, Nevis, St. Kitts and Nevis* ☏ *869/469–5505.*

Nevis Handicraft Co-op Society. The Nevis Handicraft Co-op Society, next to the tourist office, offers works by local artisans (clothing, ceramic ware, woven goods) and locally produced honey, hot sauces, and jellies (try the guava and soursop). ⊠ *Main St., Charlestown, Nevis, St. Kitts and Nevis* ☏ *869/469–1746.*

★ **Philatelic Bureau.** The Philatelic Bureau, opposite the tourist office, is the place to go for stamp collectors. St. Kitts and Nevis are famous for their decorative, and sometimes valuable, stamps. Real beauties include the butterfly, hummingbird, and marine-life series. ⊠ *Cotton Ginnery, Charlestown, Nevis, St. Kitts and Nevis* ☏ *869/469–0617.*

ACTIVITIES

GOLF

Fodor's Choice **Four Seasons Golf Course.** Duffers doff their hats to the beautiful, impeccably
★ maintained Robert Trent Jones Jr.–designed Four Seasons Golf Course: the virtual botanical gardens surrounding the fairways almost qualify as a hazard in themselves. Greens fees per 18 holes are $190 for hotel guests, $290 for nonguests. ⊠ *Four Seasons Resort Nevis, Pinney's Beach, Nevis, St. Kitts and Nevis* ☏ *869/469–1111* ⌗ *18 holes, par 72, 6,766 yd.*

HIKING

The center of the island is Nevis Peak—also known as Mt. Nevis—which soars 3,232 feet and is flanked by Hurricane Hill on the north and Saddle Hill on the south. If you plan to scale Nevis Peak, a daylong affair, it's highly recommended that you go with a guide. The **Upper Round Road Trail** is a 9-mi (14.5-km) road constructed in the late 1600s that was cleared and restored by the Nevis Historical and Conservation Society. It connects the Golden Rock Plantation Inn, on the east side of the island, with Nisbet Plantation Beach Club, on the northern tip. The trail encompasses numerous vegetation zones, including pristine rain forest, and impressive plantation ruins. The original cobblestones, walls, and ruins are still evident in many places.

★ **Peak Heaven at Herbert Heights.** Peak Heaven at Herbert Heights is run by the Herbert family, who lead four-hour nature hikes up to panoramic Herbert Heights, where you drink in fresh local juices and the views of Montserrat; the powerful telescope, donated by Greenpeace, makes you feel as if you're staring right into that island's simmering volcano (or staring down whales during their migratory season). Hike prices start at $25. ⊠ Nevis, St. Kitts and Nevis ☎ 869/469–2856 or 869/665–6926 ⊕ www.peakheavennevis.com.

Sunrise Tours. Sunrise Tours, run by Lynell and Earla Liburd, offers a range of hiking tours, but their most popular is Devil's Copper, a rock configuration full of ghostly legends. They love highlighting Nevisian heritage, explaining time-honored cooking techniques, the many uses of dried grasses, and medicinal plants. Hikes range from $20 to $40 per person, and you receive a certificate of achievement. ⊠ Nevis, St. Kitts and Nevis ☎ 869/469–2758 ⊕ www.nevisnaturetours.com.

WINDSURFING

★ **Windsurfing Nevis.** Waters are generally calm and northeasterly winds steady yet gentle, making Nevis an excellent spot for beginners and intermediates. Windsurfing Nevis offers top-notch instructors (Winston Crooke is one of the best in the islands) and equipment for $30 per hour. It also offers kayak rentals and tours along the coast, stopping at otherwise inaccessible beaches. ⊠ Oualie Beach, Nevis, St. Kitts and Nevis ☎ 869/469–9682.

BEACHES

All beaches are free to the public (the plantation inns cordon off "private" areas on Pinney's Beach for guests), but there are no changing facilities, so wear a swimsuit under your clothes.

Oualie Beach. South of Mosquito Bay and north of Cades and Jones bays, this beige-sand beach lined with palms and sea grapes is where the folks at Oualie Beach Hotel can mix you a drink and fix you up with water-sports equipment. There's excellent snorkeling amid calm water and fantastic sunset views with St. Kitts silhouetted in the background. Several beach chairs and hammocks (free with lunch, $3 rental without) line the sand and the grassy "lawn" behind it. Oualie is at the island's northwest tip, approximately 3 mi (5 km) west of the airport. ⊠ Oualie Beach, Nevis, St. Kitts and Nevis.

Pinney's Beach. The island's showpiece has soft, golden sand on the calm Caribbean, lined with a magnificent grove of palm trees. The Four Seasons Resort is here, as are the plantation inns' beach clubs and casual beach bars such as Sunshine's, Chevy's, and the Double Deuce. Regrettably, the waters can be murky and filled with kelp if the weather has been inclement anywhere within a hundred miles, depending on the currents. ⊠ Pinney's Beach, Nevis, St. Kitts and Nevis.

WHERE TO EAT

$$$

SEAFOOD

★

✕**Double Deuce.** Mark Roberts, the former chef at Montpelier, decided to chuck the "five-star lifestyle" and now co-owns this jammed, jamming beach bar, which lures locals with fine, fairly priced fare, creative cocktails, and a Hemingway-esque feel. Peer behind the ramshackle bar and you'll find a gleaming modern kitchen where Mark (and fun-loving firebrand partner Lyndeta) prepare sublime seafood he often catches himself, as well as organic beef burgers, velvety pumpkin soup, creative pastas, and lip-smacking ribs. Stop by for free Wi-Fi and proper espresso, a game of pool, riotous Thursday-night karaoke, or just to hang out with a Double Deuce Stinger. ⊠ *Pinney's Beach, Nevis, St. Kitts and Nevis* ☎ *869/469–2222* ⊕ *www.doubledeucenevis.com* ⚑ *Reservations essential* ▭ *No credit cards* ◷ *Closed Mon.*

$$
CARIBBEAN
✕ **Sunshine's.** Everything about this shack overlooking (and spilling onto) the beach is larger than life, including the Rasta man Llewelyn "Sunshine" Caines himself. Flags and license plates from around the world complement the international patrons (including an occasional movie or sports star wandering down from the Four Seasons). Picnic tables are splashed with bright sunrise-to-sunset colors; even the palm trees are painted, though "it gone upscaled," as locals say, with VIP cabanas. ⊠ *Pinney's Beach, Nevis, St. Kitts and Nevis* ☎ *869/469–1089.*

OCHO RIOS, JAMAICA

John Bigley
and Paris
Permenter

About two hours east of Montego Bay lies Ocho Rios (often just "Ochi"), a lush destination that's favored by honeymooners for its tropical beauty. Often called the garden center of Jamaica, this community is perfumed by flowering hibiscus, bird of paradise, bougainvillea, and other tropical blooms year-round. Ocho Rios is a popular cruise port, and the destination where you'll find one of the island's most recognizable attractions: the stairstep Dunn's River Falls, which invites travelers to climb in daisy-chain fashion, hand-in-hand behind a sure-footed guide. This spectacular waterfall is actually a series of falls that cascades from the mountains to the sea. That combination of hills, rivers, and sea also means many activities in the area, from seaside horseback rides to mountain biking and lazy river rafting.

ESSENTIALS

CURRENCY
The Jamaican dollar (J$85 to US$1). Currency-exchange booths are set up on the docks at Ocho Rios whenever a ship is in port. The U.S. dollar is accepted virtually everywhere; at some places change is made in Jamaican dollars. Prices given are in U.S. dollars unless otherwise indicated.

INTERNET
A growing number of facilities offer Internet service; expect to pay about US$2 for 20 minutes. At the Taj Mahal Centre, the **Cafe Express Bistro** (⊠ *Ocho Rios* ☎ *876/974–6487*) offers free Wi-Fi for customers.

TELEPHONE
Public telephones are found at the communications center at the Ocho Rios Cruise Pier. Travelers also find public phones in major Ocho Rios malls. Some U.S. phone companies won't permit credit-card calls to be placed from Jamaica because they've been victims of fraud, so collect calls are often the top option. GSM cell phones equipped with tri-band or world-roaming service will find coverage throughout the Ocho Rios region.

COMING ASHORE

Most cruise ships are able to dock at this port on Jamaica's north coast, near Dunn's River Falls (a US$10 taxi ride from the pier). Also less than 1 mi (2 km) from the Ocho Rios pier are Island Village (within walking distance), Taj Mahal Duty-Free Shopping Center, and the Ocean Village Shopping Center. If you're going anywhere else beyond Island Village, a taxi is recommended; expect to pay US$8 for a taxi ride downtown. The pier, which includes a cruise terminal with the basic services and transportation, is also within easy walking distance of Turtle Beach.

Licensed taxis are available at the pier; expect to pay about US$35 per hour for a guided taxi tour.

> ### OCHO RIOS BEST BETS
>
> ■ **Chukka Caribbean.** Any of the great adventure tours here is sure to please.
>
> ■ **Dolphin Cove at Treasure Reef.** Swim with a dolphin, stingray, or shark at this popular stop.
>
> ■ **Dunn's River Falls.** A visit to the falls is touristy, yet it's still exhilarating.
>
> ■ **Firefly.** The former home of playwright Noël Coward can be seen on a guided tour. **Mystic Mountain.** Live out your *Cool Runnings* fantasies on the bobsled ride.

Jamaica is one place in the Caribbean where it's usually to your advantage to take an organized shore excursion offered by your ship unless you just want to go to the beach or do a bit of shopping in town. Car rental isn't recommended in Jamaica due to high prices, bad roads, and aggressive drivers.

EXPLORING OCHO RIOS

Fodor's Choice ★ Dunn's River Falls. One of Jamaica's most popular attractions is an eye-catching sight: 600 feet of cold, clear mountain water splashing over a series of stone steps to the warm Caribbean. The best way to enjoy the falls is to climb the slippery steps: don a swimsuit, take the hand of the person ahead of you, and trust that the chain of hands and bodies leads to an experienced guide. The leaders of the climbs are personable fellows who reel off bits of local lore while telling you where to step; you can hire a guide's service for a tip of a few dollars. After the climb, you exit through a crowded market, another reminder that this is one of Jamaica's top tourist attractions. If you can, try to schedule a visit on a day when no cruise ships are in port. ⚠ **Always climb with a licensed guide at Dunn's River Falls. Freelance guides might be a little cheaper, but the experienced guides can tell you just where to plant each footstep—helping you prevent a fall.** ⊠ *Off Rte. A1, between St. Ann's Bay and Ocho Rios, Ocho Rios* ☎ *876/974–4767* ⊕ *www.dunnsriverfallsja.com* 🎫 *$15* ☉ *Daily 8:30–5 (last entry 4 pm).*

Mystic Mountain. This is Ocho Rios' newest attraction, covering 100 acres of mountainside rain forest near Dunn's River Falls. Visitors board the Rainforest Sky Explorer, a chairlift that soars through and over the pristine rain forest to the apex of Mystic Mountain. On top, there is a restaurant with spectacular views of Ocho Rios, arts-and-crafts shops,

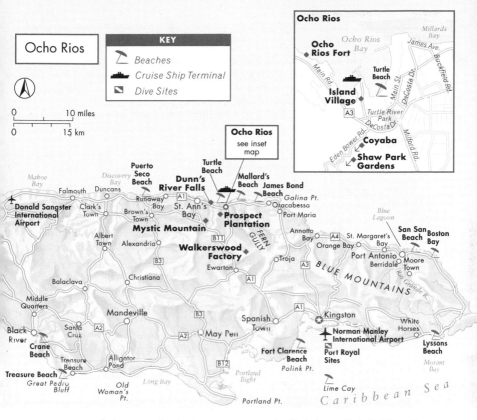

and the attraction's signature tours, the Rainforest Bobsled Jamaica ride and the Rainforest Zipline Tranopy ride. ⊠ *North Coast Hwy., Ocho Rios* ☎ *876/974–3990* ⊕ *www.rainforestadventure.com* ☒ *$42 (tram only), $62 (tram and bobsled), $104 (tram and zipline), $124 (tram, bobsled, and zipline)* ⊗ *Sun.–Thurs. 7:30–5, Fri. and Sat. 7:30 am–10 pm.*

Prospect Plantation. To learn about Jamaica's agricultural heritage, a trip to this working plantation, just east of town, is a must. It's not just a place for history lovers, however. Everyone enjoys the views over the White River Gorge and the tour in a tractor-pulled cart. The grounds are full of exotic flowers and tropical trees, some planted over the years by such celebrities as Winston Churchill and Charlie Chaplin. The estate includes a small aviary with free-flying butterflies. You can also saddle up for horseback rides and camel safaris on the plantation's 900 acres, but the actual tour times are usually geared toward the cruise-ship schedule, so call ahead. ⊠ *Rte. A1, 4 mi (3.2 km) east of Ocho Rios* ☎ *876/994–1058* ⊕ *www.prospectplantationtours.com* ☒ *$32* ⊗ *Daily 8–5; tour times vary.*

SHOPPING

Ocho Rios has several malls, and they are less hectic than the one in MoBay. Shopping centers include **Pineapple Place, Ocean Village, Taj Mahal,** and **Coconut Grove.** A fun mall that also serves as an entertainment center is **Island Village,** the place nearest to the cruise port. This open-air mall includes shops selling Jamaican handicrafts, duty-free goods and clothing, a Margaritaville restaurant, and a small beach area with a water trampoline and water sports.

ACTIVITIES

DOLPHIN-SWIM PROGRAMS

Dolphin Cove at Treasure Reef. This company offers dolphin swims as well as lower-price dolphin encounters for ages eight and up; dolphin touch programs for ages six and over; or simple admission to the grounds, which also includes a short nature walk. ⊠ *North Coast Hwy., adjacent to Dunn's River Falls, Box 21, Ocho Rios* ☎ *876/974–5335* ⊕ *www. dolphincovejamaica.com.*

GOLF

Ocho Rios courses don't have the prestige of those around Montego Bay, but duffers will find challenges at a few lesser-known courses.

Sandals Golf and Country Club. The golf course in Ocho Rios is 700 feet above sea level (green fees are $100 for 18 holes or $70 for 9 holes for nonguests; free for guests). ⊠ *5 mi (8 km) southeast of Ocho Rios, turn south at White River and continue 4 mi (6 km), Ocho Rios* ☎ *876/975–0119.*

HORSEBACK RIDING

With its combination of hills and beaches, Ocho Rios is a natural for horseback excursions. Most are guided tours taken at a slow pace and perfect for those with no previous equestrian experience. Many travelers opt to pack long pants for horseback rides, especially those away from the beach.

Fodor's Choice **Chukka Caribbean Adventures.** Ocho Rios has excellent horseback riding, ★ but the best of the operations is Chukka Caribbean's Ocho Rios stable. You don't have to be an experienced rider to enjoy its tours; horses are well trained and Chukka provides attentive guides to assist all riders along the way. The company's 2½-hour beach ride ($74, $52 for children) is a highlight of many trips to Jamaica. ⊠ *Llandovery, St. Ann's Bay* ☎ *876/972–2506* ⊕ *www.chukkacaribbean.com.*

Prospect Plantation. The plantation offers a 3½-hour ride for ages eight and older. The price ($70) includes use of helmets; advance reservations are required. For the adventurous, Prospect Plantation also offers guided camel rides. ⊠ *Rte. A1, about 3 mi (5 km) east of Ocho Rios* ☎ *876/994–1058* ⊕ *www.prospectplantationtours.com.*

WHITE-WATER RAFTING

White-water rafting is increasingly popular in the Ocho Rios area.

Chukka Caribbean Adventures. The big activity outfitter offers the Chukka River white-water rafting adventure on the White River, an easy trip that doesn't require any previous rafting experience. This tour allows you to travel in your very own tube through gentle rapids. This tour lasts for three hours and costs $63 for adults and $45 for children. ⊠ *Llandovery, St. Ann's Bay* ☎ *876/972–2506* ⊕ *www. chukkacaribbean.com.*

BEACHES

Dunn's River Falls Beach. You'll find a crowd at the small beach at the foot of the falls. Although tiny—especially considering the crowds that pack the falls—it's got a great view, as well as a beach bar and grill. Look up from the sands for a spectacular view of the cascading water, whose roar drowns out the sea as you approach. ⊠ *Rte. A1 between St. Ann's Bay and Ocho Rios.*

Turtle Beach. One of the busiest beaches in Ocho Rios is usually lively, and has a mix of both residents and visitors. It's next to the Sunset Jamaica Grande and looks out over the cruise port. ⊠ *Main St.*

WHERE TO EAT

$$ ✕ **Coconuts on the Bay.** This casual eatery, opposite the cruise pier, offers
JAMAICAN slightly upscale versions of local specialties. Start with jerk chicken wings or conch and shrimp fritters before moving on to specialties like tamarind shrimp or lobster served grilled, curried, or creole style. Complimentary transportation from local hotels is available. ⊠ *Turtle Beach Rd., Ocho Rios* ☎ *876/795–0064.*

¢ ✕ **Ocho Rios Village Jerk Centre.** This blue-canopied, open-air eatery is a
JAMAICAN good place to park yourself for frosty Red Stripe beer and fiery jerk pork, chicken, or seafood. Milder barbecued meats, also sold by weight (typically, a quarter or half pound makes a good serving), turn up on the fresh-daily chalkboard menu posted on the wall. It's lively at lunch and is popular with cruise-ship passengers. ⊠ *Da Costa Dr., Ocho Rios* ☎ *876/974–2549.*

PROGRESO, MEXICO

Marlist Kast

The waterfront town closest to Mérida, Progreso is not particularly historic. It's also not terribly picturesque; still, it provokes a certain sentimental fondness for those who know it well. On weekdays during most of the year the beaches are deserted, but when school is out (Easter week, July, and August) and on summer weekends it's bustling with families from Mérida. Progreso's charm—or lack of charm—seems to hinge on the weather. When the sun is shining, the water looks translucent green and feels bathtub-warm, and the fine sand makes for lovely long walks. When the wind blows during one of Yucatán's winter *nortes,* the water churns with whitecaps and looks gray and unappealing. Whether the weather is good or bad, however, everyone ends up eventually at one of the restaurants lining the main street, Calle 19. Across the street from the oceanfront malecón, restaurants serve cold beer, seafood cocktails, and freshly grilled fish. Most cruise passengers head immediately for Mérida or for one of the nearby archaeological sites.

ESSENTIALS

CURRENCY
The Mexican peso (MX$12.06 to US$1). U.S. dollars and credit cards are accepted by everyone at the port. There is no advantage to paying in dollars, but there may be an advantage to paying in cash.

INTERNET
The cruise terminal isn't terribly close to Progreso's downtown area, but if you take a bus or taxi into town, you'll easily find an Internet café with pretty cheap service. If you take an excursion to Mérida, you'll find that Internet cafés there are ubiquitous, particularly on the main square and calles 61 and 63; most charge $1 to $3 per hour.

TELEPHONE
Most pay phones accept prepaid Ladatel cards, sold in 30-, 50-, or 100-peso denominations. To use the card, insert it in the pay phone's slot, dial 001 (for calls to the U.S.) or 01 (for calls within Mexico), followed by the area code and number. Credit is deleted from the card as you use it, and the balance is displayed on the small screen on the phone.

COMING ASHORE

The pier in Progreso is long, and cruise ships dock at its end, so passengers are shuttled to the foot of the pier, where the Progreso Cruise Terminal offers visitors their first stop. The terminal houses small restaurants and shops selling locally produced crafts. These are some of the best shops in sleepy Progreso (a much wider selection is available in nearby Mérida). The beach lies just east of the pier and can easily be reached on foot. If you want to enjoy the sun and a peaceful afternoon, a drink at one of the small palapa-roof restaurants that line the beach is a good option.

If you are looking to explore, there are plenty of taxis around the pier. A trip around town should not cost more than $5, but ask the taxi driver to quote you a price. If you want to see more of Progresso, a cab can also take you to the local sightseeing tour bus (which departs about every 10 minutes from the Casa de Cultura), a bright blue, open-air, double-decker bus that travels through town and only costs $2. A taxi ride from Progreso to Mérida runs about $30, and most drivers charge around $15 per hour to show you around. If you plan on renting the

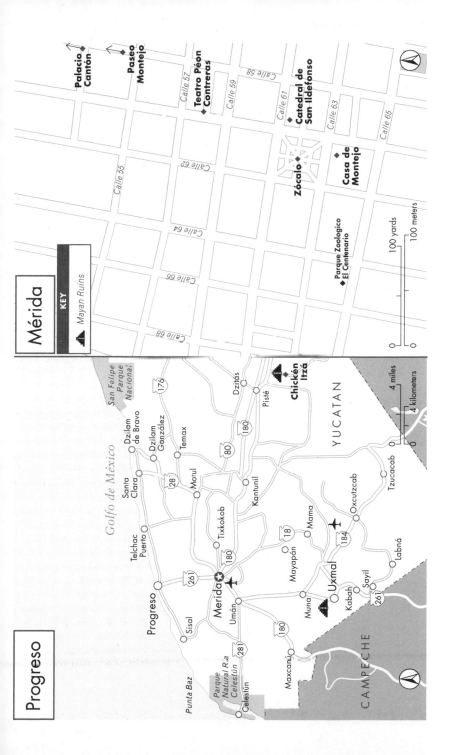

Progreso

Mérida

KEY

▲ Mayan Ruins

100 yards
100 meters

Golfo de México

San Felipe Parque Nacional

Punta Baz

Telchac Puerto

Progreso

Sisal

Santa Clara

Dzilam de Bravo

Dzilam González

Temax

Motul

Tixkokob

Umán

Mérida ★ ✈

Parque Natural Ría Celestún

Celestún

Maxcanú

Muna

Mayapán

Mama

Kantunil

Dzidzantún

Dzitás

Pisté

Chichén Itzá ▲

Oxcutzcab

Tzucacab

Uxmal

Kabah

Sayil

Labná

YUCATAN

CAMPECHE

176
180
80
28
261
180
18
184
261
281

4 miles
4 kilometers

Calle 55
Calle 62
Calle 64
Calle 66
Calle 68
Calle 57
Calle 58
Calle 59
Calle 61
Calle 63
Calle 65

Palacio Cantón ◆

Paseo Montejo

Teatro Péon Contreras ◆

Catedral de San Ildefonso ◆

Zócalo ◆

Casa de Montejo

◆ Parque Zoologico El Centenario

cab for a good part of the day, talk about the number of hours and the cost with the driver before you take off. It's difficult to rent a car, so most people just band together in a taxi.

EXPLORING MÉRIDA

Just south of Progreso (about 20 or 30 minutes by taxi), Mérida, the cultural and intellectual hub of the Yucatán, offers a great deal to explore. Mérida is rich in art, history, and tradition. Most streets are numbered, not named, and most run one-way. North–south streets have even numbers, which descend from west to east; east–west streets have odd numbers, which ascend from north to south. One of the best ways to see the city is to hire a *calesa*, a horse-drawn carriage. They congregate on the main square or at the Palacio Cantón, near the anthropology museum. Drivers charge about $20 for an hour-long circuit around downtown and up Paseo de Montejo, and $30 for an extended tour.

Casa de Montejo. Francisco de Montejo—father and son—conquered the peninsula and founded Mérida in 1542; they built their stately "casa" 10 years later. In the late 1970s it was restored by banker Agustín Legorreta, converted to a branch of Banamex bank, and now sits on the south side of the plaza. It is the city's finest—and oldest—example of colonial plateresque architecture, a Spanish architectural style popular in the 16th century and typified by the kind of elaborate ornamentation you'll see here. Even if you have no banking to do, step into the building to glimpse the leafy inner patio. ⊠ *Calle 63, Centro* ⊗ *Weekdays 9–5 and Sat. 9–1.*

Catedral de San Ildefonso. Begun in 1561, St. Ildefonso is believed to be the oldest cathedral in the Americas. It took several hundred Mayan laborers, working with stones from the pyramids of the ravaged Mayan city, 36 years to complete it. Designed in the somber Renaissance style by an architect who had worked on the Escorial in Madrid, its facade is stark and unadorned, with gunnery slits instead of windows, and faintly Moorish spires. Inside, the black Cristo de las Ampollas (Christ of the Blisters)—at 7 meters (23 feet) tall, perhaps the tallest Christ in Mexico—occupies a side chapel to the left of the main altar. ⊠ *Calles 60 and 61, Centro* ☎ *No phone* ⊗ *Daily 7–11:30 and 4:30–8.*

Palacio Cantón. The most compelling of the mansions on **Paseo Montejo,** this stately palacio was built as the residence for a general between 1909 and 1911. Designed by Enrique Deserti, who also did the blueprints for the Teatro Peón Contreras, the building has a grandiose air that seems more characteristic of a mausoleum than a home: there's marble everywhere, as well as Doric and Ionic columns and other Italianate Beaux-Arts flourishes. The building also houses the air-conditioned **Museo de Antropología e Historia,** which introduces visitors to ancient Mayan culture. Temporary exhibits sometimes brighten the standard collection. ⊠ *Paseo Montejo 485, at Calle 43, Paseo Montejo* ☎ *999/923–0469* ⊡ *$5* ⊗ *Tues.–Sat. 9 am–8 pm, Sun. 9–2.*

Paseo Montejo. North of downtown, this 10-block-long street was *the* place to reside in the late 19th century, when wealthy plantation owners sought to outdo each other with the opulence of their elegant mansions. Mansion owners typically opted for the decorative styles popular in New Orleans, Cuba, and Paris—imported Carrara marble, European antiques—rather than any style from Mexico. The broad boulevard, lined with tamarind and laurel trees, has lost much of its former panache; some of the mansions have fallen into disrepair. Many are now used as office buildings; others have been or are being restored as part of a citywide, privately funded beautification program. The street is a lovely place to explore on foot or in a horse-drawn carriage.

Teatro Peón Contreras. This 1908 Italianate theater was built along the same lines as grand turn-of-the-20th-century European theaters and opera houses. In the early 1980s the marble staircase, dome, and frescoes were restored. Today, in addition to performing arts, the theater houses the **Centro de Información Turística** (Tourist Information Center), which provides maps, brochures, and details about attractions in the city and state. The theater's most popular attraction, however, is the café-bar spilling out into the street facing Parque de la Madre. ⊠ *Calle 60 between Calles 57 and 59, Centro* ☎ *999/924–7381 or 999/928–1966 Tourist Information Center, 999/924–3843 theater* ⊙ *Tourist Information Center daily 8–9.*

Zócalo. Méridians traditionally refer to this main square as the Plaza de la Independencia, or the Plaza Principal. Whichever name you prefer, it's a good spot from which to begin a tour of the city, in which to watch music or dance performances, or to chill in the shade of a laurel tree when the day gets too hot. The plaza was laid out in 1542 on the ruins of T'hó, the Mayan city demolished to make way for Mérida, and is still the focal point around which the most important public buildings cluster. ⊠ *Bordered by Calles 60, 62, 61, and 63, Centro.*

FARTHER AFIELD

Fodor's Choice **Chichén Itzá.** One of the most dramatically beautiful of the ancient

★ Mayan cities, Chichén Itzá was discovered by Europeans in the mid-1800s, and much here remains a mystery. Experts have little information about who the Itzás might have been, and the reason why they abandoned the city around 1224 is also unknown. Unfortunately, climbing to the top of the pyramid is not permitted. ⊠ *Approximately 75 mi (120 km) east of Mérida on Carretera 180* ⊕ *www.inah.gob.mx* ▣ *Site, museum, and sound-and-light show $MX 116 (US$14); parking $2; use of video camera $3 (keep this receipt if visiting other archaeological sites on same day)* ⊙ *Daily 8–5; sound-and-light show just approximately 7 pm in fall and winter (at 8 pm in spring and summer).*

PROGRESO BEST BETS

■ **Chichén Itzá.** The famous Maya city is an easy day trip from Progreso and is home to the enormous and oft-photographed El Castillo pyramid.

■ **Mérida.** This delightful, though busy, town is full of life as people take to the streets for music, dance, food, and culture.

■ **Uxmal.** One of the most beautiful Mayan cities is reachable on a day trip from Progreso. If you've seen Chichén Itzá already, go here.

7

Fodor's Choice   **Uxmal.** If Chichén Itzá is the most expansive Mayan ruin in Yucatán,
★   Uxmal is arguably the most elegant. The architecture here reflects the
late classical renaissance of the 7th to the 9th century and is contemporary with that of Palenque and Tikal. Unfortunately, climbing to
the top of the Pyramid of the Magician is no longer allowed. ⊠ *48 mi
(78 km) south of Mérida on Carretera 261* ✉ *Site, museum, and sound-
and-light show $MX 166 (US$14); parking $1; use of video camera $2
(keep this receipt if visiting other archaeological sites along Ruta Puuc
on same day)* ⊙ *Daily 8–5; sound-and-light show just after dusk (at
7 pm in winter or 8 pm in summer, tickets to only show $5.75); official
English language tour guide $55.*

SHOPPING

In Progreso between Calle 80 and Calle 81, there is also a small downtown area that is a better place to walk than to shop. There you will
find banks, supermarkets, and shops with everyday goods for locals as
well as several restaurants that serve simple Mexican fare like *tortas*
and *tacos.*

Mérida offers more places to shop, including colorful Mexican markets
selling local goods. The **Mercado Municipal** (⊠ *Calles 56 and 67, Centro*)
has items you probably don't won't need but might find fascinating to
look at: songbirds in cane cages, mountains of mysterious fruits and
vegetables, dippers made of hollow gourds (the same way they've been
made here for a thousand years). There are also various crafts for sale,
including hammocks, sturdy leather *huaraches,* and *piñatas* in every
imaginable shape and color. ■ TIP➜ **Guides often approach tourists near
this market. They expect a tip and won't necessarily bring you to the best
deals. You're better off visiting some specialty stores first to learn about
the quality and types of hammocks, hats, and other crafts; then you'll have
an idea of what you're buying—and what it's worth—if you want to bargain
in the market. Also be wary of pickpockets within the markets.**

WHERE TO EAT

$ ✗**Café La Habana.** A gleaming wood bar, white-jacketed waiters, and
MEXICAN   the scent of cigarettes contribute to the Old European feel at this over-
whelmingly popular spot, a branch of a Mexico City café that has been
around since the 1950s. Overhead, brass-studded ceiling fans swirl the
air-conditioned air. Sixteen specialty coffees are offered (some spiked
with spirits like Kahlúa or cognac), and the menu has light snacks as
well as some entrées, including tamales, fajitas, and enchiladas. The
waiters are friendly, and there are plenty of them, although service is
not always brisk. Both the café and upstairs Internet joint are open 24
hours a day; free Wi-Fi is available downstairs for laptop-toting customers. ⊠ *Calle 59 No. 511A, at Calle 62, Centro* ☎ *999/928–6502.*

PUERTO LIMÓN, COSTA RICA

Marlise Kast

Christopher Columbus became Costa Rica's first tourist when he landed on this stretch of coast in 1502 during his fourth and final voyage to the New World. Expecting to find vast mineral wealth, he named the region "Costa Rica" (rich coast). Imagine the Spaniards' surprise eventually to find there was none. Save for a brief skirmish some six decades ago, the country *did* prove itself rich in a long tradition of peace and democracy. No other country in Latin America can make that claim. Costa Rica is also abundantly rich in natural beauty, managing to pack beaches, volcanoes, rain forests, and diverse animal life into an area the size of Vermont and New Hampshire combined. It has successfully parlayed those qualities into its role as one the world's great ecotourism destinations. A day visit is short, but time enough for a quick sample.

ESSENTIALS

CURRENCY The colón (¢498 to US$1). Most businesses in port gladly accept U.S. dollars.

INTERNET A bank of Internet computers, operated by International Telecommunication Center, is yours to use at the cruise terminal.

TELEPHONE   Telephone numbers have eight digits. Merely dial the number. There are no area codes. You'll find ample phones for use in the cruise terminal. Public phones accept locally purchased calling cards.

COMING ASHORE

Ships dock at Limón's spacious, spiffy Terminal de Cruceros (cruise terminal), one block south of the city's downtown. You'll find telephones, Internet computers, a craft market, tourist information, and tour operators' desks inside the terminal, as well as a small army of manicurists who do a brisk business. Step outside and walk straight ahead one block to reach Limón's downtown.

A fleet of red taxis waits on the street in front of the terminal. Drivers are happy to help you put together a do-it-yourself tour. Most charge $100 to $150 per carload for a day of touring. There is no place to rent a car here, but you're better off leaving the driving to someone else. Cruise lines offer dozens of shore excursions in Costa Rica, and if you want to go any farther afield than Limón or the coast south, we suggest you take an organized tour. The country looks disarmingly small on a map—it is—but hills give rise to mountains the farther inland you go, and road conditions range from "okay" to "abysmal." Distances are short as the toucan flies, but travel times are longer than you'd expect.

EXPLORING PUERTO LIMÓN

Limón. "Sultry and sweltering" describes this port community of 105,000. The country's most ethnically diverse city mixes the Latino flavor of the rest of Costa Rica with Afro-Caribbean and Asian populations, descendants of laborers brought to do construction and farming in the 19th century.

Just north and east of the cruise terminal lies the city's palm-lined central park, **Parque Vargas,** with a promenade facing the ocean. Nine or so Hoffman's two-toed sloths live in its trees; ask a passerby to point them out, as spotting them requires a trained eye.

Rain Forest Aerial Tram. This 2½-square-mi (4-square-km) preserve houses a privately owned and operated engineering marvel: a series of gondolas strung together in a modified ski-lift pulley system. (To lessen the impact on the jungle, the support pylons were lowered into place by helicopter.) The tram gives you a way of seeing the rain-forest canopy and its spectacular array of epiphyte plant life and birds from just above, a feat you could otherwise accomplish only by climbing the trees yourself. ⊠ *Braulio Carrillo National Park, 76 mi (120 km) west of Limón* ☎ *2257–5961, 866/759–8726 in North America* ⊕ *www. rainforestadventure.com* ✉ *$55 tram only; $89.50 tram, lunch, and transportation* ☉ *Daily 7–4.*

San José. Costa Rica's sprawling, congested capital sits in the middle of the country about three hours inland from the coast. Despite the distance, San José figures as a shore excursion—a long one to be sure—on most ships' itineraries. (The vertical distance is substantial, too; the capital sits on a plateau just under a mile above sea level. You'll appreciate a jacket here after so many days at sea level.) Although the city dates from the mid-18th century, little from the colonial era remains. The northeastern San José suburb of **Moravia** is chock-full of souvenir stores lining a couple of blocks behind the city's church. The **Teatro Nacional** (*National Theater* ⊠ *Plaza de la Cultura, Barrio La Soledad* ☎ *221–5341* ⊕ *www. teatronacional.go.cr* 🎫 *$10–$30 for most performances* ☉ *Mon.– Sat. 9–4*) is easily the most enchanting building in Costa Rica, and San José's must-see sight. Coffee barons constructed the Italianate sandstone building, modeling it on a composite of European opera houses, and inaugurating it in 1897. ✛ *100 mi (160 km) west of Limón.*

> ### PUERTO LIMÓN BEST BETS
>
> ■ **The Rain Forest Tram.** This attraction takes you up into the canopy of the rain forest to see it from a unique angle.
>
> ■ **Tortuguero Canals.** Whether you go on a ship-sponsored tour or arrange it on your own, you see a wild part of Costa Rica that isn't reachable by anything but boat.
>
> ■ **Zip-Line Tours.** If you have never done one of these thrilling tours, flying from tree to tree, Costa Rica is the original place to do it.

The **Museo Nacional** (*National Museum* ⊠ *C. 17, between Avs. Central and 2, Barrio La Soledad* ☎ *257–1433* ⊕ *www.museocostarica.go.cr* 🎫 *$6* ☉ *Tues.–Sat. 8:30–4:30, Sun. 9–4:30*) is housed in a whitewashed fortress dating from 1870. Notice the bullet holes: this former army headquarters saw fierce fighting during a brief 1948 civil war. But it was also here that the government abolished the country's military in 1949. ✛ *100 mi (160 km) west of Limón.*

Tortuguero Canals. The largely forested region north of Limón is one of those Costa Rican anomalies: roadless and remote, it's nevertheless one of the country's most-visited places. A system of inland canals runs parallel to the shoreline, providing safer access to the region than a dangerous journey for smaller vessels up the seacoast. Some compare the densely layered greenery highlighted by brilliantly colored flowers. Your guide will point out the abundant wildlife: sloths hang in the trees; howler monkeys let out their plaintive calls; egrets soar above the river surface; and crocodiles laze on the banks. ⊠ *North of Limón.*

☾ **Veragua Rainforest Adventure Park.** The region's newest attraction is a 4,000-acre nature theme park, about 30 minutes west of Limón. Veragua's great strength is its small army of enthusiastic, super-informed guides who take you through a network of nature trails and exhibits of hummingbirds, snakes, frogs, and butterflies and other insects. A gondola ride overlooks the complex and transports you through the rain-forest canopy. A branch of the **Original Canopy Tour** is here, too, and offers you the chance to zip from platform to platform—10 in all—through the rain-forest canopy. You have two options, the "full" package of every activity but the canopy tour, or a more expensive option including the canopy tour. ⊠ *Veragua de Liverpool* ✛ *9 mi (15 km) west of*

Limón ☎ *2296–5056 in San José* ⊕ *www.veraguarainforest.com* 🖃 *Full package $65, full package with canopy tour $89* ⊙ *Tues.–Sun. 8–4.*

Volcán Irazú. Five active volcanoes loom over Costa Rica's territory (as well as many inactive ones). Irazú clocks in at the highest at about 11,000 feet (3,700 meters) and the farthest east and most accessible from Limón, though still a three-hour drive. The volcano last erupted in 1965, but gases and steam have billowed from fumaroles on its northwestern slope ever since. You can go right up to the top, although cloudy days—there are many—can obscure the view. ⊠ *84 mi (140 km) southwest of Limón* ☎ *2551–9398, 8200–5025 for ranger station* 🖃 *$7* ⊙ *Daily 8–4:30.*

SHOPPING

The cruise-ship terminal contains an orderly maze of souvenir stands. Vendors are friendly; there's no pressure to buy. Many shops populate the restored port building across the street as well. Spelling is not its forte, but the **Caribean Banana** (⊠ *50 meters north Terminal de Cruceros, west side of Parque Vargas*) stands out from the other shops in the cruise-terminal area with a terrific selection of wood carvings.

ACTIVITIES

WHITE-WATER RAFTING

You can experience some of the world's premier white-water rafting in Costa Rica. Old standby **Ríos Tropicales** (⊠ *On hwy. in Siquirres* ☎ *2233–6455, 866/722–8273 in North America* ⊕ *www.riostropicales.com*) has tours on a Class III–IV section of the Pascua sector of the Río Reventación for experienced rafters only. Not quite so wild, but still with Class II–III rapids, is the nearby Florida section of the Reventazón. You can kick off your excursion in this part of the country at the company's operations center in Siquirres, 45 mi (75 km) west of Limón.

ZIP-LINE TOURS

Costa Rica gave birth to the so-called canopy tour, a system of zip lines that transports you from platform to platform in the rain-forest treetops courtesy of a very secure harness. Though billed as a way to get up close with nature, your Tarzan-like yells will probably scare any wildlife away. Think of it more as an outdoor amusement-park ride. The nearest zip-line tour is at **Veragua Rainforest Adventure Park** (*see the listing, above*).

BEACHES

The dark-sand beaches on this sector of the coast are pleasant enough, but won't dazzle you if you've made previous stops at Caribbean islands with their white-sand strands. Nicer beaches than Limón's Playa Bonita lie farther south along the coast and can be reached by taxi or organized shore excursion. Strong undertows make for ideal surfing conditions on these shores, but risky swimming. Exercise caution.

Playa Bonita (⊠ *1 mi [2 km] north of Limón*), the name of Limón's own strand, translates as "pretty beach," but it's your typical urban beach, a bit on the cluttered side. **Playa Blanca** (⊠ *26 mi [44 km] southeast of Limón, Cahuita*), one of the coast's only white-sand beaches, lies within the boundaries of Cahuita National Park, right at the southern entrance of the pleasant little town of Cahuita. The park's rain forest extends right to the edge of the beach, and the waters here offer good snorkeling. **Playa Cocles** (⊠ *38 m [63 km] southeast of Limón, Puerto Viejo de Talamanca*), the region's most popular strand of sand, lies just outside Puerto Viejo de Talamanca, one of Costa Rica's archetypal beach towns, with its attendant cafés and bars and all-around good times to be had.

WHERE TO EAT

$ ✕ **Brisas del Caribe.** Here's a case study in what happens when cruise
SEAFOOD ships come to town. This old downtown standby, once as charmingly off-kilter as the crooked umbrellas on its front tables, got rid of its video poker machines (and the locals who always hoped to get lucky playing them), tiled the floors, and remodeled. The food is still good— seafood and surprisingly decent hamburgers, a real rarity in Costa Rica, are the fare here—but a bit of the local color has faded. This place does it up big with a lunch buffet on cruise days. ⊠ *North side of Parque Vargas* ☎ *2758–0138.*

$ ✕ **Park Hotel.** Take refuge from the sweltering midday heat in the air-
SEAFOOD conditioned restaurant of Limón's pastel-and-pink, mid-range business-class hotel. Decent pastas, seafood, and desserts are on the menu, and the pleasant ocean view is tossed in for free. ⊠ *Av. 3, Calles 2–3* ☎ *2798–0555* ⊕ *www.parkhotelcostarica.com.*

7

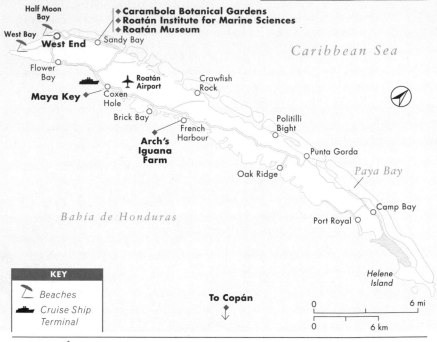

ROATÁN, HONDURAS

Marlise Kast

You'll swear you hear Jimmy Buffett singing as you step off the ship onto Roatán. The flavor is decidedly Margaritaville, but with all there is to do on this island off the north coast of Honduras, you'll never waste away here. Roatán is the largest and most important of the Bay Islands, though at a mere 40 mi (65 km) from tip to tip, and no more than 3 mi (5 km) at its widest; "large" is relative here. As happened elsewhere on Central America's Caribbean coast, the British got here first—the Bay Islands didn't become part of Honduras until the mid-1800s—and left an indelible imprint in the form of place names such as Coxen Hole, French Harbour, and West End, and of course their language, albeit a Caribbean-accented English. The eyes of underwater enthusiasts mist over at the mention of Roatán, one of the world's premier diving destinations, but plenty of topside activity will keep you busy, too.

ESSENTIALS

CURRENCY The Honduran leimpira (L18.9 to US$1). You'll find an ATM at Banco BAC in the town of Coxen Hole, where cruise ships arrive. There are also ATMs in West End at the Dolphin Resort and in West Bay at the Mayan Princess Resort. Credit cards are widely accepted, although merchants frequently add a surcharge to offset the high processing fees they are charged by card companies.

INTERNET Check your email and make international phone calls at **Paradise Computers** (✉ *Megaplaza Mall French Harbour*), in their main location inside the new Megaplaza Mall, or at their satellite location on the main drag in West End Village.

TELEPHONE Land lines in Honduras have seven digits, while cell phones have eight. There are no area codes, so just dial the number. Public phones are hard to find, but some hotels and businesses will offer phone services to walk-up users for a small fee.

COMING ASHORE

Some ships dock at the Terminal de Cruceros (cruise terminal) in the village of Coxen Hole, the island's administrative center. You'll find telephones, Internet computers, and stands with tour information inside the terminal, as well as a flea market of crafts vendors just outside the gate. Carnival completed a new cruise-ship dock in 2010, and its ships now dock at this new $80 million installation in Mahogany Bay. The new dock is not near any major towns, but it is just a few miles from the new Megaplaza Mall and the town of French Harbour.

Taxis are readily available outside the cruise-ship docks, but be prepared to pay a premium for services there. Trips to the major tourism centers like West End and West Bay beach will cost around $20. If you would like to save money on your taxi fares, you can walk out to the main highway (or into the town of Coxen Hole if you dock near there) and look for taxis marked "Colectivo." These taxis charge a flat rate of L25–L30, depending on the distance. They also pick up as many passengers as they can hold, so plan on riding with other locals or tourists. The local public-transport system consists of blue minivans that leave from Main Street in Coxen Hole to various points on the island until 6 pm.

Look for the cadre of tourist police if you need help with anything. They wear yellow shirts and dark-green trousers and are evident on cruise days. You certainly can rent a car here, but the island's compact size makes it unnecessary. Taxis will happily take you anywhere; expect to pay $60 to $120 for a day's private tour, depending on how far you wish to travel.

EXPLORING ROATÁN

Arch's Iguana Farm. West of French Harbour you'll find this farm where you can get a close look at hundreds of indigenous reptiles. There are tropical birds as well, and a marine viewing area where you can see many species of fish and live lobsters from the dock. ✉ *French Harbour* ☎ *2445–7743* ✉ *$8.*

Carambola Botanical Gardens. With one of the country's most extensive orchid collections, this is home to many different varieties of tropical plants. It is also a breeding area for iguanas. There are several trails to follow, and many of the trees and plants are identified by small signs. The longest trail leads up to the top of the hill, where you find an amazing view of the West End and Anthony's Key Resort. ⊠ *Sandy Bay, across from Anthony's Key Resort* ☎ *445–3117* ⊕ *www.carambolagardens. com* 🖃 *$10* ⊘ *Daily 8–5.*

Maya Key. One of the premier day excursions for cruisers visiting Roatán is this small, private island near Coxen Hole. The park offers a wide variety of amenities and activities, including sandy beaches, tropical gardens, a museum with cultural displays, and an animal rescue center, where you can meet the animals. Carnival and Norwegian cruise lines offer this option as a shore excursion, or you can book independently on the park's Web site. This is a great place for families with children. Maya Key is operated by Anthony's Key Resort, which is one of the oldest and most famous resorts in Honduras. ⊹ *3-minute water shuttle ride from the shuttle pier 50 yds east of Terminal de Cruceros near Coxen Hole* ☎ *9995–9589* ⊕ *www. mayakeyroatan.com* 🖃 *$70 (includes boat shuttle and lunch, advance reservations required)* ⊘ *Mon.–Sat. 7 am–4 pm.*

ROATÁN BEST BETS

■ **Diving and Snorkeling.** Roatán is one of the world's great diving destinations. There's snorkeling, too, most of it easily accessible from shore.

■ **Explore Garífuna Culture.** You'd never know it wandering West End, but the island has an original culture that predated the arrival of tourism, and which still dominates Roatán's eastern side.

■ **Hands on animal adventures.** At the Iguana Farm you can feed and touch hundreds of the famous reptiles; dolphin encounters are available at Anthony's Key Resort.

🐾 **Roatán Institute for Marine Sciences.** One of the attractions at Anthony's Key Resort, the Institute is an educational center that researches bottlenose dolphins and other marine animals. There are dolphin shows twice a day, which are free to the public. For an additional fee you can participate in a "dolphin encounter," which allows you to interact with the dolphins either swimming or snorkeling. There are also programs for children ages 5 to 14, including snorkeling experiences, and the "Dolphin Trainer for a Day" program. ⊠ *Anthony's Key Resort* ☎ *445–1327* ⊕ *www.anthonyskey.com* 🖃 *L64* ⊘ *Daily 8:30–5.*

Roatán Museum. Well worth a visit is the tiny museum, which has been called one of the best small museums in Central America. The facility, at Anthony's Key Resort, displays archaeological discoveries from Roatán and the rest of the Bay Islands. ⊠ *Anthony's Key Resort* ☎ *445–1327* ⊕ *www.anthonyskey.com* 🖃 *$4* ⊘ *Daily 8:30–5.*

West End. One of the most popular destinations for budget travelers, West End offers idyllic beaches stretching as far as the eye can see. One of the loveliest spots is Half Moon Bay, a crescent of brilliant white sand. A huge number of dive shops offer incredibly low-price diving courses. ⊠ *West End.*

SHOPPING

At the cruise ship dock in Coxen Hole you can find craft vendors, who set up shop outside the cruise-terminal gates; a small number of souvenir shops are scattered around the center of Coxen Hole, a short walk from the docks. Few of the souvenirs for sale here—or anywhere else on the island for that matter—were actually made in Roatán; most come from mainland Honduras. The new cruise-ship dock in Mahogany Bay has a shopping area as well. If you get as far as West End, there are a variety of souvenir and craft sellers in small shops lining the main sand road that runs parallel to the beach.

ACTIVITIES

DIVING AND SNORKELING

Most of the activity on Roatán centers on scuba diving and snorkeling, as well as the newest sensation, snuba, a cross between the two, whereby your mask is connected to an air tube above. Warm water, great visibility, and thousands of colorful fish make the island a popular destination. Add to this a good chance of seeing a whale shark, and you'll realize why so many people head here each year. Dive sites cluster off the island's western and southern coasts. Competition among the dive shops is fierce in West End, so check out a few. When shopping around, ask about class size (eight is the maximum), the condition of the diving equipment, and the safety equipment on the dive boat.

In West Bay, **Bananarama Dive Center** (⊠ *West Bay* ☎ *445–5005, 727/564–9058 in U.S.* ⊕ *www.bananaramadive.com*) is a top-notch dive operation. The staff are particularly good with kids and families, and they offer a variety of services for cruisers, such as snorkel rental, snacks and drinks right on the beach. Just at the entrance to West End, **Coconut Tree Divers** (⊠ *West End* ☎ *445–4081, 813/964–7214 in U.S.* ⊕ *www.coconuttreedivers.com*) is a PADI Gold Palm resort, offering a wide range of dives and dive courses. They also have cabins with air-conditioning and fridges, with a discount for their divers. **Native Sons** (⊠ *West End* ☎ *445–4003* ⊕ *www.nativesonsroatan.com*) is one of the most popular dive shops in town. It's run by a native of Roatán who really knows the area. The popular **Ocean Connections** (⊠ *West End* ☎ *445–1925 or 3372–0935* ⊕ *www.ocean-connections.com*) is a well-established dive shop. In business for more than a decade, **West End Divers** (⊠ *West End* ☎ *445–4289* ⊕ *www.westendivers.com*) has a pair of dive boats. The company is committed to protecting the fragile marine ecology.

FISHING

Early Bird Fishing Charters (⊠ *Sandy Bay* ☎ *445–3019* ⊕ *www.earlybirdfishingcharters.com*) is a great charter fishing company operated by a Roatán native. In addition to deep-sea and flats fishing, you'll have a great opportunity to see the island. Roatán has traditionally had a sea-based economy, and many of the small towns and villages look better from the vantage point of a boat.

FLIGHTSEEING

Bay Island Airways (☎ 9858–8819 or 9858–8824, 303/242–8004 in U.S. ⊕ www.bayislandairways.com) offer sightseeing tours in a multi-engine, three-seat seaplane. The experience is thrilling, since the cockpit is open and the plane takes off from the water; it is a fantastic photo opportunity. The company also offers packages that include landing near inaccessible beaches for a private picnic far from the crowds of other cruisers.

BEACHES

You almost can't go wrong with any of Roatán's white-sand beaches. Even those adjacent to populated areas manage to stay clean and uncluttered, thanks to efforts of residents. Water is rougher for swimming on the less-protected north side of the island.

Half Moon Bay, Roatán's most popular beach, is also one of its prettiest. Coconut palms and foliage come up to the crescent shoreline. The beach lies just outside the tourist-friendly West End. Crystal-clear waters offer abundant visibility for snorkeling.

Roatán is famous for the picturesque **West Bay Beach.** It's a de rigueur listing on every shore-excursions list. Once there, you can lounge on the beach or snorkel; on cruise days, most ships offer an excursion to nearby **Gumba Limba Park** (⊕ www.gumbalimbapark.com), which offeres close encounters with monkeys and birds, as well as canopy zip-line tours and other activities; to visit on a cruise-ship day, passengers must purchase an excursion from their ship that includes the park.

WHERE TO EAT

$$ ✘ **Blue Bahia Resort.** Tucked back off the road, just west of Anthony's
SEAFOOD   Key in Sandy Bay, the Blue Bahia Resort is a popular lunch and dinner destination. Their specialties are barbecue from their smoker and delicious seafood. ⊠ KM 9, Sandy Bay ☎ 445–3385.

$$ ✘ **Mangiamo Market and Deli.** With a wide selection of deli meats and
CAFÉ   imported foods, this small market is a standard shopping spot for island residents and tourists. You can get great sandwiches and soups, and it is a perfect spot to stock up on take-out food, drinks, and other necessities for your day on West Bay Beach. ⊠ West Bay Mall, West Bay ☎ 445–5035 ⊕ roatandeli.com.

SAMANÁ (CAYO LEVANTADO), DOMINICAN REPUBLIC

Eileen Robinson Smith

Samaná, the name of both a peninsula in the Dominican Republic as well as the largest town on Samaná Bay, is one of the least-known regions of the country, but the new international airport that opened in nearby El Catey in 2006, and the new highway from Santo Domingo that has cut drive-time to two hours, are changing that perception quickly. (Still, only charters fly into El Catey.) Much development is planned, so a visit now will be to a place that is not yet geared to a great deal of mainstream, mass tourism. But with the use of the port by some mega-ships, that, too, is changing rapidly. Samaná is one of the Dominican Republic's newest cruise-ship destinations, with one of the island's greatest varieties of shore excursions. You can explore caves and see an amazing waterfall. And since many humpback whales come here each year to mate and give birth, it's a top whale-watching destination from January through March. While some cruise lines still use Cayo Levantado as a private-island type of experience, for other lines it is just one of several options.

ESSENTIALS

CURRENCY The Dominican peso (RD$37.50 to US$1). Get local currency if you are touring on your own, but most places accept U.S. dollars, though any change will be in pesos. Banks and *cambios* (currency exchange offices) are plentiful.

INTERNET You'll find several convenient Internet cafés in town. The price of going online ranges between RD$40 and RD$80 per hour, inexpensive to be sure. This is still a developing destination, and electrical blackouts are not uncommon. Although most hotels and restaurants have generators, usually these shops do not. **Centro de Communications Claro** (⊠ *13 Maria Trinidad Sanchez, Samaná, across from landmark Palacio Justicia* ☎ *809/538–3538*) has just computers and phone booths for local and long-distance calls.

TELEPHONE You can call U.S. or Canadian numbers easily; just dial 1 plus the area code and number. **Centro de Communicationes Verizon** (⊠ *8 Francisco Rosario Sanchez, near market, Samaná* ☎ *809/538–2901* ⊠ *Maria Trinidad Sanchez, Samaná, next door to Pharmacia Gisella*) is a good place to make phone calls. Only cash is taken, preferably pesos. At the first location, there are public computers for checking your email; at the second, you won't be able to go online.

COMING ASHORE

Cruise ships anchor at a point equidistant between the town of Samaná and Cayo Levantado, an island at the mouth of Samaná Bay with a great beach and facilities to receive 1,500 cruise-ship passengers. Tenders will take you to one of three docks, located on the malecón, referred to as the Samaná Bay Piers. The farthest is a five-minute walk from the town center.

Renting a car, although possible, isn't a good option. Driving in the D.R. can be a hectic and even harrowing experience; if you are only in port one day, don't risk it. You'll do better if you combine your resources with friends from the ship and share a taxi to do some independent

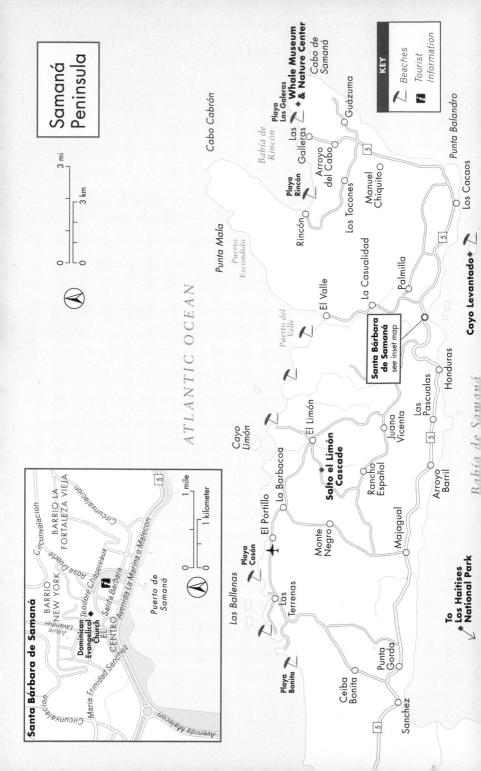

Samaná Peninsula

Santa Bárbara de Samaná

KEY

Beaches

Tourist Information

ATLANTIC OCEAN

Cabo Cabrón

Bahía de Rincón

Whale Museum & Nature Center

Playa Las Galeras

Cabo de Samaná

Las Galeras

Guázuma

Arroyo del Cabo

Manuel Chiquito

Punta Balandro

Playa Rincón

Rincón

Los Tocones

La Casualidad

Palmilla

Los Cacaos

5

5

Punta Mala

Puerto Escondido

El Valle

Puerto del Valle

Santa Bárbara de Samaná
see inset map

Cayo Levantado

Honduras

Bahía de Samaná

Cayo Limón

El Limón

Salto el Limón Cascade

Las Pascualas

Juana Vicenta

5

Arroyo Barril

La Barbacoa

Rancho Español

El Portillo

Majagual

Playa Cosón

Las Ballenas

Monte Negro

To Los Haitises National Park

Las Terrenas

Playa Bonita

Ceiba Bonita

Punta Gorda

Sanchez

5

3 mi

3 km

Santa Bárbara de Samaná

Circunvalación

BARRIO NEW YORK

BARRIO LA FORTALEZA VIEJA

Rosa Duarte

Julio Lavandier

Teodore Chásereaux

Dominican Evangelical Church

EL CENTRO

Santa Bárbara

María Trinidad Sánchez

Avenida La Marina o Malecón

Circunvalación

Puerto de Samaná

Avenida Malecón

5

1 mile

1 kilometer

exploring. Negotiate prices, and settle before getting in the taxi. To give you an idea of what to expect, a minivan that can take eight people will normally charge $90 for the round-trip to Las Terranas, including a two-hour wait while you explore or enjoy the beach. Similarly, you'll pay $80 to travel to Las Galleras or Playa Rincón. Many of the drivers speak some English. Within Samaná, rickshaws are far less costly and are also fun. Called *motoconchos de carretas,* they are not unlike larger versions of the Thai tuk-tuk, but can hold up to six people. The least you will pay is RD$10. They're fine for getting around town, but don't even think about going the distance with them.

SAMANÁ BEST BETS

■ **El Limón Waterfall.** A horse-back ride into the forest culminates in dazzling falls cascading into a natural pool.

■ **Los Haitises National Park.** The caves are filled with Taíno drawings; the mangroves are magnificent.

■ **Playa Rincón.** This rarely accessed beach offers a river, unspoiled mountainside, perfect beach, and privacy.

■ **Whale-watching.** In season, this is the top activity on the Samaná Peninsula.

EXPLORING SAMANÁ

SANTA BARBARA DE SAMANÁ

The official name of the city is Santa Barbara de Samaná; alas, that saint's name is falling into disuse, and you'll more often hear simply "Samaná" these days. An authentic port town, not just a touristic zone, it has a typical *malecón* (seaside promenade) with gazebos and park benches, ideal for strolling and watching the boats in the harbor. The main avenue that borders this zone is lined with restaurants, shops, and small businesses. A small but bustling town, Samaná is filled with friendly residents, skilled local craftsmen selling their wares, and many outdoor cafés.

Dominican Evangelical Church. The historic church is the oldest original building left in Samaná. It actually came across the ocean from England in 1881 in a hundred pieces, and was reassembled here, serving the spiritual needs of African-American freedmen who emigrated here from Philadelphia, Pennsylvania, in 1824. ⊠ *Calle Chaseurox, in front of Catholic church* ☎ *809/538–2579* ⬚ *Donations appreciated* ☉ *Daily dawn–dusk.*

Whale Museum and Nature Center. This museum is dedicated to the mighty mammals of the sea, and you will learn everything you have ever wanted to know about whales here. Samaná has one of the largest marine-mammal sanctuaries in the world, and is a center for whale-watching in the migration season. The C.E.B.S.E (Center for Conservation and Ecodevelopment of Samaná Bay and its Environment) manages this facility, which has been nicely renovated. ⊠ *Av. La Marina, Tiro Blanco* ☎ *809/538–2042* ⊕ *samana.org.do* ⬚ *RD$75* ☉ *Daily 8 noon and 2–5.*

ELSEWHERE IN THE SAMANÁ PENINSULA

Cayo Levantado. Residents of Samaná call Cayo Levantado their *pasa dia en la playa* (the place to pass the day on the beach). Today the small island in Samaná Bay has been improved to receive up to 1,500 cruise-ship passengers per day, with dining facilities, bars, restrooms, and lounge chairs on the beautiful beach. This isn't the most tranquil island, but you can quite happily spend the day here if you don't want to go into the town of Samaná. Day-use of the island will either be included in your cruise fare or will be treated as a regular shore excursion, for which the lines usually charge $40 to $60. ✉ *Samaná Bay* ☎ *No phone* 🎫 *Public beach free* ⊙ *Daily dawn–dusk.*

Los Haitises National Park. A guided tour is the only way to explore Los Haitises (pronounced Hi-*tee*-sis), which is across Samaná Bay from the peninsula. The park is famous for its karst limestone formations, caves, and grottoes filled with pictographs and petroglyphs left by the indigenous Taíno. Mangrove forests shelter many coastal bird species, including black-crowned night herons and the magnificent American frigate birds, making this a bird-watchers delight as well. Typical trips cruise the coastline dotted with small islands and spectacular cliff faces, finally docking to allow passengers to walk quietly around a mangrove swamp and visit the various caves.

Salto el Limón Cascade. Provided that you are fit, an adventurous guided trip to this spectacular waterfall is a delight. The journey is usually done mostly on horseback, but includes walking down rocky, sometimes muddy trails. The well-mannered horses take you across rivers and up mountains to El Limón, where you'll find the waterfall amidst luxuriant vegetation. Some snacks and drinks are usually included in the guided trip. ✉ *Santi Rancho, El Limón.*

SHOPPING

Rum, coffee, and cigars are popular local products. You may also find good coconut handicrafts, including coconut-shell candles. Whale-oriented gift items are particularly popular. Most of the souvenir shops are on Samaná's malecón or in the market plaza; you will find more on the major downtown streets in town, all within easy walking distance of the tender piers. A shopping mall called **Pueblo Principe** (✉ *20 Francisco Rosario Sanchez, Santa Barbara de Samaná*) is near the piers; it has a bevy of shops and food outlets (including American fast food).

ACTIVITIES

DIVING AND SNORKELING

In 1979 three atolls disappeared after a seaquake off Las Terrenas, providing an opportunity for truly memorable dives. Also just offshore from Las Terrenas are the Islas Las Ballenas (The Whale Islands), a cluster of four little islands with good snorkeling. A coral reef is off Playa Jackson, a beach accessible only by boat.

Las Terrenas Divers (✉ *At hotel Bahía Las Ballenas, Playa Bonita, Las Terrenas* ☎ *809/889–2422* ⊕ *www.lt-divers.com*) offers diving lessons and trips. A dive is $38; daily diving-equipment rentals are $10. Learn-to-dive programs are $80. It is closed Sunday.

WHALE-WATCHING

Humpback whales come to Samaná Bay to mate and give birth each year, from approximately January 15 through March 30. Samaná Bay is considered one of the top destinations in the world for watching whales. If you're here in season, this can be the experience of a lifetime. **Whale Samaná** (✉ *Av. Malecón 3, across street from cement town dock, beside park, Santa Barbara de Samaná* ☎ *809/538-2494* ⊕ *www.whalesamana.com*) is owned by Kim Beddall, a Canadian who is incredibly knowledgeable about whales and Samaná in general, having lived here for 20-some years. Kim leads the regions' best trips on board the *Pura Mia*, a 55-foot motor vessel. Trips are $58, which includes the Marine Mammal Sanctuary entrance fee. Kim welcomes cruise passengers but requires advance reservations; in most cases the trip times have been modified to accommodate cruise schedules, but be sure to ask about timing in advance to make sure it will work with your port call.

BEACHES

There are no recommendable beaches in Samaná de Santa Barbara itself. You will have to travel to one of the beautiful ones elsewhere on the peninsula, another reason why the Cayo Levantado excursion is very popular on most ships.

Fodor's Choice ★ **Playa Cusón** (✉ *Las Terrenas*) is a long, wonderful stretch of white sand and best beach close to the town of Las Terrenas. At the time of this writing, it was completely undeveloped, but there are a dozen condo developments under construction, so that sense of solitude is not going to last. One restaurant, the Beach, serves the entire 15-mi shore.

Playa Las Galeras (✉ *Las Galeras*) is within this tiny coastal town, a 30-minute drive northeast from Samaná town. It's a lovely, long, and uncluttered beach. The sand is white, the Atlantic waters generally calm. It has been designated a "Blue Flag" beach, which means that it's crystal-clean, with no pollution, though there are several small hotels here. This is a good snorkeling spot, too. That said, this is really just a departure point to the nearby virgin beaches closer to the cape to west. Hire a boat and get to them!

Fodor's Choice ★ **Playa Rincón** (✉ *5 km [3 mi] by boat, 15 km [9 mi] by road from Las Galeras*), a beautiful, white-sand beach, is considered one of the top beaches in the Caribbean. It's relatively undeveloped, and at the far-right end is a sheltered area, where you can snorkel. There are no facilities per se, but local ladies will sell you the freshest lobster and fish in coconut sauce with rice, and other creole dishes as well as cold drinks. You can reach Playa Rincón by boat or bus or car from Las Galeras. A boat is preferable; expect to pay about $15.

WHERE TO EAT

$ SEAFOOD ✕ **La Mata Rosada**. La Mata represents more than a step up in comfort and gastronomic complexity. The French owner-chef Yvonne Bastian has been luring local expats and foodies since the late 1990s. She sets tables up with white linens in an all-white interior including an army of ceiling fans to keep you cool; breezes sneak in from the bay across the street. There's a

7

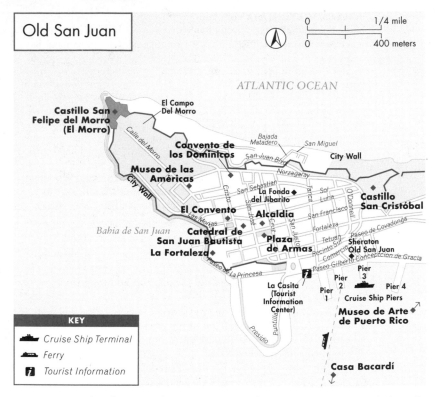

plentiful array of choices, starting with a sea and country salad of conch, potatoes, greens, and bacon; or the "gourmet" plate, a mix of grilled lobster and other shellfish. Ceviche, a specialty of this port town, is made with dorado (mahimahi) and conch. Save room: desserts are presented with pride. ⊠ *5B Av. Malecón* ☎ *809/538–2388* ⊙ *Closed Tues. June–Nov.*

SAN JUAN, PUERTO RICO

Heather
Rodino

Although Puerto Rico is a commonwealth of the United States, few cities in the Caribbean are as steeped in Spanish tradition as San Juan. Within a seven-square-block area in Old San Juan are restored 16th-century buildings, museums, art galleries, bookstores, and 200-year-old houses with balustraded balconies overlooking narrow, cobblestone streets. In contrast, San Juan's sophisticated Condado and Isla Verde areas have glittering hotels, fancy boutiques, casinos, and discos. Out in the countryside is 28,000-acre El Yunque National Forest, a rain forest with more than 240 species of trees growing at least 100 feet high. You can stretch your sea legs on dramatic mountain ranges, numerous trails, in vast caves, at coffee plantations, old sugar mills, and hundreds of beaches. No wonder San Juan is one of the busiest ports of call in the Caribbean. Like any other big city, San Juan has its share of petty crime, so guard your wallet or purse, especially in crowded markets and squares.

ESSENTIALS

CURRENCY The U.S. dollar is the official currency of Puerto Rico.

INTERNET You can check your email at **CyberNet Café** (✉ *1128 Av. Ashford, Condado* ☎ *787/724–4033* ✉ *5980 Av. Isla Verde, Isla Verde* ☎ *787/728–4195*).

TELEPHONE Calling the United States from Puerto Rico is the same as calling within the United States, and all U.S. cell phone plans work here just as they do at home. You can use the long-distance telephone service office in the cruise-ship terminal, or you can use your calling card by dialing the toll-free access number of your long-distance provider from any pay phone. You'll find a phone center by the Paseo de la Princesa.

SAN JUAN BEST BETS

■ **Casa Bacardí.** Rum lovers can jump on the public ferry and then taxi over to the factory.

■ **El Morro.** Explore the giant labyrinthine fort.

■ **El Yunque National Forest.** This rain forest east of San Juan is a great half-day excursion.

■ **Old San Juan.** Walk the cobblestone streets of Old San Juan.

■ **Shopping.** Within a few blocks of the port there are plenty of factory outlets and boutiques.

COMING ASHORE

Most cruise ships dock within a couple of blocks of Old San Juan; however, there is a second cruise pier across the bay, and if your ship docks there you'll need to take a taxi to get anywhere on the island. The Paseo de la Princesa, a tree-lined promenade beneath the city wall, is a nice place for a stroll—you can admire the local crafts and stop at the refreshment kiosks. Major sights in the Old San Juan area are mere blocks from the piers, but be aware that the streets are narrow and steeply inclined in places.

It's particularly easy to get to Cataño and the Bacardí Rum Plant on your own; take the ferry (50¢) that leaves from the cruise piers every half hour and then a taxi from the other side. Taxis, which line up to meet ships, are the best option if you want to explore beyond Old San Juan. White taxis labeled "Taxi Turistico" charge set fares of $10 to $19. Less common are metered cabs authorized by the Public Service Commission that charge an initial $1; after that, it's about 10¢ for each additional 1/13 mi. If you take a metered taxi, insist that the meter be turned on, and pay only what is shown, plus a tip of 15% to 20%. You can negotiate with taxi drivers for specific trips, and you can hire a taxi for as little as $30 per hour for sightseeing tours. If you want to see more of the island but don't want to drive, you may want to consider a shore excursion, though almost all trips can be booked more cheaply with local tour operators.

EXPLORING SAN JUAN

Old San Juan, the original city founded in 1521, contains carefully pre-served examples of 16th- and 17th-century Spanish-colonial architecture. More than 400 buildings have been beautifully restored. Graceful wrought-iron balconies with lush hanging plants extend over narrow streets paved with *adoquines* (blue-gray stones originally used as ballast on Spanish ships). The Old City is partially enclosed by walls that date from 1633 and once completely surrounded it. Designated a U.S. National Historic Zone in 1950, Old San Juan is chockablock with shops, open-air cafés, homes, tree-shaded squares, monuments, and people. You can get an overview on a morning's stroll (bear in mind that this "stroll" includes some steep climbs). However, if you plan to immerse yourself in history or to shop, you'll need a couple of days.

OLD SAN JUAN

Alcaldía. San Juan's city hall was built between 1602 and 1789. In 1841, extensive alterations were made so that it would resemble the city hall in Madrid, with arcades, towers, balconies, and an inner courtyard. Renovations have refreshed the facade of the building and some interior rooms, but the architecture remains true to its colonial style. Only the patios are open to public viewings. A municipal tourist information center and an art gallery with rotating exhibits are in the lobby. ⊠ *153 Calle San Francisco, Plaza de Armas, Old San Juan* ☎ *787/480–2548* 🖾 *Free* ☉ *Mon.–Sat. 8–4.*

Ⓒ **Castillo San Cristóbal.** This huge stone fortress, built between 1634 and 1785, guarded the city from land attacks from the east. The largest Spanish fortification in the New World, San Cristóbal was known in the 17th and 18th centuries as the Gibraltar of the West Indies. Five freestanding structures divided by dry moats are connected by tunnels. You're free to explore the gun turrets (with cannon in situ), officers' quarters, re-created 18th-century barracks, and gloomy passageways. ⊠ *Calle Norzagaray at Av. Muñoz Rivera, Old San Juan* ☎ *787/729–6777* ⊕ *www. nps.gov/saju* 🖾 *$3, $5 includes admission to El Morro* ☉ *Daily 9–6.*

Ⓒ **Castillo San Felipe del Morro** (*El Morro*). On a rocky promontory at the **Fodor's Choice** northwestern tip of the Old City is El Morro ("the promontory"), a ★ fortress built by the Spaniards between 1539 and 1786. Rising 140 feet above the sea, the massive six-level fortress was built to protect the harbor entrance. It is a labyrinth of cannon batteries, ramps, barracks, turrets, towers, and tunnels. Built to protect the port, El Morro has a commanding view of the harbor. You're free to wander throughout. The fort's small but enlightening museum displays ancient Spanish guns and other armaments, military uniforms, and blueprints for Spanish forts in the Americas, although Castillo San Cristóbal has more extensive and impressive exhibits. ⊠ *Calle del Morro, Old San Juan* ☎ *787/729–6960* ⊕ *www.nps.gov/saju* 🖾 *$3, $5 includes admission to Castillo San Cristóbal* ☉ *Daily 9–6.*

Catedral de San Juan Bautista. The Catholic shrine of Puerto Rico had humble beginnings in the early 1520s as a thatch-roof, wooden structure. After a hurricane in 1525 destroyed the church, it was rebuilt in 1540, when it was given a graceful circular staircase and vaulted

Gothic ceilings. Most of the work on the present cathedral, however, was done in the 19th century. The remains of Ponce de León are behind a marble tomb in the wall near the transept, on the north side. ⊠ *151 Calle Cristo, Old San Juan* ☎ *787/722–0861* ⊕ *www.catedralsanjuan. com* ⊠ *$1 donation suggested* ☉ *Mon.–Sat. 8–5, Sun. 8–4:30.*

Convento de los Dominicos. Built by Dominican friars in 1523, this convent—the oldest in Puerto Rico—often served as a shelter during Carib Indian attacks and, more recently, as headquarters for the Antilles command of the U.S. Army. Now home to some offices of the Institute of Puerto Rican Culture, the beautifully restored building contains the Galería Nacional, displaying santos (traditional wood carvings); artwork by José Campeche and Francisco Oller, two of the island's most important painters; as well as twentieth-century Puerto Rican art. ⊠ *98 Calle Norzagaray, Old San Juan* ☎ *787/721–6866* ⊠ *$3* ☉ *Mon.–Sat. 9–noon and 1–5.*

★ **La Fortaleza.** Sitting atop the fortified city walls overlooking the harbor, the Fortaleza was built between 1533 and 1540 as a fortress—and not a very good one. It was attacked numerous times and was occupied twice, by the British in 1598 and the Dutch in 1625. When El Morro and the city's other fortifications were finished, the Fortaleza instead became the governor's palace. Numerous changes have been made to the original primitive structure over the past four centuries, resulting in the current eclectic yet eye-pleasing collection of marble and mahogany, medieval towers, and stained-glass galleries. It is still the official residence of the island's governor and is the Western Hemisphere's oldest executive mansion in continual use. Guided tours are conducted several times a day in English and Spanish; both include a short video presentation. Call ahead to make a reservation, as the tour schedule will depend on the official functions occurring that day. ⊠ *Western end of Calle Fortaleza, Old San Juan* ☎ *787/721–7000 Ext. 2211* ⊕ *www.fortaleza.gobierno. pr* ⊠ *$3* ☉ *Weekdays.*

Museo de las Américas. On the second floor of the imposing former military barracks, Cuartel de Ballajá, the museum's permanent exhibit, Las Artes Populares en las Américas, focuses on the popular art and folk art of Latin America, including religious figures, musical instruments, basketwork, costumes, and farming and other implements. ⊠ *Calle Norzagaray and Calle del Morro, Old San Juan* ☎ *787/724–5052* ⊕ *www. museolasamericas.org* ⊠ *$3* ☉ *Tues., Wed., and weekends 10–4, Thurs. and Fri. 9–4.*

ELSEWHERE IN SAN JUAN

Casa Bacardí Visitor Center. Exiled from Cuba, the Bacardí family built a small rum distillery here in the 1950s. Today it's the world's largest, with the capacity to produce more than 100,000 gallons of spirits a day and 21 million cases a year. You can hop on a little tram to take an approximately 45-minute tour of the visitor center, though you can no longer visit the distillery itself. Yes, you'll be offered a free sample. You can reach the factory by taking the ferry from Pier 2 for 75¢ each way and then a *público* (public van service) from the ferry pier to the factory for about $2 or $3 per person. ⊠ *Rd. 165, Rte. 888, Km 2.6,*

7

Cataño ☎ 787/788–1500 *or* 787/788–8400 ⊕ *www.casabacardi.org* ✉ *Free Mon.–Sat. 9–6, last tour at 4:30; Sun. 10–5, last tour at 3:45.*

↻ **Museo de Arte de Puerto Rico.** One of the biggest museums in the Caribbean, this 130,000-square-foot building was once known as San Juan Municipal Hospital. The beautiful neoclassical building, dating from the 1920s, proved to be too small to house the museum's permanent collection of Puerto Rican art dating from the 17th century to the present. The solution was to build a new east wing, which is dominated by a five-story-tall stained-glass window, the work of local artist Eric Tabales. ⊠ *299 Av. José De Diego, Santurce* ☎ 787/977–6277 ⊕ *www. mapr.org* ✉ *$6; free Wed. 2–8* ⊗ *Tues. and Thurs.–Sat. 10–5, Wed. 10–8, Sun. 11–6.*

Fodor's Choice
★

SHOPPING

San Juan is not a duty-free port, so you won't find bargains on electronics and perfumes. However, shopping for native crafts can be fun. Popular souvenirs and gifts include *santos* (small, hand-carved figures of saints or religious scenes), hand-rolled cigars, local coffee, handmade lace, and carnival masks.

In Old San Juan—especially on Calles Fortaleza and Cristo—you can find everything from T-shirt emporiums to selective crafts stores, bookshops, art galleries, jewelry boutiques, and even shops that specialize in made-to-order Panama hats. Calle Cristo is lined with factory-outlet stores, including Coach and Ralph Lauren.

ACTIVITIES

GOLF

★ The spectacular **Río Mar Country Club** (⊠ *Río Mar Beach Resort & Spa, a Wyndham Grand Resort, 6000 Río Mar Blvd., Río Grande* ☎ 787/888–7060 ⊕ *www.wyndhamriomar.com*) has a clubhouse with a pro shop, two restaurants between two 18-hole courses, and a recently added fire pit that doubles as a place to grab a quick beverage and bite. The River Course, designed by Greg Norman, has challenging fairways that skirt the Mameyes River. The Ocean Course, designed by Tom and George Fazio, has slightly wider fairways than its sister; iguanas can usually be spotted sunning themselves near its fourth hole. If you're not a resort guest, be sure to reserve tee times at least 24 hours in advance. Fees for walk-ins range from $60 to $165.

BEACHES

San Juan does not have the island's best beaches, but anyone can rent a chair for the day at one of the public entry points.

Balneario de Carolina. When people talk of a "beautiful Isla Verde beach," this is the one they're talking about. A government-maintained beach, this *balneario* east of Isla Verde is so close to the airport that the leaves rustle when planes take off. The long stretch of sand, which runs parallel to Avenida Los Gobernadores, is shaded by palms and almond trees. There's plenty of room to spread out and lots of amenities: life-guards, restrooms, changing facilities, picnic tables, and barbecue grills. ✉ *Carolina* 🅿 *Parking $3* ⊙ *Daily 8–5.*

Playa del Condado. East of Old San Juan and west of Ocean Park, this long, wide beach is overshadowed by an unbroken string of hotels and apartment buildings. Beach bars, water-sports outfitters, and chair-rental places abound. You can access the beach from several roads off Avenida Ashford, including Calle Cervantes and Calle Candina. The protected water at the small stretch of beach west of the Conrad San Juan Condado Plaza hotel is particularly calm and popular with families; surf elsewhere in Condado can be a bit strong. The stretch of sand near Calle Vendig (behind the Atlantic Beach Hotel) is especially popular with the gay community. ✉ *Condado* ⊙ *Daily dawn–dusk.*

NIGHTLIFE

Almost every ship stays in San Juan late or even overnight to give passengers an opportunity to revel in the nightlife—the most sophisticated in the Caribbean.

CASINOS

By law, all casinos are in hotels. The atmosphere is refined, and many patrons dress to the nines, but informal attire (no shorts or tank tops) is usually fine. Casinos set their own hours, which change seasonally, but generally operate from noon to 4 am, although the casino in the Conrad Condado Plaza Hotel and Casino is open 24 hours. Other hotels with casinos include the InterContinental San Juan Resort and Casino, the Ritz-Carlton San Juan Hotel, Spa and Casino, and the Sheraton Old San Juan Hotel and Casino.

BARS AND DANCE CLUBS

Blend. This hip SoFo nightspot draws fashionistas enamored of the black walls, neon-blue lighting, and eye-candy female waitstaff. You can settle in at the marble-top bar, nestle cozily in a banquet sofa, or dance to salsa, techno, and world beat music in the dance hall to the rear. It serves late-night nouvelle native cuisine. ✉ *309 Calle Fortaleza, Old San Juan* ☎ *787/360–3681.*

The wildly popular **El Batey** (✉ *101 Calle Cristo, Old San Juan, San Juan* ☎ *787/725–1787*) won't win any prizes for its decor. Grab a marker to add your own message to the graffiti-covered walls, or add your business card to the hundreds that cover the light fixtures. The jukebox, packed with vintage 45s, has one of the best music selections on the island.

Krash. A balcony bar overlooks all the drama on the dance floor at this popular club. Most of the time DJs spin music ranging from house and hip-hop to bachata and reggaetón, but occasionally disco nights send you back to the music of the 1970s and '80s. It's open Wednesday through Saturday. ✉ *1257 Av. Ponce de León, Santurce* ☎ *787/722–1131* ⊕ *www.krashklubpr.com.*

7

WHERE TO EAT

$$$
SPANISH

✗**El Picoteo.** You could make a meal of the small dishes that dominate the menu at this tapas restaurant, on a mezzanine balcony at the Hotel El Convento. You won't go wrong ordering the sweet sausage in brandy or the grilled cuttlefish and passing them around the table. If you're not into sharing, there are two different kinds of paella that arrive on huge plates. There's a long, lively bar inside; one dining area overlooks a pleasant courtyard, whereas the other looks out onto Calle Cristo. Even if you have dinner plans elsewhere, consider stopping here for a nightcap or a midday pick-me-up. ⊠ *Hotel El Convento, 100 Calle Cristo, Old San Juan* ☎ *787/723–9202* ⊕ *www.elconvento.com.*

$–$$
CARIBBEAN
Fodor's Choice
★

✗**La Fonda del Jíbarito.** The menus are handwritten and the tables wobble, but sanjuaneros have favored this casual, no-frills, family-run restaurant—tucked away on a quiet cobbled street—for years. The shrimp with garlic sauce, goat fricassee, and shredded beef stew are among the specialties on the menu of typical Puerto Rican comida criolla dishes. The tiny back porch is filled with plants, and the dining room is filled with fanciful depictions of life on the street outside. The ever-present owner, Pedro J. Ruíz, is filled with the desire to ensure that everyone is happy. ⊠ *280 Calle Sol, Old San Juan* ☎ *787/725–8375* ⊕ *www.eljibaritopr.com* ⚠ *Reservations not accepted.*

SANTO DOMINGO, DOMINICAN REPUBLIC

Eileen Robin-son Smith

Spanish civilization in the New World began in Santo Domingo's 12-block Zona Colonial (Colonial Zone). As you stroll its narrow streets, it's easy to imagine this old city as it was when the likes of Columbus, Cortés, and Ponce de León walked the cobblestones, when pirates sailed in and out of the harbor, and when colonists first started building—the New World's largest city. Tourist brochures tout that "history comes alive here"—a surprisingly truthful statement. However, many tourists bypass the large, sprawling, and noisy city; it's their loss. The Dominican Republic's seaside capital—despite such detractions as poverty and sprawl, not to mention a population of some 2 million people—has some of the country's best hotels, restaurants, and nightlife (not to mention great casinos). Many of these are right on or near the Malecón and within the historic Zona Colonial area, which is separated from the rest of the city by Parque Independencia. If your ship calls or even embarks here, you'll be treated to a vibrant Latin cultural center unlike any other in the Caribbean.

ESSENTIALS

CURRENCY
The Dominican peso (RD$37.50. to US$1). Independent merchants willingly accept U.S. dollars, but you may need to change some money. Cambios (money exchange offices) are abundant, but you'll get the best rates at either a bank or a casino. Banco Popular has ATMS in the Zona Colonial, but you will be able to get only pesos.

INTERNET
Look up, and you will see many Internet shops on the Conde, usually with second-floor locations. Also, in the Colonial Zone, a convenient place to check your email is **Verizon Comunicaciones** (⊠ *256 Calle Conde,*

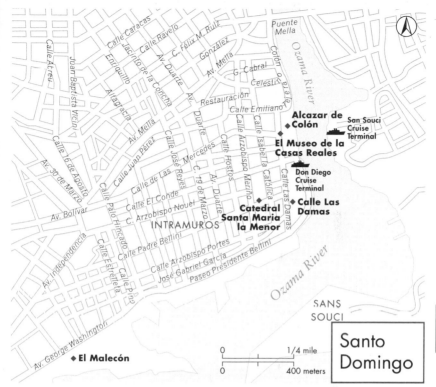

Santo Domingo

0 ———— 1/4 mile

0 ———— 400 meters

Zona Colonial ☎ 809/221–4249), where you can also make phone calls. You will have to pay cash—pesos or dollars.

TELEPHONE From the D.R. you need only dial 1 plus the area code and number to call the U.S. To make a local call, you must now dial 809 plus the seven-digit number. Phone cards, which are sold at gift shops and grocery stores, can give you considerable savings on your calls home. If you have a tri-band GSM phone, it should work on the island.

COMING ASHORE

Santo Domingo has two cruise-ship terminals. The Port of Don Diego is on the Ozuma River, facing the Avenida del Puerto, and across the street are steps that lead up to the main pedestrian shopping street of the Zona Colonial, Calle Conde. Don Diego has a lovely yellow-and-white building, with stained-glass windows and faux gas lights. It now has a small cafeteria, and potted palms soften the cordoned-off lines of passengers waiting to have their tickets checked and go through immigration. Just down the dock is an ATM machine; in front of that is a counter where you can get cold drinks and snacks. Across from it is a booth offering new self-guided audio tours. Should you want to go to the Malecón or shop in the modern city, $20 an hour is the going taxi rate. Don't rent a car; it's expensive, and traffic and parking are stressful.

The newer Sans Souci Terminal is still a work in progress, and some shops and other infrastructure are not yet finished. It is diagonally across the river from Don Diego, on Avenida Francisco Alberto Caaman. If you dock there, you will need transportation to get to the Colonial Zone.

Just a few paces in front of the Don Diego cruise terminal is the office of **Audio Guide Dominicana** (⊕ *www.jccolonialservice.com*). Tours come in three languages, and include information on more than 29 historic sites in the Colonial City and seven museums, plus a map and informative booklet. All museum entrances are included, as well as a nonalcoholic beverage at Hard Rock Café. The total cost is US$29, and credit cards are accepted. The company will also store luggage and provide airport transfers.

> ### SANTO DOMINGO BEST BETS
>
> ■ **Dining.** Some of the D.R.'s best restaurants can be found in the capital. Take advantage of them if you have any extra time to spend here.
>
> ■ **Shopping.** The country's best shopping can be found in Santo Domingo. You can go souvenir shopping right on Calle Conde, a pedestrian street that is the main drag of the Zona Colonial.
>
> ■ **Zona Colonial.** Santo Domingo's Colonial Zone is a World Heritage Site and a great place to stroll. It is a trip to the Old World; it is Spain in the 16th century.

AIRPORT TRANSFERS

If you are embarking in Santo Domingo, you should fly into Las Américas International Airport (SDQ), about 15 mi (24 km) east of downtown. Upon arrival you will have to pay $10 for a tourist tax. Transportation into the city is usually by taxi; figure on $40 to or from hotels on the Malecón or in the Zona Colonial. You'll be greeted by a melee of hawking taxi drivers and sometimes their English-speaking solicitors (who expect to be tipped, as do the freelance porters who will undoubtedly scoop up your luggage). If you are spending a night or two in Santo Domingo before a cruise, you can probably arrange a driver through your hotel, so you'll be met with someone holding a sign with your name (it's worth the extra $10 or so to avoid the hassle). If you're going straight to your cruise ship, consider taking the cruise line's prearranged transfer. When you disembark from your ship, expect long lines at check-in, and be sure to give yourself a full two hours for check-in and security. The government departure tax should be included in your airline ticket.

EXPLORING SANTO DOMINGO

History buffs will want to spend a day exploring the many "firsts" of our continent. A horse-and-carriage ride throughout the Colonial Zone costs $25 an hour. The steeds are no thoroughbreds, but they clip right along, though any commentary will be in Spanish. You can also negotiate to use them as a taxi, say down to the Malecón. The drivers hang out in front of the Hostal Nicolas de Ovando hotel.

Alcazar de Colón. The castle of Don Diego Colón, built in 1517, has 40-inch-thick coral-limestone walls. The Renaissance-style structure, with its balustrade and double row of arches, has strong Moorish, Gothic, and Isabelline influences. The 22 rooms are furnished in a style to which the viceroy of the island would have been accustomed—right down to the dishes and the viceregal shaving mug. Multilingual audio guides can be rented for RD$50 and are strongly recommended. ⊠ *Plaza de España off Calle Emiliano Tejera at foot of Calle Las Damas, Zona Colonial* ☎ *809/687–5361* ⊠ *RD$60* ☉ *Mon.–Sat. 9–5 and 8 pm–midnight, Sun. 9–4. Closed if no cruise ship in port.*

★ **Calle Las Damas.** The Ladies Street was named after the elegant ladies of the court who, in the Spanish tradition, promenaded in the evening. Here you can see a sundial dating from 1753 and the Casa de los Jesuitas, which houses a fine research library for colonial history as well as the **Institute for Hispanic Culture**; admission is free, and it's open weekdays from 8 to 4:30. If you follow the street going toward the Malecón, you will pass a picturesque alley fronted by a wrought-iron gate that has perfectly maintained colonial structures that are owned by the Catholic Church.

Catedral Santa María la Menor. The coral-limestone facade of the first cathedral in the New World towers over the south side of the Parque Colón. Spanish workmen began building the cathedral in 1514, but left to search for gold in Mexico. The church was finally finished in 1540. Its facade is composed of architectural elements from the late Gothic to the lavish plateresque style. Inside, the high altar is made of hammered silver. At this writing, a museum is being built for the cathedral's treasures. ⊠ *Calle Arzobispo Meriño, Zona Colonial* ☎ *809/689–1920* ⊠ *Free* ☉ *Mon.–Sat. 9–4; Sun. Masses begin at 6 am.*

El Malecón. Avenida George Washington, better known as the Malecón, runs along the Caribbean and has tall palms, cafés, high-rise hotels, and sea breezes.

★ **El Museo de las Casas Reales.** This is a remarkable museum that helps you understand the New World that was discovered by Columbus and the ensuing history of exploration and colonization in the 16th century. Exhibits include everything from Taíno archaeological finds to colonial artifacts, coins salvaged from wrecks of Spanish galleons, authentic colonial furnishings, and a collection of weapons. Additionally, the building in which the collection is housed is one of the most handsome colonial edifices remaining in Santo Domingo and has undergone a careful and complete restoration. ⊠ *Calle Las Damas, right before Plaza de Espana, Zona Colonial* ☎ *809/682–4202* ⊠ *RD$50* ☉ *Tues.–Sun. 9–5.*

SHOPPING

Exquisitely hand-wrapped cigars continue to be the hottest commodity coming out of the D.R. Only reputable cigar shops sell the real thing. Dominican rum and coffee are also good buys. *Mamajuana,* an herbal liqueur, is said to be the Dominican answer to Viagra. Look also for the delicate, faceless ceramic figurines that symbolize Dominican culture. Though locally crafted products are often very affordable, expect to pay for designer jewelry made of amber and larimar, an indigenous semiprecious stone the color of the Caribbean. Amber, a fossilization of resin from a prehistoric pine tree, often encasing ancient animal and plant life, from leaves to spiders to tiny lizards, is mined extensively. (Beware of fakes, which are especially prevalent in street stalls.)

One of the main shopping streets in the Zone is **Calle El Conde,** a pedestrian thoroughfare. With the advent of so many restorations, the dull and dusty stores with dated merchandise are giving way to some hip, new shops. However, many of the offerings, including local designer shops, are still of a caliber and cost that the Dominicans can afford. Some of the best shops are on **Calle Duarte,** north of the Colonial Zone, between Calle Mella and Avenida de Las Américas. **El Mercado Modelo,** a covered market, borders Calle Mella in the Colonial Zone; vendors here sell a dizzying selection of Dominican crafts.

The **Malecón Center,** the latest complex, adjacent to the classy Hilton Santo Domingo, will eventually house 170 shops, boutiques, and services plus several movie theaters. In the tower above are luxury apartments and Sammy Sosa, in one of the penthouses.

Plaza Central. This is a major shopping center with high-end shops, including a Jenny Polanco shop (an upscale Dominican designer who has incredible white linen outfits, artistic jewelry, purses, and more). ⊠ *Avs. Winston Churchill and 27 de Febrero, Piantini* ☎ *809/541–5929.*

NIGHTLIFE

Santo Domingo's nightlife is vast and ever changing. Check with the concierges and hip capitaleños. Get a copy of the free newspapers *Touring, Flow,* and *Aqui o Guía de Bares Restaurantes*—available at the tourist office and at hotels—to find out what's happening. At this writing, there is still a curfew for clubs and bars; they must close at midnight during the week, and 2 am on Friday and Saturday nights. There are some exceptions to the latter, primarily those clubs and casinos located in hotels. Sadly, the curfew has put some clubs out of business, but it has cut down on crime and late-night noise, particularly in the Zone.

WHERE TO EAT

$$ ✕ **Café Bellini.** This café has always had a panache far and above its
ITALIAN   counterparts, for the Italian owners also have the adjacent furniture design center. The modern, wicker-weave barrel chairs and the contemporary art and light fixtures are all achingly hip. It has recently had a renovation and looks refreshed. The menu is the same at lunch and dinner. The democratic pricing usually offers pasta dishes, such as the trio of raviolis (spinach, beet, and pumpkin), for about $10, which works for those on a slim budget. Main courses of meat or seafood are accompanied by pasta or grilled vegetables and potato. You can enjoy French and Italian liquors here (like pastis and grappa); dessert might be dark-chocolate mousse and fresh mango sorbet. Service is laudable, as is the music. ⊠ *Arzobispo Merino, corner of Padre Bellini, Zona Colonial* ☎ *809/686–3387* ⚱ *Reservations essential* ⊘ *Closed Sun. No lunch Mon.*

$$$
FRENCH
★

✕La Residence. This fine-dining enclave has always had the setting—Spanish colonial architecture, with pillars and archways overlooking a courtyard—and an esoteric lunch-dinner menu. The three-course, daily Menu del Chef is less than $28, including tax. It could be brochettes of spit-roasted duck, chicken au poivre, or vegetable risotto. You could start with a salad of panfried young squid and segue way to a luscious French pastry. You also get an amuse-bouche and excellent bread service. Veer from the daily specials menu and prices can certainly go higher, but they are still fair. ⊠ *Hostal Nicolas de Ovando, Calle Las Damas, Zona Colonial* ☎ *809/685–9955.*

WHERE TO STAY

Since Santo Domingo is a port of embarkation for some ships, we list these hotel recommendations for those who want or need to stay overnight.

¢
B&B/INN
★

Coco Boutique Hotel. Behind the soft, Caribbean-turquoise facade, you'll find a most untypical B&B, with earth tones and white almost everywhere—the reception and lounge, the stark wooden staircase, the grillwork on the French doors. Pros: amazingly quiet for the Zona Colonial; opposite the Plaza Pellerano Castro; rooftop terrace with Balinese sun beds and restaurant serving lunch and dinner. Cons: not steeped in creature comforts; bathrooms are small, as is one upstairs room. ⊠ *Arzobispo Porte 7, corner of Las Damas, Zona Colonial* ☎ *809/685‑8467* ⊕ *www.cocoboutiquehotel.com* ➳ *5 rooms* ὡ *In-room: a/c, no phone, no TV, no safe, Wi-Fi. In-hotel: bar, parking* ❚❂❚ *Breakfast.*

¢–$
HOTEL
★

Hilton Santo Domingo This has become *the* address on the Malecón for businesspeople, convention attendees, and leisure travelers. Pros: Sunday brunch is one of the city's top tickets; best service in Santo Domingo. Cons: little about the property is authentically Dominican; hotel can feel large and impersonal. ⊠ *Av. George Washington 500, Gazcue* ☎ *809/685–0000* ⊕ *hiltoncaribbean.com/santodomingo* ➳ *228 rooms, 32 suites* ὡ *In-room: a/c, Internet, Wi-Fi. In-hotel: restaurants, bars, pool, gym, spa, business center* ❚❂❚ *No meals.*

¢–$$
HOTEL
Fodor's Choice
★

Hostal Nicolas de Ovando. Listed as a World Heritage Site, this luxury hotel, sculpted from the residence of the first governor of the Americas, is the best thing to happen in the Zone since Diego Columbus's palace was finished in 1517. Pros: lavish breakfast buffet; beautifully restored historic section. Cons: can be pricey; no executive floor. ⊠ *Calle Las Damas, Zona Colonial* ☎ *809/685–9955 or 800/763–4835* ⊕ *www. sofitel.com* ➳ *97 rooms, 3 junior suites, 4 suites* ὡ *In-room: a/c, Wi-Fi. In-hotel: restaurant, bars, pool, gym, business center, parking, some pets allowed* ❚❂❚ *Breakfast.*

7

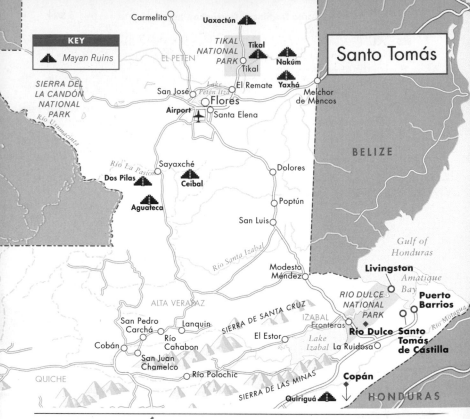

SANTO TOMÁS DE CASTILLA, GUATEMALA

Marlise Kast

Guatemala's short Caribbean shoreline doesn't generate the buzz of those of neighboring Belize and Mexico. The coast weighs in at a scant 74 mi (123 km), and this mostly highland country, which wears its indigenous culture on its sleeve and has historically looked inland rather than to the sea. You'll be drawn inland, too, with a variety of shore excursions. This is the land of the Maya, after all. But there's plenty to keep you occupied here in the lowlands. Tourist brochures tout the Caribbean coast as "The Other Guatemala." The predominantly indigenous and Spanish cultures of the highlands give way to an Afro-Caribbean tradition that listens more closely to the rhythms of far-off Jamaica rather than taking its cue from Guatemala City. Think of it as mixing a little reggae with your salsa.

ESSENTIALS

CURRENCY The Guatemalan quetzal, named for the brightly plumed bird that is the symbol of the country (Q7.69 to US$1). Take care of any banking matters in the cruise terminal in Santo Tomás de Castilla. You'll find ATMs in Puerto Barrios and Livingston but nowhere else in this region.

INTERNET The Terminal de Cruceros in Santo Tomás de Castilla has Internet computers for your use, the easiest option if you're a day visitor.

TELEPHONE Guatemalan phone numbers have eight digits. There are no city or area codes. Simply dial the number for any in-country call. Most towns have offices of Telgua, the national telephone company, where you can place both national and international calls. Avoid the ubiquitous public phones with signs promising "Free calls to the USA." The number back home being called gets socked with a hefty bill.

COMING ASHORE

Cruise ships dock at the modern, spacious Terminal de Cruceros, where you'll find a bank, post office, money exchange, telephones, Internet access, a lively craft market, and an office of INGUAT, Guatemala's national tourist office. A marimba band serenades you with its clinking xylophone-like music; a Caribbean ensemble dances for you (and may even pull you in to take part).

Taxis, both vehicular and water, take you to various destinations in the area. Plan on paying $2 to Santo Tomás de Castilla proper, and $5 to Puerto Barrios. Boats transport cruise visitors to Livingston, charging about $6 for the 20-minute trip. The Amatique Bay Resort provides water taxis from port to resort of $9 per person. Vehicular taxis charge $30 per head to travel by land to the resort.

EXPLORING SANTO TOMÁS DE CASTILLA

7

Amatique Bay. "Bahía de Amatique" denotes the large bay that washes the Caribbean coast of Guatemala and southern Belize, but for most travelers the name is inexorably linked with the **Amatique Bay Resort and Marina,** part of the Clarion chain, and the region's only five-star hotel. The 61-room resort opens itself up for day visitors, and many cruise passengers stop by for a drink, a meal, or an entire day of swimming, watersliding, kayaking, horseback riding, or bicycling. ⊠ *6 mi (10 km) north of Santo Tomás* ☎ *7948–1800, 2421–3333 in Guatemala City.*

Copán. The famous Mayan ruins of Copán lie just across the border from this region in neighboring Honduras, but are accessible enough from Santo Tomás to be an excursion on many itineraries. Bring your passport, since this entails an international border crossing. ⊠ *½ mi (1 km) east of Copán Ruinas, Honduras; 122 mi (203 km) southeast of Santo Tomás* ☎ *504/651–4018 or 504/651–4349* ⊠ *$15* ☉ *Daily 8–4.*

Livingston. Visitors compare Livingston with Puerto Barrios across the bay, and the former wins hands down, for its sultry, seductive Caribbean flavor. Wooden houses, some on stilts, congregate in this old fishing town, once an important railroad hub, but today inaccessible by land from the outside world. Livingston proudly trumpets its Garífuna heritage, a culture unique to Central America's eastern coast and descended from the intermarriage of African slaves with Caribbean indigenous people. Music and dance traditions and a Caribbean-accented English remain, even if old-timers lament the creeping outside influences, namely Spanish rap and reggae. ⊠ *15 mi (25 km) by water northwest of Santo Tomás.*

Puerto Barrios. Puerto Barrios maintains the atmosphere of an old banana town, humid and a tad down at the heels, perhaps longing for better days. Santo Tomás has replaced it as the country's largest port, and you'll likely zip through the Caribbean coast's biggest city on your way to somewhere else, but the cathedral and municipal market are worth a look if you find yourself here. Water taxis depart from the municipal docks for Livingston, across the bay, where you start your trip up the Río Dulce. ⊠ *3 mi (5 km) north of Santo Tomás de Castilla.*

Quiriguá. Construction began on the Guatemalan lowlands' most important Mayan ruins about AD 500. Its hieroglyphics tell its story: Quiriguá served at the time as a satellite state under the control of Copán, about 30 mi (50 km) away in present-day Honduras. By the height of its power in the 7th century, Quiriguá had overpowered Copán, but just as quickly fell back into submissive status. Quiriguá's ruins still today live in the shadow of their better-known neighbor across the border, and of the Tikal ruins in the northern part of Guatemala, but a visit here is rewarding for the carvings of *stelae,* the ornate sculptures depicting the city's rulers, and the largest such works in Central America. (Quiriguá's stelae stand 33 feet [10 meters] tall, dwarfing those of Copán.) Ease of access from the Caribbean coast makes Quiriguá well worth a visit, too. ⊠ *54 mi (90 km) southwest of Santo Tomás* ⊡ *$4* ⊘ *Daily 7:30–5.*

Río Dulce. The natural crown jewel of this region is the 13,000-hectare (32,000-acre) national park that protects the river leading inland from Livingston to Lago de Izabal, Guatemala's largest lake. Pelicans, herons, egrets, and terns nest and fly along the Río Dulce, which cuts through a heavily forested limestone canyon. Excursions often approach the park by land, but we recommend making the trip upriver from Livingston to immerse yourself in the entire Indiana Jones experience. ⊠ *Southwest of Livingston.*

In 1955 the Guatemalan government reconstructed the ruined fortress of **Castillo de San Felipe de Lara** (⊠ *Southwest of Fronteras* ☎ *No phone* ⊡ *$4*). Spanish colonists constructed the fortress in 1595 to guard the inland waterway from pirate incursions. It was used as a prison between 1655 and 1660. You can reach it by the road leading west from Río Dulce or by a short boat ride. A 1999 earthquake in this region destroyed the river pier as well as damaging portions of the fort. If you wish to visit, rather than simply see the structure from the water, you'll need to approach the park overland rather than upriver.

A short launch from Fronteras takes you to **Hacienda Tijax** (⊠ *Northeast of Fronteras* ☎ *7930–5505* ⊕ *www.tijax.com*), an old rubber plantation, now a reforestation project, which offers hiking and kayaking and a chance to view the cultivation of orchids and spices.

Santo Tomás de Castilla. Belgian immigrants settled Santo Tomás in the 19th century, but little remains of their heritage today, save for the preponderance of French and Flemish names in the local cemetery. Most visitors move on. Santo Tomás has experienced a small renaissance as the country's most important port, receiving growing numbers of cruise and cargo ships, and serving as the headquarters of the Guatemalan navy.

Fodor'sChoice   **Tikal.** The high point of any trip to Guatemala is a visit to Central Amer-
★   ica's most impressive ruins. There's nothing quite like the sight of the towering temples, ringed on all sides by miles of virgin forest, but you need a lot of quetzales to get here, since you'll travel by plane from the

airstrip outside Santo Tomás to the small airport in Santa Elena, near the ruins. Although this region was home to Mayan communities as early as 600 BC, Tikal wasn't established until around 200 BC. By AD 500 it's estimated that the city covered more than 18 square mi (47 square km) and had a population of close to 100,000. For almost 1,000 years Tikal remained engulfed by the jungle. Excavation began in earnest in the mid-1800s. Today, after more than 150 years of digging, researchers say that Tikal includes some 3,000 buildings. Countless more are still covered by the jungle. Temple IV, the tallest-known structure built by the Maya, offers an unforgettable view from the top. ⊠ *Parque Nacional Tikal* ☎ *No phone* ⌨ *$20* ☉ *Daily 6–6.*

SHOPPING

The rest of Guatemala overflows with indigenous crafts and art, but the famous market towns of the highlands are nowhere to be found in Caribbean region. Quite honestly, your best bet for shopping is the Terminal de Cruceros at Santo Tomás de Castilla, and you'll have plenty of opportunity to buy before you board your ship. What you'll find here comes from Guatemala's highlands—the Caribbean has never developed a strong artisan tradition—with a good selection of fabrics, weavings, woodwork, and basketry to choose from. Markets in Puerto Barrios and Livingston, the only real urban areas you'll encounter in this region, are more geared to the workaday needs of residents rather than visitors.

ACTIVITIES

BEACHES AND WATER SPORTS

A beach culture has just never developed in this region of Guatemala the way it has in neighboring Belize and Mexico. The only real beach in the region is found within the confines of the **Amatique Bay Resort and Marina** (⊠ *6 mi [10 km] north of Santo Tomás* ☎ *7913–0000 in Guatemala City* ⊕ *www.amatiquebay.net*), which is the only place here that has a resort feel to it. Day visitors partake of swimming, waterslides, and kayaking. The resort's launch will bring you over from the cruise-ship terminal in Santo Tomás.

HIKING AND KAYAKING

Hacienda Tijax (⊠ *Northeast of Fronteras* ☎ *7930–5505* ⊕ *www. tijax. com*), which is pronounced tee-*hahsh*, is inland, near the point where the Río Dulce meets Lake Izabal, and provides kayaking and hiking for day visitors.

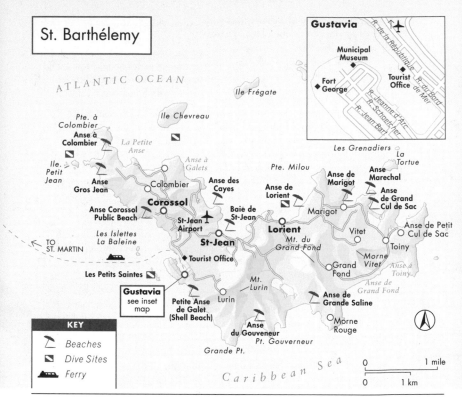

ST. BARTHÉLEMY (GUSTAVIA)

Elise Meyer

Hilly St. Barthélemy, popularly known as St. Barth (or St. Barts) is just 8 square mi (21 square km), but the island has at least 20 good beaches. What draws visitors is its sophisticated but unstudied approach to relaxation: the finest food, excellent wine, high-end shopping, and lack of large-scale commercial development. A favorite among upscale cruise-ship passengers, who also appreciate the shopping opportunities and fine dining, St. Barth isn't really equipped for mega-ship visits, which is why most ships calling here are from smaller premium lines. This is one place where you don't need to take the ship's shore excursions to have a good time. Just hail a cab or rent a car and go to one of the many wonderful beaches, where you will find some of the best lunch-time restaurants, or wander around Gustavia, shopping and eating. It's the best way to relax on this most relaxing of islands.

ESSENTIALS

CURRENCY The euro (€1 to US$1.41); however, U.S. dollars are accepted in almost all shops and in many restaurants. Credit cards are widely accepted.

INTERNET Most restaurants on the island now offer free Wi-Fi for customers, and there is also a free hotspot at the port area.

Centre Alizes. Centre Alizes offers Internet service. ⊠ *Rue de la République, Gustavia, St. Barthélemy* ☏ *0590/29–89–89.*

TELEPHONE Public telephones accept *télécartes,* prepaid calling cards that you can buy at the gas station next to the airport and at post offices in Lorient, St-Jean, and Gustavia. Making an international call using a télécarte is the best way to go.

COMING ASHORE

Even medium-size ships must anchor in Gustavia Harbor and bring passengers ashore on tenders. The tiny harbor area is right in Gustavia, which is easily explored on foot. Taxis, which meet all cruise ships, can be expensive. Technically, there's a flat rate for rides up to five minutes long. Each additional three minutes is an additional amount. In reality, however, cabbies usually name a fixed rate—and will not budge. Fares are 50% higher on Sunday and holidays. St. Barth is one port where it's really worth it to arrange a car rental for a full-day exploration of the island, including the island's out-of-the-way beaches. But be aware that during high season there is often a three-day minimum, so this may not be possible except through your ship (and then you'll pay premium rates indeed). Most car-rental firms operate at the airport; however, renting on your own is usually cheaper than what you'll get if you go with one of the ship's car rentals (you may be able to find a car for €50 per day).

EXPLORING ST. BARTH

With a little practice, negotiating St. Barth's narrow, steep roads soon becomes fun. Free maps are everywhere, roads are well marked, and painted signs will point you where you want to be. Take along a towel, sandals, and a bottle of water, and you will surely find a beach upon which to linger.

☺ **Corossol.** The island's French provincial origins are most evident in this two-street fishing village with a little rocky beach. ⊠ *Corossol, St. Barthélemy.*

Inter Oceans Museum. Ingenu Magras's Inter Oceans Museum has more than 9,000 seashells and an intriguing collection of sand samples from around the world. You can buy souvenir shells. ⊠ *Corossol, St. Barthélemy* ☏ *0590/27–62–97* ⊠ *€3* ☺ *Tues.–Sun. 9–12:30 and 2–5.*

Gustavia. You can easily explore all of Gustavia during a two-hour stroll. Most shops close from noon to 2 or 3, so plan lunch accordingly, but stores stay open past 7 in the evening.

Tourist Office. A good spot to park your car is rue de la République, alongside the catamarans, yachts, and sailboats. The tourist office on the pier can provide maps and a wealth of information. During busier holiday periods, the office may be open all day. ⊠ *Rue de la République, Gustavia, St. Barthélemy* ☏ *0590/27–87–27* ⊕ *www.saintbarth-tourisme. com* ☺ *Mon. 8:30–12:30, Tues.–Fri. 8–noon and 2–5, Sat. 9–noon.*

Municipal Museum. On the far side of the harbor known as La Pointe is the charming Municipal Museum, where you can find watercolors, portraits, photographs, and historic documents detailing the island's

7

history, as well as displays of the island's flowers, plants, and marine life. ⊠ *La Pointe, Gustavia, St. Barthélemy* ☎ *599/29–71–55* 🖃 *€2* ⊙ *Mon., Tues., Thurs., and Fri. 8:30–12:30 and 2:30–6, Sat. 9–12:30.*

Lorient. Site of the first French settlement, Lorient is one of the island's two parishes; a restored church, a school, and a post office mark the spot. Note the gaily decorated graves in the cemetery.

Le Manoir. One of St. Barth's secrets is Le Manoir, a 1610 Norman manor, now a guesthouse, which was painstakingly shipped from France and reconstructed in Lorient in 1984. Look for the entrance by the Ligne de St. Barth building. ⊠ *Lorient, St. Barthélemy* ☎ *0590/27–79–27.*

St-Jean. The half-mile-long crescent of sand at St-Jean is the island's most popular beach. A popular activity is watching and photographing the hair-raising airplane landings, but be sure to not stand in the area at the beach end of the runway, where someone was seriously injured. You'll also find some of the best shopping on the island here, as well as several restaurants. ⊠ *St-Jean, St. Barthélemy.*

SHOPPING

St. Barth is a duty-free port, and with its sophisticated crowd of visitors, shopping in the island's 200-plus boutiques is a definite delight. In Gustavia boutiques line the three major shopping streets. Quai de la République, which is right on the harbor, rivals New York's Madison Avenue or Paris's avenue Montaigne for high-end designer retail, including shops for **Louis Vuitton, Bulgari, Cartier, Chopard,** and **Hermès.** These shops often carry items that are not available in the United States. The Carré d'Or plaza is great fun to explore. Shops are also clustered in **La Savane Commercial Center** (across from the airport), **La Villa Créole** (in St-Jean), and **Espace Neptune** (on the road to Lorient). It's worth working your way from one end to the other at these shopping complexes—just to see or, perhaps, be seen. Boutiques in all three areas carry the latest in French and Italian sportswear and some haute couture. Bargains may be tough to come by, but you might be able to snag that *pochette* that is sold out stateside, and in any case, you'll have a lot of fun hunting around.

ACTIVITIES

BOATING AND SAILING

St. Barth is a popular yachting and sailing center, thanks to its location midway between Antigua and St. Thomas. Gustavia's harbor, 13 to 16 feet deep, has mooring and docking facilities for 40 yachts. There are also good anchorages available at Public, Corossol, and Colombier. You can charter sailing and motorboats in Gustavia Harbor for as little as a half day. Stop at the tourist office in Gustavia for an up-to-the minute list of recommended charter companies.

Jicky Marine Service. Jicky Marine Service offers full-day outings, either on a variety of motorboats, or 42- or 46-foot catamaran, to the uninhabited Île Fourchue for swimming, snorkeling, cocktails, and lunch. The cost starts at about $100 per person; an unskippered motor rental runs about

$260 a day. ⊠ *Ferry dock, Gustavia, St. Barthélemy* ☎ *0590/27–70–34* ⊕ *www.jickymarine.com.*

DIVING AND SNORKELING
Several dive shops arrange scuba excursions to local sites. Depending on weather conditions, you may dive at **Pain de Sucre, Coco Island,** or toward nearby **Saba.** There's also an underwater shipwreck to explore, plus sharks, rays, sea tortoises, coral, and the usual varieties of colorful fish. The waters on the island's leeward side are the calmest. For the uncertified who still want to see what the island's waters hold, there's an accessible shallow reef right off the beach at Anse de Cayes that you can explore if you have your own mask and fins.

> ### ST. BARTHÉLEMY BEST BETS
>
> ■ **Beautiful Beaches.** Pick any of the lovely, uncrowded beaches.
>
> ■ **French Food. St.** Barth has some of the best restaurants in the Caribbean.
>
> ■ **Soaking up the Atmosphere.** It's the French Riviera transported to the Caribbean.
>
> ■ **Shopping.** There is no better fashion shopping in the Caribbean, especially if you are young and slim.

Plongée Caraïbe. Plongée Caraïbe is recommended for its up-to-the-minute equipment and dive boat. ⊠ *St. Barthélemy* ☎ *0590/27–55–94* ⊕ *www.plongee-caraibes.com.*

BEACHES

There are many *anses* (coves) and nearly 20 *plages* (beaches) scattered around the island, each with a distinctive personality and each open to the general public. Even in season you can find a nearly empty beach. Topless sunbathing is common, but nudism is forbidden—although both Grande Saline and Gouverneur are de facto nude beaches.

Anse de Grand Cul de Sac. The shallow, reef-protected beach is nice for small children, fly-fishermen, kayakers, and windsurfers—and for the amusing pelicanlike frigate birds that dive-bomb the water fishing for their lunch. You needn't do your own fishing; you can have a wonderful lunch at one of the excellent restaurants. ⊠ *Grand Cul de Sac, St. Barthélemy.*

Fodor's Choice
★ **Anse de Grande Saline.** Secluded, with its sandy ocean bottom, this is just about everyone's favorite beach and is great for swimmers, too. Without any major development (although there is some talk of developing a resort here) it's an ideal Caribbean strand. However, there can be a bit of wind here, so you can enjoy yourself more if you go on a calm day. In spite of the prohibition, young and old alike go nude. The beach is a 10-minute walk up a rocky dune trail, so be sure to wear sneakers or water shoes. Although there are several good restaurants for lunch near the parking area, once you get here, the beach is just sand, sea, and sky. ⊠ *Grande Saline, St. Barthélemy.*

★ **Anse du Gouverneur.** Because it's so secluded, this beach is a popular place for nude sunbathing. It is truly beautiful, with blissful swimming and views of St. Kitts, Saba, and St. Eustatius. Venture here at the end of the day and watch the sun set behind the hills. The road here from Gustavia also offers spectacular vistas. Legend has it that pirates' treasure is buried in the vicinity. There are no restaurants or other services here, so plan accordingly. ⊠ *Anse du Gouverneur, Gouverneur, St. Barthélemy.*

Baie de St-Jean. Like a mini–Côte d'Azur—beachside bistros, terrific shopping, bungalow hotels, bronzed bodies, windsurfing, and day-trippers who tend to arrive on BIG yachts—the reef-protected strip is divided by Eden Rock promontory. You can rent chaises and umbrellas at La Plage restaurant or at Eden Rock, where you can lounge for hours over lunch. ⊠ *Baie de St-Jean, St-Jean, St. Barthélemy.*

WHERE TO EAT

A service charge is always added by law, but you should leave the server 5% to 10% extra in cash. It is generally advisable to charge restaurant meals on a credit card, as the issuer will offer a better exchange rate than the restaurant.

$$$ ✕ **Le Tamarin.** A leisurely lunch here en route to Grande Saline beach is
FRENCH   a St. Barth *must*. But new management makes it tops for dinner too.
★   Sit on one of the licorice-color Javanese couches in the lounge area and nibble excellent sushi, or settle at a table under the wondrous tamarind tree for which the restaurant is named. A unique cocktail each day, ultrafresh fish provided by the restaurant's designated fisherman, and gentle prices accommodate local residents as well as the holiday crowd. The restaurant is open year-round. ⊠ *Grande Saline, St. Barthélemy* ☎ *0590/27–72–12* ⊙ *Closed Tues.*

$$$ ✕ **Wall House.** The food is excellent—and the service is always friendly—at
ECLECTIC   this restaurant on the far side of Gustavia Harbor. The snail and spinach ravioli are out of this world, and the rotisserie duck marinated in honey from the rotisserie is a universal favorite. Local businesspeople crowd the restaurant for the bargain € 10.50 prix-fixe lunch menu. An old-fashioned dessert trolley showcases some really yummy sweets. ⊠ *La Pointe, Gustavia, St. Barthélemy* ☎ *0590/27–71–83* ⊕ *www.wallhouserestaurant. com* ⧓ *Reservations essential* ⊙ *Closed Sun. and Sept. and Oct.*

ST. CROIX (FREDERIKSTED)

Lynda Lohr   St. Croix is the largest of the three U.S. Virgin Islands (USVI) that form the northern hook of the Lesser Antilles; it's 40 mi (64 km) south of its sister islands, St. Thomas and St. John. Christopher Columbus landed here in 1493, skirmishing briefly with the native Carib Indians. Since then, the USVI have played a colorful, if painful, role as pawns in the game of European colonialism. Theirs is a history of pirates and privateers, sugar plantations, slave trading, and slave revolt and liberation. Through it all, Denmark had staying power. From the 17th to the 19th century, Danes oversaw a plantation slave economy that produced molasses, rum, cotton, and tobacco. Many of the stones you tread on in the streets were once used as ballast on sailing ships, and the yellow fort of Christiansted is a reminder of the value once placed on this island treasure. Never a major cruise destination, it is still a stop for several ships each year.

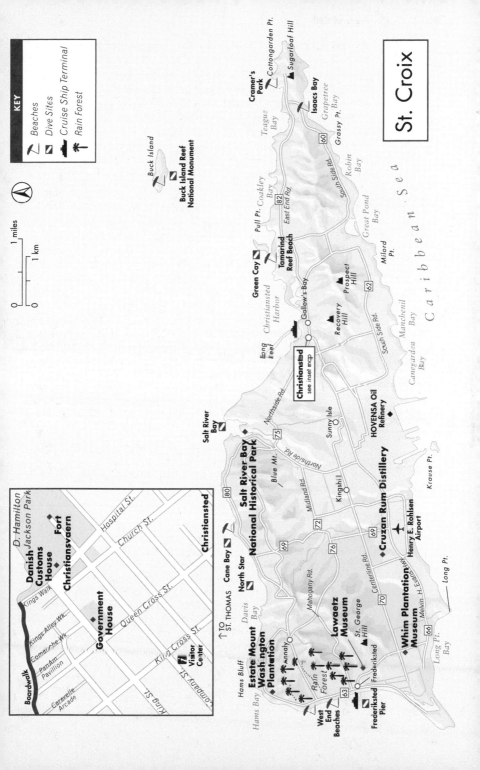

St. Croix

KEY

- Beaches
- Dive Sites
- Cruise Ship Terminal
- Rain Forest

1 miles

1 km

Inset map: Christiansted

- D. Hamilton Jackson Park
- Danish Customs House
- Fort Christiansvaern
- Government House
- Visitor Center
- Boardwalk
- Kings Walk
- Kings Alley Wk.
- Comar/the Wk.
- PanAm Pavillion
- Caravelle Arcade
- Hospital St.
- Church St.
- Queen Cross St.
- King Cross St.
- Company St.
- King St.

Christiansted

Main map labels

- Buck Island
- Buck Island Reef National Monument
- Cottongarden Pt.
- Sugarloaf Hill
- Cramer's Park
- Isaacs Bay
- Grapetree Bay
- Grassy Pt. Bay
- Teague Bay
- 60
- South Side Rd.
- Robin Bay
- Pull Pt. Coakley Bay
- 82
- East End Rd.
- Great Pond Bay
- Green Cay
- Tamarind Reef Beach
- Christiansted Harbor
- Gallow's Bay
- Milord Pt.
- Prospect Hill
- 62
- Recovery Hill
- South Side Rd.
- Manchenil Bay
- Canegarden Bay
- Long Reef
- Christiansted (see inset map)
- Northside Rd.
- Sunny Isle
- HOVENSA Oil Refinery
- Krause Pt.
- 75
- Blue Mt.
- Salt River Bay
- Salt River Bay National Historical Park
- 80
- TO ST. THOMAS
- Davis Bay
- Cane Bay
- North Star
- Hams Bluff
- Hams Bay
- West End Beaches
- Estate Mount Washington Plantation
- Rain Forest
- 63
- Frederiksted Pier
- Frederiksted
- Whim Plantation Museum
- Lawaetz Museum
- St. George Hill
- Cruzan Rum Distillery
- Henry E. Rohlsen Airport
- Kingshill
- Midland Rd.
- Mahogany Rd.
- 69
- 72
- 76
- 69
- 70
- 66
- Centerline Rd.
- Melvin H. Evans Hwy.
- Long Pt. Bay
- Long Pt.
- Annaly
- Caribbean Sea

ESSENTIALS

CURRENCY The U.S. dollar is the official currency of St. Croix.

INTERNET There's a convenient Internet café in Christiansted if you make it there during your day ashore. **A Better Copy** ✉ *52A Company St., Christiansted, St. Croix, U.S. Virgin Islands* ☎ *340/692–5303.*

TELEPHONE Calling the United States from St. Croix works the same way as calling within the U.S. Local calls from a public phone cost up to 35¢ for every five minutes. You can use your regular toll-free connections for long-distance services. Most U.S. cell phone plans include the Virgin Islands for no additional cost.

COMING ASHORE

Cruise ships dock in Frederiksted, on the island's west end. You'll find an information center near the pier, and the town is easy to explore on foot. Beaches are nearby. The only difficulty is that you are far from the island's main town, Christiansted. Some cruise lines offer bus transportation there; otherwise, you are probably better off renting a car to explore the island, since both car-rental rates and gasoline prices are reasonable; just remember to drive on the left.

Taxis of all shapes and sizes are available at the cruise-ship pier and at various shopping and resort areas. Remember, too, that you can hail a taxi that's already occupied. Drivers take multiple fares and sometimes even trade passengers at midpoints. Taxis don't have meters, so you should check the list of official rates (available at the visitor centers or from drivers) and agree on a fare before you start, but there are standard rates for most trips. A taxi to Christiansted will cost about $25 for two people for transportation only; an island tour including Christiansted will cost $110 for four people.

Car Rentals

Midwest. Midwest is outside Frederiksted, but will pick you up at the pier if you want to rent a car for the day. ☎ *340/772–0438, 877/772–0438* ⊕ *www.midwestautorental.com.*

EXPLORING ST. CROIX

Frederiksted speaks to history buffs with its quaint Victorian architecture and historic fort. There's very little traffic, so this is the perfect place for strolling and shopping. Christiansted is a historic Danish-style town that served as St. Croix's commercial center. Your best bet is to see the historic sights in the morning, when it's still cool. This two-hour endeavor won't tax your walking shoes and will leave you with energy to poke around the town's eclectic shops.

CHRISTIANSTED

In the 1700s and 1800s Christiansted was a trading center for sugar, rum, and molasses. Today there are law offices, tourist shops, and restaurants, but many of the buildings, which start at the harbor and go up the gently sloped hillsides, still date from the 18th century. You can't get lost. All streets lead back downhill to the water.

Danish Customs House. Built in 1830 on foundations that date from a century earlier, the historic building, which is near Ft. Christiansvaern, originally served as both a customshouse and a post office. In 1926 it became the Christiansted Library, and it's been a national park facility since 1972. It's closed to the public, but the sweeping front steps make a nice place to take a break. ⊠ *King St., Christiansted, St. Croix* ☏ *340/773–1460* ⊕ *www.nps.gov/chri.*

Ⓒ **Ft. Christiansvaern.** The large yellow **Fodor's Choice** fortress dominates the waterfront. ★ Because it's so easy to spot, it makes a good place to begin a walking tour. In 1749 the Danish built the fort to protect the harbor, but the structure was repeatedly damaged by hurricane-force winds and had to be partially rebuilt in 1771. It's now a national historic site, the best preserved of the few remaining Danish-built forts in the Virgin Islands. The park's visitor center is here. Rangers are on hand to answer questions. ⊠ *Hospital St., Christiansted, St. Croix* ☏ *340/773 1460* ⊕ *www.nps.gov/chri* ⌹ *$3 (includes Steeple Bldg.)* ☉ *Weekdays 8–4:30, weekends 9–4:30.*

Government House. One of the town's most elegant structures was built as a home for a Danish merchant in 1747. Today it houses offices. If you're here weekdays from 8 to 4:30, slip into the peaceful inner courtyard to admire the still pools and gardens. A sweeping staircase leads you to a second-story ballroom, still used for official government functions. ⊠ *King St., Christiansted, St. Croix* ☏ *340/773–1404.*

MID ISLAND

Cruzan Rum Distillery. A tour of the company's factory, established in 1760, culminates in a tasting of its products, all sold here at bargain prices. It's worth a stop to look at the distillery's charming old buildings even if you're not a rum connoisseur. ⊠ *West Airport Rd., Estate Diamond, St. Croix* ☏ *340/692–2280* ⊕ *www.cruzanrum.com* ⌹ *$5* ☉ *Weekdays 9–4.*

Ⓒ **Whim Plantation Museum.** The lovingly restored estate, with a windmill, **Fodor's Choice** cook house, and other buildings, will give you a sense of what life ★ was like on St. Croix's sugar plantations in the 1800s. The oval-shape greathouse has high ceilings and antique furniture and utensils. Notice its fresh, airy atmosphere—the waterless stone moat around the greathouse was used not for defense but for gathering cooling air. If you have kids, the grounds are the perfect place for them to run around, perhaps while you browse in the museum gift shop. It's just outside of Frederiksted. ⊠ *Rte. 70, Estate Whim, St. Croix* ☏ *340/772–0598* ⊕ *www.stcroixlandmarks.com* ⌹ *$10* ☉ *Mon.–Sat. 10–4.*

ST. CROIX BEST BETS

■ **Buck Island.** The snorkeling trail here is fun, but go by catamaran.

■ **Christiansted.** The best shopping on the island as well as interesting historical sights are here.

■ **Cruzan Rum Distillery.** This West End rum distillery gives you a tour and samples.

■ **Kayaking.** The Salt River, with few currents, is a great place to take a guided kayak trip.

■ **West End Beaches.** The island's best beaches are on the west end, and are just a short hop from the cruise pier.

7

FREDERIKSTED AND ENVIRONS

This town is noted less for its Danish than for its Victorian architecture, which dates from after the slave rebellion and great fire of July 1848.

Caribbean Museum Center for the Arts. Sitting across from the waterfront in a historic building, this small museum hosts an always-changing roster of exhibits. Many are cutting-edge multimedia efforts that you might be surprised to find in such an out-of-the way location. The openings are popular events. ⊠ *10 Strand St., Frederiksted, St. Croix* ☎ *340/772–2622* ⊕ *www.cmcarts.org* ⊠ *Free* ⊙ *Tues.–Sat. (and any cruise-ship day) 10–4.*

☙ **Fort Frederik.** On July 3, 1848, 8,000 slaves marched on this fort to demand their freedom. Danish governor Peter von Scholten, fearing they would burn the town to the ground, stood up in his carriage parked in front of the fort and granted their wish. The fort, completed in 1760, houses an art gallery and a number of interesting historical exhibits, including some focusing on the 1848 Emancipation and the 1917 transfer of the Virgin Islands from Denmark to the United States. It's within earshot of the Frederiksted Visitor Center. ⊠ *Waterfront, Frederiksted, St. Croix* ☎ *340/772–2021* ⊠ *$3* ⊙ *Weekdays (and any cruise-ship day) 8:30–4.*

Frederiksted Visitor Center. Across from the pier, Federiksted's visitor center has brochures from numerous St. Croix businesses, as well as a few exhibits about the island. You can stop in weekdays from 8 to 5. ⊠ *321 King St., Frederiksted Mall, Frederiksted, St. Croix* ☎ *340/772–0357* ⊙ *Weekdays 8–5.*

Fodor's Choice **Lawaetz Museum.** For a trip back in time, tour this circa-1750 farm.
★ Owned by the prominent Lawaetz family since 1896, just after Carl Lawaetz arrived from Denmark, the lovely two-story house is in a valley at La Grange. A Lawaetz family member shows you the four-poster mahogany bed Carl and Marie shared, the china Marie painted, the family portraits, and the fruit trees that fed the family for several generations. Initially a sugar plantation, it was subsequently used to raise cattle and grow produce. ⊠ *Rte. 76, Mahogany Rd., Estate Little La Grange, St. Croix* ☎ *340/772–1539* ⊕ *www.stcroixlandmarks.com* ⊠ *$10* ⊙ *Tues., Thurs., Sat. (and any cruise-ship day) 10–4.*

NORTH SHORE

Salt River Bay National Historical Park and Ecological Preserve. This joint national and local park commemorates the area where Christopher Columbus's men skirmished with the Caribs in 1493 on his second visit to the New World. Take a short hike up the dirt road to the ruins of an old earthen fort for great views of Salt River Bay. The area also encompasses a coastal estuary with the region's largest remaining mangrove forest, a submarine canyon, and several endangered species, including the hawksbill turtle and the roseate tern. A visitor center, open winter only, sits just uphill to the west. The water at the beach can be on the rough side, but it's a nice place for sunning. ⊠ *Rte. 75 to Rte. 80, Salt River, St. Croix* ☎ *340/773–1460* ⊕ *www.nps.gov/sari* ⊙ *Nov.–June, Tues.–Thurs. 9–4.*

SHOPPING

The selection of duty-free goods on St. Croix is fairly good. The best shopping is in Christiansted, where most stores are in the historic district near the harbor. King Street, Strand Street, and the arcades that lead off them compose the main shopping district and where you'll find **Sonya's**, the jewelry store that first sold the locally popular hook bracelet. The longest arcade is **Caravelle Arcade**, adjacent to the hotel of the same name. In Frederiksted a handful of shops face the cruise-ship pier.

Sonya's. This store is owned and operated by Sonya Hough, who invented the popular hook bracelet. She has added an interesting decoration to these bracelets: the swirling symbol used in weather forecasts to indicate hurricanes. ⊠ *1 Company St., Christiansted, St. Croix* ☎ *340/778–8605.*

ACTIVITIES

BOAT TOURS

Many people take a day trip to Buck Island aboard a charter boat. Most leave from the Christiansted waterfront or from Green Cay Marina and stop for a snorkel at the island's eastern end before dropping anchor off a gorgeous sandy beach for a swim, a hike, and lunch. Sailboats can often stop right at the beach; a larger boat might have to anchor a bit farther offshore. A full-day sail runs about $100, with lunch included on most trips. A half-day sail costs about $68.

Big Beard's Adventure Tours. Big Beard's Adventure Tours takes you on catamarans, either the *Renegade* or the *Adventure,* from the Christiansted waterfront to Buck Island for snorkeling before dropping anchor at a private beach for a barbecue lunch. ⊠ *Christiansted, St. Croix* ☎ *340/773–4482* ⊕ *www.bigbeards.com.*

DIVING AND SNORKELING

N2 the Blue. In Frederiksted, N2 the Blue takes divers right off the beach near Coconuts restaurant, on night dives off the Frederiksted Pier, or on boat trips to wrecks and reefs. ⊠ *Frederiksted Pier, Rte. 631, Frederiksted, St. Croix* ☎ *340/772–3483 or 888/789–3483* ⊕ *www.n2theblue.com.*

GOLF

★ **Carambola Golf Club.** The spectacular 18-hole course at the Renaissance St. Croix Carambola Resort, in the northwest valley, was designed by Robert Trent Jones Sr. It sits near Carambola Beach Resort. Greens fees are $140 for 18 holes, which includes the use of a golf cart. ⊠ *Remaissance St. Croix Carambola Resort, Rte. 18, Davis Bay, St. Croix* ☎ *340/778–5638* ⊕ *www.golfcarambola.com.*

HORSEBACK RIDING

Paul and Jill's Equestrian Stables. Well-kept roads and expert guides make horseback riding on St. Croix pleasurable. At Sprat Hall, just north of Frederiksted, Jill Hurd runs Paul and Jill's Equestrian Stables. She will take you through the rain forest, across the pastures, along the beaches, and through valleys—explaining the flora, fauna, and ruins on the way. A 1½-hour ride costs $90. ⊠ *Rte. 58, Frederiksted, St. Croix* ☎ *340/772–2880 or 340/332–0417* ⊕ *www.paulandjills.com.*

KAYAKING

Caribbean Adventure Tours. Caribbean Adventure Tours takes you on trips through Salt River Bay National Historical Park and Ecological Preserve, one of the island's most pristine areas. All tours run $450 ⊠ *Salt River Marina, Rte. 80, Salt River, St. Croix* ☎ *340/778–1522* ⊕ *www.stcroixkayak.com.*

BEACHES

West End beaches. There are several unnamed beaches along the coast road north of Frederiksted, but it's best if you don't stray too far from civilization. For safety's sake, most vacationers plop down their towel near one of the casual restaurants spread out along Route 63. The beach at the Rainbow Beach Club, a five-minute drive outside Frederiksted, has a bar, a casual restaurant, water sports, and volleyball. If you want to be close to the cruise-ship pier, just stroll on over to the adjacent sandy beach in front of Ft. Frederik. On the way south out of Frederiksted, the stretch near Sandcastle on the Beach hotel is also lovely. ⊠ *Rte. 63, north and south of Frederiksted, Frederiksted, St. Croix.*

WHERE TO EAT

$$$
ECLECTIC
Fodor's Choice
★

✗ **Blue Moon.** This terrific little bistro, which has a loyal local following, offers a changing menu that draws on Cajun and Caribbean flavors. Try the spicy gumbo with andouille sausage or crab cakes with a spicy aioli for your appetizer. A grilled chicken breast served with spinach and artichoke hearts and topped with Parmesan and cheddar cheeses makes a good entrée. The Almond Joy sundae should be your choice for dessert. There's live jazz on Wednesday and Friday. ⊠ *7 Strand St., Frederiksted, St. Croix* ☎ *340/772–2222* ⊕ *www.bluemoonstcroix.com* ☾ *Closed Mon.*

$$
CONTINENTAL
☾
Fodor's Choice
★

✗ **Rum Runners.** The view is as stellar as the food at this highly popular local standby. Sitting right on Christiansted boardwalk, Rum Runners serves everything, including a to-die-for salad of crispy romaine lettuce and tender grilled lobster drizzled with lemongrass vinaigrette. More hearty fare includes baby back ribs cooked with the restaurant's special spice blend and Guinness stout. ⊠ *Hotel Caravelle, 44A Queen Cross St., Christiansted, St. Croix* ☎ *340/773–6585* ⊕ *www.rumrunnersstcroix.com.*

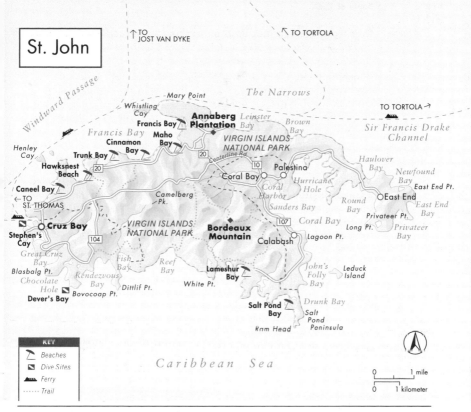

St. John

↑ TO
JOST VAN DYKE

↖ TO TORTOLA

Windward Passage

Mary Point

The Narrows

Whistling Cay

Francis Bay

Annaberg Plantation

Leinster Bay

Brown Bay

TO TORTOLA →

Sir Francis Drake Channel

Francis Bay

Maho Bay

VIRGIN ISLANDS NATIONAL PARK

Francis Bay **Cinnamon Bay**

Henley Cay

Trunk Bay

20

Centerline Rd.

10

Palestina

Haulover Bay

Newfound Bay

Hawksnest Beach

20

Coral Bay

Coral Harbor

Hurricane Hole

East End Pt.

Caneel Bay

← TO
ST. THOMAS

Camelberg Pk.

Round Bay

○ **East End**

East End Bay

Cruz Bay ○

VIRGIN ISLANDS NATIONAL PARK

Bordeaux Mountain

Sanders Bay

107

Coral Bay

Privateer Pt.

Privateer Bay

Stephen's Cay

104

Calabash

Lagoon Pt.

Long Pt.

Great Cruz Bay

Fish Bay

Reef Bay

Lameshur Bay

John's Folly Bay

Leduck Island

Blasbalg Pt.

Rendezvous Bay

White Pt.

Chocolate Hole

Dittlif Pt.

Dever's Bay

Bovocoap Pt.

Salt Pond Bay

Drunk Bay

Salt Pond

Kam Head

Salt Pond Peninsula

Caribbean Sea

KEY

⤢ Beaches
◪ Dive Sites
⚓ Ferry
····· Trail

0   1 mile
0   1 kilometer

ST. JOHN (CRUZ BAY)

Lynda Lohr

St. John's heart is Virgin Islands National Park, a treasure that takes up a full two-thirds of St. John's 20 square mi (53 square km). The park helps keep the island's interior in its pristine and undisturbed state, but if you go at midday you'll probably have to share your stretch of beach with others, particularly at Trunk Bay. The island is booming, and while it can get a tad crowded at the ever-popular Trunk Bay Beach during the busy winter season, you won't find traffic jams or pollution. It's easy to escape from the fray, however: just head off on a hike. St. John doesn't have a grand agrarian past like her sister island, St. Croix, but if you're hiking in the dry season, you can probably stumble upon the stone ruins of old plantations. The less adventuresome can visit the repaired ruins at the park's Annaberg Plantation and Caneel Bay resort. Of the three U.S. Virgin Islands, St. John, which has 5,000 residents, has the strongest sense of community, which is primarily rooted in a desire to protect the island's natural beauty.

ESSENTIALS

CURRENCY The U.S. dollar is the official currency of U.S. Virgin Islands; you'll find a few ATMs in Cruz Bay.

INTERNET **Quiet Mon Pub** ✉ *1 block up from ferry dock, across from First Bank and Julius E. Sprauve School, Cruz Bay, St. John, U.S. Virgin Islands* ☎ *340/779–4799* ⊕ *www.quietmon.com.*

TELEPHONE Both Sprint and AT&T phones work in most of St. John (take care that you're not roaming on the Tortola cell network on the island's north coast, though). It's as easy to call home from St. John as from any city in the United States. On St. John public phones are near telephone poles mid-way along the Cruz Bay waterfront.

COMING ASHORE

While a few smaller ships drop anchor at St. John, most people taking a cruise aboard a larger ship visit St. Thomas's sister island on a shore excursion or on an independent day trip from St. Thomas. If you prefer to not take a tour, ferries leave St. Thomas from the Charlotte Amalie waterfront and Red Hook. You'll have to take a taxi to reach the ferry dock.

If you're aboard a smaller ship that calls in St. John, your ship may simply pause outside Cruz Bay Harbor to drop you off or drop anchor if it's spending the day. You'll be tendered to shore at the main town of Cruz Bay. The shopping district starts just across the street from the tender landing. You'll find an eclectic collection of shops, cozy restaurants, and places where you can just sit and take it all in. The island has few sights to see. Your best bet is to take a tour of the Virgin Islands National Park. (If your ship doesn't offer such a tour, arrange one with one of the taxi drivers who will meet your tender.) The drive takes you past luscious beaches to a restored sugar plantation. With only a single day in port, you're better off just using the island's shared taxi vans rather than renting a car, but if you want to do some independent exploring, you can rent a car in Cruz Bay.

EXPLORING ST. JOHN

CRUZ BAY

St. John's main town may be compact (it consists of only several blocks), but it's definitely a hub: the ferries from St. Thomas and the British Virgin Islands pull in here, and it's where you can get a taxi or rent a car to travel around the island. There are plenty of shops in which to browse, a number of watering holes where you can stop for a breather, many restaurants, and a grassy square with benches where you can sit back and take everything in. Look for the current edition of the handy, amusing *"Road Map: St. Thomas–St. John"* featuring Max the Mongoose.

V.I. National Park Visitors Center. To pick up a useful guide to St. John's hiking trails, see various large maps of the island, and find out about current Park Service programs, including guided walks and cultural demonstrations, stop by the park visitor center, which is open daily from 8 to 4:30. ✉ *Near baseball field, Cruz Bay, St. John, U.S. Virgin Islands* ☎ *340/776–6201* ⊕ *www.nps.gov/viis.*

ELSEWHERE ON THE ISLAND

Fodor's Choice   **Annaberg Plantation.** In the 18th century, sugar plantations dotted the steep
★   hills of this island. Slaves and free Danes and Dutchmen toiled to harvest the cane that was used to create sugar, molasses, and rum for export.

Built in the 1780s, the partially restored plantation at Leinster Bay was once an important sugar mill. Although there are no official visiting hours, the National Park Service has regular tours, and some well-informed taxi drivers will show you around. ⊠ *Leinster Bay Rd., Annaberg, St. John, U.S. Virgin Islands* ☎ *340/776–6201* ⊕ *www.nps.gov/viis* 🏷 *Free* ☉ *Daily dawn–dusk.*

★ **Bordeaux Mountain.** St. John's highest peak rises to 1,277 feet. Route 10 passes near enough to the top to offer breathtaking vistas. Don't stray

into the road here—cars whiz by at a good clip along this section. Instead, drive nearly to the end of the dirt road that heads off next to the restaurant and gift shop for spectacular views at Picture Point and the trailhead of the hike downhill to Lameshur. Get a trail map from the park service before you start. ⊠ *Rte. 10, Bordeaux, St. John, U.S. Virgin Islands.*

SHOPPING

Luxury goods and handicrafts can be found on St. John. Most shops carry a little of this and a bit of that, so it pays to poke around. The Cruz Bay shopping district runs from **Wharfside Village,** just around the corner from the ferry dock, to **Mongoose Junction,** an inviting shopping center on North Shore Road. (The name of this upscale shopping mall, by the way, is a holdover from a time when those furry island creatures gathered at a nearby garbage bin.) Out on Route 104 stop in at the **Marketplace** to explore its gift and crafts shops. At the island's other end, there are a few stores—selling clothes, jewelry, and artwork—here and there from the village of **Coral Bay** to the small complex at **Shipwreck Landing.**

On St. John, store hours run from 9 or 10 to 5 or 6. Wharfside Village and Mongoose Junction shops in Cruz Bay are often open into the evening.

ACTIVITIES

DIVING AND SNORKELING

Cruz Bay Watersports. Cruz Bay Watersports actually has two locations: in Cruz Bay at the Lumberyard Shopping Complex and at the Westin St. John Resort. Owners Marcus and Patty Johnston offer regular reef, wreck, and night dives and USVI and BVI snorkel tours. The company holds both PADI five-star-facility and NAUI-Dream-Resort status. ⊠ *Lumberyard Shopping Complex, Cruz Bay, St. John, U.S. Virgin Islands* ☎ *340/776–6234* ⊕ *www.divestjohn.com.*

Low Key Watersports. Low Key Watersports offers two-tank dives and specialty courses. It's certified as a PADI five-star training facility. ⊠ *Wharfside Village, Strand St., Cruz Bay, St. John, U.S. Virgin Islands* ☎ *340/693–8999 or 800/835–7718* ⊕ *www.divelowkey.com.*

FISHING

Well-kept charter boats—approved by the U.S. Coast Guard—head out to the north and south drops or troll along the inshore reefs, depending on the season and what's biting. The captains usually provide bait, drinks, and lunch, but you need to bring your own hat and sunscreen. Half-day fishing charters run between about $750 for the boat.

Captain Byron Oliver. Captain Byron Oliver takes you out to the north and south drops. ⊠ *St. John, U.S. Virgin Islands* ☎ *340/693–8339.*

HIKING

Although it's fun to go hiking with a Virgin Islands National Park guide, don't be afraid to head out on your own. To find a hike that suits your ability, stop by the park's visitor center in Cruz Bay and pick up the free trail guide; it details points of interest, trail lengths, and estimated hiking times, as well as any dangers you might encounter. Although the park staff recommends long pants to protect against thorns and insects, most people hike in shorts because it can get very hot. Wear sturdy shoes or hiking boots even if you're hiking to the beach. Don't forget to bring water and insect repellent.

Fodor'sChoice **Virgin Islands National Park.** The Virgin Islands National Park maintains
★ more than 20 trails on the north and south shores and offers guided hikes along popular routes. A full-day trip to Reef Bay is a must; it's an easy hike through lush and dry forest, past the ruins of an old plantation, and to a sugar factory adjacent to the beach. It can be a bit arduous for young kids, however. Take the $6 safari bus from the park's visitor center to the trailhead, where you can meet a ranger who'll serve as your guide. The park provides a boat ride back to Cruz Bay for $15 to save you the walk back up the mountain. The schedule changes from season to season; call for times and reservations, which are essential. ⊠ *1300 Cruz Bay Creek, St. John, St. John, U.S. Virgin Islands* ☎ *340/776–6201* ⊕ *www.nps.gov/viis.*

BEACHES

Cinnamon Bay Beach. This long, sandy beach faces beautiful cays and abuts the national park campground. The facilities are open to the public and include cool showers, toilets, a commissary, and a restaurant. You can rent water-sports equipment here—a good thing, because there's excellent snorkeling off the point to the right; look for the big angelfish and large schools of purple triggerfish. Afternoons on Cinnamon Bay can be windy—a boon for windsurfers but an annoyance for sunbathers—so arrive early to beat the gusts. Restrooms are on the main path from the commissary to the beach and scattered around the campground. ⊠ *North Shore Rd., Rte. 20, about 4 mi (6 km) east of Cruz Bay, Cinnamon Bay, St. John, U.S. Virgin Islands.*

★ **Hawksnest Beach.** Sea grape and waving palm trees line this narrow beach, and there are restrooms, cooking grills, and a covered shed for picnicking. A patchy reef just offshore means snorkeling is an easy swim away, but the best underwater views are reserved for ambitious snorkelers who head farther to the east along the bay's fringes. ⊠ *North Shore Rd., Rte. 20, about 2 mi (3 km) east of Cruz Bay, Hawksnest Bay, St. John, U.S. Virgin Islands.*

Fodor's Choice
★

Trunk Bay Beach. St. John's most-photographed beach is also the preferred spot for beginning snorkelers because of its underwater trail. Crowded or not, this stunning beach is one of the island's most beautiful. There are changing rooms with showers, bathrooms, a snack bar, picnic tables, a gift shop, phones, lockers, and snorkeling-equipment rentals. The parking lot often overflows, but you can park along the road. ⊠ *North Shore Rd., Rte. 20, about 2½ mi (4 km) east of Cruz Bay, Trunk Bay, St. John, U.S. Virgin Islands.*

WHERE TO EAT

$
ECLECTIC

✕ **Deli Grotto.** At this air-conditioned (but no-frills) sandwich shop you place your order at the counter and wait for it to be delivered to your table or for takeout. The portobello panini with savory sautéed onions is a favorite, but the other sandwiches such as the smoked turkey and artichoke get rave reviews. Order a delicious brownie or cookie for dessert. ⊠ *Mongoose Junction Shopping Center, North Shore Rd., Cruz Bay, St. John, U.S. Virgin Islands* ☎ *340/777–3061* ▭ *No credit cards* ☉ *No dinner.*

ST. KITTS (BASSETERRE)

Jordan Simon

Mountainous St. Kitts, the first English settlement in the Leeward Islands, crams some stunning scenery into its 65 square mi (168 square km). Vast, brilliant green fields of sugarcane (the former cash crop, now slowly being replanted) run to the shore. The fertile, lush island has some fascinating natural and historical attractions: a rain forest replete with waterfalls, thick vines, and secret trails; a central mountain range dominated by the 3,792-foot Mt. Liamuiga, whose crater has long been dormant; and Brimstone Hill, known in the 18th century as the Gibraltar of the West Indies. St. Kitts and Nevis, along with Anguilla, achieved self-government as an associated state of Great Britain in 1967. In 1983 St. Kitts and Nevis became an independent nation. English with a strong West Indian lilt is spoken here. People are friendly but shy; always ask before you take photographs. Also, be sure to wear wraps or shorts over beach attire when you're in public places.

ESSENTIALS

CURRENCY

Eastern Caribbean (E.C.) dollar (EC$2.67 to US$1). U.S. dollars are accepted practically everywhere, but you'll usually get change in E.C. currency.

INTERNET

Basseterre usually has an operational Internet café, but it rarely lasts in one location. The tourist office in Pelican Mall will have the latest information.

TELEPHONE

Phone cards, which you can buy in denominations of $5, $10, and $20, are handy for making local phone calls, calling other islands, and accessing U.S. direct lines. To make a local call, dial the seven-digit number. To call St. Kitts from the United States, dial the area code 869, then access code 465, 466, 468, or 469 and the local four-digit number.

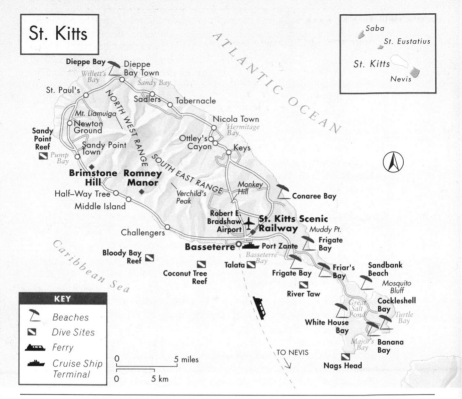

COMING ASHORE

Cruise ships calling at St. Kitts dock at Port Zante, which is a deep-water port directly in Basseterre, the capital of St. Kitts. The cruise-ship terminal is right in the downtown area, two minutes' walk from sights and shops. Taxi rates on St. Kitts are fixed, and should be posted right at the dock. If you'd like to go to Nevis, several daily ferries (30 to 45 minutes, $8–$10 one-way) can take you to Charlestown in Nevis; the byzantine schedule is subject to change, so double-check times.

Taxi rates on St. Kitts are fairly expensive, and you may have to pay $32 for a ride to Brimstone Hill (for one to four passengers). A four-hour tour of St. Kitts runs about $80. It's often cheaper to arrange an island tour with one of the local companies than to hire a taxi driver to take your group around. Several restored plantation greathouses are known for their lunches; your driver can provide information and arrange drop-off and pickup. Before setting off in a cab, be sure to clarify whether the rate quoted is in E.C. or U.S. dollars.

EXPLORING ST. KITTS

Basseterre. On the south coast, St. Kitts's walkable capital is graced with tall palms and flagstone sidewalks; although many of the buildings appear run-down, there are interesting shops, excellent art galleries, and some beautifully maintained houses. Duty-free shops and boutiques line the streets and courtyards radiating from the octagonal **Circus,** built in the style of London's famous Piccadilly Circus.

Independence Square. There are lovely gardens on the site of a former slave market at Independence Square. The square is surrounded on three sides by 18th-century Georgian buildings. ⊠ *Off Bank St., Basseterre, St. Kitts.*

St. George's Anglican Church. St. George's Anglican Church is a handsome stone building with a crenellated tower originally built by the French in 1670 and called Nôtre-Dame. The British burned it down in 1706 and rebuilt it four years later, naming it after the patron saint of England. Since then it has suffered a fire, an earthquake, and hurricanes and was once again rebuilt in 1869. ⊠ *Cayon St., Basseterre, St. Kitts.*

Port Zante. Port Zante is an ambitious, ever-growing 27-acre cruise-ship pier and marina in an area that has been reclaimed from the sea. The domed welcome center is an imposing neoclassical hodgepodge, with columns and stone arches, shops, walkways, fountains, and West Indian–style buildings housing luxury shops, galleries, restaurants, and a small casino. A second pier, 1,434 feet long, has a draft that accommodates even leviathan cruise ships. The selection of shops and restaurants (Tiffany Bar and Deli is a find for fantastic local fare, Twist for global fusion cuisine) is expanding as well. ⊠ *Waterfront, behind Circus, Basseterre, St. Kitts.*

National Museum. In the restored former Treasury Building, the National Museum presents an eclectic collection reflecting the history and culture of the island. ⊠ *Bay Rd., Basseterre, St. Kitts* ☎ *869/465–5584* ⊠ *EC$1 residents, US$1 nonresidents* ☉ *Weekdays 9–5, Sat. 9–1.*

★ **Brimstone Hill.** This 38-acre fortress, a UNESCO World Heritage Site, is part of a national park dedicated by Queen Elizabeth in 1985. After routing the French in 1690, the English erected a battery here; by 1736 the fortress held 49 guns, earning it the moniker Gibraltar of the West Indies. In 1782, 8,000 French troops laid siege to the stronghold, which was defended by 350 militia and 600 regular troops of the Royal Scots and East Yorkshires. When the English finally surrendered, they were

---

ST. KITTS BEST BETS

■ **Brimstone Hill Fortress.** Stop here for some of the best views on St. Kitts and historic ambience.

■ **Nevis.** A trip to Nevis is a worthwhile way to spend the day.

■ **Plantation Greathouses.** Stop for a lunch at Ottley's or Rawlins Plantation.

■ **Rain-forest Hikes.** Several operators on the island lead day-long hikes through the rain forest.

■ **Romney Manor.** This partially restored manor house is enhanced by the chance to shop at Caribelle Batik and watch the elaborate wax-and-dye process.

7

allowed to march from the fort in full formation out of respect for their bravery (the English afforded the French the same honor when they surrendered the fort a mere year later). The spectacular view includes Montserrat and Nevis to the southeast; Saba and St. Eustatius to the northwest; and St. Barth and St. Maarten to the north. Nature trails snake through the tangle of surrounding hardwood forest and savanna (a fine spot to catch

the green vervet monkeys—inexplicably brought by the French and now outnumbering the residents—skittering about). ⊠ *Main Rd., Brimstone Hill, St. Kitts* ☎ *869/465–2609* ⊕ *www.brimstonehillfortress.org* ⊑ *$8* ⊙ *Daily 9:30–5:30.*

★ **Romney Manor.** The ruins of this somewhat restored house (reputedly once the property of Thomas Jefferson) and surrounding replicas of chattel-house cottages are set in 6 acres of glorious gardens, with exotic flowers, an old bell tower, and an enormous, gnarled 350-year-old saman tree (sometimes called a rain tree). Inside, at **Caribelle Batik,** you can watch artisans hand-printing fabrics by the 2,500-year-old Indonesian wax-and-dye process known as batik. Look for signs indicating a turnoff for Romney Manor near Old Road. ⊠ *Old Road, St. Kitts* ☎ *869/465–6253* ⊕ *www.caribellebatikstkitts.com* ⊑ *Free* ⊙ *Daily 9–5.*

St. Kitts Scenic Railway. The old narrow-gauge train that had transported sugarcane to the central sugar factory since 1912 is all that remains of the island's once-thriving sugar industry. Two-story cars bedecked in bright Kittitian colors circle the island in just under four hours. Each passenger gets a comfortable, downstairs air-conditioned seat fronting vaulted picture windows and an upstairs open-air observation spot. The conductor's running discourse embraces not only the history of sugar cultivation but also the railway's construction, local folklore, island geography, even other agricultural mainstays from papayas to pigs. ⊠ *Needsmust, St. Kitts* ☎ *869/465–7263* ⊕ *www.stkittsscenicrailway. com* ⊑ *$89, children 4–12 $44.50* ⊙ *Departures vary according to cruise-ship schedules (call ahead, but at least once daily Dec.–Apr., usually 8:30 am).*

SHOPPING

St. Kitts has limited shopping, but there are several small duty-free shops with good deals on jewelry, perfume, china, and crystal. Numerous galleries sell excellent paintings and sculptures. The batik fabrics, scarves, caftans, and wall hangings of Caribelle Batik are well known. British expat Kate Spencer is an artist who has lived on the island for years, reproducing its vibrant colors on everything from silk pareus (beach wraps) to note cards to place mats. Other good island buys include crafts, jams, and herbal teas. Don't forget to pick up some CSR

(Cane Spirit Rothschild), which is distilled from fresh wild sugarcane right on St. Kitts. The Brinley Gold company has made a splash among spirits connoisseurs for its coffee, mango, coconut, lime, and vanilla rums (there is a tasting room at Port Zante). Most shopping plazas are in downtown Basseterre, on the streets radiating from the Circus.

> **CAUTION**
>
> Pack a small flashlight just in case there's an emergency. You don't want to be stumbling around in the dark.

ACTIVITIES

DIVING AND SNORKELING

Though unheralded as a dive destination, St. Kitts has more than a dozen excellent sites, protected by several new marine parks. The surrounding waters feature shoals, hot vents, shallows, canyons, steep walls, and caverns at depths from 40 to nearly 200 feet.

Dive St. Kitts. Dive St. Kitts, a PADI–NAUI facility, offers competitive prices, computers to maximize time below, wide range of courses from refresher to technical, and friendly, laid-back dive masters. The Bird Rock location features superb shore diving (unlimited when you book packages): common sightings 20 to 30 feet out include octopuses, nurse sharks, manta and spotted eagle rays, sea horses, even barracudas George and Georgianna. It also offers kayak and snorkeling tours. ⊠ *2 mi [3 km] east of Basseterre, Frigate Bay, St. Kitts* ☎ *869/465–1189* ⊕ *www.divestkitts.com.*

GOLF

Royal St. Kitts Golf Club. The Royal St. Kitts Golf Club is an 18-hole, par-71 links-style championship course that underwent a complete redesign by Thomas McBroom to maximize Caribbean and Atlantic views and increase the challenge (there are 12 lakes and 83 bunkers). Holes 15 through 17 (the latter patterned after Pebble Beach No. 18) skirt the Atlantic in their entirety, lending new meaning to the term sand trap. The sudden gusts, wide but twisting fairways, and extremely hilly terrain demand pinpoint accuracy and finesse, yet holes such as 18 require pure power. Greens fees are $180 for nonguests. ⊠ *St. Kitts Marriott Resort, Frigate Bay, St. Kitts* ☎ *869/466–2700 or 866/785–4653* ⊕ *www.royalstkittsgolfclub.com.*

HIKING

Trails in the central mountains vary from easy to don't-try-it-by-yourself. Monkey Hill and Verchild's Peak aren't difficult, although the Verchild's climb will take the better part of a day. Don't attempt Mt. Liamuiga without a guide. You'll start at Belmont Estate—at the west end of the island—on horseback, then proceed on foot to the lip of the crater, at 2,600 feet. You can go down into the crater—1,000 feet deep and 1 mi (1.5 km) wide, with a small freshwater lake—clinging to vines and roots and scaling rocks, even trees. Expect to get muddy. There are several fine operators (each hotel recommends its favorite); tour rates range from $50 for a rain-forest walk to $95 for a volcano

7

expedition, and usually include round-trip transportation from your hotel and picnic lunch.

★ **Duke of Earl's Adventures.** Earl of Duke of Earl's Adventures is as entertaining as his nickname suggests—and his prices are slightly cheaper ($45 for a rain-forest tour includes refreshments, $70 volcano expeditions add lunch; hotel pickup and drop-off is complimentary). He genuinely loves his island and conveys that enthusiasm. He also conducts a thorough volcano tour to the crater's rim and a drive-through ecosafari tour ($50 with lunch). ⊠ *St. Kitts* ☎ *869/465–1899 or 869/663–0994.*

Greg's Safaris. Greg Pereira of Greg's Safaris, whose family has lived on St. Kitts since the early 19th century, takes groups on half-day trips into the rain forest and on full-day hikes up the volcano and through the grounds of a private 18th-century greathouse. The rain-forest trips include visits to sacred Carib sites, abandoned sugar mills, and an excursion down a 100-foot coastal canyon containing a wealth of Amerindian petroglyphs. ⊠ *St. Kitts* ☎ *869/465–4121* ⊕ *www.gregsafaris.com.*

HORSEBACK RIDING

Trinity Stables. Guides from Trinity Stables offer beach rides ($50) and trips into the rain forest ($60), both including hotel pickup. The latter is intriguing, as guides discuss plants' medicinal properties along the way (such as sugarcane to stanch bleeding) and pick oranges right off a tree to squeeze fresh juice. Otherwise, the staffers are cordial but shy; this isn't a place for beginners' instruction. ⊠ *St. Kitts* ☎ *869/465–3226.*

ZIP-LINING

☾ **Sky Safari Tours.** Sky Safari Tours whisks would-be Tarzans and Janes through the "Valley of the Giants" (so dubbed for the towering trees) at speeds up to 50 mph (80 kph along five cable lines); the longest (nicknamed "The Boss") stretches 1,350 feet through towering turpentine and mahogany trees draped thickly with bromeliads, suspended 250 feet above the ground. Following the Canadian-based company's mantra of "faster, higher, safer," it uses a specially designed trolley with secure harnesses attached. Admission is usually $65–$75, depending on the tour chosen. It's open daily 9–6, with the first and last tours departing at 10 and 3. ⊠ *Wingfield Estate, St. Kitts* ☎ *869/466–4259 or 869/465–4347* ⊕ *www.skysafaristkitts.com.*

BEACHES

The powdery white-sand beaches of St. Kitts, free and open to the public (even those occupied by hotels), are in the Frigate Bay area or on the lower peninsula. Chair rentals cost around $3, though if you order lunch you can negotiate a freebie. Caution: The Atlantic waters are rougher.

Banana/Cockleshell Bays. These twin connected eyebrows of glittering champagne-color sand—stretching nearly 2 mi (3 km) total at the south-eastern tip of the island—feature majestic views of Nevis and are backed by lush vegetation and coconut palms. The water is generally placid, ideal for swimming. The downside is irregular maintenance, with seaweed (particularly after rough weather) and occasional litter, especially on Banana Bay. ⊠ *Banana Bay, St. Kitts.*

Friar's Bay. Locals consider Friar's Bay, on the Caribbean (southern) side, the island's finest beach. It's a long, tawny scimitar where the water always seems warmer and clearer. Several happening bars, including Shipwreck, Mongoose, and Sunset Grill, serve terrific, inexpensive local food and cheap, frosty drinks. Chair rentals cost around $3, though if you order lunch, you can negotiate a freebie. ⊠ *Friar's Bay, St. Kitts.*

Frigate Bay. The Caribbean side offers talcum-powder-fine beige sand framed by coconut palms and sea grapes, and the Atlantic side (a 15-minute stroll)—sometimes called North Frigate Bay—is a favorite with horseback riders. South Frigate Bay is bookended by Sunset Café and the popular, pulsating Buddies Beach Hut. In between are several other lively beach spots, including Cathy's (fabulous jerk ribs), the Monkey Bar, Elvis Love Shack, and Mr. X Shiggidy Shack. Most charge $3 to $5 to rent a chair, though they'll often waive the fee if you ask politely and buy lunch. Waters are generally calm for swimming; the rockier eastern end offers fine snorkeling. ⊠ *Frigate Bay, St. Kitts.*

WHERE TO EAT

$$$ ✗ **Reggae Beach Bar & Grill.** Treats at this popular daytime watering
ECLECTIC hole include honey-mustard ribs, coconut shrimp, grilled lobster, decadent banana bread pudding with rum sauce, and an array of tempting tropical libations. Business cards and pennants from around the world plaster the bar, and the open-air space is decorated with a variety of nautical accoutrements, from fishnets and turtle shells to painted wooden crustaceans. You can snorkel here, spot hawksbill turtles and the occasional monkey, visit the enormous house pig Wilbur (who once "ate" beer cans whole, then moved to "lite" beers—but feeding is no longer encouraged), laze in a palm-shaded hammock, or rent a kayak, Hobie Cat or snorkeling gear. Beach chairs are free. Locals come Sunday afternoons for dancing to live bands. ⊠ *S.E. Peninsula Rd., Cockleshell Beach, St. Kitts* ☎ *869/469–9086* ⊕ *www.reggaebeachbar. com* ☾ *No dinner.*

7

St. Lucia

ATLANTIC OCEAN

Castries

Pt. Séraphine

Port Castries

Vendor's Arcade ◆   ◆ Market

Derek Walcott Sq. ◆   ◆ Cathedral of the Immaculate Conception

Cariblue Beach

Cap Pt.

Pigeon Point   Pigeon Island National Park

Anse Lavouette

Gros Islet

Esperance Harbour

Reduit Beach   Rodney Bay

Choc Beach

Castries–Gros Islet Hwy.

Vigie Beach

Cape Marquis

Pte. Séraphine

George F.L. Charles (Vigie) Airport

Castries Harbour

Castries see inset map

Grand Anse Bay

Morne Fortune

Grande Anse

Grande Cul de Sac Bay

La Sorcière

Marigot Bay

Marigot Beach

B A R R E D E L' I S L E R I D G E

St. Lucia Channel

Roseau

Anse-la-Raye

Anse-la-Raye

Fond d'or Bay

Mt. Parasol

Dennery

Grande Caille Pt.

Canaries

Mt. Gimie

Mandéle Pt.

Praslin Bay

Anse Cochon

Anse Chastanet

Soufrière

Diamond Botanical Gardens

Fond St. Jacques

Soufrière Harbour

Petit Piton & The Pinnacles

Vierge Pt.

La Soufrière Volcano

Micoud

Petit Piton

Fond Doux Estate

Anses des Pitons

Gros Piton

Caribbean Sea

Choiseul

LaFargue   Laborie

Laborie Bay

Hewanorra International Airport

Savannes Bay

Maria Islands

Vieux Fort

Vieux Fort Honeymoon Beach

Anse de Sables

Moule à Chique Peninsula

KEY

⚑ Beaches
🚢 Cruise Ship Terminal
◼ Dive Sites
⛴ Ferry
🌴 Rain Forest

0 ____ 4 miles
0 ____ 4 km

ST. LUCIA (CASTRIES)

Jane E. Zarem   Magnificent St. Lucia—with its towering mountains, dense rain forest, fertile green valleys, and acres of banana plantations—lies in the middle of the Windward Islands. Nicknamed " Helen of the West Indies" because of its natural beauty, St. Lucia is distinguished from its neighbors by its unusual geological landmarks, the Pitons—the twin peaks on the southwest coast that soar nearly ½ mi (1 km) above the ocean floor. Named a World Heritage Site by UNESCO in 2004, the Pitons are the symbol of this island. Nearby, in the former French colonial capital of Soufrière, are a "drive-in" volcano, its neighboring sulfur springs that have rejuvenated bathers for nearly three centuries, and one of the most beautiful botanical gardens in the Caribbean. A century and a half of battles between the French and English resulted in St. Lucia's changing hands 14 times before 1814, when England established possession. In 1979 the island became an independent state within the British Commonwealth of Nations. The official language is English, although most people also speak a French Creole patois.

ESSENTIALS

CURRENCY   Eastern Caribbean (E.C.) dollar (EC$2.67 to US$1). U.S. dollars (but not coins) are generally accepted, but change is given in E.C. currency.

INTERNET   Internet cafés can be found in Castries, Soufrière, and Rodney Bay.

Office Mobile ⊠ *46 St. Louis St., Castries, St. Lucia* ☎ *758/458–2514.*
Cost-Less Rent-a-Car & Internet Café ⊠ *Harmony Suites, Rodney Bay, Gros Islet, St. Lucia* ☎ *758/458–0671.*

TELEPHONE   You can make direct-dial overseas and inter-island calls from St. Lucia, and the connections are excellent. You can charge an overseas call to a major credit card with no surcharge by dialing 811. Phone cards can be purchased at many retail outlets.

COMING ASHORE

Most cruise ships dock at the capital city of Castries, on the island's northwest coast, at either of two docking areas: Pointe Seraphine, a port of entry and duty-free shopping complex, or Port Castries (Place Carenage), a commercial wharf across the harbor. Ferry service connects the two piers. Smaller vessels occasionally call at Soufrière, on the island's southwest coast. Ships calling at Soufrière must anchor offshore and bring passengers ashore via tender. Tourist information booths are located at Pointe Seraphine and across from the commercial wharf in Castries and along the waterfront on Bay Street in Soufrière. Downtown Castries is within walking distance of the pier, and the produce market and adjacent crafts and vendors' markets are the main attractions. Soufrière is a sleepy West Indian town, but it's worth a short walk around the central square to view the French colonial architecture; many of the island's interesting natural sights are in or near Soufrière.

Taxis are available at the docks in Castries. Although they are unmetered, the standard fares are posted at the entrance to Pointe Seraphine. Taxi drivers are well informed, and can give you a full tour—often an excellent one—thanks to government-sponsored training programs.

From the Castries area, full-day island tours for up to four people cost $35 to $70 per person, depending on the route and whether entrance fees and lunch are included; sightseeing trips to Soufrière cost around $150. If you plan your own day, expect to pay the driver at least $35 per hour plus a 10% tip. Whatever your destination, negotiate the price with the driver before you depart—and be sure that you both understand whether the rate is quoted in E.C. or U.S. dollars.

EXPLORING ST. LUCIA

CASTRIES AND THE NORTH

Castries. The capital, a busy commercial city of about 65,000 people, wraps around a sheltered bay. Morne Fortune rises sharply to the south of town, creating a dramatic green backdrop. The charm of Castries lies in its liveliness rather than its architecture, since four fires that occurred between 1796 and 1948 destroyed most of the colonial buildings. Freighters (exporting bananas, coconut, cocoa, mace, nutmeg, and citrus fruits) and cruise ships come and go frequently, making Castries Harbour one of the Caribbean's busiest ports. **Pointe Seraphine** is a duty-free shopping complex on the north side of the harbor, about a 20-minute walk or two-minute cab ride from the city center; a launch ferries passengers across the harbor when cruise ships are in port. **La Place Carenage,** on the south side of the harbor near the pier and markets, is another duty-free shopping complex with a dozen or more shops and a café. **Derek Walcott Square** (formerly Columbus Square), a green oasis bordered by Brazil, Laborie, Micoud, and Bourbon streets, was renamed to honor the hometown poet who won the 1992 Nobel Prize in Literature—one of two Nobel laureates from St. Lucia (the late Sir W. Arthur Lewis won the 1979 Nobel in economic science). Some of the few 19th-century buildings that survived fire, wind, and rain can be seen on Brazil Street, the square's southern border. On the Laborie Street side, there's a huge, 400-year-old samaan (monkeypod) tree with leafy branches that shade a good portion of the square. Directly across Laborie Street from Derek Walcott Square is the Roman Catholic **Cathedral of the Immaculate Conception,** which was built in 1897. Though it's rather somber on the outside, its interior walls are decorated with colorful murals reworked in 1985, just before Pope John Paul II's visit, by St. Lucian artist Dunstan St. Omer. This church has an active parish and is open daily for both public viewing and religious services. At the corner of Jeremie and Peynier streets, spreading beyond its brilliant orange roof, is the **Castries Market.** Full of excitement and bustle, the market is open every day except Sunday. It's liveliest on Saturday morning, when farmers bring their fresh produce and spices to town, as they have for more than a century. Next door to the produce market is the **Craft Market,** where you can buy pottery, wood carvings, and handwoven straw articles. At the Vendor's Arcade, across Peynier Street from the Craft Market, you'll find still more handicrafts and souvenirs. ⊠ *St. Lucia.*

Pigeon Island National Park. Jutting out from the northwest coast, Pigeon Island is connected to the mainland by a causeway. Tales are told of the pirate Jambe de Bois (Wooden Leg), who once hid out on this 44-acre hilltop islet—a strategic point during the French and British struggles for control of St. Lucia. Now it's a national park and a venue for concerts, festivals, and family gatherings. There are two small beaches with calm waters for swimming and snorkeling, a restaurant, and picnic areas. ⊠ *Pigeon Island, St. Lucia National Trust, Rodney Bay, St. Lucia* ☎ *758/452–5005* ⊕ *www. slunatrust.org* ☑ *$5* ⊙ *Daily 9–5.*

Rodney Bay. About 15 minutes north of Castries, the natural bay and an 80-acre man-made lagoon—surrounded by hotels and many popular restaurants—are named for Admiral George Rodney, who sailed the British Navy out of Gros Islet Bay in 1780 to attack and ultimately decimate the French fleet. With 232 slips, Rodney Bay Marina is one of the Caribbean's premier yachting centers and the destination of the Atlantic Rally for Cruisers (transatlantic yacht crossing) each December. ⊠ *St. Lucia.*

ST. LUCIA BEST BETS

■ **Diamond Botanical Garden.** Stroll through this tropical paradise to Diamond Waterfall.

■ **Pigeon Island.** This national park is both a historic site and a natural playground.

■ **The Pitons.** You must see the Pitons, St. Lucia's unique twin peaks.

■ **The Rain Forest.** St. Lucia's lush rain forest is striking.

■ **Reduit Beach.** St. Lucia's nicest white-sand beach is north of Castries.

SOUFRIERE AND THE SOUTH

Ⓒ **Diamond Botanical Gardens and Waterfall.** These splendid gardens are part
Fodor's Choice of Soufrière Estate, a 2,000-acre land grant presented by King Louis
★ XIV in 1713 to three Devaux brothers from Normandy in recognition of their services to France. The estate is still owned by their descendants; Joan Du Bouley Devaux maintains the gardens. Water bubbling to the surface from underground sulfur springs streams downhill in rivulets to become Diamond Waterfall, deep within the botanical gardens. Through the centuries, the rocks over which the cascade spills have become encrusted with minerals and tinted yellow, green, and purple. A bathhouse was built nearby, but it was later destroyed. In 1930 André Du Boulay had the site excavated, and two of the original stone baths were restored for his use. Outside baths were added later. For a small fee, you can slip into your swimsuit and soak for 30 minutes in one of the outside pools; a private bath costs slightly more. ⊠ *Soufrière Estate, Diamond Rd., Soufrière, St. Lucia* ☎ *758/452–4759, 758/454–7565* ⊕ *www.diamondstlucia.com* ☑ *$5, outside bath $4, private bath $6* ⊙ *Mon.–Sat. 10–5, Sun. 10–3.*

Ⓒ **Fond Doux Estate.** One of the earliest French estates established by land
★ grant (1745 and 1763), this plantation still produces cocoa, citrus, bananas, coconut, and vegetables on 135 hilly acres; the restored 1864 plantation house is still in use, as well. A 30-minute walking tour begins at the cocoa fermentary, where you can see the drying process under way. You then follow a trail through the lush cultivated area, where a guide points out the various fruit- or spice-bearing trees and tropical flowers. Cool drinks and a creole buffet lunch are served at the

7

restaurant. Souvenirs, including just-made chocolate balls, are sold at the boutique. ⊠ *Chateaubelair, Soufrière, St. Lucia* ☎ *758/459–7545* ⊕ *www.fonddouxestate.com* 🍴 *Estate $30, includes buffet lunch* ⊘ *Daily 9–4.*

🌋 **La Soufrière Drive-In Volcano.** As you approach, your nose will pick up the strong scent of the sulfur springs—more than 20 belching pools of muddy water, multicolor sulfur deposits, and other assorted minerals baking and steaming on

---

BAG IT

A mesh laundry bag or a "pop-up" mesh clothes hamper are two fairly light items that pack flat in your suitcase. The bag can hang from the closet, but either will keep your closet neat, allow damp clothing to dry out, and help you tote dirty clothes to the self-service laundry room so you can avoid high cleaning charges.

---

the surface. Actually, you don't drive in. You drive up within a few hundred feet of the gurgling, steaming mass and then walk behind your guide—whose service is included in the admission price—around a fault in the substratum rock. It's a fascinating, educational half hour, though it can also be pretty stinky on a hot day. ⊠ *Bay St., Soufrière, St. Lucia* ☎ *758/459–5500* 🎫 *$2* ⊘ *Daily 9–5.*

Fodor's Choice   **The Pitons.** These two unusual mountains, which are, in fact, a symbol
★   of St. Lucia and were named a UNESCO World Heritage Site in 2004, rise precipitously from the cobalt-blue Caribbean Sea just south of Soufrière. Covered with thick tropical vegetation, the massive outcroppings were formed by lava from a volcanic eruption 30 to 40 million years ago. They are not identical twins since—confusingly—2,619-foot Petit Piton is taller than 2,461-foot Gros Piton, though Gros Piton is, as the word translates, broader. It's possible to climb the Pitons as long as you have permission and use a guide, but it's a strenuous trip. ⊠ *Soufrière, St. Lucia* ☎ *758/450–2231, 758/450–2078 for St. Lucia Forest & Lands Department, 758/459–9748 for Pitons Tour Guide Association* 🎫 *Guide services $45* ⊘ *Daily by appointment only.*

Soufrière. The oldest town in St. Lucia and the former French colonial capital, Soufrière was founded by the French in 1746 and named for its proximity to the volcano of the same name. The wharf is the center of activity in this sleepy town (which currently has a population of about 9,000), particularly when a cruise ship is moored in pretty Soufrière Bay. French colonial influences can be noticed in the architecture of the wooden buildings, with second-story verandas and gingerbread trim that surround the market square. The market building itself is decorated with colorful murals.

Soufrière Tourist Information Centre. The Soufrière Tourist Information Centre provides information about area attractions. Outside some of the popular attractions in and around Soufrière, souvenir vendors can be persistent. Be polite but firm if you're not interested in their wares. ⊠ *Bay St., Soufrière, St. Lucia* ☎ *758/459–7200.*

SHOPPING

The island's best-known products are artwork and woodcarvings; clothing and household articles made from batik and silk-screen fabrics, designed and printed in island workshops; and clay pottery. You can also take home straw hats and baskets and locally grown cocoa, coffee, and spices. Duty-free shopping is at **Pointe Seraphine** or **La Place Carenage**, on opposite sides of the harbor. You must show your passport and cabin key card to get duty-free prices. You'll want to experience the **Castries Market** and scour the adjacent **Vendor's Arcade** and **Craft Market** for handicrafts and souvenirs at bargain prices.

ACTIVITIES

DIVING AND SNORKELING

Fodor's Choice
★
The coral reefs at Anse Cochon and Anse Chastanet, on the southwest coast, are popular beach-entry dive sites. In the north, Pigeon Island is the most convenient site.

Dive Fair Helen. Dive Fair Helen is a PADI center that offers half- and full-day excursions to wreck, wall, and marine reserve areas, as well as night dives. ⊠ *Vigie Marina, Castries, St. Lucia* ☎ *758/451–7716, 888/855–2206 in U.S. and Canada ⊕ www.divefairhelen.com.*

Scuba St. Lucia. Scuba St. Lucia is a PADI five-star training facility. Daily beach and boat dives and resort and certification courses are offered; underwater photography and snorkeling equipment are available. Day trips from the north of the island include round-trip speedboat transportation. ⊠ *Anse Chastanet Resort, Anse Chastanet Rd., Soufrière, St. Lucia* ☎ *758/459–7755 ⊕ www.scubastlucia.com.*

FISHING

Sportfishing is generally done on a catch-and-release basis. Neither spearfishing nor collecting live fish in coastal waters is permitted. Half- and full-day deep-sea fishing excursions can be arranged at either Vigie Marina or Rodney Bay Marina. A half-day of fishing on a scheduled trip runs about $75 to $85 per person or $450 to $550 for a private charter for up to six or eight persons, depending on the size of the boat. Beginners are welcome.

Captain Mike's. Captain Mike's has a fleet of Bertram powerboats (31 to 38 feet) that accommodate as many as eight passengers; tackle and cold drinks are supplied. ⊠ *Vigie Marina, Castries, St. Lucia* ☎ *758/452–1216 or 758/452–7044 ⊕ www.captmikes.com.*

Mako Watersports. Mako Watersports takes fishing enthusiasts out on the well-equipped six-passenger *Annie Baby.* ⊠ *Rodney Bay Marina, Rodney Bay, St. Lucia* ☎ *758/452–0412.*

GOLF

St. Lucia and Country Golf Club. St. Lucia and Country Golf Club, the island's only public course, is at the northern tip and offers panoramic views of both the Atlantic and the Caribbean. It's an 18-hole championship course (6,836 yards, par 71). Depending on the season, greens fees range from $95 for 9 holes to $145 for 18 holes; carts are required and included in the

7

greens fee; club and shoe rentals are available. Reservations are essential. Complimentary transportation from your hotel or cruise ship is provided for parties of three or more people. ⊠ *Cap Estate, St. Lucia* ☎ *758/452–8523* ⊕ *www.stluciagolf.com.*

CAUTION
Germicidal hand cleaner is a must-have for adventure excursions or where water might be at a premium. Bring a small bottle you can carry along with you.

HORSEBACK RIDING

Creole horses, a breed indigenous to South America and popular on the island, are fairly small, fast, sturdy, and even-tempered animals suitable for beginners. Established stables can accommodate all skill levels and offer countryside trail rides, beach rides with picnic lunches, plantation tours, carriage rides, and lengthy treks. Prices run about $50 for one hour, $65 for two hours, and $80 for a three-hour beach ride and barbecue.

International Riding Stables. International Riding Stables offers English- and Western-style riding. The beach-picnic ride includes time for a swim—with or without your horse. ⊠ *Beauséjour Estate, Gros Islet, St. Lucia* ☎ *758/452–8139 or 758/450–8665.*

Trim's National Riding Stable. Trim's National Riding Stable, the island's oldest riding stable, offers four sessions per day, plus beach tours, trail rides, and carriage tours to Pigeon Island. ⊠ *Cas-en-Bas, Gros Islet, St. Lucia* ☎ *758/452–8273* ⊕ *www.trimsnationalridingacademy.com.*

BEACHES

All of St. Lucia's beaches are open to the public, but beaches in the north are particularly accessible to cruise-ship passengers.

Pigeon Point. At this small beach within Pigeon Island National Park ($5 admission), on the northwestern tip of St. Lucia, a restaurant serves snacks and drinks, but this is also a perfect spot for picnicking. ⊠ *Pigeon Island, St. Lucia.*

Fodor's Choice ★ **Reduit Beach.** This long stretch of golden sand frames Rodney Bay and is within walking distance of many hotels and restaurants in Rodney Bay Village. The Rex St. Lucian hotel, which faces the beach, has a water-sports center, where you can rent sports equipment and beach chairs and take windsurfing or waterskiing lessons. Many feel that Reduit (pronounced red-wee) is the island's finest beach. ⊠ *Rodney Bay, St. Lucia.*

Vigie Beach. This 2-mi (3-km) strand runs parallel to the George F.L. Charles Airport runway in Castries and continues on past the Rendez-vous resort, where it is called Malabar Beach. ⊠ *Across the street from the airport, Castries, St. Lucia.*

WHERE TO EAT

$$$
CARIBBEAN
Fodor's Choice ★
✕ **Dasheene Restaurant and Bar.** The terrace restaurant at Ladera resort has breathtakingly close-up views of the Pitons and the sea between them, especially beautiful at sunset. It's casual by day and magical at night. Executive-chef Orlando Satchell describes his creative West

Indian menu as "sexy Caribbean." Appetizers may include grilled crab claws with a choice of dips or silky pumpkin soup with ginger. Typical entrées are triggerfish seasoned and soaked in lime and fish stock and cooked in banana leaves, shrimp Dasheene (panfried with local herbs), seared duck breast with passion-fruit jus, or baron fillet of beef with sweet potato and green-banana mash. Light dishes, fresh salads, and sandwiches are served at lunchtime. ✉ *Ladera resort, 2 mi (3 km) south of Soufrière, Soufrière, St. Lucia* ☎ *758/459–7323* ⊕ *www.ladera.com.*

$$$
ECLECTIC
Fodor's Choice
★

✗ **Jacques Waterfront Dining.** Chef–owner Jacky Rioux creates magical dishes in his open-air garden restaurant (known for years as Froggie Jack's) overlooking Vigie Cove. The cooking style is decidedly French, as is Rioux, but fresh produce and local spices create a fusion cuisine that's memorable at either lunch or dinner. You might start with a bowl of creamy tomato-basil or pumpkin soup, a grilled portobello mushroom, or octopus and conch in curried coconut sauce. Main courses include fresh seafood, such as oven-baked kingfish with a white wine–and–sweet pepper sauce, or breast of chicken stuffed with smoked salmon in a citrus-butter sauce. The wine list is also impressive. ✉ *Vigie Marina, Castries, St. Lucia* ☎ *758/458–1900* ⊕ *www.jacquesrestaurant. com* ⚠ *Reservations essential* ⊙ *Closed Sun.*

ST. MAARTEN (PHILIPSBURG)

Elise Meyer

St. Martin/St. Maarten: one tiny island, just 37 square mi (59 square km), with two different accents and ruled by two sovereign nations. Here French and Dutch have lived side by side for hundreds of years, and when you cross from one country to the next there are no border patrols, no customs agents. In fact, the only indication that you have crossed a border at all is a small sign and a change in road surface. St. Martin/St. Maarten epitomizes tourist islands in the sun, where services are well developed but there's still some Caribbean flavor. The Dutch side is ideal for people who like plenty to do. The French side has a more genteel ambience, more fashionable shopping, and a Continental flair. The combination makes an almost ideal port. On the negative side, the island has been completely developed. It can be fun to shop, and you'll find an occasional bargain, but many goods are cheaper in the United States.

ESSENTIALS

CURRENCY   At this writing on the Dutch side, the NAf guilder (NAf 2.20 to US$1). On the French side, the currency is the euro (€1 to US$1.42 at this writing). U.S. currency is accepted almost everywhere on the island, and ATMs are plentiful, but you will occasionally find a restaurant or small business on the French side that accepts euros on a 1 to 1 basis. The currency on the Dutch side is expected to be changed to the Caribbean guilder in 2012.

INTERNET   There is Wi-Fi service on the boardwalk behind Front Street if you have your own laptop.

Cyber Link ✉ *53 Front St., Philipsburg, St. Maarten.*

TELEPHONE   To phone from the Dutch side to the French, you first must dial (00–590–590) for local numbers, or (00–590–690) for cell phones, then the

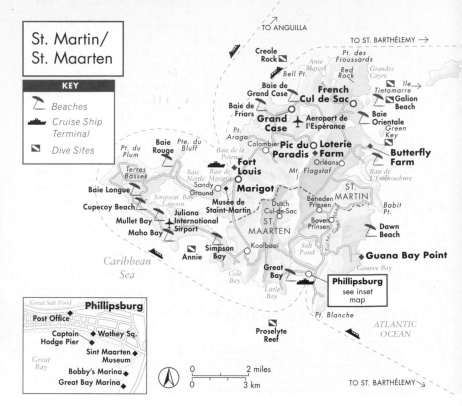

St. Martin/ St. Maarten

KEY

⤴ Beaches

🚢 Cruise Ship Terminal

◣ Dive Sites

six-digit local number. To call from the French side to the Dutch, dial "00–599" then the seven-digit local number. Remember that a call from one side to the other is an international call.

At the Landsradio in Philipsburg there are facilities for overseas calls and a USADirect phone, where you're directly in touch with an operator who will accept collect or credit-card calls. To call direct with an AT&T credit card or operator, dial 001–800/872–2881. On the French side, AT&T can be accessed by calling 080–099–00–11. If you need to use public phones, go to the special desk at Marigot's post office and buy a *télécarte*. There's a public phone at the tourist office in Marigot where you can make credit-card calls: the operator takes your card number (any major card) and assigns you a PIN, which you then use to charge calls to your card.

COMING ASHORE

Most cruise ships drop anchor off the Dutch capital of Philipsburg or dock in the marina at the southern tip of the Philipsburg harbor; a very few small or medium-size ships drop anchor in Marigot Bay and tender passengers ashore in the French capital. If your ship anchors, tenders will ferry you to the town pier in the middle of town, where taxis await passengers. If your ship docks at the marina, downtown is a 15-minute taxi ride away. The walk is not recommended. The island is small, and most spots aren't more than a 30-minute drive from Marigot or Philipsburg.

Doing your own thing will be much less expensive here than a ship-sponsored tour, and since rental cars are cheap (starting at $30 per day for a local car rental), you can easily strike out as soon as your ship docks. This is the best thing to do if you just want to see the island and spend a little time at a beach. Taxis are government-regulated and fairly costly, so they aren't really an option if you want to do much exploring. Authorized taxis display stickers of the St. Maarten Taxi Association. Taxis are also available at Marigot. You may be able to negotiate a favorable deal with a taxi driver for a two to three-hour island tour for as little as $70 for two passengers or $30 per person for more than two.

ST. MAARTEN BEST BETS

■ **Beaches.** The island has 37 beautiful beaches, all open to the public.

■ **Butterfly Farm.** The terrarium-like Butterfly Farm is a treat for all ages.

■ **The 12-Metre Challenge.** Help sail an America's Cup yacht.

■ **Loterie Farm.** On the slopes of Pic du Paradis, an amazing eco-friendly preserve with fun activities.

■ **Shopping.** Both sides of the island are a shopper's paradise.

EXPLORING ST. MAARTEN/ST-MARTIN

☺ Fodor's Choice ★ **Butterfly Farm.** If you arrive early in the morning when the butterflies first break out of their chrysalis, you'll be able to marvel at the absolute wonder of dozens of butterflies and moths from around the world and the particular host plants with which each evolved. At any given time, some 40 species of butterflies—numbering as many as 600 individual insects—flutter inside the lush screened garden and hatch on the plants housed there. Butterfly art and knickknacks are for sale in the gift shop. ⊠ *Le Galion Beach Rd., Quartier d'Orléans, St. Martin* ☎ *590/87–31–21* ⊕ *www.thebutterflyfarm.com* ⌗ *$12* ☺ *Daily 9–3:30.*

Fort Louis. Though not much remains of the structure itself, Fort Louis, which was completed by the French in 1789, is great fun if you want to climb the 92 steps to the top for the wonderful views of the island and neighboring Anguilla. On Wednesday and Saturday there is a market in the square at the bottom. ⊠ *Marigot, St. Martin.*

French Cul de Sac. North of Orient Bay Beach, the French colonial mansion of St. Martin's mayor is nestled in the hills. Little, red-roof houses look like open umbrellas tumbling down the green hillside. The area is peaceful and good for hiking. From the beach here, shuttle boats make the five-minute trip to **Ilet Pinel**, an uninhabited island that's fine for picnicking, sunning, and swimming. There are full-service beach clubs there, so just pack the sunscreen and head over. ⊠ *St. Martin.*

Grand Case. The Caribbean's own Restaurant Row is the heart of this French side town, a ten-minute drive from either Orient Bay or Marigot, stretching along a narrow beach overlooking Anguilla. You'll find a first-rate restaurant for every palate, mood, and wallet. At lunchtime, or with kids, head to the casual lolos (open-air barbecue stands) and feet-in-the sand beach bars. Twilight drinks and tapas are fun. At night, stroll the strip and preview the sophisticated offerings on the menus posted outside before you settle in for a long and sumptuous meal. If you still have the energy, there are lounges with music (usually a DJ) that get going after 11 pm. ⊠ *St. Martin.*

Guana Bay Point. On the rugged, windswept east coast about 10 minutes north of Philipsburg, Guana Bay Point is an isolated, untended beach with a spectacular view of St. Barth. Undercurrents make it more a turf than a surf destination, and locals favor the area for hiking. ⊠ *St. Maarten.*

Fodor's Choice
★   **Marigot.** It is great fun to spend a few hours exploring the bustling harbor, shopping stalls, open-air cafés, and boutiques of St. Martin's biggest town, especially on Wednesday and Saturday, when the daily open-air craft markets expand to include fresh fruits and veggies, spices, and all manner of seafood. TMarina Port La Royale is the shopping–lunch-spot central to the port, but rue de la République and rue de la Liberté, which border the bay, have duty-free shops, boutiques, and bistros. The West Indies Mall offers a deluxe (and air-conditioned) shopping experience, with such shops as Lacoste. There's less bustle here than in Philipsburg, but the open-air cafés are still tempting places to sit and people-watch. From the harborfront you can catch ferries for Anguilla and St. Barth. ⊠ *St. Martin.*

Philipsburg. The capital of Dutch St. Maarten stretches about a mile (1½ km) along an isthmus between Great Bay and the Salt Pond and has five parallel streets. Most of the village's dozens of shops and restaurants are on Front Street, narrow and cobblestone, closest to Great Bay. It's generally congested when cruise ships are in port, because of its many duty-free shops and several casinos. Little lanes called *steegjes* connect Front Street with Back Street, which has fewer shops and considerably less congestion. Along the beach is a ½-mi-long (1-km-long) boardwalk with restaurants and several Wi-Fi hot spots.

Wathey Square (pronounced watty) is in the heart of the village. Directly across from the square are the town hall and the courthouse, in the striking white building with the cupola. The structure was built in 1793 and has served as the commander's home, a fire station, a jail, and a post office. The streets surrounding the square are lined with hotels, duty-free shops, fine restaurants, and cafés. The **Captain Hodge Pier,** just off the square, is a good spot to view Great Bay and the beach that stretches alongside. ⊠ *St. Maarten.*

Sint Maarten Museum. The Sint Maarten Museum hosts rotating cultural exhibits and a permanent historical display called Forts of St. Maarten–St. Martin. Artifacts range from Arawak pottery shards to objects salvaged from the wreck of the HMS *Proselyte.* ⊠ *7 Front St., Philipsburg, St. Maarten* ☎ *599/542–4917* ⊕ *www.speetjens.com/museum* ⊠ *$1* ☺ *Weekdays 10–4, Sat. 10–2..*

Fodor's Choice
★   **Pic du Paradis.** Between Marigot and Grand Case, "Paradise Peak," at 1,492 feet, is the island's highest point. There are two observation areas. From them, the tropical forest unfolds below, and the vistas are breathtaking. The road is quite isolated and steep, best suited to

a four-wheel-drive vehicle, so don't head up here unless you are prepared for the climb. There have also been some problems with crime in this area, so it might be best to go with an experienced local guide. ⊠ *St. Martin.*

Loterie Farm. Halfway up the road to Pic du Paradis is Loterie Farm, a peaceful 150-acre private nature preserve opened to the public in 1999 by American expat B. J. Welch. There are hiking trails and maps, so you can go on your own (€5) or arrange a guide for a group (€25 for six people). Along the marked trails you will see native forest with tamarind, gum, mango, and mahogany trees, and wildlife including greenback monkeys if you are lucky. Don't miss a treetop lunch or dinner at **Hidden Forest Café** (⇨ *Where to Eat, below*), Loterie Farm's restaurant, where Julie, B. J.'s wife, cooks. If you are brave—and over 4 feet 5 inches tall—try soaring over trees on one of the longest zip lines in the Western Hemisphere. ⊠ *Rte. de Pic du Paradis, St. Martin* ☎ *590/87–86–16, 590/57–28–55* ⊕ *www.loteriefarm.net* ⊠ *€35–€55* ⊗ *Tues.–Sun. 9–4.*

SHOPPING

It's true that the island sparkles with its myriad outdoor activities—diving, snorkeling, sailing, swimming, and sunning—but shopaholics are drawn to the sparkle within the jewelry stores. The huge array of such stores is almost unrivaled in the Caribbean. In addition, duty-free shops offer substantial savings—about 15% to 30% below U.S. and Canadian prices—on cameras, watches, liquor, cigars, and designer clothing. It's no wonder that each year 500 cruise ships make Philipsburg a port of call. On both sides of the island, be alert for idlers. They can snatch unwatched purses. Prices are in dollars on the Dutch side, in euros on the French side. As for bargains, there are more to be had on the Dutch side.

Philipsburg's **Front Street** has reinvented itself. Now it's mall-like, with a redbrick walk and streets, palm trees lining the sleek boutiques, jewelry stores, souvenir shops, outdoor restaurants, and the old reliables, like McDonald's and Burger King. Here and there a school or a church appears to remind visitors there's more to the island than shopping. Back Street is where you'll find the **Philipsburg Market Place,** a daily open-air market where you can haggle for bargains on such goods as handicrafts, souvenirs, and beachwear. **Old Street,** near the end of Front Street, has stores, boutiques, and open-air cafés offering French crepes, rich chocolates, and island mementos.

On the French side, wrought-iron balconies, colorful awnings, and gingerbread trim decorate Marigot's smart shops, tiny boutiques, and bistros in the **Marina Royale** complex and on the main streets, **Rue de la Liberté** and **Rue de la République.** Also in Marigot are the pricey **West Indies Mall** and the **Plaza Caraïbes,** which house designer shops, although some shops are closing in the economic downturn.

ACTIVITIES

For a wide range of water sports, including parasailing and waterskiing, head to Orient Beach, where a variety of operators have their headquarters.

DIVING AND SNORKELING

Although St. Maarten is not generally known as a dive destination, the water temperature here is rarely below 70°F (21°C). Visibility is often excellent, averaging about 100 feet to 120 feet. The island has more than 40 good dive sites, from wrecks to rocky labyrinths. For snorkelers, the area around Orient Bay, Caye Verte (Green Key), Ilêt Pinel, and Flat Island is especially lovely, and is officially classified, and protected, as a regional underwater nature reserve. The average cost of an afternoon snorkeling trip is about $45 to $55 per person.

Dive Safaris. Dive Safaris has a shark-awareness dive on Friday where participants can watch professional feeders give reef sharks a little nosh. ⊠ *La Palapa Marina, Simpson Bay, St. Maarten* ☎ *599/545–3213* ⊕ *www.divestmaarten.com.*

Ocean Explorers Dive Shop. Ocean Explorers Dive Shop is St. Maarten's oldest dive shop, and offers different types of certification courses. ⊠ *113 Welfare Rd., Simpson Bay, St. Maarten* ☎ *599/544–5252* ⊕ *www.stmaartendiving.com.*

FISHING

You can angle for yellowtail snapper, grouper, marlin, tuna, and wahoo on deep-sea excursions. Costs range from $150 per person for a half-day to $250 for a full day. Prices usually include bait and tackle, instruction for novices, and refreshments. Ask about licensing and insurance.

Lee's Deepsea Fishing. Lee's Deepsea Fishing organizes excursions, and when you return, Lee's Roadside Grill will cook your tuna, wahoo, or whatever else you catch and keep. Rates start at $150 per person for a half day. ⊠ *Welfare Rd. 82, Simpson Bay, St. Maarten* ☎ *599/544–4233* ⊕ *www.leesfish.com.*

Rudy's Deep Sea Fishing. Rudy's Deep Sea Fishing has been around for years, and is one of the more experienced sport-angling outfits. ⊠ *14 Airport Rd., Simpson Bay, St. Maarten* ☎ *599/545–2177 or 599/522–7120* ⊕ *www.rudysdeepseafishing.com.*

BEACHES

The island's 10 mi (16 km) of beaches are all open to cruise-ship passengers. You can rent chairs and umbrellas at most of the beaches, primarily from beachside restaurants. The best beaches are on the French side. Topless bathing is common on the French side. If you take a cab to a remote beach, be sure to arrange a specific time for the driver to return for you. Don't leave valuables unattended on the beach or in a rental car, even in the trunk.

Baie des Péres (*Friars Bay*). This quiet cove close to Marigot has beach grills and bars, with chaises and umbrellas, calm waters, and a lovely view of Anguilla. Kali's Beach Bar, open daily for lunch and (weather permitting) dinner, has a Rasta vibe and color scheme. You can get lunch, beach chairs, and umbrellas there. To get to the beach, take National Road 7 from Marigot, go toward Grand Case to the Morne Valois hill, and turn left on the dead-end road at the sign. ⊠ *Friar's Bay, St. Martin.*

Fodor's Choice **Baie Orientale** (*Orient Bay*). Many consider this the island's most beauti-
★ ful beach, but its 2 mi (3 km) of satiny white sand, underwater marine reserve, variety of water sports, beach clubs, and hotels also make it one of the most crowded. Lots of "naturists" take advantage of the clothing-optional policy, so don't be shocked. Plan to spend the day at one of the clubs; each bar has different color umbrellas, and all boast terrific restaurants and lively bars. To get to Baie Orientale from Marigot, take National Road 7 past Grand Case, past the Aéroport de L'Espérance, and watch for the left turn. ⊠ *Baie Orientale, St. Martin.*

★ **Dawn Beach.** True to its name, Dawn Beach is the place to be at sunrise. On the Atlantic side of Oyster Pond, just south of the French border, this is a first-class beach for sunning and snorkeling. It's not usually crowded, and there are several good restaurants nearby. To find it, follow the signs to Mr. Busby's restaurant. ⊠ *South of Oyster Pond, St. Maarten.*

Ilet Pinel. A protected nature reserve, this kid-friendly island is a five-minute ferry ride from French Cul de Sac ($7 per person round-trip). The ferry runs every half hour from midmorning until dusk. The water is clear and shallow, and the shore is sheltered. If you like snorkeling, don your gear and paddle along both coasts of this pencil shaped speck in the ocean. You can rent equipment on the island or in the parking lot before you board the ferry for about $10. Plan for lunch any day of the week at the water's edge at a palm-shaded beach hut at **Karibuni** (except in September, when it's closed) for the freshest fish, great salads, tapas, and drinks—try the frozen mojito for a treat. ⊠ *Ilet Pinel, St. Martin.*

WHERE TO EAT

$ ✗**Enoch's Place.** The blue-and-white-striped awning on a corner of the
CARIBBEAN Marigot Market makes this place hard to miss. But Enoch's cooking is what draws the crowds. Specialties include garlic shrimp, fresh lobster, and rice and beans (like your St. Martin mother used to make). Try the saltfish and fried johnnycake—a great breakfast option. The food more than makes up for the lack of decor, and chances are you'll be counting the days until you can return. ⊠ *Marigot Market, Front de Mer, Marigot, St. Martin* ☎ *590/29–29–88* ▭ *No credit cards* ☉ *Closed Sun. No dinner.*

$$ ✗**Taloula Mango's.** Ribs are the specialty at this casual beachfront restau-
ECLECTIC rant, but the jerk chicken and thin-crust pizza, not to mention a few vegetarian options like the tasty falafel, are not to be ignored. On weekdays lunch is accompanied by live music; every Friday during happy hour a DJ spins tunes. In case you're wondering, the restaurant got its name from the owner's golden retriever. ⊠ *Sint Rose Shopping Mall, off Front St. on beach boardwalk, Philipsburg, St. Maarten* ☎ *599/542–1645* ⊕ *www.taloulamango.com.*

7

St. Thomas

Charlotte Amalie

BRITISH VIRGIN ISLANDS

TORTOLA

West End

Jost van Dyke

ATLANTIC OCEAN

ST. JOHN

Cruz Bay

Mary Pt.

Cinnamon Bay

Great Thatch Island

The Narrows

East End Pt.

Government House

Frederick Lutheran Church

Fort Christian

Emancipation Garden

Legislature Building

King's Wharf

St. Thomas Harbor

Berge Gade

Norre Gade

Veterans Dr.

Coral World Ocean Park

Coki Beach

Sapphire Beach

Thatch Cay

Pillsbury Sound

Red Hook

Great St. James Island

Little St. James Island

Nadir

Long Pt.

Bovoni Bay

St. Thomas Skyride

Charlotte Amalie
see inset map

Morningstar Beach

Frenchman Bay

Magens Bay

Big Hans Lollick

Drake's Seat

Picara Pt.

Inner Brass

Estate St. Peter Guesthouse and Botanical Gardens

Dorothea

ST. THOMAS

Cyril E. King International Airport

Brewers Bay

Water Island

Santa Maria Bay

Stumpy Bay

Botany Bay

David Pt.

Fortuna

Caribbean Sea

TO ST CROIX →

← TO PUERTO RICO

KEY

Ferry

Cruise Ship Terminal

0   3 miles
0   3 kilometers

ST. THOMAS (CHARLOTTE AMALIE)

Carol
Bareuther

St. Thomas is the busiest cruise port of call in the world. Up to eight mega ships may visit in a single day. Don't expect an exotic island experience: one of the three U.S. Virgin Islands (with St. Croix and St. John), St. Thomas is as American as any place on the mainland, complete with McDonald's and HBO. The positive side of all this development is that there are more tours here than anywhere else in the Caribbean, and every year the excursions get better. Of course, shopping is the big draw in Charlotte Amalie, but experienced travelers remember the days of "real" bargains. Today so many passengers fill the stores that it's a seller's market. On some days there are so many cruise passengers on St. Thomas that you must book a ship-sponsored shore excursion if you want to do more than just take a taxi to the beach or stroll around Charlotte Amalie.

ST. THOMAS BEST BETS

■ **Coral World Ocean Park.** This aquarium attraction is a great bet for families, and it's on one of best snorkeling beaches.

■ **Magen's Bay Beach.** St. Thomas has one of the most picture-postcard perfect beaches you'll ever see. It's great for swimming.

■ **St. John.** It's easy to hop on the ferry to St. John for a day of hiking, then relax for an hour or two on the beach afterward.

■ **Shopping.** Charlotte Amalie is one of the best places in the Caribbean to shop.

ESSENTIALS

CURRENCY The U.S. dollar is the official currency of U.S. Virgin Islands, and ATMs are plentiful.

INTERNET **Beans, Bytes and Websites** ✉ *Royal Dane Mall, behind Tavern on Water-front, Charlotte Amalie, St. Thomas, U.S. Virgin Islands* ☎ *340/775–5262* ⊕ *www.beansbytesandwebsites.com.*

Havensight Cafe ✉ *Havensight Mall, Charlotte Amalie, St. Thomas, U.S. Virgin Islands* ☎ *340/774–5818.*

TELEPHONE Both GSM and Sprint phones work in St. Thomas (and the USVI are normally included in most U.S. cell phone plans). It's as easy to call home from St. Thomas and St. John as from any city in the United States. On St. Thomas, public phones are easily found, and AT&T has a telecommunications center across from the Havensight Mall.

COMING ASHORE

Depending on how many ships are in port, cruise ships drop anchor in the harbor at Charlotte Amalie and tender passengers directly to the waterfront duty-free shops, dock at the Havensight Mall at the eastern end of the crescent bay, or dock at Crown Bay Marina a few miles west of town (Holland America almost always docks at Crown Bay).

The distance from Havensight to the duty-free shops is 1½ mi (3 km), which can be walked in less than half an hour; a taxi ride there costs $6 per person ($5 for each additional person). Tourist information offices are at

7

the Havensight Mall (across from Building No. 1) for docking passengers and downtown near Fort Christian (at the eastern end of the waterfront shopping area) for those coming ashore by tender. Both offices distribute free maps. From Crown Bay it's also a half-hour walk or a $5 per person cab ride ($4 for each additional person). V.I. Taxi Association drivers offer a basic 2-hour island tour for $25 per person for two or more people. You can rent a car in St. Thomas, but with all the tour options it's often easier and cheaper to take an organized excursion or just hop in a cab.

EXPLORING ST. THOMAS

CHARLOTTE AMALIE

St. Thomas's major burg is a hilly shopping town. There are also plenty of interesting historic sights—so take the time to see at least a few.

🕲 **Emancipation Garden.** Built to commemorate the freeing of slaves in 1848, the garden was the site of a 150th anniversary celebration of emancipation. A bronze bust of a freed slave blowing a symbolic conch shell commemorates this anniversary. The gazebo here is used for official ceremonies. Two other monuments show the island's Danish-American connection—a bust of Denmark's King Christian and a scaled-down model of the U.S. Liberty Bell. ✉ *Between Tolbod Gade and Fort Christian, Charlotte Amalie, St. Thomas, U.S. Virgin Islands.*

🕲 **Ft. Christian.** St. Thomas's oldest standing structure, this monument was built between 1672 and 1680 and now has U.S. National Landmark status. This remarkable building has, over time, been used as a jail, governor's residence, town hall, courthouse, and church. A multimillion-dollar renovation project was started in 2005 to stabilize the structure and halt centuries of deterioration. Delays have plagued the project, including the discovery of human skeletal remains buried in the walls from when the structure was used as a Lutheran church. You can see from the outside the four renovated faces of famous 19th-century clock tower. ✉ *Waterfront Hwy. east of shopping district, Charlotte Amalie, St. Thomas, U.S. Virgin Islands* 🕾 *340/776–4566.*

Frederick Lutheran Church. This historic church has a massive mahogany altar, and its pews—each with its own door—were once rented to families of the congregation. Lutheranism is the state religion of Denmark, and when the territory was without a minister, the governor—who had his own elevated pew—filled in. ✉ *Norre Gade, Charlotte Amalie, St. Thomas, U.S. Virgin Islands* 🕾 *340/776–1315* 🕙 *Mon.–Sat. 9–4.*

Government House. Built in 1867, this neoclassical white brick-and-wood structure houses the offices of the governor of the Virgin Islands. Inside, the staircases are of native mahogany, as are the plaques hand-lettered in gold with the names of the governors appointed and, since 1970, elected. Brochures detailing the history of the building are available, but you may have to ask for them. ✉ *Government Hill, Charlotte Amalie, St. Thomas, U.S. Virgin Islands* 🕾 *340/774–0294* 🎟 *Free* 🕙 *Weekdays 8–5.*

Legislature Building. Its pastoral-looking lime-green exterior conceals the vociferous political wrangling of the Virgin Islands Senate. Constructed originally by the Danish as a police barracks, the building was later used to billet U.S. Marines, and much later it housed a public school. You're welcome to sit in on sessions in the upstairs chambers. ⊠ *Waterfront Hwy. across from Ft. Christian, Charlotte Amalie, St. Thomas, U.S. Virgin Islands* ☎ *340/774–0880* ⊙ *Daily 8–5.*

ELSEWHERE ON ST. THOMAS

☾ **Coral World Ocean Park.** This interactive aquarium and water-sports cen-
Fodor's Choice ter lets you experience a variety of sea life and other animals up close
★ and personal. Coral World has an offshore underwater observatory, an 80,000-gallon coral reef exhibit, and 21 jewel aquariums displaying the Virgin Islands' coral reef habitats and unusual marine life. The park also has several outdoor pools where you can pet baby sharks, feed stingrays, touch starfish, and view endangered sea turtles. Daily feedings take place at most exhibits. In addition, the park operates several activities, both above and below the water. ⊠ *Coki Point north of Rte. 38, Estate Frydendal, St. Thomas, U.S. Virgin Islands* ⊠ *6450 Estate Smith Bay, St. Thomas, U.S. Virgin Islands* ☎ *340/775–1555* ⊕ *www.coralworldvi.com* ⊠ *$19, Sea Lion Swim $105, Sea Lion Encounter $65, Sea Trek $58, Snuba $52, Shark and Turtle Encounters $32, Nautilus $20* ⊙ *Daily 9–4. Off-season (May–Oct) hrs may vary so call to confirm.*

☾ **Drake's Seat.** Sir Francis Drake was supposed to have kept watch over his fleet and looked for enemy ships from this vantage point. The panorama is especially breathtaking (and romantic) at dusk, and if you arrive late in the day, you can miss the hordes of day-trippers on taxi tours who stop here to take a picture and buy a T-shirt from one of the many vendors. ⊠ *Rte. 40, Estate Zufriedenheit, St. Thomas, U.S. Virgin Islands.*

Estate St. Peter Greathouse and Botanical Gardens. This unusual spot is perched on a mountainside 1,000 feet above sea level, with views of more than 20 islands and islets. You can wander through a gallery displaying local art, sip a complimentary rum punch while looking out at the view, or follow a nature trail that leads you past nearly 70 varieties of tropical plants, including 17 varieties of orchids. ⊠ *Rte. 40, Estate St. Peter, St. Thomas, U.S. Virgin Islands* ☎ *340/774–4999* ⊕ *www. greathousevi.com* ⊠ *$5* ⊙ *Mon.–Sat. 8–4.*

☾ **St. Thomas Skyride.** Fly skyward in a gondola to Paradise Point, an overlook
★ with breathtaking views of Charlotte Amalie and the harbor. There are several shops, a bar, a restaurant, and a wedding gazebo; kids enjoy the tropical bird show held daily at 10:30 am and 1:30 pm. A ¼-mi (½-km) hiking trail leads to spectacular views of St. Croix. Wear sturdy shoes, as the trail is steep and rocky. ⊠ *Rte. 30, across from Havensight Mall, Havensight, St. Thomas, U.S. Virgin Islands* ☎ *340/774–9809* ⊕ *www.stthomasskyride. com* ⊠ *$21; Sky Jump $30* ⊙ *Thurs.–Tues. 9–5, Wed. 9–9.*

SHOPPING

The prime shopping area in **Charlotte Amalie** is between Post Office and Market squares; it consists of two parallel streets that run east–west (Waterfront Highway and Main Street) and the alleyways that connect them. Particularly attractive are the historic **A.H. Riise Alley, Royal Dane Mall, Palm Passage,** and pastel-painted **International Plaza.**

Havensight Mall, next to the cruise-ship dock, may not be as charming as downtown Charlotte Amalie, but it does have more than 60 shops. It also has an excellent bookstore, a bank, a pharmacy, a gourmet grocery, and smaller branches of many downtown stores. The shops at **Port of $ale,** adjoining Havensight Mall (its buildings are pink instead of brown), sell discount goods. Next door to Port of $ale is the **Yacht Haven Grande** complex, with many upscale shops.At the Crown Bay cruise-ship pier, the **Crown Bay Center,** off the Harwood Highway in Sub Base about ½ mi (¾ km), has quite a few shops.

East of Charlotte Amalie on Route 38, **Tillett Gardens** is an oasis of artistic endeavor across from the Tutu Park Shopping Mall. The late Jim and Rhoda Tillett converted this Danish farm into an artists' retreat in 1959. Today you can watch artisans produce silk-screen fabrics, candles, pottery, and other handicrafts. Something special is often happening in the gardens as well: the Classics in the Gardens program is a classical music series presented under the stars, Arts Alive is an annual arts-and-crafts fair held in November, and the Pistarckle Theater holds its performances here.

☾ **Vendors Plaza.** Here merchants sell everything from T-shirts to African attire to leather goods. Look for local art among the ever-changing selections at this busy market. ⊠ *Waterfront, west of Fort Christian, Charlotte Amalie, St. Thomas, U.S. Virgin Islands* ☉ *Weekdays 8–6, weekends 9–1.*

ACTIVITIES

DIVING AND SNORKELING

☾ **Coki Beach Dive Club.** Coki Beach Dive Club is a PADI Gold Palm outfit run by avid diver Peter Jackson. Snorkeling and dive tours in the fish-filled reefs off Coki Beach are available, as are classes from beginner to underwater photography. ⊠ *Rte. 388, at Coki Point, Estate Frydendal, St. Thomas, U.S. Virgin Islands* ☎ *340/775–4220* ⊕ *www.cokidive.com.*

Snuba of St. Thomas. Snuba of St. Thomas offers something for nondivers, a cross between snorkeling and scuba diving: a 20-foot air hose connects you to the surface. The cost is $52. Children must be eight or older to participate. ⊠ *Rte. 388, at Coki Point, Estate Smith Bay, St. Thomas, U.S. Virgin Islands* ☎ *340/693–8063* ⊕ *www.visnuba.com.*

FISHING

Charter Boat Center. The Charter Boat Center is a major source for sportfishing charters, both marlin and inshore. ⊠ *6300 Red Hook Plaza, Red Hook, St. Thomas, U.S. Virgin Islands* ☎ *340/775–7990* ⊕ *www.charterboat.vi.*

GOLF

★ **Mahogany Run Golf Course.** The Mahogany Run Golf Course attracts golfers for its spectacular view of the British Virgin Islands and the challenging three-hole Devil's Triangle. At this Tom and George Fazio–designed, par-70, 18-hole course, there's a fully stocked pro shop, snack bar, and open-air clubhouse. Greens fees and half-cart fees for 18 holes are $150. The course is open daily, and there are frequently informal weekend tournaments. It's the only course on St. Thomas. ⊠ *Rte. 42, Estate Lovenlund, St. Thomas, U.S. Virgin Islands* ☎ *340/777–6006 or 800/253–7103* ⊕ *www. mahoganyrungolf.com.*

BEACHES

Coki Beach. Funky beach huts selling local foods such as meat pates (fried
Fodor's Choice turnovers with a spicy ground-beef filling), picnic tables topped with
★ umbrellas sporting beverage logos, and a brigade of hair braiders and
taxi men give this beach overlooking picturesque Thatch Cay a Coney
Island feel. But this is the best place on the island to snorkel and scuba
dive. Ashore you can find conveniences such as restrooms and changing facilities, both of which received a much-needed renovation in 2010
as well as beefed up security. ⊠ *Rte. 388, next to Coral World Ocean
Park, St. Thomas, U.S. Virgin Islands.*

Magens Bay. Deeded to the island as a public park, this heart-shape
Fodor's Choice stretch of white sand is considered one of the most beautiful in the
★ world. The bottom of the bay is flat and sandy, so this is a place for
sunning and swimming rather than snorkeling. There's a bar, snack
shack, and beachwear boutique; bathhouses with restrooms, changing
rooms, and saltwater showers are close by. Sunfish and paddleboats
are the most popular rentals at the water-sports kiosk. If you arrive
between 8 am and 5 pm, you pay an entrance fee of $4 per person, $2
per vehicle; it's free for children under 12. ⊠ *Rte. 35, at end of road on
north side of island, St. Thomas, U.S. Virgin Islands.*

★ **Sapphire Beach.** A steady breeze makes this beach a boardsailor's paradise. The swimming is great, as is the snorkeling, especially at the reef
near Pettyklip Point. Beach volleyball is big on the weekends. Sapphire
Beach Resort and Marina has a snack shop, bar, and water-sports rentals. ⊠ *Rte. 38, Sapphire Bay, St. Thomas, U.S. Virgin Islands.*

WHERE TO EAT

$$$ ✕ **Cuzzin's Caribbean Restaurant and Bar.** This is the place to sample bona
CARIBBEAN fide Virgin Islands cuisine. For lunch, order tender slivers of conch
stewed in a rich onion-and-butter sauce, savory braised oxtail, or cur-
ried chicken. At dinner the island-style mutton, served in thick gravy
and seasoned with locally grown herbs, offers a tasty treat that's deli-
ciously different. Side dishes include peas and rice, boiled green bananas,
fried plantains, and potato stuffing. In a 19th-century livery stable on
Back Street, this restaurant is hard to find but well worth it if you like
sampling local foods. ⊠ *7 Wimmelskafts Gade, also called Back St.,
Charlotte Amalie, St. Thomas, U.S. Virgin Islands* ☎ *340/777–4711.*

$$ ✕ **Gladys' Cafe.** Even if the local specialties—conch in butter sauce, salt
CARIBBEAN fish and dumplings, hearty red bean soup—didn't make this a recom-
Fodor's Choice mended café, it would be worth coming for Gladys's smile. Her cozy
★ alleyway restaurant is rich in atmosphere with its mahogany bar and
native stone walls, making dining a double delight. While you're here,
pick up a $5 or $10 bottle of her special hot sauce. There are mustard-,
oil and vinegar–, and tomato-based versions; the tomato-based sauce
is the hottest. Only Amex is accepted. ⊠ *Waterfront, at Royal Dane
Mall, 28 Dronningens Gade, Charlotte Amalie, St. Thomas, U.S. Virgin
Islands* ⊠ *28 Dronningens Gade, Charlotte Amelie,, St. Thomas, U.S.
Virgin Islands* ☎ *340/774–6604* ⊘ *No dinner.*

7

ST. VINCENT (KINGSTOWN)

Jane E. Zarem   You won't find glitzy resorts or flashy discos in St. Vincent. Rather, you'll be fascinated by its busy capital, mountainous beauty, and fine sailing waters. St. Vincent is the largest and northernmost island in the Grenadines archipelago; Kingstown, the capital city of St. Vincent and the Grenadines, is the government and business center and major port. Except for one barren area on the island's northeast coast—remnants of the 1979 eruption of La Soufrière, one of the last active volcanoes in the Caribbean—the countryside is mountainous, lush, and green. St. Vincent's topography thwarted European settlement for many years. As colonization advanced elsewhere in the Caribbean, in fact, the island became a refuge for Carib Indians—descendants of whom still live in northeastern St. Vincent. After years of fighting and back-and-forth territorial claims, British troops prevailed by overpowering the French and banishing Carib warriors to Central America. Independent since 1979, St. Vincent and the Grenadines remains a member of the British Commonwealth.

ESSENTIALS

CURRENCY   Eastern Caribbean (E.C.) dollar (EC$2.67 to US$1). U.S. dollars (but not coins) are generally accepted, but change is given in E.C. currency.

INTERNET   **E@gles Internet Cafe** ⊠ *Kingstown, St. Vincent, St. Vincent and the Grenadines.*

TELEPHONE   Your cell phone should operate in St. Vincent, but roaming charges can be hefty. Pay phones are readily available and best operated with the prepaid phone cards that are sold at many stores. Telephone services are available at the Cruise Ship Complex in Kingstown. For an international operator, dial 115; to charge your call to a credit card, call 117.

COMING ASHORE

The Cruise Ship Complex at Kingstown, St. Vincent's capital city, accommodates two cruise ships; additional vessels anchor outside the harbor and bring passengers to the jetty by launch. The facility has about two-dozen shops that sell duty-free items and handicrafts. There's a communications center, post office, tourist information desk, restaurant, and food court.

Buses and taxis are available at the wharf. Taxi drivers are well equipped to take you on an island tour; expect to pay $25 per hour for up to four passengers. The ferry to Bequia (one hour each way) is at the adjacent pier. Renting a car for just one day isn't advisable, since car rentals are expensive (at least $55 per day) and require a $24 temporary driving permit on top of that. It's almost always more financially favorable to take a tour, though you don't have to limit yourself to those offered by your ship.

EXPLORING ST. VINCENT

Botanical Gardens. A few minutes north of downtown by taxi is St. Vincent's famous Botanical Gardens. Founded in 1765, it's the oldest botanical garden in the Western Hemisphere. Captain Bligh—of *Bounty* fame—brought the first breadfruit tree to this island for landowners to propagate. You can see a direct descendant of this original tree among the specimen mahogany, rubber, teak, and other tropical trees and

Fodor's Choice
★

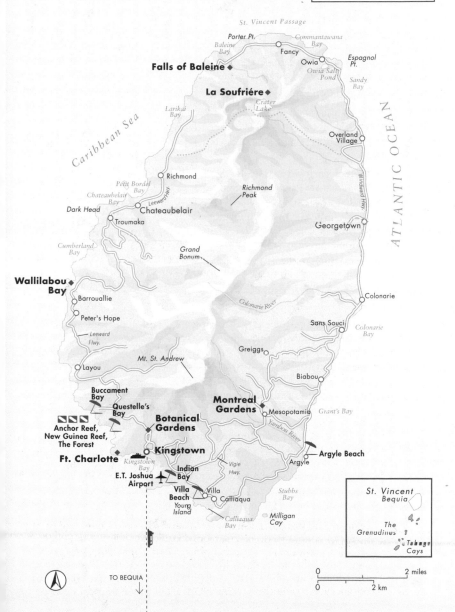

St. Vincent

KEY

Beaches

Cruise Ship Terminal

Dive Sites

Ferry

St. Vincent Passage

Porter Pt.

Baleine Bay

Commantawana Bay

Fancy

Owia

Espagnol Pt.

Falls of Baleine

Owia Salt Pond

Sandy Bay

La Soufriére

Crater Lake

Larikai Bay

Caribbean Sea

Overland Village

ATLANTIC OCEAN

Richmond

Richmond Peak

Petit Bordel Bay

Chateaubelair Bay

Leeward Hwy.

Dark Head

Chateaubelair

Troumaka

Georgetown

Grand Bonum

Cumberland Bay

Colonarie River

Wallilabou Bay

Colonarie

Barrouallie

Peter's Hope

Sans Souci

Colonarie Bay

Leeward Hwy.

Greiggs

Layou

Mt. St. Andrew

Biabou

Buccament Bay

Montreal Gardens

Questelle's Bay

Botanical Gardens

Mesopotamia

Grant's Bay

Anchor Reef, New Guinea Reef, The Forest

Yambou River

Kingstown

Ft. Charlotte

Kingstown Bay

Argyle Beach

Vigie Hwy.

Argyle

E.T. Joshua Airport

Indian Bay

Villa Beach

Villa

Catliaqua

Stubbs Bay

Young Island

Calliaqua Bay

Milligan Cay

St. Vincent

Bequia

The Grenadines

Tobago Cays

0   2 miles

0   2 km

TO BEQUIA

shrubs in the 20 acres of gardens. Guides explain all the medicinal and ornamental trees and shrubs; they also appreciate a tip at the end of the tour. ⊠ *Off Leeward Hwy., Montrose, St. Vincent, St. Vincent and the Grenadines* ☎ *784/457–1003* 🔲 *Free* ☉ *Daily 6–6.*

Fodor's Choice
★
Falls of Baleine. The falls are impossible to reach by car, so book an escorted, all-day boat trip from Villa Beach or the Lagoon Marina. The boat ride along the coast offers scenic island views. When you arrive, you have to wade through shallow water to get to the beach. Then local guides help you make the easy five-minute trek to the 60-foot falls and the rock-enclosed freshwater pool the falls create—wear a bathing suit so you can take a dip. ⊠ *St. Vincent, St. Vincent and the Grenadines.*

ST. VINCENT BEST BETS

■ **Falls of Baleine.** An all-day boat trip to the 60-foot falls is a beautiful way to spend a day.

■ **Ferry to Bequia.** Laid-back Bequia is one hour by ferry from St. Vincent.

■ **Hiking.** Whether you hike in the rain forest or do the more difficult climb of La Soufrière, it's worth exploring some of the island's rugged terrain.

■ **Island Tour.** Tour the greater Kingstown area, then travel up the leeward coast to Wallilabou.

■ **Tobago Cays.** These uninhabited islands in the Grenadines are the top destination for snorkeling.

☾ **Ft. Charlotte.** Started by the French in
★ 1786 and completed by the British in 1806, the fort was named for Queen Charlotte, wife of King George III. It sits on Berkshire Hill, a dramatic promontory 2 mi (3 km) north of Kingstown and 636 feet above sea level, with a stunning view of the capital city and the Grenadines. Interestingly, cannons face inward—the fear of attack by the French and their native allies was far greater than any threat approaching from the sea, though, truth be told, the fort saw no action. Nowadays, the fort serves as a signal station for ships; its ancient cells house historical paintings of the island by Lindsay Prescott. ⊠ *St. Vincent, St. Vincent and the Grenadines.*

Kingstown. The capital city of St. Vincent and the Grenadines is on the island's southwestern coast. The town of 13,500 residents wraps around Kingstown Bay; a ring of green hills and ridges, studded with homes, forms a backdrop for the city. This is very much a working city, with a busy harbor and few concessions to tourists. Kingstown Harbour is the only deepwater port on the island.

A few gift shops can be found on and around **Bay Street,** near the harbor. Upper Bay Street, which stretches along the bay front, bustles with daytime activity—workers going about their business and housewives doing their shopping. Many of Kingstown's downtown buildings are built of stone or brick brought to the island in the holds of 18th-century ships as ballast (and replaced with sugar and spices for the return trip to Europe). The Georgian-style stone arches and second-floor overhangs on former warehouses create shelter from midday sun and the brief, cooling showers common to the tropics.

Grenadines Wharf, at the south end of Bay Street, is busy with schooners loading supplies and ferries loading people bound for the Grenadines.

The **cruise-ship complex,** just south of the commercial wharf, has a mall with a dozen or more shops, plus restaurants, a post office, communications facilities, and a taxi-minibus stand.

An almost infinite selection of produce fills the **Kingstown Produce Market,** a three-story building that takes up a whole city block on Upper Bay, Hillsboro, and Bedford streets in the center of town. It's noisy, colorful, and open Monday through Saturday—but the busiest times (and the best times to go) are Friday and Saturday mornings. In the courtyard, vendors sell local arts and crafts. On the upper floors, merchants sell clothing, household items, gifts, and other products.

Little Tokyo, so called because funding for the project was a gift from Japan, is a waterfront shopping area with a bustling indoor fish market and dozens of stalls where you can buy inexpensive homemade meals, drinks, ice cream, bread and cookies, clothing, trinkets, and even get a haircut.

St. George's Cathedral, on Grenville Street, is a pristine, creamy yellow Anglican church built in 1820. The dignified Georgian architecture includes simple wooden pews, an ornate chandelier, and beautiful stained-glass windows; one was a gift from Queen Victoria, who actually commissioned it for London's St. Paul's Cathedral in honor of her first grandson. When the artist created an angel with a red robe, she was horrified by the color and sent it abroad. The markers in the cathedral's graveyard recount the history of the island. Across the street is **St. Mary's Roman Catholic Cathedral of the Assumption,** built in stages beginning in 1823. The strangely appealing design is a blend of Moorish, Georgian, and Romanesque styles applied to black brick. Nearby, freed slaves built the **Kingstown Methodist Church** in 1841. The exterior is brick, simply decorated with quoins (solid blocks that form the corners), and the roof is held together by metal straps, bolts, and wooden pins. **Scots Kirk** was built from 1839 to 1880 by and for Scottish settlers but became a Seventh-Day Adventist church in 1952. ✉ *St. Vincent, St. Vincent and the Grenadines.*

La Soufrière. This towering volcano, which last erupted in 1979, is 4,000 feet high and so huge in area that its surrounding mountainside covers virtually the entire northern third of the island. The eastern trail to the rim of the crater, a two-hour ascent, begins at Rabacca Dry River. ✉ *St. Vincent, St. Vincent and the Grenadines.*

Fodor'sChoice
★
Montreal Gardens. Welsh-born landscape designer Timothy Vaughn renovated 7½ acres of neglected commercial flower beds and a falling-down plantation house into a stunning yet informal garden spot. Anthurium, ginger lilies, birds-of-paradise, and other tropical flowers are planted in raised beds; tree ferns create a canopy of shade along the walkways. The gardens are in the shadow of majestic Grand Bonhomme Mountain, deep in the Mesopotamia Valley, about 12 mi (19 km) from Kingstown. ✉ *Montreal St., Mesopotamia, St. Vincent, St. Vincent and the Grenadines* ☎ *784/458–1198* ✆ *$2* ☺ *Dec.–Aug., weekdays 9–5.*

☺
★
Wallilabou Bay. The *Pirates of the Caribbean* left its mark at Wallilabou (pronounced wally-la-*boo*), a location used for filming the opening scenes of "The Curse of the Black Pearl" film in 2003. Many of the buildings and docks built as stage sets remain, giving the pretty bay (a

port of entry for visiting yachts) an intriguingly historic appearance. You can sunbathe, swim, picnic, or buy your lunch at Wallilabou Anchorage. This is a favorite stop for day-trippers returning from the Falls of Baleine and boaters anchoring for the evening. Nearby, at Wallilabou Heritage Park, there's a river with a small waterfall and pool, where you can take a freshwater plunge. ⊠ *St. Vincent, St. Vincent and the Grenadines.*

SHOPPING

The 12 small blocks that hug the waterfront in **downtown Kingstown** compose St. Vincent's main shopping district. Among the shops that sell goods to fulfill household needs are a few that sell local crafts, gifts, and souvenirs. Bargaining is neither expected nor appreciated. The **cruise-ship complex,** on the waterfront in Kingstown, has a collection of a dozen or so boutiques, shops, and restaurants that cater to cruise-ship passengers.

St. Vincent Craftsmen's Centre. St. Vincent Craftsmen's Centre, three blocks from the wharf, sells locally made grass floor mats, place mats, and other straw articles, as well as batik cloth, handmade West Indian dolls, hand-painted calabashes, and framed artwork. No credit cards are accepted. ⊠ *Frenches St., Kingstown, St. Vincent, St. Vincent and the Grenadines* ☏ *784/457–2516.*

ACTIVITIES

DIVING AND SNORKELING

Novices and advanced divers alike will be impressed by the marine life in the waters surrounding St. Vincent and the Grenadines—brilliant sponges, huge deepwater coral trees, and shallow reefs teeming with colorful fish. The best dive spots on St. Vincent are in the small bays along the coast between Kingstown and Layou; many are within 20 yards of shore and only 20 feet to 30 feet down.

Anchor Reef has excellent visibility for viewing a deep-black coral garden, schools of squid, seahorses, and maybe a small octopus. The **Forest,** a shallow dive, is still dramatic, with soft corals in pastel colors and schools of small fish. **New Guinea Reef** slopes to 90 feet (28 meters) and can't be matched for its quantity of corals and sponges. The pristine waters surrounding the **Tobago Cays,** in the Southern Grenadines, will give you a world-class diving experience.

Dive Fantasea. Dive Fantasea offers dive and snorkeling trips to the St. Vincent coast and the Tobago Cays. ⊠ *Villa Beach, St. Vincent, St. Vincent and the Grenadines* ☏ *784/457–5560 or 784/457–5577.*

Dive St. Vincent. Dive St. Vincent is where NAUI- and PADI-certified instructor Bill Tewes and his two certified dive masters offer beginner and certification courses for ages eight and up, advanced water excursions along the St. Vincent coast and to the southern Grenadines for diving connoisseurs, and an introductory scuba lesson for novices. ⊠ *Young Island Dock, Villa Beach, St. Vincent, St. Vincent and the Grenadines* ☏ *784/457–4714 or 784/457–4928* ⊕ *www.divestvincent.com.*

FISHING

Crystal Blue Sportfishing Charters. Crystal Blue Sportfishing Charters offers sportfishing charters on a 34-foot pirogue for both amateur and serious fishermen. ⊠ *Indian Bay, St. Vincent, St. Vincent and the Grenadines* ☎ *784/457–4532.*

BEACHES

St. Vincent's origin is volcanic, so its beaches range in color from golden-brown to black. Swimming is recommended only in the lagoons and bays along the leeward coast. By contrast, beaches on Bequia and the rest of the Grenadines have pure white sand, palm trees, and crystal-clear aquamarine water; some are even within walking distance of the jetty.

Indian Bay. South of Kingstown and just north of Villa Beach, this beach has golden sand but is slightly rocky; it's good for snorkeling. ⊠ *St. Vincent, St. Vincent and the Grenadines.*

Villa Beach. The long stretch of sand in front of the row of hotels and restaurants along the Young Island Channel varies from 20 to 25 feet wide to practically nonexistent. The broadest, sandiest part is in front of Beachcombers Hotel, which is also the perfect spot for sunbathers to get lunch and liquid refreshments. ⊠ *St. Vincent, St. Vincent and the Grenadines.*

WHERE TO EAT

$$$
CARIBBEAN

✗ **Basil's Bar and Restaurant.** It's not just the air-conditioning that makes this restaurant cool. Downstairs at the Cobblestone Inn, Basil's is owned by Basil Charles, whose Basil's Beach Bar on Mustique is a hangout for the vacationing rich and famous. This is the Kingstown power-lunch venue. Local businesspeople gather for the daily buffet (weekdays) or full menu of salads, sandwiches, barbecued chicken, or fresh seafood platters. Dinner entrées of pasta, local seafood, and chicken are served at candlelit tables. There's a Chinese buffet on Friday, and takeout is available that night only. ⊠ *Cobblestone Inn, Upper Bay St., Kingstown, St. Vincent, St. Vincent and the Grenadines* ☎ *784/457–2713* ☉ *Closed Sun.*

$$
CARIBBEAN
★

✗ **Cobblestone Roof-Top Bar & Restaurant.** To reach what is perhaps the most pleasant, the breeziest, and the most satisfying breakfast and luncheon spot in downtown Kingstown, diners must climb the equivalent of three flights of interior stone steps within the historic Cobblestone Inn. A full breakfast menu is available to hotel guests and the public alike. The luncheon menu ranges from homemade soups, salads (tuna, chicken, fruit, or tossed), sandwiches, or burgers and fries to full meals of roast beef, stewed chicken, or grilled fish served with rice, plantains, macaroni pie, and fresh local vegetables. Dee-licious! ⊠ *Upper Bay St., Kingstown, St. Vincent, St. Vincent and the Grenadines* ☎ *784/456–1937* ☉ *No dinner.*

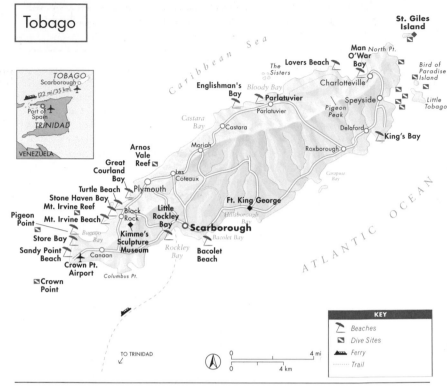

TOBAGO (SCARBOROUGH)

Vernon
O'Reilly
Ramesar

The smaller and quieter of the sister islands that make up Trinidad and Tobago offers pristine beaches and friendly people. Tobago has long been a favorite of European visitors, who enjoy the rustic feel of the island and the laid-back pace. There are numerous fine restaurants, though many are not located in Scarborough, where cruise ships dock. The culinary thrill here is exploring the local cuisine that can be found at food stalls across the island, and you could easily make eating the focus of your shore excursion and be all the happier for it. No trip here is complete without trying the quintessential Tobago dish, curry crab and dumplings. This can be a slow (and messy) experience, but it fits in perfectly with the pace of life on the island.

ESSENTIALS

CURRENCY   The Trinidad and Tobago dollar (TT$6.39 to US$1). Most places catering to tourists will accept U.S. currency, but the exchange rate may vary wildly from place to place.

INTERNET   Internet cafés spring up and disappear quickly. A quick look around the port area should reveal the latest incarnations.

TELEPHONE   Pay phones are located in the cruise terminal. To make an international call from a pay phone, you must first purchase a prepaid "companion" card, which is readily available from most convenience shops at or near the port, then simply follow the instructions on the card. Cards are available in various denominations.

COMING ASHORE

Scarborough, Tobago's lazy and hilly capital, is where all cruise ships dock. The cruise terminal is at the base of the city, near the market, many colorful shops, and fast-food restaurants. There are shops selling goods specifically marketed to tourists right at the port, but a short stroll around the streets of downtown can yield considerably more interesting treasures.

While you can easily walk into town, the island's best beaches and restaurants are in Crown Point. Because of the narrow roads and hilly terrain—not to mention aggressive drivers who like to drive very fast—it is not advisable to rent a car. But if you choose to drive yourself, remember that driving is on the left, British style. Taxis flock to the port whenever a cruise ship arrives. Authorized taxis always have a license plate starting with the letter "H" (for "hire"). Although rates are technically fixed, it is never a bad idea to negotiate with the driver.

EXPLORING TOBAGO

Ft. King George. On Mt. St. George, a short drive up the hill from Scarborough, Tobago's best-preserved historic monument clings to a cliff high above the ocean. Ft. King George was built in the 1770s and operated until 1854. It's hard to imagine that this lovely, tranquil spot commanding sweeping views of the bay and landscaped with lush tropical foliage was ever the site of any military action, but the prison, officers' mess, and several stabilized cannons attest otherwise. Just to the left of the tall wooden figures dancing a traditional Tobagonian jig is the former barrack guardhouse, now housing the small **Tobago Museum.** The **Fine Arts Centre** at the foot of the Ft. King George complex shows the work of local artists. ✉ *84 Fort St., Scarborough, Tobago, Trinidad and Tobago* ☎ *868/639–3970* ⌚ *Fort free, museum TT$5* ☉ *Weekdays 9–5.*

★ **Kimme Sculpture Museum.** The diminutive and eccentric German-born sculptress Luise Kimme fell in love with the form of Tobagonians and has devoted her life to capturing them in her sculptures. Her pieces can exceed 12 feet in height and are often wonderfully whimsical. Much of her work is done in wood (none of it local), but there are many bronze pieces as well. The museum itself is a turreted structure with a commanding view of the countryside. Most locals refer to it as "The Castle." There are numerous signs in Mt. Irvine directing visitors to the museum. ✉ *Mt. Irvine, Tobago, Trinidad and Tobago* ☎ *868/639–0257* ⊕ *www.luisekimme.com* ⌚ *TT$20* ☉ *Sun. 10–2 or by appointment.*

Scarborough. Around Rockley Bay on the island's leeward hilly side, this town is both the capital of Tobago and a popular cruise-ship port, but it conveys the feeling that not much has changed since the area was settled two centuries ago. It may not be one of the delightful pastel-color cities of the Caribbean, but Scarborough does have its charms, including several interesting little shops. Whatever you do, be sure to check out the busy Scarborough Market, an indoor and outdoor affair featuring everything from fresh vegetables to live chickens and clothing. Note the red-and-yellow Methodist church on the hill, one of Tobago's oldest churches. ⊠ *Tobago, Trinidad and Tobago.*

SHOPPING

Determined shoppers should manage to find a few things to take home. Scarborough has the largest collection of shops on the island, and Burnett Street, which climbs sharply from the port to St. James Park, is a good place to browse.

Cotton House. Cotton House is a good bet for jewelry and imaginative batik work. Paula Young runs her shop like an art school. You can visit the upstairs studio; if it's not too busy, you can even make a batik square at no charge. ⊠ *Bacolet St., Scarborough, Tobago, Trinidad and Tobago* ☎ *868/639–2727.*

ACTIVITIES

BIRD-WATCHING

★ Some 200 varieties of birds have been documented on Tobago: look for the yellow oriole, scarlet ibis, and the comical motmot—the male of the species clears sticks and stones from an area and then does a dance complete with snapping sounds to attract a mate. The flora is as vivid as the birds. Purple-and-yellow *poui* trees and spectacular orange immortelles splash color over the countryside, and something is blooming virtually every season.

Pioneer Journeys. Pat Turpin and Renson Jack at Pioneer Journeys can give you information about their bird-watching tours of Bloody Bay rain forest and Louis d'Or River valley wetlands. ⊠ *Tobago, Trinidad and Tobago* ☎ *868/660–4327 or 868/660–5175* ✉ *pturpin@tstt.net.tt.*

Rooks Nature Tours. Naturalist and ornithologist David Rooks operates Rooks Nature Tours, offering bird-watching walks inland and trips to offshore bird colonies. He's generally considered the best guide on the island. ⊠ *462 Moses Hill, Lambeau, Tobago, Trinidad and Tobago* ☎ *868/756–8594.*

BOAT TOURS

Tobago offers many wonderful spots for snorkeling. Although the reefs around Speyside in the northeast are becoming better known, **Buccoo Reef,** off the island's southwest coast, is still the most popular—perhaps too popular. Over the years the reef has been badly damaged by the ceaseless boat traffic and by the thoughtless visiting divers who take pieces of coral as souvenirs. Still, it's worth experiencing, particularly if you have children. Daily 2½-hour tours by glass-bottom boats let you snorkel at the reef, swim in a lagoon, and gaze at Coral Gardens—where fish and coral are as yet untouched. Most dive companies in the Black Rock area also arrange snorkeling tours. There's also good snorkeling near the **Arnos Vale Hotel** and the **Mt. Irvine Bay Hotel.**

Hew's Glass Bottom Boat Tours. Hew's Glass Bottom Boat Tours are perfect excursions for those who neither snorkel nor dive. Boats leave daily at 11:30 am.

✉ *Pigeon Point, Tobago, Trinidad and Tobago* ☎ *868/639–9058.*

GOLF

★ **Tobago Plantations Golf & Country Club.**
The 18-hole, PGA-designed championship par-72 course at Tobago Plantations Golf & Country Club is set amid rolling greens and mangroves. It offers some amazing views of the ocean as a bonus. Greens fees are $60 for one 18-hole round, $95 for two rounds (these rates include a golf cart and taxes). This is the newer of the two main courses on the island and is by far the most popular. The course is well maintained and contains areas of mangrove and forest that are home to many bird species. ✉ *Lowlands, Tobago, Trinidad and Tobago* ☎ *868/631–0875.*

BEACHES

You won't find manicured country-club sand here. But those who enjoy feeling as though they've landed on a desert island will relish the untouched quality of these shores.

Bacolet Beach. This dark-sand beach was the setting for the films *Swiss Family Robinson* and *Heaven Knows, Mr. Allison*. Though used by the Blue Haven Hotel, like all local beaches it's open to the public. If you are not a guest at the hotel, access to the beach is down a track next door to the hotel. The bathroom and changing facilities on the beach are for hotel guests only. ✉ *Windward Rd. east of Scarborough, Tobago, Trinidad and Tobago.*

Great Courland Bay. Near Ft. Bennett, the bay has clear, tranquil waters. Along the sandy beach—one of Tobago's longest—you can find several glitzy hotels. A marina attracts the yachting crowd. ✉ *Leeward Rd. northeast of Black Rock, Courland, Tobago, Trinidad and Tobago.*

King's Bay. Surrounded by steep green hills, this is the most visually satisfying of the swimming sites off the road from Scarborough to Speyside—the bay hooks around so severely, you can feel like you're in a lake. The crescent beach is easy to find because it's marked by a sign about halfway between the two towns. ✉ *Delaford, Tobago, Trinidad and Tobago.*

Pigeon Point Beach. This stunning locale is often displayed on Tobago travel brochures. The white-sand beach is lined with swaying coconut trees, and there are changing facilities and food stalls nearby. Although the beach is public, it abuts part of what was once a large coconut estate, and you must pay a token admission (about TT$18) to enter the grounds and use the facilities. ✉ *Pigeon Point, Tobago, Trinidad and Tobago.*

Store Bay. The beach, where boats depart for Buccoo Reef, is little more than a small sandy cove between two rocky breakwaters, but the food stands here are divine: several huts licensed by the tourist board to local ladies who sell roti, *pelau* (meat stewed in coconut milk with peas and rice), and the world's messiest dish—curried crab and dumplings. Near the airport, just walk around the Crown Point Hotel to the beach entrance. ⊠ *Crown Point, Tobago, Trinidad and Tobago.*

WHERE TO EAT

$$$

CARIBBEAN

Fodor's Choice

★

✕ **Blue Crab Restaurant.** The Sardinha family have been serving the best local lunches at their home since the 1980s. The ebullient Alison entertains and hugs diners while her husband, Ken, does the cooking. The food is hearty and usually well seasoned in the creole style. The only bad news here is that the restaurant is rarely open for dinner; the good news is that you may not have room for dinner after lunch. ⊠ *Robinson and Main Sts., Scarborough, Tobago, Trinidad and Tobago* ☎ *868/639–2737* ⊕ *www.tobagobluecrab.com* ⊘ *Closed weekends. No dinner.*

¢

CAFÉ

Fodor's Choice

★

✕ **Shore Things Café & Craft.** With a dramatic setting over the ocean on the Milford Road between Crown Point and Scarborough, this is a good spot to stop for a lunch or coffee break. Survey the view from the deck tables while enjoying a variety of freshly prepared juices (the tamarind is particularly refreshing) and nibbling on excellent sandwiches. The whole-wheat pizza here may well be the best on the island. While waiting for your meal, you can shop for local crafts in the lovely and comprehensive gift shop. ⊠ *25 Old Milford Rd., Lambeau, Tobago, Trinidad and Tobago* ☎ *868/635–1072* ⊘ *Closed Sun. No dinner.*

TORTOLA (ROAD TOWN)

Lynda Lohr

Once a sleepy backwater, Tortola is definitely busy these days, particularly when several cruise ships tie up at the Road Town dock. Passengers crowd the streets and shops, and open-air jitneys filled with cruise-ship passengers create bottlenecks on the island's byways. That said, most folks visit Tortola to relax on its deserted sands or linger over lunch at one of its many delightful restaurants. Beaches are never more than a few miles away, and the steep green hills that form Tortola's spine are fanned by gentle trade winds. The neighboring islands glimmer like emeralds in a sea of sapphire. Tortola doesn't have many historic sights, but it does have abundant natural beauty. Beware of the roads, which are extraordinarily steep and twisting, making driving demanding. The best beaches are on the north shore.

ESSENTIALS

CURRENCY

The U.S. dollar is the official currency. Some places accept cash only, but major credit cards are widely accepted. You'll find ATMs in Road Town.

TELEPHONE

To call anywhere in the BVI once you've arrived, dial all seven digits. A local call from a pay phone costs 25¢, but such phones are sometimes on the blink. An alternative is a Caribbean phone card, available in $5, $10, and $20 denominations. They're sold at most major hotels and many stores, and can be used to call within the BVI as well as all over the Caribbean, and to access USADirect from special phone-card phones. If you're coming ashore at the cruise-ship dock, you'll find pay

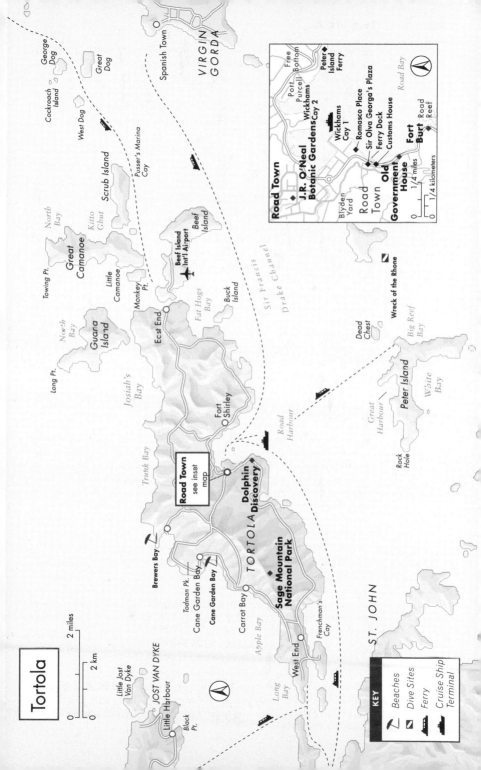

phones right on the dock. If a tender drops you right in Road Town at the ferry dock, phones are located in the terminal.

AT&T has service in nearby St. John, USVI, so it's possible to get service from there in some spots in Road Town and along the waterfront highway that leads to the West End. You may not have to pay international roaming charges on some U.S. cell-phone plans if you can connect with this network.

COMING ASHORE

Large cruise ships usually anchor in Road Town Harbor and bring passengers ashore by tender. Small ships can sometimes tie up at Wickham's Cay dock. Either way, it's a short stroll to Road Town. If your ship isn't going to Virgin Gorda, you can make the 12-mi (19-km) trip by ferry from the dock in Road Town in about 30 minutes for about $30 round-trip, but you'll still have to take a taxi to get to the Baths for swimming and snorkeling, so it's not necessarily a bad deal to go on your ship's shore excursion.

There are taxi stands at Wickham's Cay and in Road Town. Taxis are unmetered, and there are minimums for travel throughout the island, so it's usually cheaper to travel in groups. Negotiate to get the best fares, as there is no set fee schedule. If you are in the islands for just a day, it's usually more cost-effective to share a taxi with a small group than to rent a car, since you'd have to pay an agency at Wickham's Cay or in Road Town car-rental charges of at least $50 a day. You must be at least age 25 to rent a car.

EXPLORING TORTOLA

The bustling capital of the BVI looks out over Road Harbour. It takes only an hour or so to stroll down Main Street and along the waterfront, checking out the traditional West Indian buildings painted in pastel colors and with corrugated-tin roofs, bright shutters, and delicate fretwork trim. For sightseeing brochures and the latest information on everything from taxi rates to ferry schedules, stop in at the BVI Tourist Board office. Or just choose a seat on one of the benches in Sir Olva Georges Square, on Waterfront Drive, and watch the people come and go from the ferry dock and customs office across the street.

Dolphin Discovery. Get up close and personal with dolphins as they swim in a spacious seaside pen. There are three different programs that provide a range of experiences. In the Royal Swim, dolphins tow participants around the pen. The less expensive Adventure and Discovery programs allow you to touch the dolphins. ⊠ *Prospect Reef Resort, Road Town, Tortola, British Virgin Islands* ☎ *284/494–7675* ⊕ *www. dolphindiscovery.com* ⊠ *Royal Swim $149, Adventure $99, Discovery $79* ☉ *Royal Swim daily at 10, noon, 2, and 4. Adventure and Discovery daily at 11 and 1.*

Ft. Burt. The most intact historic ruin on Tortola was built by the Dutch in the early 17th century to safeguard Road Harbour. It sits on a hill at the western edge of Road Town and is now the site of a small hotel and restaurant. The foundations and magazine remain, and the structure offers a commanding view of the harbor. ✉ *Waterfront Dr., Road Town, Tortola, British Virgin Islands* ☎ *No phone* 💲 *Free* ☉ *Daily dawn–dusk.*

★ **J.R. O'Neal Botanic Gardens.** Take a walk through this 4-acre showcase of lush plant life. There are sections devoted to prickly cacti and succulents, hothouses for ferns and orchids, gardens of medicinal herbs, and plants and trees indigenous to the seashore. From the tourist office in Road Town, cross Waterfront Drive and walk one block over to Main Street and turn right. Keep walking until you see the high school. The gardens are on your left. ✉ *Botanic Station, Road Town, Tortola, British Virgin Islands* ☎ *284/494–3904* 💲 *$3* ☉ *Mon.–Sat. 8:30–4:30.*

TORTOLA BEST BETS

■ **The Rhone.** For certified divers, this is one of the best wreck dives in the Caribbean.

■ **Sage Mountain.** The highest peak in the Virgin Islands has breathtaking views and is a great hiking destination.

■ **Sailing Trips.** Because of its proximity to small islets and good snorkeling sights, Tortola is the sailing capital of the Caribbean.

■ **Virgin Gorda.** Ferries link Tortola and Virgin Gorda, making a half-day trip to the Baths quite possible (just be sure to check the ferry schedules before heading out).

Fodor's Choice
★ **Old Government House Museum.** The official government residence until 1997, this gracious building now displays a nice collection of artifacts from Tortola's past. The rooms are filled with period furniture, hand-painted china, books signed by Queen Elizabeth II on her 1966 and 1977 visits, and numerous items reflecting Tortola's seafaring legacy. ✉ *Waterfront Dr., Road Town, Tortola, British Virgin Islands* ☎ *284/494–4091* 💲 *$3* ☉ *Weekdays 9–3, Sat. 9–1.*

★ **Sage Mountain National Park.** At 1,716 feet, Sage Mountain is the highest peak in the BVI. From the parking area, a trail leads you in a loop not only to the peak itself (and extraordinary views) but also to a small rain forest that is sometimes shrouded in mist. Most of the forest was cut down over the centuries to clear land for sugarcane, cotton, and other crops; to create pastureland; or simply to use the stands of timber. In 1964 this park was established to preserve what remained. Up here you can see mahogany trees, white cedars, mountain guavas, elephant-ear vines, mamey trees, and giant bullet woods, to say nothing of such birds as mountain doves and thrushes. Take a taxi from Road Town or drive up Joe's Hill Road and make a left onto Ridge Road toward Chalwell and Doty villages. The road dead-ends at the park. ✉ *Ridge Rd., Sage Mountain, Tortola, British Virgin Islands* ☎ *284/494–3904* 💲 *$3* ☉ *Daily dawn–dusk.*

SHOPPING

Many shops and boutiques are clustered along and just off Road Town's **Main Street.** You can shop in Road Town's **Wickham's Cay I** adjacent to the marina. The **Crafts Alive Market** on the Road Town waterfront

7

is a collection of colorful West Indian–style buildings with shops that carry items made in the BVI. You might find pretty baskets or interesting pottery or perhaps a bottle of home-brewed hot sauce. An ever-growing number of art and clothing stores are opening at **Soper's Hole** in West End.

> **CAUTION**
>
> Check the balance of your shipboard account before the end of your cruise. You'll avoid a long line at the Purser's Desk that last morning after the final bill arrives.

ACTIVITIES

DIVING AND SNORKELING

The *Chikuzen,* sunk northwest of Brewers Bay in 1981, is a 246-foot vessel in 75 feet of water; it's home to thousands of fish, colorful corals, and big rays. In 1867 the **RMS *Rhone,*** a 310-foot royal mail steamer, split in two when it sank in a devastating hurricane. It's so well preserved that it was used as an underwater prop in the movie *The Deep.* You can see the crow's nest and bowsprit, the cargo hold in the bow, and the engine and enormous propeller shaft in the stern. Its four parts are at various depths from 30 to 80 feet. Get yourself some snorkeling gear and hop aboard a dive boat to this wreck near Salt Island (across the channel from Road Town). Every dive outfit in the BVI runs scuba and snorkel tours to this part of the BVI National Parks Trust; if you have time for only one trip, make it this one. Rates start at around $75 for a one-tank dive and $100 for a two-tank dive.

Blue Waters Divers. Blue Waters Divers teaches resort, open-water, rescue, and advanced diving courses, and also makes daily dive trips. If you're chartering a sailboat, the company's boat will meet your boat at Peter, Salt, Norman, or Cooper Island for a rendezvous dive. Rates include all equipment as well as instruction. Reserve two days in advance. ⊠ *Nanny Cay, British Virgin Islands* ☎ *284/494–2847* ⊕ *www.bluewaterdiversbvi.com.*

FISHING

Most of the boats that take you deep-sea fishing for bluefish, wahoo, swordfish, and shark leave from nearby St. Thomas, but local anglers like to fish the shallower water for bonefish. A half day runs about $480, a full day around $850.

Caribbean Fly Fishing. Call Caribbean Fly Fishing. ⊠ *Nanny Cay, Tortola, British Virgin Islands* ☎ *284/494–4797* ⊕ *www.caribflyfishing.com.*

SAILING

ℭ The BVI are among the world's most popular sailing destinations. **Fodor's Choice** They're close together and surrounded by calm waters, so it's fairly ★ easy to sail from one anchorage to the next.

Aristocat Charters. Aristocat Charters sets sail daily to Norman Island, the Indians, and Peter Island aboard a 48-foot catamaran. ⊠ *West End, Tortola, British Virgin Islands* ☎ *284/499–1249* ⊕ *www. aristocatcharters.com.*

White Squall II. *White Squall II* takes you on regularly scheduled day sails to The Baths at Virgin Gorda, Cooper, the Indians, or the Caves at Norman Island on an 80-foot schooner. ⊠ *Village Cay Marina, Road Town, Tortola, British Virgin Islands* ☎ *284/494–2564* ⊕ *www. whitesquall2.com.*

BEACHES

Tortola's north side has several perfect palm-fringed white-sand beaches that curl around turquoise bays and coves. Nearly all are accessible by car (preferably one with four-wheel-drive), albeit down bumpy roads that corkscrew precipitously. Facilities run the gamut from absolutely none to a number of beachside bars and restaurants as well as places to rent water-sports equipment.

Brewers Bay. Brewers Bay is good for snorkeling, and you can find a beach bar tucked in the foliage right behind the beach. An old sugar mill and ruins of a rum distillery are off the beach along the road. The beach is easy to find, but the steep, twisting paved roads leading down the hill to it can be a bit daunting. ⊠ *Brewers Bay Rd. E off Cane Garden Bay Rd., Tortola, British Virgin Islands.*

Cane Garden Bay. A silky stretch of sand, Cane Garden Bay has exceptionally calm, crystalline waters—except when storms at sea turn the water murky. Snorkeling is good along the edges. The beach is a laidback, even somewhat funky place to put down your towel. It's the closest beach to Road Town—one steep uphill and downhill drive—and one of the BVI's best-known anchorages (unfortunately, it can be very crowded). Water-sports shops rent equipment. ⊠ *Cane Garden Bay Rd. off Ridge Rd., Tortola, British Virgin Islands.*

7

WHERE TO EAT

$
ITALIAN
Fodor's Choice
★

✕ **Capriccio di Mare.** The owners of the well-known Brandywine Bay restaurant also run this casual, authentic Italian outdoor café. Stop by for an espresso, a fresh pastry, a bowl of perfectly cooked penne, or a crispy tomato-and-mozzarella pizza. Drink specialties include a mango Bellini, an adaptation of the famous cocktail served at Harry's Bar in Venice. ⊠ *Waterfront Dr., Road Town, Tortola, British Virgin Islands* ☎ *284/494–5369* ⌲ *Reservations not accepted* ⊘ *Closed Sun.*

$$$
CARIBBEAN

✕ **Village Cay Restaurant.** Docked sailboats stretch nearly as far as the eye can see at this busy Road Town restaurant. For lunch, try the grouper club sandwich with an ancho chili mayonnaise. Offerings include fish and crispy chips, as well as a savory roti made with chicken, potatoes, and a delicious curry sauce. ⊠ *Wickhams Cay I, Road Town, Tortola, British Virgin Islands* ☎ *284/494–2771.*

VIRGIN GORDA (THE VALLEY)

Lynda Lohr

Virgin Gorda, or "Fat Virgin," received its name from Christopher Columbus. The explorer envisioned the island as a pregnant woman in a languid recline with Gorda Peak being her big belly and the boulders of the Baths her toes. Different in topography from Tortola, with its arid landscape covered with scrub brush and cactus, Virgin Gorda has a slower pace of life, too. Goats and cattle own the right-of-way, and the unpretentious friendliness of the people is winning. The top sight (and beach for that matter) is the Baths, which draws scores of cruise-ship passengers and day-trippers to its giant boulders and grottoes that form a perfect snorkeling environment. While ships used to stop only in Tortola, saving Virgin Gorda for shore excursions, smaller ships are coming increasingly to Virgin Gorda directly.

ESSENTIALS

CURRENCY

The U.S. dollar is the official currency here. Some places accept cash only, but major credit cards are widely accepted. First Caribbean International, which has an ATM, isn't far from the ferry dock in Spanish Town.

TELEPHONE

To call anywhere in the BVI once you've arrived, dial all seven digits. There are no longer any pay phones on Virgin Gorda. Instead, get a Caribbean phone card, available in $5, $10, and $20 denominations. They're sold at most major hotels and many stores, and can be used to call within the BVI, as well as all over the Caribbean. Your own cell phone may work in the BVI, but you'll probably pay a hefty roaming fee.

COMING ASHORE

Ships often dock off Spanish Town, Leverick Bay, or in North Sound and tender passengers to the ferry dock. A few taxis will be available at Leverick Bay and at Gun Creek in North Sound—you can set up an island tour for about $45 for two people—but Leverick Bay and North Sound are far away from the Baths, the island's must-see beach, so a shore excursion is often the best choice. If you are tendered to Spanish Town, then it's possible to take a shuttle taxi to the Baths for as little as $4 per person each way. If you are on Virgin Gorda for just a day, it's usually more cost-effective to share a taxi with a small group than to rent a car, since you'd have to pay car-rental charges of at least $50 a day. You must be at least age 25 to rent a car.

EXPLORING VIRGIN GORDA

There are few roads, and most byways don't follow the scalloped shoreline. The main route sticks resolutely to the center of the island, linking the Baths on the southern tip with Gun Creek and Leverick Bay at North Sound. The craggy coast, scissored with grottoes and fringed by palms and boulders, has a primitive beauty. If you drive, you can hit all the sights in one day. Stop to climb Gorda Peak, which is in the island's center. Signage is erratic, so come prepared with a map.

Ⓒ
Fodor's Choice
★

The Baths. At Virgin Gorda's most celebrated sight, giant boulders are scattered about the beach and in the water. Some are almost as large as houses and form remarkable grottoes. Climb between these rocks to swim in

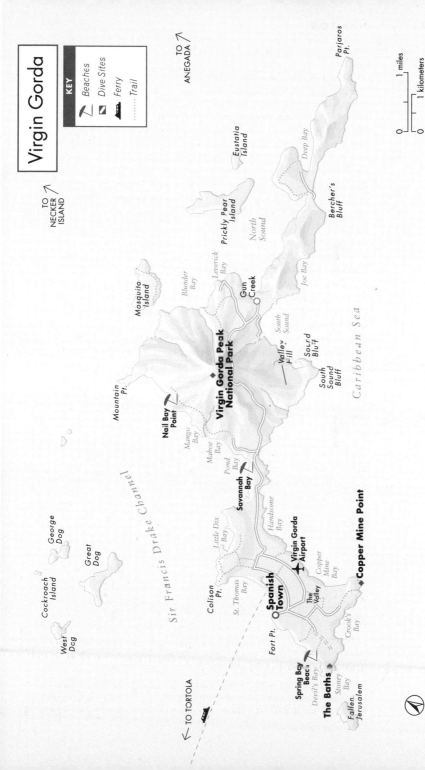

the many placid pools. If it's privacy you crave, follow the shore northward to quieter bays—Spring Bay, the Crawl, Little Trunk, and Valley Trunk—or head south to Devil's Bay. ✉ *About 1 mi [1½ km] west of Spanish Town ferry dock on Tower Rd., Spring Bay, Virgin Gorda, British Virgin Islands* ☎ *284/494–3904* 🖰 *$3* ⊙ *Daily dawn–dusk.*

Copper Mine Point. Here stand a tall stone shaft silhouetted against the sky and a small stone structure that overlooks the sea. These are the ruins of a copper mine established 400 years ago and worked first by the Spanish, then by the English, until the early 20th century. The route is not well marked, so turn inland near LSL Restaurant and look for the hard-to-see sign pointing the way. ✉ *Copper Mine Rd., Virgin Gorda, British Virgin Islands* ☎ *No phone* 🖰 *Free.*

Spanish Town. Virgin Gorda's peaceful main settlement, on the island's southern wing, is so tiny that it barely qualifies as a town at all. Also known as the Valley, Spanish Town has a marina, some shops, and a couple of car-rental agencies. Just north of town is the ferry slip. At the Virgin Gorda Yacht Harbour you can stroll along the dock and do a little shopping. ✉ *Virgin Gorda, British Virgin Islands.*

★ **Virgin Gorda Peak National Park.** There are two trails at this 265-acre park, which contains the island's highest point, at 1,359 feet. Small signs on North Sound Road mark both entrances; sometimes, however, the signs are missing, so keep your eyes open for a set of stairs that disappears into the trees. It's about a 15-minute hike from either entrance up to a small clearing, where you can climb a ladder to the platform of a wooden observation tower and a spectacular 360-degree view. ✉ *North Sound Rd., Gorda Peak, Virgin Gorda, British Virgin Islands* ☎ *No phone* 🖰 *Free.*

SHOPPING

Most boutiques are within hotel complexes or at Virgin Gorda Yacht Harbour. Two of the best are at Biras Creek and Little Dix Bay. Other properties—the Bitter End and Leverick Bay—have small but equally select boutiques.

ACTIVITIES

DIVING AND SNORKELING

The dive companies on Virgin Gorda are all certified by PADI. Costs vary, but count on paying about $100 for a one-tank dive and $130 for a two-tank dive. All dive operators offer introductory courses as well as certification and advanced courses. Should you get an attack of the bends, which can happen when you ascend too rapidly, the nearest decompression chamber is at Roy L. Schneider Regional Medical Center in St. Thomas.

Dive BVI. Dive BVI offers expert instruction, certification, and day trips. ✉ *Virgin Gorda Yacht Harbour, Spanish Town, Virgin Gorda, British Virgin Islands* ☎ *284/495–5513 or 800/848–7078* ⊕ *www.divebvi.com.*

> **CAUTION:**
> **OBSTRUCTED VIEWS**
>
> If you pick an outside cabin, check to make sure your view of the sea is not obstructed by a lifeboat. The ship's deck plan will help you figure it out.

Sunchaser Scuba. Sunchaser Scuba offers resort, advanced, and rescue courses. ✉ *Bitter End Yacht Club, North Sound, Virgin Gorda, British Virgin Islands* ☎ *284/495–9638 or 800/932–4286* ⊕ *www.sunchaserscuba.com.*

SAILING AND BOATING

The BVI waters are calm, and terrific places to learn to sail. You can also rent sea kayaks, waterskiing equipment, dinghies, and powerboats, or take a parasailing trip.

Double "D" Charters. If you just want to sit back, relax, and let the captain take the helm, choose a sailing or power yacht from Double "D" Charters. Rates are $65 for a half-day trip and $110 for a full-day island-hopping excursion. Private full-day cruises or sails for up to eight people run $950. ✉ *Virgin Gorda Yacht Harbour, Spanish Town, Virgin Gorda, British Virgin Islands* ☎ *284/499–2479* ⊕ *www.doubledbvi.com.*

Leverick Bay Watersports. If you'd rather rent a Sunfish or Hobie Wave, check out Leverick Bay Watersports. ✉ *Leverick Bay, North Sound, Virgin Gorda, British Virgin Islands* ☎ *284/495–7376* ⊕ *www.watersportsbvi.com.*

BEACHES

The best beaches are easily reached by water, although they're also accessible on foot, usually after a moderately strenuous 10- to 15-minute hike. Anybody going to Virgin Gorda should experience swimming or snorkeling among its unique boulder formations, which can be visited at several beaches along Lee Road. The most popular of these spots is the Baths, but there are several others nearby that are easily reached.

The Baths. A national park, The Baths features a stunning maze of huge granite boulders that extend into the sea, is usually crowded midday with day-trippers. The snorkeling is good, and you're likely to see a wide variety of fish, but watch out for dinghies coming ashore from the numerous sailboats anchored offshore. Public bathrooms and a handful of bars and shops are close to the water and at the start of the path that leads to the beach. Lockers are available to keep belongings safe. ✉ *About 1 mi [1½ km] west of Spanish Town ferry dock on Tower Rd., Spring Bay, Virgin Gorda, British Virgin Islands* ☎ *284/494–3904* ✉ *$3* ⏱ *Daily dawn–dusk.*

★ **Savannah Bay.** This is a wonderfully private beach close to Spanish Town. It may not always be completely deserted, but you can find a spot to yourself on this long stretch of soft, white sand. Bring your own mask, fins, and snorkel, as there are no facilities. The view from above is a photographer's delight. ✉ *Off N. Sound Rd., ¾ mi [1¼ km] east of Spanish Town ferry dock, Savannah Bay, Virgin Gorda, British Virgin Islands* ☎ *No phone* 🎫 *Free* 🕒 *Daily dawn–dusk.*

Spring Bay Beach. Just off Tower Road, Spring Bay is a national-park beach that gets much less traffic than the nearby Baths, and has the similarly large, imposing boulders that create interesting grottoes for swimming. It also has no admission fee, unlike the more popular Baths. The snorkeling is excellent, and the grounds include swings and picnic tables. ✉ *Off Tower Rd., 1 mi [1½ km] west of Spanish Town ferry dock, Spring Bay, Virgin Gorda, British Virgin Islands* ☎ *284/494–3904* 🎫 *Free* 🕒 *Daily dawn–dusk.*

WHERE TO EAT

$$ AMERICAN ✕ **Bath and Turtle.** You can sit back and relax at this informal tavern with a friendly staff—although the noise from the television can sometimes be a bit much. Well-stuffed sandwiches, homemade pizzas, pasta dishes, and daily specials such as conch soup round out the casual menu. Local musicians perform Wednesday and Sunday nights. ✉ *Virgin Gorda Yacht Harbour, Spanish Town, Virgin Gorda, British Virgin Islands* ☎ *284/495–5239* 🌐 *www.bathandturtle.com.*

$$$ AMERICAN ✕ **Top of the Baths.** At the entrance to The Baths, this popular restaurant starts serving at 8 am. Tables are on an outdoor terrace or in an open-air pavilion; all have stunning views of the Sir Francis Drake Channel. Hamburgers, coconut chicken sandwiches, and fish-and-chips are among the offerings at lunch. For dessert, the key lime pie is excellent. The Sunday barbecue, served from noon until 3 pm, is an island event. ✉ *The Valley, Virgin Gorda, British Virgin Islands* ☎ *284/495–5497* 🌐 *www.topofthebaths.com* 🕒 *No dinner.*

INDEX

Photo Credits: 9 (left), Windstar Cruises. 9 (right), Norwegian Cruise Line. 11 (left), Royal Caribbean International. 11 (right), Princess Cruises. 13 (left), Radisson Seven Seas Cruises. 13 (right), Celebrity Cruises. 15 (left), SeaDream Yacht Club. 15 (right), Windjammer Barefoot Cruises. Chapter 1: Cruising: The Basics: 17, Andy Newman/Carnival Cruise Lines. 34-35 (diagrams and photos), Celebrity Cruises. Chapter 2: Planning Your Cruise: 45, Radisson Seven Seas Cruises. Chapter 3: Getting Ready: 81, Holland America Line. Chapter 4: Enjoying Your Cruise: 101, Holland America Line. Chapter 5: Cruise Lines & Cruise Ships: 137, Radisson Seven Seas Cruises. 146 (top), Michel Verdure/Azamara Cruises. 146 (bottom) and 148 (both), Azamara Cruises. 150 (top), Fernando Diez/Celebrity Cruises. 150 (bottom), Celebrity Cruises. 151, Nick Garcia/Celebrity Cruises. 152 (top), Andy Newman/Carnival Cruise Lines. 152 (bottom), Carnival Cruise Lines. 153-63, Andy Newman/Carnival Cruise Lines. 164-68, Celebrity Cruises. 170 (top and bottom), and 171, Stephen Beaudet/Celebrity Cruises. 172 (top and bottom), Celebrity Cruises. 174-78, Costa Cruises. 180 (top and bottom), Johansen Krause/ Crystal Cruises. 181, and 182 (top and center), Crystal Cruises. 182 (bottom), Corey Weiner/Red Square/Crystal Cruises. 184 (top and bottom), Crystal Cruises. 186 (top), Crystal Cruises. 186 (bottom), Corey Weiner/Red Square/Crystal Cruises. 188-89 and 190 (top), Cunard Line. 190 (center and bottom) and 192, Michel Verdure/Cunard Line. 194-95 Cunard Images. 196-200, © Disney. 202 (top), Disney Dream Inaugural Cruise 178 by Samantha Chapnick http//www.flickr.com/photos/sierraandi/5425983156/Attribution-ShareAlike License. 202 (bottom), Disney Dream Inaugural Cruise 98 by Samantha Capnick http//www.flickr.com/photos/sierraandi/5425782064/Attribution-ShareAlike License. 204-06, Holland America Line. 208 (top), Andy Newman/Holland America Line. 208 (bottom) and 209, Michel Verdure/Holland America Line. 210 (top), Andy Newman/Holland America Line. 210 (bottom), Holland America Line. 212-15, Holland America Line. 216-20, MSC Cruises. 222-24, Norwegian Cruise Line. 226 (top and bottom), Rick Diaz/Norwegian Cruise Line, 227-29, Norwegian Cruise Line, 230-31, Michel Verdure/Norwegian Cruise Line. 232-33, Norwegian Cruise Line, 234-41, Oceania Cruises. 242-46, Princess Cruises. 247, Andy Newman/Princess Cruises. 248-53, Princess Cruises. 254-59, Regent Seven Seas Cruises. 260-62 Royal Caribbean. 264 (top), Michel Verdure/Royal Caribbean, 264 (bottom), Katherine Wessel/Royal Caribbean. 266 (top and bottom), and 267, Hugh Stewart/Royal Caribbean International. 268 (both) Johansen Krause/Royal Caribbean International. 270-77, Royal Caribbean International. 278 (top) and 279 (top), Johansen Krause/ The Yachts of Seabourn. 278 (bottom) and 279 (bottom), The Yachts of Seabourn. 280 (top), Johansen Krause/The Yachts of Seabourn. 280 (center and bottom) and 282-85, The Yachts of Seabourn. 286-91, SeaDream Yacht Club. 292-301, Silversea Cruises. 302-09, Star Clippers. 310-17, Windstar Cruises. Chapter 6: Ports of Embarkation: 319, Royal Caribbean International. Chapter 7: Ports of Call: 405, Celebrity Cruises.

NOTES

NOTES

NOTES

NOTES

NOTES